ANYWAY ANYHOW ANYWHERE
the complete chronicle of
THE WHO
1958 – 1978

ANDY NEILL & MATT KENT

DEDICATIONS

I would like to dedicate this book to my parents Warwick and Margaret, who for years endured the ear-splitting volume at which Who records were played on *their* sound system. — A.N.

The book is dedicated to my big brother Pat Kent, without whom I wouldn't have got involved in this lunacy, Jo Kent for putting up with it for so long, and Ross Halfin for giving me the encouragement to finish it! — M.K.

ACKNOWLEDGMENTS

For an epic of such scale, a considerable amount of people have to be acknowledged, so without any further ado, we'd like to thank the following interviewees, listed here in alphabetical order:

Keith Altham, Rod Argent, Jon Astley, Mick Avory, Richard "Barney" Barnes, Joe Boyd, Mick Bratby, Vernon Brewer, Arthur Brown, John "Rabbit" Bundrick, John Burgess, Anya Butler, Peter "Dougal" Butler, Neville Chesters, Dave Clarke, Richard Cole, Jeff Dexter, Mick Double, Robert Druce, Allen Ellett, Steve Ellis, Alison Entwistle, Mike Evans, Barry Fantoni, Bill Harrison, Tony Haslam, Jim Hubbard, Graham Hughes, Chris Huston, Glyn Johns, Billy Kinsley, Cy Langston, Nancy Lewis, Damon Lyon-Shaw, Jack "the Barber" Marks, Mike McInnerney, John Mears, Deirdre Meehan, Gordon "Lurch" Molland, Chris Morphet, Billy Nicholls, Alan Oates, Andrew Oldham, Bob Pridden, Noel Redding, Tony Rivers, Peter Rudge, Doug Sandom, Roger Searle, John Sebastian, Mike Shaw, Jerry Shirley, "Legs" Larry Smith, Chris Stamp, Richard Stanley, Shel Talmy, Chris Townson, Peter Tree, Peter Vernon-Kell, Chris Welch, Vicki Wickham, John "Wiggy" Wolff, and Tom Wright.

Thanks also to the following for their help, information, and/or assistance (however major or minor) over the past five years:

Barry Appleby, Paul Atkinson, Mike Baess, Glenn A. Baker, Fred Bannister, Danny Barbour, Nick Bartlett, Sandy Baynes, Danny Betesch, Bob Bickford, Steve Binder, Denis Bowler, John Brett, Mike Brewer, Geoff Brown, Tony Brown, Chris Butler, Brian Cady, Laura Campbell (Trinifold Ltd.), Chris Charlesworth, Gordon Chilvers, Arthur Chisnall, Dave Clark, June Clark, Dave Clynch (MCPS), Glenn Cornick, Bill Curbishley, Austin David, Andy Davis (*Record Collector*), Tim Derbyshire (*On The Beat*), Paul Derry (*Who's Wax*), Mary Devereux, Barry Dickens, Jeff Docherty, Peter Doggett, Mark Donovan, Andrew Easterbrook (*Twenty Twenty*), Ruth Edge (EMI archives), Steve English, Richard Evans, B.P. Fallon, Dick Fiddy, Tony Fletcher, Alberto Genero, Pat Gilbert (*Mojo*), Nick Godison, Kenny Goodless, Richard Groothuizen (AVRO), Ross Halfin, Richard & Daphne Hamilton, Linda Haslam, Mark Hayward, Jesse Hector, John Hellier, *Helter Skelter* Bookshop Ltd. (Sean and Mike), Doug Hinman, Chris Hjort, Brian Hogg, Phil Hopkins (*Generations*), Gary & Melissa Hurley, Virginia Ironside, Keith Jackson, Colin Jones, Nick Jones, Tom Kaniewski (VH-1), Jon Keeble (ITC), Pat Kent, Tom Keylock, Justin Kreutzman, Olle Lundin, Max Ker-Seymer, Uve Klee, Eric Kuhlberg & Jon Paige (Universal Media), Mark Laff, Spencer Leigh, Robert Lemkin, Simon & Tony Lordan, Alan Mair, Mike Mansfield, Bryan Mason, Paul McEvoy, Joe McMichael, Doug McLauchlan, George McManus (Polydor), Alan & Susan McMullan, Barry Miles, Kenny Mundey, Peter Neal, Peter Norris, Clare Norton-Smith (BFI), Helen Oakley, Mandy O'Connor, Ian O'Sullivan (BFI), Don Paulsen, Mark Paytress, John Peel, John Perry, Dave Petersen, Ian Pickavance (Abbey Road), Trevor Poppell (LWT), Roger Powell, Raja Prem, Sarah Prosser (BFI), Marek Pytel, Terry Rawlings, John Reed, Jan Reynaert, Jim Rodford, Brad Rodgers, Robert Rosenberg (Trinifold), Gary & Peter Ross, Henry Scott-Irvine, Greg Shaw, Keith Smart, Russell Smith, Terry Smith, Paul Southeran, David Stark, Sandy Steel, Frans Steensma, Carl Stickley, Bob Strano, Reggy Tan, Veronica Taylor (BFI), Andrea Thompson (Trinifold), Ronald Thorp, Mark Tilson, Ralph & Cathy Titterton, Steve Tollivay (BFI), Ted Tuksa, Dave van Staveren, Hugh Wallace, Dana & Martin Wiffen, Richard Williams, Phil Windeatt (LWT), Birte Zwyko (Studio-Hamburg), and to anyone else we've unintentionally omitted...

We'd also like to express our appreciation to the group of talented and dedicated professionals whose hard work helped make this book a reality:

At Friedman/Fairfax—Kevin Baier, Chris Bain, Jeff Batzli, Betsy Beier, Richela Fabian Morgan, and Nathaniel Marunas. At Barnes & Noble—Steve Riggio. At SMAY Vision—Stan Stanski and Phil Yarnell.

Special thanks to Ed Hanel for preparing the discography, Mark Lewisohn for sleuthing addresses, Keith Badman for the BBC research, the photographers featured here, and lastly, but by no means least, Roger, John, Pete (and in spirit, Keith), without whom...

First published in Great Britain in 2002 by Virgin Books Ltd.
Thames Wharf Studios, Rainville Road
London, W6 9HA

Published in the USA in 2002 by Barnes & Noble, Inc.

© 2002 Michael Friedman Publishing Group, Inc.

A catalogue record for this book is available from the British Library.

ISBN 1 85227 904 4

Editors: Nathaniel Marunas and Betsy Beier
Art Director: Jeff Batzli
Photography Editor: Chris Bain
Production Manager: Richela Fabian Morgan
Design: SMAY Vision
Production Artist and Additional Layout: Kevin Baier

Color separations by Bright Arts Graphics (S) Ptc Ltd
Printed in China by C & C Offset Printing Co., Ltd

1 3 5 7 9 10 8 6 4 2

Virgin
BOOKS

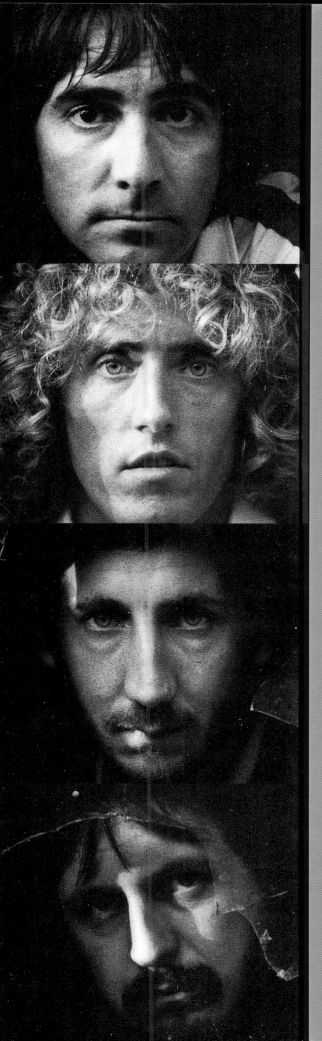

FOREWORD

IT NEVER CEASES TO AMAZE ME

how four young prats (aren't we all at that age?) with such diverse personalities ever came to be in the same band. To make matters worse, we were four megalomaniacs, with all the traumas, insecurities, and paranoia that make adolescence such a joy. Looking back on those years, what is so amazing, here at the pinnacle of our decline, is that the bond that connects us is stronger than ever. I always knew it was special. This was brought home to me when I was sacked from the band in 1965. It was then that I realised that this was the most important thing in my life. I've actually had it proven to me that music conquers all!

The Who were quirky from the start. The Beatles and the Stones were much more broad based, but we were individual, in a league of our own—distinctly British. We were the bloke's band and thank God for that because they've stuck with us. They identified with the songs that Pete was writing from a bloke's perspective. He was obviously making contact at a very deep level; it must have taken a lot of courage to write with such honesty.

We were in the spotlight, but the truth is that everyone involved with us from those early days was an important part of the jigsaw. Helmut Gorden kept us in a van for a year. Pete Meaden recognised the value of the Mod movement and got

us noticed. Kit Lambert and Chris Stamp were the fifth and sixth members of the Who: Kit, with his outrageous behaviour and ideas on how to manipulate the media, and Chris, the expert in cool, menace, and scams! Their contribution to the band should never be underestimated, and neither should the input of our manager since the 1970s, Bill Curbishley.

One of my greatest frustrations with the Who was that we never really achieved our full potential in recorded sound. We had the songs, we had the talent—but our sound was too big for the grooves! If only 5.1 sound had been around in those days.

It hasn't all been a bed of roses. We took casualties. Keith Moon's death cast a giant shadow. What made it worse was that somehow we were expecting it. He was our funny bone and, as Pete has said, our alter ego. Although not here in body, his spirit still lives on in everything we do. Kit Lambert's slow death through drugs and alcohol left a creative void, especially as far as Pete is concerned, which is very difficult to fill.

With all the shit that went down in the early years (and occasionally the latter ones!), for me, I'm never as happy in my life as I am when the Who are working. It's the ultimate highlight; the inner feeling of purpose, struggle, success, and failure—all these things rolled into one. My other careers I enjoy, but it could never be the same. Maybe that's why I like acting so much, because I go from one production to another searching for another Who—but of course there isn't one.

A great deal of misinformed rubbish has been written about the Who. Yes, we had our differences—and still have. But it's the differences that make it work. Thanks to Andy and Matt for making the effort to get it down as accurately and in as much detail as possible, talking to all the people that matter while we're all still here and before senility sets in. A lot of it I didn't know, a lot of it I've forgotten, but most of it reminds me just why the Who are the best fucking rock 'n' roll band in the world.

ROGER DALTREY
LONDON
JANUARY 2002

DURING THE SUMMER OF 1964

Kit Lambert and I were two young filmmakers looking for a rock group for our first independent film. Our idea was to find a group that somehow represented the emerging ideas of our time. They would be rebellious, anarchistic, and uniquely different from the established English pop scene. We would then manage them to success, all the while filming, cinema verité–style, all that happened. The film would be in stark contrast to the pop film fodder that existed at the time.

After interminable months of scouting ballrooms, clubs, and pubs, we saw The High Numbers. They brought into being what had only been in our minds, and more. We made a film called *High Numbers*, which amounted to a filmic good-bye to that name. New multimedia concepts emerged as Kit and I gave over our hearts, minds, and souls to our new roles as managers of the Who.

We were six very different people, but over the next ten years, our differences worked to our benefit. We sparked each other to reach into previously untapped parts of ourselves. Struggles became creative adventures. The powerful dynamics that held us together threatened to explode us apart at any moment. We stayed the course. Every idea was cheered or jeered until it was accepted by the group, and the more we trusted this process the more the creative centre grew. The united strength combined with the challenging weaknesses seemed to be in sync with the time we were living in. The success was sometimes more difficult to handle than the failure but we could always rely on the strength of the group.

It often felt like two worlds, the united, dynamic, creative struggle of the group that transcended everything and everyone, in contrast with the day-to-day reality of a rock 'n' roll family system with its rivalries, fighting, and emotional growth.

The first few years were meteoric. Time seemed to speed up; emotional and psychic changes took place every day. These inner changes were soon manifested outwardly; even our appearances changed. As we wandered wide-eyed into the 1970s, the pace slowed down. New ideas were talked about more, as opposed to the spontaneity of the earlier happenings. Our adulthood was struggling with our youth.

With success came more money. At first the money fuelled creativity, but this soon fragmented into a search for luxury. This was fun for awhile, but became ultimately unfulfilling, a distraction from our real path. The centre began to weaken and some of us lost our grip. Over time, some of us became dependent on the strength of the group, while some of us fell away. My years with the force that is known as the Who were more than magnificent, they were about untethered love.

CHRIS STAMP
NEW YORK
6 APRIL, 2001

INTRODUCTION

Who, what, where, when, and more importantly, why? In 1971, the first Who-related biography was published. Since then, a plethora of titles have hit the shelves, a few authorised, the bulk not, and most with a frustrating lack of definitive information relating to the Who's lengthy career. The idea for this exhaustive tome initially sprang from that void.

As fans of the group since the early 70's, we were both hopeful of seeing such a volume appear during our lifetimes. When it failed to materialise, it seemed

the maxim "if you want something done properly..." was going to apply.

Before commencing the gargantuan amount of work required for such an undertaking, an approach was made in 1997 to Bill Curbishley, the Who's manager, to gauge whether the band would object to an in-depth chronicling of Who history from their formation up to the untimely death of Keith Moon. After consulting each respective individual, Curbishley gave his approval by stating, "At last, I'm looking forward

to reading a factually accurate account of the Who's history." Work began in earnest in April 1997.

While God may have created the earth in seven days, it soon became apparent that this endeavour was to take a little longer!

During the course of researching the group's professional career, we were fortunate to be given access to various official archives, many of which had not been exhumed or examined in more than thirty years. This in turn led us to many of the connected individuals, some of whom had not previously spoken about their association with the Who.

As for John, Pete, and Roger, they have helped in varying degrees to either confirm, deny, or (occasionally) confuse different issues. However, without their input, for which we are indebted, there would be several unresolved holes in the book you now hold. In most instances, all quotes contained within were given directly to the authors, unless otherwise stated. We apologize to any sources that remain uncredited. Inevitably, inaccuracies are prone to arise when relying on memories of events that took place up to four decades ago. The information provided herein has been cross-checked as much as humanly possible, but we accept the possibility that there are errors. (Nobody's perfect, least of all us.) A complete and exhaustive document remains frustratingly unattainable; it would be false to claim otherwise.

The Who continue to sporadically function as a working unit, but this reference work steadfastly concentrates on the period up to Keith Moon's death in 1978, when the group were still considered a working, creative entity. Throughout the 80's and beyond, the Who's reputation suffered as the result of lucrative "reunion" tours and record company indifference. Now, at the time of this writing, thanks to the advent of Britpop and grunge (in which their influence is tangible), exposure gained through films and television, and recent faith-affirming live shows, the Who have reached a new generation. Their reputation as *the* greatest live act has been firmly re-established.

In closing, we both hope this book aids in enhancing the enjoyment of the Who's timeless music because ultimately, that's what it's all about. And to those who kept asking "Where's the book?" here it is, finally!

Andy Neill & Matt Kent
(London, 2002)

GUIDANCE NOTES

This book chronicles the Who's professional activities from their West London beginnings as the Detours to Keith Moon's 1978 demise and the end of the Who as they are best known. It is by no means complete or exhaustive. Such a document remains out of reach.

Unlike peers such as the Beatles, Bob Dylan, or the Rolling Stones, the minutiae of the Who's activities were never reported with the same degree of detail or fascination. This is particularly true of the group's early incarnations, where frustratingly large amounts of information from 1961 to 1964 sadly appears lost to the passage of time. However, a considerable wealth of new information from those years is presented here for the first time.

Basically, all known concerts, radio and television broadcasts, recording activities, and record release dates by the group and its individual members are presented in chronological order, using the British configuration of day, month, year.

CONCERTS

For the most part, a concert is defined here as a live performance in front of a paying audience. Early engagements where the group were booked at private functions are documented where known, as are specially arranged concerts such as the Young Vic experiments (early 1971), Portsmouth (22/5/74), Kilburn (15/12/77), and Shepperton (25/5/78). Because these were essentially closed events, they have been excluded from the "Who Concerts" appendix.

Similarly, impromptu jam sessions involving band members have been excluded, as most went unreported. However, those that occurred at billed shows (e.g., the Beach Boys on 12/11/70) have been included. Concerts that were advertised or booked in advance but were subsequently either cancelled or rescheduled, have been duly noted under "Engagements Not Played" in the same appendix.

For a more in-depth examination of the Who's live performances, the authors recommend *The Who Concert File* by Joe McMichael and "Irish" Jack Lyons (Omnibus Press, 1998) as a companion volume.

RADIO, TELEVISION, AND FILMS

These appearances are defined as engagements for the purposes of radio/television broadcasts (either live or recorded for subsequent transmission) or a promo/feature film. These include all principal U.K. and U.S. media appearances by the group as individuals up to September 1978, though this list remains illustrative, not exhaustive.

Local radio and TV coverage have been excluded due to the sheer impossibility of chronicling all the appearances in detail, particularly in the United States, where minor press interviews were given in most cities and states. The odd exception, such as *Look North* (6/11/73), has been included due to surrounding circumstances. The transmission dates and times relate to the relevant region, though different broadcasters may have aired a particular programme at different times or dates.

RECORDING SESSIONS

These group activities are defined as recording and/or mixing sessions involving the group or its individual members. Unfortunately, the Who's work in the studio was not documented as thoroughly, for example, as the Beatles' work at Abbey Road. Because the Who weren't tied to an organisation like EMI, where all work had to be accounted for (ironically, written records of the Who's audition for this very company cannot be found!), the band utilised a number of independent studios around London and, in the odd instance, the United States. Details of take numbers, overdubs, etc., remain vague and often non-existent. A producer like Kit Lambert was more intent on capturing a definitive performance than keeping administrative records. Therefore, many of the studio references are based upon limited information from personal diaries, written sources, and the Who's official tape archive.

In some cases, a date written on a tape box may refer to the actual mixing (i.e., when the recording in question was mixed down from a multitrack tape for the purposes of acetate cutting, tape copying, and/or mastering).

It's widely known within Who circles that from the outset of the group's career, Pete Townshend recorded demonstration tapes, usually at his home studios, as a means of presenting material for group consideration. To a lesser degree, so did John Entwistle. Because no details, specifically dates, are available in the main for this type of material, they are not addressed in the book.

UNOFFICIAL RECORDINGS

Many of the Who's appearances were illicitly recorded by spectators on basic audio and visual equipment, leading to a thriving circulation of illegal "bootleg" tapes, records, videos, and CDs over the years. This book details only legal activities, unless the film or tape in question was subsequently integrated into an authorised venture (e.g., the Cow Palace footage from 20/11/73) or has a specific historic importance (e.g., the first U.S. *Tommy* performance on 9/5/69).

PUBLIC ACTIVITIES

An examination of the Who's private affairs is beyond the scope of this book, but slotted between the group's hectic professional career is a public log of births, deaths, marriages, divorces, court cases, and the like. Once again, this part of the work is illustrative, not exhaustive.

I'm a BOY

ROGER DALTREY

Roger Harry Daltrey was born at Hammersmith Hospital, West London, on 1 March 1944, during a heavy World War II bombing raid. Both parents were staunchly working class. His father Harry worked as an insurance clerk, while mother Irene was a sickness beneficiary due to losing a kidney and contracting polio prior to Roger's birth.

When Harry was drafted overseas, Irene and her three-month-old baby were evacuated to a farm in Scotland. With the end of the war, the family was reunited back at 15 Percy Road, Shepherd's Bush. Roger's sisters, Gillian and Carol, were born in 1945 and 1947 respectively.

In 1957, the Daltreys moved to 135 Fielding Road, Bedford Park, part of the more affluent suburb of neighbouring Acton. Having passed the all-important 11-plus examination at Victoria Junior Boys School, Shepherd's Bush, Roger attended Acton County Grammar School, situated on Gunnersbury Lane, near Acton Town station.

Initially promising as a student, Roger's Cockney accent and street attitude stood out among the more refined pupils. Consequently, any thoughts of scholastic achievement were abandoned by the rebellious lad dressed in Teddy boy threads. Besides, the invigorating sounds of early rock and roll and skiffle had reached his impressionable teenage ears.

Unable to afford a proper guitar and inspired by skiffle's do-it-yourself raison d'être, Roger made his own acoustic model, carving the body from a solid piece of plywood with his father's tools. (In much the same fashion, he went on to design the Who's early guitars, which Pete Townshend remembered as being "quite good except the necks kept folding up.") Roger's skiffle group came first in a local talent contest, winning £10 worth of record vouchers—a hollow victory, as none of the band members owned a record player.

Audible sighs of relief were no doubt heard in the staff room at Acton County Grammar when the disruptive fifteen-year-old was expelled, ostensibly for being caught smoking in the lavatories. His despairing parents packed him off to his first job as a £2-a-week electrician's mate on a local building site.

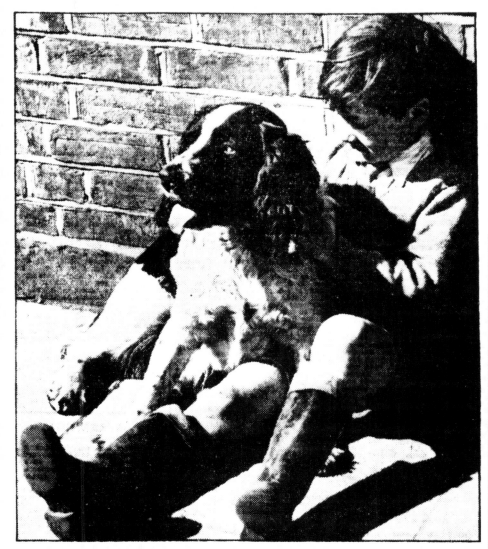

This sun really makes you tired! Five-year-old Peter Townsend takes it easy with his dog Bruce.

PETE TOWNSHEND

Peter Dennis Blandford Townshend was born on 19 May 1945 at Nazareth House, a convent in Isleworth that had been requisitioned as an annex to the nearby West Middlesex Hospital for use as a maternity ward during the war.

He arrived into a musical family. Pete's grand-father Horace had performed in the Jack Shepherd concert revue. His parents, Clifford and Betty, were part of the RAF dance orchestra, later known as the Squadronaires and regarded as Britain's most popular showband. Clifford was alto saxophonist and star-billed as "Cliff Townshend and His Singing Saxophone." His wife, Betty Dennis, had sung with the Sidney Torch Orchestra. After the war, Cliff continued with the Squadronaires, and at the age of only thirteen months, Pete first saw his father perform during a summer season at Butlin's Holiday Camp, Clacton.

While on holiday on the Isle of Man, he met a performing Texan cowboy. "He promised me a har-monica, which I never got," Pete recalled, "and in the end I think I had to shoplift one a couple of years later." With both parents absent for long periods, the five-year-old was uprooted from the family home at 22 Whitehall Gardens, Acton, and spent a year living in Kent with his maternal grandmother, Denny.

The Townshend family resettled into a large house at 20 Woodgrange Avenue, off Ealing Common. Pete's younger brothers, Paul and Simon, were born in 1957 and 1960 respectively. Surprisingly, there was little music to be heard around the household, "apart from my dad practising clarinet in the back room," said Pete. "We didn't have a very good record player, and we had a shitty radio, and there was no piano in the house."

While a pupil at Berrymede Junior School, South Acton, Pete sang in the local choir. An auntie encouraged him to learn piano, but it wasn't until the summer of 1956 that his musical aspirations coa-lesced. On 28 July, during a Squadronaires' season on the Isle of Man, Cliff took Pete and his childhood chum, Graham "Jimpy" Beard, along to a Saturday morning preview of *Rock Around The Clock* at the Gaiety Theatre, Douglas. "*Rock Around The Clock* did it for me," Pete told Richard Green. "I hadn't been into rock and roll before that. After a while, I decided the guitar was what I wanted."

First, however, Pete went through a brief period trying to follow in his father's foot-steps as a saxophonist. Watching his red-faced son struggle unsuccessfully to get a note out of a reed, Cliff suggested what was then his second instrument: the guitar. At twelve, Denny bought Pete his first woefully inadequate model as a Christmas present. He spent a year struggling with it before conceding defeat. Temporarily abandoning the guitar and rock and roll, Pete got a five-string mandolin banjo from a friend of his father's, and in the mold of Acker Bilk, learned to play trad jazz and bluegrass.

JOHN ENTWISTLE

John Alec Entwistle was born at Hammersmith Hospital, Acton, on 9 October 1944. His father Herbert was in the Royal Navy, and mother Maud (known to all as "Queenie") worked as a tax clerk. An only child, John's parents separated when he was just eighteen months. Maud took John to live with his grandparents at 81a Southfield Road, where he was raised. At a time when broken homes were uncommon, especially in suburban Acton, this early displacement undoubtedly contributed to John's reserved nature.

Herbert taught John trumpet, and thanks to his mother making him take piano lessons (under considerable duress), he was able to read music from the age of seven. The lad made his first public appearance in the Boys' Brigade at Hendon Town Hall at age eleven. With a surfeit of trumpet players already in the school orchestra, John took up the less glamorous French horn, joining the 200-piece Middlesex Youth Orchestra for two years as lead horn player.

At twelve, John met fellow student and struggling banjo player Peter Townshend at Acton County Grammar. Both shared a similar sense of humour and a liking for traditional Dixieland jazz, which was unusually popular in the area. Together, they attended gigs by the likes of Cy Laurie and Ken Colyer at the Chiswick Jazz Club, which hosted trad sessions every Sunday evening.

John invited Pete to join his band, the Confederates, featuring schoolmates Phil Rhodes on clarinet and Chris Sherwin on drums. "I'd been buggering about for two years on guitar without getting anywhere," Townshend told Richard Green in *New Musical Express*. "I knew they expected me to play, so I rushed out and got a chord book. They were fairly impressed, which I couldn't work out. Perhaps they thought if you could play three chords, you could play the rest!"

Keith moon

Keith John Moon was born at Central Middlesex County Hospital, Willesden, North West London, on 23 August 1946. He was raised in Wembley by his father Alfred, a motor mechanic, and mother Kathleen ("Kitty"), a part-time domestic cleaner. Keith's two sisters, Linda and Lesley, were born in 1949 and 1958 respectively.

At Barham Primary School, Keith was already displaying extrovert tendencies: he was a hyperactive boy with a restless imagination. In 1957, after failing the 11-plus, he attended Alperton Secondary School For Boys. However, schoolwork came a poor second to the antics that reduced his teachers to fits of apoplexy but had his classmates in stitches (which to Keith was far more important).

After an early interest in boxing, Keith's musical rumblings began at twelve, when he joined the local Barham Sea Cadets, blowing a bugle one week, a trumpet the next. This in turn led to the acquisition of a bass drum. At sixteen, he received his first proper kit, a £25 pearl blue Premier kit, with help from his father, Alfie, who signed the hire purchase forms. Practice sessions in the family sitting room at 134 Chaplin Road became a regular endurance test for the neighbours.

The cocky teenager received some tutelage from local hero Carlo Little, of Screaming Lord Sutch's backing group, the Savages; the rest he picked up from watching and listening to other skinsmen. In a 1971 interview, Moon claimed his main influences to be DJ Fontana, Ringo Starr, and Tony Meehan (the Shadows' original drummer), choosing them over jazzers like Elvin Jones or Buddy Rich. Still, Shelly Manne and the visually flamboyant style of Gene Krupa, who single-handedly turned the drums into a solo instrument, were undoubtedly important inspirations.

Keith sat in with a succession of Wembley bands, including schoolmates' bands the Altones and the Escorts, before joining his first serious group, Mark Twain and the Strangers, featuring singer Peter Tree, guitarist Barry Foskett, and bassist Michael Evans. Tree and Evans had answered an ad in *Melody Maker*. "It was for a singer," recalled Evans, "but we used that as a ruse to find ourselves a drummer. This audition was being held in somebody's front room up in Rickmansworth, and there was Keith behind the drums. I thought this kid's young, but then he started playing... Peter asked me, 'Well, what do you think?' I said, 'If you can get hold of that drummer, I'll join a band with you!'"

Foskett found a rehearsal hall in East Hill, Wandsworth, South West London, where the group rehearsed twice a week for the usual round of pubs, dances, and functions. At fifteen, Keith left Harrow Technical College and was employed briefly in the printing room at the National Council of Social Services in Bedford Square. As well as recording a demo tape, Mark Twain and the Strangers auditioned for the Light Programme at the BBC's studio at 201 Piccadilly on 5 September 1962. Unfortunately, they were passed over in favour of a Tottenham combo, the Dave Clark Five.

When the band were offered six months' work playing U.S. Army bases around Germany, Keith's age precluded him from going and the group eventually disbanded. Keith then unsuccessfully auditioned for Shane Fenton and the Fentones (future Hollies drummer, Bobby Elliott got the gig), before answering an ad placed in the *Harrow Observer*, dated 25 April 1963. The Beachcombers were a semi-professional outfit from Wembley, comprised of Ron Chenery (a.k.a. Clyde Burns) on vocals, Norman Mitchener on lead guitar, John Schollar on rhythm guitar, and Tony Brind on bass.

At the time, Keith was holding down a day job as a trainee electrician at a government sponsored firm, Ultra Electronics. "That was the first of twenty-three jobs I started within two years," he recalled years later to *Rolling Stone*'s Jerry Hopkins in typically exaggerated fashion. "With my knowledge and personality, I was always considered 'management material.'"

RIGHT: MARK TWAIN
AND THE STRANGERS
(FROM LEFT: BARRY FOSKETT, KEITH,
PETER TREE, MIKE EVANS).

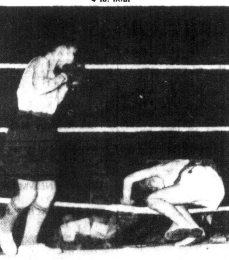

C. Hartley of Copland, in dark shorts, shoots a right to the chin of D. Caisley (Claremont) who won the Junior 5 st. 4 lb. bout

K. Moon (Alperton) who won the 5 st. 10 lb. fight, looks on as his opponent, R. Gibson (Claremont) tries to recover after being almost knocked through the ropes.

BEACHCOMBERS require good, reliable rock drummer, regular work. — Tel. WOR 7185.

BASF

"THE DETOURS"

PILOT TRACKS

SPEED: 7½.

Leerspule Nr. 10

für

MAGNETOPHONBAND BASF

Badische Anilin-& Soda-Fabrik AG.
LUDWIGSHAFEN AM RHEIN

THE KIDS ARE ALRIGHT
1958-1963

On Saturday, 6 December 1958, the Congregational Church Hall on Churchfield Road, Acton, opened a "Youth Club" each Thursday and Saturday, known as the "Congo Club." Each night, local amateur skiffle and trad jazz hopefuls could attack their favourite Lonnie Donegan or Acker Bilk tunes (or at least the ones they could play) in a mighty bid for the sometimes embarrassingly scanty audiences' attention. It was such a night, during the summer of 1959, that Acton County Grammar schoolboys, John Entwistle and Pete Townshend, made their first public appearance together as part of the Confederates. Pete, for one, was nervous. "We stood up there with about five people in the room, and I really blushed," he told Richard Green. "It was the only time in my whole life that I've been nervous on a stage."

With the Confederates in a constant state of flux, John was lured off to a rival trad band. Pete was ostracised after a violent altercation with drummer Chris Sherwin, and subsequently diverted his attentions away from the banjo to the £3 Czechoslovakian acoustic guitar he had acquired from his parents' antique shop, "Miscellania," on Ealing Common.

Besides, the tide was turning on trad jazz and, thanks to Bert Weedon's *Play In A Day Guitar Guide*, Britain was starting to produce its own indigenous (albeit watered down) version of invigorating American rock and roll.

In 1958, Cliff Richard scored with "Move It," England's first bona fide rock and roll single. Townshend was more impressed with the song's distinctive guitar work—played by Hank Marvin, the nerdish guitarist in Cliff's backing band, the Shadows—than with any charisma the singer possessed. The withdrawn fourteen-year-old was acutely aware of the large proboscis that was making his adolescence hellish. "This seemed to be the biggest thing in my life; my fucking nose, man," he told *Rolling Stone*'s Jann Wenner years later. "It was the reason I did everything. It's the reason I played guitar—because of my nose..."

After flirting briefly with the guitar, John Entwistle had discovered the electric bass, inspired by the "twanging" sound and bass string solos of Duane Eddy. "I was playing trumpet in a dance band, playing at interesting venues like Joe Lyons and social clubs," he told Tony Jasper. "I was quite interested in the guitar in the band, but the guitarist kept breaking strings. I think he must have tuned it wrong. Anyway, I had a guitar-playing friend who had made his own amp, and he wanted me to join him in a group playing trumpet. When we got together, he was louder than me, so I thought I'd better enquire into this guitar thing! I looked at 6-strings, but I found bass was much easier—mainly because the strings are further apart. There were only two or three you could buy in England in those days, Tuxedo, Star and Lucky 7, and they were all too expensive. I wanted a Fender, but they just weren't available. I think Jet Harris of the Shadows was the only person who had one then."

Ever practical, John, like Roger, resolved to build his own. "I had one made up, same sort of shape, but not really very good. It had a great, square-backed neck, just glued on to the body. One day when I was playing it, the glue gave out and I had an instant four-string harp!" He replaced it with a similar, cheaply-made model that Townshend remembered as sounding "pretty good," although Entwistle's estimation of "diabolical" was probably nearer the mark.

The pair played in groups like the Aristocrats and the Scorpions, formed by guitarist Pete Wilson

and drummer Mick Brown. The group rarely ventured out of their East Acton practices, although a second ill-rehearsed gig did occur at the Congo Club sometime in the early part of 1960. "The Congo wasn't just a place where we got together and entertained the troops, as it were," Pete recalled to Richard Green. "There was a lot of violence and sex and stuff going on... We played Shadows numbers, which must be the cliché story, but that's the way it was... There just weren't any other groups around. I was terribly happy with it, people quite liked us, and it was incredibly exciting when we appeared in front of an audience. It gave me a new confidence... I was getting into the guitar and it became an obsession."

Meanwhile, sixteen-year-old Roger Daltrey was busy playing lead guitar with his group, the Detours, in between graduating from tea boy to apprentice sheet metal worker at a factory on Colville Road, South Acton. Daltrey met John Entwistle carrying his home-made bass, with girlfriend Alison lugging his amplifier, as they returned from a Scorpions rehearsal to the Entwistle residence on Southfield Road. "I remember Roger said, 'I hear you play bass,'" said John, "which I thought was funny considering I was carrying one without a case!"

Roger casually invited John to a rehearsal being held the following week at drummer Harry Wilson's house on Yew Tree Road, Shepherd's Bush. Entwistle knew of the Detours, but was wary of Daltrey's Teddy boy reputation, which preceded him from Acton County Grammar. "Roger told me they had some gigs coming up, which was a lie, and that they were making money, which was a lie, but I went along to the rehearsal anyway." Afterwards, Daltrey enquired of John, "Do you think we're any good?" Entwistle decided there was nothing to lose by leaving the Scorpions (and Pete) to throw in his lot with the Detours.

The Detours featured an ever changing line-up that, along with Roger and John, was comprised of vocalist Colin Dawson, drummer Harry Wilson, and rhythm guitarist Reg Bowen, whose family home was used for band rehearsals. "I didn't have an amp," Entwistle recalled, "so I used to plug into his radio-gram." Originally, there was an additional rhythm guitarist, Roy East, whose inclusion had been justified by his expensive Vox 15s amplifier; it became the group's after he tragically drowned on holiday.

After six months, with Bowen's abilities as a rhythm player limited at best ("he only knew three

Wilson and his father were conveniently away on holiday, Sandom joined the Detours as their permanent drummer during the summer of 1962.

The Detours were indistinguishable from any other Shadows-influenced band in the area, performing in matching suits, with Colin Dawson crooning à la Cliff Richard in a dapper navy blue blazer and light grey slacks. Between the whirl of youth clubs, weddings, and company dances, Dawson was a sales rep for a Danish bacon company, Sandom a bricklayer for a joinery firm, and Daltrey still earning £7 a week at the sheet metal factory. "I used to get up at eight o'clock, work in the factory until six o'clock at night, and then the group from seven till midnight," Roger recalled.

After sitting for their GCEs, John and Pete left Acton County Grammar, John to start work as a trainee tax officer for Inland Revenue at it's Bromyard Avenue office, East Acton. "I had a choice when I left school of either going to art school or music school," he remembered, "but there was some trouble from my family about the music thing, and I didn't particularly want to go to art school. So my mother got me a job at the tax office, where at least I was starting to earn money."

Pete enrolled in a four-year graphic design course at Ealing Art College, on St. Mary's Road. His mother, Betty, solved the Detours' eternal transport problem by driving their gear to gigs in the yellow Ford van used for her antiques business. The group

chords," according to Entwistle), John began pitching his schoolfriend Pete Townshend as a replacement. Daltrey remembered the gangly youth in the year below as "a nose on a stick," but when the two met in the corridor at Acton County Grammar, Roger invited him to join. Pete had a Harmony single pickup Stratocruiser guitar, which he'd sprayed red, and was won over by John's promise of the use of the Vox amp. "What I didn't tell him was he'd be sharing with Roger," said Entwistle. "Meanwhile, I was plugged into the other AC15 with the PA!"

With Bowen's house now unavailable for rehearsals, the fledgling group resorted to subterfuge. While Roger's parents were out for the evening, their bed would be pushed against the wall, allowing space for a few hours of illicit band practice in the front room. Like any other aspiring combo of the period, the Detours' repertoire included an all-encompassing pot-pourri of Shadows and Ventures instrumentals, current pop hits, and even trad jazz,

featuring Pete on banjo, John on trumpet, and Roger blowing trombone.

"It became a good social thing," Pete told Richard Green. "The drummer's father ran us about in his Dormobile, and we got a lot of seaside gigs. We did an audition at Peckham Paradise Club for £7 a night, which we thought was very good."

Roger had chanced upon drummer Doug Sandom, from South Acton, outside a rehearsal hall on Beaumont Road. At twenty-six, Sandom was some eight years older—a fact he swiftly concealed by knocking several years off his age. He was also married, with a child on the way. However, these deficiencies were overlooked in recognition of his proficiency and experience; he had played semi-pro for the past two years. "Dougie" first met his future bandmates outside Acton Town Hall, as they waited for the Dormobile to deliver them to the Paradise, where he "sat in" on certain numbers. While Harry

would then travel separately by train, or if this proved impractical, they would squeeze uncomfortably into the back of the van.

As well as providing wheels, Betty was adept at procuring work by calling in favours with various contacts in the business. She arranged several important auditions on the group's behalf, the first at the Castle Hill Hotel, Richmond. After reading of his successful dances at Acton's White Hart Hotel in the *Ealing and Acton Gazette*, Betty hustled an audition through sheer persistence with local promoter Robert Druce at the Oldfield Hotel, 1089 Greenford Road, Greenford.

Druce ran Commercial Entertainments Ltd. with partner Barry Foran from his home at 58 Abbotts Drive, North Wembley, and was responsible for booking exclusive "Club Druane" dances around a widespread pub circuit. On any given night, one could catch his stable of bands, including Peter Nelson and the Travellers, Bobby King and the Sabres, the Images, the Corvettes, the Riversiders, the Presidents, the Federals, and the Bel-Airs, gigging in the hall's adjoining pubs like the White Hart, 264 High Street, Acton, as well as at the Goldhawk Social Club, 205 Goldhawk Road, Shepherd's Bush. Druce also ran promotions further afield—in the West End at the Notre Dame Hall, Leicester Square, and in South London at St. Mary's Ballroom, Hotham Road, Putney, and the Glenlyn Ballroom Dance Club, 15a Perry Vale, Forest Hill.

The Bel-Airs were appearing at the Oldfield on a Tuesday night when the Detours nervously auditioned during the interval, borrowing their equipment to play several numbers. "What do you

RIGHT: PETER VERNON-KELL.

think of the lads?" asked regular compère Louie Hunt. "Do you want them back?" Audience reaction was favourable; the Detours had passed the acid test. The Detours were on Commercial Entertainments' books with the group agreeing to pay Druce 10% commission on all work he offered. If a booking came from outside the agency, the promoter in question deducted a further 10%. As acting manager, Druce paid for the group's own van—a Dewhurst grocery model Roger found for £115—by deducting £10 from their weekly earnings.

By the end of 1962, the sound of electrified Chicago rhythm and blues was replacing trad jazz around London's hipper clubs. Alexis Korner's legendary Blues Incorporated were the forefathers of this new music, and the Ealing Club, directly opposite Ealing Broadway station, became its mecca. Pete got his first glimpse of the embryonic Rolling Stones on the station platform, and the bohemian sensibility they exuded was not lost on the image-conscious art student. Suddenly, the social scene at college was buzzing around this charismatic bunch of urchins playing such obscure but exciting music.

The Detours were slow to make changes, playing it safe with trad jazz and conventional Top Twenty covers. Thanks to mutual acquaintance Phil Rhodes (the clarinet player in John and Pete's school band, the Confederates), Peter Vernon-Kell, from Acton Vale, joined for a short period to play lead guitar and Claviolene. He eventually left to form the Macabre, another regular group on the Druce circuit, and became a record producer in the 70's, forming his own PVK Records. By this time, Colin Dawson, newly-engaged, was increasingly looked upon as being too straight and therefore, expendable. When he finally quit after one argument too many, Roger, who in Townshend's words "really was the balls in the band and ran things the way he wanted them," stepped into the breach by taking on the extra role of lead vocalist.

Art school in early sixties Britain became a veritable breeding ground for the prime movers behind the 60's "Beat Boom." John Lennon, Keith Richards, Eric Clapton, Ray Davies, Ron Wood, David Bowie, Dick Taylor, and Phil May were just some who served art college apprenticeships before moving on to musical careers. "I didn't learn much about art in art school, but I did learn a lot about guitar playing" was Richards' succinct (and accurate) summation.

Pete Townshend's time at Ealing Art College was undoubtedly the most important component in his personal and creative development. "I soon decided that I was going to get nowhere as an introvert and that I'd become an extrovert," he told his friend, fellow graphic artist Richard "Barney" Barnes, "and that's what I did."

As well as sharpening his social skills, Pete's mind was broadened by the unorthodox curriculums, which aimed to break down all preconceived notions about art. There were important and often controversial lectures and displays given by jazz musicians, film writers, and artists such as Peter Blake and Jasper Johns (whose pop art symbolism utilising targets and badges was later adopted by the Who so effectively), Larry Rivers, Robert Brownjohn, and radical playright David Mercer. Some lessons were spent simply listening to jazz or classical music.

After hearing about Pete's guitar playing from fellow student Tim Bartlett, Tom Wright, an Ealing photography student from Alabama, introduced himself and asked for lessons. It would prove a seminal encounter. While his family was stationed at the U.S. airbase in nearby West Ruislip, Wright roomed with a friend from Oklahoma, Campbell "Cam" McLester, in a second story flat at 35 Sunnyside Road, around the corner from the college. Pete soon became a constant fixture there. The worldly Southerners introduced the neophyte to the potent influences of jazz, soul, and black American R&B, along with the insidious delights of

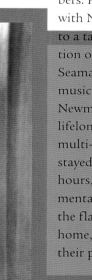

ABOVE: TOM WRIGHT.
RIGHT: "CAM" McLESTER AT EALING ART COLLEGE.

marijuana—then a rare commodity in Britain.

Cam and Tom's stunning record collection encompassed everything from the rural folk of Leadbelly to the urban Chicago blues of Bo Diddley, Jimmy Reed, and John Lee Hooker, and the cool jazz of Ray Charles, Barney Kessel, and Mose Allison. For the first time, Pete heard Chuck Berry, whose songwriting vistas left an impression, as did Steve Cropper's stinging leads on Booker T and the M.G.'s "Green Onions."

Listening to these revelatory sounds was made even more attractive by the aromatic and verdant herb. "When I first got into pot, I was involved in the environment more," Pete told Zigzag. "There was a newness about art college, having beautiful girls around for the first time in my life, having all that music around me for the first time, and it was such a great period, with the Beatles and all that exploding all over the place."

In December 1962, Pete attended a lecture/slide demonstration by Austrian artist Gustav Metzger entitled "Auto-Destructive Art, Auto-Creative Art: The Struggle For The Machine Arts Of The Future." At another such event, jazz bassist Malcolm Cecil ritually demolished a double bass by sawing through it. One lunch hour, eccentric pianist and GPO telephone engineer Andrew "Thunderclap" Newman played bizarre arrangements of various jazz numbers. Pete became intrigued with Newman after listening to a tape on the recommendation of a mutual friend, Dick Seaman. Unable to read music, Pete followed Newman's example, starting a lifelong infatuation with multi-track recording. He stayed up into the small hours, making bizarre, experimental sound montages in the flat above his parents' home, the volume testing their patience to the limit.

In early 1963, a lucrative Sunday afternoon engagement came up at the Douglas House, a private hotel off Bayswater Road. The Detours were offered £20 for two hours entertainment, playing country and western music for American servicemen—good work for the time if you could find it. Although Pete's Chet Atkins-style fingerpicking was ideally suited, Roger (now the vocalist) was no Jim Reeves. Enter Gabby Connolly, from West Acton, previously the singer and bassist with the Bel-Airs, (ironically the group whose instruments the Detours

had borrowed for the Bob Druce audition). Over the three month stint, Connolly alternated vocals with Roger, playing bass when John switched to trumpet and Roger blew trombone for a Dixieland spot.

As Daltrey's confidence grew, Gabby was eased out, but not before providing John with his first proper bass. "He had a '61 Fender Precision, but he had some HP [hire purchase] troubles," Entwistle recalled. "He kept the guitar hidden under his girlfriend's bed. He said I could have it if I paid off his £50 HP debt. Roger thought it kept blowing up the speakers and convinced me to get rid of it, and like a fool, I later sold it."

On occasion, Druce booked the Detours as support to such names as Screaming Lord Sutch and the Savages, Cliff Bennett and the Rebel Rousers, and Shane Fenton and the Fentones. (Fenton went on to achieve fame in Britain during the early 70's as Alvin Stardust.) Opening for Johnny Kidd and the Pirates at St. Mary's Ballroom in Putney, the musicians came away with their minds blown by the simplicity and sheer power of the Pirates four-man singer-guitar-rhythm section configuration. Willesden-born Kidd (née Fred Heath) became a seminal figure from the barren pre-Beatles era in England with "Please Don't Touch" (1959) and "Shakin' All Over" (1960). "My favourite group was Johnny Kidd and the Pirates, with Mick Green on guitar," said Pete. "That's where we first heard R&B second-hand."

ABOVE: JOHNNY KIDD & THE PIRATES, FEATURING MICK GREEN (RIGHT).

Green, like Townshend, was a great admirer of James Burton's unique string bending style, used to such great effect on Ricky Nelson records. From the impact of seeing the Pirates, the Who's unique ensemble approach gradually developed. Following Green's lead, Townshend concentrated on combining rhythm and lead to partly compensate for the lack of a second guitar in the band—an unorthodox,

1
9
6
2

yet effective part of the group's dynamics. "I couldn't play properly, and I built up a style around chords," Pete admitted. Entwistle's trebly bass now underpinned the sound by acting largely as a melodic instrument.

Roger's fingers were often split from sheet metal work, so he sold the Epiphone solid his father had bought him to Pete on an instalment basis, becoming the singer full-time. The group dropped songs that his vocal range couldn't handle, and as a result, were sometimes forced to repeat numbers. John often went to work at the tax office with no voice after straining his larynx on repeated requests for "I Saw Her Standing There" and "Twist And Shout."

Although impressed by the Lennon-McCartney self-sufficiency and already introduced to the work of Bob Dylan, songwriting was still of only marginal interest to Townshend at this point. However, one Sunday evening, circa autumn 1963, the Detours tentatively recorded two of his earliest compositions. The father of Pete Wilson, a former Scorpions bandmate of Townshend and Entwistle's, knew Barry Gray, the musical director of the popular children's TV series *Fireball XL5*. Thanks to both the Wilsons' influence, the Detours got the opportunity to record a demo at Gray's home studio, which was simply two downstairs rooms converted into a studio and control room.

"That was a one-track mono tape machine," Entwistle remembered, "with just a string reverb unit and a Baby Binson." With Gray engineering, the group laid down a cover of Chuck Berry's (via the Rolling Stones) "Come On," featuring Roger on harmonica. They also recorded two of Pete's songs, "It Was You" and "Please Don't Send Me Home," both lightweight Merseybeat offerings, with the latter featuring John on lead vocal. "It Was You" stayed in the group's repertoire for a brief period, and they recorded the song again as the Who the following year. It was eventually given away to an Essex group, the Naturals.

In December 1963, Cam McLester and Tom Wright were busted for possession of hemp and recommended for deportation. At short notice, Tom asked Pete and Richard Barnes to take over their flat and the Aladdin's cave of a record collection. (Wright would become the Who's American tour manager in the late 60's.) Constantly exposed to such great sounds, Pete subtly introduced certain numbers into Detours' rehearsals, which were held in the back

room of the Durbanwater Social Club, on Strafford Road, South Acton. Initially, this met with stubborn resistance from the surly singer, who sensed his leadership being challenged. The fact that this layabout art student wasn't working for a living rankled the blue-collar Daltrey, who resented Townshend's hipster sneering and waspish putdowns. Entwistle and Sandom confined themselves impassively to the sidelines.

"We played Beatles songs for about six months and then we completely forgot that and went on a really heavy blues trip," Daltrey told Gary Herman. "That gave us our freedom, that's when we really started putting out any sort of new music... Playing pop before, you just copied a record, and that was it. If we got near to the record we were happy. But blues was a completely different thing altogether. There was so little in a blues song that you had to do something different, improvise."

The decision to play R&B exclusively came after the group played a short notice fill-in spot at the Oldfield, as a favour for Bob Druce. "We lost all the fans we had at the time by playing blues," Daltrey told Herman. "It took about six months for them all to come back, but when they did, we found that we had three times as many fans as we'd had six months before." By the end of 1963, the Detours had become one of Druce's most popular draws, playing up to five nights a week, earning on average £12 a night.

On one of these dates in December, the Detours supported the Rolling Stones at St. Mary's Ballroom, Putney, playing Howlin' Wolf, Jimmy Reed, Muddy Waters, and John Lee Hooker numbers with Roger on harmonica. For Pete, the Stones' appearance was nothing short of a revelation: "I think we learned more about rock theatre that night than any other. I mean, Jagger walked on stage and was a star to me. It did me in." However, it was Keith Richards who inadvertently gave Townshend one of his most visually distinctive trademarks. As the curtains were about to part, Pete noticed Richards stretch his right arm up in an arc over his guitar as a limbering-up exercise. From then on, Townshend's exaggerated display of swinging his arm like a windmill, before crashing it down across the strings, earned him a nickname: "The Birdman."

RIGHT: A CLIPPING FROM THE SOUTH WESTERN STAR, DATED 10 AUGUST, 1962.

THEN one day he heard the strains of pop music coming from a hall in East Hill, looked in, and found Mark Twain and the Strangers — I'd never heard of them either — rehearsing their repertoire.

He got chatting with the leader of the group — this Twain did meet — and found out that what were needed was some original compositions and a manager.

Brian fulfilled the first requirement with four numbers, the first he has written and all were accepted by the group. He was then offered the job of manager.

Well, one or two dates followed and these led to others and so on until now there's quite a busy time ahead for the Strangers, and they, of course, are becoming better known every day.

German tour

BUT the plum booking of the lot so far is a six months' tour of U.S. Army bases in Western Germany, commencing in October. Brian leaves next week to make the final arrangements.

Recording and television prospects for the group are improving and Brian's confident tip is: "They're going straight to the top of the tree."

Before leaving for the continent there are a couple of West End dates to be fulfilled.

Mark Twain — with a name like that he's the one who should be writing stories for the American magazines — is 19 and comes from Burgess Hill in Sussex. He, of course, is the vocalist. Two members of the group, 18-year-old guitarists Barry Foskett and Michael Evans, are from East Hill. The group is completed by 16-year-old drummer Keith Moon, from Wembley.

Of Brian's four compositions two are songs: "Margie" and "You're Breaking My Heart." The other two, "Blue" and "Rock," are instrumentals for guitars and drums.

1962

(THE DETOURS)

CIRCA JULY/AUGUST

Paradise Club, 3 Consort Road, Peckham, South East London.

The fledgling Detours played at least five Friday night gigs at this ironically-named ballroom in the borough of Southwark. "I had to study to pass another couple of GCEs to become a fully-fledged tax officer," recalled John Entwistle. "Every Wednesday, they sent me to this day school in Holborn, where I made friends with this kid from Peckham who attended all the same classes as me. We used to go to lunchtime dances at the Lyceum and skip the afternoon economics lesson to go window shopping at Jennings and Selmer music shops down Charing Cross Road. This guy was a regular at this place [the Paradise], and he got us the gig. It was all word-of-mouth, there were no posters up.

"The first time we turned up to play, there was hardly anybody there, just some girls. Around 10 o'clock, their boyfriends all turned up with bloody noses and black eyes. It turns out they'd been at another club and started a brawl. What we didn't know is that the other club would come by the following week, and it would be our turn to get our gear trashed. So we figured we'd do one more and not bother turning up the following week! We got paid around £7 per night, but after we paid for the Dormobile, we only had about £2 between the five of us."

SATURDAY, 1 SEPTEMBER

Town Hall, Acton, West London.

At a "Gala Ball" to mark the re-opening of the venue, "The Detours Jazz Group" supported the Ron Cavendish Orchestra. Local promoter Robert Druce was in the audience, persuaded by Betty Townshend to see her son's group. Druce came away distinctly underwhelmed, but through sheer persistence on Betty's part, an audition was arranged at the Oldfield Hotel, Greenford.

Two band impact!

TOWN HALL DANCE GALA SWINGS WITH NEW LOOK

SOFT lights, hot music, and big names brought about a "spectacular increase in attendance from the usual figure of a hundred-plus to more than 317" at the Gala Ball at the Town Hall on Saturday.

Glad to see so many stepping out on the first night of the new season was Mr. George Scott, Town Hall Entertainments Manager.

He put the success down to the two bands — the Ron Cavendish Orchestra and the "Detours" Jazz Group — which supplied music for all ages, the display by Peter Eggleton and Brenda Winslade, this year's international professional dancing champions, and the redecoration of the hall.

Licence

Six revolving lights, adding glamour to the scene in six colours, floral decorations for the stage, foyer and tables, and a licence, extending until 11.30, have all been added to ensure the success of the Council's Entertainment Committee's weekly dances and special Christmas and New Year Balls.

Attractions like Saturday's demonstration pair, who danced an encore, and the additional group which supplied the gist of the twist are hoped to be included as often as possible.

The buffet, run by the Council Catering Committee, and the novelty and prize spots will be maintained.

The Chris Stone, Fred Hedley and Phill Spurr orchestras are among the attractions this side of Christmas.

Acton jazz and jive group, the "Detours," at last found their way to a local booking on Saturday when they were the second band at Saturday's Gala Ball at the Town Hall. Left to right : Roger Daltrey (18), Colin Dawson (19), Peter Townsend (17), Doug Sandon (18), and John Johns (17)

FRIDAY, 23 NOVEMBER

Grand Ballroom, Broadstairs, Kent.

Bob Druce tested the water by providing a regular Friday night booking. The band played two sets at this coastal town near Margate and were paid £20, including expenses. The band either travelled with the gear in Betty Townshend's van, or were driven by Brian Taylor, the doorman at the White Hart, Acton. "Broadstairs usually had an audience of twenty five and that was every kid in the area," said Entwistle. "We didn't realise it was a place you went to retire. It was the same twenty-five kids every week.

"I remember the first time we played there, we were running late, and there was nobody around. As we were unloading the equipment, this coach turned up, and we thought 'great, this must be our audience.' The driver got out and started unloading all these wheelchairs!"

FRIDAY, 30 NOVEMBER

Grand Ballroom, Broadstairs.

1963

FRIDAY, 4 JANUARY

Grand Ballroom, Broadstairs.

FRIDAY, 11 JANUARY

The Fox and Goose Hotel, Hanger Lane, Ealing, West London.

FRIDAY, 18 JANUARY

Grand Ballroom, Broadstairs.

SATURDAY, 19 JANUARY

"New Years Rave," CAV Sports Ground, Northolt, Middlesex.

SUNDAY, 17 FEBRUARY

A regular Sunday double booking commenced at the Douglas House, 14 & 16 Clanricarde Gardens, Bayswater, West London, during the afternoon, followed by an evening gig at the White Hart Hotel, Acton.

MONDAY, 18 FEBRUARY

White Hart Hotel, Acton.

A Monday night residency for which the group was paid £10.

THURSDAY, 21 FEBRUARY

Oldfield Hotel, Greenford.

FRIDAY, 22 FEBRUARY
Grand Ballroom, Broadstairs.

SATURDAY, 23 FEBRUARY
Oldfield Hotel, Greenford.

SUNDAY, 24 FEBRUARY
Douglas House, Bayswater/White Hart Hotel, Acton.

MONDAY, 25 FEBRUARY
White Hart Hotel, Acton.

THURSDAY, 28 FEBRUARY
Oldfield Hotel, Greenford.

SUNDAY, 3 MARCH
Douglas House, Bayswater/White Hart Hotel, Acton.

MONDAY, 4 MARCH
White Hart Hotel, Acton.

THURSDAY, 7 MARCH
Oldfield Hotel, Greenford.

SATURDAY, 9 MARCH
Osterley Hotel, Isleworth, Middlesex.

SUNDAY, 10 MARCH
Douglas House, Bayswater.

MONDAY, 11 MARCH
White Hart Hotel, Acton.

WEDNESDAY, 13 MARCH
Mazenod Church Hall, Kilburn, North West London.

THURSDAY, 14 MARCH
Oldfield Hotel, Greenford.

SUNDAY, 17 MARCH
Douglas House, Bayswater.

MONDAY, 18 MARCH
White Hart Hotel, Acton.

THURSDAY, 21 MARCH
Oldfield Hotel, Greenford.

FRIDAY, 22 MARCH
Grand Ballroom, Broadstairs.

SUNDAY, 24 MARCH
Douglas House, Bayswater.

MONDAY, 25 MARCH
White Hart Hotel, Acton.

THURSDAY, 28 MARCH
Oldfield Hotel, Greenford.

FRIDAY, 29 MARCH
College of Distributive Trade, Charing Cross Road, London, in place of Grand Ballroom, Broadstairs. Two sets, 7:30—9:00 pm and 10:00—10:30 pm, paid £25.

SUNDAY, 31 MARCH
Douglas House, Bayswater.

MONDAY, 1 APRIL
White Hart Hotel, Acton.

THURSDAY, 4 APRIL
Oldfield Hotel, Greenford.

SATURDAY, 6 APRIL
CAV Sports Ground, Northolt.

SUNDAY, 7 APRIL
Douglas House, Bayswater.

MONDAY, 8 APRIL
White Hart Hotel, Acton.

THURSDAY, 11 APRIL
Oldfield Hotel, Greenford.

SATURDAY, 13 APRIL
Oldfield Hotel, Greenford.

SUNDAY, 14 APRIL
Douglas House, Bayswater.

MONDAY, 15 APRIL
White Hart Hotel, Acton.

THURSDAY, 18 APRIL
Oldfield Hotel, Greenford.

SUNDAY, 21 APRIL
Douglas House, Bayswater.

MONDAY, 22 APRIL
White Hart Hotel, Acton.

THURSDAY, 25 APRIL
Oldfield Hotel, Greenford.

SATURDAY, 27 APRIL
Oldfield Hotel, Greenford.

SUNDAY, 28 APRIL
Douglas House, Bayswater.

MONDAY, 29 APRIL
White Hart Hotel, Acton.

TUESDAY, 30 APRIL
Oldfield Hotel, Greenford.

SUNDAY, 5 MAY
Douglas House, Bayswater/White Hart Hotel, Acton.

THURSDAY, 9 MAY
White Hart Hotel, Acton.

SATURDAY, 11 MAY
Oldfield Hotel,
Greenford.

SUNDAY, 12 MAY
Douglas House,
Bayswater.

FRIDAY, 17 MAY
Park Hotel, Carnival Ballroom, Hanwell,
West London.

SATURDAY, 18 MAY
Oldfield Hotel, Greenford.

SUNDAY, 19 MAY
Douglas House, Bayswater.

Direction: Ron Edwards

Bob Druce Management
(Licensed by the Westminster City Council)

Sole Agents for Bands & Artistes

244 EDGWARE ROAD, MARBLE ARCH, LONDON. W.2
723-0135/5602

THURSDAY, 23 MAY
Oldfield Hotel, Greenford.

FRIDAY, 24 MAY
Grand Ballroom, Broadstairs.

SUNDAY, 26 MAY
Douglas House, Bayswater/White Hart Hotel, Acton.
This final Sunday double booking marked Gabby Connolly's last gig with the Detours.

TUESDAY, 28 MAY
Oldfield Hotel, Greenford.

FRIDAY, 31 MAY
Grand Ballroom, Broadstairs, supporting Freddie
and the Dreamers.

SATURDAY, 1 JUNE
Oldfield Hotel, Greenford.

THURSDAY, 6 JUNE
White Hart Hotel, Acton.

FRIDAY, 7 JUNE
Goldhawk Social Club, Shepherd's Bush.

SATURDAY, 8 JUNE
Oldfield Hotel, Greenford.

SUNDAY, 9 JUNE
White Hart Hotel, Acton.

THURSDAY, 13 JUNE
White Hart Hotel, Acton.

FRIDAY, 14 JUNE
GEC Pavilion, Preston Road, Wembley, North
West London.

SATURDAY, 15 JUNE
Oldfield Hotel, Greenford.

THURSDAY, 20 JUNE
Oldfield Hotel, Greenford.

SATURDAY, 22 JUNE
The Detours were paid £15 to play a wedding recep-
tion at the Millet Arms, Perivale, booked by one S.
Baker through Bob Druce.

SUNDAY, 23 JUNE
White Hart Hotel, Acton.

THURSDAY, 27 JUNE
Oldfield Hotel, Greenford.

SATURDAY, 29 JUNE
Oldfield Hotel, Greenford.

SUNDAY, 30 JUNE
White Hart Hotel, Acton.

THURSDAY, 4 JULY
Oldfield Hotel, Greenford.

FRIDAY, 5 JULY
Goldhawk Social Club, Shepherd's Bush.

SATURDAY, 6 JULY
Oldfield Hotel, Greenford.

SUNDAY, 7 JULY
White Hart Hotel, Acton.

THURSDAY, 11 JULY
Oldfield Hotel, Greenford.

S. BAKER.
25 DEACON Rd
WILLESDEN
N.W.2.

6th July 1963

Dear Sir,

Please find enclosed one cheque for payment of the hire of "the Detours" on the 22ND of last month. I must congratulate them on their playing that night, it was the best they have ever played. But unfortunately I can't say the same for their behaviour at one time, especially towards one of the married women — believe me our parents soon told us off. but still it was probably the beer that done it! We are hoping to have another party about xmas time and would like to hire them again if we do, providing you come along too.

All the Best
S. Baker.

P.S. SORRY FOR THE DELAY Sir.

THE DETOU

FRIDAY, 12 JULY
Goldhawk Social Club, Shepherd's Bush.

SUNDAY, 14 JULY
White Hart Hotel, Acton.

THURSDAY, 18 JULY
Oldfield Hotel, Greenford.

SATURDAY, 20 JULY
Oldfield Hotel, Greenford.

SUNDAY, 21 JULY
White Hart Hotel, Acton.

TUESDAY, 23 JULY
Oldfield Hotel, Greenford.

THURSDAY, 25 JULY
Oldfield Hotel, Greenford.

FRIDAY, 26 JULY
Notre Dame Church Hall, 5 Leicester Place, off Leicester Square, London.
    A regular Friday night "Notre Dame De Danse," from 8:00 pm—12 midnight, paid £16.

SATURDAY, 27 JULY — FRIDAY, 9 AUGUST
A fortnight's holiday.

SATURDAY, 10 AUGUST
Oldfield Hotel, Greenford.

SUNDAY, 11 AUGUST
White Hart Hotel, Acton.

THURSDAY, 15 AUGUST
White Hart Hotel, Acton.

FRIDAY, 16 AUGUST
Goldhawk Social Club, Shepherd's Bush.

SATURDAY, 17 AUGUST
Oldfield Hotel, Greenford.

SUNDAY, 18 AUGUST
White Hart Hotel, Acton.

TUESDAY, 20 AUGUST
Oldfield Hotel, Greenford.

THURSDAY, 22 AUGUST
Oldfield Hotel, Greenford.

SUNDAY, 25 AUGUST
White Hart Hotel, Acton.

TUESDAY, 27 AUGUST
Oldfield Hotel, Greenford.

THURSDAY, 29 AUGUST
Oldfield Hotel, Greenford.

FRIDAY, 30 AUGUST
Notre Dame Church Hall, London.

SUNDAY, 1 SEPTEMBER
White Hart Hotel, Acton.

THURSDAY, 5 SEPTEMBER
Oldfield Hotel, Greenford.

FRIDAY, 6 SEPTEMBER
Goldhawk Social Club, Shepherd's Bush.

SATURDAY, 7 SEPTEMBER
Oldfield Hotel, Greenford.

SUNDAY, 8 SEPTEMBER
White Hart Hotel, Acton.

FRIDAY, 13 SEPTEMBER
Glenlyn Ballroom, Forest Hill, South East London.

SUNDAY, 15 SEPTEMBER
White Hart Hotel, Acton.

THURSDAY, 19 SEPTEMBER
Oldfield Hotel, Greenford.

SUNDAY, 22 SEPTEMBER
White Hart Hotel, Acton.

THURSDAY, 26 SEPTEMBER
Oldfield Hotel, Greenford.

FRIDAY, 27 SEPTEMBER
Notre Dame Church Hall, London.

SATURDAY, 28 SEPTEMBER
Oldfield Hotel, Greenford.

SUNDAY, 29 SEPTEMBER
White Hart Hotel, Acton.

The Beachcombers, a local "beat" group, with the van they bought to carry their instruments. The guitarists are (left-right) Tony Brind, John Schollar and Norman Mitchener. On top of the van is the group's drummer, Keith Moon, and their singer, Clyde Burns—real name, Ron Chinnery. The group is starting a tour of London dance halls. Past engagements have included "backing" singer Gene Vincent on a cross-channel ferry show

Fan club president at work : Angela Dives answers letters from admirers the Detours

Town Hall twisting

● LUNCHTIME rock 'n' roller Denny Piercy, the man whose " Parade of the Pops " cry kicks off radio's mid-day music show, is booked for an Acton date in the evening.

He has agreed to compere a parade of musical talent at Acton Town Hall. It's designed to give local groups a look at new instruments and playing techniques.

Doing the playing and instructing will be Geoff Love, drummer Bobby Kevin, Bob Miller, guitar man Eric Ford, B.B.C. accordionist Jack Emblow, Kenny Baker's pianist Lawrie Holloway, harmonica player Harry Pitch and Vic Kettle's modern jazz group.

Acton twist and shout group The Detours have found their way into the programme and will be providing some of the music. The show is set for November 26 and, what do you know, admission is free.

The swinging Detours from Acton (left to right): Roger Daultry, Peter Town John Entwistle and Doug Sandom

...RS ARE FINDING
WAY
TO FAME

● ARE YOU getting fed-up with the Beatles? Then try screaming for a homegrown group: The Detours. I'm sure they would appreciate it.

Twenty - year - old Angela Dives, of Gibbon-road, East Acton, is the girl to contact for information about the Detours. She is the President of their fan club (over 30 members and growing fast).

And she has no doubts about the top-pop quality of her favourite group, though she wasn't quite sure what made them so special.

"They have a good sense of humour," she said after a little thought. "They laugh and crack jokes on the stage. And they can play very good harmonies."

The Detours are apparently a versatile group, too. They all sing, they all play the harmonica, one of their guitarists plays the trumpet as well and the vocalist plays the trombone.

The founders of the group got their experience years ago in the dark days of skiffle Then they formed the Detours guitar group in the summer, 1961 — and went steadily from success to success. Now the group, originally a five-man organization, consists of two guitarists, a drummer and a singer: Peter Townsend (19), John Entwistle (20), Doug Sandom (25) and Roger Daultry (21).

Roger, the vocalist, and Jonn, the bass guitarist, were with the group when it was founded. The others have joined since.

What happens when you join the Detours' fan club, I asked?

"We send you a photograph of the group and a letter of welcome," said blonde Angela, who operates an accounting machine when she's not dealing with the Detours' fan mail. "And we're planning to send out a news letter as well, though nothing has come of that yet."

Applications for membership are, I'm told, coming in fairly steadily. The average is three a day.

"And nearly all of them are from outside Acton," said Angela jubilantly. "We have members in Tunbridge Wells in Kent, in East London — all over the place!"

That's nice. But the time to start really celebrating will be when the fan mail starts pouring in from Liverpool!

Pearce

THURSDAY, 3 OCTOBER
Oldfield Hotel, Greenford.

FRIDAY, 4 OCTOBER
Glenlyn Ballroom, Forest Hill.

SUNDAY, 6 OCTOBER
St. Mary's Ballroom, Putney, South West London.

THURSDAY, 10 OCTOBER
Oldfield Hotel, Greenford.

FRIDAY, 11 OCTOBER
Glenlyn Ballroom, Forest Hill.

SATURDAY, 12 OCTOBER
Oldfield Hotel, Greenford.

THURSDAY, 17 OCTOBER
Oldfield Hotel, Greenford.

THURSDAY, 24 OCTOBER
Oldfield Hotel, Greenford.

FRIDAY, 25 OCTOBER
Goldhawk Social Club, Shepherd's Bush.

SATURDAY, 26 OCTOBER
Oldfield Hotel, Greenford.

SUNDAY, 27 OCTOBER
St. Mary's Ballroom, Putney.

THURSDAY, 31 OCTOBER
Oldfield Hotel, Greenford.

FRIDAY, 1 NOVEMBER
Glenlyn Ballroom, Forest Hill.

THURSDAY, 7 NOVEMBER
Oldfield Hotel, Greenford.

FRIDAY, 8 NOVEMBER
Goldhawk Social Club, Shepherd's Bush.

SATURDAY, 9 NOVEMBER
Oldfield Hotel, Greenford.

THURSDAY, 14 NOVEMBER
Oldfield Hotel, Greenford.

FRIDAY, 15 NOVEMBER
Feathers Hotel, Ealing Broadway.

SUNDAY, 17 NOVEMBER
St. Mary's Ballroom, Putney.

THURSDAY, 21 NOVEMBER
Oldfield Hotel, Greenford.

FRIDAY, 22 NOVEMBER
Goldhawk Social Club, Shepherd's Bush.

SUNDAY, 24 NOVEMBER
White Hart Hotel, Acton.

TUESDAY, 26 NOVEMBER
Town Hall, Acton.

THURSDAY, 28 NOVEMBER
Oldfield Hotel, Greenford.

FRIDAY, 29 NOVEMBER
Goldhawk Social Club, Shepherd's Bush.

SATURDAY, 30 NOVEMBER
Railway Hotel, Greenford.

SUNDAY, 1 DECEMBER
St. Mary's Hall, Putney.

THURSDAY, 5 DECEMBER
Oldfield Hotel, Greenford.

FRIDAY, 6 DECEMBER
Glenlyn Ballroom, Forest Hill.

SATURDAY, 7 DECEMBER
California Ballroom, Dunstable, Bedfordshire, supporting Wayne Fontana and the Mindbenders.

SUNDAY, 8 DECEMBER
St. Mary's Hall, Putney.

THURSDAY, 12 DECEMBER
Oldfield Hotel, Greenford.

FRIDAY, 13 DECEMBER
Evershed and Bignoles Apprentice Association Social Club Dance, Feathers Hotel, Ealing Broadway, West London.

SATURDAY, 14 DECEMBER
Oldfield Hotel, Greenford.

SUNDAY, 15 DECEMBER
St. Mary's Hall, Putney.

THURSDAY, 19 DECEMBER
Oldfield Hotel, Greenford.

On this date, Pete filled out an official audition form on the Detours' behalf for the BBC Light Programme. Their respective roles were listed as: Drums—D. Sandom; Bass—J. Johns; Lead—P. Townshend; and Rhythm—R. Daltrey. Manager: Mr. R.A. Druce, Wembley, Middlesex.

FRIDAY, 20 DECEMBER
Glenlyn Ballroom, Forest Hill.

SUNDAY, 22 DECEMBER
St. Mary's Hall, Putney, supporting the Rolling Stones.

Recording engineer and singer with the Presidents, Glyn Johns took Pete backstage to meet the headliners. "Mick Jagger was very polite and so was Brian Jones, who was very complimentary about the Detours, and offered to help the band if he could," Townshend remembered, while Keith Richard was "completely sardonic and arrogant and unapproachable, basically."

SUNDAY, 29 DECEMBER
White Hart Hotel, Acton.

1
9
6
3

If Pete Townshend was largely responsible for the Detours' change in musical direction, it was Roger Daltrey who still called the shots. He drove the van, collected the others for gigs, dealt with the gear, planned the act, and was band go-between with Bob Druce. "You've got to remember that, left to his own devices," Daltrey recalled, "Pete would have laid in bed all day when he was at art college. If we're honest, he would have laid in bed with a joint and got up whenever he'd fancy it, and would never have made the gig! Someone had to go out and bang on the bloody door and do all that side of it, and I used to do it. I'd set the gear up because it was unbelievable in those days, you could barely get them to carry one amplifier out. We had no roadies, it was me."

Despite an uneasy alliance, Townshend and Daltrey were united in their ruthless quest forward. "I couldn't wait to get out of the fucking factory," said Daltrey. "As soon as I was out, I just wanted to get on the stage and play, anything to take you out of that world."

On 1 February, Pye recording act Johnny Devlin and the Detours appeared on the network television pop show *Thank Your Lucky Stars*. Consequently, rethinking the band's name was suddenly deemed necessary. After the following Friday night gig at the Goldhawk, the group returned to Pete's Sunnyside Road flat to rack their brains for a replacement. Various names, some serious, many not so, were put forward before a hemp-fuelled Richard Barnes suggested the Who. It was gimmicky but memorable, and being short, it would stand out distinctively on posters. The matter was settled the following day when Daltrey came by to collect Townshend. "It's the Who, 'innit?" he said to Barnes.

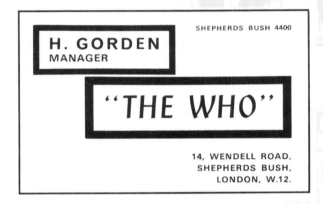

SHEPHERDS BUSH 4400

H. GORDEN
MANAGER

"THE WHO"

14, WENDELL ROAD,
SHEPHERDS BUSH,
LONDON, W.12.

In addition to a new name, the group found themselves an unlikely backer. Doug Sandom's sister-in-law Rose worked for Helmut Gorden, a German-Jewish doorknob manufacturer who owned a Shepherd's Bush brass foundry and, in Entwistle's words, "fancied himself as another Brian Epstein." Gorden expressed an interest after Doug invited him to see the Detours perform at the White Hart, Acton. Like the Beatles' svengali before him, Gorden had no music business experience, but he had enthusiasm, and more importantly, finances. He also rashly promised to secure a record deal.

Gorden formed a partnership with Bob Druce as Gorden-Druce Enterprises, Ltd., and a management agreement was drawn up and signed at the Sandom residence at 64 Wharf Court, Vincent Road, South Acton. Since most of the group were under twenty-one, Roger,

Saturday
5.45 News
The latest from the newsroom of ITN

5.50 Thank Your Lucky Stars
INTRODUCED
BY
BRIAN MATTHEW
The latest pops from the top stars on record
Tonight's *Lucky Stars* hit parade brought to you by
ADAM FAITH
and
THE ROULETTES
DICKIE VALENTINE
JACKIE TRENT
MANFRED MANN
KRIS JENSEN
HEINZ
DARYL QUIST
JOHNNY DEVLIN
and
THE DETOURS
JANICE NICHOLLS
heads a panel of teenagers who comment on the latest American releases in
Spin-a-Disc
GUEST
DISC JOCKEY
DOUG ARTHUR
DESIGNER
TONY BORER
DIRECTED
BY
MARK STUART
ABC Television Network Production

John, and Pete's guardians were required as co-signatories. Cliff and Betty Townshend's show business background made them study the fine print more closely, however, and they wisely elected not to countersign. Gorden immediately set out to impress. He paid for a new van, better equipment, and a set of leather stage outfits designed by Pete.

Gorden regularly got his hair cut by Jack Marks at the Barber Shop at 97a Edgware Road off Marble Arch. While Jack "the Barber" snipped, Gorden would regale him with stories of "ze group" and how they were poised to be the next big thing, if only they had a recording contract. Marks mentioned the Who to his other customers, including Pye producer Tony Hatch, who politely declined, having his hands full with Petula Clark and the Searchers. After having his ear bent by Marks, Chris Parmeinter, a young A&R man with the Fontana label, went to see the group perform at the Oldfield. Parmeinter was impressed, but told Gorden he had reservations about the drumming.

Dougie's wife Lillian resented the group's dominance in her husband's life, and the strain was starting to affect his playing. On top of this, there were growing musical differences, as Sandom was less than enthused with the R&B numbers the others were unapologetically in favour of playing night after night. Events accelerated after Rose casually mentioned Dougie's true age during a conversation with Gorden. Even the easy-going Entwistle, to whom Sandom was closest, noticed the growing targeting of Dougie and warned the drummer he was being "set up." Things came to a head at a recording audition held before Parmeinter on 9 April. The group ran through three numbers, including Bo Diddley's "Here 'Tis." Again, the question of the drumming was raised.

Seeing their big chance evaporating, Townshend, who was having second thoughts about the older man anyway, turned on Dougie in a rather unsubtle outburst. The normally placid drummer had reached the end of his tether. When auditioning at the White Horse pub in Willesden a year earlier, he had insisted it was "all of us or nothing" when the group had been offered a regular gig provided they lose "that gangly guitarist."

His confidence in tatters, Dougie announced he was quitting and stormed out, humiliated, to stew in a nearby cafe. Daltrey and Entwistle followed in quick pursuit to smooth things over, but he had made up his mind. With a full band workload ahead, Sandom agreed to serve out several days notice while a replacement was found. His final gig with the Who was at the 100 Club on 13 April. The experience left a bitter aftertaste, and he retired from music shortly thereafter.

Several replacement drummers were considered, including seventeen-year-old Ealing child prodigy John "Mitch" Mitchell, who worked as a part-time assistant in Marshall's Music Shop in Hanwell. (Mitchell went on to join the Riot Squad and Georgie Fame and the Blue Flames before finding success with the Jimi Hendrix Experience.) In a bind, the group employed the temporary services of session drummer Dave Gold from Marshall's, whose £4 fee ate into their earnings.

In late April, a seventeen-year-old, baby-faced trainee salesman for the plaster manufacturing company British Gypsum was watching and waiting expectantly at the Oldfield. Since joining the Beachcombers in April 1963, Keith Moon had followed the same trail of pubs, clubs, and dance halls that had kept both groups gainfully employed. Indeed, they had occasionally crossed paths on the Druce circuit. (Ironically, one of Doug Sandom's last jobs at the White Hart was filling in for Moon with the Beachcombers.) The Beachcombers never harboured any ambitions beyond being a semi-professional outfit, so Keith's ears pricked up when Oldfield emcee Louie Hunt happened to mention the Who's drummer problem.

John Entwistle recounted how the final piece fell into place. "We were playing in Greenford one night with a session drummer, and this fellow walked up to us and said, 'My mate can play better than your drummer.' So we said, 'Well, let's hear him then. Bring him up.' So he brought up this little ginger-bread man, and it was Keith with dyed ginger hair and a brown shirt, brown tie, brown suit, brown shoes. He got up on the kit, and we said, 'Can you play "Road Runner?"' because we actually hadn't come across a drummer that could play 'Road Runner' with us. So we played 'Road Runner' and he broke this drummer's bass drum pedal and mucked up the hi-hat. We thought, 'This is the fella!'"

According to Entwistle, Keith moonlighted with the Beachcombers for a short while, uncertainly weighing his options. "They didn't ask me to join the group but said they were having a rehearsal at some West Indian club," Moon told Chris Charlesworth in

a 1972 interview. "This chap from Philips [Fontana] Records, Chris Parmeinter, turns up with another drummer because they had been offered a record deal by Philips... He set his kit up, and I set mine up, and nobody was saying anything. The rest of the band just didn't care. They were tuning up in one corner, and it was dead embarrassing. Then they asked me to play in the first number, but the man from Philips wanted to play. I can't remember if he played or not, but the group said they didn't want him."

Keith was referring to Brian Redman, a drummer from Liverpool, who had played with the Fourmost in their original guise as the Four Jays. Through Bill Harry (editor of *Mersey Beat* newspaper), Redman was told of the drummer vacancy, and

ABOVE: PETER MEADEN.

an all-expenses-paid trip to London was arranged with Helmut Gorden. After sitting in at a gig at the Glenlyn, Forest Hill, Parmeinter arranged a formal audition the following day in the same Edgware Road basement where Doug Sandom had been ousted. Both Gorden and Parmeinter were impressed with Redman's abilities, but, like Sandom, Redman wasn't an R&B acolyte, while the group had reservations about his not looking the part. The Liverpudlian packed his drums into his car and headed back up North.

With Keith Moon in the group, the transformation was remarkable. "From the point we found Keith, it was a complete turning point," Townshend declared. "He was so assertive and confident. Before then, we had just been fooling about."

By coincidence, another of Jack Mark's regular customers was Peter Meaden, a nineteen-year old freelance publicist who'd helped his flamboyant colleague, Andrew Loog Oldham, with the Rolling Stones publicity. Like Oldham, Meaden was a natural born hustler, unwilling to play second fiddle. He had already tried his hand at managing an East London group, the Moments (featuring seventeen-year-old singer, Steve Marriott), and was doing Georgie Fame's press when Jack mentioned Helmut Gorden and this band of his. Suitably intrigued, Meaden met Gorden at his office and accepted an on-the-spot offer of £50 a week to "put the Who together."

"I had this dream of getting a group together that would be the focus, the entertainers for the mods," Meaden told Barbara Charone ten years later, "a group that would actually be the same people onstage as the guys in the audience."

Mod (from "modernist") had gradually turned from an elitist cult, centred around a few Soho tailoring and garment shops, into a fully-fledged youth subculture. In its 1964 incarnation, Mod had it's own music (R&B, American soul, Tamla-Motown, West Indian rhythm, and blue beat), transport (Italian motor scooters), fashion (cycling shirts, turned-up Levi's, Fred Perry shirts, Madras cotton jackets, bowling shoes, etc.), and drugs (Drinamyl, i.e., purple hearts, and other amphetamines mandatory for a weekend's non-stop activity). What distinguished it from other British post-war styles was its obsessive attention to just that: style.

This cool individualism clashed with the more reactionary style it superseded—that of the leather clad "rocker," who remained faithful to 50's Americana, rock and roll, Harley Davidsons, and black leather biker jackets. Clashes in image and lifestyle sparked the legendary "Mods and Rockers" Bank Holiday skirmishes in the seaside resorts of coastal Britain, although much of it was a product of media manipulation rather than full-blooded warfare. These same Fleet Street distortions awoke the rest of the country to what was happening, but in so doing, helped to bury the original movement.

Even in the depths of spiritualism, Pete Townshend was quick to acknowledge the impact Mod had on him. "It was a great show of solidarity, and you felt that you belonged to something," he told Ray Tolliday in 1971. "This was when I first became aware of the force of rock as a reflection of what was going on in the streets... But we, the Who, were never in any danger of getting obsessed with the mod image, because we were not so much a part of it as a mirror. When we were on stage, we reflected the mood of the kids and caught their frustration and aggression."

Meaden set about transforming the Who from Stones clones to his own mod-obsessed image. "He didn't have to force his ideas on us very hard," admitted Daltrey. "He thought we could pick up on the Mod thing and was very right because Mods had no focal point at all, and the Who became that, even though we were a little bit old to be a real part of it." Although enthusiastically supported by the arty Townshend, Meaden's style-mongering met with some resistance. "He [Meaden] had us all in the barbers, and they cut our hair off and took us around all these shops and dressed us up in skating jackets, T-shirts, and jeans with one-inch turn-ups, and boxing boots," Entwistle told Steve Turner. "He dressed Roger in an Ivy League seersucker suit. I mean we rebelled against that more or less straight away. I walked through a puddle in my boxing boots and the soles fell off. I think I only wore the skating jacket once." Little wonder Meaden referred to Entwistle in his press handout as John Allison, "the most conservative member of the group." The stage name was a reference to John's girlfriend (and future wife) Alison Wise. (During the Detours period, he occasionally called himself "John Johns", his father-in-law's surname, and throughout the first half of 1965, "John Browne.")

Meaden's next bold move was persuading the group to change their name yet again, because "we're all into pills, into a bit of pot, and when we're hip, we've got to dress hip, and we're going to be called the High Numbers." ("Number" was hip-slang for a regular street type of mod, "blocked" on "blues." The "high" was self-explanatory.) He appropriated the tunes from the Showmen's "Country Fool," and Slim Harpo's "Got Love If You Want It," re-writing hipster lyrics, laden with self-conscious mod references, to create "Zoot Suit" and "I'm The Face," respectively as their first release. For all the publicity he could hustle, including features in *Record Mirror*, *Boyfriend*, and *Fabulous*, the single sold a dismal 500 copies, with around fifty allegedly bought by Meaden in a misguided attempt to hype it into the charts. While the record was faithfully bought by the band's loyal following (including Entwistle's grandmother), most saw it for what it was: blatant opportunism. Fontana,

who had signed the group on a one-off option, saw the poor returns and decided against a follow-up.

By the time of the record's release on 3 July, the group (bar John) had given up their vocations to pursue uncertain futures as professional musicians. Gorden was paying the group a £20 weekly wage and assuming a managerial position, although they preferred to regard Meaden in this role. By this time, most bands around London and, indeed, the whole country were hooked on rhythm and blues as a route to success, thanks to the examples set by the Rolling Stones, the Yardbirds, Manfred Mann, and the Animals.

At Meaden's urging, the group dropped the more obvious numbers from their act in favour of the black American pop of the Tamla-Motown labels—still relatively obscure in Britain, though it was creeping over on the Oriole and Stateside

The High Numbers . . . now under new management as *The Who*

OLYMPIA
LONDON STREET, READING   Tel. 50687

Saturday, 14th November   7.30 pm—11 pm
LEO'S CAVERN
By Public Demand
Return of "THE WHO"   Plus Discs, etc.

Sunday, 15th November   7.30 pm—10.30 pm
RICKY TICK
JIMMIE REED   Plus John Lee and The Ground Hogs

Monday, 16th November   7.30 pm
PARAMOUNT BINGO
Jackpot £50.   Membership 1/-   Applications to: 34 Minster Street, Reading

Tuesday, 17th November   7.30 pm—10.30 pm
LEO'S CAVERN
London's 2nd Top R. & B. Group
THE BIRDS

Thursday, 19th November   7.30 pm—11 pm
THURSDAY BLUES CLUB
JOHN MYALL'S BLUES BREAKERS

THE WHO
MAXIMUM R & B

WEDNESDAY NIGHTS AT THE FLORIDA

ADMISSION 3/- & 4/-

OLYMPIA

FRIDAY, OCT. 9   8 pm–2 am

TONIGHT—S.L.Y. BALL

Admission 10/6

Dancing to Two Bands

SATURDAY, OCT. 10   7.30 pm—11 pm

LEO'S CAVERN CLUB

The fabulous HIGH NUMBERS

Admission : 4/- before 8 pm, 5/- after

SUNDAY, OCT. 11

PARAMOUNT BINGO 7.30 pm

Jackpot £50 Membership 1/-
Applications to 34 Minster Street, Reading

TUESDAY, OCT. 13   7.30 pm—10.30 pm

LEO'S CAVERN CLUB

R & B RAVE

First time here—   Admission 3/-

The Fabulous
COPS 'N ROBBERS

---

labels. Tamla artists such as the Miracles, Martha and the Vandellas, the Temptations, and Marvin Gaye were being championed in such hip joints as the Flamingo, La Discotheque, and the Scene—the absolute focal point of the urban Mod movement—all located within a square mile of Soho. That

Easter, the Scene's owner, Ronan O'Rahilly, started Britain's first all-music pirate station, Radio Caroline, and DJ Guy Stevens had his finger on the pulse, making tapes available (for a fee) from his formidable record collection. It was Stevens that Meaden approached with the unrealised idea of the High Numbers releasing a cover of the Miracles' "I Gotta Dance To Keep From Crying" on Stevens' own Sue label imprint.

If the young musicians were happy to let Meaden chart their direction, they were disillusioned by their record's failure to sell and Gorden's hopelessly archaic ideas about presentation. Because of show business connections at the Stork Club at 66 Regent Street, Gorden arranged an audition for impresario Bunny Lewis and, after a brief spell with the Harold Davison Organisation, got the group placed with the Arthur Howes agency. Howes was Britain's leading "old school" promoter, whose clients included the Beatles, the crown jewels in a cavalcade of acts that the High Numbers supported in a series of package shows over late summer. But by then, the group was under new management.

On a fortuitous July evening, Christopher "Kit" Lambert, a twenty-six-year-old assistant film director, saw a multitude of kids on scooters hovering outside the Railway Hotel, Harrow. He pulled up in his Volkswagon Beetle for a closer inspection, telling promoter Richard Barnes he was looking for a suitable group to appear in a documentary he and an associate were making. Barnes in turn directed him to Pete Meaden. Lambert later set the scene for George Tremlett: "The atmosphere in there was fantastic. The room was black and hot. Steaming hot. And the audience seemed hypnotised by the wild music, with the feedback that Pete Townshend was already producing from his guitar and amplifier."

That evening, Lambert enthusiastically telephoned his partner Chris Stamp in Ireland. To finance their documentary, Stamp was working on location as assistant director on John Ford's *Young Cassidy*. Lambert urged him to return post-haste to witness the band for himself.

Lambert and Stamp had formed their partnership while discontented assistant film directors working on such films as *Of Human Bondage*, *The L-Shaped Room*, and *I Could Go On Singing* at Shepperton Studios. At first glance, the two didn't seem ideally suited. Knightsbridge-born Lambert went to public

school (Lancing and Trinity College) and Oxford, followed by film school in France and explorations in Brazil. His father, the classical composer Constant Lambert, was musical director at Sadlers' Wells and Covent Garden; his grandfather was landscape painter George Washington Lambert.

Stamp was working class, a barrow boy from Plaistow, East London. His father worked on a Thames tugboat and his brother was budding film star Terence Stamp. However, such a dichotomy proved ideal in handling as volatile a combination as the Who. The two were renting a central London flat at 113 Ivor Court, Gloucester Place, and had spent the past few months on a fruitless search across England looking for the right unknowns for their film, which required something financially less problematic than an already established group. Additionally, Stamp brought in his schoolfriend, Mike Shaw, who had been working the footlights at the Bristol Hippodrome, to assist in their venture.

Like Lambert before him, Stamp was overwhelmed when catching the last part of the High Numbers' act at Watford Trade Hall. "I was knocked out," he told *The Observer* in 1966. "But the excitement I felt wasn't coming from the group. I couldn't get near enough. It was coming from the people blocking my way." Lambert and Stamp initially signed the group to appear in a twenty minute documentary, charting their progress from obscurity to success. However, it swiftly dawned on them that they should become managers, despite knowing next to nothing about how the music business operated. The pair sought advice, arranging a clandestine meeting with David Jacobs, the Beatles' lawyer, who asked to meet the group personally. They needed little urging.

Gorden, for all his capital and connections, had only succeeded in proving how out-to-sea he was at moulding a modern pop group. Meaden, thanks to a debilitating speed habit, was out-to-sea, *period*. Lambert and Stamp were offering an equivalent contract guaranteeing each member £1000 per year. When returning from a holiday in the Seychelles, Gorden was informed by letter that his services were no longer required. He instantly took legal action—unsurprisingly, in view of the time and expenditure invested in his "little diamonds." When the dubious legality of the contract was pointed out, Gorden in turn sued his solicitors for negligence.

ABOVE: CHRIS STAMP (LEFT) AND KIT LAMBERT.

Shortly after their introduction, Lambert unexpectedly turned up at an audition Meaden arranged for his erstwhile partner Andrew Oldham at the New Carlton Irish Club, 308–310 Uxbridge Road, Shepherd's Bush. When Oldham deferred taking the High Numbers on, the way was clear for Lambert and Stamp to act. Even though he had no legal position as their publicist, Meaden wasn't about to take his usurpation lying down. For a while, he turned up at band rehearsals accompanied by a menacing character named Phil the Greek, until Lambert took the expedient of offering Meaden the buy-out sum of £250 cash.

The High Numbers signed an agreement with New Action, Lambert and Stamp's limited company, giving the management a substantial 40% split (20% each), with the remaining 60% divided four ways. In preparation for the Arthur Howes dates, Mike Shaw hired the Granada Theatre in Wandsworth, South West London, over successive afternoons for the group to rehearse in and for Shaw to practice his pioneering stage lighting—something yet to be fully developed in rock presentation.

Already, the group had gained a local reputation as being the loudest band around. "In them days, it was all psychological warfare being in a group," Roger told John Swenson, "so we hit on the idea of having the biggest cabinets you've ever seen in your life—yet inside we'd have this little 12-inch speaker in the bottom." Thanks to being frequent habitués of Marshall's, both Entwistle and Townshend started exploring the sonic possibilities of their equipment.

In the process, they were indirectly responsible for the invention of the Marshall stack, which evolved quite accidentally out of a spirit of one-upmanship. Townshend explained: "Jim Marshall started manufacturing amplifiers, and somebody in his store came up with the idea of building a 4 x 12 cabinet for bass. John bought one and he suddenly doubled in volume. So I bought one, and then later on I bought another one, and I stacked it on top of the first one."

Marshall's were outraged at the way their products were being treated. When company technician Ken Bran complained to Pete that the top cabinet of "the stack" risked getting damaged when the sheer volume shifted it to the verge of falling off, Townshend sneered, "so what?" and knocked it over. "I was using a 12-string Rickenbacker at the time," Pete said, "which I packed with paper, and when the pickup was right in line with the speakers, I was instantly getting feedback on certain harmonics. I discovered it by accident because I wanted my amps to be bigger than I was; this was image consciousness again."

Intimidated by the virtuosity of contemporaries such as Eric Clapton of the Yardbirds, and Jeff Beck (then of the Tridents), whom he claims to have never seen, Townshend channelled his frustration into expressing himself visually. "I tried to make playing the guitar look lethal," he recalled to Jann Wenner. "My whole absurdly demonstrative stage act was worked out to turn myself into a body instead of a face. Most pop singers were pretty, but I wanted people to look at my body, and not have to bother looking at my head if they didn't like the look of it."

While Pete was swinging his arm and inducing feedback over Roger's menacing growl and Keith's merciless pounding, John, by contrast, stood resolutely still. "I think the different stage presences of the group happened partly by accident and partly by design," he said. "I found that I could always play better when I wasn't actually moving about. I had to spend an awful lot of time standing at the microphone because I was doing some lead vocals and an awful lot of backing vocals in the early days. I started getting paranoid because the girls in the front row weren't screaming out my name, so I figured, 'Well,

I'll try moving.' So I tried moving and they screamed my name out, so I thought to myself, 'Well, now I know, I'll stop moving again.' So I stopped moving. Once I knew that they'd scream at me if I started moving, it didn't matter anymore. I could go back to playing bass and trying to hold the band together, which I could do better from a standing position." This steady role as anchorman earned John his sobriquet: the Ox.

Perhaps the Who's most distinctive trademark developed by accident, as Entwistle recalled: "Pete had a thing in the act where he used to put his fingers on a chord and smash the guitar into the speaker cabinet so that it would resound in a crash. He had another thing where he used to put his guitar above his head and spin round and then spin back again. We were doing a gig at the Railway, which had a high stage made out of beer crates and a rather low ceiling. The guitar that Pete was using was a Rickenbacker, which had been considerably weakened by him hitting it into the amplifier for so long. He forgot it was a low ceiling and put his guitar above his head, and the neck fell off. He got into a bit of a temper and smashed it to smithereens with a mike stand. He had a guitar spare, a 12-string Rickenbacker. He picked that up and carried on as if he'd meant to do it."

Word spread and the following week, a large crowd gathered for a repeat performance. When Townshend didn't oblige, Moon wrecked his kit to compensate. Lambert's initial horror at the expense soon gave way to a realisation that there was audience demand for such antics, as well as

enormous publicity value involved. Within three months, his personal savings of £6000 were soaked up like a sponge.

Lambert and Stamp set up their own production company from an office at 84 Eaton Place. "It was the only slum in Belgravia," Lambert told *The Observer*, "but it got us credit."

New Action Ltd. consisted of themselves, production manager Mike Shaw, and a friend of Stamp's from Chelsea, Anya Butler, who became Lambert's PA. Shortly thereafter, the group's name reverted back to the Who. "The High Numbers was a nothing name," Stamp explained. "It implied the Top Twenty, but the Who seemed perfect for them. It was impersonal, it couldn't be dated." (Whether they knew it or not, an R&B group from Sheffield continued calling themselves the Who well into the following year.)

Unsuccessful attempts were made to break the group out of their regular constituency into uncharted territories around suburban London. A stronghold in the West End was sorely needed, where word could spread beyond the converted. In March, the Marquee Jazz Club had moved from its original site at 165 Oxford Street to nearby 90 Wardour Street. Stamp buttonholed Blue Beat Records' boss, Ziggy Jackson, into giving the Who a Tuesday night try-out at the Marquee, traditionally the club's "dead" night.

Lambert and Stamp set to work. £300 was spent on printing 1500 flyposters around the Shepherd's Bush area and 2500 handbills for distribution in clubs. A strikingly distinctive white on black poster, with the slogan "Maximum R&B"(coined by Lambert), was designed by Brian Pike, an art school friend of Pete's. The band name featured an arrow extending from the "o," resembling the biological symbol for male. In the top left-hand corner was a high-contrast image of Townshend, arm outstretched, having struck a power chord on his Rickenbacker Fireglo. A secret society, the "100 Faces," was formed from the group's hardcore Goldhawk Social Club following, with key members receiving free tickets and even more receiving half-price admission.

On opening night, 24 November, only a desultory thirty braved pouring rain to see them. Within three weeks, though, the group's Tuesday night slot had broken house attendance records set by Manfred Mann and the Yardbirds. Lambert and Stamp's next hurdle was securing a recording contract.

In October, the group had auditioned for EMI as the High Numbers, but the company was after acts playing solely original material. A friend of Anya's happened to be married to one Sheldon Talmy. Shel Talmy was a twenty-three-year-old independent producer from Chicago who had worked as an engineer in L.A. on records by the Checkmates, the Marquettes, Little Richard, and Billy Eckstine, among others. Arriving in England

ABOVE: SHEL TALMY.

in 1962, he was hired by Decca and his first production for the company, "Lollipops And Roses" by Doug Sheldon, was followed by the Bachelors' hit, "Charmaine." On the lookout for the right act, he had unsuccessfully offered Georgie Fame and the Blue Flames and Manfred Mann to Decca before being vindicated with the Kinks, recording them as an independent for Pye. It was Talmy's work with that North London group that made Kit Lambert make contact.

"I went to see the Who at some funny little church hall somewhere in Shepherd's Bush, and they were great," Talmy told Bob Edmands. "You just listened to them for five minutes, and you knew these guys had something. Their energy, their attack, which groups [in Britain] did not have then."

Talmy arranged a proper audition in the basement of the legendary 2 I's Coffee bar at 59 Old Compton Street, Soho, before going into the studio. "When we recorded," he said, "I just tried to get down to translating their live sound to record... I heard 'I Can't Explain' as a one minute, 90-second

demo [cut at the Marquee's studio and played down the phone to him by Mike Shaw]. Just a collection of chords stuck together."

Townshend willingly admits he structured the song as a Kinks derivative to attract Talmy's interest: "Talmy came down, heard 'I Can't Explain' and said that's the one. We did other numbers, 'Call Me Lightning' being one, but that was the only real original we had, and he wanted something that sounded original."

Upon entering Pye Studios, the group were alarmed to find hired session musicians on hand. "Jimmy [Page] was there to play lead. He nearly played the solo on the A side, but it was so simple, even I could play it," Townshend asserts. According to Entwistle, Pete played on "I Can't Explain," while the B-side, "Bald Headed Woman," featured Page's fretwork since Page refused to lend Townshend his Roger Mayer-patented fuzzbox.

For a debut conceived in such trying circumstances, "I Can't Explain" sounds remarkably self-assured. Daltrey, who styled himself on the growl of Howlin' Wolf and the soulful yelp of James Brown, harboured misgivings about the group's commercial leanings. "That leap was painful for me," he admitted, "because it was such a different style of singing, and I had to really reinvent myself vocally." Such fears of the Who becoming a pop group appear to have bypassed Townshend completely. "From my point of view," Townshend told Alan di Perna, "when British kids who were in bands discovered R&B, what they discovered was a new way to write pop songs which was purely British."

Talmy signed a one-off deal to record the Who for American Decca, with Brunswick as their British outlet, after U.K. Decca had turned him down. In November, Lambert and Stamp, operating under the mistaken belief that U.S. and U.K. Decca were one and the same, willingly signed a one-year production contract with Talmy's company, Orbit Music, giving Talmy a valid four-year option on the group, considered the maximum lifespan of any successful pop group. It was to be a costly mistake for Lambert, Stamp, and the Who.

1964

(THE DETOURS)

THURSDAY, 2 JANUARY
Oldfield Hotel, Greenford.

FRIDAY, 3 JANUARY
Glenlyn Ballroom, Forest Hill, supporting the Rolling Stones for the second time. (See 22 December 1963.)

Pete temporarily dropped his arm-swinging act. "I thought I was copying Keith Richards," he told Steve Peacock, "so I didn't do it all night, and I watched him and he didn't do it all night either. 'Swing me what?' Keith said. He must have got into it as a warming up thing... but he didn't remember, and it developed into my sort of trademark."

SUNDAY, 5 JANUARY
St. Mary's Hall, Putney.

SATURDAY, 11 JANUARY
Oldfield Hotel, Greenford.

SUNDAY, 12 JANUARY
White Hart Hotel, Acton.

TUESDAY, 14 JANUARY
Oldfield Hotel, Greenford.

THURSDAY, 16 JANUARY
Oldfield Hotel, Greenford.

SATURDAY, 18 JANUARY
Oldfield Hotel, Greenford.

SUNDAY, 19 JANUARY
White Hart Hotel, Acton.

TUESDAY, 21 JANUARY
Oldfield Hotel, Greenford.

THURSDAY, 23 JANUARY
Oldfield Hotel, Greenford.

FRIDAY, 24 JANUARY
Glenlyn Ballroom, Forest Hill, supporting the Hollies.

Who is Who? Hey?

● EARNING a place in the new edition of "Who's Who" published this week —"The Who."

Who the heck's "The Who?" I couldn't find the answer in the big red book of top people.

So I asked an Acton guitar group that used to be called "The Detours."

Yes, they said, they were "The Who."

Why the change of name? It sounds slicker.

The group play one of their first concerts under the new name at the Goldhawk Social Club, Shepherds Bush, tomorrow night (Friday).

Also on the bill are "The Undertakers" — from Liverpool. The where? Sorry, Beatleville.

SATURDAY, 25 JANUARY
Oldfield Hotel, Greenford.

SUNDAY, 26 JANUARY
St. Mary's Hall, Putney.

THURSDAY, 30 JANUARY
Oldfield Hotel, Greenford.

FRIDAY, 31 JANUARY
Glenlyn Ballroom, Forest Hill, supporting the Big Three.

SUNDAY, 2 FEBRUARY
St. Mary's Hall, Putney, supporting Dave Berry and the Cruisers.

THURSDAY, 6 FEBRUARY
Oldfield Hotel, Greenford.

FRIDAY, 7 FEBRUARY
Goldhawk Social Club, Shepherd's Bush, supporting an up-and-coming North London group, the Kinks.

SUNDAY, 9 FEBRUARY
St. Mary's Hall, Putney, supporting the Big Three for the second time. (See 31 January.)

THURSDAY, 13 FEBRUARY
Oldfield Hotel, Greenford.

FRIDAY, 14 FEBRUARY
Glenlyn Ballroom, Forest Hill, supporting Carter Lewis and the Southerners.

(THE WHO)

THURSDAY, 20 FEBRUARY
Oldfield Hotel, Greenford.

SATURDAY, 22 FEBRUARY
Oldfield Hotel, Greenford.

SUNDAY, 23 FEBRUARY
St. Mary's Hall, Putney, supporting Brian Poole and the Tremeloes.

THURSDAY, 27 FEBRUARY
Oldfield Hotel, Greenford.

FRIDAY, 28 FEBRUARY
Goldhawk Social Club, Shepherd's Bush.

SATURDAY, 29 FEBRUARY
Evershed Sports Pavilion, Harlequin Avenue, Brentford, West London.

SUNDAY, 1 MARCH
St. Mary's Hall, Putney.

WEDNESDAY, 4 MARCH
Pete filled in a second BBC Light Programme audition form, now listing the group's name as "The Who."

THURSDAY, 5 MARCH
Oldfield Hotel, Greenford.

FRIDAY, 6 MARCH
Goldhawk Social Club, Shepherd's Bush, supporting the Undertakers.

SATURDAY, 7 MARCH
Mead Hall, Ealing.

According to The Who Concert File, the group additionally played the wedding reception of Joan Wilson, the sister of their former drummer Harry Wilson, Jr., at the Old Oak Common Institute, Shepherd's Bush.

SUNDAY, 8 MARCH
St. Mary's Hall, Putney.

SATURDAY, 14 MARCH
Melody Maker carried a feature, "Massive Swing To R&B," by Bob Dawbarn, on the increasing popularity of the R&B scene. Among the emergent new groups mentioned were the Who—their first name-check in the national music press.

SUNDAY, 15 MARCH
White Hart Hotel, Acton.

MONDAY, 16 MARCH
Glenlyn Ballroom, Forest Hill.
The start of an extra Monday night booking.

TUESDAY, 17 MARCH
Oldfield Hotel, Greenford.

THURSDAY, 19 MARCH
Oldfield Hotel, Greenford.

MONDAY, 23 MARCH
Glenlyn Ballroom, Forest Hill.

THURSDAY, 26 MARCH
Oldfield Hotel, Greenford.

FRIDAY, 27 MARCH
Goldhawk Social Club, Shepherd's Bush.

SATURDAY, 28 MARCH
At Wandsworth Registry Office, Roger married his sixteen-year-old girlfriend, Jacqueline Rickman, witnessed by John Reader, a friend of Roger's from the Merchant Navy who helped out as the Who's first roadie in his spare time. A reception was held at the Rickman residence in Putney with guests including Johnny Kidd and the Pirates. The couple's son, Simon, was born on 22 August at the Downs, Wimbledon, but the marriage did not last. In a 1972 *Observer* feature, Roger confessed, "I knew that if I didn't move away from her in those early days, I would be a sheet metal worker forever." (Jacqueline applied for a divorce in January 1968, which was granted in May 1970.)

SUNDAY, 29 MARCH
Florida Rooms (adjoining Brighton Aquarium), Brighton, Sussex, supported by the Mark Leeman Five. The first Who gig at "The Scene"—a regular residency at the Aquarium, promoted by Bob Druce, and later Bonni Manzi.

THURSDAY, 2 APRIL
Oldfield Hotel, Greenford.

FRIDAY, 3 APRIL
Glenlyn Ballroom, Forest Hill.

SATURDAY, 4 APRIL
California Ballroom, Dunstable, supporting the Tony Meehan Combo. The group were still billed as the Detours.

SUNDAY, 5 APRIL
White Hart Hotel, Acton.

MONDAY, 6 APRIL
Glenlyn Ballroom, Forest Hill.

THURSDAY, 9 APRIL
An important day of assignments and a fateful one for Doug Sandom. Firstly, the Who went to a restaurant on Edgware Road, where a formal audition for Chris Parmeinter, an A&R man for Fontana Records, took place in the basement cafe. The group ran through several numbers including Bo Diddley's "Here 'Tis." Parmeinter was impressed but made it clear that he considered Sandom's drumming unsuitable. Under pressure, Sandom announced his departure, but agreed to serve out the weekend.

At 8:10 pm, the group (with Sandom) went on to audition for the BBC Light Programme at Studio S2 in the sub-basement of Broadcasting House, three floors below Portland Place. Pete had listed the group as the Detours on the original application form (dated 19 December 1963), which confused the corporation to no end. Their paperwork demanded, "Which name do you wish to continue to be known by?" A letter dated 13 April apologised for the mix-up and confirmed the new name as the Who. (See 28 April.)

FRIDAY, 10 APRIL
Glenlyn Ballroom, Forest Hill, supporting the Undertakers for the second time. (See 6 March.)

SATURDAY, 11 APRIL
Goldhawk Social Club, Shepherd's Bush, supporting Wee Willie Harris.

SUNDAY, 12 APRIL
White Hart Hotel, Acton.

MONDAY, 13 APRIL
100 Club, 100 Oxford Street, London, supporting the Mike Cotton Sound.

Doug Sandom's final appearance with the Who, almost two years after joining them.

THURSDAY, 16 APRIL
Oldfield Hotel, Greenford.
The first gig employing the services of session drummer Dave Gold, from Marshall's Music Shop, in the wake of Sandom's departure. Gold received £4 a week, paid out of the group's earnings.

FRIDAY, 17 APRIL
Goldhawk Social Club, Shepherd's Bush.

SATURDAY, 18 APRIL
Florida Rooms, Brighton.

MONDAY, 20 APRIL
Glenlyn Ballroom, Forest Hill.

THURSDAY, 23 APRIL
Oldfield Hotel, Greenford.

FRIDAY, 24 APRIL
Glenlyn Ballroom, Forest Hill, supporting the Merseybeats.

SUNDAY, 26 APRIL
White Hart Hotel, Acton.

MONDAY, 27 APRIL
100 Club, London, supporting the Mike Cotton Sound.

TUESDAY, 28 APRIL
The BBC prepared and dispatched an official letter turning the Who/Detours down for radio programmes, signed by David Dore, Assistant to Light Entertainment Booking Manager.

A re-application didn't occur until 15 January 1965.

THURSDAY, 30 APRIL
Oldfield Hotel, Greenford.
The *probable* occasion where Keith Moon made his highly original entrance, sitting in on Bo Diddley's "Road Runner" to open the second set.

california Pool ★★★★
Ballroom · Dunstable
WHIPSNADE ROAD

WRESTLING TONIGHT, 7 p.m. for 7.45. Adm. 3/6 to 10/-
Fri., 3rd Apr., SCREAMING & SHOUTING, 8 to 11.30 p.m. Adm. 6/6
KENNY LYNCH & GROUP   THE RAMBLERS
BARRY NOBLE & SAPPHIRES   THE FUGITIVES
Sat., 4th Apr., SONG OF MEXICO, 8 p.m. to midnight. Adm. 7/-
THE TONY MEEHAM COMBO
THE CHEROKEES   THE DETOURS
THE STORMBREAKERS
Bar extension. Car park. Late bus to Luton. Doors close 10.30 p.m.

A previously undocumented demo session, financed by Bob Druce and Helmut Gorden, took place during the month. "I'm The Face" and Pete's earliest composition, "It Was You," were recorded. Precise studio/session details have proved untraceable, although it may have taken place at IBC Studios, 35 Portland Place, London, where mono tape copies of both were made by engineer Alan Florence on 11 May and 4 June, respectively.

The first version of "I'm The Face" features the zoom bass line played on guitar, rather like a slide part, and there is no harmonica on the fade. Pete Meaden plays percussive clicks on a clapperboard, and Roger sings "all the cats down the Scene, baby" in imitation of Meaden's hip jargon. "I'm The Face" was selected to be re-recorded at the company's studio. (See June.)

SATURDAY, 2 MAY

Keith's first gig with the Who, a twenty-first birthday in the upstairs of a pub on the North Circular, for which they were paid the princely sum of £25. "The first gig that Keith turned up to with us was this girl's 21st," remembered John. "He put his little blue drum kit up and then got this huge coil of rope and tied it all together. We couldn't understand why until he went into a drum solo, and everything started to sway backwards and forwards!"

MONDAY, 4 MAY

Glenlyn Ballroom, Forest Hill.
This gig featured Liverpool drummer Brian Redman (formerly of the Fourmost) sitting in without rehearsal, as a warm-up for the following day's audition.

TUESDAY, 5 MAY

The group auditioned again for Philips Records' Chris Parmeinter and Jack Baverstock at the same basement restaurant on Edgware Road (See 9 April.) Keith Moon was present and both he and Brian Redman played on versions of "I'm The Face." Despite Helmut Gorden's protestations, Redman was deemed unsuitable by the group. Redman received £40 for two days of expenses and returned to Liverpool, where he joined the Merseyside C&W outfit, the Hillsiders.

THURSDAY, 7 MAY
Oldfield Hotel, Greenford.

FRIDAY, 8 MAY
Goldhawk Social Club, Shepherd's Bush.

SUNDAY, 10 MAY
Florida Rooms, Brighton.

MONDAY, 11 MAY
Glenlyn Ballroom, Forest Hill.

THURSDAY, 14 MAY
Oldfield Hotel, Greenford.

FRIDAY, 15 MAY
Glenlyn Ballroom, Forest Hill, supporting the Interns.

SATURDAY, 16—SUNDAY, 17 MAY
Florida Rooms, Brighton.

In addition to the Saturday gig, held during the Whitsun Bank Holiday Mod-Rocker disturbances, the Who were paid £20 to play the following night's "All-Nite Rave."

MONDAY, 18 MAY
Glenlyn Ballroom, Forest Hill.

THURSDAY, 21 MAY
Oldfield Hotel, Greenford.

SUNDAY, 24 MAY
Majestic Ballroom,
Luton, Bedfordshire.

MONDAY, 25 MAY
Glenlyn Ballroom,
Forest Hill.

THURSDAY, 28 MAY
Oldfield Hotel, Greenford.

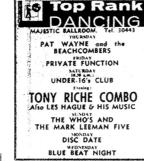

FRIDAY, 29 MAY
Corporation Hotel, Derby, Derbyshire.

One of the Who's first known bookings outside the general London area, the gig paid £25 and was arranged through the Harold Davison agency. On the return journey, their Dormobile blew up. Helmut Gorden shelled out for a woefully inadequate replacement, a low-powered Commer diesel. This too eventually met its fate on the A1.

SUNDAY, 31 MAY
White Hart Hotel, Acton.

JUNE
After two days of rehearsals supervised by Pete Meaden at Dineley Rehearsal Studio, 4 Blandford Street, London, the Who's first proper recording session took place over an afternoon at Philips' studio, Stanhope Place, off Marble Arch, with producers Jack Baverstock and Chris Parmeinter.

At least five takes of "I'm The Face" were recorded with Baverstock, while Parmeinter supervised sixteen takes of Bo Diddley's "Here 'Tis" and seven takes of "Zoot Suit." Roger played harmonica and Richard Barnes, maracas on "Here 'Tis." Allen Ellett, an associate of Pete Meaden who'd played piano with Steve Marriott's Moments and had backed Jerry Lee Lewis with the Nashville Teens, contributed piano trills throughout "I'm The Face," while an unidentified associate produced a cracking whip sound by folding and unfurling a leather belt. (Ellett later sat in on Who gigs at the Scene Club and the Railway Hotel.) Meaden also roped in such unlikely associates as Helmut Gorden and Jack "The Barber" Marks to provide handclaps.

"Zoot Suit" was chosen for the A-side of the single, released by the High Numbers on Friday, 3 July. For the B-side, "Here 'Tis" was passed over in favour of "I'm The Face." (See 21 May 1974.)

In his book *Maximum R&B*, Barnes states that the group additionally taped a version of Eddie Holland's "Leaving Here" (released that month in the U.K. on the *R & B Chartbusters Vol. 3* EP). This has yet to surface, and contrary to the track annotation for the *Thirty Years of Maximum R&B* box set, the version included therein was produced by Shel Talmy. (See 19 March, 1965.)

MONDAY, 1 JUNE
Glenlyn Ballroom, Forest Hill.

THURSDAY, 4 JUNE
White Hart Hotel, Southall, Middlesex.
A regular Thursday night Druce booking for the usual £12.

SUNDAY, 7 JUNE
Florida Rooms, Brighton.

MONDAY, 8 JUNE
Glenlyn Ballroom, Forest Hill.

THURSDAY, 11 JUNE
White Hart Hotel, Southall.

MONDAY, 15 JUNE
Glenlyn Ballroom, Forest Hill.

THURSDAY, 18 JUNE
White Hart Hotel, Southall.

FRIDAY, 19 JUNE
The Who Concert File lists the Who appearing on the bill at the "Kinky Ball," Granby Halls, Leicester, based on an eye witness account, although they are not mentioned in the advertising.

SATURDAY, 20 JUNE
Regency Ballroom, Bath, Somerset, with Dave Davani and the D Men and the Falling Leaves. The Who headlined the final R&B night of the four-day 1964 Bath Jazz Festival.

MONDAY, 22 JUNE
Glenlyn Ballroom, Forest Hill.

THURSDAY, 25 JUNE
White Hart Hotel, Southall.

FRIDAY, 26 JUNE
The Refectory, Golders Green, North West London.
Jack Marks recalls "The Who's" were not invited back, after they turned up their amps in response to appeals for the volume to be lowered!

SUNDAY, 28 JUNE
Florida Rooms, Brighton.

MONDAY, 29 JUNE
Glenlyn Ballroom, Forest Hill.

TUESDAY, 30 JUNE
The first documented gig in a regular Tuesday night residency at the Bluesday R & B Club, situated in the basement of the Railway Hotel, Wealdstone, Harrow, Middlesex. It was co-promoted by Lionel Gibbins and Richard Barnes. An official capacity was fixed at 180, but more than three times that many regularly packed into the tiny club. The group usually played two sets from 8:00 pm—1:00 am, receiving the sum of £20, which was later upped to £25.

on their first disc outing,
four hip young men
from london say:

i'm the face

and wear:
zoot suit

(the first _authentic_ mod record)

the four hip young men?

the high numbers

fontana tf 480
release date july 3rd 1964

TUESDAY, 14 JULY

Railway Hotel, Wealdstone.

The _probable_ date that Kit Lambert first set eyes on the Who. His partner, Chris Stamp, had taken a job as assistant director on John Ford and Jack Cardiff's MGM film, _Young Cassidy,_ which had gone into production on location in Ireland the previous day.

SATURDAY, 18 JULY

Trade Union Hall, Watford.

Stamp flew back from Ireland and joined Lambert in time to catch the last twenty minutes of the High Numbers act.

SUNDAY, 19 JULY

Florida Rooms, Brighton.

At Holland Park Comprehensive School, Campden Hill Road, West London, an informal audition took place, witnessed by Stamp and associate Mike Shaw, in a gymnasium hired by Lambert, (who arrived characteristically late).

TUESDAY, 21 JULY

Railway Hotel, Wealdstone.

WEDNESDAY, 22 JULY

Scene Club, Ham Yard, 41 Great Windmill Street, Soho.

A _Record Mirror_ article (dated 25 July) mentioned that the High Numbers were appearing every Wednesday for the next three months.

SATURDAY, 25 JULY

Trade Union Hall, Watford.

(THE HIGH NUMBERS)

FRIDAY, 3 JULY

Fontana Records released "Zoot Suit" B/W "I'm The Face," with just 1000 copies pressed. Despite Pete Meaden's best efforts, the record failed to enter the Top 50, making the single a valuable collector's item.

In his 1971 "Meaty, Beaty, Big, and Bouncy" essay for _Rolling Stone_, Pete mentioned plans for the record to be re-released on the Rolling Stones label. A limited picture sleeve reissue on Back Door (via Polydor) did occur in March 1980.

TUESDAY, 7 JULY

Railway Hotel, Wealdstone. Billed as the Who.

SATURDAY, 11 JULY

Trade Union Hall, Watford, Hertfordshire. Billed as the Who, supporting Chris Farlowe and the Thunderbirds. This 1000-person capacity venue, opposite Watford Junction railway station, became a Who stronghold. A sure sign of their popularity came when, swapping the billing around the following week, the promoter found the first half sparsely attended, with the second near full.

SUNDAY, 12 JULY

Florida Rooms, Brighton.

Currently creating a storm in London's "Scene" club on Wednesday nights are the HIGH NUMBERS, the first really mod group to hit the group scene. The boys have been the centre of interest for pressmen and agents for several weeks since their sensational debut at the "Scene" club, in Ham Yard off Great Windmill Street in the heart of London's Soho. The High Numbers have been signed up by Arthur Howes and Jimmy O'Day for a series of Sunday dates starting on August 9 at Brighton Hippodrome where they will be appearing with Gerry and The Pacemakers. Other dates so far negotiated include the Blackpool Opera House with the Beatles on August 16, and Kelvin Hall Glasgow with the Animals and the Yardbirds on September 4. An autumn tour for the boys is being planned but the High Numbers will be playing at the "Scene" on Wednesday nights for the next three months. Their disc "I'm The Face" was last week given a Top Fifty Tip by RM Pop Jury. (RM pic Bill Williams).

SUNDAY, 26 JULY
White Hart Hotel, Acton.

TUESDAY, 28 JULY
Railway Hotel, Wealdstone.

WEDNESDAY, 29 JULY
Scene Club, Soho.

FRIDAY, 31 JULY
Goldhawk Social Club, Shepherd's Bush.

SATURDAY, 1 AUGUST
Trade Union Hall, Watford.

SUNDAY, 2 AUGUST
"All Nite Rave," Florida Rooms, Brighton.

TUESDAY, 4 AUGUST
Railway Hotel, Wealdstone.

WEDNESDAY, 5 AUGUST
Scene Club, Soho.

THURSDAY, 6 AUGUST
White Hart Hotel, Southall.

SATURDAY, 8 AUGUST
All Saints Hall, Whetstone, Barnet, Hertfordshire.

SUNDAY, 9 AUGUST
Hippodrome, Brighton. Two shows, 6:00 & 8:30 pm, supporting Gerry and the Pacemakers, the Nashville Teens, and Elkie Brooks with the Quotations. The first support slot in a series of Sunday concerts promoted by Arthur Howes.

As well as playing their own ten minute spot, the group reluctantly adhered to Howes' added proviso of backing female singer, Valerie McCullam.

TUESDAY, 11 AUGUST
Railway Hotel, Wealdstone.

WEDNESDAY, 12 AUGUST
The Mine, Carpenders Park Station, South Oxhey, near Watford.

A regular Wednesday night booking started at this mod venue, situated behind "The Pheasant" public house, from 7:30—11:00 pm, followed by a late engagement at the Scene Club.

SATURDAY, 15 AUGUST
Thames Riverboat Shuffle (departing Charing Cross Pier), London. A summer dance for Hoover (the vacuum cleaner company.)

The support group, the South Beats, featured guitarist Alan Oates, who joined Cyrano Langston as the Who's assistant road manager in April 1965.

SUNDAY, 16 AUGUST
Opera House, Blackpool, Lancashire. Two shows, 6:20 & 8:15 pm, opening for the Beatles and with the Kinks, who closed the first half.

As the Detours, the Who had supported the now chart-ready Kinks at the Goldhawk in February. Although unimpressed with their image of matching red hunting jackets, Pete was particularly taken with the staccato riff used for their latest single, "You Really Got Me."

TUESDAY, 18 AUGUST
Railway Hotel, Wealdstone.

1 9 6 4

Looking for information on your favourite stars?
Then you've found the page that gives you it.

"I'M the Face" is a funny sort of title for a record—the one made by the Hi Numbers. What's it supposed to mean? Any information on this group, Billy? I've never heard of them before they released this.—**Kathleen Burton (Hants.).**

"Face" was a word used a lot in London at one time to describe a person who was always around. Someone who was in on everything that happened. Now it's being used to describe Mods. The Hi Numbers are a new group to me, too. This is their first record. Roger Daltrey (20) lives in Wimbledon and was once a sheetmetal worker. Peter Townshend, from Ealing, came straight from art school into show-business. John Allison was a tax officer! Now he plays bass guitar. The drummer, Keith Moor, is 17, studied at Harrow Technical College and was once a trainee salesman.

Letters and postcards to Billy, Mirabelle, Tower House, Southampton St., London, W.C.2.

aiming high - the hi numbers

ANY news of what Gerry and the Pacemakers are doing in the next few months? I think they're terrific, and I'd love to see them.—**Geraldine Stoke (Glos.).**

Gerry will be doing an autumn tour, but I haven't got the actual dates and places yet. I'll let you know if he's coming your way, Geraldine. At Christmas he's doing a show in Liverpool called Gerry's Christmas Cracker—which should be an absolute riot. But of course at the moment he's got his mind on his film Ferry Across The Mersey. Apparently he loves filming. Everybody working with him said they had a fantastic time—even the camera crew enjoyed themselves. They shot some scenes in the Cavern Club, which went like a bomb, and others on location in Liverpool. "I got some lovely early nights," Gerry told us. "But I was up at the crack of dawn!"

WEDNESDAY, 19 AUGUST

Scene Club, Soho.

THURSDAY, 20 AUGUST

Majestic Ballroom, Luton.

Prior to the gig, the Who (still called the High Numbers) rehearsed and taped their debut television appearance on BBC-2's *The Beat Room* in Studio 3, at the BBC Television Centre, Wood Lane. It was broadcast Monday 24 August, from 7:35 to 8:00 pm.

Introduced by Pat Campbell, the group appeared in "The Beat Room Audition Spot," performing live versions of Bo Diddley's "Bring It To Jerome" and the Miracles' "Gotta Dance To Keep From Crying." Produced by Barry Langford, this edition also featured Brenda Lee, the Swinging Blue Jeans, Tommy Tucker, and resident group, Wayne Gibson with the Dynamic Sounds.

SATURDAY, 22 AUGUST

Trade Union Hall, Watford.

SUNDAY, 23 AUGUST

Hippodrome, Brighton. Two shows, 6:00 & 8:30 pm, supporting Dusty Springfield, Eden Kane, and the Interns.

TUESDAY, 25 AUGUST

Railway Hotel, Wealdstone.

WEDNESDAY, 26 AUGUST

Scene Club, Soho.

SUNDAY, 30 AUGUST

Queen's Theatre, Blackpool. Two shows, 6:00 & 8:10 pm, supporting the Searchers and the Kinks.

WEDNESDAY, 2 SEPTEMBER

The Mine, Carpenders Park Station, followed by the Scene Club, Soho.

A forty minute film, simply entitled *High Numbers*, shot on 16-mm by Kit Lambert (assisted by Mike Shaw) at the Scene and on location around Soho (exact filming dates unknown) was designed as a promotional tool to attract outside interest in the group. Thirteen years later, some of the surviving footage was blown up to 35-mm and used by Jeff Stein in his 1979 biopic, *The Kids Are Alright*. The synched mag track has since appeared on bootleg recordings, erroneously attributed to the Marquee Club.

The surviving reel features the Miracles' "I Gotta Dance To Keep From Crying," Mose Allison's "Young Man" (a.k.a. "Blues"), Don Covay's "Long Tall Shorty," Bo Diddley's "Pretty Thing" and "Here 'Tis," an extended version of Howlin Wolf's "Smokestack Lightning" (featuring experimental feedback passages), Barrett Strong's "Money," and a series of improvisations, one incorporating the "You Really Got Me" riff, being fresh from the recent Kinks' support slots.

FRIDAY, 4 SEPTEMBER

"Fab '64—The Big Beat Show," Kelvin Hall Arena, Glasgow, Scotland. Two shows, 6:00 & 8:15 pm, supporting Dave Berry and the Cruisers and Lulu and the Luvvers, promoted by Enterprise Scotland '64.

SUNDAY, 6 SEPTEMBER

Queens Theatre, Blackpool. Two shows, 6:00 & 8:10 pm, supporting the Swinging Blue Jeans and the Nashville Teens.

TUESDAY, 8 SEPTEMBER

Railway Hotel, Wealdstone.

TUESDAY, 15 SEPTEMBER

Railway Hotel, Wealdstone.

SATURDAY, 19 SEPTEMBER

Trade Union Hall, Watford.

TUESDAY, 22 SEPTEMBER

Railway Hotel, Wealdstone.

WEDNESDAY, 23 SEPTEMBER

Town Hall, Greenwich, South East London.

Local promoter Bryan Mason booked the High Numbers for his weekly dance after working with Bob Druce at the Glenlyn. DJ Jeff Dexter, whose path was to cross with the Who's on numerous occasions, first encountered them here: "I first heard about the Who through Pete Meaden. He'd told me about this mod band from Shepherd's Bush, which at that time, was like the other side of the world to me. Bryan booked them to play at our record show, which we held at the Town Hall one night a week. They had made up these bizarre flyers saying 'The High Numbers—The Worst In Family Entertainment.' Some of their West London mob came over and they all stood at the front.

"Ian 'Sammy' Samwell [composer of Cliff Richard's 'Move It'] introduced them, and I remember sitting upstairs watching them, thinking they were crap! However, I admired what they were trying to do. There was plenty of feedback from Pete, and Keith was astonishing to watch even then. They had this pop art–style drape, which I thought was quite arty, but they didn't really fulfil what Pete Meaden had told me."

Mason went on to promote the Who at the Starlite, Crawley; Bromel Club, Bromley; and Eltham Baths, Eltham Hill.

TUESDAY, 29 SEPTEMBER

Railway Hotel, Wealdstone.

WEDNESDAY, 30 SEPTEMBER

Town Hall, Greenwich.

FRIDAY, 2 OCTOBER

Shandon Hall Dance Club, Romford, Essex.

MONDAY, 5 OCTOBER

Corn Exchange, Rochester, Kent.

TUESDAY, 6 OCTOBER

Railway Hotel, Wealdstone.

WEDNESDAY, 7 OCTOBER

The Mine, Carpenders Park Station.

SATURDAY, 10 OCTOBER

Olympia Ballroom, Reading, Berkshire.

The first of a string of gigs at "Leo's Cavern," run by local entrepreneur Leo de Clerck, who operated clubs under the same name at Maidenhead and Windsor. (The Who very likely played these also, but the dates cannot be traced.)

Fabulous magazine ran an article on the High Numbers written by June Southworth, along with a full-page colour photo taken by Fiona Adams. John was cited as John Allison who "plays rhythm guitar."

SUNDAY, 11 OCTOBER

Wolsey Hall, Cheshunt, Hertfordshire.

The group were a popular attraction at this Waltham Cross youth club, which opened on 26 August. The group returned on 18 November after reverting back to the name the Who.

TUESDAY, 13 OCTOBER
Trade Union Hall, Watford.

WEDNESDAY, 14 OCTOBER
Town Hall, Greenwich.

SUNDAY, 18 OCTOBER
Trade Union Hall, Watford.

MONDAY, 19 OCTOBER
Corn Exchange, Rochester.

TUESDAY, 20 OCTOBER
Railway Hotel, Wealdstone.

During this time, Kit Lambert shot 16-mm film stock of the group and their audience at one of the regular Tuesday night sessions, designed to be shown as an interval feature at gigs. Surviving footage (showing Daltrey wearing dark shades and Moon in a striped top) was used in *The Kids Are Alright*.

Lambert and Stamp hired cameramen and technicians from Better Sound Ltd., a company based at 33 Endell Street, Covent Garden, and run by brothers Michael and Jack Colomb. "Kit and I made their lives hell over the years," Stamp remembered. "We rented their equipment and people and always expected to get hold of them at short notice because we'd only owe the company and not the individuals. Such was our credit system; we couldn't afford to pay them, but we were always giving them work!"

THURSDAY, 22 OCTOBER
On this date, John Burgess, an A&R man at EMI, formally replied to Kit Lambert concerning the High Numbers' "test session," cautiously asking for more material after listening to the "white labels" cut. (Unfortunately, a thorough search through EMI's meticulous written archive and tape library log could provide no record of the session.)

Certainly, an audition did take place in Studio 3 at EMI Recording Studios, 3 Abbey Road, St. John's Wood, North West London. As Burgess recalled: "I got to hear about the group through Russ Conway [a popular British light entertainment pianist], who asked me to audition them as a favour. I think they'd met in his dressing room at the Palladium when there was vague talk of them backing him! I was working for Norman Newell at Abbey Road at the time. The band ran through three or four numbers, and I remember Keith's drums being far too loud, but they were very good." As the letter, later reproduced without his permission in *Live At Leeds*, stated, Burgess was interested in hearing any other material the band might have to offer. Townshend elaborated: "They [EMI] said, 'we think you're a great little R&B band, but the Beatles have set a trend of groups writing their own material you've just really got to do it.' So away we walked and about eight to ten weeks later, a song I'd written, 'I Can't Explain' was in the charts."

SATURDAY, 24 OCTOBER
Olympia Ballroom, Reading.

TUESDAY, 27 OCTOBER
Olympia Ballroom, Reading.

WEDNESDAY, 28 OCTOBER
Town Hall, Greenwich.

FRIDAY, 30 OCTOBER
Ricky-Tick Club, Windsor, Berkshire.

SATURDAY, 31 OCTOBER
Waterfront Club, Cliff Hotel, Woolston, Southampton, Hampshire.

(THE WHO)

EARLY NOVEMBER
The Who's debut session with producer Shel Talmy took place over two hours at Pye Records Ltd. Studio, ATV House, Great Cumberland Place, Marble Arch. "I Can't Explain" and "Bald Headed Woman," a Talmy "trad-arranged" composition that had recently been recorded by his other clients, the Kinks, were recorded and mixed on three-track tape.

Like many studio debuts of the era, the session had tried and trusted session musicians on hand, including twenty-year-old guitarist, Jimmy Page, who played fuzz box on "Bald Headed Woman." Roger played percussion on "I Can't Explain" and harmonica on "Bald Headed Woman." The distinctive, high register backing vocals on "I Can't Explain" were provided by the Ivy League, a three-man harmony trio from Birmingham, consisting of John Carter, Perry Ford, and Ken Lewis. Ford also played piano on "Bald Headed Woman."

The Who's official Fan Club was founded under the pseudonym "Jane Who" at 74 Kensington Park Road, West London. This was the residential address of Robert Fearnley-Whittingstall, an army colleague of Lambert's. His wife Jane became the group's first Fan Club president, later replaced by Island Records' secretary Deirdre Meehan in mid-1965.

MONDAY, 2 NOVEMBER
Railway Hotel, Wealdstone.

WEDNESDAY, 4 NOVEMBER
The Mine, Carpenders Park Station.

SATURDAY, 7 NOVEMBER
Trade Union Hall, Watford.

MONDAY, 9 NOVEMBER
Corn Exchange, Rochester.

SATURDAY, 14 NOVEMBER
Olympia Ballroom, Reading.

WEDNESDAY, 18 NOVEMBER
Wolsey Hall, Cheshunt.

FRIDAY, 20 NOVEMBER
"Look At Me Now" B/W "It Was You" was released by the Naturals on Parlophone. The B-side, one of Pete's earliest compositions, carried the co-written credit: "Townshend—[Eula] Parker—[Barry] Gray." As a result of an agreement signed on Wednesday, 14 October, which placed the song with Beatles' publisher Dick James, the publishing royalties were split, with Parker and Gray each receiving 25%. As Pete was still a minor, Cliff Townshend acted as co-signatory, with Pete's address given as 30 Disraeli Road, Ealing W5.

SATURDAY, 21 NOVEMBER
Ealing Club, Ealing Broadway, West London. The first documented Who gig at this legendary venue below the ABC bakery, opposite Ealing Broadway station.

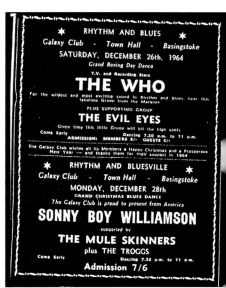

TUESDAY, 24 NOVEMBER

Marquee Club, Soho, London.

This gig was the commencement of the Who's important Tuesday night residency at this central London club, situated at 90 Wardour Street. Despite the poor turn-out, promoter Ziggy Jackson was impressed enough to book the group for a run of sixteen weeks—extended to a further seven when their popularity broke house attendance records. The Who usually played two sets, from 8:45–9:15 pm and from 10:00–11:00 pm. Coincidentally, the support group, the Sneekers, had just issued their version of "Bald Headed Woman," produced by Shel Talmy on Columbia Records.

WEDNESDAY, 25 NOVEMBER

Florida Rooms, Brighton.

SATURDAY, 28 NOVEMBER

Corn Exchange, Chelmsford, Essex.

SUNDAY, 29 NOVEMBER

Trade Union Hall, Watford.

TUESDAY, 1 DECEMBER

Marquee Club.

WEDNESDAY, 2 DECEMBER

Florida Rooms, Brighton.

TUESDAY, 8 DECEMBER

Marquee Club.

WEDNESDAY, 9 DECEMBER

Florida Rooms, Brighton.

SATURDAY, 12 DECEMBER

Technical College, Harrow. Students' Christmas Dance at Keith's old alma mater.

Cathy McGowan, a compère on British television's most "with-it" pop programme, *Ready, Steady, Go!*, was present, and no doubt reported back to the show's producers. (See 29 January 1965.)

MONDAY, 14 DECEMBER

The Red Lion, Leytonstone, East London.

Lambert and Stamp's obsession to launch the Who in solid working class areas continued with a trial Monday night stint at this large, draughty East End pub, found for them by journalist associate Ray Tolliday. There was a strong Mod following in the area, but without a record or promotion, virtually nobody had heard of the group. At least four Monday night bookings followed.

TUESDAY, 15 DECEMBER

Marquee Club.

WEDNESDAY, 16 DECEMBER

Florida Rooms, Brighton.

FRIDAY, 18 DECEMBER

Waterfront Club, Cliff Hotel, Southampton.

SATURDAY, 19 DECEMBER

Xmas Ball, London College of Printing, Elephant and Castle, South East London.

The American record industry journal *Cashbox* reviewed the Who's first Decca single, "Bald Headed Woman" B/W "I Can't Explain," (the B-side was considered the "plug side") almost six weeks before its U.K. release on 15 January 1965. The record only barely squeezed into the *Billboard* Hot 100, reaching #93 on 3 April.

MONDAY, 21 DECEMBER

The Red Lion, Leytonstone.

TUESDAY, 22 DECEMBER

Marquee Club. Supported by the North London group the Boys, who renamed themselves the Action the following year. Bassist Mike Evans had played with Keith in Mark Twain and the Strangers. (See "I'm a Boy," Keith.)

WEDNESDAY, 23 DECEMBER

Florida Rooms, Brighton.

SATURDAY, 26 DECEMBER

Galaxy Club, Town Hall, Basingstoke, Hampshire.

SUNDAY, 27 DECEMBER

Ealing Club.

MONDAY, 28 DECEMBER

The Red Lion, Leytonstone.

TUESDAY, 29 DECEMBER

Marquee Club.

THURSDAY, 31 DECEMBER

New Year's Eve Dance, Pinner, Middlesex.

BALD HEADED WOMAN (2:10) [Duchess, BMI—Talmy]
I CAN'T EXPLAIN (2:05) [Champion, BMI—Townsend]
THE WHO (Decca 31725)

The Who, a new English group, bows on Decca with a wild-sounding affair that could bust loose in the coming weeks. It's a blues-styled hand-clapper, tagged "Bald Headed Woman," that starts off slow and picks up steam along the way—building into a 'pull-out-all-the-stops' throbber. Side was produced in England by Shel Talmy. Under half's an attention-getting shuffle-rock'er.

my generation 1965

THE WHO
Brunswick

"I Can't Explain" was released one year into the so-called "British Invasion." The Beatles, the Rolling Stones, the Animals, the Kinks, and Manfred Mann had successfully brought coals to Newcastle by reintroducing America to its own indigenous roots. The Mersey Sound faded away, to be replaced by R&B groups sprouting like mushrooms all over England.

The single slipped out on 15 January among a slew of Decca releases that week, with approximately 1000 copies initially pressed. Since its salad days of scoring hits with Bill Haley, Buddy Holly, Brenda Lee, and Ricky Nelson, the American arm of Decca had become less enamoured with rock and roll. The burden of pushing the record automatically fell upon Kit Lambert and Chris Stamp, who were horrified to learn that the company's promotional policy was unimaginative at best, non-existent at worst.

As film men, both rightly believed the visual medium was imperative in breaking the Who's unorthodox sound and image. Since it's inception in August 1963, *Ready, Steady, Go!* had established a reputation as the most stylish and innovative pop music programme on British television, carrying the immortal tag: "The Weekend Starts Here!" The show's production team were one step ahead in tirelessly pursuing the most exciting music and fashion trends from week to week. Lambert met with programme editor Bob Bickford, a former record reviewer for the *Daily Mail*, who, by coincidence, knew of the Who's reputation from the Marquee. Bickford booked them for their first *RSG!* appearance on 29 January. A week before transmission, the studio was found to be around 150 dancers short of its usual quota. In a stroke of managerial genius, Lambert advised the floor manager to scout the Marquee on a Tuesday night. Come the day of the taping, the audience was half-full of the Who's devoted following. When Lambert exhorted the faithful to shower their scarves around the studio, the effect was galvanising. Anyone watching that week would have remembered it and immediately associated it with the Who.

Lambert next turned his sights to offshore pirate radio, whose influence was inestimable in breaking a record—at a price. Radio London's Dave Dennis started plugging the record as a "climber," but it was rival Caroline who succeeded in breaking it when Stamp (working in Norway on Anthony Mann's *The Heroes Of Telemark*) bombarded station boss Ronan O'Rahilly with calls to have it played. Several *Top Of The Pops* appearances later, "I Can't Explain" finally broke into the U.K. Top Ten, reaching # 8 in April.

When the dust settled, the record had grossed approximately £35,000. Out of this, the retailers took £10,000, Decca £16,000, the taxman £5,000. Townshend and his publisher, David Platz of Essex Music, took £2000 in composer royalties, and the group ended up with about £250 each. Lambert and Stamp failed to break even. Realising the hopelessness of the situation, the pair fought for three weeks with Talmy and Decca to raise the group's pitiful royalty rate from 2.5 to 4 per cent in England and Europe, but it was still a pittance. Keeping their investment ticking over was going to be a precipitous business. By year's end, it was estimated the Who were already £60,000 in debt.

Journalist and associate Ray Tolliday perfectly encapsulated the organised chaos that was New Action Ltd. in an article for *Cream*: "Money matters were always tight, to say the least, and one feature of the group's headquarters at Eaton Place was an accountant slowly going demented as the bills piled up and the money didn't. At one point, only the money Chris Stamp was sending to England from

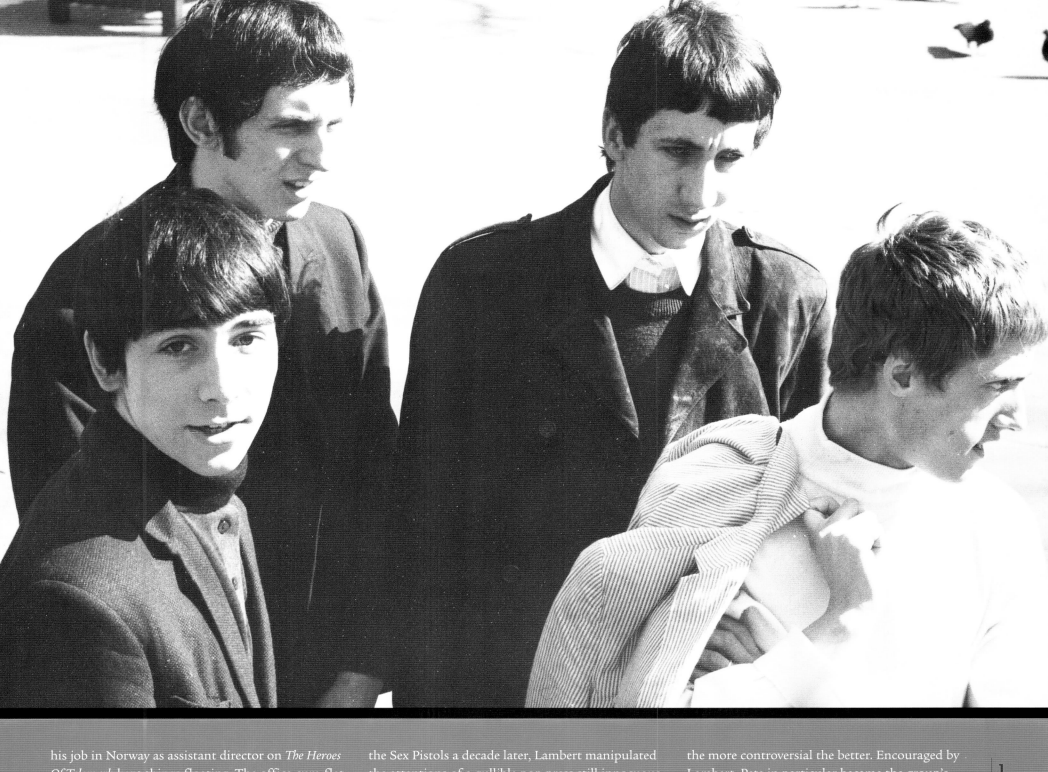

his job in Norway as assistant director on *The Heroes Of Telemark* kept things floating. The office-cum-flat generally looked as though Oscar Madison [from Neil Simon's *The Odd Couple*] lived there, and droves of people drifted in and out, reporting parking tickets and stolen gear."

With little money coming in, publicity, good or bad, was invaluable. Like Malcolm McLaren behind the Sex Pistols a decade later, Lambert manipulated the attentions of a gullible pop press still innocuous enough to faithfully report a musician's height and favourite colour. With the Who, they found they weren't dealing with the same industry-tamed puppets. Journalists from the music weeklies and national dailies would squeeze into dressing rooms to hear the group expound their outspoken views, the more controversial the better. Encouraged by Lambert, Pete in particular became the group's enfant terrible, willing to provide quotable copy to provoke the most hardened hack. "Kit used to brief us before we went into interviews about what to say," he told *The Observer* in 1972, "...to be as objectionable, arrogant and nasty as possible. And oh, those outrageous lies we told! I remember telling

Jonathan Aitken [of the *Evening Standard*], 'I've got four cars, a Lincoln Continental, a Jag XK 150, a Cortina GT, and a London taxi' and all I had was an old banger. Then I said to somebody else that I was spending between £40 and £50 a week on clothes, and had to borrow money to go to Carnaby Street and buy a jacket in order to pose for a picture."

Townshend described the Who as the group with a "built-in hate," combining "tremendous fire and aggression." "We don't allow our instruments to stop us doing what we want," he sneered. "We smash our instruments, tear our clothes, and wreck everything. The expense doesn't worry us because that would get between us and our music. If I stood on stage worrying about the price of a guitar, then I'm not really playing music. I'm getting involved in material values." Having been drawn into the web, the journalist was invited to witness the theory of "pop art" being put into practice on stages almost too small to contain the group. Exploiting the power of amplification

to its limits, the Who used its deafening possibilities to project a brilliantly cohesive blend of rage, frustration, tension, and fury.

A typical Marquee set incorporated an eclectic mix of R&B (elongated workouts on Bo Diddley's "I'm A Man" and Howlin Wolf's "Smokestack Lightning"), soul (Derek Martin's "Daddy Rolling Stone," Rufus Thomas's "Jump Back," Chris Kenner's "Land Of 1000 Dances," and Jesse Hill's "Oo Poo Pah Doo"), jazz

(Mose Allison's "Young Man" and Phil Upchurch's "You Can't Sit Down"), Motown (Martha and the Vandellas' "Dancing In The Street," "Heatwave," and "Motorin'," Eddie Holland's "Leaving Here," and Marvin Gaye's "Baby Don't You Do It"), and James Brown ("Please, Please, Please," "I Don't Mind," and "Shout And Shimmy.") "I think in some ways, that was the most interesting period of our career," said Daltrey, "because we made all those songs our own as just a three instrument and vocal band."

The smashing of the instruments climaxed the act as the final cathartic release of aggression. As a concession to purism, the hit record was rarely played. "'Can't Explain' was written as a commercial number to introduce us to the charts," Pete told the BBC's Brian Matthew, "but we want to try and get rid of all that and show what we're really trying to do."

The Who's anarchic image still needed to be brought through on wax for maximum impact. The arrogant, strutting braggadocio of "Anyway, Anyhow, Anywhere" was just the ticket—two and a half minutes of "orderly disorder," as Townshend described it.

The song's existentialist feel was inspired by his love of the free jazz of Albert Ayler and Charlie Parker, reflected in Townshend's rhythmic flipping of the guitar's toggle switch to produce the solo's morse code bleeps and machine gun fire. During a Marquee rehearsal, Daltrey changed Townshend's verses to toughen the song up to suit his temperament, the sole example of any credited collaboration between the two. Kit Lambert, in atypically florid fashion, described it as "a pop art record, containing pop art music. The sounds of war and chaos and frustration expressed musically without the use of sound effects."

Upon it's release on 24 May, "Anyway, Anyhow, Anywhere" neatly polarised opinion. Its brashness was perfectly suited to the visual pop art of *Ready,*

Steady, Go! Indeed, the show adopted the song as it's signature tune for a spell.

Pop art was *in*. Ideas were concocted from Pete's art school experience in earnest discussions with Lambert. "We stand for pop art clothes, pop art music, and pop art behaviour," Townshend declared. "This is what everybody seems to forget. We don't change offstage. We live pop art." Pete's jackets were festooned with badges and medals found in his parent's antique shop; Roger created makeshift designs on sweaters with black adhesive tape; Keith wore T-shirts emblazoned with a coloured target, the word "POW!" or hip slogans such as "Elvis For Everyone"; and John's bush jackets had RAF stripes or chevron motifs on the sleeves, an idea copied from Bridget Riley. Townshend draped a Union Jack flag over his speaker cabinet, which he symbolically speared at the end of a show, and now, with the help of a Savile Row tailor, the sanctified symbol of British royalty was designed into a jacket to his specifications.

With a non-conformist image and two Top Ten hits under their belts, the Who were finding acceptance from their more discerning peers. Brian Jones befriended Pete, telling journalists the Who occupied the position that the Stones had held after their first few hits. "They are the only young group doing something new both visually and musically," Jones said. "Originality usually means success." The more gregarious Keith rubbed shoulders with the premier group in rock royalty, the Beatles. Paul McCartney called the Who "the best thing to happen on the 1965 scene."

If Mod was dying in London, no one told the provinces, where the Who found a ready-made audience that was experiencing the short, sharp shocks from the group's regular *Ready, Steady, Go!* appearances. The group were getting bigger and better bookings further afield, and the year was spent travelling ridiculous distances around Britain. "We used to play up North and dash back in the furniture van to play the Noreik in Tottenham," John reminisced to Richard Green. "We were complete pill heads, and we'd often still be playing when the other group went on. Then we got used to drunken playing, and I'd often forget I'd done a gig. Moon would pass out before a gig, sober up just before we went on, play like a maniac, and go back to the bottle as soon as we finished!"

While Stamp was away for six weeks working on *The Heroes Of Telemark*, Lambert persuaded Pete to

1965

move from Ealing into the flat he and Stamp rented above New Action's office. Once installed, Lambert took the art school drop-out under his worldly wing, introducing Pete to all manner of sophistication, which also appealed to Keith's tastes. In June, Pete moved into a two room, £12 per week flat at nearby 8 Chesham Place, found for him by Anya Butler. Lambert's faith in Townshend's songwriting abilities was demonstrated when he invested more than £1,000 in recording equipment: two Vortexions (upgraded to a pair of stereo Revoxes), a Nagra portable recorder, and two Marshall stage speakers. Out of this environment, Pete recorded and presented demos to the band for consideration.

Lambert often came to listen and make suggestions, encouraging his protégé to make a grand statement—something sweeping, "something Wagnerian!" When Townshend's beloved 1935 Packard hearse was towed away, supposedly because it represented an affront to the Queen Mother, who passed it from nearby Buckingham Palace, his revulsion at the incident and his disdain for the haughty residents of Belgravia provided the appropriate inspiration.

"'My Generation' was written as a talking blues thing," Townshend recalled, "something like Jimmy Reed's 'Talkin' New York Blues.' In fact, 'Generation' started off as my folk song single. Dylan affected me a lot. Then it went through six or seven changes." The demo was very nearly discarded as lightweight, but Chris Stamp thought otherwise and used heavy persuasion to get the group to record it. "We tried it a couple of times," said Townshend, "and it got more like a Who number. Then Kit came up and rapped with me about how I should alter this and that—and then I came up with the stutter."

The actual sessions for "My Generation" were acrimonious ("near punch-ups" according to Daltrey) and for Entwistle, expensive. As he remembered it, "I bought this Danelectro bass, and it had these tiny, thin wirewound strings on. They were so thin, they sounded just like a piano, an unbelievably clear sound. The only thing was that you couldn't buy these strings. When we recorded 'My Generation,' I ended up with three of these Danelectros just for the strings. The last one I had, the string busted before we actually got into the studio to re-record it, so I did it on a Fender Jazz in the end with tape-wound La Bella strings."

The song surged forward through three key changes (an idea pilfered again from the Kinks) before exploding to a climax of feedback and distortion. Even if the Who had not recorded another note, which at that point remained a distinct possibility, "My Generation" would have ensured their immortality. It was a rallying cry for the disaffected, the first truly subversive rock song to come out of Britain. It was also a provocative statement and one which the group, and Townshend in particular, would have difficulty coming to terms with over successive years.

Violence and frustration were an integral part of the Who's image, and now internal dissension spilled out into the open. "Roger causes a lot of trouble because he is never satisfied with the sound, and he is the only one who will speak about it," Townshend told *Disc*. Both he and Moon thought Daltrey's vocal abilities suspect and delighted in stating so publicly. For his part, Daltrey felt the group had lost touch with its earthy roots, and had little empathy with Townshend's arty-farty ideas or Moon's daft passion for surf music. Entwistle just never bothered to take sides. Added to this, the others were consuming speed with great alacrity, which Daltrey felt adversely affected their playing.

Tensions finally snapped during a particularly fraught European jaunt in September. As Keith told Jerry Hopkins: "Roger blew up: 'You're all fucking junkies! I'm not having any truck with ya!'" When Daltrey made his point by flushing Moon's pill

stash, the diminutive drummer attacked the wiry frontman with a tambourine, resulting in a full-on punch-up. That night, the group unanimously elected to fire their singer.

With the Who effectively in limbo, fate intervened. A heavy workload beckoned when "My Generation" was released on 29 October, jumping straight into the *New Musical Express* chart at #16. Estranged from his wife and son and living in the back of the group van, Roger swallowed his pride and meekly asked to be allowed to rejoin, promising to curb his temper. Lambert and Stamp persuaded the others he should be re-admitted, but for years afterward, Daltrey continued to fret as to the extent of his re-acceptance. Had the others forgiven him, or were they planning to replace him at the earliest convenience?

In December, the group's long-awaited debut album, *My Generation*, was unleashed. Despite perfectly encapsulating the early Who rawness, the group disowned it, mainly due to their growing disenchantment with Shel Talmy. Townshend's disparaging review appeared in *Record Mirror* under the self-explanatory verdict: "I Hate It... Rubbish!... It's Crap." "That was after playing blues for two years," Daltrey told Gary Herman. "...and it was very scrappily done... It wasn't like we were on stage... That album was recorded very quickly and very cheaply, and it wasn't really what we were all about then, but it came out in the period when we were getting into Pete Townshend more, you know."

My Generation signified the end of the Who's Mod phase. It was also the last in a series of perceptive statements that mirrored their audience. "I was able to achieve it," Townshend told Nick Logan in 1972, "by actually being involved! What was so great was the unanimity of it, the way I could blend in and be one of them. There was no class thing... The point was that I was involved in it, and I could write songs as a pilled-up Mod that were straight from the heart, involvement songs like 'Can't Explain,' 'Anyway, Anyhow, Anywhere,' 'My Generation.' But I think that's where they stopped."

Daltrey gave a more realistic slant: "I think if he had stuck with writing for that group of kids in Shepherd's Bush, what would ever have been written? I think he was always writing about bigger things, for me anyway, being the interpreter of it."

1965

SATURDAY, 2 JANUARY
Ealing Club.

MONDAY, 4 JANUARY
The Red Lion, Leytonstone.

TUESDAY, 5 JANUARY
Marquee Club.

SATURDAY, 9 JANUARY
Ealing Club, followed by the first of several appearances at the "All Nite Rave," held from midnight— 6:00 am at the Club Noreik, a bingo hall situated on Tottenham High Road, North London.

TUESDAY, 12 JANUARY
Marquee Club.

WEDNESDAY, 13 JANUARY
Wolsey Hall, Cheshunt.

FRIDAY, 15 JANUARY
"I Can't Explain" B/W "Bald Headed Woman" was released on Brunswick, American Decca's U.K. subsidiary (see 19 December 1964). This same day, Pete filled in a third BBC Light Programme audition form (see 19 December 1963 and 4 March 1964), now listing Keith Moon on drums and "John Brown" (another Entwistle nom de plume) on bass.

SUNDAY, 17 JANUARY
New Theatre, Oxford, Oxfordshire.
Two shows, 6:15 & 8:30 pm, supporting P.J. Proby with the Mike Cotton Sound, Cliff Bennett and the Rebel Rousers, and Sandra Barry and the Boys.

MONDAY, 18 JANUARY
Technical College, Westminster, London.

TUESDAY, 19 JANUARY
Marquee Club.

LEFT: First appearance on *Ready, Steady, Go!*, 29 January.

FRIDAY, 22 JANUARY
From 8:15—8:45 pm, the Who pre-taped their first appearance on Radio Luxembourg's *Ready, Steady, Radio!*—the Sunday evening waveband equivalent to Rediffusion's popular television programme, *Ready, Steady, Go!*
The show involved guest artists interviewed from the stage of the Marquee and then miming to their latest release before an invited live audience. Hosted by *RSG!* presenter Keith Fordyce and Luxembourg's Dee Shenderey, it was broadcast over the 208 waveband on 31 January, from 9:30—10:00 pm.

SATURDAY, 23 JANUARY
Corn Exchange, Chelmsford, followed by the "All Nite Rave," Club Noreik, Tottenham, with the Muleskinners, featuring future Small Faces keyboardist, Ian McLagan.

TUESDAY, 26 JANUARY
Marquee Club.

FRIDAY, 29 JANUARY
The Who's memorable first appearance on Rediffusion's Friday evening pop show *Ready, Steady, Go!*, which was transmitted live over the ITV region from 6:08—7:00 pm. Although usually presented from Studio Nine, Television House, Kingsway, this edition was staged at the larger Studio One in Wembley, where the production eventually moved to from 2 April.
The group spent the afternoon in rehearsal, and as well as miming "I Can't Explain," were allowed to play one other (unknown) number because of a programming slip-up. Fellow guests were the Animals, the Hollies, Donovan, Ron and Mel, Elkie Brooks, Goldie and the Gingerbreads, Rick and Sandy, and Rhythm and Blues Inc.

SATURDAY, 30 JANUARY
Ealing Club.

TUESDAY, 2 FEBRUARY
Marquee Club.

TUESDAY, 9 FEBRUARY
Marquee Club.
The group were billed as "The Who London 1965" until 20 April.

THURSDAY, 11 FEBRUARY
Ealing Club.
Billed as "The Who London 1965" for the next four Thursdays.

FRIDAY, 12 FEBRUARY
At 9:00 am, the Who's second audition for the BBC Light Programme took place at Studio S2, Broadcasting House, Portland Place, the same studio where they had (unsuccessfully) auditioned on 9 April 1964. (The corporation's paperwork took great pains to note that two members of the group arrived 25 minutes late!)
The group performed "Baby Don't You Do It," "Luby [sic] Come Home," and "Shout And Shimmy." The group narrowly passed on a 4/3 majority. "Ponderous and unentertaining," "at the limit of their capabilities," and "lead guitar seemed more sure of himself than the rest. Overall not very original and below standard" were some of the harsher verdicts delivered. One of the group's four allies noted: "With the right material and production, they could very easily make a hit." The tape was passed by J.E. Grant on Thursday 18 February, and a letter informing the group of their successful application was written and delivered the following day—just as "I Can't Explain" entered the week's *Record Mirror* chart (compiled by *Record Retailer*) at #45.

SATURDAY, 13 FEBRUARY
Waterfront Club, Cliff Hotel, Southampton.

TUESDAY, 16 FEBRUARY
Marquee Club.
Excerpts from six numbers, plus film shot in Shepherd's Bush and Hammersmith, formed a documentary about Mods by French television producers, Alain de Sedouy and André Harris, both acquaintances of Chris Stamp. The film was shown as part of the weekly programme *Seize Millions de Jeunes*, transmitted Thursday 18 March, 9:00—9:30 pm, on ORTF TV 2. Sedouy described the Who as having "a logical musical expression of the bewilderment and anarchy of London's teenagers."
Marquee footage of the Who from this time appeared for all of eight seconds in *Carousella*, a 25 minute "X" certificate documentary about three Soho strippers, directed by John Irvin (*The Dogs Of War*) for Mithras Films.

THURSDAY, 18 FEBRUARY
Ealing Club.

SUNDAY, 21 FEBRUARY
St. Joseph's Hall, Wembley.

TUESDAY, 23 FEBRUARY
Marquee Club.
"I Can't Explain" entered the *NME* chart at #28.

THURSDAY, 25 FEBRUARY
Ealing Club.

FRIDAY, 26 FEBRUARY
Lynx Youth Club, Boreham Wood, Hertfordshire.

SUNDAY, 28 FEBRUARY
Agincourt Ballroom, Camberley, Surrey.

TUESDAY, 2 MARCH
Marquee Club.

WEDNESDAY, 3 MARCH
Le Disque a Go!Go! Club, Lansdowne, Bournemouth, Hampshire.
Keith met his future wife, sixteen-year-old local model Kim Kerrigan at the gig.

THURSDAY, 4 MARCH
Ealing Club.

FRIDAY, 5 MARCH
Granby Halls, Leicester. "Rag Rave" with Manfred Mann and Mike Berry and the Le Roys.
On the bill were the Contacts, featuring singer and harmonica player, Christopher Morphet, a film student at the College of Arts and Technology. Morphet struck up a close friendship with Pete and photographed the Who on numerous occasions throughout the 60's.

MONDAY, 8 MARCH
"I Can't Explain" had climbed to #26 on the previous week's *NME* chart, but then, alarmingly, dropped out completely. During this week, Lambert and Stamp spent three days (and £350) shooting and editing a 16-mm promotional film featuring location scenes, a promotional appearance inside the Harlequin Record Store at 96 Berwick Street, Soho, and studio shots with the band miming to playback in front of their

RIGHT: FILMING THE "I CAN'T EXPLAIN" PROMO AT HARLEQUIN RECORDS, SOHO, 8 MARCH.

Marshall set-up at the rear of the Marquee studio.
Lambert then sold the clip for the inclusive sum of £25 to the producers of Rediffusion's *That's For Me*, a weekly viewer's request programme. The 2 min 6 secs film was inserted into the 15 March edition, introduced by future BBC Radio 1 disc jockey Anne Nightingale from Studio One, Wembley, and transmitted live from 6:08—7:00 pm over certain ITV regions. Nightingale also talked to fans in the audience who had written in asking for the group to appear. Part of the "I Can't Explain" promo was used in the video *Who's Better, Who's Best*.
Thirty seconds of Marquee footage (shot this week) appeared during "In Search Of Constant Lambert," part of BBC-2's *Workshop* series. Broadcast Monday 26 July, 9:40—10:40 pm, and narrated by Francis Coleman, the documentary painted "a portrait of the man and his music by friends and colleagues." The Who were seen miming to "I Can't Explain" under the watchful eye of Kit Lambert (seen in the video *Thirty Years of Maximum R&B Live*), who also talked about his composer father.

TUESDAY, 9 MARCH
Marquee Club.

WEDNESDAY, 10 MARCH
Ealing Club.

THURSDAY, 11 MARCH
Fate dealt Lambert and Stamp a lucky hand when the Who were booked as last-minute replacements in the "Tip For The Top" slot on the prime time BBC-1 programme *Top Of The Pops*. The group were flown to Manchester, their fares paid for by the BBC, to record their first appearance at the corporation's studio, a converted church in Dickenson Road, Rusholme. Following camera rehearsals running from noon in Studio A, the group mimed "I Can't Explain," broadcast live from 7:30—8:00 pm.

FRIDAY, 12 MARCH
Goldhawk Social Club, Shepherd's Bush.

SATURDAY, 13 MARCH
"All Nite Rave," Club Noreik, Tottenham.

SUNDAY, 14 MARCH
Starlite Ballroom, Sudbury, Greenford. The first documented Who gig at this popular Allendale Road venue, which opened on 25 September 1964.

MONDAY, 15 MARCH
Rehearsals commenced at 10:30 am inside Television Theatre, Shepherd's Bush, for BBC-2's *Gadzooks! It's All Happening*, the successor to *The Beat Room*, on which the Who had made their television debut as the High Numbers. (See 20 August 1964.) The group played live versions of "Shout and Shimmy" and "I Can't Explain," receiving a standard BBC performance fee of £42.

CLUB NOREIK
HIGH RD., TOTTENHAM, N.15
SAT. MAR. 13
THE WHO
PLUS
THE CANDLES
ADMISSION - 7/6

Introduced by Alan David and Christine Holmes, the programme was transmitted live, 7:00—7:30 pm, and featured comedian Peter Cook, the Three Bells, Dorris Henderson, the Countrymen, Alexis Korner's Blues Incorporated, Donovan, and Judi Johnson and the Perfections.

By lucky coincidence, if viewers switched to the programme from rival channel ITV, they would have just caught the Who on *That's For Me* (see 8 March.) What with a last-minute *Top Of The Pops* appearance (11 March), it was the kind of exposure Lambert and Stamp could only have dreamed of. Within the week, "I Can't Explain" re-entered the *NME* Top Thirty at #23.

TUESDAY, 16 MARCH
Marquee Club.

According to a New Action call sheet, the group were scheduled to rehearse at the club for Shel Talmy from 12:00—6:00 pm. Around this time, a session at Pye Studios with Talmy included versions of Eddie Holland's "Leaving Here" and Marvin Gaye's "Baby Don't You Do It." The master tapes appear lost, but both tracks were remastered (from an acetate source) and released on the revamped *Odds and Sods* CD in 1998.

WEDNESDAY, 17 MARCH
Ealing Club.

The Who spent the afternoon being photographed around various West End sites by Decca lensman David Wedgbury, ostensibly for their first U.S. album sleeve. Wedgbury photographed in both colour and black-and-white at Piccadilly Circus, Regent Street, and Trafalgar Square. A shot of the group sitting among the lion statues at the foot of Nelson's Column would later be included in the *Live At Leeds* packaging in 1970. Wedgbury also photographed them standing, using Nelson's Column as a sky backdrop. The group then walked to nearby Westminster Bridge for the same idea, utilising the Big Ben clocktower. Although the album didn't eventuate in its intended form, U.S. Decca chose one of the latter striking shots to grace *The Who Sings My Generation* sleeve.

FRIDAY, 19 MARCH
Public Baths, Royston, Hertfordshire.

From 2:00—5:00 pm, the group recorded at IBC (International Broadcasting Company) Sound Recording Studios, 35 Portland Place, London, with producer Shel Talmy, engineer Glyn Johns, and session pianist Nicky Hopkins. Tracks cut included a second version of Eddie Holland's "Leaving Here" and Bo Diddley's "I'm A Man." In a *Disc* interview (dated 27 February), Pete mentioned the group might be cutting a Townshend original, "You Don't Have To Jerk" (a popular dance step), as their next single, but Talmy's tape log does not mention this title.

SATURDAY, 20 MARCH
Goldhawk Social Club, Shepherd's Bush.

Beforehand, all of the group attended the opening show of the Tamla Motown Revue at the Astoria, Finsbury Park, North London.

SUNDAY, 21 MARCH
Trade Union Hall, Watford.

BELOW: Edmonton, 25 March.

MONDAY, 22 MARCH
Parr Hall, Warrington, Lancashire.

TUESDAY, 23 MARCH
Marquee Club.

WEDNESDAY, 24 MARCH
Ealing Club.

That morning, the Who pre-recorded their second appearance on BBC-1's *Top Of The Pops* in Manchester, transmitted the following evening, 7:30—8:00 pm.

THURSDAY, 25 MARCH
Blue Opera R&B Club, Cooks Ferry Inn, Edmonton, North London.

FRIDAY, 26 MARCH
Ealing Club.

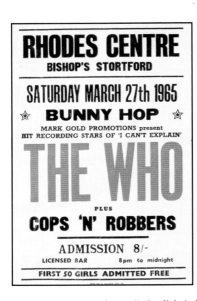

THE QUESTION IS 'WHO'?
THE ANSWER IS HERE . . .

WHOEVER? Who cares? Who knows? Who are you? The Who. The What? The Who group. A new-sound group. A strange group. A moving group. A noisy group. A spontaneous group, whose performance is without love or sentiment. We can't explain.

It's different. It's dangerous. You dig it. You don't. Wild. Way-out. Their sound rings through you. Bursting your eardrums. Exciting. Bewildering. Appalling. Gripping. You leave the Marquee Club where they play, wondering. Perhaps doubtful. Perhaps joyful. Their sound is your sound or it isn't.

In the London streets again, you walk and remember. Lead guitarist, Peter Townsend, tall, thin; long, spiky, expressive hands, a red spotlight shining on him in the darker than half-light, crashes across the strings of a guitar. Twists the amplifiers so that the feed-back keeps coming through and he brutally bangs his guitar forward, hitting the speaker, smashing through the canvas screen. He

jerks back, convulses forward. There is a stiffness and an abandon. What is happening?

Drummer, Keith Moon, dark fringe falling into his eyes, the hair separated with perspiration. Almost maniacal, rolling his drum sticks, going wild, opening his mouth, closing his eyes.

Bass guitarist, Johnny Entwhistle, stands tall and sinister, unmoved by the movement around him. He stands looking powerful and strong.

Roger Daltry, singer, wields and pulls at the microphone, almost performing to it alone. Wriggling and reeling, singing words you can't hear, frighteningly.

A mass of movement in the crowded Marquee on a Monday night.

The Who gathered round and straight-talked. "We hate weak sounds like many of the groups have." They looked surprisingly harmless after their gyrations on stage.

Keith looked as if butter wouldn't melt in his

SATURDAY, 27 MARCH
Rhodes Centre, Bishop's Stortford, Hertfordshire.

SUNDAY, 28 MARCH
The Brum Kavern Club, Small Heath, Birmingham.

TUESDAY, 30 MARCH
Marquee Club.

Regular supporting band the Boys fell afoul of Kit Lambert's manoeuvrings. "Kit didn't like the fact we were going down as well as the Who," Mike Evans remembered. "But even though we were doing the same sort of stuff, we didn't consider ourselves as competition. That was just his paranoia."

The Who shared the duration of their residency with either Gary Farr and the T-Bones, Jimmy James and the Vagabonds, or the Mark Leeman Five supporting.

WEDNESDAY, 31 MARCH
Bromel Club, Bromel Court Hotel, Bromley Hill, Kent.

THURSDAY, 1 APRIL
Harrow Technical College Students Rag Week Dance, Town Hall, Wembley.

Billed as "The Who London 1965," the group supported Donovan, with Rod Stewart and the Soul Agents. The event raised £350 for local charities, marred only by angry students storming the gate because of a reported ticket forgery.

That morning, the Who flew to Manchester to record their third consecutive appearance on BBC-1's *Top Of The Pops*, transmitted from 7:30—8:00 pm. A fortnight later, "I Can't Explain" finally cracked the Top Ten, reaching it's highest position of #8 (#10 on the *NME* chart) on 17 April. It sold 104,000 copies.

FRIDAY, 2 APRIL
Youth Centre, Loughton, Essex.

The Who rehearsed at 10:00 am for their BBC Light Programme lunchtime radio debut, replacing Freddie and the Dreamers on *The Joe Loss Pop Show* for a fee of £30. Introduced by Tony Hall, the group performed Martha and the Vandellas' "Heat Wave," "I

Can't Explain," plus James Brown's "Please, Please, Please" and "Shout And Shimmy." The show was transmitted live, in front of an audience, 1:00—3:00 pm, from the Playhouse Theatre, Northumberland Avenue, near Charing Cross Station.

SATURDAY, 3 APRIL
London College of Printing, Elephant and Castle, South East London.

SUNDAY, 4 APRIL
Plaza Ballroom, Newbury, Berkshire.

MONDAY, 5 APRIL
The Lakeside R&B Scene, "Old Welsh Harp," Hendon, Middlesex. Promoted by Bob Druce.

TUESDAY, 6 APRIL
Marquee Club.

WEDNESDAY, 7 APRIL
Dacorum College, Hemel Hempstead, Hertfordshire.

THURSDAY, 8 APRIL
Olympia Ballroom, Reading.

Kit Lambert invited Virginia Ironside (from the *Daily Mail*) and writer Nik Cohn along to this gig and briefed Pete to create an impression by smashing his £400 Rickenbacker, despite the expense. This he duly did, and Keith joined in by smashing his drums. However, Lambert had been waylaid in the bar with the journalists when this grand spectacle occurred and was reportedly horrified to find he had been taken at his word.

FRIDAY, 9 APRIL
Stamford Hall, Altrincham, Cheshire.

SATURDAY, 10 APRIL
The Cavern, Notre Dame Hall, Leicester Square, London.

SUNDAY, 11 APRIL
Majestic Ballroom, Luton.

TUESDAY, 13 and WEDNESDAY, 14 APRIL
Two-day recording schedule at IBC, produced by Shel Talmy and engineered by Glyn Johns, with Nicky Hopkins on piano. Three-track masters cut included James Brown's "Please, Please, Please," "I Don't Mind" (two versions), and "Shout And Shimmy"; Martha and the Vandellas' "Heat Wave" (two versions) and "Motorin'"; Derek Martin's "Daddy Rolling Stone"; Garnett Mimms and the Enchanters' "Anytime You Want Me" (two versions); Paul Revere and the Raiders' "Louie Go Home" (amended to "Lubie (Come Back Home)"; and a Townshend original, "You're Going To Know Me (Out In The Street)."

Talmy recorded the Who's second single, "Anyway, Anyhow, Anywhere," during the sessions. As he recalled it, "I used three mikes to ensure that I could capture the natural room reverb and signal delays: one right on the amp, one three to four feet away and another angled way back into the room. Then I mixed the inputs to mono and compressed it. When I sent the tape to Decca in America, they said I delivered a faulty master because there were all these strange noises on it. I had to assure them that was the way it was meant to sound!"

The evening of the 13th, the Who played their usual Marquee date, while on the 14th, they made an excursion north to Leicester to play the Il Rondo, a Mod stronghold on Silver Street, packed to its 400 capacity.

THURSDAY, 15 APRIL
Victoria Ballroom, Chesterfield, Derbyshire.

FRIDAY, 16 APRIL
Goldhawk Social Club, Shepherd's Bush.

SATURDAY, 17 APRIL
"Big Easter Rave," The Florida, Brighton.

SUNDAY, 18 APRIL
Civic Hall, Town Hall, Crawley, Sussex.

MONDAY, 19 APRIL
Botwell House, Hayes, Middlesex.

TUESDAY, 20 APRIL
Marquee Club.

THURSDAY, 22 APRIL
Waterfront Club, Cliff Hotel, Southampton.

Dave "Cyrano" Langston was hired at this gig, assisting Mike Shaw as the Who's first regular road manager. Langston first met the group as the Detours while playing lead guitar with his band, Phil Allen and the Chessmen (renamed Cyrano and the Bergeracs) on the Bob Druce circuit.

At IBC, Shel Talmy prepared mono mixes of "Heat Wave," "Lubie," "Leaving Here," and "Motorin'."

FRIDAY, 23 APRIL
Oasis Club, Manchester.

SATURDAY, 24 APRIL
Lynx Youth Club, Boreham Wood, followed by the "All Nite Rave," Club Noreik, Tottenham.

SUNDAY, 25 APRIL
Trade Union Hall, Watford.

MONDAY, 26 APRIL
Town Hall, Bridgwater, Somerset.

TUESDAY, 27 APRIL
Marquee Club.
    The end of the Who's sixteen-week residency.

WEDNESDAY, 28 APRIL
Bromel Club, Bromley Court Hotel, Bromley.

THURSDAY, 29 APRIL
At IBC, "Anyway, Anyhow, Anywhere," "Anytime You Want Me," and "Shout and Shimmy" were mixed into mono by Shel Talmy in Studio A. The master for "Anyway..." was extracted on Tuesday 11 May.

FRIDAY, 30 APRIL
Town Hall, Trowbridge, Wiltshire.

SATURDAY, 1 MAY
College of Arts and Technology, Leicester.

Film student Richard Stanley screened his experimental films onto (literally) the group. Pete was fascinated and the two got talking, leading to a long-standing friendship. Stanley later worked on several Who-related film projects with mutual friend Chris Morphet. (See 5 March.)

SUNDAY, 2 MAY
Dungeon Club, Nottingham, Nottinghamshire.

MONDAY, 3 MAY
Majestic Ballroom, Newcastle-upon-Tyne.

THURSDAY, 6 MAY
Two Red Shoes Ballroom, Elgin, Morayshire, Scotland.

FRIDAY, 7 MAY
Raith Ballroom, Kirkcaldy, Fifeshire, Scotland.

SATURDAY, 8 MAY
New Palladium Ballroom,

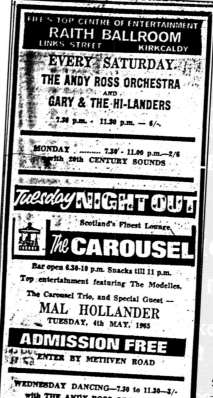

Greenock, Strathclyde, Scotland, with Studio Six and the Jaygars.

The latter group featured twelve-year-old guitarist Jimmy McCulloch and his elder brother Jack on drums, both later sidemen for Townshend protégés, Thunderclap Newman.

SUNDAY, 9 MAY
De Montfort Hall, Leicester. Two shows—5:40 & 8:00 pm.

The Who appeared third on the bill, supporting Tom Jones and Marianne Faithfull, with the Naturals, the Squires, the Hustlers, Jon Mark, and Al Paige.

TUESDAY, 11 MAY
Radio Luxembourg's *Ready, Steady, Radio!* was pre-recorded onstage at the Marquee, from 8:15–8:45 pm. A tape of "Daddy Rolling Stone" was played, which the Who truculently refused to mime to. The programme was broadcast 16 May, 9:30–10:00 pm.

WEDNESDAY, 12 MAY
On his evening off, while visiting girlfriend Kim in Bournemouth, Keith sat in with the Action (formerly Marquee support band the Boys) at the Le Disque a Go! Go! club.

THURSDAY, 13 MAY
Public Hall, Barrow-in-Furness, Lancashire.

Pop art didn't translate well in the provinces. The Who played their first set to a half-empty hall, and during the second, were heckled and showered with bottles and pennies by a bunch of "closing-time" drunks from the pub next door.

FRIDAY, 14 MAY
Civic Hall, Dunstable, Bedfordshire.

SATURDAY, 15 MAY
Neeld Hall, Chippenham, Wiltshire.

SUNDAY, 16 MAY
Town Hall, Stratford, East London.

MONDAY, 17 MAY
The Pavilion, Bath.

Promoted by Frederick Bannister, the Who became a regular attraction at Bannister's dances in Bath, Bristol, Worthing, Malvern, Stourbridge, and Kidderminster.

TUESDAY, 18 MAY
McIlroy's Ballroom, Swindon, Wiltshire.

The Who were booked for Granada Television's *Scene at 6.30* on this date, but according to company documentation, they did not appear.

WEDNESDAY, 19 MAY
Corn Exchange, Bristol.

THURSDAY, 20 MAY
Town Hall, Kidderminster, Worcestershire.

The Who appeared on Southern ITV's regional news programme, *Three Go Round*, playing at the Caribbean Hotel, which catered to teenagers in the coastal resort of Bognor Regis. (Filming date and further details are unknown.) The item was transmitted from 5:25—5:55 pm in the Southern ITV, Anglia and Channel regions only.

FRIDAY, 21 MAY
Ricky-Tick Club, Plaza Ballroom, Guildford, Surrey.

The Who's second single, "Anyway, Anyhow, Anywhere" B/W "Daddy Rolling Stone" was released, reaching #10 and selling a total of 88,000 copies. Its American release followed on 5 June, with "Anytime You Want Me" the B-side, but it failed to make the *Billboard* Hot 100.

To plug "the first pop art record," the group appeared on *Ready, Steady, Goes Live!*, which was transmitted across the ITV network from 6:08—7:00 pm. As of 2 April, *RSG!* had moved from Television House, Kingsway, to Rediffusion's Studio One on Wembley Park Drive, with an increased production budget to match its new, progressive live format— hence the new (albeit temporary) name. This edition, hosted by Cathy McGowan with David Goldsmith, also featured the Four Tops, Connie Francis, and Ronnie Jones.

SATURDAY, 22 MAY
Astoria Ballroom, Rawtenstall, Lancashire.

RIGHT: MARQUEE MEMORIES, SUMMER 1965. (NOTE ROGER ON DRUMS AND KEITH ON ORGAN.)

In *Record Mirror*, Pete talked about "Anyway, Anyhow, Anywhere" with Richard Green: "If this record doesn't get in the charts, we're going to slam it up with another. We're not giving it as long as 'I Can't Explain,' and we won't go back to the other style for our next record either, we'll do two or three more this way."

SUNDAY, 23 MAY

The Who pre-recorded their only appearance on ABC Television's Saturday evening pop show, *Thank Your Lucky Stars*, from Alpha Television Studios, Aston, Birmingham, transmitted 29 May, 5:50—6:35 pm. Introduced by DJ Brian Matthew, the group mimed to "Anyway, Anyhow, Anywhere" on a programme featuring Billy Fury, the Nashville Teens, the Rockin' Berries, Chad Stuart and Jeremy Clyde, the Four Tops, Paul Dean, the Three Bells, and Connie Francis.

MONDAY, 24 MAY

Majestic Ballroom, Reading.

From 2:00—6:30 pm, the Who pre-recorded a session for the BBC Light Programme's *Top Gear* at Studio Two, Aeolian Hall, 135/137 New Bond Street, London.

Introduced by influential DJ Tony Hall, the group taped versions of the Olympics' "Good Lovin'" (a U.S. hit for the Young Rascals the following year), James Brown's "I Don't Mind," "Anyway, Anyhow, Anywhere," and Derek Martin's "Daddy Rolling Stone" for the 19 June broadcast. Also in session were Who favourites, the Marvellettes and Solomon Burke.

Despite proving an enormous success, thanks largely to producer Bernie Andrews' innovative efforts, *Top Gear* had been cut from two hours and moved from its Thursday night slot to Saturday afternoons, 4:00—5:00 pm. The show was axed at the end of June, to be later resurrected in a radical new format two years later. (See 10 October 1967).

TUESDAY, 25 MAY

Marquee Club.

The Who pre-recorded Radio Luxembourg's *Ready, Steady, Radio!* at the club from 8:15—8:45 pm, transmitted 30 May, 9:30—10:00 pm.

From 4:00—6:30 pm, in Studio Five at the BBC's Delaware Road studios in Maida Vale, the Who had rehearsed and recorded the first of numerous appear-

ABOVE: *Thank Your Lucky Stars*, 23 May.

ances on *Saturday Club*, produced by Jimmy Grant and engineered by Brian Willey. "Good Lovin,'" "Anyway, Anyhow, Anywhere," "Leaving Here," and James Brown's "Please, Please, Please" and "Just You And Me, Darling," as well as an interview with Pete by host Brian Matthew, were transmitted on 29 May, 10:00 am—12:00 noon. The last half-hour of the two-hour show was simultaneously transmitted on short-wave frequencies by the BBC's General Overseas Service. The programme also featured Peter and Gordon, Unit 4 Plus 2, the Walker Brothers, Ottilie Patterson, and the Chris Barber Band in session.

Although unindicated by BBC documentation, the versions of "Good Lovin'" and "Anyway, Anyhow, Anywhere" were, in all probability, the same as recorded for *Top Gear* the previous day.

WEDNESDAY, 26 MAY

The Who went to the TWW Television Centre, Bath Road, Bristol, to tele-record a scheduled appearance on the regional programme, *Discs A Go Go*, for transmission on Tuesday 1 June, 7:00—7:30 pm. However, due to a miming dispute with the show's producer Christopher Mercer, the group walked out and did not appear.

THURSDAY, 27 MAY

Assembly Hall, Worthing, Sussex.

FRIDAY, 28 MAY

Ricky-Tick Club, Windsor.

SATURDAY, 29 MAY

Pavilion Gardens Ballroom, Buxton, Derbyshire.

SUNDAY, 30 MAY

The King Mojo Club, Sheffield, Yorkshire. The Who's first gig in Sheffield, co-promoted by Peter Stringfellow.

ABOVE: First French EP.

TUESDAY, 1 JUNE

The Who's first European jaunt involved a two-day promotional trip to Paris, marking the release of their first EP. (France released extended plays in preference to 45 rpm singles until 1967.)

WEDNESDAY, 2 JUNE

Le Club au Golf Drouot, Paris, France.

The group were specially invited to play a musique concrète event organised by "Le Club des Rockers." Despite the language barrier, the appearance marked the beginning of the Who's popularity in France, a market generally resistant to English acts.

FRIDAY, 4 JUNE

Trentham Gardens, Stoke-on-Trent, Staffordshire.

The group arrived, but were unable to play as their equipment van broke down in Coventry.

SATURDAY, 5 JUNE

Loyola Hall, Stamford Hill, North London.

Melody Maker ran a feature headed "Every So Often, A Group Is Poised On The Brink Of A Breakthrough. Word Has It It's...The Who." "There is no suppression within the group," Pete declared. "You are what you are, and nobody cares. We say what we want when we want. If we don't like something someone is doing, we say so. Our personalities clash, but we argue and get it all out of our system. There's a lot of friction, and offstage we're not particularly matey, but it doesn't matter. If we were not like this it would destroy our stage performance. We play how we feel."

SUNDAY, 6 JUNE

St. Joseph's Hall, Highgate, North London.

MONDAY, 7 JUNE

Marquee Club, with Jimmy James and the Vagabonds, who were being managed by Pete Meaden.

Prior to the gig, the Who rehearsed from 10:00 am, miming "Anyway, Anyhow, Anywhere" on BBC-2's *Gadzooks! It's The In-Crowd*, transmitted live from BBC Television Centre, Wood Lane, from 7:00—7:30 pm. Hosted by Alan David and singer Lulu, the programme also featured Marianne Faithfull, Gene Pitney, and Dana Gillespie.

TUESDAY, 8 JUNE

Wallington Public Hall, Wallington, Surrey.

From 8:15—8:45 pm, the Who pre-recorded their third appearance within a month on Radio Luxembourg's *Ready, Steady, Radio!* at the Marquee, broadcast 13 June, 9:30—10:00 pm.

WEDNESDAY, 9 JUNE

Il Rondo, Leicester.

THURSDAY, 10 JUNE

The Who rehearsed at the BBC's Dickenson Road TV studios, Manchester, miming "Anyway, Anyhow, Anywhere" live on *Top Of The Pops*, which was broadcast 7:30—8:00 pm.

FRIDAY, 11 JUNE

Co-Op Ballroom, Nuneaton, Warwickshire.

SATURDAY, 12 JUNE

Town Hall, Dudley, Worcestershire.

SUNDAY, 13 JUNE

Manor Lounge Club, Stockport, Cheshire.

TUESDAY, 15 JUNE

Town Hall, High Wycombe, Buckinghamshire.

WEDNESDAY, 16 JUNE

Town Hall, Stourbridge, Worcestershire.

Chris Stamp "piggybacked" his first flight to New York to represent the Who's American affairs, thanks to brother Terence downgrading his first-class ticket to attend the premiere of *The Collector*.

THURSDAY, 17 JUNE

Bowes Lyon House Youth Centre, Stevenage, Hertfordshire.

The Who flew to Manchester for *Top Of The Pops*, broadcast live from 7:30—8:00 pm. Once the show was completed, the group were whisked to Ringway Airport for a chartered flight to Luton Airport and then driven by fast car to Stevenage. More than 1200 packed into the venue, breaking the house attendance record. Many had watched the group's earlier *TOTP* appearance on television sets specifically installed for the occasion. Forty bouncers formed a chain to help carry fifty reported fainting cases backstage into the dressing room, while many more were passed outside to revive.

Of all the towns and cities the early Who played in Britain, Stevenage boasted perhaps the group's most devout fan base. "We used to like playing Stevenage," Pete recalled, "because our audience there was 80 per cent female, and they used to scream. When we used to come out, the girls would push me aside to get at Keith Moon. I used to bloody despise them because they didn't know how much it hurt. I was on a vengeance trip after that."

FRIDAY, 18 JUNE

Floral Hall Ballroom, Morecambe, Lancashire.

SATURDAY, 19 JUNE

1965 Uxbridge Blues and Folk Festival, Uxbridge,

Middlesex, 3:00—11:30 pm, with Cliff Bennett and the Rebel Rousers, Long John Baldry and the Hoochie Coochie Men, the Ray Martin Group, John Mayall's Bluesbreakers, Zoot Money's Big Roll Band, Solomon Burke, the Spencer Davis Group, Marianne Faithfull, and the Birds.

The Who appeared before an audience of more than 4000 from 3:45—4:15 pm and then went on to a gig in the evening at the Cavern, Notre Dame Hall, London.

SUNDAY, 20 JUNE

Blue Moon Club, Hayes, Middlesex.

THURSDAY, 24 JUNE

Town Hall, Greenwich, London.

FRIDAY, 25 JUNE

Ricky-Tick Club, Windsor.

SATURDAY, 26 JUNE

Town Hall, High Wycombe, followed by the "All Night Rave," Club Noreik, Tottenham.

But mo. children on other ideas.

...ned Mrs. Hannaford.
The jolt broke his leg, but he kept on driving.

he wor

'THE WHO' CAUSE A HOO-HA

SUNDAY, 27 JUNE
Starlite Ballroom, Greenford.

MONDAY, 28 JUNE
Manor House Ballroom, Ipswich, Suffolk.

TUESDAY, 29 JUNE
Burtons Ballroom, Uxbridge, supported by the Mark Four. A year later, vocalist Kenny Pickett, drummer Jack Jones, and guitarist Eddie Phillips evolved into the Creation. Bassist John Dalton replaced Pete Quaife in the Kinks.

WEDNESDAY, 30 JUNE
Town Hall, Farnborough, Hampshire.

JULY
Beat Instrumental magazine reported the Who had completed recording their first album, originally scheduled for June release in the U.S. Columnist John Emery was played a nine-track acetate by Shel Talmy, featuring "I'm A Man," "Heatwave," "I Don't Mind," "Lubie," "You're Going To Know Me (Out In The Street)," "Please, Please, Please," "Leaving Here," "Motorin'" and one other (probably "Shout And Shimmy").

Partly due to Emery's adverse comments about the lack of originality, the album was shelved. "The Who are having serious doubts about the state of R&B," Kit Lambert told *Melody Maker*. "Now the LP material will consist of hard pop. They've finished with 'Smokestack Lightning'!"

THURSDAY, 1 JULY
The Who pre-taped a special *Ready, Steady, Go!* devoted to groups "discovered at various clubs" at Studio One, Wembley, featuring Manfred Mann, the Ad-Libs, the Majority, Kenny Lynch, Peter Cook and the Dudley Moore Trio, and the Nina Simone Trio. Introduced by Cathy McGowan, the group performed "Anyway, Anyhow, Anywhere" and "Shout And Shimmy." The programme was transmitted the following evening, 6:08–7:00 pm.

As of this writing, this is the sole surviving Who film insert out of a total of seventeen *RSG!* appearances. (Previous reports have erroneously claimed the footage came from the 21 May appearance.) The "Anyway, Anyhow, Anywhere" performance was featured in *The Kids Are Alright* movie and soundtrack.

Boyfriend   July 3rd, 1965

A BOYFRIEND SPOTLIGHT FEATURE

KEITH   JOHN   PETE

THE BIG WHO

Once they were just a small-time group—

THEY'RE growing. Fantastically and furiously carrying with them, attracting towards them, the Mods, who go to the clubs and buy the records. And like the great, growing wave that the young cling to, the wave that's never still for a moment, the Who are becoming more and more part of the flood. Unlike so many other groups, they are not just riding the wave, they are doing the steering and helping the new scene on its far-reaching and endless way.

The Who are everything that is 1965 to their wild, pushing audiences. You may think their music phoney or gimmicky, but it's no more that way than the action painters who sling their material violently on to the canvas instead of using neat perfect strokes and a pallet. One is as wild, like the Who are wild, propelling into their drums, guitars and voices, the feel of the buildings, the jets flying over them, the cars roaring along the new motorway. And they call this pop art music because the sounds are not purely musical, but full of the noises of the streets and lives around them.

Same with clothes. Fashion never stays in a rut for long. Because the young have too little time to wait for the shops to come up with new ideas and they're adapting and making new styles of their own. It saves money, it's original. So, too, the Who wear pop art gear. John has a jacket made out of a Union Jack. Keith has a white polo-neck sweater with a target marked on the front, the idea coming from the wing of a jet. Roger wears a leather belt decorated with insulating tape. All you do is sit on the floor at home and do it yourself.

The Who are weirdly weird and ordinarily ordinary. Probably the only time that something happens between them is when they're on stage. Off stage they lead lives of their own when they can.

now their talent is making them grow

WEDNESDAY, 7 JULY
The Manor House, Manor House, North West London.

The Who played the "Gala Opening" of this blues club, upstairs above the Manor House pub. Due to the oppressive heat, an exhausted Keith collapsed and had to be carried outside to revive.

THURSDAY, 8 JULY
Olympia Ballroom, Reading.

FRIDAY, 9 JULY
Locarno Ballroom, Basildon, Essex.

SATURDAY, 10 JULY
Winter Gardens, Ventnor, Isle of Wight.

SUNDAY, 11 JULY
Birdcage Club, Savoy Ballroom, Southsea, Portsmouth, Hampshire.

MONDAY, 12 JULY
Rehearsal at the group's old stomping ground, the White Hart on Acton Hill.

TUESDAY, 13 JULY
Marquee Club.

WEDNESDAY, 14 JULY
Locarno Ballroom, Stevenage.

THURSDAY, 15 JULY
Ritz Ballroom, Skewen and Glen Ballroom, Llanelli, Wales.

The Who's first Welsh gigs near Swansea, supported by the Iveys. The group were later signed to the Beatles' Apple label, and Paul McCartney renamed them Badfinger in 1969.

FRIDAY, 2 JULY
The Maple Ballroom, Northampton, Northamptonshire.

SATURDAY, 3 JULY
The Gaiety Ballroom, Ramsey, Huntingdonshire.

SUNDAY, 4 JULY
Community Centre, Southall, West London.

MONDAY, 5 JULY
Assembly Rooms, Tunbridge Wells, Kent.

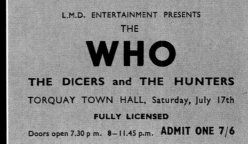

L.M.D. ENTERTAINMENT PRESENTS
THE
WHO
THE DICERS and THE HUNTERS
TORQUAY TOWN HALL, Saturday, July 17th
FULLY LICENSED
Doors open 7.30 p.m. 8–11.45 p.m. ADMIT ONE 7/6

FRIDAY, 16 JULY
Town Football Ground, Whaddon, Cheltenham, Gloucestershire, as part of the 1965 Cheltenham Festival.

The bill also featured the Yardbirds,

1965

Shades Of Blue, and the Hellions. The latter group featuring future members of Traffic and Spooky Tooth.

SATURDAY, 17 JULY
Town Hall, Torquay, Devonshire.

SUNDAY, 18—SUNDAY, 25 JULY
One clear week off from a hectic schedule. A week of rehearsals followed at the Marquee to change the Who's stage repertoire.

TUESDAY, 27 JULY
From 8:15—8:45 pm, the Who pre-taped Radio Luxembourg's *Ready, Steady, Radio!* from the Marquee stage for broadcast 1 August, 9:30—10:00 pm.

WEDNESDAY, 28 JULY
Pontiac Club, Zeeta House, Putney, London.

The Who played only one set after the PA blew up. An early version of "My Generation" was performed for possibly the first time. Richard Cole, a roadie working for Unit Four Plus Two, approached Mike Shaw looking for work. He replaced Cyrano Langston in October.

At IBC Studios, Glyn Johns prepared tape copies of "Anyhow, Anywhere, Anyway" [sic] and "Anytime You Want Me" for Australasian release.

FRIDAY, 30 JULY
New Fender Club, Kenton, Middlesex.

SATURDAY, 31 JULY
Wilton Hall, Bletchley, Buckinghamshire.

"We'll be cutting the new disc soon, which I expect will be one of my compositions, 'My Generation,'" Pete told *Disc*. "It's a more uptempo number and it talks about old people and young married people. The fellow who's telling the story can't really express himself properly and stutters. In a way, I'm trying to stop the group getting old. It's the one serious thing we're always talking about."

SUNDAY, 1 AUGUST
Britannia Theatre, Brittania Pier, Great Yarmouth, Norfolk. Two shows, 6:30 & 8:45 pm.

A season of Sunday concerts, promoted by Austin Newman, commenced at the venue on 20 June and extended through until 5 September. The Who were co-billed for the next four Sundays with Donovan. Pete missed one show; roadie Alan Oates took his place.

TUESDAY, 3 AUGUST
The Who videotaped three songs for the U.S. ABC network's syndicated pop show, *Shindig!* at Twickenham Film Studios. Due to work permit restrictions imposed by the American Federation of Musicians, many "British Invasion" acts were excluded from appearing in America personally. The problem was partially resolved by recording inserts specifically for entertainment programmes such as *Shindig!*. Producer Jack Good, the pioneer of 50's British rock television behind *6.5 Special* and *Oh Boy!*, regularly included new acts to satisfy ravenous demand for all things English. Thus, *Shindig!* inadvertently provided America with its first glimpse of the Who.

From 10:00 am, the group rehearsed and taped live versions of "Daddy Rolling Stone," "I Can't Explain," and "My Generation" on Stage 3. The performances (additionally dubbed with an audience track) were spread over different editions of the bi-weekly show, each introduced by host DJ Jimmy O'Neill. "I Can't Explain" was first broadcast Saturday 2 October (8:30—8:59 pm EST), and repeated, along with "My Generation," on the last-ever *Shindig!*, Thursday 6

January 1966 (same times). Footage was later used in *The Kids Are Alright* movie and soundtrack. "Daddy Rolling Stone" was shown Thursday 30 December (same times).

The *Shindig!* crew remained in London to videotape the National Jazz and Blues Festival, held in neighbouring Richmond, three nights later.

WEDNESDAY, 4 AUGUST
The Witchdoctor Club, St. Leonards, Hastings, Sussex.

BBC-TV cameras filmed a four minute sequence for the pilot of *A Whole Scene Going*, a forthcoming series about teenagers views on holidays, clothes, sport, and music. The Who were included "as giving a true impression of the current beat music scene." The programme was not aired until 5 January 1966—a full five months later.

FRIDAY, 6 AUGUST
Another live slot on *Ready, Steady, Go!* from Studio One, Wembley, with Brian Poole and the Tremeloes, the Byrds, and Sonny and Cher, transmitted 6:08—

ABOVE: Camera rehearsal for *Ready, Steady, Go!*, 6 August.

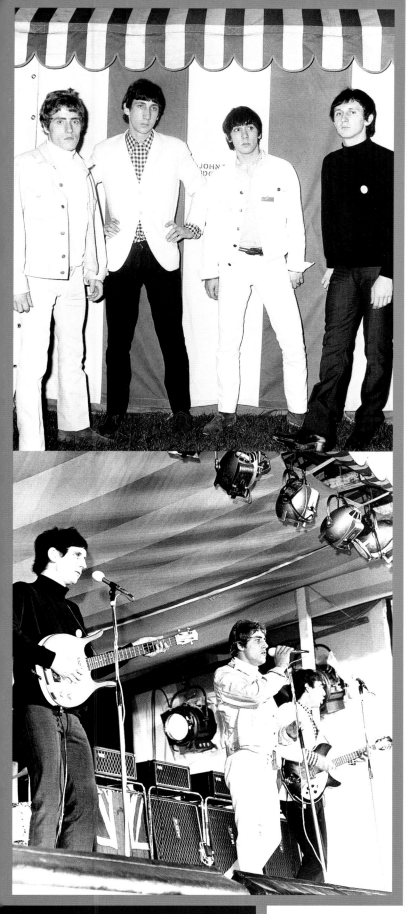

7:00 pm. This particular appearance was notable because the Who performed as a three-piece without Roger, who had taken ill and been ordered home from rehearsals by the show's doctor.

He was well enough to appear with the rest of the group that evening at "Ready, Steady, Richmond," the first night of the Fifth National Jazz and Blues Festival, held in the Richmond Athletic Association Grounds, Surrey. The Who were billed with the Mike Cotton Sound, the Yardbirds, and the Moody Blues. Marquee compère, Hamish Grimes, introduced them with a feeble rhyme: "Hey diddle diddle, the Who are on the fiddle, Entwistle jumped over Keith Moon, young Roger laughed to see such fun, while Pete ran away with the tune."

Film rights for the event were bought jointly by Leon Mirrell, executive producer of Selmur Productions, the U.S. company videotaping English acts for ABC's *Shindig!* (see 3 August) and Brian Epstein's Subafilms Ltd. "Anyway, Anyhow, Anywhere" and "Shout And Shimmy" appeared in the second of a two-part *Shindig Goes To London!* special, transmitted Thursday 9 December, 8:30—8:59 pm EST.

Part of "Shout and Shimmy" reappeared in *The Kids Are Alright*, while "Anyway, Anyhow, Anywhere" was featured in *Thirty Years of Maximum R&B Live*.

SATURDAY, 7 AUGUST
Loyola Hall, Stamford Hill, London.

SUNDAY, 8 AUGUST
Britannia Theatre, Brittania Pier, Great Yarmouth. Two shows, 6:30 & 8:45 pm.

WEDNESDAY, 11 AUGUST
Blue Moon Club, Cheltenham.

THURSDAY, 12 AUGUST
Dreamland Ballroom, Margate, Kent.

FRIDAY, 13 AUGUST
Marine Ballroom, Central Pier, Morecambe.

SATURDAY, 14 AUGUST
The New Georgian Club, Cowley, Uxbridge.

SUNDAY, 15 AUGUST
Britannia Theatre, Britannia Pier, Great Yarmouth. Two shows, 6:30 & 8:45 pm.

MONDAY, 16 AUGUST
During the week, the first attempts were made at recording "My Generation." "Kit Lambert was 'practising' record production at the time," Pete told Roy Carr. "He used to take us all down to a studio called City of London Studios [Osborn House, 9—13 Osborn Street, Aldgate East], which at the time was mono. It was small and poorly equipped, but it had something no other studio in Britain could offer at that time—an engineer who could understand what Kit was saying."

Over the following month (exact dates unknown), two versions were cut at Marquee Sound Studios, situated behind the club, in Richmond Mews, Dean Street, and a further remake at Lansdowne Recording Studios, Lansdowne Road, Notting Hill Gate. The final master was captured at IBC on 13 October. *Record Mirror* (dated 21 August) mentioned a premature 24 September release date.

THURSDAY, 19 AUGUST
Assembly Hall, Worthing.

FRIDAY, 20 AUGUST
Pavilion Ballroom, Bournemouth.

LEFT AND ABOVE: RICHMOND JAZZ AND BLUES FESTIVAL, 6 AUGUST.

SATURDAY, 21 AUGUST

Palais de Danse, Peterborough, Northamptonshire.

SUNDAY, 22 AUGUST

Brittania Theatre, Brittania Pier, Great Yarmouth.
Two shows, 6:30 & 8:45 pm.

MONDAY, 23 AUGUST

"4 Hour Rave," Corn Exchange, Colchester, Essex.

TUESDAY, 24 AUGUST

Town Hall, High Wycombe.

THURSDAY, 26 AUGUST

City Hall, Salisbury, Wiltshire.

It was one of those days for Roger. On the journey, his Austin Westminster hit the back of another car, causing damage estimated at £100 to his car and £300 to the other vehicle. He and passengers John Entwistle and Mike Shaw were shaken but unhurt. Then, at the gig, fans pulled his microphone stand into the crowd. As he went to retrieve it, he was pulled from the stage, resulting in a strained back.

FRIDAY, 27 AUGUST

Rang-A-Tang Club, The Carnival Hall, Basingstoke.

SATURDAY, 28 AUGUST

Matrix Hall, Coventry, Warwickshire.

SUNDAY, 29 AUGUST

The King Mojo Club, Sheffield.

MONDAY, 30 AUGUST

Sophia Gardens, Cardiff, Glamorganshire, Wales.

A Bank Holiday concert promoted by the group's new agent, Australian impresario Robert Stigwood. The Who were supported by the Merseybeats, whose management had been taken over by Lambert and Stamp, and the Graham Bond Organization.

WEDNESDAY, 1 SEPTEMBER

Top Rank Suite, Hanley, Stoke-on-Trent.

THURSDAY, 2 SEPTEMBER

The Who's van was stolen with £5000 worth of gear inside. It had been parked outside Battersea Dogs' Home, where, ironically, Cyrano Langston, Mike

WHO STOLE THE WHO'S POP GEAR?

—As they shopped for a guard dog

BY SALLY MOORE

THE WHO pop group went shopping yesterday for a fierce-looking dog to guard their van.

But no sooner had they started looking at Alsatians at London's Battersea dogs' home, than someone STOLE the van outside plus the £5,000-worth of musical gear in it.

And last night the group were frantically trying to find new equipment for their "live" appearance on ITV's "Ready Steady, Go" time tonight.

"We got the guard-dog idea just too late," said Roy Tollisay, The Who's publicity manager.

"All our guitars, drums, and amplifiers were taken."

The dark-grey van—it is

A DEAD GIRL SETS RIDDLE

ABOVE: Roadie Neville Chesters tests the mike before "curtain-up."

Shaw, and assistant Alan Oates had been enquiring about buying an Alsatian guard dog! The van was eventually recovered in Grafton Square, Clapham, South London, minus a door, but with none of the equipment left except for two broken speakers. Police later found the gear during a raid on an East End flat full of stolen property and held it as evidence.

FRIDAY, 3 SEPTEMBER

California Ballroom, Dunstable.

Support acts included Mike Sheridan and the Nightriders, featuring future Move, E.L.O., and Wizzard maestro, Roy Wood.

Cyrano hired brand-new Vox gear from the Jennings factory in Dartford, Kent, in time for the

Who's live *Ready, Steady, Go!* appearance, transmitted 6:08–7:00 pm. The group performed "My Generation" and "Dancing In The Street" on a show featuring Big Dee Irwin, Lou Johnson, the Walker Brothers, the Zombies, and the Honeycombs. When interviewed by Cathy McGowan, Keith appealed for the return of his personal briefcase he'd left inside the stolen van.

SATURDAY, 4 SEPTEMBER
Spa Royal Hall, Bridlington, Yorkshire.

WEDNESDAY, 8 SEPTEMBER
Town Hall, Farnborough.

SATURDAY, 11 SEPTEMBER
Imperial Ballroom, Nelson, Lancashire.

SUNDAY, 12 SEPTEMBER
Oasis Club, Manchester.

FRIDAY, 17 SEPTEMBER
Gaiety Ballroom, Grimsby, Lincolnshire.

SATURDAY, 18 SEPTEMBER
Drill Hall, Grantham, Lincolnshire.

SUNDAY, 19 SEPTEMBER
Savoy Ballroom, Southsea, Portsmouth.

MONDAY, 20 SEPTEMBER
The Who travelled by boat from Harwich to Amsterdam, Holland, to record their own AVRO TV special at Studio Bellevue, produced by Bob Rooyens. The programme took the form of a typical live show, with the group performing Chris Kenner's (via Cannibal and the Headhunters) "Land Of 1000 Dances," "Daddy Rolling Stone," Rufus Thomas's "Jump Back," "I Can't Explain," Martha and the Vandellas' (via the Everly Brothers) "Dancing In The Street," "Bald Headed Woman," "Anyway, Anyhow, Anywhere," "Please, Please, Please," "Shout And Shimmy," the Everly Brothers' "Love Hurts," "I Don't Mind," "Just You And Me, Darling," "The Kids Are Alright," the Everly's "Man With Money," and "My Generation."

The Who was transmitted the following evening, 8:01–8:20 pm, over the Nederland 2 channel. The latter seven songs were later transmitted as a separate

Tiener TV Nederland 1 special on Saturday 9 October, 4:40–4:55 pm.

TUESDAY, 21 SEPTEMBER
De Marathon Club, The Hague, Holland.

The Who had played eight songs on borrowed equipment from support group, the Hajues, before the amps broke down. They continued on gear hastily borrowed from the Golden Earrings (later signed to Track Records) and the Empty Hearts.

SATURDAY, 25 SEPTEMBER
Folkets Hus, Helsingor, followed by a midnight gig at the KB Hallen, Frederiksberg, Copenhagen, Denmark. At the latter show, the Who borrowed equipment from support group, the Lee Kings.

SUNDAY, 26 SEPTEMBER
Aarhus Hallen, Aarhus followed by the Fredrikstorv, Aalborg.

The Aarhus gig was terminated after only four minutes when the audience overran the stage. Fans stormed out of the hall into the town, causing approximately £10,000 worth of damage. While in Denmark, an ugly backstage incident involving Roger and Keith resulted in Daltrey being unanimously

fired from the group. He was reluctantly reinstated initially on a trial basis due to the Who's sheer workload.

During this time, Cyrano Langston left the Who's employ to join Gary Farr and the T-Bones as their lead guitarist. Mike Shaw hired Richard Cole as his replacement (see 28 July) and additional help followed in the form of Merseybeats road manager, Neville Chesters. Tragically, Shaw suffered a serious motor accident on 15 October which left him paralysed. After a period of recovery in Cornwall, he moved back to London in 1967 to work for Track Records in an administrative role.

SATURDAY, 2 OCTOBER
Agincourt Ballroom, Camberley.

SUNDAY, 3 OCTOBER
"The Twisted Wheel" Club, Manchester.

WEDNESDAY, 6 OCTOBER
Kinema Ballroom, Dunfermline, Fifeshire, Scotland.

FRIDAY, 8 OCTOBER
City Halls, Perth, Perthshire, Scotland.

ABOVE: STOCKHOLM, 10 OCTOBER.

SATURDAY, 9 OCTOBER
Market Assembly Hall, Carlisle, Cumberland.

SUNDAY, 10 OCTOBER
The Who made a whirlwind trip to Sweden to headline three shows, the first at the Johanneshovs Isstadion, Stockholm, at 2:00 pm. Because the group's equipment had been sent on to Gothenburg, they were forced to use equipment borrowed from support act, the Moonjacks. There followed two shows at the Cirkus, Lorensbergsparken, Gothenburg, 7:00 & 9:00 pm. The group flew back to England the following morning.

TUESDAY, 12 and WEDNESDAY, 13 OCTOBER
A frantic recording schedule at IBC with Shel Talmy and Glyn Johns, with Nicky Hopkins on piano. Tracks recorded: "It's Not True," "A Legal Matter," "Much Too Much," "La La La Lies," "The Good's Gone," and "The Ox," an instrumental based on the Surfaris' "Waikiki Run" credited to Townshend-Moon-Entwistle-Hopkins.

A midnight session on the 13th produced the masters for "My Generation" and "The Kids Are Alright." "We recorded the entire first album in six hours," said Pete. "It wasn't our club act, but we spent a week rehearsing. Kit shaped the songs, got rid of the lousy verses, and coached Roger's vocals. Then we went in, laid it on a plate, and Shel Talmy gave us our sound. I was only allowed into the control room to hear playbacks. Glyn had told Shel I was interested in recording. John, Roger and Keith didn't get in."

During this time at IBC, Keith and Nicky Hopkins played on "I Stand Accused" by the Merseybeats, released as a single by Fontana on Friday, 3 December. Bass player Billy Kinsley recalled: "Keith said, 'I don't just want to hang around. I want to play something. I know I'll bang the gong at the end!'"

THURSDAY, 14 OCTOBER
Skating Rink, Camborne, Cornwall.

At IBC, in Studio A, Glyn Johns made tape copies of "Shout And Shimmy," the master of "My Generation," and the 2:42 U.S. edit of "The Kids Are Alright."

FRIDAY, 15 OCTOBER
Hillside Ballroom, Hereford, Worcestershire.

SATURDAY, 16 OCTOBER
Baths Ballroom, Scunthorpe, Humberside.

WEDNESDAY, 20 OCTOBER
Top Rank Ballroom, Southampton.

FRIDAY, 22 OCTOBER
Pill Social Centre, Milford Haven, Pembrokeshire.

SATURDAY, 23 OCTOBER
Rhodes Centre, Bishop's Stortford.

SUNDAY, 24 OCTOBER
Carlton Ballroom, Slough, Buckinghamshire.

MONDAY, 25 OCTOBER
Trade Union Hall, Watford.

THURSDAY, 28 OCTOBER
Locarno Ballroom, Swindon.

FRIDAY, 29 OCTOBER
Starlite Ballroom, Greenford.

"My Generation" B/W "Shout And Shimmy" was released, initially with distribution problems by Decca. "There has been a huge demand in the shops, but the records aren't there," Kit Lambert complained to *Melody Maker*. The single went on to sell over 300,000 copies and eventually reached #2 in the charts, kept off the coveted pole position by the Seekers' ballad, "The Carnival Is Over." "Out In The Street" (subtitled "You're Gonna Know Me") became the U.S. B-side on 20 November. It could only manage a disappointing # 74 in the *Billboard* Hot 100, (no) thanks to Decca's lack of promotion.

SATURDAY, 30 OCTOBER
University, Manchester.

SUNDAY, 31 OCTOBER
Cavern Club, Liverpool.

The Who's only appearance at this legendary venue, which went into liquidation the following February.

MONDAY, 1 NOVEMBER
"Bluesville" Club, the Baths Hall, Ipswich.

TUESDAY, 2 NOVEMBER
Marquee Club.

Billed as "The Return of the Who" after an absence of nearly four months.

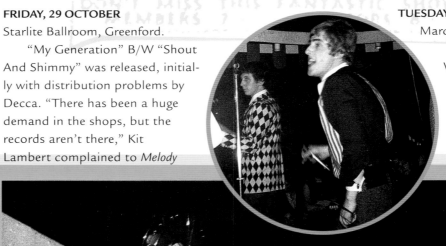

LEFT AND BELOW: MARQUEE CLUB, 2 NOVEMBER.

..1..day(s) at..Marquee..Club,..90..Wardour..St...on..Tuesday..21st..December!65
......day(s) at....London,..W.1.............................on..
......day(s) at..on..

ABOVE: "GLAD RAG BALL," WEMBLEY, 19 NOVEMBER.

WEDNESDAY, 3 NOVEMBER

Locarno Ballroom, Stevenage.

THURSDAY, 4 NOVEMBER

Queen's Hall, Barnstaple, Devonshire.

Cancelled because Roger suffered from a throat infection. Hall manager Mr. Gordon claimed the group made no effort to let him know that they would not be fulfilling the engagement. At 10:15 pm, it was announced the Who wouldn't be appearing, and 450 disappointed punters were given voucher tickets redeemable for five shillings. Support group the Spartans played the whole evening.

FRIDAY, 5 NOVEMBER

Roger's tonsils were fit enough to sing "My Generation" on *Ready, Steady, Go!*, transmitted live from Studio One, Wembley, 6:08—7:00 pm, with the Sir Douglas Quintet, Lesley Duncan, and Paul and Barry Ryan.

SATURDAY, 6 NOVEMBER

St. George's Ballroom, Hinckley, Leicestershire.

SUNDAY, 7 NOVEMBER

The King Mojo Club, Sheffield.

WEDNESDAY, 10 NOVEMBER

At IBC, in Studio A, Glyn Johns and editing/dubbing engineer Michael Weighell prepared mono tape copies of "The Good's Gone," "Lies" [sic], "It's Not True," and "Much Too Much." On the 12th, they prepared "Legal Matter"[sic] and "The Ox."

THURSDAY, 11 NOVEMBER

The Who were flown to Manchester to plug "My Generation" on *Top Of The Pops*, broadcast live from 7:30—8:00 pm. Their appearance fee was hiked up five pounds to £52.

SATURDAY, 13 NOVEMBER

La Locomotive Club, Paris, France. Two shows, 5:00 pm & 12:00 am.

The Who were now using 8" x 12" Marshall cabinets. Roger Vadim, Jane Fonda, and Catherine Deneuve were among the audience at the midnight show. "['My Generation'] was written at the height of our Mod time," Pete told *Disc*. "It's been a long time coming out and so now it's rather nostalgic. We're scared of growing old. I personally wouldn't

mind growing old in a Picasso sort of way or Charlie Chaplin, but growing old doing routine things after living a routine life really scares me."

MONDAY, 15 NOVEMBER

The Pavilion, Bath.

TUESDAY, 16 NOVEMBER

Winter Gardens, Malvern, Worcestershire.

At Decca Studios, Broadhurst Gardens, West Hampstead, Glyn Johns prepared mono mixes of "Out In The Street" and "The Kids Are Alright."

THURSDAY, 18 NOVEMBER

Another flight to Manchester, again paid for by the

BBC at a cost of £46-8-0 for *Top Of The Pops* (7:30—8:00 pm).

FRIDAY, 19 NOVEMBER

The Who appeared on *Ready, Steady, Go!* with the Kinks, Gerry and the Pacemakers, the Searchers, Chris Andrews, the Beatstalkers, Keith Powell, and Gillian Hills, broadcast live, 6:08—7:00 pm. Pete borrowed Gerry Marsden's Rickenbacker (it's price tag still dangling from the machine heads!) for "Shout and Shimmy," which was faded early due to the show running over time.

The group then dashed the short distance to the Empire Pool (now Wembley Arena) to rehearse for their appearance at the annual "Glad Rag Ball."

Organised by the London Students Carnival Ltd., in association with Radio Caroline and Immediate Records, the event was staged from 9:00 pm—4:00 am, before a rowdy audience of around 3000, with all proceeds going to five different charities.

Compèred by Cathy McGowan, BBC DJ Denny Piercy and Radio Caroline's Tom Lodge and Ugli Ray Terret, the bill also featured Donovan, the Hollies, Georgie Fame and the Blue Flames, the Barron Knights, Wilson Pickett, Geno Washington and the Ram Jam Band, the Birds, the Masterminds, the Golden Apples of the Sun, and the Merseybeats.

The Kinks were supposed to headline but didn't appear, while John Lee Hooker was replaced at the last minute by an unknown eighteen-year-old Dylan-influenced folk singer, Marc Bolan.

Although successful, the show was not without incident. Roger stormed off stage mid-set due to the inadequate sound system, leaving the others to carry on while the Who's own gear was hastily installed. Daltrey eventually returned and the show continued.

Like the previous year, Rediffusion arranged a four-camera shoot of the concert for a television special, *Glad Rag Ball*, broadcast Wednesday, 8 December, 9:40—10:25 pm.

SATURDAY, 20 NOVEMBER
The Florida, Brighton.

The Who were banned from reappearing at the Aquarium after fans caused hundreds of pounds worth of damage. As "My Generation" entered the Top Five at #4, *Melody Maker* carried a front-page story called "The Who Split Mystery." The report suggested that Roger was leaving the group to be replaced by singer Boz Burrell of the Boz People (later the bassist with King Crimson and Bad Company). Despite going as far as to audition, Burrell refuted the rumour, acidly commenting that the Who "are children playing with electronic toys." ("Yes, but rich children!" was Moon's cheeky and patently untrue quip.)

An additional drummer—Ray Stock, of Flamingo club houseband the Shevelles—was also said to be joining to enable Keith to "explore other forms of percussion." Chris Stamp dismissed these rumours as "..c-c-crap! Quite seriously I've never heard such a lot of rubbish. Does anybody in their right mind think the Who would split at a time like this?"

MONDAY, 22 NOVEMBER
From 7:00—9:30 pm, the Who recorded their fourth BBC radio session at Studio Four, Maida Vale, for the Light Programme's *Saturday Club*, produced by Jimmy Grant and Brian Willey. Tracks recorded included "It's Not True," "The Good's Gone," "La La La Lies," "My Generation," and "Baby Don't You Do It," plus an interview with Pete by host Brian Matthew. The show, featuring Tom Jones and the Squires, Donovan, the Fourmost, and the Settlers, was broadcast 27 November, 10:00—12:00 am.

TUESDAY, 23 NOVEMBER
Dorothy Ballroom, Cambridge, Cambridgeshire.

WEDNESDAY, 24 NOVEMBER
Town Hall, Stourbridge, Worcestershire.

THURSDAY, 25 NOVEMBER
The Who pre-recorded another *Ready, Steady, Go!* appearance, broadcast the following evening, 6:08—7:00 pm. Because their gear was in transit, they performed on equipment borrowed from fellow guests the Animals. Cover versions known to have been performed by the Who on the show during this time included the Everly Brothers' "Love Hurts" and Dion and the Belmonts' "Runaround Sue."

FRIDAY, 26 NOVEMBER
Wimbledon Palais, Wimbledon, South West London.

SATURDAY, 27 NOVEMBER
Community Centre, Hanwell, West London, followed by the London School of Economics Ball, Aldwych, London.

SUNDAY, 28 NOVEMBER
Oasis Club, Manchester.

MONDAY, 29 NOVEMBER
St Andrew's Hall, Norwich, Norfolk.

The Who were unable to appear as their journey from Manchester was halted by snow in the Pennines. Support groups Mike Patto and the Continentals and Lucas and the Emperors played the whole evening. Promoter Howard Platt assured fans that tickets would be valid for a make-up show on 13 December.

TUESDAY, 30 NOVEMBER
Town Hall, High Wycombe.

WEDNESDAY, 1 DECEMBER
Wolsey Hall, Cheshunt.

THURSDAY, 2 DECEMBER
With "My Generation" at its highest position of #2, the Who were flown to Manchester by the BBC to make a further live *Top of the Pops* appearance, from 7:30—8:00 pm. On top of their expenses, the Who were paid an appearance fee of £63. (From 20 January 1966, all *TOTP* appearances were made from London.)

FRIDAY, 3 DECEMBER
The Who's first album, *My Generation*, was belatedly released, reaching #5 in the U.K. album charts. When released for the American market in April 1966, it was re-titled *The Who Sings My Generation* by Decca, with a different sleeve and amended track listing.

To mark the occasion, the group appeared yet again on *Ready, Steady, Go!*, broadcast live from Wembley, 6:08—7:00 pm, with Fontella Bass, the Walker Brothers, the Hollies, Wayne Fontana, Ketty Lester, Major Lance, and the Toys. Keith, suffering from what was eventually diagnosed as whooping cough, was late for rehearsals and went on to miss two weeks of gigs.

Directly afterwards, the group paid homage to their roots by returning to play one last triumphant gig at the Goldhawk Social Club, Shepherd's Bush. Among the packed audience was film director, Michelangelo Antonioni, scouting for the right group to appear in his forthcoming murder mystery, *Blow Up*, to be shot in London the following summer.

Antonioni had read press reports about the Who, and after witnessing Townshend ritually smash a Rickenbacker, the director made tentative arrangements for a screen test. Before this ever occurred, the fiery Italian and an uncompromising Townshend were in disagreement over how the Who's scene would be shot, while other sources point to the high fee that foreign film buff Kit Lambert was expecting for his charges. "What the Who do is too meaningful," Antonioni said by way of excuse. "I wanted something utterly meaningless, so I couldn't use them." Antonioni went looking for a less problematic band, eventually deciding on the Yardbirds, who shot their scene, a contrived version of the Who's act, the following October at Elstree Film Studios.

SATURDAY, 4 DECEMBER
Corn Exchange, Chelmsford.

SUNDAY, 5 DECEMBER
The White Lion, Edgware, North London.
Promoted by Bob Druce. The Who's final pre-taped appearance on Radio Luxembourg's *Ready, Steady, Radio!* was transmitted from 9:30—10:00 pm.

MONDAY, 6 DECEMBER
Eltham Baths, Eltham Hill, South East London.
The first of several gigs that Keith missed because of illness. Looking for a suitable replacement at short notice, the perfect candidate was found in Vivian 'Viv' Prince, whose lunatic behaviour had recently gotten him fired from the Pretty Things. Keith attended early Pretty Things' gigs to study Prince's unique drumming style.

WEDNESDAY, 8 DECEMBER
Corn Exchange, Bristol.

THURSDAY, 9 DECEMBER
The Guildhall, Plymouth, Devonshire.

SATURDAY, 11 DECEMBER
University, Southampton, with the Zombies.

SUNDAY, 12 DECEMBER
New Barn Club, Brighton.

MONDAY, 13 DECEMBER
Federation Club, Norwich.
People holding tickets from the cancelled St.

ABOVE: *READY, STEADY, GO!*, 3 DECEMBER.

Andrew's Hall gig on 29 November were admitted to the Federation Club show. A letter from a local group, published in *Record Mirror* the following month, illustrated that not every musician was smitten with the Who: "In view of the widespread publicity and popularity of the Who, we expected an excellent performance. But after an irritating 20 minute wait while vast and totally unnecessary speakers were staggered into place, obscuring the whole stage, the group made an appearance. After some token hysterics by some half-wits in the front, we were treated to some of the most appalling, sound-soaked, electronic drivel we have ever heard. Musical sense, professionalism, sound balance, entertainment value were nil. The whole object seems to be to make as much painful sound in a small place as was physically possible. If this truly laughable performance is the ultimate to be achieved from Marshall amps, Rickenbacker guitars, and Fender basses, we'll have much pleasure in selling ours to the first person to send us a five shilling postal order."

WEDNESDAY, 15 DECEMBER
University College, Swansea, Wales.
"Going Down Ball," with Chris Farlowe and the Thunderbirds.

The Who Concert File suggests that John "Twink" Alder may have filled in at this gig, but Alder himself confirms that he never sat in with the Who on any occasion in their career.

THURSDAY, 16 DECEMBER
Town Hall, Kidderminster.
A film of the Who made in Battersea Park, South West London (filming date unknown), featuring "My Generation" was shown on Southern's *Three Go Round* programme, transmitted 5:25—5:55 pm over the Southern ITV, Anglia, and Channel regions only.

FRIDAY, 17 DECEMBER
Ricky-Tick Club, Windsor.
Keith felt sufficiently recovered to rejoin the group in pre-recording a Christmas Eve *Ready, Steady, Go!* special, transmitted at the later hour of 8:00—8:55 pm. Also taking part were the Animals, the Hollies, the Kinks, Herman's Hermits, and Chris Farlowe.
The programme, hosted by Cathy McGowan and Cilla Black, was divided into three parts. The first was allocated to guests plugging their latest records

1965

live, with the Who performing a brief eight second "My Generation" before going straight into "The Kids Are Alright."

An all-star pantomime of *Cinderella* occupied the second. Cathy McGowan appeared as Cinderella, Peter Noone as the Prince, Eric Burdon and Chas Chandler, respectively, as the Fairy Godmother and Dandini, and Keith as "Buttons," with all characters miming to a current pop record. Pete hammed it up to Peter Cook and Dudley Moore's "Goodbye-e."

The final segment incorporated Christmas carols, including the Who's zany version of "Jingle Bells," featuring "John on French horn, Roger on bell, Keith on kazoo, and Pete on feedback," according to Keith Althams's contemporary *NME* report. The entire cast sang "White Christmas" as the end titles rolled.

Following the recording, the Who went straight on to Windsor. After half an hour onstage, Keith complained of feeling ill. A decision was made to prematurely terminate the act with "My Generation," but Keith collapsed before they managed to finish and was carried off. Viv Prince was again deputized at the following gigs in Portsmouth and Guildford.

SATURDAY, 18 DECEMBER
Birdcage Club, Portsmouth.

SUNDAY, 19 DECEMBER
Ricky-Tick Club, Guildford.

TUESDAY, 21 DECEMBER
Marquee Club.

THURSDAY, 23 DECEMBER
Pavilion Ballroom, Worthing.

FRIDAY, 24 DECEMBER
Pier Ballroom, Hastings.

SATURDAY, 25 DECEMBER
In *Melody Maker*, Chris Stamp confirmed that "[the

ABOVE: *Ready, Steady, Go!*, 17 December.

Who] will be in the studios next week to record their next single, which should be released at the end of January. It will be another Pete Townshend composition, probably 'Circles' or 'The Magic Bus.'"

FRIDAY, 31 DECEMBER
Since the Who had participated in the Christmas edition of *Ready, Steady, Go!*, they were the popular choice for its New Year's Eve counterpart, *The New Year Starts Here*, broadcast live from Studio One, Wembley, from 10:52 pm (pausing to catch the chimes of Big Ben) until it was closed down in the early hours of 1966.

With there being no set running order to follow, the transmission wound up when all acts had finished their spots. Hosted by Keith Fordyce and Cathy McGowan, the bill read like a "Who's Who" of the 1965 pop scene, featuring the Animals, Chris Andrews, Dave Berry, the Dave Clark Five, Tom Jones, Chris Farlowe, the Kinks, Lulu, Kenny Lynch, the Searchers, Dusty Springfield, and the Rolling Stones.

Keith used Dave Clark's sparkle Premier kit during rehearsals, but his own kit arrived in time for the live broadcast. Although *Ready, Steady, Go!* continues to spark affectionate memories today, by this time, its popularity had waned, and both Yuletide specials were intended as the programme's final curtain. (Indeed, the Rediffusion cameras carried "Ready To Go in '66!" slogans.) Until it's final demise on 23 December 1966, the show was given a temporary reprieve, cut from 52 to 27 minutes, and screened only on Fridays in London and on Thursdays in the North and East of England.

a legal matter

1966

1966 was dominated by a drawn-out battle over the Who's recording contract. On 12 January, Chris Stamp flew to New York on a two week promotional mission to shake up, with the help of adviser Lloyd Greenfield, the apathy that greeted each new Who release at Decca. After being stonewalled at every turn, Stamp despairingly phoned Lambert to review the situation. The managers decided to cut their losses. Stamp consulted his American solicitor, Joe Vigoda, who saw a possible legal loophole and arranged a meeting with Sir Edward Lewis, the head of British Decca, who happened to be in town. The question of the recording contract was raised, and Sir Edward agreed to wield his influence, but ultimately, to no avail. Stamp phoned Lambert and directed him to force the issue by breaking the contract.

Lambert and Stamp were taking a considerable gamble. "Shel Talmy had to be gotten rid of," Townshend told *Zigzag*, "and the only guy who was really powerful enough, who was connected with the Who in any way whatsoever at the time, and who wouldn't suffer by it was Robert Stigwood." Believing they had a case against the contractual terms, the group jumped ship, as a temporary measure, to Reaction, the label Stigwood set up for the purpose as an independent within the Polydor organisation in Europe. While in New York, Stamp negotiated a one-off U.S. deal via Atlantic subsidiary, Atco.

At the same time, Talmy had started his own label, Planet Records, distributed through Philips. One of his signings, the Creation, played a brand of musical pop art similar to the Who. Townshend was a fan and allegedly considered asking guitarist Eddie Phillips (whom Talmy maintains was the true pioneer of guitar feedback) to join the Who as deputy axeman. Another Planet Records act, the Untamed, covered "It's Not True," while A Wild Uncertainty copied the Who's stage cover of the Everly Brothers' "Man With Money."

The roster on Stigwood's label included the Birds, featuring eighteen-year-old guitarist Ron Wood, and the South London group the Cat, which boasted guitarist and future record producer Chris Thomas, as well as drummer John "Speedy" Keene, a friend of Townshend's from Hanwell. "I think we were, at the time, both searching for the same thing," Keene reflected to Allan Jones. "I saw him as a mirror of myself—a more together mirror, I suppose." Pete got Speedy signed to his publishers, Fabulous Music, where a nineteen-year-old David Jones (soon to be Bowie) worked as a songwriter. Keene's first song, "Club Of Lights," was released by labelmate Oscar, the son of the Who's lawyer, Oscar Beuselinck. Later, under the stage name Paul Nicholas, he appeared with Keith Moon in *Stardust* and played Cousin Kevin in Ken Russell's film adaptation of *Tommy*.

The legal battle got fully underway when "Circles," recorded with Talmy and widely reported in the music press as the intended follow-up to "My Generation," was suddenly withdrawn by the band in favour of a new Townshend composition, "Substitute." The move had the desired effect. Talmy immediately filed suit in the High Court, claiming copyright infringement on the record's B-side "Instant Party," which was actually a version of "Circles" re-recorded for Reaction. Since Talmy's injunction prevented the Who from recording, the record was hastily withdrawn and the B-side replaced with "Waltz For A Pig"—a thinly veiled one-finger instrumental salute performed by labelmates, the Graham Bond Organisation.

"Substitute" started life as a Rolling Stones parody—Townshend affecting a Jaggeresque vocal on the demo—allied with a 12-string acoustic hook and his cleverest lyrics yet. The Motown riff in the verses was lifted from "Where Is My Girl" by Robb Storme and the Whispers, an obscure single Townshend heard when reviewing new releases for *Melody Maker*'s "Blind Date" column. With Talmy's presence banished from the studio, Townshend assumed production duties. The live mix gave Entwistle the opportunity to notch up his bass level during the solo, and such was Moon's pilled-up state that he didn't recognise his own playing when he heard the finished cut. So paranoid was he that he believed the others had resorted to replacing him.

"Substitute" was a Top 5 hit in England, but in America, it failed to trouble *Billboard*'s Hot 100. Unable to record, live work became the Who's sole means of survival. Thanks to a run of four Top Ten singles, the group could command upwards of £300 a night in Britain. Yet the business uncertainties threatened to sever their shaky alliance at any point. "I always used to work with the thought in my mind that the Who were gonna last precisely another two minutes," Townshend told Jann Wenner two years later. "If the tax man didn't get us, then our own personality clashes would."

By May, these personality clashes came as close to breaking up the Who as they ever would. Daltrey temporarily quit to consider his options, while the others stoically soldiered on as a three-piece. Back in February, Keith had made overtures to join the Animals after John Steel vacated the drum stool. When Barry Jenkins of the Nashville Teens got the gig, Keith in turn pitched himself as Jenkins' replacement. Meanwhile, Entwistle considered replacing bassist Clint Warwick in the Moody Blues. ("It could have been 'Nights In Black Satin!" he said later.)

Opposites attracting, the rhythm section had the closest thing to a friendship within the group and despaired at the constant bickering. Both stated their intention to quit after a tension-fraught gig at Newbury, when Moon was on the receiving end of Townshend's guitar. "I saw myself writing film scores," Townshend told Chris Welch, "while Keith and John saw themselves forming a group called Led Zeppelin."

ABOVE: FILMING *WHERE THE ACTION IS*, 18 MARCH.

LEFT: PETE CHECKS THE CHART PROGRESS OF "SUBSTITUTE" IN *DISC*. NOTE THE AD FOR REACTION LABELMATE OSCAR.

Despite his recent marriage and the responsibility of fatherhood, Keith swanned around swinging London clubland, usually with John in tow, in search of the next party. When their driver, Richard Cole, racked up three speeding tickets, his services had to be dispensed with. The pair bought a maroon and silver Bentley and hired John "Wiggy" Wolff, who had previously worked for the Walker Brothers, as Cole's replacement. Wiggy was eventually promoted to the position of the Who's production manager.

In June, a way out of the contractual mess was offered by Rolling Stones' manager Andrew Oldham

and his business adviser, the notorious Allen Klein, who saw the chance of getting his claws into the Who. In return for extricating the group from Talmy, Klein was offering a lucrative $500,000 recording deal with MGM Records via his company, ABKCO. Klein may have been smart, but luckily, Lambert and Stamp were smarter. They got Klein to sign a document agreeing to a twenty-one-day time limit in which to fix the deal. "All we had to do was come back to England and wait out the time," said Stamp. "Klein couldn't get it together in time because we kept changing the terms to stall him."

Lambert and Stamp were forced back to Davenport-Lyons, Talmy's solicitors, and an out-of-court settlement was finally reached. The Who got creative freedom, but at a price. As part of the agreement, Talmy continued to receive an override of 5% on all Who recordings for the next five years—an

1
9
6
6

unexpected windfall. With the future uncertain for such a combustible outfit, it seemed ludicrous to suggest he would substantially benefit from the deal. Decca tripled the Who's percentage of retail earnings, advanced Lambert and Stamp £25,000 and retained the Who for America, but released them for the rest of the world. In Britain, Lambert and Stamp signed with the Polydor Organisation for an advance of £50,000. This allowed them free reign to follow their next scam. If the likes of Shel Talmy and Robert Stigwood could set up their own independent record label, why couldn't they?

On 26 August, "I'm A Boy" was released. It was the Who's first single in almost six months, a wait that was usually certain career death for a successful band in the mid-sixties. It showed Townshend's songwriting continuing to swing away from anger to situational vignettes about modern characters with adolescent traumas. "'I'm A Boy' came from a musical I'd written about the year 2000 called *Quads*," he later revealed, "when you can order the sex of your children, and this woman orders four girls and one of them turns out to be a boy, so she pretends it's a girl... horrifying!"

Like "The Kids Are Alright," the bridge's chordal structure was inspired by English baroque composer, Henry Purcell, particularly his short piece "Fantasia Upon One Note," which Lambert had played to Townshend as a form of inspiration. (The Purcell influence would rear it's head again within the opening chords to "Pinball Wizard.")

"I'm A Boy" was also the first Who release to be produced by Lambert, marking the start of an unorthodox but inspired arrangement. "We were short of money," Entwistle recalled, "so when our second album was due, Chris Stamp somehow got this publishing deal with Essex Music, where if we all wrote two songs, they'd give us a cash advance of £500 each. Keith managed his two, and Roger managed one, and I composed my first song 'Whiskey Man,' which I'd got from the film *Night Of The Tiger* [1965]. At the end, the villain, who's also the town drunk, gets shot, and he says, 'Whiskey man, they got us both.' I still had one more number to write, and I was down at the Scotch of St. James with Bill and Charlie from the Stones, and we started making up stupid names for animals, and I came up with this name for a spider, Boris, as in Boris Karloff.

"A few days later, while we were rehearsing at the White Hart in Acton, Pete asked me if I'd written my second song, which I hadn't, but I said, 'Yeah, I have.' He said, 'What's it about, then?' I suddenly remembered that conversation, so I said to Pete, 'It's about a spider.' 'What's it called?' 'Oh, uh, "Boris The Spider!"' He said, 'How does it go?' and I kind of panicked and made it up as I went along. Then I rushed home and demoed it on my old Vortexian tape machine. Once I had the idea, it only took me ten minutes." The novelty Who single-that-never-was, "Boris" went on to become John's signature tune and one of the Who's most popular stage numbers.

"Basically, *A Quick One* [the resulting album] was a scream from start to finish," Pete told Alan di Perna. "Running around the studios banging bass drums, playing penny whistles, going out in the street and coming back in with the poor engineer trying to follow us with a microphone. It was a good, good period for the Who. That album was when we realised that studios were the greatest places."

With the album still requiring some ten minutes to fill, Lambert suggested the idea of linking several different stories within the narrative structure of one track—a "mini-opera." Townshend's initial scepticism was enthusiastically subsumed in meeting Lambert's challenge. "A Quick One (While He's Away)" took six different themes ("Her Man's Been Gone," "Crying Town," "We Have A Remedy," "Ivor The Engine Driver," "Soon Be Home," and "You Are Forgiven") to tell a tale of infidelity and ultimate forgiveness, even concluding with an over-the-top aria. Originally, each theme was to be linked with a semi-narrative libretto, but the idea was rejected for being too unwieldy.

Despite its slight nature, the experiment got the Who noticed and was successful in pointing the way forward. *A Quick One* reflects the boutique culture of the swinging London scene in which it was created—right down to its Alan Aldridge–designed sleeve.

The album appeared in time for the Christmas market alongside a new single, "Happy Jack." "My father used to play saxophone in a band for the summer season on the Isle of Man when I was a kid," Pete explained. "There was no character called Happy Jack, but I played on the beach a lot, and it's just my memories of some of the weirdos who live out on the sand." "Happy Jack" rewarded the Who with another Top 5 hit, but their failure to break through in

ABOVE: MFF STADION, MALMÖ, SWEDEN, 23 OCTOBER.

America continued to rankle. If the Who were considered third in the pecking order behind the Beatles and the Rolling Stones in Britain, continuing homegrown success could consolidate but not sustain that position.

Because of their success across the water, the Beatles and the Stones could now largely eschew personal appearances, yet the Who's reputation lay as a formidable live act. Unlike those groups, the Who had no easily marketable angle and thanks to an archaic record company, their music remained unheard beyond a small hardcore group of converted Anglophiles. With the exception of the Kinks, the Who were *the* quintessential English group, but, paradoxically, America held the key to their survival.

In December, publicist Nancy Lewis flew to New York on a ten day promotional blitz for "I'm A Boy." With the help of U.S. representative Pete Kameron, Chris Stamp demanded, and eventually got, Decca's rock department reorganised with three switched-on

promo men working non-stop on the Who's behalf, including Detroit rep Pete Gidion. When the company released "Happy Jack" the following March, it wouldn't be met with the same wall of stony indifference all previous Who releases had suffered. Now all they needed was an agent.

Stamp flew to Texas on a mission to interest Radio England boss Don Pearson in backing a tour, but this was merely a base-covering excercise. Stamp had already set his sights on an ideal New York firm, Premier Talent, though the company's director, Frank Barselona, wasn't interested in the Who.

Barselona had worked as an agent for the GAC company, which had promoted the Beatles' first American tour, before breaking away to form his own visionary Premier Talent Ltd. Stamp had unsuccessfully tried to place the Who with Premier during his January visit, but Barselona wasn't buying. Finding Barselona absent on business on his later trip, Stamp seized the moment and did the hard sell on Barselona's partner, Dick Friedberg. Stamp returned to England having inked a unilateral deal, leaving Barselona fuming about what Premier had lumbered themselves with. A concentrated American assault was planned for the following year.

1966

SATURDAY, 1 JANUARY
Trade Union Hall, Watford.

During the afternoon, Chris Stamp directed a short film designed for American television, featuring the Who playing four numbers, live inside the empty Marquee Club. On 12 January, Stamp left for New York on a two-week promotional jaunt and tried to interest the producers of NBC's *Hullabaloo* in the film, to no avail.

SUNDAY, 2 JANUARY
"Ultra Club," the Downs, Hassocks, Sussex.

The gig was negotiated as a favour to promoter Peter Tree, Keith's old bandmate from Mark Twain and the Strangers. (See "I'm A Boy," Keith.)

WEDNESDAY, 5 JANUARY

The Who received £105 to appear on the inaugural edition of a new youth television series, *A Whole Scene Going*, hosted by cartoonist/satirist Barry Fantoni and actress Wendy Varnals. The programme was pre-recorded at 4:00 pm in Studio 7, Television Centre, and transmitted on BBC-1, from 6:30—7:00 pm.

The Who mimed to "Out In The Street" and "It's Not True" and were shown seated before Keith's drumkit, as jazz singer/critic George Melly named them as his "brightest hope for 1966." The latter part of the programme was given over to the "Hot Seat," where Pete was grilled by both presenters and a panel of chosen teenagers. This was preceded by a 16-mm film insert, shot by Nat Cohen the previous August, showing Pete in his Belgravia flat and the Who at the Witchdoctor Club, Hastings (see 4 August 1965). It also featured live versions of "Heat Wave" and "The Kids Are Alright."

The footage was overlaid with Pete's narration concerning the Who and their audience, pop art fashions, his relations with the other members, his own musical background and ambitions, and how musical quality shouldn't affect a group's outlook. This segued into the discussion forum, chaired by Fantoni and Varnals, where Pete, perched upon a stool, neatly, sometimes arrogantly, parried the questioning put

ABOVE: STEVENAGE, 26 JANUARY.

forward for approximately five minutes. Clips from the programme were used in *The Kids Are Alright*.

The Who (and Pete's frankness about drug use in particular) created enough of a stir that producer Elizabeth Cowley was keen for them to reappear, which they duly did on 15 June.

Fantoni and Townshend both appeared in *Keep The Faith Baby*, a 16mm, B&W, 15-minute film on the pop scene made by Chris O'Dell and distributed by the London Film School in 1967.

FRIDAY, 7 JANUARY
"Mister McCoy's" Club, Middlesbrough, Yorkshire.

SATURDAY, 8 JANUARY
Jigsaw Club, Manchester.

Disc ran an article entitled "Who Are Growing Up Fast," in which John declared: "We'll jump out of '65 like we jumped out of the Mod scene to the Pop Art scene." Pete added, "We intend dropping Pop Art right away, it's impractical for a start. The material we use for clothes is all wrong. We're sick of it. We still dress as individuals, but we won't be so anxious about it… we nearly split up towards the end of

last year. Our rows were nasty ones. But when 'My Generation' took off, we became so involved in our career, we suddenly got on fine again. As soon as we communicate with the fans, we feel mates again."

SUNDAY, 9 JANUARY
Cosmopolitan Club, Carlisle.

WEDNESDAY, 12 and THURSDAY, 13 JANUARY
Mixing/tape copying at IBC: Glyn Johns made mono mixes of "Instant Party Mixture" and "Circles" (featuring John on French horn.) During the ensuing legal dispute between Shel Talmy and the group, this first version of "Circles" was confusingly titled "Instant Party" when released in the U.K. as the B-side to "A Legal Matter" and in the U.S. on *The Who Sings My Generation* album. "Instant Party Mixture," a Dion and the Belmonts–style pastiche, remains unreleased.

THURSDAY, 13 JANUARY
Ritz Ballroom, Skewen and Regal Ballroom, Ammanford, Glamorgan, Wales.

FRIDAY, 14 JANUARY
Municipal Hall, Pontypridd, Wales.

SATURDAY, 15 JANUARY
"Big Beat Club," Two Puddings Pub, Stratford, followed by the In Crowd Club, Hackney, East London.

"Professionalism doesn't count," Pete told the *NME*. "For example, the Who don't mind leaving a few gaps between numbers, and we don't mind keeping an audience waiting, or playing badly. It doesn't worry us to do this. We aren't so professional that we fall head over heels just because of a few mistakes."

SUNDAY, 16 JANUARY
Agincourt Ballroom, Camberley.

FRIDAY, 21 JANUARY
Glenlyn Ballroom, Forest Hill.

SATURDAY, 22 JANUARY
Adelphi Ballroom, West Bromwich, followed by a 10:15 pm gig at the Smethwick Baths Ballroom, Smethwick, Staffordshire.

SUNDAY, 23 JANUARY
Co-Operative Hall, Warrington.

WEDNESDAY, 26 JANUARY
Locarno Ballroom, Stevenage.

THURSDAY, 27 JANUARY
The Who pre-recorded "Circles" for *Ready, Steady, Go!* from Studio One, Wembley. The show, featuring the Small Faces, Sandie Shaw, and Paul and Barry Ryan, was broadcast the following night over certain ITV regions, from 6:08–6:35 pm.

FRIDAY, 28 JANUARY
University, Edgbaston, Birmingham.

SATURDAY, 29 JANUARY
Imperial Ballroom, Nelson.

SUNDAY, 30 JANUARY
Beachcomber Club, Leigh, Lancashire.

MONDAY, 31 JANUARY
Coed Eva Community College, Cwmbran, Gwent, Wales.

TUESDAY, 1 FEBRUARY
Brittania Rowing Club, Nottingham.

FRIDAY, 4 FEBRUARY
Astoria Cinema, Finsbury Park, North London.
Two shows, 6:40 & 9:10 pm.

Opening night of a three date trial package tour with the Fortunes, the Merseybeats, Hamilton and the Hamilton Movement (featuring ex-Detours' guitarist Peter Vernon-Kell), the Graham Bond Organisation, and Screaming Lord Sutch and the Savages. The dates were organised by Lambert and Stamp and promoted by Robert Stigwood, with a view to a future four or five week tour. "If these shows are successful, we are going to do another three day tour taking in another cross section of the country," Lambert told the *NME*.

SATURDAY, 5 FEBRUARY
Odeon Cinema, Southend-on-Sea, Essex.
Two shows, 6:30 & 8:45 pm.

The *NME* reported that the planned release of the next Who single, "Circles," had now been cancelled altogether. The song was "given away" to the Fleur-De-Lys, whose version was released by Immediate Records on 18 March.

SUNDAY, 6 FEBRUARY
Empire Theatre, Liverpool.
Two shows, 5:40 & 8:00 pm.

FRIDAY, 11 FEBRUARY
Wimbledon Palais, Wimbledon, London.

SATURDAY, 12 FEBRUARY
Dreamland Ballroom, Margate. Recording "Substitute" at Olympic Sound Studios, Carton Hall, Carton Street, off Marble Arch.

"That was the first Who-produced session," Townshend told *Zigzag*. "Kit didn't slide naturally into the seat of producing the Who—he kind of arrived in the position of producing the Who because we desperately needed a producer."

The mix designated for the U.S. was noticeably different, featuring an alternate vocal and the offending line "I look all white but my dad was black" replaced with "I try going forward but my feet walk back" to placate sensitive radio programmers.

SUNDAY, 13 FEBRUARY
Community Centre, Southall.

MONDAY, 14 FEBRUARY
Valentine's Panto Dance Ball, University, Liverpool.

TUESDAY, 15 FEBRUARY
Esquire Club, Sheffield.

THURSDAY, 17 FEBRUARY
Club A Go-Go, Newcastle.

FRIDAY, 18 FEBRUARY
Volunteer Hall, Galashiels, Scotland.
Melody Maker reported that the Who were moving to Robert Stigwood's newly formed Reaction

label, whose records would be released by Atlantic in the U.S. and by Polydor throughout the rest of the world.

SATURDAY, 19 FEBRUARY
Memorial Hall, Northwich, Cheshire.

SUNDAY, 20 FEBRUARY
Oasis Club, Manchester.

MONDAY, 21 FEBRUARY
Beachcomber Club, Preston, Lancashire.

TUESDAY, 22 and WEDNESDAY, 23 FEBRUARY
Rehearsals at the White Hart, Acton, and recording instrumentals at Olympic Studios, intended for a French EP. (Further details unknown.)

THURSDAY, 24 FEBRUARY
Victoria Ballroom, Chesterfield.
    The Who didn't play because of Roger's laryngitis—a form of apology appeared in the Sheffield paper, *The Star*. With time on their hands, Keith and John sat in as part of the Merseys backing group, the Fruit Eating Bears, at the City Hall, Sheffield. Roger's laryngitis caused him to miss the following gigs in Wellington, Boston, and Eltham. The group performed without him as a three-piece, with Pete and John sharing vocal duties.

FRIDAY, 25 FEBRUARY
Majestic Ballroom, Wellington, Shropshire.

SATURDAY, 26 FEBRUARY
Starlight Room, Gliderdrome, Boston, Lincolnshire.
    "New Action are the production company for the Who now," said Kit Lambert in *Disc*, "but in fact, actual production in the studios will be done by the group themselves."

MONDAY, 28 FEBRUARY
Eltham Baths, Eltham Hill, London.

WEDNESDAY, 2 MARCH
Wolsey Hall, Cheshunt.

THURSDAY, 3 MARCH
Victoria Ballroom, Chesterfield.
Re-scheduled from 24 February.

FRIDAY, 4 MARCH
British Nylon Spinners Club, Pontypool, Gwent, Wales.
    To 35,000 advance orders, "Substitute" B/W "Circles" and "Substitute" B/W "Instant Party" were released simultaneously in the U.K. on Robert Stigwood's Reaction label.
    The B-sides were, in fact, identical, the same re-recorded version of "Circles" in a vain attempt at hoodwinking Shel Talmy. (This faster, self-produced version was recorded at Olympic around the end of January.) On Tuesday, 8 March, he successfully applied in the High Court for a temporary injunction, claiming infringement of copyright.
    "It's Alright" (loosely derived from "The Kids Are Alright") was released on CBS by the Rockin' Vickers. Included among their ranks was guitarist Ian Kilminster, who went on to perform with Sam Gopal, Hawkwind, and Motorhead, under his better known nickname "Lemmy."

SATURDAY, 5 MARCH
Marcam Hall, March, Cambridgeshire.

MONDAY, 7 MARCH
At Granada TV Centre, Manchester, the Who mimed "Substitute" in Studio Three for the Northern news magazine programme *Scene at 6.30*, broadcast across the Granada ITV region from 6:30—7:00 pm.
    To counteract potential sales of "Substitute," Decca rush-released "A Legal Matter"—an ironic choice from *My Generation*—onto the market with "Instant Party," the original version of the song at the root of the dispute, as its B-side. The single could only rally to #32 without the group to promote it. A vengeful Talmy continued to cull a further two singles from *My Generation* as a counter measure to new Who product appearing on the market.

WEDNESDAY, 9 MARCH
Town Hall, Farnborough.
    "Substitute" entered the *NME* chart at #19 as Polydor was served with a notice to cease distribution after pressing 50,000 copies of the record. That afternoon, a judge refused an application from counsel to lift the court order and extended it to the following Friday.
    Orbit Music, Talmy's company, agreed to provide a surety of £3000 to cover damages that could be awarded to Polydor if the injunction was found to be wrongfully awarded.

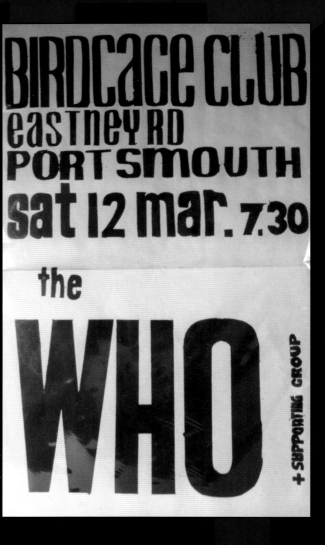

THURSDAY, 10 MARCH
The Ram Jam Club, Brixton, South West London.

FRIDAY, 11 MARCH
The Cavern, Leicester Square, London, preceded by a rehearsal at the White Hart, Acton.

SATURDAY, 12 MARCH
Birdcage Club, Portsmouth.

SUNDAY, 13 MARCH
Starlite Ballroom, Greenford.

MONDAY, 14 MARCH
In order to beat the temporary ban and to cope with outstanding orders, Polydor re-pressed "Substitute" over the weekend with a different B-side. "Waltz For A Pig," an instrumental credited to the Who Orchestra, was performed by the Graham Bond Organisation, as Talmy's injunction prevented the

ABOVE: ON LOCATION AT CHARING CROSS PIER, 18 MARCH.

the Small Faces, and the Yardbirds around familiar London landmarks.

Surrounded by a crowd of extras and curious bystanders, the Who mimed to "I Can't Explain" and "Bald Headed Woman" at Potter's Fields, near the southern entrance to Tower Bridge, and "Substitute" at Charing Cross Pier, Westminster. "I Can't Explain" and "Substitute" aired Monday, 16 May, while "Bald Headed Woman" was slotted into the 27 June programme (times varied between each ABC region).

That evening, the Who made another of their regular *Ready, Steady, Go!* appearances from Studio One, Wembley, playing live versions of "Barbara Ann" and "Substitute." The show, featuring Barbara Lewis, Billy Fury, Irma Thomas, and Bob Lind, was broadcast 6:07—6:35 pm.

Reaction were due to have issued the Cat's "Run, Run, Run," written and produced by Pete, on this date. However, the single was inexplicably withdrawn. Fellow labelmates the Birds also recorded an unissued version. The Who's own version appeared on *A Quick One* nine months later.

Who from recording until 4 April. A BBC embargo was subsequently lifted after the Corporation was satisfied the record complied with legal regulations. Despite these impediments, "Substitute" eventually reached #5 in the U.K. charts, selling 200,000 copies. Its release in America appeared on a stopgap label, Atlantic Records subsidiary Atco, on 2 April, but failed to chart.

TUESDAY, 15 MARCH

The Who recorded a session for the BBC Light Programme's *Saturday Club* at Studio One, Aeolian Hall, London, produced by Jimmy Grant and Brian Willey. The Regents' "Barbara Ann" (featuring Keith on lead vocal), "Substitute," an "Ox"-like instrumental entitled "You Rang," stage versions of the Everly Brothers' "Man With Money" and the Everly's

arrangement of Martha and the Vandellas' "Dancing in the Street," together with an interview with Pete by host Brian Matthew, were broadcast in the 19 March edition, 10:00—12:00 am. Also in session were the Small Faces, Freddie and the Dreamers, the Bachelors, Valerie Masters, John Mayall's Bluesbreakers, pianist Ted Taylor, the Ladybirds, and the Les Reed Orchestra.

FRIDAY, 18 MARCH

Locarno Ballroom, Basildon.

The day was spent making television recordings. During the morning, the Who were filmed on location for American television's *Where The Action Is!*—a weekday, half-hour syndicated ABC show, produced and hosted by media personality Dick Clark and featuring musical acts miming in external settings. Clark and his crew came over on a week's shoot, also filming Them, the Mindbenders, Dave Berry, the Action,

SATURDAY, 19 MARCH

King's Hall, Stoke-on-Trent.

Disc revealed Keith's impending engagement to seventeen-year-old *Ready, Steady, Go!* dancer Sandra Serjeant. Keith had met her at the show some six months earlier, "but we won't be getting married for a very long time yet." This was nothing more than an effective smokescreen to conceal the fact he'd married his seventeen-year-old girlfriend, Kim Kerrigan, amid great secrecy at Brent Register Office on 17 March. Their daughter, Amanda Jane, was born on 12 July at Central Middlesex Hospital.

SUNDAY, 20 MARCH

"The Making Of The Who" profile appeared in the *Observer* Colour Supplement, written by John Heilpern, who followed the group, as well as Lambert and Stamp, to Manchester, Stevenage, and

The prediction business (2)

MONDAY, 21 MARCH
A Chris Stamp-directed promotional clip of "Substitute" was made for American television at a rented film studio in Neal's Yard, Covent Garden. The group, resplendent in pop art regalia, mimed to the censored U.S. single against a plain white backdrop. The clip was also sent to Europe and later shown in a Belgian BRTN documentary, *Contrastes*, on 18 May, and on German NDR TV's *Beat Club* on 28 May. It appeared, redubbed, in *The Kids Are Alright* and *Who's Better, Who's Best*.

WEDNESDAY, 23 MARCH
Tower Ballroom, Great Yarmouth.

In a spot of japery, roadie Neville Chesters joined the group onstage to sing an impromptu version of Crispian St. Peters' current hit, "You Were On My Mind."

New York. The article mentioned that Lambert and Stamp received 40% of the group's earnings, on top of which they paid a further 10% to agent Robert Stigwood. The classic cover shot was taken by Colin Jones in a hotel near Manchester Airport. "Looking back, I wonder how I ever managed to get it done," Jones recalled. "I'd never met a band that were so antagonistic towards each other, and it was a case of having to keep them still for long enough to take the picture. I knew there was no way I could keep them together for long, so I didn't bother setting up my lights. We just used natural daylight."

Both photo and article were subsequently updated as "Who's Still Who" in the *Observer* supplement, dated 19 March 1972.

THURSDAY, 24 MARCH
Starlight Ballroom, Crawley.

Prior to the gig, the Who taped an insert for "Substitute" at Studio 2, Television Centre, Wood Lane, broadcast on BBC-1's *Top Of The Pops*, 7:30—8:05 pm. It was repeated the following week (same times).

FRIDAY, 25 MARCH
Corn Exchange, Hertford, Hertfordshire.

"Substitute" went back on sale in its original form. On 18 March, the injunction restraining Polydor from selling it with "Instant Party" as the B-side had been removed by a High Court judge, and the company were able to issue a remaining stock of 40,000 copies with the original coupling.

In *NME*, Paul Samwell-Smith of the Yardbirds mentioned the Who when discussing the touchy subject of who invented feedback: "Our Jeff Beck was using feedback when we used to play at Richmond Athletic Ground, and Pete Townshend and the rest of them used to come along and watch. Pete Townshend literally copies us now, and though he's pretty good, he still doesn't do it that well. This isn't mean't as a big knock of the Who, but I think it's only fair that credit should go where it's due."

Townshend has always denied this: "Somehow we became aware of the Yardbirds and we incorporated the things they were doing into our act without ever seeing them; it was done by word of mouth."

SATURDAY, 26 MARCH
St. George's Ballroom, Hinckley.

That morning, Pete went to Caroline House, 6 Chesterfield Gardens (where New Action Ltd relocated offices in August) to be interviewed by pop critic Penny Valentine for a special "Sound of the Stars" flexi-disc. John Maus and Gary Leeds of the Walker Brothers were also interviewed, and the single was offered free with the 23 April launch edition of *Disc and Music Echo*.

Fifty-five seconds of the conversation (taped in the basement studio by DJ Tom Lodge) was included, alongside interviews with Cilla Black, Dusty Springfield, Sandie Shaw, Cliff Richard, the Hollies, Spencer Davis, and the Beatles, among others.

SUNDAY, 27 MARCH
Marine Ballroom, Central Pier, Morecambe.

TUESDAY, 29 MARCH
Roger, John, and Pete arrived in Paris (Keith had flown over in advance) for television rehearsals.

THURSDAY, 31 MARCH
The Who recorded their appearance on an ORTF spectacular *Music Hall de France* at d'Ailleurs, Issy-les-Moulineaux, transmitted TV2, Thursday, 9 April, 10:20—11:15 pm. Presented by Michele Arnaud, the group performed live versions of "Substitute," "Dancing In The Street," "Man With Money," "Barbara Ann," and "My Generation." Guests included the Fortunes and the Ikettes.

FRIDAY, 1 APRIL
The Who, with the Yardbirds, appeared in a special *Ready, Steady, Go!* assignment—*Ready, Steady, Allez!*—

hosted by Cathy McGowan and French singer Dick Rivers. The show went out live over the Eurovision link, 7:00–7:30 pm (U.K. time), from La Locomotive Club, situated in the Moulin Rouge. The broadcast was made doubly difficult by an uncooperative French crew and a nationwide phone strike, which made the one open line to London virtually unusable. Hence, it was almost impossible to ascertain if England was actually receiving the transmission!

Rehearsals commenced at 2:00 pm with guest French artists Huges Aufray, Antoine, Eddy Mitchell, and Mirelle Mathieu. The Who performed live versions of "My Generation" (which opened the show) and "Substitute." Surprise guests among the crowd were Rolling Stones Brian Jones and Bill Wyman. According to producer Vicki Wickham, for the finale, the cameras followed both groups running out of the club into the back courtyard, only to catch them urinating against a wall. Later the same evening, the Who appeared in a live Radio Luxembourg 208 broadcast from the Locomotive, compèred by singer Ronnie Bird.

SATURDAY, 2 APRIL

La Locomotive Club, Paris, France. Two shows, 2:00 pm & 12 midnight.

MONDAY, 4 APRIL

Town Hall Theatre, Chatham, Kent.

The first hearing in the London High Court for Shel Talmy's claim to exclusive recording rights for the Who. An interim injunction was granted restraining the group from recording.

FRIDAY, 8 APRIL

Queen's Hall, Leeds, Yorkshire.

SATURDAY, 9 APRIL

Pavilion Gardens Ballroom, Buxton.

THURSDAY, 14 APRIL

Gaumont Cinema, Southampton.
Two shows, 6:15 & 8:40 pm.

The Who embarked on their second British package tour, promoted by Robert Stigwood, featuring the Spencer Davis Group, guest stars the Merseys (backed by the Fruit Eating Bears), the Band Of Angels, Jimmy Cliff and the Sound System, Oscar B. Hamilton, and compère Mike ("Come Outside") Sarne.

Prior to this, the group recorded another *Top Of The Pops* insert for "Substitute" at Television Centre, broadcast that evening, 7:30–8:00 pm.

FRIDAY, 15 APRIL

Fairfield Hall, Croydon, Surrey.
Two shows, 6:45 & 9:00 pm.

SATURDAY, 16 APRIL

Odeon Cinema, Watford.
Two shows, 6:30 & 8:45 pm.

SUNDAY, 17 APRIL

Regal Theatre, Edmonton, North London.
Two shows, 6:00 & 8:30 pm.

TUESDAY, 19 APRIL

Town Hall, Walsall, Staffordshire.

THURSDAY, 21 APRIL

Benington Football Club Gala Ball, Locarno Ballroom, Stevenage.

FRIDAY, 22 APRIL

Odeon Cinema, Derby.
Two shows, 6:15 & 8:40 pm.

SATURDAY, 23 APRIL

Odeon Cinema, Rochester, Kent.
Two shows, 6:15 & 8:45 pm.

SUNDAY, 24 APRIL

Birmingham Theatre, Birmingham.
Two shows, 5:30 & 8:00 pm.

On the way to the gig, while pulling away from the kerb outside Keith's home in Chaplin Road, Wembley, a passing vehicle struck driver Richard Cole's Humber Hawk, causing serious damage. Keith and John were shaken but unhurt.

MONDAY, 25 APRIL

The Pavilion, Bath.

TUESDAY, 26 APRIL

Links International Club, Boreham Wood, with Bluesology.

"I got friendly with their keyboard player and we were both drowning our sorrows," Entwistle remembered. "He was pissed off they wouldn't let him sing, and I was pissed off that I wasn't singing enough." The nineteen-year-old Pinner pianist, Reginald Dwight, had better luck under his alter ego, Elton John.

THURSDAY, 28 APRIL

The Witchdoctor, Savoy Rooms, Catford, South East London.

FRIDAY, 29 APRIL

Tiles Club, 79–89 Oxford Street.

More than 500 fans were turned away when 2500 queued for admission, breaking the house record for this central London club, which opened on 28 February. The group's 45 minute act was cut by half after fans twice rushed the stage. The Who returned on 29 July.

SATURDAY, 30 APRIL

Corn Exchange, Chelmsford.

SUNDAY, 1 MAY

The Who appeared at the fourth annual *New Musical Express* "Poll Winners Concert," held as usual at the Empire Pool, Wembley, before an audience of 12,000. The bill featured (in order): Sounds Incorporated, the Overlanders, the Small Faces, the Spencer Davis Group, Roy Orbison, the Walker Brothers, the Yardbirds, the Seekers, the Alan Price Set, Cliff Richard and the Shadows, the Fortunes, Crispian St.Peters, Herman's Hermits, Dave Dee, Dozy, Beaky, Mick and Tich, Dusty Springfield, the Who, the Rolling Stones, and the Beatles.

The Who's two-song set consisted of "Substitute" and "My Generation," the latter concluding with Keith toppling his kit. Like the previous two years, ABC-TV cameras were on hand to cover the event, but because of both the Beatles' and the Rolling Stones' contractual refusal to be filmed, the resulting two-part special *Poll Winners Concert* was only shown in selected ITV regions (excluding London). The Who were featured in Part One, broadcast Sunday 8 May, 3:50—5:00 pm.

TUESDAY, 3 MAY

The Who were due to appear at the Winter Gardens, Malvern, a booking made in February. With the gear sent on ahead, a spokesman rang at 7:00 pm warning of a possible late arrival, explaining that the van was experiencing brake failure. At 9:30 pm, they rang again from Oxford to say the van was still undergoing repairs, but they would start out immediately, knowing full well the group would arrive only in time for the final curtain.

With Roger being the only one to turn up, promoter Fred Bannister was forced to announce the Who's non-appearance, although tickets were valid for a make-up show on 21 June. Support group the Deep Feeling, featuring future Traffic members Dave Mason on guitar and Jim Capaldi on drums, played the remainder of the evening.

In reality, the van story was nothing more than a hastily concocted cover-up. "Roger was gonna leave the group," Pete admitted to *Zigzag*. "It was just an amazing time in the Who's career. We were more or less about to break up. Nobody really cared about the group. It was just a political thing. Kit and I used to go for long walks in Hyde Park and talk about combining what was gonna be left of the Who with Paddy, Klaus, and Gibson."

Paddy Chambers, Klaus Voormann, and Gibson Kemp were a Liverpudlian-German amalgam (managed by Brian Epstein and signed to Pye Records) that released three flop singles in 1965–66. Bassist Voormann went on to join Manfred Mann and designed the Beatles' *Revolver* sleeve. During Roger's absence, Pete and John shared vocal chores.

WEDNESDAY, 4 MAY

Town Hall, Stourbridge.

THURSDAY, 5 MAY

Town Hall, Kidderminster.

"Robert Plant talks about the fact that when he first saw us, I was the singer," Pete told *Musician*. "He came to see us and offered himself for the job, as did Steve Gibbons when he came to see us... Obviously none of them thought I was any good!"

ABOVE: POLLWINNERS CONCERT, 1 MAY.

Smashed windows in a huff

THERE was a spate of window smashing in Malvern on Tuesday night by a gang of disgruntled youths after The Who had failed to turn up at a teenage dance at the Winter Gardens.

Weekly teenage rock sessions are run at the Winter Gardens by Bannister Promotions Ltd., and when it was announced that The Who, the group which had been engaged to play, were unable to get to Malvern because their car had broken down, there were boos and hisses from a crowd of 1,000 teenagers.

After the dance a gang of between ten and 15 youths, believed to be from the Cheltenham area, apparently decided to "take it out on someone" and smashed windows at the Winter Gardens and Festival Theatre.

In Church-street a milk bottle was thrown through the window of the Sports Depot and both windows at the nearby Dorothy Café were broken.

Pol.-Insp. J. Rowberry said lots of people must have seen the window smashing but it had been difficult to get descriptions of the culprits.

The Deep Feeling, who played in place of The Who, got a good reception from the teenagers.

Chris Stamp, manager of The Who, told the "Gazette" yesterday that the group were sorry to have let Mr. Bannister down. They would like to come to Malvern again as soon as possible.

"Their car broke down coming out of London," he explained. "The brakes kept jamming, and they did not get to Oxford until about 9 o'clock."

FRIDAY, 6 MAY

Top Hat Ballroom, Lisburn, Northern Ireland.

An uneasy truce prevailed as Roger rejoined the Who for their first visit to the Emerald Isle.

SATURDAY, 7 MAY

National Stadium, Dublin, Ireland.

Disc reported the IRA's supposed threat to blow up the stage (situated in the round) if the Who appeared wearing Union Jack attire. This appears to have been exaggerated, as local support band, the Next-In-Line, regularly wore Union Jack T-shirts. Pete did bring his jacket, but opted instead for a specially tailored one made up of the Irish tricolour of green, gold, and white. All in all, the Who did not go down well with the 2500 crowd members, whose allegiance lay with the local acts on the bill. A reception was held at the Intercontinental Hotel, where Pete was interviewed by journalist B.P. Fallon for *Spotlight* magazine. He spoke frankly about the use of feedback and drugs, although the latter remarks were unsurprisingly edited from the finished article.

SUNDAY, 8 MAY

Arcadia Ballroom, Cork, Ireland.

WEDNESDAY, 11 MAY

Corn Exchange, Bristol.

THURSDAY, 12 MAY

Pavilion Ballroom, Worthing.

FRIDAY, 13 MAY

Wimbledon Palais, Wimbledon.

Roger missed this and the following night's gig in Bury. He returned to the Who in time for their next gig on 20 May, only for Keith to quit in more dramatic circumstances. That afternoon, the three-man line-up performed "A Legal Matter," Ma Rainey's "See See Rider" (based on Mitch Ryder's "Jenny Take A Ride" interpretation), and "Dancing in the Street" on the BBC Light Programme's *The Joe Loss Show*. They were introduced by Tony Hall, and the performance was broadcast live from the Playhouse Theatre, 1:00–1:50 pm.

SATURDAY, 14 MAY

Palais de Danse, Bury, Lancashire.

MONDAY, 16 and TUESDAY, 17 MAY

Keith played drums at two Jeff Beck sessions at IBC Studios, organised amid great secrecy by Yardbirds' manager Simon Napier-Bell and engineered by Glyn Johns. One of the tracks cut by Beck and heavy session friends Jimmy Page (guitar), John Paul Jones (bass), and Nicky Hopkins (piano) was a rock arrangement of Ravel's "Bolero," released the following March as the B-side to "Hi Ho Silver Lining," with Mickie Most claiming an updated production credit. When the track reappeared on Beck's *Truth* album in July 1968, the liner notes credited Keith as playing timpani under the pseudonym "You Know Who".

"The thing is that when Keith did Beck's 'Bolero,'" Townshend told *Zigzag*, "that wasn't just a session, that was a political move. It was at a point when the group was very close to breaking up. Keith was very paranoid and going through a heavy pills thing. He wanted to make the group plead for him because he'd joined Beck."

WEDNESDAY, 18 MAY

Keith and Beach Boy Bruce Johnston, in town to publicise *Pet Sounds*, were surprise guests at a Tony Rivers and the Castaways gig at Romford County Technical School, Essex. Rivers had known Keith since 1964, thanks to their mutual love of surf music. "I used to go round to Keith's house in Wembley to listen to records," Rivers recalled, "and you could hear the Beach Boys' *Shut Down Vol.2* from three blocks away! I met Keith, Bruce, and L.A. scenester Kim Fowley that morning at the Waldorf Astoria and told them about the gig that night, not thinking for a minute they'd turn up. Once they were on, we couldn't get them off! It was a great night, the kids couldn't believe it. It was only a pound to get in, but because the promoter had an unexpected bonus, it was an extra pound to get out!"

FRIDAY, 20 MAY

Corn Exchange, Newbury, Berkshire.

An evening that could be described as anything but uneventful. Firstly, Keith accompanied Bruce Johnston to *Ready, Steady, Go!*, broadcast live, 6:07–6:35 pm. The following gig at Newbury's "Ricky-Tick" became the site of perhaps the most explosive Who rumpus of all. At 10:10 pm, Keith and John nonchalantly arrived more than two hours late from an *RSG!* party and were angered to find a fuming Daltrey and Townshend had already started the set,

using bassist Colin Standring and drummer Geoff Brown from support group, the Jimmie Brown Sound.

As the rightful rhythm section resumed their places, words were exchanged. During "My Generation," palpable frustration boiled over into violence. Keith sustained a black eye and a leg injury requiring three stitches, after being bodily injured by Pete's guitar and Roger's mike stand. The melee spilled into the upstairs dressing room, where a window and chair were broken and glasses smashed.

Moon told an *NME* journalist present that he and Entwistle were leaving the Who to appear in the future as a duo. The pair sped back to London and informed an astonished Kit Lambert and Robert Stigwood of their intention. Keith, at least, was as good as his word and quit for a week.

SATURDAY, 21 MAY

Floral Hall, Southport, Lancashire.

While Keith nursed a grudge (and a fractured ankle from the previous night's skirmish), it was business as usual with a string of gigs booked up North. At each date, a drummer from the local support group was asked to fill in at short notice.

MONDAY, 23 MAY

Locarno Ballroom, Blackburn, Lancashire.

WEDNESDAY, 25 MAY

Robert Stigwood announced that Keith had withdrawn his threat to leave the Who: "Everything has been sorted out."

THURSDAY, 26 MAY

Locarno Ballroom, Ashton-under-Lyne, Lancashire.

FRIDAY, 27 MAY

Granby Halls, Leicester.

SATURDAY, 28 MAY

South Pier, Blackpool. Two shows, 6:15 & 8:30 pm, with the Rockin' Vickers, the Birds, and Oscar. Keith was back in the fold, debuting his new-look Premier double bass drum kit.

SUNDAY, 29 MAY

Winter Gardens, Morecambe. Two shows, 6:15 & 8:30 pm, with the Merseys, the Fruit Eating Bears, Mike Berry and the Innocents, Philip Goodhand-Tait and the Stormsville Shakers, She Trinity, and Oscar.

Driving back to London, Pete's Lincoln Continental was involved in a five car pile-up on the M1 at Gayhurst, near Newport Pagnell, Buckinghamshire. Apart from some bruising, he escaped without injury. (See 21 September.) However, this didn't halt inaccurate radio bulletins reaching certain European stations that Roger had died. "Somehow the overseas stations got hold of the wrong story," Kit Lambert reassured *Melody Maker*.

MONDAY, 30 MAY

Lincoln Pop Festival, Lincoln City Football Club.

An early prototype of the open-air rock festival, staged by *The Lincolnshire Chronicle* in association with the L.C.F.C, staged 12 midday—10:30 pm, admission just £1. The floodlights were turned on at 10:00 pm for the Who's bill-topping appearance over the Kinks, the Small Faces, the Yardbirds, Georgie Fame and the Blue Flames, Screaming Lord Sutch, Crispian St. Peters, Dave Dee, Dozy, Beaky, Mick and Tich, the Alan Price Set, She Trinity, and the Creation. Despite such an impressive line-up, Bank Holiday attendance levels failed to reach expectation and the club suffered serious financial setbacks as a result.

WEDNESDAY, 1 JUNE

The Who flew into Arlanda Airport, Stockholm, Sweden at 12:15 pm to commence a week-long Scandanavian tour.

THURSDAY, 2 JUNE

Grona Lund, Tivoli Garden, Stockholm. More than 15,000 fans stood in pouring rain to watch this afternoon show.

LEFT: LEICESTER, 27 MAY, WITH A MYSTERY DRUMMER REPLACING KEITH.

FRIDAY, 3 JUNE

Two Swedish shows: Liljekonvaljeholmen, Uppsala, at 8:00 pm, followed by Kungsparken, Kungsör, at 11:30 pm.

The Who spent most of the day rehearsing and taping six songs for Sverige Television's *Popside*, produced by Peter Goldmann, who went on to direct the Beatles' "Penny Lane" and "Strawberry Fields Forever" promotional films.

The Who's twenty minute segment commenced with them smashing through a paper Union Jack to the strains of "The Ox," before taking their positions upon a slanted ramp. The group mimed to playback (linked by spoken introductions): "Daddy Rolling Stone," "It's Not True," "Bald Headed Woman,"

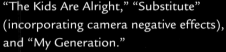
LEFT AND ABOVE: TIVOLI GARDEN, STOCKHOLM, 2 JUNE.
RIGHT AND BELOW: *POPSIDE*, 3 JUNE.

"The Kids Are Alright," "Substitute" (incorporating camera negative effects), and "My Generation."

The insert was included in the programme broadcast two days later, from 6:00—6:40 pm. Goldmann worked with the Who again in London. (See 14 October.)

SATURDAY, 4 JUNE
Two Swedish shows: Berget, Söderhamn, at 4:00 pm, followed by a one hundred mile (161km) drive to Högbo Bruk, Sandviken for an 8:00 pm appearance.

SUNDAY, 5 JUNE
Two Swedish shows: At Träffen, Nyköping, as part of a local pop festival before an afternoon audience of 2500, followed by a drive to Örebro to headline an eight-hour, sixteen-band package at the Idrottshuset. Enroute, they stopped at the residence of Gunnel Larsson in Vrena to watch their pre-taped *Popside* appearance. (See 3 June.)

With the concert running behind schedule, the Who's act was terminated by local police, who cut the power when the crowd rioted. As John recalled: "Once when we were in Sweden, I was in a temper for some reason, and I smashed my guitar through a speaker. It came out the other side and just stuck there—I couldn't get it out. Eventually it took two people to pull it out."

ABOVE: Söderhamn, Sweden, 4 June.

TUESDAY, 7 JUNE
Hit House, Copenhagen, followed by Fyens Forum, Odense, Denmark.

The Who flew back to England the following day.

TUESDAY, 14 JUNE
Recording/mixing on four-track at IBC and Pye Studios: "Disguises" and "I'm A Boy." A tape copy of a rough mono mix of "Disguises" was made to be mimed to on the following day's television recording. Both tracks were completed at IBC on 31 July.

WEDNESDAY, 15 JUNE
Having appeared on the maiden broadcast of BBC-1's youth series, *A Whole Scene Going* (see 5 January), the Who were also booked for the final edition (Show 24), receiving a fee of £63. Also appearing were Chris Farlowe and bluesman Jimmy Witherspoon. (Mick Jagger was due to appear, but had collapsed the previous morning from nervous exhaustion.)

Rehearsals began at 2:30 pm in Studio 2, Television Centre, for the live transmission, aired from 6:30—7:05 pm. The Who mimed to "Disguises," with Townshend sporting a false, villainous handlebar moustache, and Entwistle a tuba christened "Gladys." In addition, a one minute extract from Pete's inter

view on the first show was shown as part of a look back on the series.

THURSDAY, 16 JUNE
University, Hull, Yorkshire, with the Mike Cotton Sound, whom the Who had supported at the 100 Club, just two short years before.

FRIDAY, 17 JUNE
City Halls, Perth, Scotland.

SATURDAY, 18 JUNE
Market Assembly Hall, Carlisle.

SUNDAY, 19 JUNE
Recording/mixing: backing track to "I'm A Boy" (long version).

MONDAY, 20 JUNE
Gay Tower Ballroom, Edgbaston, Birmingham.

TUESDAY, 21 JUNE
Winter Gardens, Malvern. A rescheduled show from 3 May, filmed in colour by CBS-TV as part of an hour-long documentary on British teenagers. The show

RIGHT: *A Whole Scene Going*, 15 June.

was broadcast as a *CBS Reports* special, transmitted during the week of 14–18 November.

Also during this time, Chris Stamp filmed and conducted a twenty minute interview with the group at Pete's Wardour Street flat, intended for transmission on Dick Clark's *Where The Action Is!* (a five minute extract was inserted into the 22 November show). Clips showing Pete tugging John's ear and discussing the importance of volume to the Who's act were used in *The Kids Are Alright*.

THURSDAY, 23 JUNE

University, Leeds. Student Rag Ball with John Mayall's Bluesbreakers, Wayne Fontana, the Alan Price Set, and the Swinging Blue Jeans.

FRIDAY, 24 JUNE

University, Salisbury.

SATURDAY, 25 JUNE

College Of Further Education, Chichester, Sussex.

SUNDAY, 26 JUNE

Brittania Theatre, Brittania Pier, Great Yarmouth. Two shows, 6:30 & 8:45 pm, with the Merseys, Oscar, the Fruit Eating Bears, the Herd, and Genevieve.

The second in a series of Sunday concerts stretching from 19 June through to 4 September. Although the music press reported that the Who would be appearing throughout (barring 7 and 14 August for holidays), promoter Robert Stigwood decided that "attractions with family appeal would be more suitable." This diplomatic statement to the *NME*

covered up the fact that the Who were out of favour with the venue's general manager, John Powles, because of lateness and an incident where one of Keith's drumsticks hit an audience member. The Searchers and Wayne Fontana replaced them for the duration of the run.

MONDAY, 27 JUNE

Pete made a quick first trip to New York to rendezvous with Rolling Stones manager Andrew Oldham and Allen Klein, Oldham's American business adviser. The pair were interested in taking over the Who's recording contract. Pete flew over first class (his return fare paid for by Klein), travelling incognito with Herman's Hermits, whom Klein represented in America. As the group was commencing a U.S. tour, Pete attended a press luncheon in their honour at the Americana Hotel on 7th Avenue at West 53rd St, where he was photographed by Linda Eastman (the future Mrs. McCartney) and interviewed by Danny Fields for *Datebook* magazine.

WEDNESDAY, 29 JUNE

The Who were contracted to play Sheffield University with Tony Rivers and the Castaways. Roger, Keith, and John duly turned up, but did not perform due to the absence of a severely jet-lagged Pete, who having arrived from New York that afternoon, had fallen asleep on the hard shoulder of the M1. Rivers and his band ended up playing the whole evening.

JULY

To remedy the Who's heard but not seen situation in the States, Chris Stamp directed a series of promotional clips designed for American television. A B&W film of the group miming their current U.S. single "The Kids Are Alright" was shot near the Serpentine in Hyde Park. (The clip later appeared in *Who's Better, Who's Best*.) A colour short, made on location around the West End, showed the band emerging from Foubert's Place into Carnaby Street and onto a hired jeep, driven by Pete and chased by a late arriving Keith. (This was used in *The Kids Are Alright*.)

FRIDAY, 1 JULY

The Winter Garden, Eastbourne, Sussex.

MONDAY, 4 JULY

Marina Ballroom, Ramsgate, Kent.

THURSDAY, 7 JULY

Locarno Ballroom, Streatham, South West London.

FRIDAY, 8 JULY

Top Rank Suite, Cardiff, Wales.

SATURDAY, 9 JULY

Technical College, Westminster, London.

The show was filmed by Canadian television for a special "British Pop Groups" edition of the magazine programme *Take 30*, which was broadcast Thursday, 6 October over the CBC network, 3:00–3:25 pm. In addition to interviews with fashion designer Ossie Clark and Manfred Mann singer Paul Jones (filmed elsewhere), the show featured the following Who-related material: Keith and John arriving at the gig in their 1950 R Type Bentley with new driver John 'Wiggy' Wolff; host Adrienne Clarkson interviewing Pete, Keith, and John backstage; and excerpts from "Substitute," "Baby Don't You Do It," "See See Rider," and "My Generation."

WEDNESDAY, 13 JULY

Recording/mixing IBC: Pete produced the Merseys' version of "So Sad About Us," though the credit went to Kit Lambert. It was released by Fontana on Friday 29 July. (The Who's version, recorded in October, didn't appear until *A Quick One* in December.) John played French horn on the B-side, "Love Will Continue."

ABOVE: FILMING WITH CHRIS STAMP IN HYDE PARK.

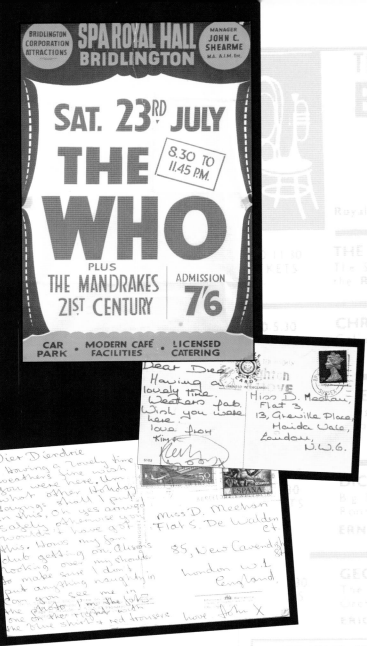

ABOVE: KEITH AND JOHN'S HOLIDAY POSTCARDS FROM SPAIN TO FAN CLUB SECRETARY, DEIRDRE MEEHAN.

THURSDAY, 14 JULY
Liberal Hall, Yeovil, Somerset.

FRIDAY, 15 JULY
Starlite Ballroom, Greenford.

SATURDAY, 16 JULY
Civic Hall, Barnsley, Yorkshire.

THURSDAY, 21 JULY
Locarno Ballroom, Bristol.

FRIDAY, 22 JULY
Marine Ballroom, Central Pier, Morecambe.

SATURDAY, 23 JULY
Spa Royal Hall, Bridlington.

WEDNESDAY, 27 JULY
Flamingo Club, Redruth, Cornwall.

THURSDAY, 28 JULY
Queen's Hall, Barnstaple.

FRIDAY, 29 JULY
Tiles Club, London.

SATURDAY, 30 JULY
Sixth National Jazz and Blues Festival, Balloon Meadow, Windsor.

The annual three-day event had moved from its regular Richmond site to Windsor Racecourse after complaints from the local council about fan behaviour. The Who topped the second night over the Summer Set, Jimmy James and the Vagabonds, Gary Farr and the T-Bones, and the Move. The Yardbirds and Chris Farlowe and the Thunderbirds were billed but cancelled because of illness.

The Who's forty minute set climaxed in a frenzy of destruction. Lambert and Stamp stood in the wings, lighting and throwing smoke bombs onto the stage. A dry-ice machine created artificial mist as Pete smashed his guitar and pushed amplifiers over, Keith scattered his kit, and Roger threw microphones and kicked in the footlights. A section of the crowd broke chairs and damaged canvas screens in response to the group's antics, while others were exuberantly celebrating England's victory in that day's 1966 World Cup Final.

SUNDAY, 31 JULY and MONDAY, 1 AUGUST
Recording/mixing IBC, Studio A: "I'm A Boy," "Disguises," and "In The City," produced by Kit Lambert (his first credited Who production) and engineered by Paul Clay.

"I'm A Boy" B/W "In The City" was released by Reaction on Friday 26 August, eventually reaching the #2 position on 30 September, though Jim Reeves' "Distant Drums" refused to budge from the first slot. On the *Melody Maker* chart, it actually reached the #1 position "for about half an hour," as Pete wryly remembered. The record was not released in the U.S. until 10 December.

TUESDAY, 2—SUNDAY, 14 AUGUST
A fortnight's holiday. John and Keith went to

ABOVE: THE AFTERMATH OF THE WHO'S PERFORMANCE AT WINDSOR, 30 JULY.

Torremolinos, Spain, Pete to Israel, while Roger remained in London.

FRIDAY, 12 AUGUST
"The Kids Are Alright" B/W "The Ox," from *My Generation*, was released. In the final stages of the legal dispute over their recording contract, the Who disowned the disc, which stalled at #41 in the *NME* chart. The 2:42 edit (from the U.S. album), paired with "A Legal Matter," had been released the previous month by Decca in America and became a regional hit in Detroit and Chicago.

The *NME* reported that the proposed recording deal between the Who and Andrew Oldham and Allen Klein had collapsed that week. Sometime in July, Pete, Lambert, Stamp, and their lawyer, Edward Oldman of Wright & Webb Solicitors, briefly returned to New York with Keith in tow for unproductive business negotiations. "[Oldman] just took two looks at Klein and said 'we're leaving,'" Townshend told *Zigzag*, "so we ate his caviar, had a

TOWN HALL
TORQUAY

L.M.D. ENTERTAINMENTS PROUDLY PRESENTS

BY DEMAND THE RETURN OF

✶ **THE** ✶

WHO

HIT RECORDS "I CAN'T EXPLAIN", "ANYWAY, ANYHOW, ANYWHERE", "MY GENERATION" and "SUBSTITUTE" — LATEST HIT "DISGUISES"

THE STAGGERLEES
THE HUNTERS ✶ THE EMPTY VESSELS
★ ★ ★ MOD FASHION PARADE ★ ★ ★

SATURDAY 20TH AUG.

8 P.M. - 11.45 P.M. **FULLY LICENSED BAR** TICKETS 10/-

ADVANCE TICKETS FROM John Conway, Mens Fashion Shop, Abbey Road, Torquay, 27322 or send P.O. and S.A.E. to Impact House, 31, Market Street, Torquay. Tel. 22585

LEFT AND **ABOVE:** FELIXSTOWE PIER PAVILION, 9 SEPTEMBER.

vocal), the Everly Brothers' "Man With Money," Neal Hefti's "Batman Theme" (two versions, one an instrumental), and a remake of Martha and the Vandellas' "Heat Wave." The tracks were earmarked for the Who's second album, carrying the working title *Jigsaw Puzzle.*

In *Disc* (dated 10 September), a report mentioned the group were to record "King Rabbit," a Townshend original in similar vein to "Happy Jack" "about king concepts and ruling concepts and ceremonies and things like that." The song got as far as demo stage, but it does not appear in the Who's tape log.

THURSDAY, 1 SEPTEMBER
Locarno Ballroom, Coventry.

FRIDAY, 2 SEPTEMBER
Locarno Ballroom, Basildon.

SATURDAY, 3 SEPTEMBER
Drill Hall, Grantham.

SUNDAY, 4 SEPTEMBER
New Elizabethan Hall, Belle Vue, Manchester.

TUESDAY, 6 SEPTEMBER
Palais, Ilford, Essex.

From 6:15—7:00 pm, the Who pre-recorded *Ready, Steady, Go!* from Studio One, Wembley, performing "I'm A Boy" and "Heat Wave." The programme, featuring Eddie Cave and the Fyx, Zoot Money, David

---

look at the Statue of Liberty from his yacht, shat in his toilet, and went back to England."

THURSDAY, 18 AUGUST
Palace Ballroom, Douglas, Isle of Man.

Contrary to *The Who Concert File*, Keith did play this date on the offshore isle. He missed a gig at the venue on 10 June 1967.

FRIDAY, 19 AUGUST
The Who performed "A Legal Matter" and (a week before its release) "I'm A Boy" on *Ready, Steady, Go!* from Studio One, Wembley. The show, featuring Salena Jones, Twice As Much, Cliff Bennett, and Manfred Mann, was transmitted live from 7:00—7:30 pm.

SATURDAY, 20 AUGUST
Town Hall, Torquay.

SUNDAY, 21 AUGUST
Pier Ballroom, Hastings.

TUESDAY, 23 AUGUST
Sherwood Rooms, Nottingham.

WEDNESDAY, 24 AUGUST
Orchid Ballroom, Purley, Surrey.

THURSDAY, 25 AUGUST
Dreamland Ballroom, Margate.

TUESDAY, 30—
WEDNESDAY, 31 AUGUST
Recording/mixing IBC/Pye No.2: Producer Kit Lambert and engineer Paul Clay oversaw covers of the Regents' "Barbara Ann" (with Keith on lead

WHO'S WHO?

OUT NOW — a sure-fire hit from the Who, the Pete Townshend composition "I'm A Boy", on Reaction. And also doing well, on the boys' old label Brunswick, is "The Kids Are Alright", an old recording taken from their album "My Generation".

This sort of situation, the old label vying with the new, usually causes caustic comment and heated words. Even Juke Box Jury panellists have been known to moan about it. But the Who, and the Who management, seem unmoved. Said co-manager Chris Stamp: "We're not worried; just glad that both discs are doing so well — it underlines the popularity of the group. Our only grouse is one of timing. If 'kids' had come out mid-way between our new releases, it would fill the gap and sell more. It would have added continuity . . ."

But, somewhat naturally, the Who are concentrating on "I'm A Boy" for their television appearances.

Garrick, Twice As Much, and Peter and Gordon, was broadcast three nights later, 7:00–7:30 pm.

In the *NME* dated 21 October, Brian Jones praised the Who's appearance to Keith Altham: "I saw them on *Ready, Steady, Go!* a few weeks back. They were unbelievably good. Townshend is incredible. Really, the Beatles, the Who, and ourselves are the only British groups to evolve something completely original in visual and musical production—from our own compositions."

WEDNESDAY, 7 SEPTEMBER
Locarno Ballroom, Stevenage.

THURSDAY, 8 and FRIDAY, 9 SEPTEMBER
By arrangement with Chris Stamp, a French ORTF television crew filmed the Who over two days for the weekly TV2 programme *Seize Millions De Jeunes*, which was broadcast Tuesday, 18 October, 8:30–9:00 pm. The Who's sixteen minute segment featured the following content: Lambert and Stamp watching Roger, Keith, and John depart from New Action's offices in Chessington Gardens for Felixstowe on the Suffolk coast (the soundtrack featured an alternate take of "Barbara Ann"); DJ Emperor Rosko and Lambert (with Stamp) discussing the Who in French at Radio Luxembourg's Paris studio; John, Roger, Keith, and Wiggy's antics inside the Bentley during the drive;

and Rosko introducing live footage of "Heat Wave," "So Sad," "I'm A Boy," "Substitute," and "My Generation" from the Pier Pavilion gig on the 9th. The remainder of the programme featured the Merseys, filmed in Morecambe and Liverpool, and Georgie Fame in London.

SATURDAY, 10 SEPTEMBER
Corn Exchange, Bedford, Bedfordshire.

Disc reported the Who were cutting down their appearances to major ballrooms only. Chris Stamp explained: "Not only is it impossible for the smaller places to pay, but the group gets bad representation being dragged off stage and so on. So from now on, they will only appear at absolutely top ballrooms."

SUNDAY, 11 SEPTEMBER
Ultra Club, the Downs, Hassocks. Rescheduled from 28 August.

TUESDAY, 13 SEPTEMBER
The Who recorded a session for the Light Programme's *Saturday Club* at the Playhouse Theatre, London, produced by Jimmy Grant and Brian Willey. "Disguises," "I'm A Boy," "Heat Wave," "So Sad," and a stage cover of the Lovin' Spoonful's "On The Road Again" were taped, as was an interview with Pete by host Brian Matthew. During the brief exchange, Pete revealed plans for a forthcoming visit to America, which

would result in the cancellation of most of a booked theatre tour. (See 16 September.) The programme, featuring Peter and Gordon, the Searchers, Paul Ritchie, and the Cryin' Shames, was transmitted 17 September, 10:00 am—12 midday.

THURSDAY, 15 SEPTEMBER
Gaumont Cinema, Hanley, Stoke-on-Trent. Two shows, 6:35 & 9:00 pm.

The opening night of the Who's third scheduled U.K. package tour, featuring the Merseys, the Cream, Oscar, the M.I. Five, and compère Max Wall.

At 11:00 am, the Who pre-recorded "I'm a Boy" for that evening's *Top Of The Pops* at the BBC's Lime Grove studio, broadcast 7:30—8:00 pm.

FRIDAY, 16 SEPTEMBER
Odeon Cinema, Derby. Two shows, 6:15 & 8:40 pm. The Magic Lanterns replaced Cream.

With the Who's planned departure for a ten-day American promotional trip slated for 23 September, no effort was made to find a replacement at short notice, and these shows consequently marked the tour's premature cancellation. All tickets were refunded.

Despite all that, the U.S. visit was delayed and then cancelled altogether due to visa problems and legal difficulties over the release of the Who's records there. Instead, all energies were directed to completing their second album in time for October release.

RIGHT AND BELOW:
TOP OF THE POPS,
21 SEPTEMBER.

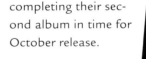

ABOVE: RECORDING AT CBS STUDIOS, 3 OCTOBER.

SATURDAY, 17 SEPTEMBER

"Whatever anyone says, I regard myself as the first person to do feedback and I was naturally disappointed when the credit went on several occasions to the Beatles and Yardbirds," Pete told *Disc*. "So I called it off and concentrated more on writing. I prefer to be called a showman and writer. Although I can play the guitar as well as most guitarists on the scene, I only specialise in big chords played very loud, which has got nothing to do with music. It's more to do with volume and impact."

WEDNESDAY, 21 SEPTEMBER

With "I'm A Boy" at #4 in the week's *NME* chart, the Who recorded a further *Top Of The Pops* insert at Lime Grove. It was first transmitted the following evening, 7:30–8:00 pm, and repeated the following week at the same time.

Prior to the taping, Pete appeared at Newport Pagnell court, Buckinghamshire, and was fined £25 with £26-16-0 costs, after being found guilty of dangerous driving, stemming from the M1 pile-up incident on 29 May. The court was told how he ignored a comprehensive system of warnings, before his Lincoln Continental ploughed into a Jaguar, which in

turn had crashed into the back of a lorry trailer. Townshend explained he thought the warning signals were part of the roadworks.

THURSDAY, 29 SEPTEMBER

By this date, Keith's "Showbiz Sonata" (the working title for "Cobwebs And Strange") had been recorded at Pye No.2. The tune, based on British jazzman Tony Crombie's "Eastern Journey" from the 1959 U.S. NBC television series *Man From Interpol* soundtrack, featured John on cornet, tuba, and trumpet, Keith on orchestral cymbals, Roger on trombone, and Pete on recorder, penny whistle, and maracas.

"Kit wanted to get a marching effect," said Entwistle, "so he had us marching back and forth in front of the mike. It worked O.K. until we came to double-track it. We started marching up and down again but once we passed the monitor, we couldn't hear the track. By the time we came back, we were hopelessly out, so we had to stand in one place and record."

During this time, Roger's Buddy Holly-ish composition "See My Way" was demoed at Pete's top-floor flat-cum-studio at 87 Wardour Street. The basic four-track recording was beefed up by Keith additionally overdubbing cymbal crashes and a

rhythm beat out on cardboard boxes to replicate the sound of Crickets' drummer, Jerry Allison.

SATURDAY, 1 OCTOBER

Imperial Ballroom, Nelson, booked as last minute replacements for the Kinks.

MONDAY, 3 OCTOBER

Recording/mixing at CBS Recording Studios, 104 New Bond Street, London: "Don't Look Away" and John's "Whiskey Man."

Pete went to the BBC's studio at 1 Kensington House, Shepherd's Bush, to record an interview for the radio programme, *Dateline London* (Show 205). The conversation was included in a BBC Transcription Disc intended for overseas broadcast only.

During the week, "Run Run Run" and a longer remake of "I'm A Boy" were recorded at IBC. (The latter was eventually released on the 1971 compilation *Meaty, Beaty, Big, and Bouncy*.) Kit invited an unfamiliar visitor to the studio, as Pete recalled to Curtis Knight: "Jimi Hendrix wandered in looking peculiar... I mean, he really did look pretty wild, and very scruffy." Hendrix's manager, ex-Animal Chas Chandler, accompanied him and enquired of Townshend and Entwistle what amplifiers to use. "Anyway," Pete continued, "[Jimi] walked around for a bit and gave me a sort of lukewarm handshake, and then I never saw him again for a little while. I didn't know anything about his playing, and I never heard his music until I first saw him live." (See 21 December.)

TUESDAY, 4 OCTOBER

Recording/mixing Pye: John's "Boris The Spider" and Keith's "I Need You (Like I Need A Hole In My Head)." "I Need You," featuring John on harpsichord, was Moon's paranoid swipe at the Beatles' double-talk. "The bit in the middle was meant to sound like a night at the Scotch [of St James]," said Entwistle. "We got 'Lurch,' our Liverpudlian roadie [Gordon Molland], to do a Lennon impersonation, and you can hear Kit ordering a table for four."

FRIDAY, 7 OCTOBER

"Join My Gang," an early Townshend "pro-feminist" composition, was released by Oscar on Reaction. "'Join My Gang' was a self-conscious thing," said Pete. "The reason the Who never recorded it was because it was very much an exercise. You know who

WHO are they looking at?

GIRLS FAINT IN BATH POP FRENZY

HUNDREDS of pop fans provided just the right atmosphere for a concert by The Who at Bath Pavilion last night—as a film unit took candid camera shots for a television documentary.

Teenage girls fainted in the crush of bodies against the stage and the group's wild man at the drums, mop-haired Keith Moon beat out a frenzy of emotion through the packed hall. All the time the movie cameras whirred on.

Athletic attendants dived off stage into the screaming throng and passed the girls who had been overcome to backstage exits, and fresh air.

The show climax came with The Who best-seller "I'm a boy," featuring lead guitarist Pete Townshend—in a blinding red-and-white striped sweatshirt.

DOORS CLOSED

It was also the climax for the film unit from American C.B.S. Films. The crew had spent all afternoon setting out high power arc lights and cables for the cameramen. Shots from their reels will feature in the finished documentary, which deals with British pop groups.

... and the centre of their interest was Peter Townshend, the lead guitarist.

camera rolls and fans strain their eyes ...

...NNED MAN ...TOOK CAR

who took his ...red from drivin... ...s sudden irrespo... ...ered to take a ... ...ates were told

100 WANT TO ...OIN CAST

ABOVE: Recording "Bucket T" at IBC, 11 October.

used to rave about that song? David Bowie. He actually heard it in the publishing office—he used to work in an office that had a lot of my stuff then."

SATURDAY, 8 OCTOBER
Palais de Danse, Peterborough.

MONDAY, 10 OCTOBER
The Pavilion, Bath.

The group's set was filmed in colour, with additional footage shot in London by CBS-TV for a *CBS Reports* documentary on British pop groups. It was to be broadcast later that month, although whether the footage was incorporated with the material shot at Malvern (see 21 June) remains unclear.

TUESDAY, 11 OCTOBER
Recording/mixing IBC/Pye: The IBC session for Jan and Dean's "Bucket T," with Keith on vocal and an Entwistle French horn solo lifted from "Linda," was filmed by producer Peter Goldmann (see 3 June) and cameramen Peter Fisher and Anthony Stern. The segment was part of a Sverige Television special, *My Generation—Popreportage fran London*, broadcast in two 30 minute segments. The Who appeared at the end of Show One, transmitted 2 February 1967, 7:30—8:00 pm, featuring the Small Faces, Manfred Mann, producer Mickie Most, Donovan, designer Mary Quant, and an interview with Pete conducted at the session by Inga-Lill Palm.

WEDNESDAY, 12 OCTOBER
The Who flew to Zestienhoven, Holland, to play a poorly attended gig at the Club 192, Scheveningen, near the Hague. The group played to approximately 1000 people and were paid 7000 guilders. During the afternoon, they pre-taped an appearance, miming "I'm A Boy" for the television show *Waauw*, in Bellevue Studios, at the Leidseplein, Amsterdam, broadcast 8:01—8:30 pm on Nederland 2.

FRIDAY, 14 OCTOBER
Queen's Hall, Leeds. A marathon ten group, ten-and-a-half-hour "all-night dance and barbecue," staged from 8:00 pm—6:30 am.

The Who arrived in an ambulance and very nearly left in one when 6000 fans rioted during their midnight performance.

Prior to the trip north, recording continued at IBC. A bizarre medley incorporating "My Generation" and Edward Elgar's "Land Of Hope And Glory" was taped for a *Ready, Steady, Go!* special. For the filming on 18 October, "Rule Brittania" was substituted.

SATURDAY, 15 OCTOBER
Corn Exchange, Chelmsford.

"I like all the smashing up," John told *Record Mirror*. "But it's part of the act. I stand there and look amazed and horrified as the others smash up valuable equipment. Then at the end of the song, on my last note, I adjust the feedback to keep the note going and drop the guitar heavily on the stage. It makes a terrific sound, and that's the end of the number."

TUESDAY, 18 OCTOBER
The Who pre-recorded their own sixteen-minute *Ready, Steady, Go!* segment ("based on the Theatre of the Absurd ideas that the Who have," Kit Lambert loftily informed *Melody Maker*) at Studio One, Wembley, directed by Daphne Shadwell.

Camera rehearsals commenced at 11:15 am, and the show was taped before an audience from 6:15—7:00 pm. The Who appeared lip-synching to "Batman" (featuring extra Larry Viner cavorting as the Caped Crusader), sending up Cliff Richard's "Summer Holiday" in a mime sequence, performing an edited "Showbiz Sonata" ("Cobwebs And Strange"), as well as "Bucket T," "I'm A Boy," "Disguises," and the auto-destructive finale of "My Generation"/ "Rule Brittania" (see 14 October).

"The Hofner violin bass that I broke on the show," revealed Entwistle, "I bought for £50 off Billy Kinsley of the Merseys who'd bought it off Paul McCartney. I filled the body with feathers and confetti, and during rehearsals, I banged it lightly on the floor, making out I was going to smash it, and the neck broke. When I smashed it on the actual show, the carpenter screwed it back together, but the neck came off again. All the stuff we'd smashed up, he swept away and put into a guitar case." (The fragments were sold in a Sotheby's auction in 1987.)

The Who occupied the entire second half of the programme—the first featured Lee Dorsey and Georgie Fame—broadcast across certain ITV regions on 21 October, 6:08—6:35 pm. Legal problems prevented the group from using the actual soundtrack for their *Ready, Steady, Who* EP, so normal studio cuts were substituted for its release on Friday 11 November. It would go on to reach #1 on the *Record Mirror* EP chart.

LEFT: *KLAR I STUDIET*, DENMARK, 20 OCTOBER.

ABOVE: JÄGERSBO-HÖÖR, SWEDEN, 22 OCTOBER.

WEDNESDAY, 19 OCTOBER

Roger, Keith, John, and Kit Lambert arrived in Copenhagen, Denmark, without Pete, who had missed the flight. A press reception was held in his absence at the Star Club.

THURSDAY, 20 OCTOBER

The Who's second Scandanavian tour of the year commenced with a riotous show before 2000 at the Herlev Hallen, Copenhagen. During the morning, the group taped a segment for the television show *Klar i Studiet* ("Ready in the Studio"), broadcast Saturday, 5 November, 5:00—5:45 pm. "I'm A Boy," "Substitute," and "My Generation" were mimed on instruments borrowed from the Swedish group, the Tages.

FRIDAY, 21 OCTOBER

Konserthallen, Liseberg, Gothenburg, Sweden. Two shows, 7:00 & 9:00 pm.

SATURDAY, 22 OCTOBER

Two Swedish shows: Gislövs Stjärna, Simrishamn (8:00 pm), followed by Jägersbo-Höör, Höör (11:15 pm).

SUNDAY, 23 OCTOBER

MFF-Stadion, Malmö, Sweden at 3:00 pm, followed by a chartered flight to Denmark for an 8:00 pm gig at the Fyens Forum, Odense.

MONDAY, 24 OCTOBER

Folkparken, Halmstad, Sweden.

TUESDAY, 25 OCTOBER

Club Nalen, Stockholm, Sweden.

FRIDAY, 28 OCTOBER

Palais d'Hiver de Lyon, Villeurbanne, Lyon, France.

The Who and Screaming Lord Sutch and the Stormsville Shakers represented England at the British Trade Fair gala.

SUNDAY, 30 OCTOBER

Sportpalast, Berlin, West Germany.

The Who were severely criticised for letting the audience of 10,000 down by playing for only twelve minutes and were thrown out of the Berlin Hilton because of "bad behaviour." The group were supposed to travel on to Bremen to tape a contracted television appearance for the 19 November edition of *Beat Club*. Instead, they flew back to London to continue recording, as it was only a month before the desired release date of their second album. Producer Michael Leckebusch was not amused. "The Who do what they want, including their manager," he said. "We twice had a fixed contract. The Who twice accepted, and twice they couldn't be bothered. But we are not running after them. If they want to come, then okay."

An initial acoustic version of "Happy Jack," featuring Pete on cello, was recorded during this time as were the song fragments for "A Quick One (While He's Away)," variously taped at IBC, Pye, and Regent Sound Studio A, 164—166 Tottenham Court Road, and edited together by Kit Lambert.

SATURDAY, 5 NOVEMBER

Messehalle, Saarbrücken, West Germany.

SUNDAY, 6 NOVEMBER

Kongresshalle, Cologne, West Germany. Two shows, 4:00 & 8:00 pm.

MONDAY, 7 NOVEMBER

Rheinhalle, Düsseldorf, West Germany.

Instead of flying to Switzerland the following day as intended, the group returned to London to continue recording.

TUESDAY, 8—THURSDAY, 10 NOVEMBER

The backing track to a remake of "Happy Jack" was recorded in a single session at Regent Sound Studio A. Vocals and mixing were done at CBS. "A lot of the time, Keith would try and join in on the backing vocals, and we'd try and get rid of him," said John. "After a time, he knew that once he had finished playing the backing track, he should go and get out of there, but he tried creeping back in for 'Happy Jack' and that's when Pete said, 'I saw yer!' as he was trying to creep back round to the microphone."

1966

ABOVE: CHELSEA BARRACKS, 12 NOVEMBER.

John's "I've Been Away" was recorded at Regent Sound. "We did that in thirty minutes," he recalled, "it was just me on piano and Keith. The others had gone to the pub, and we did the B-side." (It's possible this is the session normally attributed to "In The City," where a track was cut merely because Moon and Entwistle were the only ones aware of the booked session.)

FRIDAY, 11 NOVEMBER
Decca extracted the last of three opportunistic releases from *My Generation*, "La La La Lies" B/W "The Good's Gone." Unsurprisingly, in light of the Who's musical advancement, it failed to chart.

SATURDAY, 12 NOVEMBER
From 7:00—10:30 am, the Who were filmed in colour for American television, performing five songs live at the Duke of York's Barracks, Kings Road, Chelsea. (Originally the group had planned to perform on a specially constructed stage in Carnaby Street.) Clips were included in a special "Swinging London" edition of the daily *Today* show, including interviews with fashion designers Mary Quant and John Stephen, broadcast over the NBC network on Tuesday 15 November, 7:00—9:00 am EST.

SUNDAY, 13—WEDNESDAY, 16 NOVEMBER
A four-day break in Neuschnee, Grindelwald, a village at the base of the Jungfraujoch mountain range in Switzerland. Publicity shots were taken in the snow.

THURSDAY, 17 NOVEMBER
Locarno Ballroom, Glasgow, Scotland.

FRIDAY, 18 NOVEMBER
City Halls, Perth, Scotland.

SATURDAY, 19 NOVEMBER
Market Assembly Hall, Carlisle.

ABOVE: ARRIVING FOR NOVEMBER GERMAN DATES.

THURSDAY, 24 NOVEMBER
Pavilion Ballroom, Worthing.

SATURDAY, 26 NOVEMBER
Spa Royal Hall, Bridlington.

TUESDAY, 29 NOVEMBER
Winter Gardens, Malvern.

SATURDAY, 3 DECEMBER
"All-Nighter," Midnight City, Birmingham, with the Family, who shortened their name to Family the following year.

FRIDAY, 9 DECEMBER
Assembly Rooms, Dumfries, Scotland.

After being delayed a week because of technical difficulties, "Happy Jack" and *A Quick One* were released in Britain. Polydor put on extra staff at their factory to cope with advance orders on the single, which reached #3 in the charts. Despite the demand, the Who resolved not to plug it via TV appearances. "It's just not a visual number and in any case they don't want to suffer from overexposure," said a spokesman; (see 19 December). The album reached #4 and was re-titled to the less risqué *Happy Jack*, when released in America the following May.

SATURDAY, 10 DECEMBER
Empire Theatre, Sunderland, Durham.

Two shows, 6:00 & 8:30 pm, with Dave Berry, She Trinity, the Kool, the Slade Brothers, and the Peddlers. Promoted by Mervyn Conn.

THURSDAY, 15 DECEMBER
Locarno Ballroom, Streatham, London.

Twenty-one-year-old Bob Pridden, from Ickenham, Middlesex, who had previously worked with the Alan Bown Set, received his baptism by fire as head road manager. "I came down in the afternoon," he remembered, "and they were rehearsing a few numbers from *A Quick One* to play that night. It was all fine, the gear went up and then when they went on stage, I was stunned... At the end of the act, everything got smashed to pieces. The group walked off, and they turned the revolving stage round, and Roger just said to me 'get it fixed for the next gig.'" Pridden graduated to the position of the Who's chief sound technician in 1969, a position he still holds.

ABOVE: HEAD ROAD MANAGER BOB PRIDDEN.

FRIDAY, 16 DECEMBER
The Who pre-recorded versions of "I'm A Boy" and Johnny Kidd and the Pirates' "Please Don't Touch" (over the original choice of Bill Haley and the Comets' "Rock Around The Clock") at Ryemuse Sound Studios, 64 South Molton Street. "Please Don't Touch" was the group's affectionate tribute to Kidd, who died in a car accident on 7 October. The recordings were designed to be mimed to on the farewell edition of *Ready, Steady, Go!* on 20 December.

SATURDAY, 17 DECEMBER
Imperial Ballroom, Nelson.

MONDAY, 19 DECEMBER
Inside New Action's offices at Caroline House, 6 Chesterfield Gardens, a zany, 35-mm black and white promotional film to accompany "Happy Jack" was shot for *Top Of The Pops* by ex-*Ready, Steady, Go!* director Michael Lindsay Hogg. The clip, depicting the group as bungling cat burglars, premiered three nights later (BBC-1, 7:30–8:00 pm) and reappeared in *The Kids Are Alright*.

TUESDAY, 20 DECEMBER
The Who assembled at Studio One, Wembley, for midday camera rehearsals to record their appearance on the final *Ready, Steady, Go!*—aptly retitled *Ready, Steady, Goes!*—the show that had established them above any other.

Produced by Francis Hitching, directed by Daphne Shadwell, and introduced by Cathy McGowan, an impressive roll-call of past performers were on hand to bid a fond farewell, namely Paul Jones, Dave Dee, Dozy, Beaky, Mick and Tich, Eric Burdon and Alan Price, Donovan, Lulu, Mick Jagger and Chris Farlowe, Keith Relf and Paul Samwell-Smith (representing the Yardbirds), Julie Felix, Cat Stevens, the Merseys, Peter and Gordon, the Small Faces, and the Spencer Davis Group.

ABOVE: FINAL *READY, STEADY, GO!*, 20 DECEMBER.

Nodding back to their Detours past, the Who opened with a 1 min 25 secs version of Johnny Kidd's "Please Don't Touch" (see 16 December) and later performed a 47 second burst of "I'm A Boy" (chosen over "Happy Jack"). Like the previous year, Kenny Lynch led the cast in a rendition of "White Christmas" to end the show and an era. *Ready, Steady, Goes!* was transmitted over the London region on 23 December, 6:08–6:35 pm. (Tuesday 27 December in other ITV areas.)

WEDNESDAY, 21 DECEMBER
The Upper Cut, Forest Gate, East London.

The Who opened boxer Billy Walker's new club, a converted roller-skating rink at Forest Gate Centre. Following the gig, Pete, John, and Roger drove to Blaise's in Queens Gate, Kensington, to witness the Jimi Hendrix Experience for the first time. Upon entering the club, Pete met Jeff Beck coming out, as Townshend later told Curtis Knight: "Jeff said to me, 'He's [Jimi] banging his guitar against the amp. You'll just have to tell him that's your thing.' So I went in and listened, and of course he was doing a lot of the things I used to do, like banging his guitar around, and he was using lots of high feedback. But he was also playing in a way that I couldn't hope to approach."

THURSDAY, 29 DECEMBER
Despite the "no television plugs" decision (see 9 December) and a promotional clip at their disposal, the Who went to Studio 2, Television Centre, to mime "Happy Jack" in person on BBC-1's *Top Of The Pops*, broadcast 7:30–8:00 pm.

FRIDAY, 30 DECEMBER
Baths Hall, Cheam, Surrey.

SATURDAY, 31 DECEMBER
"Psychedelicamania," The Roundhouse, Chalk Farm, North West London. "Giant New Year's Eve Freak Out All Night Rave!" held from 10:00 pm till dawn. The Who appeared sandwiched between the Pink Floyd and the Move. Ironically, the "liquid crystal light projections" were provided by Gustav Metzger, Pete's art school muse.

The Who took the stage an hour late amid a hail of smoke bombs. The strobe lights in use interfered with Pete's playing, and three power cuts and several lighting failures didn't improve his mood. This resulted in a particularly savage guitar and amp smashing display, prompting a flurry of aggrieved letters to *Melody Maker*.

— PSYCHEDELICAMANIA —
THE ROUNDHOUSE, CHALK FARM, N.W.1
NEW YEARS EVE
SATURDAY 31st DECEMBER 1966
ALL NIGHT RAVE - 10 p.m. on
THE WHO
THE MOVE
THE PINK FLOYD   No. 2364
Admission 15/-

I can see for

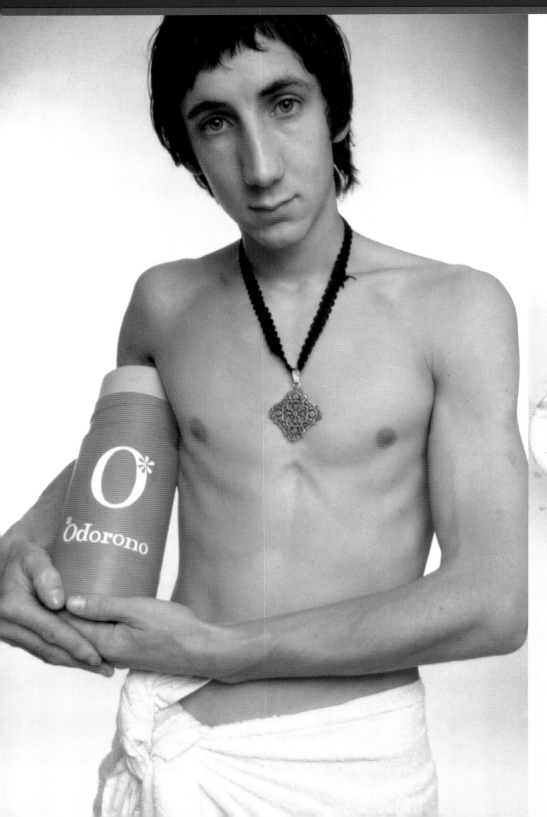

MILES 1967

Despite having six British Top 5 singles to their credit, the Who were buried perilously in debt. So what better time for their inventive managers to launch their own record label?

Track Records came into being after Lambert and Stamp studied the production methods of biscuit and washing powder firms that marketed goods roughly the same size as a box of records. After two months research, they nailed what it cost to manufacture, distribute, and advertise such a product,

drew a parallel with the record industry, and marched triumphantly into the boardroom of Polydor, offering them a partnership.

"This is the biggest thing in our career so far," Lambert told *Disc*. "I've always dreamt of having my own record company—I would like to turn it into a hip EMI and be very big. I've spent my life having rows with record companies and the only solution was to start my own."

The Who were on the label almost by default. The first signing was a twenty-four-year-old, black American guitarist without precedent, James Marshall Hendrix. Jimi had arrived in Britain the previous September and was playing a showcase at the Scotch of St. James club when, according to his manager Chas Chandler, "Kit nearly knocked all the

tables over... wanting Jimi to be on the new label he was launching." Not only was he technically proficient, Hendrix's flamboyant showmanship extended to guitar bashing and feedback histrionics, previously the unspoken domain of a certain English guitarist. "Hendrix was the first man to walk all over my territory," Townshend told Richard Green. "I felt incredibly intimidated by that."

Lambert and Stamp put each member of the Who in charge of a musical department. Pete looked for jazz and new sounds; Keith, surf and good-time music; John, orchestral; and Roger, soul and rhythm and blues. If successful, they were each promised a share of Track's profits, a promise that was ultimately reneged upon, with far-reaching consequences.

As a talent scout, Townshend narrowly missed signing the between-labels Bonzo Dog Doo-Dah Band. On a Friday night, he often frequented the UFO club at 31 Tottenham Court Road, championing the burgeoning London "underground" scene by paying twice the normal admission. (The extra profit helped keep the UFO's broadsheet, *International Times*, afloat.) Entranced by the psychedelic experiments of the Pink Floyd and Tomorrow (both already signed to EMI), Pete was particularly taken with the anarchic ravings of an ex-Reading University philosophy student, Arthur Brown. "People kept coming up and saying why didn't I do something about him," Pete remembered. "So I eventually signed and produced some demos on behalf of Track. I thought he had great potential with a fantastic stage presence and a voice every bit as good as Hendrix's guitar, but he needed controlling because he was a bit of a lunatic!" (Brown's first single, the unhinged "Devil's Grip," was co-produced by Townshend and Lambert.)

In April, the Who's first piece on the new label appeared: "Pictures Of Lily," an ode to the joys of masturbation. "Really it's just a look back to that period in every boy's life when he has pin-ups," Townshend explained to Keith Altham. "The idea was inspired by a picture my girlfriend had on her wall of an old vaudeville star, Lily Bayliss. It was an

RIGHT: PETE BACKSTAGE WITH GUITARS AT THE RKO 58TH STREET THEATRE, NEW YORK.

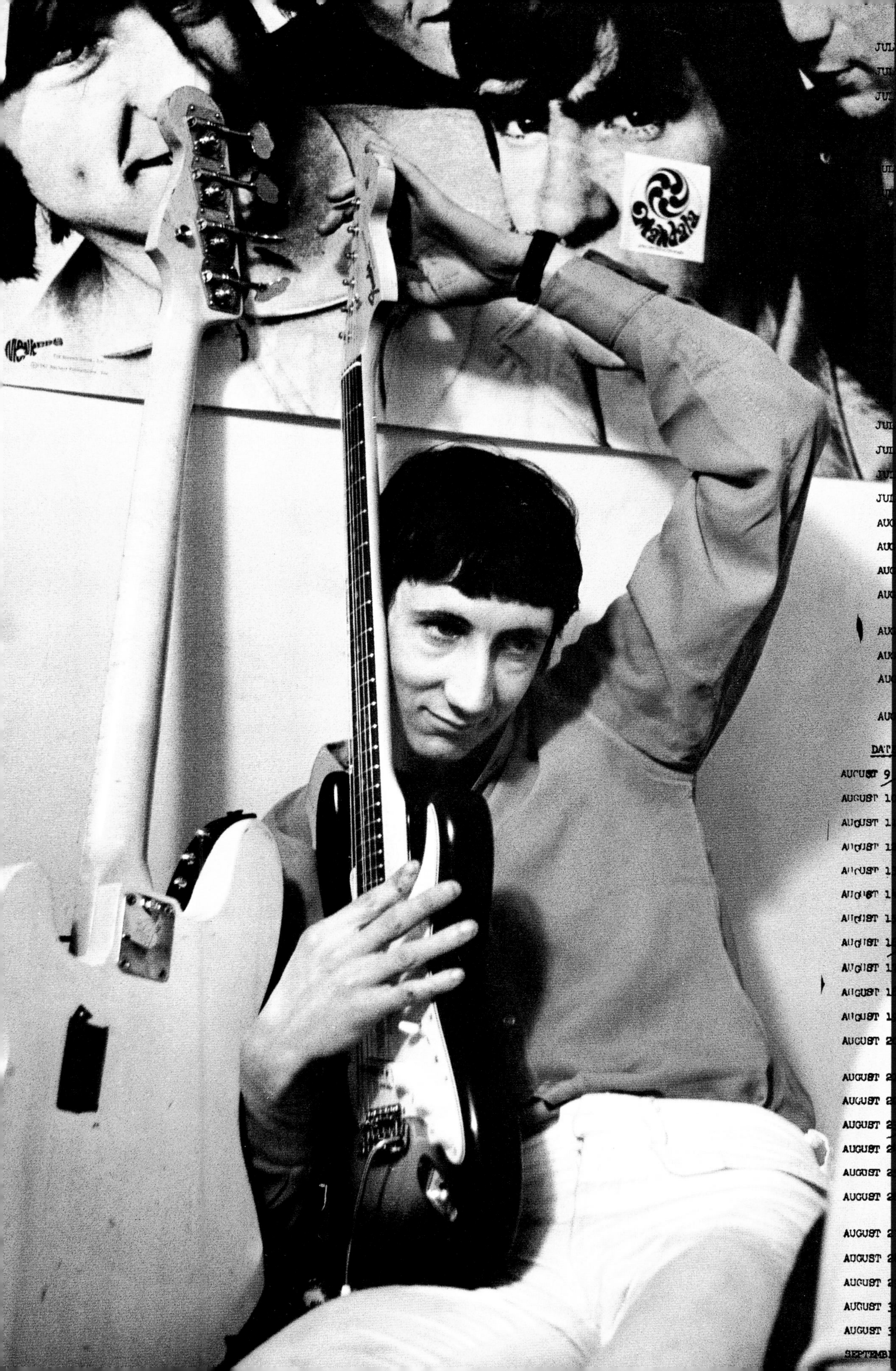

old 1920s postcard and someone had written on it, 'Here's another picture of Lily—hope you haven't got this one.'"

With the release of another finely crafted single, the group were inadvertently straddling a great pop divide. Unlike contemporaries such as Cream and Hendrix, the Who didn't look upon the three minute single as a necessary evil. On the contrary, they thrived upon it. With pop and rock divided accordingly, the Who uncomfortably refused to nail their colours to either mast.

A relentless work schedule was necessary to keep the ever-present financial wolves from the door. Despite the threat of penury, the group still insisted on all the pop star trappings. Roger would drive to gigs in his new Aston Martin; Pete temporarily employed "Speedy" Keene in often tempestuous Lincoln Continental driving arrangements; while Keith and John were driven by "Wiggy" Wolff in a blue and silver Rolls, complete with portable record player and speaker hidden behind the radiator grille. There were continental tours of Italy, Germany, and Scandinavia, where no better illustration of the Who's popularity came when their perverted rendition of Jan and Dean's "Bucket T" occupied the top position of the Swedish charts in February, much to Moon's undisguised delight!

At the end of March, the group played the States for the first time, arriving in New York as part of a cavalcade of acts booked by self-styled "fifth Beatle" Murray Kaufman ("Murray the K") at the RKO 58th Street Theatre. Local DJs had started to rotate "Happy Jack," but an inane ditty about an Isle of Man donkey couldn't possibly prepare audiences for the sensory overload of seeing the Who in the flesh for the first time. Whereas England may have felt the group's destructive dynamics were becoming a tad passé, their colonial cousins had never experienced anything like it. Throughout a week of shows, the group got through twenty-two microphones, five guitars, four speaker cabinets, and a ten-piece Premier kit. America's love affair with the Who had begun. While in New York, Townshend caught an unknown, ukelele-wielding "singer" at the Scene club, almost getting Tiny Tim signed to Track. With his hands already full with Arthur Brown, though, it seemed reasonable one madman was enough.

In June, the Who returned to appear at the prestigious Monterey International Pop Festival. "We shall draw our repertoire from our American hits,"

1
9
6
7

Keith told *Melody Maker*, "all one of them!" While most of the festival's performers were bathed in acid-drenched vibes, by stark contrast, the Who, came across like a chainsaw through flowers. Flower power never looked convincing to a bunch of Shepherd's Bush mods dressed in psychedelic threads, and their act left the Love Crowd dumbstruck. However, John Entwistle, for one, was unhappy with the Who's performance: "Kit didn't want to pay for us to bring our own equipment over. We used Vox equipment and sounded dire. Then after we'd smashed it up, Jimi Hendrix came on with big Marshall stacks, set fire to his guitar and completely

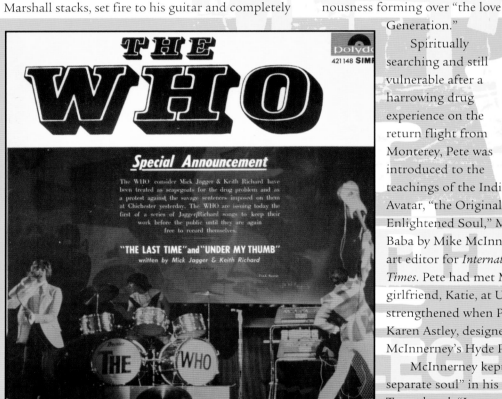

upstaged us." The question of "who upstaged who" is ultimately irrelevant as both acts left Monterey as newly established rock forces in America—a fact well illustrated by D.A. Pennebaker's film of the event.

Returning to England, the Who found London in the midst of a cause célèbre. On trial for drug offences, Rolling Stones Mick Jagger and Keith Richards were convicted and imprisoned on slender grounds. As a show of solidarity (and with Kit Lambert's keen eye for publicity), the group (sans a honeymooning Entwistle) hastily convened to record

two Stones classics, "The Last Time" and "Under My Thumb," as a rush-released single.

An ad placed by Lambert in the London *Evening Standard* pledged further support, stating the Who's intention to continue recording Rolling Stones songs for as long as the two remained incarcerated. Fortunately, the "glimmer twins" had their sentences quashed before the Who could get "Satisfaction" into the shops!

With hindsight, Monterey can now be seen as the cultural highwater mark of the Summer of Love, before exploitation and disillusionment set in. For all the lip service he paid to the underground, Pete's renowned cynicism made him among the first to notice a dark cloud of disingenousness forming over "the love Generation."

Spiritually searching and still vulnerable after a harrowing drug experience on the return flight from Monterey, Pete was introduced to the teachings of the Indian Avatar, "the Original Enlightened Soul," Meher Baba by Mike McInnerney, the art editor for *International Times*. Pete had met McInnerney and his girlfriend, Katie, at UFO and their bond strengthened when Pete's girlfriend, Karen Astley, designed the clothes for the McInnerney's Hyde Park wedding.

McInnerney kept referring to "the separate soul" in his conversations with Townshend. "I went and read this book called *The God Man*," Townshend told Michael Watts, "and everything fit. It was an intellectual appeal at first... Baba's coming was directly coincidental with a lack of available things to turn to."

Meher Baba (meaning "compassionate father") was born Merwan S. Irani in Poona, India. From 10 July 1925, he undertook a vow of complete silence, which he kept until his death on 31 January 1969. His disciples (Mandali) believe him to be a messianic figure, espousing a simple and moral philosophy of life, best summed up by his most familiar teaching: "Don't worry, be happy." By year's end, Townshend

was smitten. "Baba is the avatar of the age—the Messiah. He can't do anything but good. He has completely and utterly changed my whole life, and through me, the group as a whole." (The other Who members' views on Pete's mystical beliefs could best be described as tolerant.)

With faith restored and immersed in Baba's directives, which included the renunciation of dope, Townshend felt inspired to write an ambitious piece that would extend the limitations of the pop song format, "without making it pompous or pretentious and without making it sound like classical music." Intending the piece to operate on several levels—as a fairy tale for young people, as intellectual entertainment, and as a work with a spiritual message—Pete originally envisaged Arthur Brown, with his operatic range, as the ideal person to sing it. The first song written for the project, "The Amazing Journey," became the focal point for all of the ideas that were subsequently incorporated into what would become *Tommy*.

An earlier experiment, "Rael," set in the year 1999, about the population overspill of the Red Chinese, ended up in condensed form on the group's third album, *The Who Sell Out*. The song's bridge contained motifs that reared their heads again within "Sparks" and "Underture" on *Tommy*.

On 15 August, the Marine Broadcasting Bill was passed, ringing the death knell for Pirate Radio, which had revolutionised the British music industry and was instrumental in breaking groups like the Who. Radio 1, the BBC's new national pop network promised increased needle time for pop music, with a cast of DJs who had cut their broadcasting teeth with the pirates. Ironically, the Who's first radio session for the new regime featured tracks destined for *The Who Sell Out*, an endearing tribute to the floating stations now sadly vanquished under the new bureaucracy. The majority of tracks were linked with crass Radio London jingles and American advertisements, an idea concocted by Pete with Chris Stamp, although the concept wasn't sustained throughout. Stamp fixed up two art directors for the sleeve and attempted to sell the space between tracks to advertisers. This ambitious scheme foundered when, with

ABOVE: INDIAN SPIRITUAL LEADER MEHER BABA.

anticipated album sales at less than 50,000 copies, the companies approached were unwilling to cover it.

"It all started with this number I had written called 'Jaguar,'" Townshend explained to *Melody Maker*. "The number was a really powerful and loose thing, something like 'The Ox' from our first album, with Keith thrashing away like hell and us all pumping out 'Jag-u-a-r,' like the Batman theme tune. At this time we were working on new ideas for the album. As it stood, I could see that we just had an album of fairly good songs, but there was nothing to differentiate it from our last LP, *A Quick One*. It needed something to make it stand out. We thought of using a powerful instrumental number that we made for Coca Cola, and then I linked it up with the number 'Jaguar,' and then of course, we thought, 'Why not do a whole side of adverts?' As things progressed, we realised the whole album could be built around this aspect of commercial advertising. At the same time, Radio London and the pirates were being outlawed. You don't realise how good something like the pirates are until they've gone, so to give the album that ethereal flavour of a pirate radio station we incorporated some 'groovy' jingles. And so *The Who Sell Out*."

Unfairly overlooked upon its release, time has matured *The Who Sell Out* into one of the finer albums of the period. Included was the single many consider to be the Who's finest moment, "I Can See For Miles." Written the previous year, Townshend had kept it back as a potential "ace-in-the-hole" should the Who's hit streak run dry. Moreover, his original demo had an intimidating majesty the band felt unable to replicate. Ultimately, it was Kit Lambert's decision to record it.

The track, started in London, was imaginatively produced and mixed by Lambert during breaks from the Who's first exhausting, ten-week American trek, on a hilariously mismatched bill supporting Herman's Hermits. The group debuted the record in September with an anarchic *Smothers Brothers Comedy Hour* network television appearance, which ended with an exploding drum kit, singed hair, and perforated eardrums.

For all its magnificence, "I Can See For Miles" failed to capture the imagination of the British record-buying public. Although it did in fact reach the lowest rung of the Top 10 (hardly a flop), Townshend felt it was a poor showing by the Who's standards, as he made plain to Ray Tolliday: "The day I saw it was about to go down without reaching any higher, I spat on the British record-buyer. To me, this was the ultimate Who record, and yet it didn't sell."

The group returned from the States to find the British charts polarised between the schmaltzy balladeering of Engelbert Humperdinck and Tom Jones and the treacly pop of the Herd and the Tremeloes. The Who teamed up with both of these groups and Traffic on a British theatre tour in October. Finding themselves increasingly marginalised in their homeland, the group diverted their attention to cracking America, returning for a further two weeks in November, while "I Can See For Miles" climbed to #9 in *Billboard*, the Who's highest ever Stateside chart placing.

THE WHO
TRAFFIC
THE HERD
The Marmalade
Compere RAY CAMERON
SPECIAL GUEST STARS
THE TREMELOES

1967

WEDNESDAY, 4 JANUARY

The Who went to Television Centre to record a further *Top Of The Pops* insert for "Happy Jack" in Studio 2. It was shown the following evening, 7:30—8:00 pm. The group's BBC appearance fee had risen to £84.

FRIDAY, 6 JANUARY

Marine Ballroom, Central Pier, Morecambe.

Pete didn't arrive after an accident enroute on the M6. Mike Dickinson, a member of support group the Doodlebugs, sat in for part of the set, with Roger playing additional guitar. "I think we did 'Boris The Spider' twice that night," John remembered. "It was a weird sound without Pete. Roger would sidle over to me and mutter 'Take over the solo.'" For the "My Generation" finale, roadie Alan Oates played guitar while Roger and Keith smashed some of the gear.

SATURDAY, 7 JANUARY

In *Disc*, a four-part "Who Are The Who?" series commenced with Roger.

"I don't hate anyone now," he said. "It's a waste of time. Me and Keith, we didn't understand each other, but when you're with someone 24 hours a day, there's not much point in getting annoyed with them, is there?"

WEDNESDAY, 11 JANUARY

The Who pre-recorded a third *Top Of The Pops* insert for "Happy Jack" at the BBC's Lime Grove studio, broadcast the following evening (usual times).

Following the taping, Pete and John were among the musician-packed audience to see the Jimi Hendrix Experience perform at the Bag O'Nails, Kingly Street, Mayfair. Earlier that day, the Experience signed a recording contract with Lambert and Stamp's independent label, Track Records, at the New Action offices. Pete went to the gig with Eric Clapton, and the following evening, the incredulous guitarists attended another Experience performance at the "7 1/2" club, Whitehorse Street, off Piccadilly Circus.

FRIDAY, 13 JANUARY

Festival Hall, Kirkby-in-Ashfield, Nottinghamshire.

SUNDAY, 15 JANUARY

The Who flew to Hamburg, Germany, with Eric Burdon and the Animals. Both groups appeared in a NDR-TV *Beat Club* special "Dag Swing Time Party," filmed at the Planten und Blomen. Introduced by presenter Uschi Nerke, the Who mimed to "I'm A Boy," "Heat Wave," and "Happy Jack," featured in Show 16, transmitted 21 January. The appearance helped to give the Who their only #1 record in Germany with "Happy Jack."

TUESDAY, 17 JANUARY

From 2:30—5:00 pm, the Who recorded their fifth consecutive *Saturday Club* for the BBC Light Programme at the Playhouse Theatre, produced by Bill Bebb and Jimmy Grant. "Run, Run, Run," "Boris The Spider," "Happy Jack," "See My Way," "Don't Look Away," and an interview with Pete by Brian Matthew, were taped for the 21 January programme, broadcast 10:00—12:00 am. Also featured in session were Paul Jones, Brian Poole, the Tremeloes, the Settlers, Brian Connell and the Round Sound, Sue and Sunny, and the Johnny Arthey Orchestra.

WEDNESDAY, 18 JANUARY

Orchid Ballroom, Purley.

SATURDAY, 21 JANUARY

University, Leeds.

Pete showed up more than an hour late, after his Lincoln Continental ran out of fuel on the A1. Old Detours acquaintance Peter Vernon-Kell, who was playing guitar with support group the Hamilton Movement, stood in during the first set. "Pete ended up having to forfeit his guitar to get petrol as he didn't have any money on him," Vernon-Kell remembered. "Consequently, [roadie Alan] Oates practically begged me to let Pete use my six-string Rickenbacker, promising nothing would happen to it. Of course, I got it back with the neck snapped in half!"

WEDNESDAY, 25 JANUARY

Kingsway Theatre, Hadleigh, Essex.

Two shows presented by Radio London, 6:15 & 8:45 pm, with the Roulettes, Sounds Around and She Trinity. Compère: DJ Tony Blackburn.

THURSDAY, 26 JANUARY

Locarno Ballroom, Bristol.

SATURDAY, 28 JANUARY

Toft's Club, Folkestone, Kent.

Disc announced that Brian Epstein's NEMS Enterprises had amalgamated with the Robert Stigwood Organisation roster of artists (including the Who) and the Reaction record label. Stigwood would become joint managing director of NEMS with Epstein, who remained as chairman, but Epstein would continue to manage his own artists.

SUNDAY, 29 JANUARY

Saville Theatre, London.

Two "Soundarama" shows, 6:00 & 8:30 pm, with the Jimi Hendrix Experience, the Koobas, and the Thoughts. Compère: Mike Quinn.

This was part of a series of ambitious Sunday night concerts at this prestigious venue on Shaftesbury Avenue, staged by leaseholder Brian

The cream of London's pop elite were out in force, including John Lennon and Paul McCartney, who observed from Epstein's private box. Maverick filmmaker Peter Whitehead, present to film a colour promo of the Jimi Hendrix Experience to accompany their debut single, "Hey Joe," additionally shot backstage footage of the Who.

TUESDAY, 31 JANUARY
Palais, Ilford.

WEDNESDAY, 1 FEBRUARY
The Who were the first guests in a revamped model of Granada Television's *Scene At 6.30*—now simply titled *Scene*—screened (in the north only) from 10:25—11:00 pm. Producer Johnny Hamp wanted to make the daily programme "more controversial" with an audience of young people in discussion with the artists, plus a non-pop personality. The programme was recorded at the Granada TV Centre, Manchester, with prominent Tory politician Quintin Hogg.

THURSDAY, 2 FEBRUARY
Locarno Ballroom, Coventry.

SATURDAY, 4 FEBRUARY
Birdcage Club, Portsmouth.

The music press confirmed the Who were to star in their own television series to be produced by Brian Epstein's Subafilms Ltd. Like the Monkees, the group would act and sing several new Townshend compositions for the first half-hour pilot programme, to be offered to the BBC or ITV.

After initial talks, the idea went no further. "We found that the Monkees series itself lost money, and the networks weren't really interested," Roger explained to *Record Mirror*. "So it was too much of a gamble. Our ideas for the films were really good, the ideas alone would have made us more popular than the Monkees, but for how long? We didn't think it would be good for us. We want a lasting career, and we don't think that a series like that would particularly make us more popular than we are. A feature film would do

OPPOSITE: *Beat Club* TELEVISION APPEARANCE, 15 JANUARY.

ABOVE: REHEARSALS AND LIVE AT THE SAVILLE THEATRE, 29 JANUARY.

LEFT: THE SHOW'S SOUVENIR PROGRAMME.

Epstein (for NEMS Enterprises) and the Robert Stigwood Organisation.

It was rumoured the Who had threatened to raze the building to the ground with a new act. Indeed, publicist Nancy Lewis had reportedly warned fire attendants to be on their guard. The only sparks that flew, however, were from miniature mechanical robots being booted into oblivion by John and Pete as the curtain rose. The group's set included a non-destructive "My Generation" and ended with the debut live performance of the "mini-opera," "A Quick One."

much more good, and we're going to do one this year. Kit has got a couple of scriptwriters, and we've got a strong story."

A science fiction script was apparently worked on by Keith and Pete involving four rulers of an alien nation living beneath another planet. Pete and Keith were to play dual roles as scientists who travel to the planet, which threatens Earth!

FRIDAY, 10 FEBRUARY

Gaiety Ballroom, Grimsby.

Luckily, Roger ended up missing this gig, as part of the venue's glass roof collapsed onto the stage where he would have stood.

SATURDAY, 11 FEBRUARY

Royal Links Pavilion, Cromer, Norfolk.

SUNDAY, 12 FEBRUARY

Starlite Ballroom, Greenford.

Eric Clapton was present, as was local mod Peter Butler, who approached Bob Pridden about the possibility of work. "Dougal," as Butler was rechristened by Pete Townshend (after a character in the U.K. children's show *The Magic Roundabout*), was initially hired to drive the Who's equipment van, starting with some Scottish dates in October.

FRIDAY, 17 FEBRUARY

Chris Stamp flew to New York, setting up office in the same building as Premier Talent, the Who's U.S. agents, at 200 West 57th Street. He was on a mission to whip up Decca's promotional campaign in time for the 18 March release of "Happy Jack" and the Murray the K shows. On 5 March, Nancy Lewis left Southampton docks on the Queen Mary to work as the Who's U.S. publicist.

FRIDAY, 17—SUNDAY, 19 FEBRUARY

The scheduled shoot dates at Woburn Abbey for the pilot of an independently produced Subafilms television special *Cathy In Wonderland*, starring ex-*Ready, Steady, Go!* presenter Cathy McGowan. Artists suggested to appear were the Who, Paul Jones, Julie Felix, Rita Pavone, and the Dave Clark Five. The programme, intended for CBS television screening in May, failed to materialise.

TUESDAY, 21 FEBRUARY

The Who flew to Italy with Kit Lambert, missing a

booking at the Town Hall, High Wycombe. The gig was put back to 28 March and then to 25 April.

THURSDAY, 23 FEBRUARY
Palazzetto dello Sport, Torino, Italy.
Two shows, 4:00 & 9:15 pm.

FRIDAY, 24 FEBRUARY
Palazzetto dello Sport, Bologna, Italy.
Two shows, 4:00 & 9:15 pm.

SATURDAY, 25 FEBRUARY
Palalido, Milan, Italy, 4:30 pm, followed by a 9:15 pm show at the city's Piper Club.

Backstage at the Palalido, the group were interviewed for Italian radio, during which Pete broke into an impromptu "Happy Jack" on piano, with the others joining in on vocals.

SUNDAY, 26 FEBRUARY
Palazzetto dello Sport, Rome, Italy.

Originally two shows were scheduled, but because of poor ticket sales, the afternoon show was rolled into one 7:00 pm concert. The Italian tour, generally considered an unsuccessful affair, ended at the city's Piper Club, with a half hour gig at 10:30 pm, before approximately 300 people.

MONDAY, 27 FEBRUARY
The Who flew back to London to begin recording at De Lane Lea Music Ltd's basement studio at 129 Kingsway (a.k.a. Kingsway Recording Studio), opposite the Holborn tube station, as well as rehearsing at the Saville Theatre. A German television crew filmed their airport arrival as part of a documentary, *Die jungen Nachtwandler—London Unter 21*, which was screened Monday, 3 July on station BR (Bayerischen Rundfunks).

The Who content in the 54 minute film, directed by Edmund Wolf, revolved around the activities of Kit Lambert and Chris Stamp. These included the *Beat Club* Marquee special taping on 2 March (introduced by Lambert in German), Lambert and Stamp conducting a Track Records press conference, Pete demoing "Glittering Girl" on acoustic guitar at his Wardour Street flat for their approval as a possible single, and the Who rehearsing the song onstage at the Saville.

Out-takes from the documentary, including the group and Lambert walking through Heathrow arrivals lounge, the Who signing autographs for wait-

ing fans (some sporting Who Fan Club T-shirts), and Wiggy Wolff driving John and Keith away in their Bentley, were used in *The Kids Are Alright* and *Thirty Years of Maximum R&B Live*.

THURSDAY, 2 MARCH
During the afternoon, the Who returned to a familiar haunt, the Marquee Club, to videotape an NDR German television special *Beat Club aus London*. Introduced by ex-Radio Caroline DJ David Lee Travis and presenter Uschi Neurke, the show also featured Geno Washington and the Ram Jam Band, Cliff Bennett and the Rebel Rousers, the Smoke, and the Jimi Hendrix Experience.

The Who performed "Happy Jack," "So Sad About Us," and "My Generation" live before an invited audience of dancing Teutonic teens. During a run-through of "My Generation," Pete let off a thunder-flash, fusing the Marquee power supply in the

process. The 26 minute programme (Show 18) was first transmitted Saturday 11 March and repeated 22 May. Clips were used extensively in *The Kids Are Alright*, *Who's Better*, *Who's Best*, and *Thirty Years of Maximum R&B Live*.

SATURDAY, 4 MARCH
California Ballroom, Dunstable, supported by David Essex and Mood Indigo. Essex later appeared with Keith Moon in the films *That'll Be The Day* and *Stardust*.

FRIDAY, 10 MARCH
Top Rank Suite, Cardiff, Wales, supported by the Herd, featuring sixteen-year-old guitarist Peter Frampton. The two groups toured as part of a British theatre package in October.

OPPOSITE, BELOW: Piper Club, Rome, Italy, 26 February.
ABOVE: Leicester, 13 March.

MONDAY, 13 MARCH

"Rag Rave," Granby Halls, Leicester, with the Alan Price Set, Zoot Money, and Dick Morrisey.

THURSDAY, 16 MARCH

Track Records launch party at the Speakeasy, 48 Margaret Street, London. Guests included Michael Caine, Terence Stamp, Jean Shrimpton, Bobby Moore, Elizabeth d'Ercy, and Simon and Garfunkel. Colour promotional films of the Who, the Jimi Hendrix Experience, and John's Children were also shown.

FRIDAY, 17 MARCH

University, Exeter, Devonshire.

SATURDAY, 18 MARCH

Forum Cinema, Devonport.

TUESDAY, 21 MARCH

At 4:00 pm, the Who caught flight TW 701 to New York. The group checked into the Drake Hotel on East 56th Street. (Later, a horror-struck Chris Stamp uprooted them to the less ostentatious Gorham on 55th Street, after discovering Keith and John's room service bills.) Spare time was spent phoning WMCA and other local stations for exclusives. DJs started rotating "Happy Jack," which entered the *Billboard* chart at #47 with a bullet, the Who's highest American chart entry to date. (It eventually reached #24, selling 300,000 copies in the U.S.)

"We worked hard on propaganda for the first three days before we played," Pete said, "and I had two stock quotes: 'We want to leave a wound' and 'We won't let our music stand in the way of our visual act!' I think I was doing about twenty or thirty interviews per day, and each one had to be a little different or important than the last."

The young Englishman was obviously unhip to the escalating situation in Vietnam when he recorded an unlikely radio jingle endorsing the U.S. Air Force (date and session/studio details have proved untraceable, though in all probability, it occurred during this initial visit.) Using "Happy Jack" as its musical backdrop, Pete's thirty second message exhorted potential recruits to find out how "you too can fly the skies, reach for the moon, and touch the stars in the United States Air Force."

FRIDAY, 24 MARCH

"Lazy Fat People," written by Pete and originally offered to Pye group Episode Six, was released as a single on Columbia by comedy outfit, the Barron Knights.

SATURDAY, 25 MARCH—SUNDAY, 2 APRIL

After two days of dress rehearsals, the Who made their U.S. concert debut, joining the multi-artist bill lined up for Murray the K's "Music in the Fifth Dimension." The concert was at the RKO Radio Theatre on 58th Street and Third Avenue, Brooklyn, New York.

"I was having a conversation with Brian Epstein," Murray Kaufman recalled, "and he was describing this group that broke their instruments to me, who I'd also heard about from Paul Simon. It was quite an experience having the Who. First of all, it was an experience for them because I ran a very tight ship and didn't tolerate stageweights. When you're doing five shows a day, and you have people waiting outside, you know that if you go past 75 minutes in your show, you're paying the bands overtime. That didn't bother me so much, but the people standing in line did. So they had to learn discipline, which they weren't used to. The Who blew out the entire electrical system of the theatre at least once a day!"

The artist roster featured the Hardly-Worthit Players (a comedy troupe sharing the Who's dressing room), Jim and Jean, the Chicago Loop, Mandala, Jackie and the "K" Girls (Kaufman's wife, Jackie Hayes, in a ten-minute fashion spot), the Blues Project, the Young Rascals, Wilson Pickett, Mitch Ryder (from the 27th), and Cream, the only other English act on the bill. Smokey Robinson and the Miracles were originally billed to appear on the 26th and 27th but didn't show. Robert Stigwood negotiated a joint booking fee with Kaufman of $7,500 for both Cream and the Who, divided 70/30 in the latter's favour.

For nine days of shows, the artistes were required to give five performances per day, starting at 10:15 am. "Originally, we were supposed to do four numbers, but we complained and said it was

RIGHT: The Who relaxing at the Gorham Hotel, New York City, with Pete sporting his "electric" jacket.

OPPOSITE: In the Black Forest during the April Germany tour.

impossible to put the act over with only four numbers, so they cut it to two!" Pete told Keith Altham. "It was ridiculous," Roger remembered with hilarity. "I mean, how can you ever put the Who on stage and say, 'play two songs, work the audience into a frenzy, and smash all your gear!'"

Pete wore a self-designed "electric" jacket, consisting of flashing fairy lights connected to the same circuit as his guitar. Offstage, they worked off a normal battery. As the Who performed "Happy Jack," the promotional film (see 19 December 1966) was projected as a backdrop. Despite the event's being marred by poor attendances, disputes over billing, and acts running over, the Who stole each show, receiving overdue exposure as a result.

"We really worked the destruction bit to a fine art in our spot," Pete told Altham. "I developed a great thing where I hit myself on the head with my guitar which had absolutely no visual impact, but made me see stars, and I thought, 'that's nice!' One time, I noticed Keith throwing his big bass drum at me with the spike protruding, and Roger hurling the mike stand at me from another direction. I made myself very thin and the mike shattered to pieces in front of me, while the spike from the drum ripped my shirt down the back. The stage hands got tired of sweeping up the equipment and went on strike. Most of the things we broke had to be repaired by us afterwards for the next house.

"I discovered Fender Stratocaster guitars are very strong and cheap out in the States. Once I chopped a Vox Super Beatle amplifier in half with one. They're made out of chipboard, little bits of wood that they

glue together, and I chopped right through the whole thing. It was a 4 x 12 cabinet, and it fell into two bits. I picked up the Stratocaster and carried on playing... and it was still perfectly in tune!" Townshend personally experienced their strength after fluffing a catch, requiring three stitches to a head wound. The Who flew back to London on Monday 3 April.

Note: While in New York, the Who were scheduled to tape an invaluable *Ed Sullivan Show* television appearance, but because of a CBS newsreaders strike, the group felt obliged to drop out in support. The Who never did appear on this long-running, network variety programme, which finally went off the air in 1972.

WEDNESDAY, 5 APRIL
Recording/mixing IBC/Pye: "Pictures Of Lily" and John's "Doctor, Doctor." The "Lily" session at Pye No.2, with Kit Lambert and engineer Alan McKenzie, was filmed by French ORTF television for the programme *Bouton Rouge*, screened Sunday, 21 May. The group were seen discussing and practising their har-

monies with Pete on piano, while Roger was taped recorded his vocal track. Footage also included the recording of overdubs onto the basic track, along with a playback of an early mono mix. On 7 April, mono mixes for both tracks were made at Ryemuse Sound and released as the Who's first single on Track Records on 21 April, reaching #4 in the U.K. and #51 in *Billboard* when released in the U.S. on 24 June.

FRIDAY, 7 APRIL
The Who arrived in Essen (without Keith, who missed the flight) to commence a riotous, two-week German tour, initially with Track labelmates John's Children, featuring nineteen-year-old guitarist/lyricist Marc Bolan. At a press reception, the Who were interviewed for the BBC's German Service programme *Hit '67*.

Accompanying them were Kit Lambert and *NME* writer, Richard "the Beast" Green, in his brief tenure as Who publicist. Pete's friends from the Royal

College of Art, Richard Stanley and Chris Morphet, were also along for the jaunt, hired by Lambert to shoot a fifteen minute colour film intended for American and European television.

As well as concert footage, film was shot offstage and in the countryside, including: Keith eating flowers and juggling a bunch of oranges, John and Pete using their guitars as cricket bats while splashing around in a stream, and the group running up and rolling down a hill, playing leapfrog and larking about in the Schwartzwald (Black Forest). Some of the footage, which was later edited together by Stanley to form an unseen promotional film for "Pictures Of Lily," was used in *The Kids Are Alright* and *Who's Better, Who's Best*.

SATURDAY, 8 APRIL
Messehalle, Nuremberg, West Germany.

SUNDAY, 9 APRIL
Thalia-Theater, Wuppertal, West Germany.

MONDAY, 10 APRIL
Jaguar-Club, Herford, West Germany.

TUESDAY, 11 APRIL
Rheinhalle, Düsseldorf, West Germany.

Arriving at the venue, the group were set upon by a mob who tried to push Keith's head through a car window, before Roger pulled him to safety. When the same bunch of youths attempted to climb onstage, Keith threw his floor toms at them and hit one over the head with a cymbal. Pete bashed his guitar onto the stage, sending it into the second row of stalls. A bouncer ran across to retrieve it, punching the poor unfortunate in whose lap it had landed!

WEDNESDAY, 12 APRIL
Friedrich-Ebert-Halle, Ludwigshafen, West Germany.

John's Children were proving a nuisance with their stage antics. Despite stern warnings from Kit Lambert of being thrown off the tour, they finally succeeded in doing just that by inciting a full-scale riot, which almost prevented the Who from playing.

THURSDAY, 13 APRIL
Circus-Krone-Bau, Munich, West Germany.
Two shows, 5:15 & 8:30 pm.

FRIDAY, 14 APRIL
Münsterland Halle, Münster, West Germany.

SATURDAY, 15 APRIL
Siegerlandhalle, Siegen followed by Rhein-Main Halle, Wiesbaden, West Germany.

SUNDAY, 16 APRIL
Oberschwabenhalle, Ravensburg, followed by Donauhalle, Ulm, West Germany.

WEDNESDAY, 19 APRIL
Stadthalle, Bremen, West Germany.

The Who videotaped an insert at Radio Bremen studios for NDR TV's *Beat Club*, miming to an advance tape of their new single "Pictures Of Lily." It was slotted into Show 19, transmitted Monday 1 May, 1:15–2:00 pm, and repeated 20 May. It also appeared in both *The Kids Are Alright* and *Who's Better, Who's Best*.

THURSDAY, 20 APRIL
The Who flew back to England. "We had to give up playing on the Continent," John explained, "because if we smashed up our equipment, the audience went wild and smashed up the hall, and if we didn't do

ABOVE AND **RIGHT:** *Top Of The Pops* TAPING, 26 APRIL.

the violence bit, they smashed up the hall anyway in a temper!"

FRIDAY, 21 APRIL
Brighton Dome, Brighton.

As part of the Brighton Arts Festival, the Who topped a bill featuring Crispian St. Peters, the Merseys, and Cream. While the Who's gear was being set up, compère Tony Hall stalled the audience for 15 minutes, by interviewing surprise guests Graham Nash and Allan Clarke of the Hollies onstage. Keith snapped sticks and skins, and ended by toppling his kit—a display that was not reviewed favourably by *The Evening Argus*.

MONDAY, 24 APRIL
The Pavilion, Bath.

Between gigs, the group squeezed in a week of recording a proposed all-instrumental EP at De Lane Lea. "The instrumental market now is pretty nil, and there's such a lot we do instrumentally anyway which we used to do a long time ago," Roger told *Record Mirror*. "I'm getting a trombone, and John plays a lot of brass. It's wide open."

Harking back to their Detours days, the group taped a powerful version of Edvard Grieg's "Hall Of The Mountain King" (from *Peer Gynt*), inspired by the arrangement they'd seen performed by Johnny Kidd and the Pirates. From these sessions, "Instrumental—No Title" (a.k.a. "Sodding About"), featuring John at the fore on French horn and a pounding bass solo, was mixed on 5 June. In 1998, it was remixed for the revamped *Odds and Sods* CD, but didn't make the final selection because of restrictions.

1967

During this period, the group recorded an American radio advert for Coca Cola. Two different jingles for the sugary black liquid were taped and submitted, but, according to company records, were never aired. They eventually appeared (with "Hall Of The Mountain King") as bonus tracks on *The Who Sell Out* CD in 1995.

TUESDAY, 25 APRIL

Town Hall, High Wycombe.

At Ryemuse Sound, two mono mixes of "Pictures Of Lily," with and without John's French horn solo, were made to be mimed to on the following day's *TOTP* taping.

WEDNESDAY, 26 APRIL

The Who pre-recorded a *Top Of The Pops* insert at Lime Grove, miming "Pictures Of Lily," broadcast the following evening, 7:30—8:00 pm, and repeated the following week at the same time.

FRIDAY, 28 APRIL

U.K. Decca released "The Magic Bus" by the Pudding. The song would not be recorded or released by the Who for a full year.

SATURDAY, 29 APRIL

Disc revealed the Who were to appear at the three-day Monterey International Pop Festival in June. A similar "underground" event, the 14-Hour Technicolour Dream, was held this evening at the Alexandra Palace, North London, to raise legal funds for *International Times*. Pete went along to film and record acts for an unreleased Track venture, among them the Crazy World of Arthur Brown. Although advance publicity listed the Who among the acts appearing, only Pete was present in this capacity.

SUNDAY, 30 APRIL

The Who, with Chris Stamp, flew into Helsinki, Finland, to commence an eight-day Scandanavian tour. 16-mm B&W film was shot by Timo Aarniala. Footage included their arrival at Vantaa Airport, interviews with Pete, John, and Keith at the Hotel Vaakuna, and parts of the evening concert at the Jäähallissa (Ice Hall), featuring John, for reasons best

INSET: ROADIE ALAN OATES TO THE RESCUE IN MALMÖ, 7 MAY. ABOVE: STEVENAGE, 17 MAY.

known to himself, sporting a false moustache. Clips were used in *Thirty Years of Maximum R&B Live*.

TUESDAY, 2 MAY

Njardhallen, Oslo, Norway.

WEDNESDAY, 3 MAY

Cirkus, Lorensbergsparken, Gothenburg, Sweden. Two shows, 7:00 & 9:15 pm.

THURSDAY, 4 MAY

Mässhallen, Norrköping, followed by an 8:00 pm concert at the Rigoletto, Jönköping, attended by 1700, a house record until broken by Cream in November.

FRIDAY, 5 MAY

Sporthallen, Eskilstuna, Sweden.

Because of Pete's dissatisfaction with the stage arrangements the group played a shortened five-song set.

few weeks recording as well as rehearsing at the Saville Theatre. During that time, "Early Morning Cold Taxi," co-written by Roger with Dave "Cyrano" Langston, was recorded at CBS, while Keith's "Girl's Eyes" was tracked at Sound Techniques Ltd, 46a Old Church Street, Kensington.

Kit Lambert made 8-track masters of both tracks at CBS on 7 June, although both remained unreleased until 1994 when they were remixed and remastered for the *Thirty Years of Maximum R&B* box set and *The Who Sell Out* expanded CD. Daltrey and Langston went as far as making a demo of another co-composition, "Blue Caravan," but felt it unsuitable for the Who.

WEDNESDAY, 17 MAY

Locarno Ballroom, Stevenage.

The venue's general manager, Mr. Maurice de Jonghe, was not impressed. "Ridiculous," he whined to *Stevenage News*. "If they have to smash everything to get a reaction, then you certainly won't see them here again…We would certainly think twice about booking them again." Backstage, John broke a finger on his right hand after punching the dressing room wall, apparently taking exception to a poster of the leader of "a well-known band."

Prior to the gig, during a recording session, a group interview for Show 237 of the BBC's Transcription radio programme *Dateline London* was taped for overseas broadcast only.

SATURDAY, 20 MAY

Woluwe Festival, Woluwe, Brussels, Belgium.

The Who flew into Zaventum airport at 10:30 am to film an insert for RTB's *Vibrato* programme. Introduced by Georges Prades, the group mimed to "Happy Jack" and "Pictures Of Lily" on location at Texas City, a cowboy theme town at Tremelo, near Brussels. The show was broadcast 8:30—9:15 on Tuesday, 30 May and repeated 6 June at the same time.

TUESDAY, 23 MAY

A recording session was curtailed because of John's injury. During this time, the backing track to his composition "Someone's Coming" was recorded, with the horns and vocals being over-dubbed in Nashville. (See 17 August.) The group also recorded a one-minute American radio jingle for "Great Shakes" at City of London Studios, featuring John on trumpet and Keith endorsing

ABOVE: KIM AND KEITH AT OXFORD, 27 MAY. HE COLLAPSED WITH A SUSPECTED HERNIA TWENTY-FOUR HOURS LATER.

the instant milkshake mix manufactured by General Foods Corporation.

WEDNESDAY, 24 MAY

Recording/mixing De Lane Lea: Eddie Cochran's "Summertime Blues." This unreleased version was taken at a considerably faster pace than the remake taped on 10 October and released in 1998 on the *Odds and Sods* CD. The tape box annotation "4-track master single" confirms its intended release as a possible follow-up to "Pictures Of Lily," with John's "Someone's Coming" as the B-side.

SATURDAY, 27 MAY

Pembroke College May Ball, Oxford, co-billed with Cream.

The Who were unaccustomed to playing the Grand Marquee before a stuffy audience of debutantes and undergraduates. Keith threw his drums around, severely straining a stomach muscle in the process. Initially unaware of the injury, he collapsed in agony at an overnight recording session during the small hours of the 28th and was rushed to St. George's Hospital on Hyde Park Corner for an emergency hernia operation. He was ordered to rest for a fortnight and discharged on Sunday, 4 June.

MONDAY, 29 MAY

Locarno Ballroom, Glasgow, Scotland.

Julian Covey, of club band Julian Covey and the Machine, stood in for Keith at short notice. Covey,

SATURDAY, 6 MAY

Kungliga Tennishallen, Stockholm, Sweden.

SUNDAY, 7 MAY

Sommarlust, Kristianstad, followed by an 8:00 pm concert at the MFF-Stadion, Malmö.

MONDAY, 8 MAY

The Who flew back to London, spending the next

who had drummed with Ronnie Scott, Ronnie Ross, and the original Brian Auger Trinity, recalled his urgent recruitment: "I had a frantic phone call from Roger that morning, asking if I could stand in. He picked me up in his Aston Martin, and we made it to the airport with literally minutes to spare." The Who spent an unproductive week trying to record in Keith's absence. "They were hoping to add [Keith's] drums at a later date," Kit Lambert told *Melody Maker*, "but it didn't work. We hope he should be able to do some drumming in about a week's time, but until then all recording sessions have been postponed."

THURSDAY, 1 JUNE

Keith's injury prevented the Who's scheduled appearance as part of *Festival*, a French television and radio special, broadcast live from the Palais des Sports, Paris. Appearing were the Troggs, Dave Dee, Dozy, Beaky, Mick and Tich, Cream, the Pretty Things, John Walker, and Johnny Halliday.

SATURDAY, 3 JUNE

Floral Hall, Southport.

With Julian Covey unavailable, Chris Townson, drummer with John's Children, was approached to deputise. "It was all arranged between Kit and our manager, Simon Napier-Bell," Townson recalled. "When it was agreed I'd be filling in for Keith, Pete turned up at Simon's flat with a pile of Who singles saying, 'This is the act.'

"The next morning I went down to Pye Studios, where Pete was recording, and showed the roadies how I wanted Keith's kit set up. Pete picked me up, and we drove to the gig in his Lincoln Continental. As we got to the stage door near this high wall, there was a gang of kids lined up along it, shouting insults and spitting on us. Pete was furious, trying to run up there, offering to take them all on. They were shouting things at me like, 'Keith Moon, you pillhead!,' so they obviously didn't recognise I wasn't him!

"The first show went O.K, there was no rehearsal or anything. Somehow I got through without too many blank bits, with the roadies crouching behind the amps signalling to me. I was conscious of being slagged off as imitating Keith, so at the end, I wasn't sure what to do. Roger solved that one for me by pushing part of the kit over, so I finished it off!"

THURSDAY, 8 JUNE

Ulster Hall, Belfast, Northern Ireland. Two shows, 7:45 & 10:30 pm.

FRIDAY, 9 JUNE

Golden Slipper Ballroom, Magilligan, Co. Derry, Northern Ireland.

SATURDAY, 10 JUNE

Palace Ballroom, Douglas, Isle of Man.

Chris Townson's tour of Who duty ended memorably with this show. "It was a real anticlimax going back to John's Children. I'd been earning £40 a night with the Who and spending twice that in the casinos when we played the Isle of Man. For the last show, they decided I was going to go out with a bang—literally! While my back was turned, the roadies put flashpowder under my stool. We got to 'My Generation' and suddenly 'BOOM!' I didn't know what hit me, and there they all were, pissing themselves laughing. I went to swing for Townshend, but he blocked me with his guitar, saying, 'Remember Germany?!' when we'd [John's Children] been a right pain."

MONDAY, 12 JUNE

Christ's College Summer Ball, Cambridge, with Georgie Fame, the Moody Blues, Françoise Hardy, the Herd, and the Humphrey Lyttleton Band. The bill was organised by Student Union representative Peter Rudge, a seventeen-year-old undergraduate whose career was to take an unexpected turn exactly a year later. Keith, still bearing stapled stitches from

his operation, played against doctor's orders as a warm-up for the Who's impending American shows.

TUESDAY, 13 JUNE

The Who flew to Detroit via New York, with Neville Chesters returning to stand in for Bob Pridden. (Chesters went on to become a roadie for the Jimi Hendrix Experience.)

Nancy Lewis took them to the Roostertail, the city's top nightclub, where a special Hawaiian dinner was prepared in their honour with Frank Sinatra, Jr. providing the floorshow. The group hung out with Mitch Ryder, who had appeared on the Easter Murray the K package and had recently met up with them again in London.

WEDNESDAY, 14 JUNE

The Fifth Dimension Club, Ann Arbor, Michigan.

Detroit was an early American stronghold for the Who and enthusiastic fans wouldn't let them leave the stage, demanding an encore, despite the group having demolished most of their equipment.

ABOVE: THE WHO IN CAMBRIDGE, 12 JUNE, WITH PETER RUDGE (INSET LEFT, WEARING TIE) AND (INSET ABOVE, FROM LEFT) CYRANO LANGSTON, BOB PRIDDEN, "WIGGY" WOLFF, AND RICHARD STANLEY.

THURSDAY, 15 JUNE
The Cellar, Arlington Heights, Illinois, with H.P. Lovecraft.

FRIDAY, 16 and
SATURDAY, 17 JUNE
Fillmore Auditorium, San Francisco, California.

Both shows were promoted by Bill Graham in the start of a mutually beneficial professional relationship that lasted throughout the Who's career. Expecting to do their normal 45-minute act, the group hadn't reckoned on Graham, who told Chris Stamp: "We want two one-hour spots. No repetition because we have virtually the same audience in from eight in the evening to two o'clock in the morning!"

With only an hour to spare, a panic-stricken Stamp was despatched to find a portable record player and copies of the group's records for an emergency rehearsal at their hotel. Working well under pressure, both shows helped to consolidate the Who's reputation on the West Coast. As Townshend enthused to *Melody Maker*'s Nick Jones: "Now I understand why every group comes away [from the Fillmore] saying, 'That's the best gig we've ever played.' The P.A. system is fantastic. The whole place is very well built for sound and acoustics. It's a rock group's paradise. And the audience want to listen and take in all you've got to offer. I don't want to sound pretentious, but the vibrations are something else!"

SUNDAY, 18 JUNE
The Who flew from San Francisco to Peninsular Airport, Monterey, to appear on the closing third day of the First Monterey International Pop Festival. Also appearing were the Blues Project, Big Brother and the Holding Company, Buffalo Springfield, the Grateful Dead (following the Who), the Jimi Hendrix Experience, and the Mamas and Papas.

RIGHT: ROGER AT MONTEREY, 18 JUNE.

Co-promoted by Alan Pariser and Ben Shapiro, the non-profit event was held in the 7000 seater open-air ampitheatre at the Monterey Fairgrounds, situated on the edge of the Pacific.

"The first thing I felt when I got there was it was fantastically big," Pete told Nick Jones. "The whole conception of the festival was so big, much bigger than the Technicolour Dream at Alexandra Palace. It was the kind of thing that everyone knew about. The whole of America was talking about it. The press coverage was phenomenal."

After checking out the standing ovation given to Ravi Shankar's afternoon recital, Townshend went to confront a familiar adversary, as he told Joe Boyd. "Before the show, we were starting to talk about the running order, more for Brian Jones who was introducing Hendrix and Eric Burdon who was introducing us, and they wanted to know what was gonna come first. So I said to Jimi, 'We're not going to follow you on,' and he said, 'Well, I'm not going to follow you on.' I said, 'Listen, we are not going to follow you on and that is it. You know, as far as I'm concerned, we're here ready to go on now, our gear's gonna be there, that's the end of it.'"

Matters were apparently resolved by Papa John Phillips flipping a coin. Pete won the toss, but, as he recalled, "there was a certain look in [Jimi's] eye, and he got on a chair, and he played some amazing guitar, just standing on a chair in the dressing room underneath the stage. Janis Joplin was there, Mama Cass, Brian Jones, Eric, and me and a few other people, just standing around, and then he got down off the chair and turned round to me and just said, 'If I'm gonna follow you, I'm gonna pull out all the stops!'"

The Who took the stage as Burdon introduced them with "... and this is a group that will destroy you completely in more ways than one...." The group's half hour set climaxed with a display of exploding coloured smoke bombs, while Daltrey knocked over microphones, and Townshend beat his Stratocaster into splinters before attacking the amps. Moon concluded proceedings by kicking his whole kit over, nonchalantly throwing his sticks into the crowd, as stagehands scuttled to retrieve the microphones.

D.A. Pennebaker specialised in cinema verité-style documentaries, including two Bob Dylan English tour films, *Don't Look Back* (1965) and *Eat The Document* (1966, unreleased), to his credit. His crew filmed activities both on and offstage throughout the weekend, utilising hand-held Eastmancolor cameras, as well as tripods placed strategically around the main rostrum. Over 45 hours of 16-mm footage, originally destined for an ABC television special, was shot, edited, and blown up to 35-mm, to produce *Monterey Pop*, which was first released to U.S. cinemas in May 1969.

Although all five cameras whirred throughout the Who's set, only "My Generation" was included in the finished film. Alternate camera footage of the song was featured in *The Kids Are Alright*. "A Quick One (While He's Away)" was included in *Thirty Years of Maximum R&B Live*, while "Substitute" and "Summertime Blues" belatedly appeared as part of the (U.S.) VH-1 cable special, *Monterey: The Lost Performances*, in June 1997.

The Who's complete set, recorded on Wally Heider's 4-track mobile unit, was made officially available as part of Rhino's *The Monterey International Pop Festival* 4-CD package in 1992.

MONDAY, 19 JUNE

Reviews of the Who's Monterey performance appeared in the local press. *Monterey Peninsular Herald*: "The Who were effective as a crowd pleaser, but it seemed more theatrics than intense musical involvement. Jimi Hendrix outdid the Who by focusing his passions on his guitar." *San Francisco Examiner*: "The Who, the most impressive British group, has an out-a-sight drummer in Keith Moon. Their lyrics are imaginative, and they have a hard Beatles-Stones sound." *San Francisco Chronicle*: "Their music is hard-driving and wildly performed. The songs are interesting—kind of electronic fairy tales... Their decadent, destructive, cynical ending is really a Roman circus spectacle and has nothing at all to do with music. In fact, it's really anti-music and disgraceful."

TUESDAY, 20 JUNE

The Who flew back to London from Los Angeles. For Pete, it was a most terrifying journey: "On the plane, I looked through my pockets, and I found a pill, which had been given to me by Owsley [Augustus Stanley Owsley III, the Grateful Dead's notorious pharmaceutical dispenser] which was called STP, a very powerful hallucinogenic supposedly twenty times more powerful than acid. Keith Moon produced a similar one and said, 'Let's while away the hours with a trip!' I thought, 'I can't leave him to go off on his own,' so I swallowed mine.

About fifteen minutes later, I was having visions of the most unbelievable nature.

"Now, I'd had LSD before many times and I'd had bad trips on LSD many times, but nothing like this. At one point, I was so disgusted with what I was and what I was thinking and my body and the way I felt, that I actually left my body. I was looking down at myself in the seat, and in the end I realised I must go back otherwise I was gonna die. About three weeks later, I thought about it, and I thought it really did happen, I really did leave my body to avoid these horrible sensations. And I did avoid them, and yet I could still see, and I could still hear, and I still existed, and then I went back in again. I would never have touched acid again after that, because the shock of that bad trip was so stunning and so awful. I didn't even smoke a cigarette again for four years."

FRIDAY, 23 JUNE

John married childhood sweetheart Alison Wise in an afternoon ceremony at the Congregational Church, Acton, where, as schoolboys, he and Pete had first performed together eight years earlier. The couple embarked upon their honeymoon the following Thursday, sailing aboard the Queen Elizabeth to New York, where the others were to rendezvous for the commencement of the Herman's Hermits tour.

SUNDAY, 25 JUNE

Keith, with wife Kim and driver 'Wiggy' Wolff, went to a Beatles session at EMI Studios, 3 Abbey Road, St. John's Wood, London. They appeared as guests singing back-up on the chorus to "All You Need Is Love." The occasion was beamed live from Studio One, as part of the first global satellite link-up for the programme *Our World*. Other choristers included Mick Jagger, Marianne Faithfull, Keith Richards, Graham Nash, and Eric Clapton. The single was released by Parlophone on Friday 7 July.

WEDNESDAY, 28 JUNE

Rolling Stones' Mick Jagger and Keith Richards were being tried on drugs charges at West Sussex Quarter Sessions, Chichester. This afternoon, Jagger was found guilty of illegal possession of amphetamines. Hearing the verdict, Pete, Roger, and Keith hastily convened at De Lane Lea to record covers of "The Last Time" and "Under My Thumb" as a spontaneous gesture of support should the two go to prison.

ABOVE: JOHN'S WEDDING, 23 JUNE.

The session was produced by Kit Lambert, engineered by Damon Lyon-Shaw, and filmed by Chris Stamp for an unscreened *Top Of The Pops* clip. As well as playing guitar, Pete overdubbed keyboards, backing vocals, and bass. A honeymooning Entwistle was contacted at 3:00 am via the Queen Elizabeth ship-to-shore phone for his approval. "I had to go to the radio room just to hear that," Entwistle remembered. "I thought somebody had died!"

The following afternoon, Jagger received three months and £100 costs and Richards one year and £500 costs for allowing his premises to be used for smoking hemp. Keith and wife Kim joined the throng demonstrating outside the Bouverie Street offices of *The News Of The World*, the tabloid paper widely

ABOVE: KEITH AND KIM PROTEST THE PRISON SENTENCES GIVEN TO ROLLING STONES MICK JAGGER AND KEITH RICHARDS, 29 JUNE.

suspected of setting up the bust after Jagger issued a libel suit against them. On the 30th, a Track-paid advertisement appeared in the *Evening Standard*: "The Who consider Mick Jagger and Keith Richards have been treated as scapegoats for the drug problem and as a protest against the savage sentences imposed on them at Chichester yesterday, the Who are issuing today the first of a series of Jagger/Richards songs to keep their work before the public until they are again free to record themselves."

It was a magnanimous gesture, but by the time the single reached the shops and entered the Top 50 the following week at #44, Jagger and Richards had received bail pending appeal. "We made this record and released it in 24 hours flat before we knew they'd got bail," said Lambert. "It's just a simple gesture, and we are not trying to cash in at all. All royalties will go to charity."

SATURDAY, 1 JULY

Disc reported the Who were continuing work on their next album, provisionally titled *Who's Lily?*, in the hope of having it completed before the opening of their American tour. Eight Townshend compositions

were to be included together with six tracks written by the rest of the group.

WEDNESDAY, 5 JULY

Mixing at De Lane Lea, with Kit Lambert/Dave Siddle: "I Can't Reach You," "Relax," "Glittering Girl," and "Rael" (backing track). "Glittering Girl," featuring Pete's guide vocal, was mixed into mono by Kit Lambert, but remained unreleased until *The Who Sell Out* CD in 1995.

During this period, Pete was interviewed in London by writer Hans Verhagen for *Hoepla*, a controversial Dutch youth television programme, transmitted Friday 28 July between 7:25–7:55 pm, on Nederland 1.

FRIDAY, 7 JULY

Malibu Beach and Shore Club, Lido Beach, Long Island, New York.

SATURDAY, 8 JULY

The Village Theatre, 2nd Avenue at 6th Street, New York City, supporting the Blues Project, with Chrysalis, the New Life, and Richie Havens.

Prior to the commencement of the Herman's Hermits tour, three days of studio time were booked at Talentmasters Studio, 126 West 42nd Street, with engineer Chris Huston. (Huston, originally from Liverpool, had played with the Undertakers when the Who supported them at the Glenlyn Ballroom and Goldhawk Club in early 1964.)

The sessions were occupied with cutting a new backing track and multi-layered vocals to a condensed version of "Rael," which now had a running time of 6 mins 45 secs. Early American Who champion Al Kooper from the Blues Project played organ.

"By the end of this particular session, we were all pretty tired," Huston recalled to Brian Cady. "As was customary, if the session would be continuing the next day, I put the tapes on top of a small side shelf in the control room. This evening, for some reason, I neglected to put the tape in its box. Back then, to save money, many studios bought tape on 'flanges.' That is, the tape was on a metal hub, but didn't have the protective metal side flanges. Talentmasters was one of those studios.

"When I came in the next day, an hour or so before the session, I could not find the 'Rael' four-track master. I searched every nook and cranny, including the obvious places like the tape library. It

was only then that I thought to contact our janitor, who wasn't on the phone. I eventually got in touch with him through a relative and found out he'd taken it upon himself to declare the tape garbage and had taken it down to 41st St. [the back of the building] and put it in the dumpster, but not before breaking it off at the hub. Panic ensued. I searched frantically through the dumpster to retrieve all the pieces. The take itself was in four or five sections that I was able to splice together. However, the intro section of tape was stretched beyond redemption.

"Fortunately, I'd taken home a mono mix the night before, and we ended up copying the mono intro onto a track for the master. Pete was angry and rightly so, but he did not throw a chair through the Control Room window, as Al Kooper would have it. Furthermore, Al saying that the window and related damage was around $12,000 makes me laugh. The truth is, the whole Control Room didn't cost that much to build, and there was only a lone pane of 3/8" glass in the window!"

THURSDAY, 13 JULY

The Who commenced a ten week, coast-to-coast American and Canadian tour, as support to Herman's Hermits, with "Special Guest Stars" the Blues Magoos, at the Stampede Corral, Calgary, Canada. Two shows, 2:30 & 8:30 pm.

The groups travelled via a chartered DC7 with their names painted on the side. Such a disparate bill was bound to raise a few eyebrows. "It got us around America," said Daltrey, "but it did us no good at all." The experience did help in bringing the group closer together. "We had no responsibilities," he conceded. "We weren't headlining, and we could just roll up and do our bit in half an hour."

Unlike previous visits, the Who were able to bring their own equipment over. Keith debuted his customised Premier "Pictures Of Lily" kit, comprised of three mounted toms, three 16" floor toms, a 14" snare, a semi-locked hi-hat, three cymbals, and a pair of 22" bass drums. Each was emblazoned with Day-glo designs showing the Who logo, "Lily" nudes, and an image of Keith bearing the legend: "Keith Moon—Patent British Exploding Drummer."

FRIDAY, 14 JULY

Memorial Coliseum, Portland, Oregon.

SATURDAY, 15 JULY
Center Coliseum, Seattle, Washington.

SUNDAY, 16 JULY
Memorial Auditorium, Sacramento, California. Two shows, 7:00 & 9:30 pm.

MONDAY, 17 JULY
The Agrodome, Vancouver, British Columbia, Canada.

Keith almost got left behind when he mislaid his passport with his laundry in New York. An urgent call was made to Nancy Lewis, who sent it on by air freight. When it still hadn't arrived, several frantic calls traced it to Seattle, where the group's chartered plane had to be specially diverted to pick it up. At that evening's show, Pete smashed his guitar to fragments, thinking he had a replacement. Lewis was again pressed into service, and a guitar was waiting for him in Salt Lake City.

WEDNESDAY, 19 JULY
The Lagoon Terrace Ballroom, Salt Lake City, Utah. Two shows, 7:00 & 9:30 pm.

FRIDAY, 21 JULY
Oklahoma State Fair, Oklahoma City, Oklahoma.

SATURDAY, 22 JULY
Sam Houston Coliseum, Houston, Texas.

SUNDAY, 23 JULY
Dallas Memorial Auditorium, Dallas, Texas.

With the unauthorised sale of explosives illegal in the States, Chris Stamp frantically phoned back to England, as the group had run out of smoke bombs. When the air freight company refused to allow them on board, the Who had to make do with smoke powder

Premier Talent.
c/o Gorham Hotel
136. W 55th. NY. NY.

July 14. 1967.
Richard Stanley.

Dear Richard.

How's business? I didn't get time to come and see you and J.L. on Wednesday sorry!

We seem to be moving a lot of earth at this time here. KRLA — a very big nation station in Los Angeles is playing 8 of our records very regularly. Terence Stamp, (Chris's brother) has a half hour show on another L.A. station and he played our whole album end to end — as the stations in Cities play themselves against themselves

they're all playing it now. We also have the honor of the title 'Best group in the World' in a competition run by KWVB another L.A. station.

I finished writing the new opera for the groups next single in England and we recorded it over here. We didn't use the lushest of studios but nevertheless in 3 days really got some terrific things done. Its down to 3 parts now and runs for only 6.45. minutes. Unfortunately we don't have enough air-play status yet to release it here, so I rewrote a number called 'Relax' which was to lead the L.P. We hope to record it in Atlantics 8-track studio in August.

I'm writing this in

a plane over the Mid-West, waiting for my plastic meal.

I've been fairly worried about whether the move toward some sort of sanity over the dress situation in England is still happening. I suspect its all over, and the newspapers are back to their old standpoint — a reflection of public legal opinion. Some of the things which happen here are horrifying! In a greenwich Village newspaper I read an account of an L.A. love-in which the police tried to incite to riot. Nobody rioted but none-the-less 200,000 happily tore into 200,000 men, women and lots of kids in riot trucks and with guns and truncheons. Three children and two women are missing and the

local hospitals are full of lovable broken heads.

We're due to play Texas soon and I must admit I'm scared enough to be extra careful. The stories one hears about long hair and it's effect on the average Texan (who carries not just a gun but a SHOTGUN) are pretty worrying. I think coolness will help.

Everyone over here is hot for Arthur Brown and I think the situation is sufficiently hot enough (Atlantic Records want him) to merit a LOT of thought and work and also capital being poured into them. We'll see.

I hate to use an oldie but U.S.A is so BIG.

I don't remember it you've been to New York but a word about would not be out of place. I've made so many real friends in such a short time it's not true.

The thing is that there are about a hundred or more groups covering all age-groups (each one) with absolutely fixed preconceived attitudes to life. You really can't win 'em all. Because of this one quickly finds ones own group and practically instantly realise one's position as a functional part of the group, making friends with everyone.

The Greenwich Villagers are another race. Very un-hippy and fairly un-love but very intelligent. (I got on well with them) Ha Ha.

Anyway!

Look forward to welcoming you to my New Home when I get back.

Give my fondest regards to Chris and his dogs, harmonicas, WW (vw) and also to cunt who lives with you — storm and his party.

See you later.

Pete.

P.S. How did Storm's epic work out — his star looked very moving in a dated sort of way.

Also — don't hesitate to move that Harmonium when neccessary now — Karen knows the score.

ABOVE: Lagoon Terrace Ballroom, 19 July.

which was difficult to obtain and not quite so effective. Apparently, at the end of one Southern show, after everything had been demolished, Keith picked up his snare and walked off playing a marching rhythm, with the others falling into formation behind. At another, they waved large confederate flags.

WEDNESDAY, 26 JULY
Redemptorist High School Football Stadium, Baton Rouge, Louisiana.

FRIDAY, 28 JULY
Garrett Coliseum, Montgomery, Alabama.

SATURDAY, 29 JULY
Auditorium, Birmingham, Alabama.

An extra 2:00 pm matinee show was arranged, as well as the two 6:00 & 9:00 pm shows, and an additional six acts appeared on the bill: Sam the Sham and the Pharoahs, Lou Christie, Jim "Harpo" Valley, Every Mother's Son, Billy Joe Royal, and the Rockin' Rebellions.

The tour had been advised to stay close to the hotel or preferably not to go out at all, for fear of Southern redneck behaviour. Sound advice for any meek mortal, but encouragement for Keith Moon, who went into an adjacent restaurant. "It was like a scene from those Al Capone films," Keith told *Disc.*

"These guys had two cars waiting for them with the motors running, and as soon as I walked out, they grabbed me and pushed me right through the plate glass door. By the time I got up, they were gone." Fortunately, the shaken drummer suffered only minor cuts.

SUNDAY, 30 JULY
Miami Beach Convention Hall, Miami, Florida.

MONDAY, 31 JULY
Bayfront Center, St. Petersburg, Florida.

Pete was reunited with his old friend from art college, Tom Wright. As Wright recalled it, "I'd spent a couple of years in Europe and then went back to the States. I was working as an underwater photographer in Florida. The Who came to Florida, and that was the end of the underwater photography career!" The group needed publicity pictures, so Wright initially travelled with them as photographer, before graduating to the position of tour manager.

TUESDAY, 1 AUGUST
Mississippi State Coliseum, Jackson, Mississippi.

THURSDAY, 3 AUGUST
Dane County Memorial Coliseum, Madison, Wisconsin.

FRIDAY, 4 AUGUST
Rosenblatt Stadium, Omaha, Nebraska.

SATURDAY, 5 AUGUST
International Amphitheatre, Chicago, Illinois.

SUNDAY, 6 and MONDAY, 7 AUGUST
Recording/mixing Mirasound and Talentmasters Studios, NYC with Kit Lambert and Chris Huston: "Relax," "Mary Anne With The Shaky Hand" (two versions, both featuring Al Kooper on organ), "Summertime Blues," and the intriguingly titled "Bob Sings Soul," a joke piece featuring road manager Bob Pridden on vocals, intended for *Sell Out*.

At Talentmasters, "Relax," featuring Pete on organ, received further overdubs, and the guide vocals to "I Can See For Miles" were replaced, with the backing track recorded at CBS, London (circa May). Engineer Chris Huston made a reduction mix, leaving two vacant tracks onto which the vocals were double-tracked.

WEDNESDAY, 9 AUGUST
Maple Leaf Gardens, Toronto, Ontario, Canada.

FRIDAY, 11 AUGUST
Civic Center, Baltimore, Maryland.

SATURDAY, 12 AUGUST
Convention Hall, Asbury Park, New Jersey. Two shows, 8:00 & 10:15 pm.

SUNDAY, 13 AUGUST
Constitution Hall, Washington DC. Two shows, 3:00 & 8:00 pm.

MONDAY, 14 AUGUST
Rhode Island Auditorium, Providence, Rhode Island.

Following the show, the tour party boarded their chartered flight heading south. Engine trouble forced an emergency landing on a foam-covered runway. "That was a bleedin' nightmare," Entwistle told Roy Carr. "Two blokes on the plane were out of their heads on acid. Actually, it was probably that incident that inspired Townshend to write 'Glow Girl.'" "I never regarded myself as a person afraid of travelling by air," Townshend told Jann Wenner. "When we did the Herman's Hermits tour in an old charter plane, I wrote so many songs about plane crashes, it was incredible."

THURSDAY, 17 AUGUST
Memorial Auditorium, Chattanooga, Tennessee. Two shows, 6:00 & 9:00 pm, with added attraction Neil Diamond.

At Columbia Recording Studio, 6121 Sunset Boulevard, Hollywood, Kit Lambert made four-track mono transfers of "Mary Anne With The Shaky Hand" (single version), "Summertime Blues," "Someone's Coming" (an intended single, see 24 May), "Our Love Was," and "Relax."

While in Tennessee, Lambert arranged a session at Bradley's Barn, Nashville, previously used by the Everly Brothers and Buddy Holly and the Crickets. Vocals and backing vocal overdubs were added to certain tracks, as well as John's brass overdubs on "Someone's Coming."

SATURDAY, 19 AUGUST
With the Who receiving rave notices on the Hermits tour, Atco re-released "Substitute" in a calculated effort to gain a piece of the action. *Billboard* picked it as that week's "Sure Shot," but again, it failed to chart.

SUNDAY, 20 AUGUST
The first of three twin bookings (i.e., two gigs in two different towns on the same date), with a 2:30 pm show at the Civic Auditorium, Fargo, North Dakota, followed by a 7:30 pm show at the Minneapolis Auditorium, Minneapolis, Minnesota.

MONDAY, 21 AUGUST
New Edmonton Gardens, Edmonton, Alberta, Canada.

TUESDAY, 22 AUGUST
Winnipeg Arena, Winnipeg, Manitoba, Canada.

WEDNESDAY, 23 AUGUST
Atwood High School Stadium, Flint, Michigan.

The tour avoided riot-torn Detroit, playing some sixty miles (97km) north of the city, where the local Holiday Inn became the setting for Keith's legendary twenty-first birthday party.

Reports vary in their exaggeration as to what exactly happened. What is beyond dispute is how things got swiftly out of hand. The sheriff's office was notified after fire extinguishers were turned on cars in the parking lot, television sets were thrown into the swimming pool, and two changing cubicles were damaged. Thanks to Nancy Lewis, Premier and Decca Records had presented Keith with a five-tiered drum-shaped cake, which he proceeded to hurl around. According to Entwistle, Keith "never drove a car into a swimming pool! He couldn't even drive! He hit the sheriff with the cake, because the person he threw it at ducked, and he started running, except he was so pissed, he tripped and fell over and smashed his two front teeth. So the sheriff drove him to the dentist, and we all waited while they operated on him without any anaesthetic, because he was drunk. He was whimpering for two days. He didn't even see a swimming pool that night!"

Eardrums Take A Beating From Teens, Hermits

By SAMUEL L. SINGER
Of The Inquirer Staff

The Who, mop-headed foursome from England making their local debut in support of Herman's Hermits, set an example at the Civic Center on Thursday night that it is devoutly hoped all rock 'n' roll groups will follow.

At the conclusion of their ear-splitting act, so torrid that smoke began to come from the stage amplification equipment, the drummer tossed his drumsticks (dozens of them) and his drums to the winds, and the two guitarists broke up their instruments.

ONLY AN ACT

The youngsters in the front rows vainly looked for pieces of guitar as souvenirs. But, alas, it was only an act. The boys put their guitars together again (out of sight) for their next show. Too bad it's only an act.

Herman's Hermits, who were first heard here in 1965 in support of the Rolling Stones, starred on their own this time, and the police were prepared for anything. Mobile communications unit, fire rescue squad outside; scores of policemen and policewomen, and barricades inside.

The police were kept busy keeping teenage photographers,

1
9
6
7

ABOVE: Keith's uproarious twenty-first birthday party, 23 August, with Peter Noone (centre).

THURSDAY, 24 AUGUST
Convention Hall, Philadelphia, Pennsylvania.

Keith missed the flight, so a plane had to be chartered by tour manager Ed McCann, bringing the total cost of his twenty-first to $5,000, paid for with the help of contributions from members of the touring party.

FRIDAY, 25 AUGUST
Kiel Opera House, St. Louis, Missouri. Two shows, 6:30 & 9:00 pm.

SATURDAY, 26 AUGUST
Two shows straddling the Canadian—American border, with a 2:00 pm show at the Fort William Gardens, Fort William, Ontario, followed by an 8:00 pm show at Duluth Arena, Duluth, Minnesota.

SUNDAY, 27 AUGUST
Music Hall, Cincinnati, Ohio. Two shows, 3:00 & 8:00 pm.

MONDAY, 28 AUGUST
Sioux Falls Arena, Sioux Falls, South Dakota.

TUESDAY, 29 AUGUST
Municipal Auditorium, Atlanta, Georgia. Two shows, 4:00 & 8:30 pm.

WEDNESDAY, 30 AUGUST
War Memorial Auditorium, Rochester, New York.

THURSDAY, 31 AUGUST
Public Music Hall, Cleveland, Ohio. Two shows, 6:30 & 9:00 pm. On the bill were local group the Choir, who later evolved into the Raspberries.

FRIDAY, 1 SEPTEMBER
Indiana State Fair Coliseum, State Fairgrounds, Indianapolis, Indiana. Two shows, 4:00 & 8:30 pm.

SATURDAY, 2—MONDAY, 4 SEPTEMBER
Ohio State Fairgrounds, Columbus, Ohio.

The Hermits tour played three days at the State Fair, giving two performances at 1:00 and 4:00 pm each day, except Sunday the 3rd. On that date, they played two shows at 3:00 & 5:00 pm, before travelling to Pittsburgh, Pennsylvania, for an 8:00 pm show at the Civic Arena. The Blues Magoos had to pull out of the remaining dates due to injury.

TUESDAY, 5 SEPTEMBER
With a break in the tour, the Who flew on to Los Angeles, checking into the Beverly Hills Hilton. Kit Lambert brought the four-track tapes of "I Can See For Miles" and "Rael" to Gold Star Studios at Santa Monica and Vine, Hollywood, for mixing and mastering, utilising the studio's famed echo chamber. Safety copies were made on 8 September.

FRIDAY, 8 SEPTEMBER
Convention Center, Anaheim, California, promoted by KRLA and Bob Eubanks. The Sundowners and the Strawberry Alarm Clock appeared on the bill.

The show was notable for the extraordinary sight of John Entwistle smashing his bass. "I started to smash the bass after all the rest of the group had finished smashing their equipment," he recalled. "But it took about ten minutes to smash the thing and all in complete silence, with just the rest of the group shouting encouragement and the damn thing just wouldn't break!"

SATURDAY, 9 SEPTEMBER
Honolulu International Center Arena, Honolulu, Hawaii.

The final show on the exhaustive Hermits tour, after which the band returned to L.A.

SUNDAY, 10 SEPTEMBER
Final mixing of "I Can See For Miles" at Gold Star. U.S. Decca rush-released the single on 18 September B/W the electric version of "Mary Anne With The Shaky Hand" (see 6 August.) A second electric version remained unissued until 1995, when it was included as a bonus track on *The Who Sell Out* CD. The acoustic *Sell Out* arrangement was taped in London. "I Can See For Miles" was not released in Britain until Friday, 13 October.

FRIDAY, 15 SEPTEMBER
The Who went to the CBS Television Studios on Sunset Boulevard, Hollywood, to record their American network debut on *The Smothers Brothers Comedy Hour*. (The comic duo had caught the group at the Monterey Festival.) During the afternoon dress rehearsal, one of Keith's bass drums simply ignited and smouldered with flash powder. Unbeknownst to most, between rehearsals and showtime, he had filled the drum with an amount well in excess of safety levels.

After Tommy Smothers' introduction, the Who mimed to a prepared 2:45 edit of "I Can See For Miles" before a psychedelic coloured backdrop. Tommy then walked on to introduce each of the group in turn. Several scripted exchanges later, the Who mimed to a specially re-cut "My Generation," complete with feigned smash-up ending, with Roger's live vocal.

At the auto-destructive climax, the resulting explosion literally shook the cameras, blowing out all the studio monitors. Pete, who was closest to the blast, took the full brunt, his hearing temporarily shattered. (He later attributed much of his subsequent hearing loss to this moment.) Keith rolled around the floor, concussed and bleeding, a three inch gash in his arm. Tommy Smothers emerged dumbstruck from the wings with an acoustic guitar strapped around his neck. Townshend, hair still smouldering, seized the instrument and reduced it to matchwood with four mighty whacks onto the studio floor. Legend has it that Bette Davis, awaiting her cue in the wings, fainted clean away into the arms of fellow guest Mickey Rooney.

```
(TOM WALKS PAST ROGER...DOES A TAKE...
APPROACHES JOHN)
              TOM
     And you're...
              JOHN
(DEEP VOICE)
     John.
              TOM
     From?
              JOHN
     London.
(TOM TURNS TO ROGER)
              TOM
     You must be Roger.
              ROGER
     I must be.
              TOM
     And you're from London.
              ROGER
     No, Duluth, Minnesota...
     No, I'm a Londoner too.
(TOM GOES TO KEITH)
              KEITH
     I'm Keith.  I'm from London too.
              TOM
     Have you met these guys?  They're
     from London too.
     What are you going to sing?
```

This classic piece of anarchic television was first screened two nights later over the CBS network, 8:00–9:00 pm EST. "My Generation" (and its preceding dialogue) was rightly chosen to open *The Kids Are Alright* movie and soundtrack album.

SATURDAY, 16 SEPTEMBER

"Pete Townshend has written this opera called 'Rael,'" Chris Stamp told *Disc*, "and they've now cut it down to about seven minutes, which we could just squeeze onto a single. If we choose one of the other tracks for the new single then we'll put it on the new album, which we hope to issue in October."

SUNDAY, 17 SEPTEMBER

The Who arrived back from the Hermits tour, $5000 in the red. Keeping up appearances, John actually borrowed $100 to fly home first class rather than economy!

OCTOBER

The Who spent the month rehearsing a new act at the Saville, including song introductions for the forthcoming Herd-Tremeloes-Traffic theatre tour, while *Sell Out* sessions continued, engineered by Damon Lyon-Shaw, with Pete on keyboards.

The satirical photos for the album sleeve were designed by Track art directors, David King and Roger Law, and photographed by David Montgomery at the latter's studio at 11b Edith Grove, Chelsea. "Roger did his pose in the beans in good spirits" remembered Pete. "The thing was the beans were ice cold and had come right out of the fridge!"

MONDAY, 2 OCTOBER

At CBS, four-track mono master copies were made of "I Can See For Miles," "Armenia (City In The Sky)," "Early Morning Cold Taxi," and "Girl's Eyes."

FRIDAY, 6 OCTOBER

Ballerina Ballroom, Nairn, Nairnshire, Scotland.

SATURDAY, 7 OCTOBER

The Beach Ballroom, Aberdeen, Grampian, Scotland.

SUNDAY, 8 OCTOBER

Kinema Ballroom, Dunfermline, Fife, Scotland.

TUESDAY, 10 OCTOBER

Recording/mixing at De Lane Lea: a special radio session for the revamped *Top Gear*, which had begun 1 October on the BBC's new flagship station, Radio 1.

This session set a precedent in that it was the first to be recorded outside the corporation's own studios. The Who insisted on using stereo facilities (despite there still being only AM outlets in Britain), rather than suffer the Beeb's arcane procedures and time restrictions. The powers that be reluctantly agreed after a persuasive battle on the group's behalf by BBC producer Bernie Andrews.

In two sessions produced by Kit Lambert, starting at 12:30 pm and 5:30 pm respectively, versions of "Pictures Of Lily" (with Pete on organ), "A Quick One (While He's Away)," Eddie Cochran's "Summertime Blues," and "My Way" were recorded, along with five irreverent, one-off jingles: two for *Top Gear* and three for Radio 1 to the tunes of "Happy Jack," "Boris The Spider," and "My Generation" ("my favourite station").

Remix mono tape copies were also made (and taken away by Andrews) of "Our Love Was," "Relax," "I Can't Reach You," and "I Can See For Miles," the last featuring John's bass track re-recorded in compliance with a Musicians Union ruling on miming.

The majority of tracks were first broadcast in the third edition of *Top Gear* on Sunday, 15 October, from 2:00—5:00 pm, and introduced by Pete Drummond and Tommy Vance.

"My Way," "Someone's Coming," a repeat of "I Can't Reach You," "I Can See For Miles," "A Quick One," "Relax," and three of the jingles were included in the 15 November *Top Gear* (same times). "Our Love Was," "I Can See For Miles," "Pictures Of Lily," and "Summertime Blues" were repeated on the 28 October edition of *Saturday Club* (10:00—12:00 midday), as were the latter three on *The David Symonds Show*, broadcast daily 13—17 November, 5:33—7:30 pm.

According to BBC documentation, the Who offered to re-record some of the jingles for regular use on Radio 1, but were prevented from doing so by the fact that there was "no MU/BBC agreed basis for a contract."

WEDNESDAY, 11 OCTOBER

Recording/mixing De Lane Lea/IBC: "Heinz Baked Beans," "Odorono," "Top Gear," and several other linking adverts for *The Who Sell Out*.

"Pete's jingles were sort of like the long ones, and mine and Keith's were like short jokes," Entwistle explained. "Most of the jingles went on, whether they were good or bad. The short ones like 'Rotosound Strings' and 'Premier Drums' were made up by me and Keith in the pub near Kingsway Studios. And the thing that goes out on the run-off groove, 'Track Records, Track Records..,' we phoned that one in from the pub. We did it over the telephone, and they recorded it with a microphone. Obviously, 'Heinz Baked Beans,' 'Medac,' and 'Silas Stingy' I'd written before. I actually did demos for them."

THURSDAY, 12 OCTOBER

Recording/mixing IBC: "Tattoo."

FRIDAY, 13 OCTOBER.

Keith went to Southern Television's studios in Northam, Hampshire, representing the Who on the second "test" programme of *New Release*, produced by Mike Mansfield and presented by DJ Tony Blackburn. The show consisted of artists miming to their latest disc (appearances coincided with its release date), before they joined Blackburn in a forum to discuss the record's merits. Artists then remained to comment on the others. Camera rehearsals and taping commenced at 6:30 pm. The Who appeared by way of a specially filmed insert shot in Scotland the previous weekend, filmed to "I Can See For Miles." Appearing in the studio were Anita Harris, Paul and Barry Ryan, Long John Baldry, and Barry Mason.

Keith helpfully explained that the Who's latest was "originally recorded for an LP, but taken off because we liked it better than those that were on before we took those off that were on there before those that we took off—if you get me?!" The programme was screened Monday, 16 October, 9:30—10:00 pm, over most Southern ITV areas (screening dates varied for each region), with the 13-part series properly commencing on Tuesday, 2 January 1968.

SUNDAY, 15 OCTOBER

At Lime Grove, the Who recorded an insert for the first in a new BBC-1 Saturday night comedy series *Twice A Fortnight*, broadcast 21 October, 11:00—11:30 pm. Devised by *Observer* critic/film producer Tony Palmer, the show featured Bill Oddie and Graeme Garden (later of *The Goodies*), the team who made *Sorry I'll Read That Again*, a popular radio series; Jonathan Lynn; Dilys Watling and Ronald Fletcher; and future *Monty Python's Flying Circus* alumni Michael Palin and Terry Jones.

Each week, music was provided by a contemporary group of Palmer's choosing. From 4:30 pm the programme, sub-titled "Match Of The Day Part 2," was taped virtually non-stop before an audience in Studio G. For "I Can See For Miles," the cameras utilised frenzied, intercutting "zoom-in" shots of each group member, creating a disorientating effect. American viewers were able to see the clip when it was extracted and broadcast on 30 December over the ABC network on *American Bandstand*. The Who received a payment of £84 and reappeared in the final *Twice A Fortnight*, taped 17 December.

MONDAY, 16 OCTOBER

Mixing IBC: Mono masters of "Tattoo," "Odorono," and "Rael (1&2)." The final chorus of "Odorono" was trimmed off and sat unused until it appeared as a bonus track on the expanded *Sell Out* CD in 1995.

FRIDAY, 20 OCTOBER

Recording/mixing IBC Studio A: "Rael (1&2)," "Jaguar," and "Armenia City In The Sky" (arm and ear), written by John "Speedy" Keene. Unusually, the latter two tracks featured Keith on lead vocal. "Jaguar" remained unreleased until *The Who Sell Out* expanded CD reissue in 1995.

Around this time, Pete played an acetate of a rough mix of "Armenia" to Radio 1 DJ John Peel

ABOVE: The Who appearing on *Twice a Fortnight*, 15 October.

while being interviewed for Dutch television at Track's Old Compton Street office. Townshend displayed the proposed artwork for *The Who Sell Out* and discussed the album's thematic advertising link, as well as the difference between selling records and playing concerts. This "John Peel Special Report" appeared in *Vjoew*, transmitted Monday, 30 October, 7:03—7:55 pm on Nederland 2.

SATURDAY, 21 OCTOBER
New Century Hall, Manchester.

The following week, Pete told the *NME*'s Keith Altham: "We played 'Rael' on stage in Manchester and Scotland [6-8 October], and everyone just looked at us with their mouths open—the complication was too much."

SUNDAY, 22 OCTOBER
Saville Theatre, London, with Studio Six and Vanilla Fudge, compèred by Peter Stringfellow. Two shows.

Vanilla Fudge were particularly hot, and the Who had difficulty following them, as Pete admitted to Altham: "We've tried this semi-intellectual approach. We did it at the first house at the Saville and died a death, because we were following an overwhelming act like the Vanilla Fudge. We were like a cream tea! Kit was so worried he tried to way-lay all the journalists in a pub over the road so they would only see the end of the show, but we put things right in the second house. We did a Brian Poole routine—Roger split his trousers, Keith wore a jester's hat and knocked his drums about, and I kept falling over. They loved it." During one introduction, Pete sent himself up,

THIS PAGE:
SCENES FROM THE SAVILLE THEATRE PERFORMANCES, 22 OCTOBER.

ABOVE LEFT:
THE EARLY SHOW AT THE SAVILLE, 22 OCTOBER, WITH KEITH'S EXTRA BASS DRUM!

LEFT AND **ABOVE:** WALTHAMSTOW, 4 NOVEMBER.

saying, "This is the bit where I kick things around the stage!" Reviewers noted the conspicuous absence of any such behaviour.

Backstage, Townshend was filmed discussing the drug scene by Australian director Peter Clifton. He claimed he was only admitting drug use on television to cause an upset and referred to the Rolling Stones' recent misdemeanours. Part of the interview appeared in Clifton's *Superstars In Concert*, released 1973.

TUESDAY, 24 OCTOBER

Recording/mixing De Lane Lea: Premier Drums, Speakeasy, Charles Atlas, and Track Records jingles plus an acoustic remake of "Mary Anne With The Shaky Hand."

From 1:00—1:55 pm, Pete appeared as a guest on the Light Programme's *Pop Inn*, with the Troggs and John Walker, broadcast live from the BBC's Paris Studios on Lower Regent Street.

THURSDAY, 26 OCTOBER

Mixing IBC: Mono masters of "Jaguar"and "Rael" (1 only: the 2 coda had been subsequently dropped. It wasn't reinstated until the 1994 box set and the 1995 *Sell Out* CD). At Studio G, Lime Grove, the Who plugged "I Can See For Miles" live on *Top Of The Pops*, transmitted that evening from 7:30—8:00 pm.

SATURDAY, 28 OCTOBER

City Hall, Sheffield. Two shows, 6:20 & 8:50 pm.

The opening night of a British theatre tour, promoted by the Who's new Manchester-based agents Kennedy Street Enterprises, featuring Traffic, the

Herd, Marmalade, and the Dream. Special guests: the Tremeloes. Compère: Ray Cameron.

The Who played a full twelve-song set for the first house, but their set was cut to just three numbers when the second show ran over by 75 minutes. Enraged, Pete smashed two speakers and some of the Herd's lighting gear, which had been left onstage. The rampage extended backstage, with a trestle table over-turned and a coat stand kicked over and trampled on.

SUNDAY, 29 OCTOBER

Coventry Theatre, Coventry. Two shows, 6:00 & 8:30 pm.

The violent opening night scenes repeated themselves. Because sound problems had made the first house run over, the curtain was dropped behind the Who while they were still performing. Pete and Roger were left on stage as the National Anthem played. Townshend shouted for the curtain to be raised. When it wasn't, he threw his guitar down, toppled his amps over, and kicked the footlights out. He then picked up a footlight and used it to hammer the floats. He also swung at the lights with a mike stand, before throwing punches and an amplifier at the theatre manager.

MONDAY, 30 OCTOBER

City Hall, Newcastle. Two shows, 6:00 & 8:30 pm.

Mixing De Lane Lea: *The Who Sell Out* stereo mastering.

WEDNESDAY, 1 NOVEMBER

Empire Theatre, Liverpool. Two shows, 6:15 & 8:35 pm.

THURSDAY, 2 NOVEMBER

The Who went to Studio G, Lime Grove, plugging "I Can See For Miles" live on *Top Of The Pops*, 7:30–8:00 pm, ironically dressed as leather-clad rockers with Pete sporting a blacked out tooth. The insert was repeated on the 23 November edition (same time).

Recording IBC: "Sunrise," taped solo by Pete. "Keith didn't want that on the record," he revealed. "At the time I was studying Mickey Baker jazz methods, and I had two of his tutors, both of which were magnificent. It's all that I've ever needed to get into slightly more complex chord work. I played that song on a Harmony 12-string. It was written for my mother to show her I could write real music."

Mixing De Lane Lea: *The Who Sell Out* mono mastering. After Kit Lambert worked out the running order, discs were cut and banded by Damon Lyon-Shaw at IBC Studio A on 20 November; lacquers were rushed to the pressing plant; the sleeve was quickly printed; and finished copies of the LP were in the shops by Friday, 15 December.

FRIDAY, 3 NOVEMBER

Granada Cinema, Kingston-on-Thames, Surrey. Two shows, 7:00 & 9:10 pm.

SATURDAY, 4 NOVEMBER

Granada Cinema, Walthamstow, London. Two shows, 6:30 & 9:00 pm.

Backstage, Chris Morphet shot mute 8-mm monochrome footage of the group (and Bob Pridden) in their dressing room applying stage make-up, later blown up to 35-mm by Jeff Stein for inclusion in *The Kids Are Alright*.

SUNDAY, 5 NOVEMBER

Theatre Royal, Nottingham. Two shows, 5:30 & 8:00 pm.

MONDAY, 6 NOVEMBER

Town Hall, Birmingham. Two shows, 6:30 & 8:45 pm.

WEDNESDAY, 8 NOVEMBER

Granada Cinema, Kettering, Northamptonshire. Two shows, 7:00 & 9:10 pm.

THURSDAY, 9 NOVEMBER

Granada Cinema, Maidstone, Kent. Two shows, 6:20 & 8:30 pm.

A "wild track" film insert of the Who (a series of mute images onto which "I Can See For Miles" could be dubbed) appeared in the 200th edition of

ABOVE: *Top Of The Pops* taping, 2 November.

1967

Top Of The Pops, 7:30—8:00 pm. The programme's viewing figures had doubled to around twelve million since it's debut on New Year's Day 1964.

FRIDAY, 10 NOVEMBER
Adelphi Cinema, Slough. Two shows, 6:40 & 8:50 pm.

With the Who-Traffic tour drawing 90% capacity audiences, promoter Danny Betesh's plans to repeat the package the following February were thwarted by the Who's tour of North America.

SATURDAY, 11 NOVEMBER
Imperial Ballroom, Nelson.

WEDNESDAY, 15 NOVEMBER
The Who flew to America for a two-week visit, which had originally been expected to last four weeks. In that week's *Billboard*, "I Can See For Miles" was at its highest position of #9, staying in the chart for five weeks.

FRIDAY, 17 NOVEMBER
Shawnee Mission South High School Gymnasium, Overland Park, Kansas, Missouri, supporting the Buckinghams.

SATURDAY, 18 NOVEMBER
"Festival of Music," Cow Palace, San Francisco, California.

As "special guest stars," the Who closed the first half following the Sopwith Camel and the Sunshine Company. Eric Burdon and the Animals, the Everly Brothers, and the Association occupied the second. "People may have thought that 'I Can See For Miles' was about acid," said Pete, "but it wasn't in my mind. It's the case of the writer being taken for something he didn't say or rather mean. I mean someone said to me, 'Hey man, very groovy those lyrics, what are you getting at?' Eric Burdon was there at the time, and in his broad Newcastle accent with firm deliberation, he said, 'It's about a guy with great eyesight!'"

SUNDAY, 19 NOVEMBER
"Festival of Music," Hollywood Bowl, Los Angeles, California, same bill as 18 November.

Fire authorities had asked the group to forego using smoke bombs, but neglected to tell Bob Pridden. "I was behind the amps, letting these flashes off and smoke was going everywhere," he recalled. "The group left and two policemen came and carted me off. They arrested me for breaking six counts of the Hollywood fire laws, which was very scary because I was in a little room, and they wouldn't let me out, and the group didn't know where I was."

TUESDAY, 21 NOVEMBER
Civic Auditorium, Fargo, North Dakota.

WEDNESDAY, 22 NOVEMBER
Southfield High School Gymnasium, Southfield, Michigan.

THURSDAY, 23 NOVEMBER
The New Barn, Lions Delaware County Fairgrounds, Muncie, Indiana.

FRIDAY, 24 NOVEMBER
The Swinging Gate, Fort Wayne, Indiana.

Following the gig at this small club, the Who, Bob Pridden, tour manager Tom Wright, and their bus driver accepted an invitation to sample Thanksgiving dinner at promoter Linda Wren's apartment, following which, they drove through the night to New York.

SATURDAY, 25 and SUNDAY, 26 NOVEMBER
The Village Theatre, New York City. Two shows, 8:00 & 10:30 pm, on the 25th, and one 3:00 pm matinee on the 26th. Promoted by Gary Kurfist.

After the late show on the 25th, Pete's guitar was completely beyond repair, sending Pridden dashing around for a replacement in time for the afternoon matinee. Supports were the Rich Kids and the Vagrants. The latter's guitarist Leslie West (née Weinstein), later of Mountain, played on the New York sessions for *Lifehouse*. (See 15 March 1971.)

Rival promoter Bill Graham later upgraded the Village, re-opening it as the classier Fillmore East on 8 March, 1968, in time for the Who's return the following April. U.S. Who fan Jon Rubin shot silent 8-mm colour footage at the Village, Commack Arena, and the Fillmore East, clips of which appeared in the Who's *Better, Who's Best* laserdisc and VH1's *Legends: The Who*.

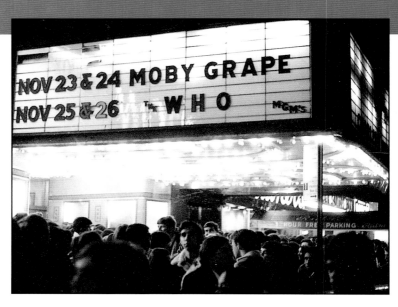

WEDNESDAY, 29 NOVEMBER
Union Catholic High School Gymnasium, Scotch Plains, New Jersey.

FRIDAY, 1 DECEMBER
Long Island Arena, Commack, New York, with Vanilla Fudge.

SUNDAY, 3 DECEMBER
The Who flew back to London.

"I honestly feel that in America we have reached the same measure of success it's taken us three years to attain in Europe," Pete told the *NME*. "The group has been getting a great feeling of satisfaction from the dates we've played. We'd like to reach the stage where our record success becomes secondary to concerts, and I think we might be getting there."

TUESDAY, 5 DECEMBER
Keith and wife Kim were among the guests at the opening of the Beatles' Apple boutique at 94 Baker Street, London. News cameras were on hand to cover the star-studded party, and footage of the Moons' arrival was included in a three minute B&W Movietone newsreel.

WEDNESDAY, 6 DECEMBER
University, Hull.

FRIDAY, 8 DECEMBER
University, Durham.

FRIDAY, 15 DECEMBER
The Who Sell Out was released in the U.K., reaching no higher than #13. The intended release date of 17

November had been put back while Track awaited written agreement from the firms mentioned on the album, namely Heinz Baked Beans, Odorono deodorant, Medac germicidal cream, and Charles Atlas. The jingles company responsible for the Radio London ads filed a lawsuit claiming unauthorised use; it was settled out of court. Initial copies of the record came with a psychedelic poster, designed by artist Adrian George for Osiris Visions. The album was released in the U.S. on 6 January 1968, reaching #48 and spending a total of twenty-three weeks on the *Billboard* chart.

SATURDAY, 16 DECEMBER

Disc announced the Who were to make their film debut in a Hollywood black comedy the following summer. "We've received offers from America," said Chris Stamp, "and if the right script comes along, it could be that they will make a film at the end of their six-week American tour in March. The Who couldn't possibly make the usual pop comedy film, which is pretty frivolous. They're too macabre. I see them in black comedy, and that's what we are looking for at the moment." The paper also revealed another unrealised Who venture, the publication of a monthly American comic book to reach Britain in March. Lambert and Stamp were to appear as Mr. Sourpuss and Mr. Killjoy, two evil exploiters who "make the Who's life a misery."

Meanwhile, at 8:30 pm, the Who pre-recorded the annual Christmas edition of *Top Of The Pops*, miming to "I Can See For Miles" at Television Centre, Wood Lane. "The Best of '67," hosted by DJs Jimmy Savile, Alan Freeman, and Pete Murray, was screened in two parts, with the Who appearing in Part One, broadcast Christmas Day, 2:05—3:00 pm. The group were also glimpsed in a year-end survey, via silent film supplied by Filmfinders.

SUNDAY, 17 DECEMBER

As they had appeared in the pilot of *Twice A Fortnight* (see 15 October), so the Who were invited back to Lime Grove to record the final programme (Show 10, sub-titled "Now Or Never") at 4:30 pm in Studio G. The group mimed to a pre-recorded version of "Mary Anne With The Shaky Hand," similar to the acoustic *Sell Out* arrangement, with added camera effects. The show was broadcast Saturday, 23 December, 11:05—11:35 pm. Palmer later used a 40 second extract for his *All My Loving* documentary. (See 10 March 1968.)

MONDAY, 18 DECEMBER

The Pavilion, Bath.

SATURDAY, 30 DECEMBER

Pier Ballroom, Hastings.

LEFT: PETE STRIKES A POSE AT NEW YORK'S VILLAGE THEATRE, 25 NOVEMBER.

AMAZING JOURNEY
1968

spent more than £5000 on equipment, but neglected to supply adequate microphones. Australian PAs couldn't hope to compete with the sophisticated sound systems the Who took for granted, and consequently, the shows were a murky din. Sir Henry Bolte, the Australian Premier, condemned both groups as "a mob of crummy hooligans" and promoters got cold feet about booking overseas rock acts for some time. Pete Townshend publicly vowed never to return, a promise he has kept to this day.

Two exceptionally gruelling coast-to-coast American and Canadian treks occupied the spring and summer. The group played everywhere from ballrooms and stadiums to school gymnasiums and outdoor state fairs, while shows in San Francisco and New York were recorded by Kit Lambert for a shelved live album. The surviving reels from the Fillmore East prove, beyond any doubt, the Who's visceral power as a live act without equal.

Off the road, each member returned to some semblance of normality, or in Keith's case, tried to. He, Kim, and two-year-old Mandy resided in upmarket Highgate Village, but cosy domesticity made Moon feel like a caged tiger. If he wasn't busy taking advantage of what London's nightlife had to offer, he moped around the flat, blowing the windows out with his antique shotgun.

In May, Pete married his girlfriend, Karen Astley, the eldest daughter of composer/arranger Ted Astley, and the couple moved into a three-storey Georgian townhouse overlooking the River Thames in Twickenham. Inside, the walls were filled with portraits of Meher Baba, with one Baba picture even given pride of place in the new Lincoln Continental Pete had shipped over from San Francisco. As with his bachelor pads, Townshend spent around £8000 installing his own studio, equipped with two organs, various guitars, a jumbled drum-kit (a gift from Keith), bongos, an upright piano, and 8-track recording equipment. On the bookshelf, next to countless records stacked against giant speakers, Baba's *The Everything and the Nothing* rubbed shoulders with *The Art Of Counterpoint*, *Rhythmic Structure*, and the scores to *Faust* and Verdi's *La Traviata*. Within these confines, Pete conceived and recorded the demos for *Tommy*, still being referred to under such guises as *The Amazing Journey*, *The Brain Opera*, and *The Deaf, Dumb And Blind Boy*.

John and wife Alison finished decorating their semi-detached near Gunnersbury Park, Acton.

"We'd had that tremendous two years of success and then something had gone wrong. We were masters of the art. We were the best Who type band around..." —Pete Townshend

Apart from some sporadic recording, ostensibly to produce a single sorely needed to restore their standing in Britain, the Who spent the bulk of the year touring abroad.

An Australasian jaunt in January with the Small Faces and ex-Manfred Mann singer Paul Jones was an unhappy one for all concerned. Before the artists had even set foot on antipodean soil, there was considerable bad press regarding foreign entertainers taking funds out of the economy. An incident on

board a commercial flight involving an air hostess was exaggerated out of all proportion in the media. Tensions finally snapped in Wellington, New Zealand, when a twenty-first birthday party for Faces singer Steve Marriott turned into a destructive vent of revenge. It became perhaps the first example of hotel smashing, that dubious road pastime perfected throughout the next decade.

Not only was the group plagued with negative publicity, their music also suffered. The promoter

Visitors to the house were greeted by "Henry," a complete suit of armour in the hallway, and Jason, an enormous Irish wolfhound. Opening local fêtes and charity bazaars became second nature to "the mayor of Ealing," as he was playfully dubbed by the others. Following Pete's lead, John installed his own home studio. In the wake of "Boris The Spider" and "Silas Stingy," Lambert had encouraged him to write an album's worth of songs for children. "I wrote about fifteen songs for this album," John said. "I wrote a song about a bogey man and a witch called Horrid Olive, scary things like that. A lot of my songs were left over from that period when I got into writing these horror songs for kids!"

ABOVE: JOHN AND THE GARGANTUAN JASON.

Roger had changed markedly from the volatile bossman of three short years before. Although still capable of arguing his side in group policy, verbally or otherwise, his fiery temperament had cooled enough for him to be nicknamed "Peaceful Perce," a nod to his Percy Road origins. Part of this new-found placidness could be attributed to a change in lifestyle. Daltrey was now more likely to be found renovating his fifteenth-century cottage at Hurst, in the Berkshire countryside, than driving up to London in his Corvette for an evening's clubbing. Having separated from his first wife Jacqueline, he met American model Heather Taylor while on tour. She abandoned her career to be with him and the two settled into rural domesticity, marrying three years later.

In June, the Who returned to the States for a nine week tour, receiving slightly better fees.

"I think it was America that really brought us together," Daltrey told Gary Herman. "It was like the four of us and a couple of road managers on a desert island, so we just had to come together 'cause there was nobody else." Reaching San Francisco, *Rolling Stone* editor Jann Wenner awarded them "Group of the Year," a supreme accolade coming from an influential rock paper that normally extolled the virtues of the Bay Area's acid rock. Following one of three Fillmore West shows Townshend gave the first and perhaps, most important of many intelligent,

self-critical, and often contradictory interviews to Jann Wenner, which sealed his status as one of rock's most eloquent spokesmen. During the course of the long (and wired) conversation, Townshend articulated the storyline for *Tommy* in detail for the first time—a blueprint which once made public, he later found frustratingly hard to deviate from.

A similar interview was given to the *San Francisco Express Times*. "The album will open as Charlie and Elsie Snerd gave birth to a boy called Tommy who was born deaf, dumb, and blind," Pete explained. "The mother and the father and the family and everybody is very fucked up because they've given birth to a deaf, dumb, and blind kid. And he doesn't know this. All he gets is feeling, this thing which we as musicians are giving him... He hears his own name which I'd like to be Tommy or Colin and he bases a whole thing around his name."

Much of that summer was spent discussing the idea with the rest of the group in hotel rooms and aeroplanes. "Roger seemed to quite like the idea, Keith would always go along with whatever I suggested, and John quite liked the idea and was quite keen on writing something for it," Townshend told Richard Barnes. To his surprise and gratitude, the others generously left him to work unaided on the project upon returning to England.

While the Who's stock continued to rise in America, it was a different state of affairs in their homeland. "The English scene for us, unfortunately, doesn't compare with America," Pete told *Melody Maker*. "The States offers us more money, fans, and excitement." Remarks like this didn't help, but the indignity of accepting bookings for a vastly reduced rate—sometimes as low as £50 a night , mostly at universities—became a harsh reality as the debts continued to mount.

In a fickle marketplace, where a group was measured by the success of its last single, the Who were floundering. "Dogs," Townshend's bizarre but endearing comic tribute to the White City dog track, inspired by his friend Chris Morphet's obsession with greyhound racing, stalled at #25. Like "I Can See For Miles" before it, "Magic Bus" was dragged out of mothballs when the group required an "instant" single. "['Magic Bus'] was written about the same time as 'My Generation,'" he told Keith

RIGHT: Pete established a reputation as one of rock's most astute interviewees.

Altham. "It was recorded at a time when we had just returned from our first [sic] trip to America, having been conned left, right, and centre, and no one really wanted to make a single except Kit Lambert, whose job was to see that we did. We all got absolutely paralytic drunk one lunch time and by the time we arrived at the studio, no one cared what we did." Townshend later cited "Magic Bus" as the song he most enjoyed playing live with the Who.

Impatient for new product and with the group safely 6000 miles (9656km) out of the picture, U.S. Decca unleashed in September the deceptively titled *Magic Bus: The Who On Tour*, the ultimate in record company exploitation. When some form of repackaging had been hinted at earlier by Decca, the group had pushed for a collection of early singles that had been either overlooked or were long since unavailable in America, light-heartedly calling it *The Who's Greatest Flops*. Ignoring this sound advice, an indifferent grab-bag of B-sides, EP tracks, and already-issued album cuts—anything but the live tracks the title alluded to—was given the nod. For all of Chris Stamp's valiant attempts at bringing U.S. Decca drastically up-to-date, it seemed this particular leopard couldn't change its spots. The Who and their audience were not amused.

The release was "a culmination of all the most terrible things American record companies ever get up to," Townshend told Chris van Ness. "Plus the fact that they made it look like a live album. I mean, that's the worst thing that's ever gone down, and there are a few people in the L.A. part of Decca that I won't even look at, because they were there at the photo session, knowing it was for an album cover."

Despite the relative failures of "I Can See For Miles," "Dogs," and "Magic Bus," Townshend passionately felt the art of the rock single could be expanded and made to do more. He had rashly talked to anyone that would listen about his grand moves towards composing a larger, conceptual piece—a series of three-minute vignettes with linked story lines that could stand alone as singles, but could also be listened to as a continuous whole.

In danger of being overshadowed by the latest underground Johnny-come-latelys, in September the Who started recording—a last-ditch, make or break attempt at reversing their fortunes. Under Kit Lambert's pervasive influence, Pete's idea gradually metamorphosed into the more theatrical concept of "Rock Opera." Early attacks on the publicised idea

made Pete both defensive and defiant. "I don't consider the album to be sick at all," he told *Disc* in November. "In fact, what I was out to show is that someone who suffers terribly at the hands of society has the ability to turn all these experiences into a tremendous musical awareness. Sickness is in the mind of the listener, and I don't give a damn what people think." Initially intended as a single

album of related tracks, the band scrapped the first attempt and virtually started again from scratch.

At year's end, the group undertook a final British package tour with the Small Faces, Joe Cocker, and the Crazy World of Arthur Brown, and also appeared as guests on *The Rolling Stones Rock And Roll Circus*. This ambitious television special represented the last true gasp of open camaraderie among the 60's rock hierarchy. Having performed it relentlessly for the better part of a year around the globe, the Who turned in a tour-de-force performance of "A Quick One" that arguably outshone their hosts. The Stones, with a fast-fading Brian Jones,

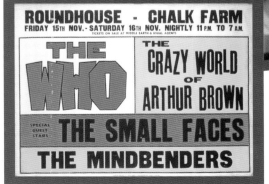

ABOVE: FILMING
*The Rolling Stones
Rock And Roll Circus.*

had been off the road for eighteen months and didn't appear until the early hours to a tired and depleted audience—one of the many reasons for the film's ignominious fate, sitting unseen until the *Circus* finally came to town in 1996.

1
9
6
8

1968

WEDNESDAY, 3 JANUARY
Bal Tabarin Club, Downham Way, Bromley.

THURSDAY, 4 JANUARY
Recording/mixing CBS: "Faith In Something Bigger,"
completed 14 January. The track lay unissued until
John remixed the mono 4-track master into stereo in
1973 for inclusion on *Odds and Sods*.

FRIDAY, 5 JANUARY
Recording/mixing IBC: "Dr. Jekyll And Mr. Hyde,"
John's ode to rooming with Keith on the Herman's
Hermits tour, completed 14 January.

SATURDAY, 6 JANUARY
Civic Hall, Nantwich, Cheshire.

MONDAY, 8 JANUARY
Silver Blades Ice Rink, Bristol.

TUESDAY, 9 JANUARY
The Brave New World Club, Southsea, Portsmouth.

THURSDAY, 11 JANUARY
Assembly Hall, Worthing.

FRIDAY, 12 JANUARY
Royal Ballroom, Tottenham, North London.

SATURDAY, 13 JANUARY
Dreamland Ballroom, Margate.

Recording/mixing IBC Studio A: "Glow Girl," a
plane crash reincarnation story (see 14 August
1967), completed 11 February.

In an *NME* interview with Keith Altham (dated
20 January), Pete mentioned the group was "working
along the lines of a very slow ballad-type number, like
'Strangers In the Night,' with a wild guitar sound laid
over the top" for English release.

An interview with Pete appeared in controversial
pop pundit Jonathan King's weekly chat show *Good
Evening*, transmitted live from 5:50—6:15 pm over certain ITV regions.

ABOVE: Arriving in Wellington, New Zealand, 30 January. From left are Bob Pridden, John, Steve Marriott, Keith, Pete, Roger (with female friend), "Wiggy" Wolff, and Ronnie Lane.

FRIDAY, 19 JANUARY
A jet-lagged Who, with Bob Pridden and John Wolff,
arrived at Mascot Airport, Sydney, Australia, after a
36-hour Qantas flight from London via Cairo, Bombay,
Karachi, and Singapore. "I think it all started when we
rolled off the plane and weren't very co-operative with
the press," said Wolff. "They herded us into a room
and the boys were all shattered from the long flight
and just didn't want to know." It was an ill omen for a
ten-day trouble-plagued tour of the antipodes, titled
"The Big Show." Jointly promoted by Aztec Services,
Stadiums, and Harry M. Miller Attractions, the Who
topped the bill over the Small Faces, ex-Manfred Mann
singer Paul Jones (in place of John Walker who was
originally booked), and Australian group, the
Questions. They had barely enough time to rest before
catching a connecting flight north to Brisbane, arriving
at 1:55 pm Australian time.

SATURDAY, 20 JANUARY
Festival Hall, Brisbane, Queensland. Two shows, 6:00
& 8:45 pm.

MONDAY, 22 and TUESDAY, 23 JANUARY
Stadium, Sydney, New South Wales. Two shows per
night, 6:00 & 8:45 pm.

During the early show on the 22nd, the venue's
revolving stage stuck as a result of the sheer weight
of the equipment. Consequently, a large part of the
audience had an obstructed view. Promoter Harry Miller
allowed these people to stay on for the second house,
but the stage was still stuck fast for that performance.
On the 23rd, both the Small Faces and Who were
accused of using obscene language onstage, warranting
a police investigation.

THURSDAY, 25 and FRIDAY, 26 JANUARY
Festival Hall, Melbourne, Victoria. Two shows per
night, 6:00 & 8:45 pm.

SATURDAY, 27 JANUARY
Centennial Hall, Adelaide, South Australia. Two
shows, 6:00 & 8:45 pm.

The early show started an hour late as Pete remained
in Melbourne to look for an emergency guitar replacement.

SUNDAY, 28 JANUARY

The entourage boarded a 7:00 am internal Ansett flight to Sydney via Melbourne. Without explanation, air hostess Susan Jones served refreshments to the passengers seated adjacent to the tour party, but ignored their demands for service. When Bob Pridden rose to complain, he was addressed, "Sit down, you scruffy little man!" An off-duty pilot in uniform, Captain L. Jacobs, accused the groups of being drunk and using foul language. When the hostesses complained of the group's alleged behaviour, pilot Captain Douglas Way radioed ahead some 127 miles (204km) to Melbourne, and as the aircraft taxied into Essendon Airport, two lines of State and Commonwealth police escorted the party of nineteen off the plane. The groups were held in the VIP lounge by police and airport security, accused of "behaving in such a manner as to constitute a risk to the aircraft."

The pilot of the connecting flight, Captain R. Stanton, refused to allow them on board his plane. Eventually, after a delay of more than three hours and assurances of good behaviour, the party were allowed to leave at 4:15 pm and escorted to a chartered Electra by four Department of Civil Aviation officers, two of whom remained on board for an uneventful flight to Sydney. The whole sorry affair was immortalised in John Entwistle's "Postcard" the following year. Upon arrival at Kingsford Smith Airport, the English musicians were taken by bus across to the International Terminal to board a 6:15 pm flight to New Zealand, arriving in Auckland at 11:00 pm.

MONDAY, 29 JANUARY

Town Hall, Auckland, New Zealand. Two shows, 6:00 & 8:30 pm.

Pete Townshend publicly announced he would never set foot in Australia again. "The final humiliation came when the police turned up at the airport," he said. "We were victims. The crew set out to humiliate us and they succeeded." Between shows, the Who stormed back to the Logan Park Motor Lodge, threatening to pull out due to the inferior P.A. system provided. The late show was delayed 45 minutes while technicians found replacement microphones. By show's end, a total of seven mikes had been smashed beyond repair. The tour flew south to Wellington the following day, celebrating Steve Marriott's twenty-first birthday in riotous fashion at the Waterloo Hotel.

WEDNESDAY, 31 JANUARY

Town Hall, Wellington, New Zealand. Two shows, 6:00 & 8:30 pm.

THURSDAY, 1 FEBRUARY

The Who and the Small Faces flew out of New Zealand, travelling home via Auckland, Fiji, Honolulu, and San Francisco. *The Truth*, a New Zealand tabloid, printed its own invective-filled epitaph on 6 February, entitled "Paul Rodgers Boos Who." According to the article, "They're the scruffiest bunch of Poms that ever milked money from this country's kids... they took nearly 8000 teenagers for $2.60 to $3.60 each. All the kids got for their money was an ear-splitting cacophony that was neither musical nor funny... They did more to harm the British image in a few days than Harold Wilson or Edward Heath could do in ten years. I'm ashamed to have come from the same country as these unwashed, foul-mouthed, booze swilling no-hopers. Britain can have them."

SATURDAY, 10 FEBRUARY

"Valentine '68," Essex University, Colchester, Essex.

SUNDAY, 11 FEBRUARY

Starlight Ballroom, Crawley.

Recording/mixing IBC Studio A, with Kit Lambert and Damon Lyon-Shaw: "Glow Girl," plus backing tracks for "Call Me Lightning" (written and demoed by Pete in late-1964) and "Little Billy's Doing Fine." Copies of both tracks were made at De Lane Lea on 14 February, to be completed and mixed at Gold Star, Hollywood, on 26 February. Like "Faith In Something Bigger" (see 4 January), "Glow Girl" remained unreleased until *Odds and Sods* in 1974. The song's coda ("It's a girl, Mrs. Walker") was reworked as "It's A Boy" for *Tommy*.

FRIDAY, 16 FEBRUARY

University, Sheffield, with the Bonzo Dog Doo-Dah Band.

1 9 6 8

ABOVE: HOLLYWOOD HILLS PHOTO SHOOT, 26 FEBRUARY.

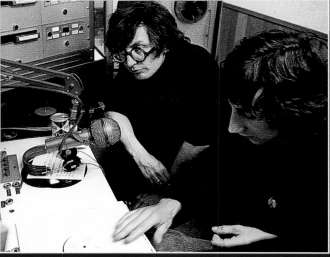

ABOVE: PETE WITH "UNCLE RUSS" GIBB AT RADIO STATION WKNR IN DETROIT.

SATURDAY, 17 FEBRUARY
Faculty of Technology Union, Students' Union Building, Manchester.

WEDNESDAY, 21 FEBRUARY
The Who commenced a six-week American and Canadian tour with an 8:00 pm show at the Civic Auditorium, San Jose, California, supported by Sagittarius and Blue Cheer.

THURSDAY, 22 FEBRUARY
Fillmore Auditorium, San Francisco, California, with the Nice (replacing the Vagrants) and jazz-player Cannonball Adderley and his Sextet. For three shows, promoter Bill Graham paid the Who the highest artist fee to date for appearing at the venue, in which he'd installed a $35,000 P.A. system.

Kit Lambert flew over to supervise the recording of this show and the following two nights at Winterland for a proposed live album, engineered by Bill Halverson, tentatively titled *The Who—Live At The Fillmore Auditorium* for June release.

Unfortunately, the tapes no longer reside in the Who's archive.

FRIDAY, 23 and SATURDAY, 24 FEBRUARY
Winterland Ballroom, San Francisco, California.

MONDAY, 26 FEBRUARY
Recording at Gold Star Studios, Los Angeles, with Kit Lambert and engineer Jim Hilton.

"Call Me Lightning" and "Little Billy's Doing Fine," commenced in London, were completed and mixed. The latter was commissioned by the American Cancer Society (despite all the Who being smokers!), who shared the same publicity firm, but remained unused as the organisation considered it too long. A similar jingle for the same purpose, "Do You Want Kids, Kids?" was supposedly submitted also, but only "Little Billy" was registered for U.S. copyright purposes on 3 March.

The Who didn't play the City of Angels on this tour, but found time to make a zany, Monkees-style

promotional clip for "Call Me Lightning," with director Austin John Marshall. Tom Wright took a series of stills of the group wearing World War I tin trench helmets and using props such as an explosives detonator. Pete described the shoot for the *NME*: "We found an old deserted warehouse in Hollywood and overcame resistance from the officious watchman by putting money in his hand. It looked very much like the factory used in the closing scenes of *The Ipcress File*." The slapstick film, starring Keith as a life-size wind-up toy being chased by the others, first aired in America on *Happening '68*, a syndicated variety show, on Saturday 27 April, and was later used in *The Kids Are Alright*, with "Cobwebs and Strange" providing the music for the Keith Moon sequence.

FRIDAY, 1 MARCH
The Agrodome, Vancouver, Canada.

The journey from California took three days via the group's hired coach.

SATURDAY, 2 MARCH
New Edmonton Gardens, Edmonton, Alberta, Canada.

FRIDAY, 8 MARCH

Metropolitan Sports Center, Bloomington, Minneapolis, Minnesota.

SATURDAY, 9 MARCH

Grande Ballroom, Detroit, Michigan.

SUNDAY, 10 MARCH

Opera House, Exposition Gardens, Peoria, Illinois.

BBC producer/director Tony Palmer, who had previously worked with the Who on his *Twice A Fortnight* series (see 15 October and 17 December 1967) was producing a serious, analytical documentary on pop and had arranged with Kit Lambert to film the Who for a fee of £210. Lambert himself was interviewed in Hollywood, while the group were filmed in less luxurious surroundings on their chartered Greyhound.

In a volte-face from his comments about musical quality on *A Whole Scene Going* (see 5 January 1966), Pete now earnestly insisted pop should be treated as a higher art form. (The full transcript of Lambert and Townshend's interviews appeared the following year in Palmer's book spin-off, *Born Under A Bad Sign*.)

All My Loving was first broadcast in black and white on Sunday, 3 November, 10:40–11:35 pm, as part of BBC-1's *Omnibus* arts series and repeated in colour on BBC-2, 18 May 1969, 9:30–10:25 pm. The Who's five minute segment featured archive film from the Railway Hotel, "Mary Anne With The Shaky Hand" from *Twice A Fortnight* (17 December 1967) and 1 min 53 secs of "My Generation" from this afternoon's Peoria show. The segment was repeated in Part 15 ("All Along The Watchtower—Sour Rock") of Palmer's ambitious 17-part follow-up, *All You Need Is Love*, first transmitted over the LWT network, 11:10—12:10 pm, 21 May 1977.

As a postscript to the Peoria show, promoter Hank Skinner withheld the balance of the group's fee, claiming they overplayed!

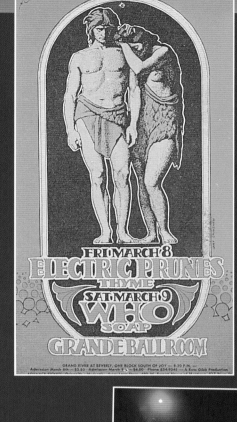

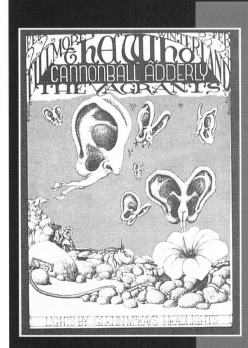

"That was the kind of world we were suddenly thrown into," Pete told Chris van Ness, "and we couldn't figure the whole thing out... The bus bill. That seemed like a fundamentally good sense thing to do. It cost us about nine thousand dollars or something. There were incredible sort of money things going on. We tipped the bus driver a hundred, and he tore it up because everybody thought that we were earning like millions of dollars."

FRIDAY, 15 MARCH

Municipal Auditorium, San Antonio, Texas.

SATURDAY, 16 MARCH

City Auditorium, Beaumont, Texas. Two shows, 3:00 & 8:00 pm.

"Call Me Lightning" B/W "Dr. Jekyll And Mr. Hyde," originally scheduled for 26 February, was rush-released as a U.S. single, but peaked at only a modest #40 on the *Billboard* chart.

SUNDAY, 17 MARCH
Music Hall, Houston, Texas. Two shows, 2:30 & 7:30 pm.

A story persists that while in Houston, the Who recorded at Sir Douglas Quintet producer Huey P. Meaux's studio. Tom Wright denies this happened, as the band flew to his parents' farm in Florida for several days' break before continuing the tour.

FRIDAY, 22 MARCH
Curtis Hixon Hall, Tampa, Florida.

SATURDAY, 23 MARCH
Code 1, Fort Lauderdale, Florida.

SUNDAY, 24 MARCH
Orlando Coliseum, Orlando, Florida.

WEDNESDAY, 27 MARCH
The Forum, Montreal, Quebec, Canada, with the Troggs.

FRIDAY, 29 MARCH
Baldwin Gymnasium, Drew University, Madison, New Jersey, with Orpheus.

SATURDAY, 30 MARCH
Westbury Music Fair, Westbury, Long Island, New York.

SUNDAY, 31 MARCH
Constitution Hall, Washington DC, with the Troggs, Orpheus, and the Beacon Street Union.

FRIDAY, 5 and SATURDAY, 6 APRIL
Fillmore East, New York City. Promoted by Bill Graham, supported by Free Spirits and Buddy Guy, with B.B King.

As at the Fillmore West, both shows were recorded on four-track. Despite being the first English group to headline over two nights at this prestigious venue, the Who's stay in New York was not a pleasant one. Civil unrest stemming from Martin Luther King's assassination on 4 April cast a pall over the concerts, which were combined into one per night at a profit loss. The entourage were shuttled between hotels, thanks to Moon's cherry bombs antics, blowing off the doors at the Gorham and the Waldorf Astoria. Pete and girlfriend Karen Astley ended up at Tom Wright's apartment, while the others slept on the tour bus.

On the morning of the 5th, the group draped themselves under a Union Jack for a photoshoot with Art Kane at the foot of Grant's Tomb, on Riverside Drive and 122nd Street, Manhattan. These photos would go on to appear in the June issue of *Life* magazine. Kane's shots later adorned *The Kids Are Alright* soundtrack and *BBC Sessions* sleeves.

While in New York, Richard Cole met up with his old employers, Keith and John, at the Salvation Club and found them considering their options. Talk centred on the possibility of forming a "supergroup" that "would go down like a lead zeppelin" (a slang variation on "going over like a lead balloon.") Various names were bandied about, including Steve Marriott, Steve Winwood, and Jimmy Page. A record sleeve was even planned to feature a German airship exploding into flames. At the time, Cole was working, off-and-on, for the Jimmy Page–era Yardbirds, and the rest, as Entwistle says, is "theft! We were always good at naming groups and designing album covers."

SUNDAY, 7 APRIL
C.N.E. Coliseum, Toronto, Canada. Promoted by Russ Gibb with the Troggs, MC5, and Raja.

MONDAY, 8 APRIL
The Who returned from the U.S. having grossed $100,000 (£30,000), though after deducting expenses, they had earned scarcely £1,000 each. The group made plans to start rehearsing and recording a (later aborted) BBC pilot for *Sound And Picture City*, produced by Tony Palmer, with Radio 1 DJs Chris Denning and Kenny Everett, as well as Caroline Coon, founder of "Release," the drug charge aid organisation. The

Who were to sing a different song each week, and at the end of the series, an album of the tracks would be released.

MONDAY, 15 APRIL
Marquee Club, London, with the Bonzo Dog Doo-Dah Band.

The Who's first gig since returning from America was a hastily arranged show at their old stomping ground (replacing Jethro Tull, who were moved to the support slot on 23 April). Keith and Pete had attended a celebratory party there on 10 April to mark the club's tenth anniversary and were interviewed by Johnny Moran for Radio 1's *Scene And Heard*, broadcast Saturday, 13 April, 6:32–7:30 pm, and repeated the following day, 4:00–5:00 pm.

TUESDAY, 23 APRIL
Marquee Club, London, with Jethro Tull. Billed as "The Return of the Fabulous Who."

"I enjoyed the Marquee show very much," Pete told *Melody Maker*'s Chris Welch. "For the first few minutes, I was very scared the whole thing was going to go wrong, but the audience was lovely. Although we've played there hundreds of times, it seemed strange to play such a small place after the States. I smashed up two guitars at the end of the show, because one I was using had recently been repaired and broke as I came on stage, so I played another one I use for recording. At the end, I thought, 'What the hell,' and smashed them both. The Gibson Stereo cost £200 and the amps, which were borrowed, will

RIGHT: Marquee Club, 23 April.

cost about £20 each to repair. I can't put it down to tax because when I say I use 70 guitars a year, they don't believe me."

SATURDAY, 27 APRIL

The Who were billed among the guests appearing in a special edition of BBC-1's *Dee Time*, introduced by host Simon Dee, live from the 1968 Golden Rose of Montreux Television Festival, but the transmission sheets reveal the Who did not appear.

MONDAY, 29 APRIL

Top Rank Suite, Watford, with Geno Washington's Ram Jam Band and the Free Expression.

FRIDAY, 3 MAY

University, Hull.

For the "Pre-Rag Ball," the Who appeared in place of the Crazy World Of Arthur Brown, who had been sought to replace the original choice of the Jimi Hendrix Experience.

SATURDAY, 4 MAY

University, Liverpool.

In an interview with *Disc*, Pete revealed that the Who's next ten-week American tour could well be their last: "It's alright onstage and the audiences are quite incredible. But you just keep slogging away, travelling the highways and the freeways and the byways and the airways... You can't work, you can't think—your mind's blanked out." (The Who were currently the fourth biggest American draw behind Cream, the Jimi Hendrix Experience, and the Doors.)

The same issue reported that the group's U.S. single, "Call Me Lightning," due for release in Britain the previous day, had been withdrawn, as it felt "unrepresentative of our current sound. In the next few weeks, we hope to record an opera as a complete LP, and we'll probably take a single off that. I've been talking about doing opera for so long. It's called *The Amazing Journey*, and the single might very well be 'I Am A Farmer,' but we're not quite sure about that yet."

WEDNESDAY, 8 MAY

Pete was filmed as a guitar-playing cowboy in Wallingford, Oxfordshire, for the end credit stills sequence to *Lone Ranger*, scripted and directed by Richard Stanley for his diploma at the Royal College of Art. The 22 minute, 16-mm, black-and-white film was photographed by Chris Morphet, edited by Alfreda Benge, with assistant directors Storm Thorgerson (later Pink Floyd's designer) and David Gale—all fellow RCA film students.

Shot around South Kensington and Knightsbridge during January and February, the film featured Matthew Scurfield as Beaky, a young drifter, Chris Cornford as his father, and Pete as a musician friend. "We edited the film roughly without sound," Stanley remembered, "then Pete wrote and recorded the incidental music, which the film was then fine cut to."

The soundtrack, recorded throughout April in Pete's studio in his top floor flat at 20 Ebury Street, Victoria (where Stanley was temporarily lodging), featured Townshend (guitar, bass, drums, organ, tape effects, vocals), Morphet (harmonica, vocals), Stanley (tape effects, vocals), and Scurfield (lead vocal on "Lone Ranger Theme").

Distributed through The Other Cinema, Wardour Street, *Lone Ranger* went on to win prizes at the prestigous Chicago and Nyons festivals. (See 6 September 1969.)

SATURDAY, 11 MAY

Strathclyde University, Glasgow, Scotland.

"America is like the Marquee Club in London, only ten million times larger," Keith told *Record Mirror*, describing how the Who's following was spreading in America by the same word-of-mouth process. "We're in an interim sort of position at the moment, both over here and in America, because although we've established a name for ourselves in both countries, we're not really an established group.

What the Who really need is a million seller, and I think we ought to stay in England and just flood the U.S. market with records until we achieve that... I think that at the moment we're losing out both in America and England, because we're not spending enough concentrated time in each country."

MONDAY, 20 MAY

In a noon ceremony at Didcot Registry Office, Oxfordshire, Pete married his fiancée, twenty-year-old dress designer Karen Astley, whom he'd met five years earlier at Ealing Art College. A reception was held at the Astley residence, but there was to be no honeymoon as Pete was "too engrossed in completing a new British single for the Who."

WEDNESDAY, 22 MAY

Recording/mixing at Advision Sound Recording Studios, 83 New Bond Street, London: "Dogs," with Pete on piano.

FRIDAY, 24 MAY

The City University, Clerkenwell, East London.

WEDNESDAY, 29 MAY

Recording/mixing: "Melancholia," Benny Spellman's "Fortune Teller," and Johnny Kidd's "Shakin' All Over."

ABOVE: Pete filming "The Lone Ranger" with Chris Morphet and Richard Stanley (back) and Matthew Scurfield.

ABOVE: Pete's wedding, 20 May.

"At Advision, we spent hours getting a sound done," said Pete. "At the end, we'd finished recording and Kit Lambert turned around to the engineer and said, 'That'll do for a demo!'"

While at Advision, a demo of "Magic Bus," and a backing track for "Now I'm A Farmer" were laid down. "Magic Bus," featuring Jess Roden, singer with the Alan Bown!, on backing vocals, was recorded at IBC—on more than one occasion as Damon Lyon-Shaw recalled: "The band wanted to do the track all live. So we miked everything up, and it sounded just dynamic. Kit went off with the 8-track master and left it in a taxi, and that's the last we saw of it." Most, if not all of these tracks were possibly short-listed for *Who's For Tennis?*—a straw-clutching idea of Lambert's to release an album in time for Wimbledon fortnight.

While in the studio, Pete was interviewed for a colour CBS documentary on the contemporary rock scene, although title and broadcast details are unknown. A clip was extracted and used in an ABC network special *The Heroes Of Rock'n'Roll*, broadcast 9 February 1979.

FRIDAY, 31 MAY
University, Manchester.

TUESDAY, 11 JUNE
The Who were originally booked to headline the St. John's College Ball, Cambridge, with Spooky Tooth and the Scaffold.

Student Union representative Peter Rudge (who'd booked the group a year earlier on 12 June), was given insufficient notice that the Who would not be appearing. "I got this phone call telling me that Keith was ill, and the band couldn't appear," Rudge remembered. "I thought they were up to something, so I jumped on the train and came down to London to have it out with Kit. On the noticeboard in his office, I saw my gig was crossed out, and instead, they were going to make a promotional film at the Walthamstow dog racing track."

Rudge made a forcible enough impression on Lambert to walk out with a job offer. After graduating, he started work as Track office boy on 1 October. Thanks to his skills in arranging the Who's opera house concerts a year later, Rudge was promoted to the role of tour organiser, a position he held until 1976.

FRIDAY, 14 JUNE
University, Leicester, with P.P. Arnold.

"Dogs" B/W "Call Me Lightning" was released, becoming the Who's first British single (discounting the unauthorised Talmy Brunswick releases) to fail to reach the Top Ten. It peaked at #25.

SATURDAY, 15 JUNE
London College of Printing, Elephant and Castle, London, supported by the Alan Bown! Jess Roden came back to sing backing vocals on "Magic Bus," as he had done on the original recording.

MONDAY, 17 JUNE
The Who pre-recorded a *Top Of The Pops* insert for "Dogs" at Studio G, Lime Grove, broadcast 20 June, 7:30—8:00 pm.

FRIDAY, 21 JUNE
University, Durham, with Status Quo, the Nashville Teens, and Ray McVay and His Orchestra.

SATURDAY, 22 JUNE
The Who were guests of honour at the annual Greyhound Derby, where Yellow Printer and Camera Flash (the canines immortalised in "Dogs") were running. The previous weekend, the group had gone to Waltham Abbey for a photo opportunity, watching Yellow Printer train with owner Pauline Wallace.

FRIDAY, 28 and SATURDAY, 29 JUNE
The Who's fourth American and Canadian tour, extended from three to nine weeks, commenced with two standing-room only Pinnacle Dance Concerts at the Shrine Exposition Hall, Los Angeles. The acts also included Peter Green's Fleetwood Mac, the Crazy World Of Arthur Brown, and the Single Wing Turquoise Bird light show. The Steve Miller Band was an added attraction on the 29th, as Arthur Brown played only one set after breaking two bones in his foot. As well as the usual song-list, the Who's sets included "Mary Anne With The Shaky Hand" and "Silas Stingy." 8-mm mute colour footage shot at the

Shrine was used during the "Magic Bus" sequence in the 1997 VH-1 cable special *Legends: The Who*.

MONDAY, 8 JULY
Memorial Auditorium, Sacramento, California, with Iron Butterfly, and the Neighbourhood Children, with lights by the Light Brigade.

WEDNESDAY, 10 JULY
Stampede Corral, Calgary, Alberta, Canada. Two shows, 2:00 & 8:30 pm.

THURSDAY, 11 JULY
Saskatoon Arena, Saskatchewan, Canada.

FRIDAY, 12 JULY
Indiana Beach Ballroom, Monticello, Indiana. Two shows, 8:45 & 10:30 pm.

SATURDAY, 13 JULY
Grande Ballroom, Detroit, Michigan.

Two shows promoted by Russ Gibb, 6:00—9:00 pm, supported by the Frost, featuring future Lou Reed and

ABOVE: KEITH AND BOB PRIDDEN PERFORM "MAGIC BUS" AT THE GRANDE BALLROOM, 13 JULY.

Alice Cooper guitarist Dick Wagner, and 10:00—1:00 am, with the Psychedelic Stooges, featuring Iggy Pop.

SUNDAY, 14 JULY

Musicarnival, Cleveland, Ohio.

The Who were dissatisfied with the Sunn sound system provided and started smashing gear early in the set at this 2500 seat theatre-in-the-round tent, sparking a minor riot. The group continued on borrowed equipment from support act Cyrus Erie, featuring singer Eric Carmen (later of the Raspberries).

MONDAY, 15 JULY

Memorial Centre, Kingston, Ontario, Canada.

The group had trouble entering Canada after Roger and Pete's passports were stolen in Cleveland.

TUESDAY, 16 JULY

Civic Centre, Ottawa, Canada, with the Troggs and the Ohio Express.

WEDNESDAY, 17 JULY

Autostade Stadium, Montreal, Canada. Two shows, 2:00 & 7:00 pm.

THURSDAY, 18 JULY

Rhode Island Auditorium, Providence, Rhode Island, with Blood, Sweat and Tears.

SATURDAY, 20 JULY

Civic Center (a.k.a., the Dome), Virginia Beach, Virginia. Two shows, 8:00 & 10:30 pm, with the Troggs.

SUNDAY, 21 JULY

Oakdale Music Theatre, Wallingford, Connecticut.

TUESDAY, 23 JULY

The Mosque, Richmond, Virginia. Two shows, 7:00 & 9:30 pm, with the Troggs.

WEDNESDAY, 24 JULY

JFK Stadium, Philadelphia, Pennsylvania, with Pink Floyd and the Troggs.

FRIDAY, 26 JULY

Saint Bernard Civic Auditorium, Chalemette, Lousiana. Two shows with the People.

SATURDAY, 27 JULY

Orlando Sports Stadium, Orlando, Florida, with the People.

To capitalise on the tour, Decca rush-released "Magic Bus" B/W "Someone's Coming," which

reached #25 in *Billboard*. The group performed it live with "Ben Pump" (Bob Pridden) on claves and backing vocals. Its release in the U.K. didn't occur until Friday, 11 October. Like its predecessor "Dogs," "Magic Bus" failed to make a significant impression on the British charts, reaching #26 (#22 on the *NME* chart.)

SUNDAY, 28 JULY

Marine Stadium, Miami, Florida, with the Ohio Express and the People.

MONDAY, 29 JULY

Tamarack Lodge, Ellenville, New York.

WEDNESDAY, 31 JULY

The New Place, Algonquin, Illinois.

THURSDAY, 1 AUGUST

The 'Lectric Theatre, Chicago, Illinois.

FRIDAY, 2 AUGUST

Singer Bowl, Flushing Meadows, Queens, New York City, with the Doors and the Kangaroo.

The first of a three-concert package, promoted by Shelley Finkel and Gary Kurfist. A near sell-out crowd of 16,000 attended the show, held on a 50-foot (15m) revolving stage, which broke down. This, a late start, and the extended intermission between bands contributed to a hostile atmosphere.

Tensions were further raised between the Who and the Doors road crews over some of the latter's gear being trashed when the Who closed the first half. Pete demolished his amps and guitar, while Keith kicked his drums across the stage and threw his cymbals high in the air. 8-mm colour footage was used during the "Magic Bus" sequence in VH-1's *Legends: The Who*.

Watching Jim Morrison's dark theatrics incite an already restless crowd to riot, Pete was simultaneously appalled and fascinated when a girl was badly injured, falling head first from the stage while trying to elude stagehands. The incident inspired "Sally Simpson" for *Tommy*.

SATURDAY, 3 AUGUST

Majestic Hills Theater, Lake Geneva, Wisconsin.

SUNDAY, 4 AUGUST

Melody Fair, Wurlitzer Park, North Tonawanda, Buffalo, New York.

TUESDAY, 6 AUGUST

Music Hall, Boston, Massachusetts. Two shows, 7:30 & 9:30 pm.

Jon Rubin shot an 8-mm colour film showing Keith smashing his kit. Director Jeff Stein later used this in *The Kids Are Alright*, with dubbed smashing effects and crowd noise.

WEDNESDAY, 7 AUGUST

The Schaefer Music Festival, Wollman Skating Rink, Central Park, New York City, with The Mandala. Two shows, 8:00 & 10:30 pm, promoted by Ron Delsener, before 10,500.

FRIDAY, 9 AUGUST

Illinois State Fairgrounds, Springfield, Illinois, with the Association.

SATURDAY, 10 AUGUST

Jaguar Club, St. Charles, Illinois.

ABOVE: SINGER BOWL, NEW YORK CITY, 2 AUGUST.

TUESDAY, 13—THURSDAY, 15 AUGUST

Fillmore West, San Francisco, California. One show per night, supported by the James Cotton Blues Band and Magic Sam.

FRIDAY, 16 AUGUST

Selland Arena, Fresno, California, with Quicksilver Messenger Service.

SATURDAY, 17 AUGUST

Municipal (Giants) Stadium, Phoenix, Arizona, with Quicksilver Messenger Service.

SUNDAY, 18 AUGUST

Kelker Junction Concert Hall, Colorado Springs, Colorado.

THURSDAY, 22 AUGUST

Music Hall, Kansas City, Missouri.

Returning from the gig, the group's car was badly rammed by another vehicle, requiring an overnight hospital stay. Although shaken, none of the band were seriously injured.

FRIDAY, 23 and SATURDAY, 24 AUGUST

Wedgewood Village Amusement Park, Oklahoma City, Oklahoma.

On the 24th, the Who played a 3:15 pm matinee, in addition to the 8:15 pm show.

MONDAY, 26 AUGUST

Civic Auditorium, San Jose, California.

TUESDAY, 27 AUGUST

Community Concourse, San Diego, California.

"We were booked into the basement of the San Diego Civic Center," Pete remembered. "It looked like a parking garage. Some photographer took a picture of us mutilating our instruments. He sold it to *Newsweek*, and we were on our way."

WEDNESDAY, 28 AUGUST

Civic Auditorium, Santa Monica, California, with the James Cotton Blues Band.

Two shows were originally scheduled at 7:00 pm & 10:00 pm, but because of poor ticket sales, only the early show went ahead.

THURSDAY, 29 AUGUST
Earl Warren Showgrounds, Santa Barbara, California.

The Who returned to England on Sunday 1 September.

THURSDAY, 5 SEPTEMBER
Local lad Keith was one of a number of celebrities participating in a Wembley charity scooter race. Coverage was included in BBC-1's arts/sketch programme *How It Is*, broadcast Friday 13 September, 6:00—6:40 pm. Johnny Moran took the opportunity to interview Keith for Radio 1's *Scene And Heard*, intended for broadcast on 21 September, but delayed until the 28th, 6:32—7:30 pm, and then repeated two days later, 7:45—8:45 pm.

THURSDAY, 19 SEPTEMBER
The Who commenced recording sessions for *The Deaf, Dumb And Blind Boy*—the working title for *Tommy*—in Studio A at IBC. The studio was block-booked Monday through Friday from 2:00—10:00 pm, though sessions often extended into the following morning. Sessions produced by Kit Lambert and engineered on eight-track by Damon Lyon-Shaw.

In addition to their regular instruments, Pete played piano and organ and John, French horn. Having exhausted Premier's tolerance, Keith used a new double kit belonging to roadie Tony Haslam.

Pete's younger brothers, Paul and Simon, were enlisted to contribute some of the higher backing vocals.

Among the first tracks recorded was Mose Allison's "Young Man Blues," a live favourite intended to somehow be incorporated into the opera's framework. When this proved impracticable, the track was considered as a stop-gap single while the group toiled on *Tommy*. This didn't occur either, and it sat unissued until appearing on *The House That Track Built* sampler in July 1969. A slower, alternate take appeared on the *Odds and Sods* CD (1998).

SUNDAY, 22 SEPTEMBER
An interview with Pete appeared in *The New York Times*. "I know people want something new," he told Michael Lydon. "They want a new reason to go to a rock and roll concert. What we're going to try is opera, not something trashy like the pompous arty types do. They do fancy things because they can't play. We've done mini-operas, now we want a long thing around a theme. I've been thinking of a story—about a deaf, dumb and blind kid, with dialogue, action, and an incredible finale. I want to get into stuff that will leave the smashing way behind."

FRIDAY, 27 SEPTEMBER
Pete talked about the Who's plans for overseas radio broadcast only via the BBC's Transcription Service at Bush House, Aldwych, London.

SATURDAY, 5 OCTOBER
The Roundhouse, Chalk Farm, London. "Middle Earth" show with Blossom Toes and the Fox.

The Who's first show since returning from the States. Originally booked for a 45 minute spot, they ended up playing for over an hour and a half, concluding with Pete snapping his guitar across his knee, pounding it with a mike stand, and finally kicking his speakers off the back of the stage.

Earlier that day, to help jumpstart "Magic Bus," the Who hired a one-hundred-year-old, green, open-topped London Transport double decker bus and packed it with a lion, a baby elephant, a parrot, and models hired by the Annie Walker agency (who provided the nudes for Jimi Hendrix's *Electric Ladyland* sleeve). The bus set out at 11:00 am from the BBC's Lime Grove studio in the direction of Porchester Place and Bayswater Road, making its way through Oxford Street, Regent Street, Shaftesbury Avenue,

Trafalgar Square, Fleet Street, and Holborn before returning via Haymarket, Piccadilly, Knightsbridge, and stopping in Chelsea's Kings Road to let Pete off.

Chris Stamp filmed the journey, intended to be shown on the BBC's *How It Is* as a promotional clip for the single. (The 16-mm colour film was not used, as the group ended up appearing personally on 11 October.) When the bus arrived back at the BBC, Keith prophetically yelled, "I bet the record doesn't even make the charts after this!" A repeat journey via the same route occurred on 18 October.

MONDAY, 7 OCTOBER
The Who made a flying visit to Bremen, Germany, to record an insert for "Magic Bus" on NDR- TV's *Beat Club* for a fee of £60. Introduced by Dave Lee Travis, Keith's particularly frenetic miming sent his toms crashing over as the song concluded. It was transmitted on Saturday, 12 October (Show 36), repeated on 16 November (Show 37), and appeared in *The Kids Are Alright*.

FRIDAY, 11 OCTOBER
University, York, with Spooky Tooth.

In Studio G, Television Centre, the Who performed "Magic Bus" on Show 13 of BBC-1's *How It Is*, an early evening, mixed-media programme "by the young for the young at heart." Produced by Tony Palmer and presented by Angela Huth, *Oz* editor Richard Neville, DJ John Peel, and Palmer himself, the show was broadcast from 6:00—6:40 pm.

SATURDAY, 12 OCTOBER
University, Sheffield, with the Crazy World Of Arthur Brown.

An interview with John appeared in *Record Mirror*. "'Magic Bus' was not really intended to be a throwback to an early R&B sound or anything, though it does sound a bit that way," he said. "It was written about the same time as 'My Generation'—we listened to it then, but didn't really think a lot of it. But we heard it again more recently and liked it, so we released it."

FRIDAY, 18 OCTOBER
Lyceum Ballroom, London.

Brunel University Students Union "Midnite Rave," 12:30 pm—7:00 am. "Pilot" concert for the forthcoming U.K. mini-tour with the Crazy World Of Arthur Brown, the Alan Bown!, Elmer Gantry's Velvet Opera, and Skip Bifferty.

Track released *Direct Hits*, the first Who compilation, which suffered from poor mastering and the unavailability of early material as a result of the Shel Talmy settlement.

SATURDAY, 19 OCTOBER

California Ballroom, Dunstable.

Disc reported that the New Yardbirds "will change their name to Lead [sic] Zeppelin next week—by courtesy of the Who's Keith Moon." (See 5 April.)

FRIDAY, 25 OCTOBER

Granby Halls, Leicester. "Middle Earth" show with Joe Cocker and Family.

The Who were scheduled to pre-tape the following evening's edition of Southern ITV's *Time For Blackburn*, but their appearance was put back to 15 November.

WEDNESDAY, 30 OCTOBER

Eel Pie Island, Twickenham, Middlesex, with East Of Eden, Proteus, and David Booth.

FRIDAY, 1 NOVEMBER

John was interviewed on *Radio 1 Club*, presented by Pete Drummond and Kenny Everett, from the BBC's Paris Studios, Lower Regent Street, broadcast live from 12:00—2:00 pm.

MONDAY, 4 NOVEMBER

A flu-ridden Keith appeared in Clerkenwell Magistrates Court, charged with being drunk and disorderly, and was fined £2. In summing up, magistrate Mr. J.D. Purcell admonished, "Now we don't want you playing in the traffic anymore, Mr Moon." "Absolutely," he replied, "they already have a drummer."

FRIDAY, 8 NOVEMBER

Granada Cinema, Walthamstow, London. Two shows, 7:00 & 9:10 pm, with the Crazy World Of Arthur Brown, Joe Cocker and the Grease Band, the Mindbenders, and Yes. Compère: Tony Hall.

The first shows on a nine-date British theatre tour, promoted by Lambert and Stamp in conjunction with Kennedy Street Enterprises. Each band's gear was sound checked at 10:30 am and all tour personnel (including the Small Faces, who were joining the tour at a later date) assembled for a full dress rehearsal at 1:30 pm.

The Who's set ran to just 35 minutes, but at the late show, the curtain was unexpectedly pulled

during an extended "Magic Bus." The group continued playing as the curtain was forcibly opened again by a Who roadie. In a frenzied state, Keith tore his shirt and trousers while hammering away, and Pete rammed his mike into his guitar and into the floor. "I closed the curtains because I get a bit tired of violence onstage," John Arm, booking manager for the Granada circuit, explained to *Melody Maker*. "It's not necessary. I've told the Who that before. They say violence is a big part of their act in America, but I said what they do in America is one thing, and what they do in England is entirely different."

SATURDAY, 9 NOVEMBER

Adelphi Cinema, Slough. Two shows, 6:00 & 8:30 pm, with Free in the warm-up slot.

SUNDAY, 10 NOVEMBER

Colston Hall, Bristol. Two shows, 5:30 & 7:45 pm, with Free opening and the Alan Bown! replacing Joe Cocker.

TUESDAY, 12 NOVEMBER

Sherwood Rooms, Nottingham.

FRIDAY, 15 NOVEMBER

The Who pre-taped an appearance, plugging "Magic Bus" on *Time For Blackburn*, hosted by BBC Radio 1 personality Tony Blackburn, with the Crazy World of Arthur Brown, Anita Harris, Force West, and Gene Pitney. The show was first broadcast the following night in the Southern and Ulster ITV regions, Tyne-Tees on the 18th, and London on the 22nd.

FRIDAY, 15 and SATURDAY, 16 NOVEMBER

The Roundhouse, Chalk Farm, London.

Two all-night "Middle Earth" shows, 10:30 pm—6:00 am, with the Small Faces joining the tour as "Special Guest Stars." Yes appeared on the 15th, and Tea and Symphony replaced Joe Cocker on the 16th. Because of the lack of time restrictions, the Who were able to perform their normal set, appearing from 2:45—4:00 am.

"It's very difficult to know just what is going to be a hit for us now," Pete told Keith Altham, "especially in America where we were not able to do those discs like 'Happy Jack,' 'Pictures Of Lily,' and 'I'm A

Boy,' which were a novelty in England because they had the strange attraction of being 'sweet songs' sung by a violent group."

SUNDAY, 17 NOVEMBER

Birmingham Theatre, Birmingham. Two shows, 5:30 & 8:00 pm, with Free. Because it was a Sunday, the Who's act was cut to 30 minutes.

MONDAY, 18 NOVEMBER

City Hall, Newcastle. Two shows, 6:15 & 8:35 pm, with Yes and Joe Cocker re-joining the bill. Now that all artists were appearing, the Who's act was cut further to 25 minutes.

TUESDAY, 19 NOVEMBER

Paisley Ice Rink, Glasgow, Scotland. 8:00 pm—1:00 am show, with Free. The Who played during the final hour.

WEDNESDAY, 20 NOVEMBER

Empire Theatre, Liverpool. Two shows, 6:15 & 8:35 pm. As in Newcastle, all artists appeared on both shows, with the Who's act cut again to 25 minutes. The final show ran far behind schedule, so a unique eight man Who–Small Faces amalgam occurred with Keith and Kenny Jones sharing the same kit. For "Magic Bus," the entire tour personnel (including the coach driver) came on stage to contribute percussion and handclaps. The backing chorus also included an old music-hall entertainer Keith had discovered in the nearby Lord Nelson pub who could play miniature harmonica and smoke a cigarette at the same time!

THURSDAY, 21 NOVEMBER

No better illustration of the Who's current standing can be provided than their appearance on BBC-1's *Crackerjack*, a popular afternoon children's television programme hosted by Michael Aspel. Unlike most of their contemporaries, the Who had successfully steered clear of this type of presentation. Now, a sense of desperation seems to have crept in as they mimed "Magic Bus" in front of a young audience at Television Theatre, Shepherd's Bush, for transmission the following day, 4:55—5:40 pm.

FRIDAY, 22 NOVEMBER

City Hall, St. Albans, Hertfordshire.

The Who recorded their second appearance on

OPPOSITE: All aboard the Magic Bus, 18 October.

How It Is (Show 19) at the BBC's Riverside Studios, Hammersmith, broadcast 6:00—6:40 pm the same evening.

SATURDAY, 23 NOVEMBER
Corn Exchange, Devizes, Wiltshire.

Earlier that day, John returned to his old alma mater with wife Alison to open the annual Acton County Grammar Christmas charity bazaar, getting a quick plug in during his speech by saying, "I hope you manage to raise the money for your Magic Mini-Bus."

TUESDAY, 26 NOVEMBER
University, Southampton, with the Freddie Mack Show, Savoy Brown, and Chris Shakespeare.

SATURDAY, 30 NOVEMBER
University, Manchester.

SATURDAY, 7 DECEMBER
University, Bristol.

MONDAY, 9 DECEMBER
The Pavilion, Bath.

During the afternoon, a cast rehearsal for the *Rock and Roll Circus* television special took place in the mezzanine ballroom at the Londonderry House Hotel on Park Lane.

TUESDAY, 10—WEDNESDAY, 11 DECEMBER
The Rolling Stones and guests the Who, John Lennon, Yoko Ono, Eric Clapton, Mitch Mitchell, Marianne Faithfull, Jethro Tull, Taj Mahal, French avant-garde violinist Ivry Gitlis, classical pianist Julius Katchen, and fashion model Donyale Luna rehearsed and taped *The Rolling Stones Rock and Roll Circus* over two days at the studios of InterTel (VTR

Services), Stonebridge Park, Wembley.

Directed by Michael Lindsay-Hogg, photographed by Tony Richardson, and produced by Sanford Lieberson, the special was financed by the Stones themselves to the tune of £50,000. The 10th was occupied with rehearsals, a press call, and initial filming. Half a circus tent was draped around one end of the studio, with a circus ring that came apart in the centre. Sawdust was spread around the ring, while at the opposite end, an archway covered with bare light bulbs became the artists' entranceway. An 8-track unit hired from IBC, manned by Glyn Johns and assistant engineer Damon Lyon-Shaw, recorded activities for a proposed charity soundtrack album.

The Who were allocated a ten minute spot, and with *Tommy* still gestating, the "mini-opera," "A Quick One," became the favoured choice. Entering into the spirit of the occasion, Keith turned up to rehearsals dressed as a clown, complete with full face make-up.

On the 11th, all were at the studio by noon for an exhausting eighteen hours filming. A specially invited audience, including 800 winners of an *NME* ticket draw, were present to add atmosphere to the proceedings. Each was given a brightly coloured poncho and felt hat to wear and was seated in stands, arranged in a horseshoe around the ring. The day had been divided up into three separate two-and-a-half hour filming sessions (morning 12:30—3:00 pm; afternoon 3:30—6:00 pm; and evening 7:00—9:30 pm), although technical complications made things drag on much longer.

With Lindsay-Hogg giving the signal, the line-up parade for the title sequence was first to be filmed. The cast were lead out by acrobats, midgets, and a cowboy on horseback. Each costumed musician was playing an uncharacteristic instrument (John Lennon a trumpet, Keith Richard a tuba, Pete Townshend a saxophone, etc.) The scene had to be re-taken several times, a portent of the problems that hampered production throughout the day.

At around 4:00 pm, the Who's equipment was set up by roadies Bob Pridden and Tony Haslam. Keith Richard, dressed as a circus dandy with monocle and cigar, introduced them simply: "And now,

ladies and gentleman... dig the Who!" The group ran through three successive takes, each more powerful than the last. Moon poured water over his kit, the spray damaging an expensive overhead microphone, and flung his floor tom over his shoulder.

The Rolling Stones didn't appear until some nine hours later, by which time, the remaining audience were completely dispirited. Unprompted, the Who contingent enlivened proceedings, with Pete dancing around with two large cushions attached to his head like a Pope's diadem, while Keith tied himself to people with a spare cape.

As the clock ticked towards 6:00 am, a shattered Jagger thanked the audience and bid viewers goodnight over the opening bars of the finale, "Salt Of The Earth." Everybody joined in on the dawn chorus, swaying from side to side, reading the words off a gigantic board. As the last notes faded, all stood and waved a frantic farewell.

A 54 minute cut, intended for possible television transmission during the early part of 1969, ran as follows: Part One—Entrance Of The Gladiators and Mick Jagger's Introduction/ Jethro Tull/ Donyale Luna/ The Who. Part Two—Taj Mahal/ Clown routine/ Marianne Faithfull. Part Three—Julius Katchen/ Trapeze act/ John Lennon, Yoko Ono, and the Dirty Mac (with Ivry Gitlis.) Part Four—the Rolling Stones.

The Stones, and Jagger in particular, were unhappy with the finished result and made grandiose, unrealised plans to reshoot their segment the following June at the Colosseum in Rome. "The circus thing was actually meant to go out on the road after that," Townshend told *Zigzag*. "Mick had an incredible amount of plans. Arrangements with American circuses. He'd gone into it very deeply. Hired trains and everything, but, in the end, I think it fell apart because the Stones weren't together." In 1971, there was vague talk of a feature film release for theatrical distribution, but a key factor that influenced its destiny was the Stones severance of all business ties with Allen Klein, who technically owned the film. At one point, Klein apparently considered re-editing the footage in a vain attempt to sell it to the Who as *The Who's Rock And Roll Circus featuring The Rolling Stones*.

In September 1977, Pete contacted Jagger and persuaded him to allow Jeff Stein to view the Who's segment, during production work on *The Kids

Are Alright. It was used in the movie (edited and surrounded by theatrical light bulbs) and soundtrack. Finally, in 1996, after twenty-eight years of rumour and conjecture, Klein's company ABKCO simultaneously released a re-edited, 65 minute version of the film, with accompanying soundtrack, restoring the Who's contribution to its full glory.

THURSDAY, 12 DECEMBER
University, Reading.
    Jess Roden appeared again to sing on "Magic Bus."

SATURDAY, 14 DECEMBER
Bubbels Club, Brentwood, Essex.

TUESDAY, 17 DECEMBER
"The Who's Xmas Party," Marquee Club, London, with Yes supporting.

THURSDAY, 19 DECEMBER
Pavilion Ballroom, Worthing.

SATURDAY, 21 DECEMBER
Gaiety Ballroom, Ramsey, Huntingdon.

MONDAY, 30 DECEMBER
The Who flew to Paris to tape three songs for a multi-artist four-hour ORTF New Year's Eve colour television special, *Surprise Partie*, at the Radiodiffusion Television studios. Directed by Guy Job and presented by Dany Saval and model Zouzou, the show also featured the Troggs, Joe Cocker, Aphrodite's Child, Fleetwood Mac, the Small Faces, P.P. Arnold, Booker T and the M.G.s, Pink Floyd, and the Equals. French artists included Marie Laforet, Jacques Dutronc, Françoise Hardy, Antoine, Johnny Hallyday, Michel Polnareff, Hughes Aufray, Herbert Leonard, Eric Charden, Freddy, Nicoletta, the Irresistibles, and the Variations.
    "Les Who" mimed to the longer album version of "I Am A Boy" [sic], "I Can't See For Miles" [sic!], and "Magic Bus" before an enthusiastic, *Top Of The Pops*–style dancing audience.

LEFT AND BELOW: MARQUEE CLUB, "THE WHO'S XMAS PARTY," 17 DECEMBER.

DEAF, DUMB, AND BLIND BOY 1969

With the benefit of hindsight, the Who were at a career crossroads. The group had produced only three albums in four years, a pace too lethargic to meet the demands of the contemporary marketplace where albums were now outselling singles. Effectively, 1969 signalled the end of the Who "Mark One" and the transformation of a Mod, Op-Art, pop art, quasi-psychedelic singles band into a bona fide "rock" act. It was all down to one Thomas...

Universally regarded as Townshend's baby, *Tommy* was a genuine product of group unity, loosely pieced together in the studio. "Pete used to come in some days with just half a demo," Daltrey told Gary Herman. "We used to talk for hours, literally. We probably did as much talking as we did recording, sorting out arrangements and things."

"I didn't write *Tommy* in any kind of chronological order," Townshend confirmed. "I already had some of the material—'Sensation,' 'Welcome,' 'Sparks,' and 'Underture.' 'We're Not Gonna Take It' was a kind of anti-fascist statement. The first run-down of the idea I put on a graph. It was intended to show *Tommy* from the outside and the impressions going on inside him."

Pete put in a certain amount of research, writing letters to different organisations, including a foundation in Los Angeles that put on concerts for the psychosomatically impaired. Like its forebear *Sgt. Pepper*, *Tommy* took six months to produce (although Daltrey later claimed the actual studio time was "only about eight weeks") at IBC, costing an exorbitant $36,000. Weekend gigs became a necessity, not only in covering costs but to road-test new ideas. Halfway through the sessions, it was

decided to make the album a double so the storyline, typed up in script form and subtitled "1914–1984" by Kit Lambert, could naturally unfold without being pruned unnecessarily. Even then, after constant rewrites and revisions, the plot seemed vague and disjointed.

Lambert was instrumental in keeping the band focused and structuring Pete's flights of fancy, as well as suggesting many of his own, including a formal overture. Thankfully, his grandiose plan of saturating the work with overlush orchestration was vetoed by the band. Because of time and budget constraints, parts of the finished recording sound unpolished and rough hewn. "It was at the time, very un-Wholike," said Moon. "A lot of the songs were soft. We never played like that." Townshend agreed: "When you listen to the early stuff, it's incredibly raucous, high energy, but this was fairly laid back, and Kit deliberately mixed it like that, with the voices up front. The music was structured to allow the concept to breathe..."

The story follows the central character's evolution, from birth through childhood to young adulthood, in his quest for spiritual enlightenment. Tommy Walker is born during World War I ("It's A

Boy"), while his father is declared missing in action. Tommy's mother takes another lover in his father's absence, but their happiness ("1921") is shortlived when Captain Walker returns to find the couple en flagrante. Enraged, he kills the lover, which the traumatised boy witnesses in the reflection of a mirror, much to his parents' horror ("you didn't hear it, you didn't see it, you won't say nothing to no one"). The shock overwhelms Tommy's senses, leaving him deaf, dumb, and blind. Despite his sensory deprivation, he finds that he can communicate through vibrations ("Amazing Journey") and by gazing at his own reflection.

During the course of his parents' increasingly desperate attempts to cure him, Tommy experiences violence from a bullying cousin ("Cousin Kevin"), drugs ("The Acid Queen"), and sex, at the hands, literally, of his wicked Uncle Ernie ("Fiddle About"). Thanks to his uncanny ability to feel and touch, he reaches a state of grace by becoming a teenage pinball champion. A local specialist finally discovers Tommy's only method of communication is via his mirror image ("Go To The Mirror"). Irate at this narcissistic

OPPOSITE: *TOMMY* PRESS LAUNCH, RONNIE SCOTT'S JAZZ CLUB, 1 MAY.

obsession, his mother smashes the mirror, and in so doing, restores Tommy's senses ("I'm Free").

A miracle cure is announced, and Tommy starts his own religion. The mercenary Uncle Ernie sets up "Tommy's Holiday Camp" to cater to those desperate to attain the same level of awareness that Tommy has reached. Disillusioned with the blind devotion he has attracted, Tommy deliberately changes the rules by making the short cut to the panacea they crave all the more difficult. Realising this, his followers rebel and discard him ("We're Not Gonna To Take It"). The ambiguous ending leaves Tommy poignantly finding himself isolated but self-aware, as he was at the start.

Pete commissioned Mike McInnerney to design and paint the elaborate album sleeve and libretto illustrations, which helped emphasise the spiritual aspect of the work. "By the time Pete came to me, *Tommy* was pretty well resolved," McInnerney told *Radio Times*. "I listened to the cassette recordings, track after track, and that was enough to get the gist." To remove any doubt, the "Avatar" was given a discreet name check at the foot of the sleeve credits.

Sensitive to charges of pretentiousness, the most obviously commercial track, "Pinball Wizard" was written with journalist (and pinball enthusiast) Nik Cohn in mind—a ploy to ensure a favourable review in his *New York Times* column. (A pop purist to the end, Cohn viewed such lofty concepts as rock opera with the utmost suspicion.) "Kit used to be extraordinarily funny on the subject," Townshend told David Fricke. "He said, 'You've got to be pretentious, you've got to go for gold, you've got to be over the top.' So as a kind of agitator in the music business, he was wonderful, because instead of devaluing the whole thing, he was actually making it real."

Four years earlier, reactionary forces at the BBC had found "My Generation" detrimental to stutterers, and now, "Pinball Wizard" was branded "distasteful" when released as a "taster" in March. Radio 1 DJ Tony Blackburn, an expert on these things, publicly labelled Townshend "sick." For the opera's most masochistic moments, Townshend passed the buck to the Who's laconic bassist. "I remember being in Detroit on the 'Magic Bus' tour," Entwistle explained, "and we had a *Tommy* meeting. Pete suggested that I write two songs he felt he couldn't write. Basically the brief I got was to write a song about a homosexual experience with a nasty uncle, and a bullying experience by…I don't know whether

a cousin was actually mentioned, but I figured that it might as well be the son of Uncle Ernie. I wrote those songs very quickly. If someone gives me a subject to write about, I get it done."

The idea for a holiday camp setting came from the fertile imagination of Keith Moon. Townshend actually wrote the song, but credited Moon for his brainwave in creating the backdrop for Tommy's religous establishment and felt "it turned out just as he himself would have written it."

Given the Who's volatile history, what is perhaps most surprising about *Tommy* was how the rest of the group were completely sympathetic to Townshend's ideas, unselfishly giving him complete artistic freedom at a critical time in their careers. Moon's drumming was at its unpredictable best, and Entwistle's horn embellishments hit the spot at the appropriate junctures. But perhaps the most stellar contribution was Daltrey's vocal performance, easily his most confident and assured to date.

If convincing his bandmates to give his ideas full rein was comparatively stress free, persuading Decca's conservative executives to finance them was another matter. "We told them they were going to have a five million-copy album on their hands, and they refused to even listen," Townshend told Chris Van Ness. "I mean I was going up to people and shaking them by the lapels, saying, 'Look, this album is going to sell more copies than any other fucking album in history so get your fucking brains together.'" Eventually, the positive sales response to "Pinball Wizard" helped to sway things.

Because *Tommy* had taken an inordinate amount of time, it was beaten into the shops by the Small Faces' *Ogden's Nut Gone Flake*, the Pretty Things' *S.F. Sorrow*, and *The Kinks Are The Village Green Preservation Society*, albums similar in execution. "Their approach was exactly the same, and it was a natural evolution for rock at the time," Pete told Chris Welch ten years later.

On 1 May, *Tommy* entered the world with an ear-splitting press launch at Ronnie Scott's Jazz Club in Soho. The album followed two weeks later, accompanied by dozens of explanatory, often contradictory, Townshend interviews given to the music and underground press. Yet despite its idiosyncratic nature,

Tommy initially met a disappointingly lukewarm response in Britain, where the Who were still perceived as a gimmicky, albeit highly superior, singles act. It was a different story across the water. Thanks to the group's touring presence, certain American underground FM stations took the unprecedented step of playing all four sides non-stop from beginning to end. Within a fortnight, *Tommy* had sold more than 200,000 copies and gained the group their first Gold Record for a million dollars worth of U.S. sales.

If, as some argued, the rock opera hadn't realised its full potential on record, it took on a whole new mantle when performed on the concert platform. Moon thrashed away like a dervish behind his outsized Premier kit; Entwistle stood in the shadows, resplendent in a series of outlandish self-mocking suits; Townshend leapt, windmilled, and scissor-kicked in a functional boiler suit; while Daltrey, in a fringed buckskin jacket, his hair grown out into a naturally curly mane, swung his microphone like a lariat. Many observers were quick to note how his new stage persona seemed to transform him into the Deaf, Dumb, and Blind Boy character.

If Moon wasn't up to his usual mayhem, then Townshend could be relied upon to be at the centre of an incident. In May, at New York's Fillmore East, he unwittingly assaulted a plain clothes police officer who had rushed onstage to warn of the neighbouring property being ablaze. He was fined $75.

During a brief respite from the road, each member continued nurturing talent for Track. Pete brought Thunderclap Newman together as a vehicle for the disparate talents of Andy Newman, John "Speedy" Keene, and Jimmy McCulloch. "Independently all three of them came to me, or I got involved with them with a view to helping them," Pete told *Zigzag*. "... it was Kit Lambert who said to me, 'You haven't got time for all of them, why not try them together.'" "Revolution" was one of three songs demoed at Pete's Twickenham studio in an effort to impress Lambert, who originally wanted to call the band "My Favourite Freaks."

Further tracks were produced at IBC during spare *Tommy* recording time, with Pete playing bass under the pseudonym "Bijou Drains." (This role was handed to Keene's friend, Jim Pitman-Avory, who later formed Track outfit Third World War.) Lambert gave them his Hampshire cottage to rehearse in and within three weeks, "Revolution,"

now called "Something In The Air," was a deserved #1. Roger produced tracks for Scottish group, Bent Frame, which included Jimmy McCulloch's elder brother, Jack, on drums. Keith found a kindred spirit in New York comedian Murray Roman. John gathered song ideas together for a solo album. (In the interim, Track collected his Who compositions together as part of their budget Backtrack series.)

America lured the group back in August for two specially contracted appearances at Tanglewood, Massachusetts, and the legendary Woodstock Music and Arts Fair in Bethel, upstate New York. The Who's taut, disciplined, and blazingly direct style clashed with the drug-induced self-indulgence of many of the acts at the three-day event. Tired, tripping, and furious, Pete made his entrance by forcibly clearing the stage of photographers, including Michael Wadleigh and his film crew, busily documenting events for a Warner Brothers picture. Halfway through *Tommy*, Yippie politico Abbie Hoffman unwisely elected to walk onstage, ranting about fellow activist John Sinclair's recent incarceration for marijuana possession. "Fuck off my fucking stage," an enraged Townshend yelled, before swatting Hoffman into the camera pit with his Gibson SG ("the most political thing I ever did!").

As the group reached the climactic "See Me, Feel Me" finale, dawn's rays enveloped the festival site, an unplanned stage effect. The spectacle was spellbinding. As Entwistle pithily remarked, "God was our lighting man!" "When the sun came up, I just didn't believe it," Townshend told Jonathan Cott. "It was just incredible. I really felt we didn't deserve it, in a way. We put out such bad vibes." Daltrey called it one of the Who's worst shows, and Townshend in particular loathed Woodstock's blind excesses. "I said to some guy, 'Listen, this is the fucking American dream, it's not my dream,'" he told Dave Schulps. "I don't want to spend the rest of my life in fucking mud, smoking fucking marijuana. If that's the American dream, let us have our fucking money and piss off back to Shepherd's Bush where people are people." Despite such scorn, he was forced to concede that Woodstock was a turning point. The Who were understandably paranoid that groups such as Hendrix, Cream, the Jeff Beck Group, and newcomers Led Zeppelin had capitalised on their blueprint.

The Who returned to England for a triumphant appearance at the 2nd Isle of Wight Festival, and in September, unveiled *Tommy* at the Concertgebouw, Amsterdam, the first concert of its kind. This was followed by a tour of European opera houses, most never having played host to rock music—nor would they again. The Who's sets had generally lasted more than an hour, but now, the envelope was pushed to a marathon two and a quarter hours. Townshend later described the concerts from this time as tripartite: the first third consisted of a mixture of stage favourites and early hits to warm the audience up for section two, *Tommy*, which was then played through virtually non-stop (sans "Cousin Kevin," "Underture," and "Welcome"). Without pausing for breath, the group would plunge into the last section, with "Summertime Blues" and "Shakin' All Over" deflating any air of pomposity the opera may have attracted. The home stretch consisted of an elongated "My Generation," weaving in reprises of *Tommy* to indicate where the Who had come from and where they were at. Occasionally, "Magic Bus" was performed as an encore if band or audience had any energy left. For Lambert, taking a beast like rock and roll and placing it within the sanctified confines of high art was the ultimate masterstroke. He now talked excitedly of inveigling enough of Universal Pictures' money to turn his *Tommy* script into a reality.

The Who finished the year with successful tours of America and Britain, including an unprecedented week at the Fillmore East, where *Tommy* was lauded by no less a figure than Leonard Bernstein, and a show at the London Coliseum, home of the Sadlers Wells Opera in Covent Garden.

As a gamble, *Tommy* had paid off handsomely, but already there were worrying signs that its significance was being taken out of all proportion by the new audiences it attracted. Townshend put the situation into perspective for Richard Green: "We were going down the drain—we needed something challenging after putting out corny singles like 'Magic Bus' and 'Dogs.' Making *Tommy* really united the group, and that was the good thing about it. The problem is that it elevated the Who to heights they hadn't attained... It was highly overrated because it was rated where it shouldn't have been, and it wasn't rated where it should have been. I don't listen to it... I enjoyed making it very, very much."

Surely the audience would tire of *Tommy*, and demand something more?

1969

JANUARY—MARCH

Tommy sessions continued in Studio A at IBC. With some studio time left over, Pete produced and played bass on three Thunderclap Newman tracks: "Accidents," "Wilhemina," and "Something In The Air," under the pseudonym "Bijou Drains," with Damon Lyon-Shaw engineering.

SATURDAY, 18 JANUARY

Civic Hall, Nantwich.

SUNDAY, 19 JANUARY

Mothers Club, Erdington, Birmingham.

The first of three Who appearances at this underground venue, introduced by John Peel.

TUESDAY, 21 and WEDNESDAY, 22 JANUARY

Tommy sessions at IBC.

On the 22nd, a nine minute interview for Dutch television by John Peel, filmed at Regents Park Zoo (date unknown), was screened on *Later*, 7:13—7:55 pm, on Nederland 2.

"We were told that the Dutch can't say 'Who,' so could we say 'Woo!'" Peel explained. "'Tell me, Pete, what are the plans for the Woo?!' 'Well, John, the Woo aren't merely a singles group and I'm working on a rock opera especially for the Woo!' 'A Woo opera, eh Pete? Strong stuff,' and so on."

FRIDAY, 24 JANUARY

Civic Hall, Wolverhampton, Staffordshire.

At Luton Court, Roger was fined £11 for minor motoring offences. His counsel David Harter told the Court his client was "a busy man in the same sense as the Chairman of ICI. He probably earns as much [sic!] and is about as big a dollar earner for this country."

SATURDAY, 25 JANUARY

New Year's Ball, Borough Road College, Isleworth, Middlesex, with the Aynsley Dunbar Retaliation, Terry Lightfoot's Jazz Band, the Pyramids, and Almond Marzipan Abbottfield Dance Orchestra.

MONDAY, 27—FRIDAY, 31 JANUARY

The Who spent the week rehearsing at the Whitehall

ABOVE: PETE'S TYPEWRITTEN LYRICS TO "SALLY SIMPSON" (FROM *TOMMY*) WITH HIS HANDWRITTEN AMENDMENTS.

Theatre, Whitehall, booked between 1:00—6:00 pm daily.

SATURDAY, 1 FEBRUARY
Union Ballroom, University, Newcastle, with Free and the Love Affair.

The *NME* reported the Who had rejected an offer of a guest spot on Tom Jones' forthcoming ATV series. A spokesman said, "The money wasn't right and in any case this show would not have been in keeping with the Who's image." (See 16 April.)

SUNDAY, 2 FEBRUARY
The Redcar Jazz Club, Coatham Hotel, Redcar, Yorkshire.

MONDAY, 3—FRIDAY, 7 FEBRUARY
Tommy sessions at IBC.

A Track Records call sheet reveals the sessions throughout the month were originally to have been filmed.

FRIDAY, 7 FEBRUARY
Top Rank Suite, University, Bath.

The Who appeared during the infamous student sit-ins, which were occurring at universities throughout the country. "Pinball Wizard" was completed and mixed in an afternoon session at Morgan Studios, 169/171 High Road, Willesden, North West London. The song was released as a single on Friday 7 March, restoring the Who to the U.K. Top 5, where it climbed to #4. It was released in the U.S. on 22 March, reaching #19 in *Billboard*.

SATURDAY, 8 FEBRUARY
Regent Polytechnic, London, with Family.

SUNDAY, 9 FEBRUARY
The original date scheduled for a Roundhouse benefit to help pay the legal fees for thirteen London School of Economics students who had writs served against them after recent sit-ins. Pete had invited the Small Faces and several other acts to appear, but the show was put back to the 23rd after problems in securing the venue.

MONDAY, 10—FRIDAY, 14 FEBRUARY
Tommy sessions at IBC.

"Dogs Part Two," originally titled "The Dark Side Of," a non-album, nonsensical jam credited to "Moon—Towser [Pete's Spaniel]—Jason [John's wolfhound]" was recorded on the 12th and released as the B-side to "Pinball Wizard."

FRIDAY, 14 FEBRUARY
Lanchester College, Coventry.

MONDAY, 17—FRIDAY, 21 FEBRUARY
Tommy sessions at IBC.

FRIDAY, 21 FEBRUARY
University, Birmingham, with the Idle Race and Honeybus.

SATURDAY, 22 FEBRUARY
University, Liverpool.

Disc reported the Small Faces had been recording that week without Steve Marriott, who had left the group. "We recorded at my home studio," said Pete. "Ronnie asked me to play lead guitar for them as a favour. They don't quite know what's happening. They were making the discs to see how things would work out without Steve. Although Ronnie's voice lacks Steve's projection, they still sound very like the Small Faces... I think that if Ronnie, Kenny, and Mac don't find another guitarist they really like, they will break up completely."

SUNDAY, 23 FEBRUARY
The Roundhouse, London. LSE Benefit, re-scheduled from 9 February, held from 4:00 pm—12 midnight. The Who appeared at 9:00 pm on a bill featuring Cat Stevens, Circus, Pete Brown's Battered Ornaments, Third Ear Band, and Occasional Word Ensemble.

MONDAY, 24—FRIDAY, 28 FEBRUARY
Tommy sessions at IBC.

SATURDAY, 1 MARCH
Mothers Club, Erdington, Birmingham.

MONDAY, 3—FRIDAY, 7 MARCH
Tommy sessions at IBC.

The following week, Kit Lambert flew to Cairo, leaving the arduous task of mixing *Tommy* to Damon Lyon-Shaw and assistant engineer Ted Sharp. "Studio B at IBC was not a good studio to mix the album," said Lyon-Shaw. "We never knew what was wrong with it, and Kit left it to us to finish it off."

FRIDAY, 7 MARCH
Technical College, Headington, Oxfordshire.

FRIDAY, 14 MARCH
Corn Exchange, Cambridge.

During the afternoon, in Studio G, Television Centre, the Who rehearsed and taped their unbilled appearance, performing "Pinball Wizard," on the pilot of BBC-1's *How Late It Is*—the successor to *How It Is*, on which they had previously appeared (see 11 October and 22 November 1968), broadcast 10:50—11:30 pm.

TUESDAY, 18 MARCH
Following rehearsals at 12:45 pm, the Who were briefly interviewed by Stuart Henry at the BBC's Paris Studios for *Radio 1 Club*, broadcast live during its 12:00—2:00 pm slot.

WEDNESDAY, 26 MARCH
The Who commenced a period of rehearsals at Bickersteth Memorial Hall, Grove Place, off New End, Hampstead, North West London. These generally commenced from 1:00—1:30 pm, lasting until approximately 6:30 pm.

THURSDAY, 27 MARCH
For a fee of £30, the Who mimed to a pre-recorded version of "Pinball Wizard" on *Top Of The Pops* at Television Centre, broadcast 7:30—8:00 pm. BBC documentation states the Corporation acquired audio rights for the "sole purpose of sound broadcasting from transmitters outside the British Isles."

FRIDAY, 28 MARCH
Pete's eldest daughter Emma Kate was born at Queen Charlotte's Maternity Hospital, Hammersmith.

The Who appeared live on Thames Television's *Today* show, presented by Eamonn Andrews, broadcast from Television House, Kingsway, to the London ITV region only, from 6:04—6:30 pm.

MONDAY, 31 MARCH
Recording at Pan Sound, 23 Denmark Street, London, from 2:00 pm onwards. During a break, the band adjourned to the rooftop for a publicity photo shoot.

TUESDAY, 1 APRIL

Rehearsal at the Community Centre, Westcott Crescent, Hanwell.

WEDNESDAY, 2 APRIL

Pavilion Ballroom, Bournemouth. Poole College social with the Third Ear Band.

THURSDAY, 3 APRIL

Rehearsal, Hanwell.

TUESDAY, 8—THURSDAY, 10 APRIL

Rehearsals, Hanwell.

On the 10th, the group went to Television Centre for 2:00 pm rehearsals, miming "Pinball Wizard" on *Top Of The Pops*, broadcast 7:30—8:00 pm. The appearance helped push the single to #10 on the following week's *NME* chart.

Keith did his best to disrupt proceedings, much to director Colin Charman's reported consternation. For the Who's next appearance on the show, their contract jokingly stipulated they would appear only if their drummer remained sober throughout the day.

FRIDAY, 11 APRIL

Rehearsal, Hanwell.

From 12:00—12:30 pm, Pete taped a short radio interview for the BBC's Transcription Service at Studio 2, Kensington House, Richmond Way, West London. (Part of the conversation was released on the U.S. *Live At The BBC* bonus disc.)

WEDNESDAY, 16 APRIL

Perhaps realising the value of a prime time plug (see 1 February), the Who recorded an appearance on the first in a new series of ATV's *This Is... Tom Jones* at Elstree Studio Centre, Borehamwood. Due to Musicians Union regulations, the group had to pre-record a new backing track for "Pinball Wizard," which they mimed to with live vocals before an audience in Studio C.

Shot on videotape for colour transmission in America (Friday 18 April over the ABC network), the programme, featuring Fran Jeffries, Mirelle Mathieu, comedian Pat Paulsen, and flamenco guitarist Manitas De Plata, was shown in monochrome in Britain over the ITV region on Sunday, 20 April, 10:20—11:20 pm.

MONDAY, 21 APRIL

1:00 pm rehearsals resumed at the Community Centre, Hanwell.

During the week, stereo mastering of *Tommy* occurred at IBC Studio A. Of the material discarded, "Cousin Kevin Model Child," a linking piece erroneously credited to Entwistle but actually written by Townshend and sung by Moon, appeared almost thirty years later on the expanded *Odds and Sods* CD.

TUESDAY, 22 APRIL

Institute of Technology, Casino Club, Bolton, Lancashire.

WEDNESDAY, 23 APRIL

The final *Tommy* rehearsal at the Community Centre, Hanwell.

"I remember when Keith and I went to a pub on the way back," Pete told Chris Welch, "and we sat there, both incredulous at how quickly it had come together. We noted how suddenly Roger had become something else, and we debated what would happen, and how it would change everything. We knew we had something cohesive and playable and that had a story." A full rehearsal from this period (or possibly later in the year) was recorded for reference purposes, and at least one set of single-sided acetates was cut at Trident Studios.

THURSDAY, 24 APRIL

The Who appeared on *Top Of The Pops* from Television Centre, 7:30—8:00 pm. Taking over the resident DJ spot on the programme, Tony Blackburn had his baptism by fire when Keith flicked drumsticks at him as he hypocritically introduced the Who live on air. (Blackburn had branded "Pinball Wizard" "distasteful" on his Radio 1 programme.)

FRIDAY, 25 APRIL

Strathclyde University, Glasgow, Scotland.

The first extended airing of *Tommy* material before an audience.

LEFT and BELOW: *Top Of The Pops*, rehearsals, 10 April. **OPPOSITE:** *This Is... Tom Jones*, 16 April.

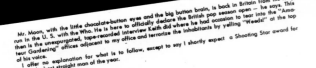

"Our Albums Are Junk" Says Who Drummer KEITH MOON

H: What kind of reaction did you get on this last U. S. tour?
Keith: It was the kind of reaction we had in the early days here when we had the big mod bit going for us. We got standing ovations wherever we went, with the exception of the War Memorial Hospital.

HP: Are you thought of there as an "underground group?
Keith: More overland really — the more ordinary, there-you-are-sir pop group.

HP: Do you fall into the category of people like the Doors?
Keith: No, they fall into their own. The category that we fall into is the Who.

HP: There does seem to be a tendency for hotel doors to mysteriously blow off their hinges when you are resident — were there any incidents of this nature?
Keith: No. All in all our road managers were very good. We've imposed a fine system, you see, and anything that they do is taken off their bonus at the end of the tour. We've decided that this must stop, categorically must stop, because it is a danger to living people. I mean it's very nasty.

HP: So how are you received now in hotels?
Keith: Open arms — open arms. A friend of mine drives us to most of the hotels, a colored chap who knows most of the managers and of course they are only too pleased to see him. And whenever he arrives they say: "Hello...Hello Sunshine," they say, because that's his name. "Come in," they say — and we do.

HP: Were you present at any of the riots in places like Chicago?
Keith: Unfortunately we organized them rather badly and most of them got started too early. They were not supposed to begin until we got there.

HP: Is your act still the same "smashing" routine?
Keith: We've tried to stop that, but wherever we go there are always some little kids yelling, "Smashyerguitar smashyerguitar" and you can't let them go away disappointed, can you?

23

SATURDAY, 26 APRIL
Community Centre, Auchinleck, Ayrshire, Scotland.

SUNDAY, 27 APRIL
Kinema Ballroom, Dunfermline, Fifeshire, Scotland.

MONDAY, 28 APRIL
Whitburn Bay Hotel, Sunderland, Durham.

THURSDAY, 1 MAY
Ronnie Scott's Jazz Club, Soho, London.
    An hour-long press preview of *Tommy*, played at deafening volume before an invited audience. "No matter what Auntie thinks, it's not sick. In fact, the sickest thing in this country is Auntie herself!" announced Townshend to prolonged applause.

FRIDAY, 2 MAY
The Who (minus Pete who flew out separately the following week), with Bob Pridden, John Wolff, and roadies Tony Haslam and John "Bumper" East, flew to New York. Pete and Pridden stocked up on guitars

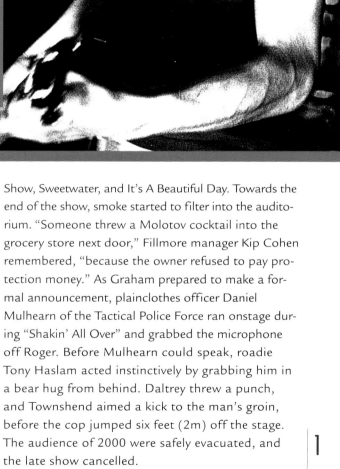

LEFT and ABOVE: RONNIE SCOTT'S JAZZ CLUB, 1 MAY.
RIGHT: PETE AT THE GRANDE BALLROOM, DETROIT, 9 MAY.

at Manny's, a well known instrument shop on 156 West 48th Street, Manhattan.

FRIDAY, 9—SUNDAY, 11 MAY

The first of two 1969 North American tours opened with a three-night stand, supported by Joe Cocker and the Grease Band, at the Grande Ballroom, Detroit, Michigan. Promoted by Russ Gibb.

This legendary venue was now being managed by ex-Who tour manager, Tom Wright, who, aware of the sense of occasion, crudely recorded the opening night on his portable Nagra recorder.

TUESDAY, 13—THURSDAY, 15 MAY

The Boston Tea Party, Boston, Massachusetts, supported by Roland Kirk.

FRIDAY, 16 MAY

Fillmore East, New York City.

The first of a three-night stand, promoted by Bill Graham, with the Joshua Light

BILL GRAHAM PRESENTS IN NEW YORK

THE WHO
SWEETWATER
IT'S A BEAUTIFUL DAY
JOSHUA LIGHT SHOW

FILLMORE EAST
May 16-17, 1969

Show, Sweetwater, and It's A Beautiful Day. Towards the end of the show, smoke started to filter into the auditorium. "Someone threw a Molotov cocktail into the grocery store next door," Fillmore manager Kip Cohen remembered, "because the owner refused to pay protection money." As Graham prepared to make a formal announcement, plainclothes officer Daniel Mulhearn of the Tactical Police Force ran onstage during "Shakin' All Over" and grabbed the microphone off Roger. Before Mulhearn could speak, roadie Tony Haslam acted instinctively by grabbing him in a bear hug from behind. Daltrey threw a punch, and Townshend aimed a kick to the man's groin, before the cop jumped six feet (2m) off the stage. The audience of 2000 were safely evacuated, and the late show cancelled.

While angry police searched Loew's Midtown Hotel, Graham harboured the band in his apartment at 71 East Seventh. The following day, Daltrey and Townshend voluntarily went to the Ninth Precinct, where they were formally charged with assaulting a

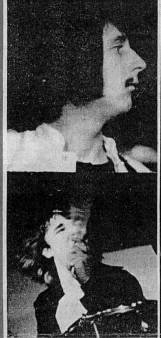

RECORD MIRROR

Largest selling colour pop weekly newspaper.

Price 6d. No. 426.

Every Thursday

Week ending May 10, 1969

PETE DOESN'T DIG THOSE AWE-STRUCK CROWDS

"FIFTEEN thousand screaming Germans at a Who pop concert may sound good to you, but I'd rather not be there" exclaimed lazily dressed Pete Townsend with an attempted flutter of his heavy eyelids.

Pete was hurriedly explaining the difference between images developed by the Who in various countries. Hurriedly, because he and the rest of the group were due any moment for their spot on everybody's favourite show, Top Of The Pops.

"I'd rather play to Americans or here in Britain than anywhere else. In Germany, the kids turn out to see you and the responses aren't bad, but the reasons for their attention are not the same as ours here. They are awe-struck by the spectacle of British revolutionary youth. They are more concerned with what we represent than what we are or can do with musical instruments. They're just not our people. That may sound a little hard, but I think it's true."

"There simply aren't other countries to compare with England or the United States. I don't care for the outlook in Germany, but in Sweden, I don't think there ARE any young people. At least I never saw any."

"We do have separate images in the separate countries. In the U.S. we are regarded as part of the British underground. This, I think, is due to the point and way in which we were introduced in the first place. During the early days, a Who album in the States was a rare thing. People were crying to get one. Because we were not that easily obtainable, we and our records became exclusive and everyone wanted to know more. A lot of artistes are still making it in that manner today. Sometimes a slight beginning pays off in the long run. Your image is often established then and carries on while you change. The fact that you're exotic must be lived up to, but we've never tried to maintain an image."

Being a noteworthy reporter, I queried as to whether success in the colonies ever alienated anyone . . .

"Yes, often the fans here tend to feel we have deserted them by going off to where the money is. We really haven't, because we do play at home and release our material".

What about other groups?

"That's another thing. All groups want to make it in the States and when one manages it, most others are pleased for them. The States are the big market and all of pop music wants to get there. To stay there can be touchy. We dropped the violent side of our act in favour of a new outlook. In England, we remain just a good pop group now concerned with writing and composing instead of carefully moulding an image."

The Who have a pretty solid position in both countries. In the States, they are one of the most sought after British underground acts. Be it the Fillmore, or the American Legion Indoor Putting green, you can bet it will be a sellout.

In Britain, they are considered one of our finest products. Rather than be upset about their popularity abroad, I'd think it better to consider them ambassadors at large and doing a grand job representing British talent. They've come a long way — Pete droops a little now; Roger Daltry is beginning to resemble Hawkeye in Chingachgook's gear, but the music goes round and round and despite America, it still comes out here.

LON GODDARD

And they preview LP at Ronnie's . . .

FROM twelve o'clock onwards, an influx of journalists, publicists and assorted ravers were to be seen conglomerated in deepest Soho, preparing themselves with liquid medication for an occasion most rare and beautiful (and likely to go berserk). This was Thursday the first of May and the Who were going to lay it on big at Ronnie's.

The evening reception was to be in honour of their forthcoming album, entitled simply, 'Tommy'. At six sharp, the pubs in the city of bright lights and lit people, began to drain. By six-thirty, there existed a severe retail booze depression outside and the scattered tables within Ronnie Scott's club were seething with the pop industry. Crawling over Hors d'Oeuvres and threatening to over-run the bar in great teeming hordes, they distributed hellos and what-are-you-havings, then meticulously selected tables and sat waiting, gorged and heavy.

There were affectionate cries of "blank off" as Pete Drummond, Roger Daltry, Keith "Mooney" Moon and John Entwistle assumed their positions. Pete began to explain the nature of the LP.

"There is a story to the music; it's the story of Tommy. Tommy is born and with the advent of the war, his father goes off to fight. Tommy's mother, meanwhile, gets randy and takes a lover. One day, Tommy sees something he shouldn't and is told to keep quiet about it. The shock causes him to go deaf, dumb and blind."

Exclamations of "sick!", "sick!"

"No, it's not sick, ha, ha," replies Pete as Keith confirms this from the drums in back. "The next scene introduces Tommy to Gypsy the Acid Queen, who declares that she will take him into a room for awhile and make a man out of a boy. Following this episode, Tommy becomes renowned as a 'Pinball Wizard'."

The LP ends with what appears to be a musical philosophical question; what happens to Tommy after his disturbed childhood? Where went the Pinball Wizard? The Who gave us a good solid hour's worth of quality listening and excellent showmanship, leaving amid chortles of "more!", "get off!" and "to the bar!" All in all, it was a great pop-religious happening and ends of the scale from Dave Dee to John Peel turned up to urge the play on. Then the pubs became enormously popular once again.

LON GODDARD

ALL RM PIX BY DEZO HOFFMAN

plainclothes police officer and remanded on bail until 27 May. (The case was further adjourned to 20 June.)

SATURDAY, 17 and SUNDAY, 18 MAY
Fillmore East, New York City.

The Who performed two shows on both dates, with an afternoon show on the 18th making up for the cancelled show on the 16th. The group were interviewed outside the theatre on the 18th by visiting *NME* journalist Keith Altham for Radio 1's *Scene And Heard*. The 7 min 30 sec segment (interspersed with records) was included in the Tuesday, 27 May broadcast, 7:45—8:45 pm.

Tommy was issued in the U.S. on the 17th, and in the U.K on the 23rd, after missing its original April release date. The delay was partly caused by the manufacture of the elaborate triptych sleeve and eleven-page booklet, designed by Mike McInnerney, which was to have originally included Kit Lambert's synopsis. *Tommy* eventually reached #2 in the U.K. and #4 in the *Billboard* album chart.

MONDAY, 19 MAY
Rock Pile Club, Toronto, Canada. Two shows, 8:00 & 11:00 pm.

WEDNESDAY, 21 MAY
The Who were scheduled to play two shows at the Capitol Theatre, Ottawa, but because the road distance from Toronto had been severely misjudged, the group's equipment did not arrive in time.

FRIDAY, 23 and SATURDAY, 24 MAY
Electric Factory, Philadelphia, Pennsylvania.

SUNDAY, 25 MAY
Merriweather Post Pavilion, Columbia, Maryland, with Led Zeppelin—the only occasion the two groups appeared together, although Zeppelin were billed to appear at St. Louis the following Sunday. At least one member of the Who's crew was happy this unique coupling was never repeated. "I had the unenviable task of throwing Zeppelin off

the stage," recalled John Wolff. "They were playing over time, stringing it out, and there was a curfew, so I was saying, 'I've got to get you off!' I had to pull the plug on them, otherwise we were never going to go on!" The following day, the Who flew from Baltimore to New York for a three-day break.

THURSDAY, 29—SATURDAY, 31 MAY
Kinetic Playground, Chicago, Illinois.

Another eclectic bill, featuring Buddy Rich and His Orchestra—watched intently from the wings each night by Keith—and Joe Cocker and the Grease Band. On the 31st, Rich was replaced by Wisconsin group Soup.

These shows raised the Who's awareness of how audiences were reacting to *Tommy*, as Townshend told Richard Barnes: "Halfway through, all of a sudden everybody realised that something was working. I don't know quite what it was, but everybody all at the same time, just stood up and stayed standing up. From that moment on they

RIGHT: ROGER IN FULL FLIGHT AT THE FILLMORE WEST, SAN FRANCISCO, 17–19 JUNE.

would always stand up at exactly the same point... It was the first time that we'd created a theatrical device that worked every time."

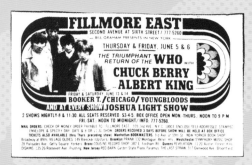

SUNDAY, 1 JUNE
Kiel Auditorium, St Louis, Missouri, with Joe Cocker and the Grease Band.

THURSDAY, 5 and FRIDAY, 6 JUNE
Fillmore East, New York City.

A return to the venue by popular demand with two shows per night, 8:00 & 11:30 pm, featuring Chuck Berry, Albert King, and the Joshua Light Show.

SATURDAY, 7 JUNE
Majestic Hills Theater, Lake Geneva, Wisconsin.

SUNDAY, 8 JUNE
Tyrone Guthrie Theatre, Minneapolis, Minnesota. Two shows, 7:00 & 9:30 pm.

The Who flew to L.A. the following day, checking into the notorious Continental Hyatt House (better known as "the Riot House") on Sunset Strip. Pete avoided the madness by staying at a friend's apartment.

FRIDAY, 13 JUNE
"Magic Circus," Hollywood Palladium, Los Angeles, California, with Poco and the Bonzo Dog Band. Fellow musicians in the

RIGHT: John and Pete at the Fillmore West, 17–19 June.

audience for the premiere show at this new rock club included Janis Joplin, Spirit, Cass Elliot, David Crosby, Peter Tork, and the Turtles.

TUESDAY, 17—THURSDAY, 19 JUNE
Fillmore West, San Francisco, California, with the Woody Herman Jazz Band.

The Who played two shows per night, except for the 19th, as an 11:30 pm night flight to New York was scheduled for Roger and Pete's 9:00 am court appearance the following day. Despite pleas for an encore, Pete explained this was impossible due to the impend-

ing court proceedings. A recording of this dialogue appeared on the *Thirty Years of Maximum R&B* box set.

FRIDAY, 20 JUNE
At the Supreme District Court, Manhattan, Pete was fined $75 on a reduced charge of harassment following the hearing of accusations that he had obstructed a plainclothes policeman at the Fillmore on 16 May. The charges against Roger were summarily dismissed.

The group remained in New York for a week, flying home on Friday 27 June. That morning, at Frank Barselona's apartment on West 57th Street, the terms for the Who's Woodstock appearance were thrashed out during the early hours between Barselona and John

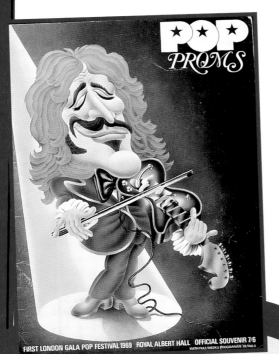

FIRST LONDON GALA POP FESTIVAL 1969 ROYAL ALBERT HALL OFFICIAL SOUVENIR 7/6
WITH FULL WEEKS PROGRAMME DETAILS

Morris of Premier Talent Associates Inc. and John Wolff representing New Action Ltd.

"Pete was really pissed off with the whole thing," Wolff recalled. "He was outnumbered, and he was doing a bit of a number. I think we were getting twelve and a half grand from Bill Graham to do Tanglewood, and all that was going to do was cover the expense of our flights, the gear, and stuff like that. So for Woodstock, I held out for the same amount."

SATURDAY, 5 JULY
Royal Albert Hall, Kensington Gore, London. Two shows, 5:30 & 8:30 pm, promoted by Roy Guest of NEMS Enterprises. The final night of a week of "Pop Proms" concerts, featuring the Who, Chuck Berry, and Bodast.

After an inevitable dispute over billing, the Who agreed to a compromise of letting Berry headline the first house, while they closed the second. During the first show, the Teddy boys in the audience tried to prevent the Who appearing by jamming the stage, trashing seats and indulging in fisticuffs with police and Albert Hall attendants. After some choice Townshend comments, sharpened coins were thrown onstage, one cutting Daltrey's forehead.

"When the Teds started yelling and being menacing down the front," remembered MC Jeff Dexter, "Tony Haslam, one of the Who's roadies, picked up a mace gun he'd got in America and fired it into the front row. I emceed from the centre of the stage, behind both amps, so at the time he fired, I was actually sitting just behind him when this whole thing started. Cans and these huge pennies started flying up on to the stage, and like a fool, I walked back to my podium, grabbed the microphone and started preaching peace and love!

"I said something like, 'Look, we all love rock and roll, we all love Chuck Berry, and the Who all love Chuck Berry. The Who have done something new, now you've got to try and dig it.'"

Police and Albert Hall staff managed to evict most of the troublemakers, while the less demonstrative were appeased with "Summertime Blues" and "Shakin' All Over." At the second show, the Who had the entire audience on their feet; most of whom had come directly from the Rolling Stones' free concert at nearby Hyde Park.

Backstage, Pete revealed to *Melody Maker* the first tentative plans for *Tommy* to be immortalised on celluloid. Universal International Pictures had made an offer, with the group having a hand in the screenplay but not in the direction. "We'll be working with a scriptwriter," he said, "but at the moment we haven't really got anybody lined up at all. All we've got is the budget of a couple of million dollars."

SUNDAY, 6—WEDNESDAY, 9 JULY
Thunderclap Newman album sessions, arranged and engineered by Pete at Eel Pie Sound.

"Some of [the album] was actually done on two Revox stereo recorders, not on 8-track," Townshend told *Zigzag*. "We didn't get the 8-track until halfway through the sessions." Under the pseudonym Bijou Drains, Pete played bass on each track and pedal steel on the instrumental "Hollywood Dream."

LEFT: *Vogue* PHOTOSHOOT, JULY 1969.

1
9
6
9

ABOVE: The Who with Chuck Berry at the Royal Albert Hall, London, 5 July.

THURSDAY, 10 and FRIDAY, 11 JULY

Keith accompanied "Legs" Larry Smith to two Bonzo Dog Doo-Dah Band gigs in the West Country. On the 10th, at the Locarno, Bristol, Keith appeared as "The Lone Arranger," replacing Larry behind the drums, while he performed front of stage. The act was repeated the following night at the Van Dike club, Devonport.

TUESDAY, 15—THURSDAY, 17 JULY

Further Thunderclap Newman sessions at Eel Pie Sound and IBC.

The group were currently at #1 in the U.K. charts with "Something In The Air." The sessions continued in August after Pete returned from the States. During the same time at IBC, Roger produced a version of "Accidents" by his protégés, Bent Frame, for a pro-

jected Track single. The band featured John Hetnerington (guitar/lead vocals), Robbie Patterson (bass), Dave McDougall (keyboards) and Who roadie Tony Haslam on vocals.

SATURDAY, 19 JULY

Mothers Club, Erdington, Birmingham.

Overcome by the sweltering heat, Keith collapsed

		Dunkley	2.20 - 2.50	Breakthru.
5.30 - 6.30	Gypsy		2.50 - 3.35	Roy Harper
6.45 - 7.30	Dry Ice		3.35 - 4.15	Strawbs
7.30 - 8.15	Wallace Collection		4.25 - 5.25	BONZO DOG BAND
8.15 - 8.55	Groundhogs		6.30 - 7.15	Aynsley Dunbar
8.55 - 9.35	Steamhammer		7.15 - 7.55	John Surman
9.35 - 10.15	King Crimson		7.55 - 8.25	John Morgan
			8.55 - 9.25	Yes
			8.25 - 8.55	Fat Mattress
			9.25 - 10.05	Chicken Shack
			10.15 - 11.15	THE WHO

Sunday 10th August

VILLAGE			ARENA	
Noon - 2.00	Discs· D J Andy		2.00 - 2.45	Ro...
		Dunkley	2.45 - 3.30	M...
5.30 - 6.30	Hardin & York		3.30 - 4.15	Jo... Kelly
6.30 - 7.15	Circus		4.25 - 5.25	P...ANGLE
7.15 - 8.00	Cuby's Blues Band		6.30 - 7.15	Kee... Hartley
8.00 - 8.40	Babylon		7.15 - 7.45	Eclection
8.40 - 9.15	Hard Meat		7.45 - 8.15	Blodwyn Pig
9.15 - 9.55	Affinity		8.15 - 8.35	Clouds
9.55 - 10.25	Julian...Treati...		8.35 - 9.05	Chris Barber
			9.05 - 9.45	Family
			9.50 - 10.20	Hair
			10.25 - 11.25	THE NICE

and was carried backstage to revive. After approximately an hour's wait, the gig continued.

SUNDAY, 20 JULY
Pier Ballroom, Hastings.

SUNDAY, 27 JULY
The Redcar Jazz Club, Coatham Hotel, Redcar.

MONDAY, 28 JULY
Fillmore North, Locarno Ballroom, Sunderland.

The Who opened this club, which was set up by Jeff Docherty, who had promoted the Who's show at Whitburn Bay on 28 April and all of their Tyneside club gigs up to 1971.

SATURDAY, 2 AUGUST
The Winter Garden, Eastbourne.

MONDAY, 4 AUGUST
The Pavilion, Bath.

THURSDAY, 7 AUGUST
Assembly Hall, Worthing.

SATURDAY, 9 AUGUST
9th National Jazz and Blues Festival, Plumpton Racecourse, Lewes, Sussex.

For a fee of £600, the Who topped the bill on the second night over Chicken Shack, Fat Mattress (who arrived late and didn't play), Yes (with jazzman Jon Hendricks), the Jazz Sound of John Surman, Roy Harper, Aynsley Dunbar Retaliation, the Bonzo Dog Doo-Dah Band, Strawbs, and Breakthru.

During the afternoon, Keith guested as "The Lone Arranger" with the Bonzos. "We're now going to do some art," announced Viv Stanshall, the group's singer. "Art with a capital 'F,'" as a masked Keith walked on, carrying three pints of beer, one of which he poured over "Legs" Larry Smith. After a few parodic bars of "Pinball Wizard," Keith tore the mask aside and continued to drum for the rest of the set.

SUNDAY, 10 AUGUST
The Who flew to New York to honour contracted appearances at the Tanglewood and Woodstock music festivals.

TUESDAY, 12 AUGUST
Tanglewood Music Festival, Music Shed, Tanglewood, Lenox, Massachusetts.

Promoted by Bill Graham, the Who supported Jefferson Airplane as special guest stars, with B.B. King. It was the first occasion that rock music had been presented at this classical music venue in the Berkshire Mountains of West Massachusetts.

THE PAVILION - BATH

MON JULY 21 — THUNDERCLAP NEWMAN — SOMETHING IN THE AIR — ADM. 5/6

MON JULY 28 — BONZO DOG — ADM. 6/6

MON AUG 4 — THE WHO — ADM. 6/6

7·30-10·30 P.M. | 2 GROUPS at EVERY SESSION

SATURDAY, 16 and SUNDAY, 17 AUGUST

Woodstock Music and Art Fair, Bethel, New York.

The legendary three day festival became a free event, after an estimated 450,000 had gathered, "a nation within a nation." Seeing the television reports and sensing the importance of the occasion, Pete brought along Karen and their six-month-old daughter, Emma, while Roger was accompanied by his girlfriend, New York model Heather Taylor. John's wife Alison remained at the hotel. Their journey took some six hours, flying part of the way by helicopter from New York, then joining a tailbank of cars, finally walking the final mile through thick mud.

Backstage, tensions mounted during a tedious fourteen-hour wait, not helped by the group's drinks being spiked with acid and the fact that the balance of their performance fee was being withheld.

John Wolff was given the thankless task of dealing with the organisers. As he recalled, "I told John Morris, 'Look, we're not waiting anymore. Where's the money?!' He said, 'I'll give you a cheque.' I said, I'm not interested in a cheque!' So he avoided me for several hours. By now, it was getting closer and closer to the band going on. They then tried the 'You'll *have* to go on' routine, like '*You won't* be able to not play in front of all these people.'

"I said, 'Don't care, not interested, they're not going on.' Anyway, they kept on stalling until, in the end, they had to get a helicopter to get the bank manager up, because the safe was on a time-lock

and he was the only person that could open it. They got the cash, paid me, and suddenly I was surrounded by all these other band managers who hadn't been paid. Sly and the Family Stone had been on for three hours and the band before that had overplayed. The Who were supposed to have been on at about ten o'clock at night, and ended up onstage at 4:00 in the morning. It was just a joke."

Michael Wadleigh and his six-man crew shot 120 hours of film (costing some $600,000) which was cut to it's eventual three hour length by Thelma Schoonmaker, whose editing team included film student, Martin Scorsese. Film techniques incorporated triple screens to enable whole groups to be seen at the same time, over-laid pictures, close-ups, zoom lenses, and colour tints.

Warner Brothers' costs were swiftly recouped when *Woodstock* simultaneously premiered at the Trans-Lux East Theater, New York, and at the Fox-Wilshire, Hollywood on Thursday 26 March 1970. (In England, it debuted at the Empire Cinema, Leicester Square, London, on 25 June 1970.)

"See Me, Feel Me," "Summertime Blues," and the "My Generation" finale were a featured highlight of the movie. "Summertime Blues" first screened on British television during BBC-2's *The Old Grey Whistle Test* on 12 October 1971. "Sparks," "Pinball Wizard," "See Me, Feel Me" (sans split-screen effects), and the finale appeared in *The Kids Are Alright*.

"My Generation" appeared in edited form in the second of a three-part television documentary, *Woodstock Diary*, broadcast twenty-five years later in 1994. The entire festival was recorded and engineered on 8-track by Eddie Kramer. Decca permitted "We're Not Gonna Take It" to be included on

the first triple disc soundtrack, released by Atlantic Records in May 1970.

FRIDAY, 22 AUGUST

Music Hall, Shrewsbury, Shropshire.

SATURDAY, 23 AUGUST

Marquee Meadow Festival, Grays, Essex.

The Who didn't perform because Keith broke his right ankle after falling down the stairs at his Highgate home—the result of a birthday lark with "Legs" Larry Smith. "The Who won't play without me so we had to cancel the gig," Keith told *Record Mirror*. "We went on stage, though, and got our money."

TUESDAY, 26 and THURSDAY, 28 AUGUST

As a measure of the attention *Tommy* was already attracting, the Who flew to Hamburg, Germany, to videotape a *Beat Club* segment over two days at Radio Bremen's studio, screened (as Show 47) on Saturday, 27 September.

The group mimed to playback on "Overture," "Pinball Wizard," "Smash The Mirror," "Sally Simpson," "Tommy Can You Hear Me?," "I'm Free," "Tommy's Holiday Camp," and "We're Not Gonna Take It." Background graphics from Mike McInnerney's sleeve art, together with filmstock and subtitles, were superimposed for the 40 minute programme, which also featured a serious, analytical Townshend interview subtitled between songs.

The Who were impressed with the finished production, as Keith told the *NME*'s Richard Green: "*Beat Club* has an amazing geezer there, Mike Leckebusch. I like him, he's got the right ideas, he's got the *Ready, Steady, Go!* ideas. He was a constant figure at *Ready, Steady, Go!*, and what he's done is go back and use their ideas. The BBC institution is like a government, they won't let any of their members be tarred, they'll cover up. But Radio Bremen with one man has the right idea."

"Tommy Can You Hear Me?" and a humorous extract from the interview appeared in *The Kids Are Alright*. With the announcement of the "world premiere" of *Tommy* taking place at Amsterdam's Concertgebouw on 29 September, a pre-recorded interview with Pete in London (filming date unknown) appeared in the Dutch television programme *Televizier*, which was screened 26 August, Nederland 1, 8:20—8:45 pm.

FRIDAY, 29 AUGUST
Pavilion Ballroom, Bournemouth.

SATURDAY, 30 AUGUST
2nd Isle of Wight Festival of Music, Woodside Bay, Isle of Wight.

Co-promoted by brothers Raymond and Ronald Foulk and Rikki Farr of Fiery Creations Ltd., the Who appeared during the second afternoon on a bill featuring Fat Mattress, Joe Cocker and the Grease Band, the Bonzo Dog Doo-Dah Band, Gypsy, Marsha Hunt and White Trash, Aynsley Dunbar Retaliation, the Pretty Things, Blodwyn Pig, Free, Blonde On Blonde, and King Crimson.

"The Who arrived by helicopter," recalled MC Jeff Dexter. "A landing pad had to be laid out, so somebody had the bright idea to lay these wooden boards down. Of course, as they landed, one of these huge boards just lifted off the ground and went straight into the propeller. It was a total disaster, because the Who intended leaving straight after they'd finished playing."

The group used one of the biggest PAs available in the U.K. at that time, with notices boldly warning the audience not to stand within 15 feet (5m) of the speakers, which blasted at over 2500 watts. Although most media attention was focused on a reclusive Bob Dylan, who was making his first British appearance in three years the following evening, the Who stole the show.

"It was a great concert for us," Pete confirmed to Richard Barnes, "because we felt so in control of the whole situation. We were able to just come in, do it and not need to know anything about what was going on. In other words, we didn't spend time at the festival getting into the vibrations, didn't stay to see

OPPOSITE: ONSTAGE AT WOODSTOCK.

ABOVE: ARRIVING AT THE ISLE OF WIGHT FESTIVAL.

Bob Dylan, didn't care what was going on. We knew that the stage act we had, with *Tommy* in it, would work under any circumstances because it had worked many times on tour."

A French film crew filmed part of the Who's set, first shown later that year as part of an ORTF television documentary on the festival. Keith had to be administered pain-killing injections in his ankle before he could play. While the group waited to go on, he and "Legs" Larry Smith amused themselves by commandeering their new-found toy: the helicopter.

"Track sent over this other helicopter to replace the broken one," Dexter remembered, "and it had extra seats. I think Peter Rudge was offering them at 25 quid a go to anyone who wanted to fly back to the Speakeasy for the night!"

SATURDAY, 6 SEPTEMBER
Kinema Ballroom, Dunfermline, Fifeshire, Scotland.

The previous night, Keith and John attended the 8:00 pm screening of Richard Stanley's *Lone Ranger* (see 8 May 1968), entered as part of a season of U.K. student films at the International Film Festival, Edinburgh.

SUNDAY, 7 SEPTEMBER
Cosmopolitan Club, Carlisle.

SATURDAY, 13 SEPTEMBER
The Belfry, Sutton Coldfield, Birmingham.

SUNDAY, 21 SEPTEMBER
Fairfield Hall, Croydon.

The Who's two and a quarter-hour act now featured the majority of *Tommy*. In a 1971 *Zigzag* interview,

Pete rated this show as perhaps their best performance of the work.

MONDAY, 29 SEPTEMBER
Concertgebouw, Amsterdam, Holland. Co-promoted by Paul Acket and New Action Ltd., the "world premiere" of *Tommy* at one of the world's foremost opera houses.

Moon made a typically unorthodox entrance, as Entwistle recalled: "We came down some carpeted stairs onto the stage. Keith started running and didn't stop. He careered across the stage and over the edge, knocking over two speaker cabinets... the crowd burst out laughing, but when he got to his feet, he was covered in blood."

There was inevitably considerable media interest in such a prestigious occasion. A brief interview with Pete by Jan Gerritsen, shots of the stage set-up, Keith's tumble, and part of "A Quick One" and "Smash The Mirror" were included in *Journaal*, broadcast the following evening, 8:00—8:15 pm. The entire concert was recorded and broadcast (with additional

BELOW: ONSTAGE AT THE ISLE OF WIGHT FESTIVAL, WITH JEFF DEXTER (LEFT), 30 AUGUST.

commentary) by AVRO on 30 September and 1 October, produced by Karel van de Graaf.

FRIDAY, 10 OCTOBER
The Who commenced a five-week American and Canadian tour at the Commonwealth Armory, Boston, Massachusetts, supported by the Flock.

SATURDAY, 11 and SUNDAY, 12 OCTOBER
Grande-Riviera Ballroom, Detroit, Michigan, supported by Alice Cooper and the Sky (featuring future Knack frontman Doug Fieger) on the 11th; All The Lonely People and the Amboy Dukes (with Ted Nugent) on the 12th.

During Cooper drummer Neal Smith's solo in "Ballad Of Dwight Frye," Keith joined in from his own kit set up behind.

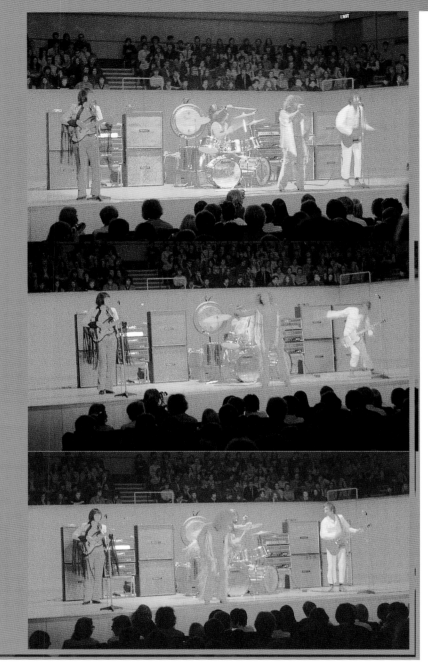

ABOVE: FAIRFIELD HALL, CROYDON, 21 SEPTEMBER.

TUESDAY, 14 OCTOBER
CNE Coliseum, Toronto, Canada.

WEDNESDAY, 15 OCTOBER
Capitol Theatre, Ottawa, Canada.

FRIDAY, 17 OCTOBER
Holy Cross College Gymnasium, Worcester, Massachusetts, with Ascension.

SATURDAY, 18 OCTOBER
New York State University Gymnasium, Stony Brook, New York, with the Flock.

SUNDAY, 19 OCTOBER
Electric Factory, Philadelphia, Pennsylvania. Two shows, 4:00 & 8:00 pm.

MONDAY, 20—SATURDAY, 25 OCTOBER
Fillmore East, New York City.

Six-night stand promoted by Bill Graham, with the Joshua Light Show. On the 24th and 25th, there were two shows per night, 8:00 & 11:30 pm.

"We tried doing a residency once at the Fillmore East," Entwistle recalled. "We did a week and every night the front row was the same people." Like the majority of shows on the tour, the concerts were recorded in stereo by Bob Pridden using just two mikes and a small recorder.

Audiences included Bob Dylan and Leonard Bernstein. "Leonard Bernstein came with his daughter," said Townshend. "...and he was incredibly excited. He grabbed me by the shoulder, shook me and said, 'Do you realize what you are doing? Do you realize how wonderful this is?' He was interested in music being accessible and popular. And that's what really excited him."

SUNDAY, 26 OCTOBER
Syria Mosque, Pittsburgh, Pennsylvania.

Pete was impressed enough with support group the James Gang, featuring guitarist Joe Walsh, to invite them to support the Who the following year. A four day break in the tour afforded Pete and John Wolff an opportunity to unwind with Tom Wright at his father's farm in Central Florida, 50 miles (80km) north of Clearwater.

"I wrote ["The Seeker"] when I was drunk standing in a swamp in Florida," Townshend told Jonathan Cott. "I was just covered in sand spurs. I kept falling, and they stick in your skin, and you can't get them out, screaming with pain and singing this song and it just came out, 'I'm looking for me, you're looking for you, we're looking at each other and we don't know what to do.'"

MONDAY, 27 OCTOBER
Pete's title music for a documentary film about CERN (European Council for Nuclear Research) high-energy physics, directed by Denis Postle of Tattooist International Films, was broadcast in BBC-2's *Horizon* series, 9:40—10:25 pm.

FRIDAY, 31 OCTOBER
Kinetic Playground, Chicago, Illinois, with the Kinks and Adrian Henri's Liverpool Scene.

The Who were due to return on 9 November, but the venue was destroyed in the interim by fire.

SATURDAY, 1 NOVEMBER
Veterans Memorial Auditorium, Columbus, Ohio.

SUNDAY, 2 NOVEMBER
McDonough Gymnasium, Georgetown University, Washington D.C.

MONDAY, 3 NOVEMBER
Westchester County Center, White Plains, New York.

TUESDAY, 4 NOVEMBER
Bushnell Auditorium, Hartford, Connecticut.

THURSDAY, 6 NOVEMBER
Livingston Gymnasium, Dennison University, Granville, Ohio.

FRIDAY, 7 NOVEMBER
Ohio State University, Athens, Ohio.

SATURDAY, 8 NOVEMBER
Kiel Opera House, St. Louis, Missouri.

MONDAY, 10 NOVEMBER
Palace Theater, Albany, New York, with the Flock.

TUESDAY, 11 and WEDNESDAY, 12 NOVEMBER
The Boston Tea Party, Boston, Massachusetts, with Tony Williams' Lifetime.

THURSDAY, 13 NOVEMBER
New York State University Gymnasium, New Paltz, New York, with the Flock.

FRIDAY, 14 NOVEMBER
Public Music Hall, Cleveland, Ohio.

SATURDAY, 15 NOVEMBER

Kleinhans Music Hall, Buffalo, New York.

SUNDAY, 16 NOVEMBER

Onondaga War Memorial Auditorium, Syracuse, New York, with Silk.

The Who flew back to England on 18 November.

THURSDAY, 4 DECEMBER

Hippodrome Theatre, Bristol.

A troublesome opening concert of an English mini-tour, co-promoted by John and Tony Smith, in conjunction with Track. Towards the end of the show, two smoke bombs were thrown from one of the boxes. The first exploded away from the stage, but the second landed in front of John, billowing out thick, choking smoke. Daltrey's voice became affected, and he stormed off-stage. A spotlight was swung onto the culprit, who dropped his trousers and "mooned" the audience. "And did you see those pimples?!" Townshend quipped.

Each of the five concerts was recorded and filmed by New Action for possible use in a pro-jected *Tommy* feature. *Disc* revealed tentative plans for a cartoon version, to be made by *Yellow Submarine* animator George Dunning, as well as for an expanded version in ballet form. "It [the film] will not just be a straight, narrative version of *Tommy*, but an extension of the album," the article read. "Pete might write some new material for it, and the name might even be changed."

FRIDAY, 5 DECEMBER

Palace Theatre, Manchester.

FRIDAY, 12 DECEMBER

Empire Theatre, Liverpool.

SUNDAY, 14 DECEMBER

Coliseum Theatre, St. Martin's Lane, London.

Except for the royal box, all 2500 seats were filled at the home of the English National Opera. "I'm a bit embarrassed to use the term opera here in the Coliseum," announced a self-deprecating Townshend, "I went to Covent Garden last night... Not bad, but not so good as us. Now we're going to take over!"

Under Chris Stamp's direction, three cameras were positioned in the stalls, pit, and on stage, but the footage was never utilised at the time—sound and lighting problems being a contributing factor. "Young Man Blues" appeared in *The Kids Are Alright* movie and soundtrack. "I'm Free" and "Happy Jack" were included in *Who's Better, Who's Best* and *Thirty Years of Maximum R&B Live*, respectively.

After the show, Kit Lambert threw a champagne celebration in a reception room at Sadlers Wells. "Legs" Larry Smith, Jimmy McCulloch, and the Rascals were among the guests.

MONDAY, 15 DECEMBER

Keith made a special appearance, drumming in the all-star aggregation of the Plastic Ono Band's "War Is Over...If You Want It" UNICEF benefit concert at the Lyceum, London. Billed as "Peace For Christmas," the line-up was assembled by John and Yoko Lennon at 48 hours notice and included George Harrison, Eric Clapton, Klaus Voormann, Bobby Keys, Delaney and Bonnie, Billy Preston, Alan White, Jim Gordon, and "Legs" Larry Smith.

Only two songs were performed: "Cold Turkey" and "Don't Worry Kyoko (Mummy's Only Looking For Her Hand In The Snow)." The entire concert was recorded by EMI and eventually released as Side Three ("Live Jam") of John and Yoko's *Sometime In New York City* album in June 1972.

TUESDAY, 16 DECEMBER

The Who rehearsed and recorded their appearance on BBC-1's end of the decade celebratory special *Pop Go The Sixties!*, a BBC/ZDF British-German co-production presented by DJ Jimmy Savile and Elfi von Kalckreuth, videotaped in Studio E, Television Centre.

With no new product to plug—and perhaps, two years on, still smarting from the churlish way it had been overlooked—the group chose to mime "I Can See For Miles," surrounded by a frenetic, go-go style audience. The Who were the first act appearing in the colour programme, which featured the Bachelors, Kenny Ball and his Jazzmen, the Beatles (on film), Cilla Black, Adam Faith, the Hollies, the Kinks, Lulu, Cliff Richard, the Rolling Stones, the Shadows, Helen Shapiro, Sandie Shaw, the Tremeloes, the Ascot Bros., and Johnny Harris & the Breakaways, transmitted Wednesday, 31 December, 10:40—11:50 pm.

FRIDAY, 19 DECEMBER

City Hall, Newcastle.

"I really enjoyed our *Tommy* tour," Pete told Chris Welch the following month, "although I felt uncomfortable every night when we went on stage, because we play at such a fantastic pitch now, and it was so loud in those theatres which seemed so little after the States, that you couldn't really hear it."

SUNDAY, 28 DECEMBER

Keith and Aynsley Dunbar were unannounced guest drummers during the premiere of the Bonzo Dog Doo-Dah Band's "Outrage Review" presentation at the Lyceum. Rather than unveiling a new phase in their career, Viv Stanshall announced the group's surprise split from the stage.

During this time, "Legs" Larry Smith, under the pseudonym Topo D. Bil, recorded a version of an old Indian chant, "Witchi Tai To" at Trident Studios, 17 St. Anne's Court (off Wardour Street), London. Musicians included Tom Cross, Tony Kaye, and Roger Ruskin Spear. Keith contributed percussion. The single was released by Charisma on Friday, 9 January 1970.

Kit Lambert and Track Records in association with John and Tony Smith present

THE WHO

A TWO - HOUR NON - STOP CONCERT

TO INCLUDE "TOMMY"

Palace - Manchester

Chairman: Prince Littler, C.B.E.   Managing Director: Leslie A. Macdonnell, O.B.E.   Manager: Tim Tillson

FRIDAY, 5th DECEMBER at 7.30 p.m.

Be Advised ... Book Early

Seats: 20/- 17/- 15/- 13/- 8/- 7/-

Bookable in advance from: Palace Box Office, Tel. CENtral 0184

1969

DEAF, DUMB, AND BLIND BOY   **171**

The Who created a monster, and they called it *Tommy*—a blessing and a curse.

"Lot's of air hostesses on airplanes said, 'I know you all; you're Tommy the Who,'" Townshend told Chris van Ness. "It was that much of a complete picture. 'The Who play *Tommy*.' Then *Tommy* even got bigger than us. '*Tommy* and the Who.' I've seen that on posters."

"We were better known for doing *Tommy* than we were for all the rest of the stuff," Entwistle lamented. "I mean all of the guitar smashing and stuff completely went out the window. We turned into snob rock, we were the kind of band that Jackie Onassis would come and see, and I didn't particularly like that. I felt we should have played opera houses and smashed them up." Townshend also balked at the idea of playing rock in such hallowed havens. "The thing I didn't dig about it is that we didn't play big enough places," he told *Rolling Stone*. "Only about a hundredth of the kids who wanted to see us could. And we'd go in and play and like the first 20 rows would be Polydor people. Or Prince Rainier and his

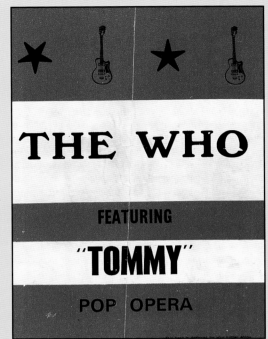

royal family, and honestly it was such a bad scene."

In March, a new Who single appeared. "'The Seeker' had nothing to do with Baba lovers, or Krishna devotees, or whatever," Townshend told Al Clark. "It was a song glorifying the ordinary man in the street, who's like hitting people with bottles but still, believe it or not, looking for god realisation even though he doesn't know it." Unfortunately, all the superlatives were still being lavished on the Deaf, Dumb, and Blind Boy.

Townshend reacted with a mixture of chagrin and bravado, telling Richard Green: "To be honest, I'm a bit disappointed in that single. It's the kind of mistake the Who often make at the most obvious time. It was meant to bridge the gap between the old Who sound and the new Who sound. It was the first record in the limbo after *Tommy* and it excited us all. But when I heard it again I thought it was a bit cumbersome."

The dilemma of following *Tommy* was partially resolved by the classy holding operation that was *Live At Leeds*, an adrenalised aural assault, recorded at Leeds University on Valentine's Day. "What hits you when you listen to it is you realise how much you need to see the Who," Townshend told Jonathan Cott. In his *New York Times* column, Nik Cohn called it "the best live rock album ever made." The bootleg-style packaging and inclusion of facsimiles relating to bygone gigs, hire purchase demands, and scribbled lyrics reveal a group already self-consciously obsessed with its past. Above all, *Live At Leeds* perfectly encapsulates the Who at the pinnacle of their prowess. "There was a point, at the time of *Live At Leeds*, when I was getting very dextrous," Townshend told Jill Eckersley. "I practised every day, the Who were working on the road a lot, and I was using a Gibson SG that I'd had a long time. It was a very fast instrument, and we really hit it off. I found my hands going faster than my head and when I listened to tapes of the shows, I was

playing some really blinding stuff, but I thought, 'What's the point?' There's always someone who can play faster, always someone who can play better."

The Who arrived in America in June for a month-long tour, comprising twenty-three appearances in nineteen cities, commencing with two concerts at New York's Metropolitan Opera House. Setting standards for sound and presentation, this was the Who's first meticulous juggernaut around America, requiring three tons of specially built Charlie Watkins gear to be flown in, including a 4000 watt stereo system, designed by Townshend and Bob Pridden, that incorporated mixers placed at the front and back of each venue. A special custom-built truck, with a five man crew, transported it across the continent.

For better or worse, the Who were pioneering that dubious animal, stadium rock. But unlike such contemporaries as Led Zeppelin, who were gearing up to play Madison Square Garden and other such cavernous auditoriums, the group gave their original promoters and fans a break on this tour by deliberately playing smaller venues for fees between $7500 and $10,000, when they could have easily demanded $15,000 or more per concert. Even after such charitable gestures, the Who ended the 1970 U.S. tour as millionaires, with *Live At Leeds* and *Tommy* pulling down over $1 million and $5 million worth of American sales respectively.

"We became a really extraordinary machine," Townshend marvelled to Alan di Perna. "We were briefly called 'The Greatest Rock snd Roll Band in the World,' and we were. There was no question about it. I used to wake up on the stage every night and think, 'Oh my God, I'm riding this horse again!'"

In August, the Who made a second memorable appearance at the 3rd Annual Isle of Wight Festival. Roger screamed in tie-dyed buckskin; Keith thrashed away in virgin white; Pete, with newly grown beard, leapt and windmilled in trademark boiler suit; while John stood resplendent in a skintight skeleton suit. On the final night, Jimi Hendrix played one of his last concerts, dying in London on 18 September. Pete paid tribute to the musician who had affected him so deeply. "Jimi doesn't need musical obituaries. It was either going to be a bomb dropping or Jimi Hendrix happening; people knew, they felt something was going to happen. The impact he made was enormous. He was there, you didn't have to see or hear him to know that it was a point in musical history."

Just as the band were laying *Tommy* to rest, interest was being generated from various theatrical companies who saw its potential within the arts. From 16-18 October, an ambitious, multi-media ballet adaptation was staged by Les Grands Ballet Canadiens in Montreal, Canada, while a thesis production by the University of Southern California opened in March 1971. MCA/Universal Pictures, who now owned Decca, had an option on the screen rights and were prepared to bankroll a film. One report had Ray Stark (*Funny Girl*) producing, while another named Joe Strick (*Ulysses*) to direct, with either Warner or MGM distributing.

Kit Lambert prepared a script, but when Townshend lost interest and rejected the idea, it marked the beginning of their estrangement. "Our relationship drifted," Townshend told *Zigzag*. "I think it was *Tommy* that destroyed the relationship. It was so exhausting. It was incredibly long and drawn out. It took about two years of active involvement. Kit's real contribution will never, ever be known because, of course, it wasn't production at all, it was far deeper... Kit was much more involved in the overall concept of the thing—much more than people imagine. Not all that much, in fact, with the overall sound. Although he did produce it and mix it, and he did make us work at it—still the main thing was that he thought of the idea of Rock Opera."

Lambert and Stamp favourably renegotiated the Who's contract with MCA getting an eight-album deal for $750,000 per album, considered not bad for the time, although the band were still tied to the same company they'd crossed swords with in the past. Each member had different ways of dealing with this new-found affluence. Roger sold his Berkshire cottage to production manager John Wolff and bought a thirty-five-acre country estate, Holmhurst Manor in Burwash, East Sussex, spending his spare hours renovating the six-bedroom, Jacobean mansion built on the property in 1610. With a backlog of songs he felt unsuitable for the

Who, John financed his own album. Keith let his irrepressible "Moon The Loon" persona effectively conceal a pit of guilt and depression he sank into after a tragic accident in the new year that left his driver Neil Boland dead beneath the wheels of his Bentley. Tired of being barred from pubs, he and neighbour Ron

ABOVE: "BAH HUMBUG!" MOON THE LOON.

Mears invested a £16,000 stake each in their own, "The Crown and Cushion," a fourteenth century hostelry in Oxfordshire's Chipping Norton. (Mears son, John, became Keith's new driver.)

Moon's antics became increasingly more bizarre. The residents of Winchmore Hill became accustomed to the sight of him wandering around the neighbourhood dressed as anything from a vicar to a gorilla. His close friendship with fellow lunatics "Legs" Larry Smith and Vivian Stanshall of the Bonzo Dog Band, lead to much amusing tomfoolery, usually perpetrated around Soho's watering holes. A typical incident involved Moon and Stanshall dressed as Adolf Hitler and Heinrich Himmler, being thrown out of a German bierkeller. Hours later, the

pair were chased around Golders Green by an angry Jewish shopkeeper wielding a meat axe. They were inseparable and their practical jokes extended to them making a record together, an insane remake of Terry Stafford's hit, "Suspicion."

While Moon spent money like water, Townshend gave away large sums to any charity or idea he felt deserving, while continuing to establish a reputation as an astute theoretician. In a lengthy editorial regarding drug use in the *Sunday Telegraph*, he bravely put his counterculture credibility on the line by emphasising Baba's dim views on the subject and was given his own monthly *Melody Maker* column, "The Pete Townshend Page," which first appeared in the 22 August issue.

Over the following eight months, his often controversial views were expounded in such thought-provoking articles as "Is Rock Dead?" and "Change—by taking people UP." At the same time, Pete became deeply involved with *Guitar Farm*, a film script written by Mike Myers of Tattooist Films, to be produced by Herb Solow (*Star Trek*) for MGM, until Lambert, still smarting from the rejection of his *Tommy* script, jealously pressured Pete into withdrawing from the project.

Ideas were buzzing around for the next Who album, including talk of a double with each member having a side to himself, an exercise exhausted by lesser talents. Over the winter, Pete's burgeoning interest in film and modern technology led to him investing in an VCS3 organ and programmable ARP 2500 synthesiser. He wrote and demoed a set of songs intended for a script involving "an experiment in relationship involving film and music between group and audience." In October, Townshend went looking for a suitable theatre that could function as a studio cum workshop, similar to Creedence's "Cosmo's Factory."

Like his lengthy 1968 *Rolling Stone* interview, in which the storyline for *Tommy* was articulated, Townshend roughly crystallised the basis for his next opus in a *Disc and Music Echo* interview with Roy Shipston, published 24 October: "It's about a set of musicians, a group who look and behave remarkably like the Who, and they have an idealistic roadie, Bobby... Anyway, this guy finds a musical note which basically creates complete devastation. And when everything is destroyed, only the real note, the true note that they have been looking for, is left."

1970

SATURDAY, 3 JANUARY

Melody Maker reported that John and Tony Smith had been refused permission to stage a Who concert at Glasgow's Kelvin Hall on Sunday, 22 March after the hall management heard adverse reports from both the Palace Theatre, Manchester, and the Hippodrome, Bristol. Who publicist Brian Somerville countered that neither the group nor any of their representatives had made an approach: "Perhaps that's why the management didn't hear both sides of the story."

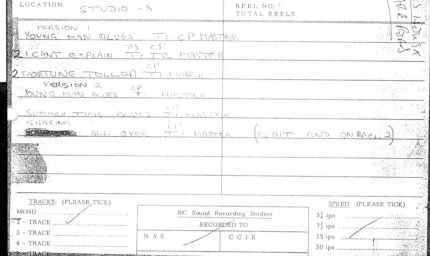

ABOVE: KEITH WITH NEIL BOLAND.

SUNDAY, 4 JANUARY

Keith was invited to open a discotheque at the Cranbourne Rooms (adjoining the Red Lion pub), Hatfield, Hertfordshire. Keith, wife Kim, "Legs" Larry Smith, and companion Jean Battye were driven to the party by the Moons' driver, twenty-four-year-old Cornelius "Neil" Boland. As they departed

at 10:45 pm, a group of around twenty-five jeering skinheads started to kick and throw pennies at the Bentley. Boland jumped out to clear a path and was attacked by some of the youths. According to an eyewitness account, "suddenly the Bentley shot out of the carpark down the A1000 [Great North Road]. I followed in a friend's car, but when we got to the Bentley, we found a man pinned beneath it."

Boland was taken to Queen Elizabeth Hospital, Welwyn Garden City, but was found dead on arrival. Moon was released the following morning, after being interviewed by local police. "I have been helping police with enquiries and have made a statement. I will not be seeing the police again," he told waiting press. On the 5th, two youths, aged eighteen and fifteen, were remanded in custody for a week at Hatfield court, accused of causing an affray. While Keith kept a low profile, recording sessions scheduled to begin during the week were cancelled.

TUESDAY, 6 JANUARY

Mixing IBC, Studio A: Damon Lyon-Shaw prepared a master reel for a proposed Who live album from 2-track tapes recorded by Bob Pridden on the October 1969 U.S. tour. Tracks: "Young Man Blues" #1, "I Can't Explain," "Fortune Teller," "Young Man Blues" #2, "Summertime Blues," "Shakin' All Over," "Tattoo," and "My Generation."

FRIDAY, 16 and SATURDAY, 17 JANUARY

Theatre des Champs Elysses, Paris, France.

The Who were given the supreme accolade of being the first rock act ever allowed to appear at each hallowed venue in a short tour of European opera houses. "The European tour is very political," said tour manager Peter Rudge. "We were turned down in Austria, Italy, Switzerland and got the cold shoulder in Spain. We've been working on the tour for four or five months, and the Germans were very groovy, so were the Dutch. But for some of the others it was a bit too much for them to contemplate the Who in their sacred opera houses." The show on the 17th was broadcast live at 9:00 pm on Europe 1 as a *Musicorama* special.

MONDAY, 19 and TUESDAY, 20 JANUARY

Recording/mixing IBC: A remake of "The Seeker," with Pete on piano, engineered by Damon Lyon-Shaw. "[Kit] had a tooth pulled, breaking his jaw, and we did it ourselves," Townshend wrote in *Rolling*

Stone. Lambert was still given the production credit, but from then on, his role greatly diminished.

"Kit thoroughly understands the Who," Townshend told Steve Peacock a year later, "but we don't understand him at all, which puts us in a very difficult position. We knew that his pride was going to be hurt by us producing ourselves, but at the same time, we knew that it was the only thing that could be done. Before that, we'd been working in my studio trying to get singles and bits and pieces together, and when it didn't work, we called Kit back in again, but he's always known on what basis he was being called in."

SATURDAY, 24 JANUARY

Det Kunglige Teater, Royal Theatre, Copenhagen, Denmark.

The *NME* reported the future of rock concerts at the Royal Albert Hall was in jeopardy from the Musicians Union after the management refused to book a 17 March charity event in aid of "Release" and the National Council for Civil Liberties. The event was to feature John Lennon, the Who, the Incredible String Band, and King Crimson.

The same issue revealed plans for a colour TV spectacular starring the Who to be made by Granada's Jo Durden-Smith, producer of *The Doors Are Open* and *The Stones In The Park*. Co-produced with other European countries, the completed fifty-minute documentary would be shown in early summer throughout Europe and also possibly the U.S. It became, however, yet another in a frustrating list of Who-related film projects that failed to get off the ground.

MONDAY, 26 JANUARY

Stadt Opernhaus, Cologne, West Germany.

President Heinemann of the West German Republic and Chancellor Willy Brandt watched the show after attending a private reception backstage. All German concert proceeds went to the Save The Children Fund, of which Heinemann was 1970 World President.

TUESDAY, 27 JANUARY

Stadt Opernhaus, Hamburg, West Germany.

THIS PAGE: Recording "The Seeker" at IBC, 19 January, with Bob Pridden, top right.

(in samenwerking met Track Records)

"tommy"

de door Pete Townshend gekomponeerde Rock

ABOVE: GERMANY, JANUARY TOUR.

WEDNESDAY, 28 JANUARY
Stadt Opernhaus, Berlin, West Germany.

FRIDAY, 30 JANUARY
Concertgebouw, Amsterdam, Holland.
  In his quest for a follow-up to *Tommy*, Pete composed "I Don't Even Know Myself" backstage.

FEBRUARY
To mark what would have been Baba's seventy-sixth birthday, Pete and a group of followers put together *Happy Birthday*, a 2500 limited edition album including a twenty-eight-page booklet, featuring Baba-inspired drawings and poems. The album was only available from the Universal Spiritual League, London, and the Meher Baba Information office,

Berkeley, California, with proceeds going to the Baba Foundation.
  Townshend-related tracks were "Content" (based on a poem written by Maud Kennedy and later included on 1972's *Who Came First*), "Day Of Silence," "Mary Jane," "The Love Man," "The Seeker" (his original Who demo), and a rendition of Cole Porter's Jubilee showtune, "Begin The Beguine," a

Baba personal favourite. Pete also played acoustic guitar on "Evolution," written and sung by Ronnie Lane of the Faces, included (in edited form) on *Who Came First*.

TUESDAY, 10 FEBRUARY

Recording/mixing Studio B IBC: Roger's composition "Here For More," engineered by Damon Lyon-Shaw. The track was released as the B-side to "The Seeker" on Friday, 20 March (25 April in the U.S.) The Who's first material since *Tommy* reached #19 and #44 in each respective territory.

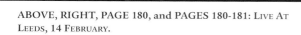

ABOVE, RIGHT, PAGE 180, and PAGES 180-181: LIVE AT LEEDS, 14 FEBRUARY.

SATURDAY, 14 FEBRUARY

University, Leeds.

"I'd been planning a live album for ages," Pete told the *NME*'s Richard Green, "and we recorded all the shows on the last American tour thinking that would be where we would get the best material. When we got back, we had eighty hours of tape, and, well, we couldn't sort that lot out, so we booked the Pye mobile studio and took it to Leeds. It turned out to be one of the best and most enjoyable gigs we've ever done."

(According to Townshend, the American concert tapes were destroyed to eliminate bootlegging. However, some recordings appear to have escaped the purge.)

An attempt was later made to overdub lost vocals. "We tried, but it didn't work," said John. "The only thing we added was a bit of tape delay. It sounded too clean for a live recording. Once we added the delay and cut the audience out, it sounded fine. There was a bit in 'Magic Bus' where we couldn't get it to flow properly, so Pete just edited the tape, cut a bit out and turned it backwards."

SUNDAY, 15 FEBRUARY
City Hall, Hull.

Recorded by the Pye eight-track as a standby operation in case of any technical imperfections arising from the Leeds recording. "We got the mikes and sound balance and things sorted out during the last American tour," Keith told Richard Green. "Moving mikes backwards and forward a bit until the recordings sounded okay... We sat Bob [Pridden] at the control panel on stage

and left him to get on with the balance. The Hull one was quite good, but the Leeds one was really good. Bob worked well that night, bless him!"

FRIDAY, 20 FEBRUARY
At Welwyn Garden City, the jury at Neil Boland's official inquest (adjourned from 9 January) recorded a verdict of accidental death. On Monday, 23 March, at Hatfield Magistrates Court, Keith pleaded guilty to charges of drunken driving and being in charge of a vehicle without insurance or a license. Due to mitigating circumstances, he was given an absolute discharge.

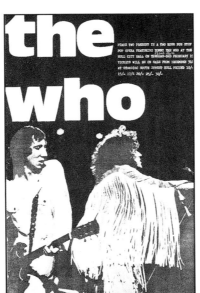

MARCH—MAY
Recording commenced sporadically at Eel Pie Sound Studios, The Embankment, Twickenham, with Pete engineering on eight-

track. Tracks known to have been taped include John's "Postcard," "I Don't Even Know Myself," "Water," "Now I'm A Farmer," and "Naked Eye." John played brass and Pete electric piano, organ, and percussion.

Pete: "We're working on an album now; well at least we keep going into the studio, but Keith demands curtains, and then a rostrum so he can feel like he's on stage, and all that takes time to set up. You see he likes to pull the curtains across when I say, 'Take Three' or something and then a roadie whips them apart, and Keith starts playing!"

John: "We're recording the album at Pete's. It's much better there, and it doesn't cost as much. It costs thirty pounds an hour to hire a studio, and we'd book it for, say, three till twelve. But we'd all arrive late, then sit about, and by that time, the pubs were open so we'd all go out for a drink..."

THURSDAY, 26 MARCH
The Who went to Television Centre to plug "The Seeker" on *Top Of The Pops*, broadcast 7:15—8:00 pm. Like the *TOTP* version of "Pinball Wizard," the BBC

ABOVE RIGHT: *Top Of The Pops*, 26 March.

acquired audio rights for the "sole purpose of sound broadcasting from transmitters outside the British Isles." (This version was released on the U.S. *Live At The BBC* bonus disc.)

"When we did *Top Of The Pops* the other week, I got so annoyed I was going to go home, the cameras just weren't on me at all," Entwistle told Richard Green. "It was all Roger and Pete and Moon. I had to kick up about it before they got shots of me. In the end, I got three or four shots, which was good for me."

He fared little better in the accompanying promotional film, made by Richard Stanley for Tattooist International Productions in a Wardour Street studio. Using a grey colorama paper backdrop, Stanley shot several group performances to playback from a Quad Electrostatic speaker, followed by individual performances in the same fashion—all on one camera. The final cut was a combination of many separate takes, one of which featured lyrics titles shot on a handheld camera, utilising single-frame pixellated footage taken at the Palace Theatre, Manchester (5 December 1969). According to Stanley, neither ver-sion was screened in Britain as Kit Lambert disliked the results, although it was distributed overseas. *The Seeker* was shown in October at the ICA (Institute of Contemporary Arts) as part of a programme of Tattooist productions.

SATURDAY, 11 APRIL

Melody Maker, who awarded *Tommy* "Album Of The Year," announced a 1 May release date for *Live At Leeds*. The Graphreaks-designed sleeve, a parody of the infamous Rolling Stones bootleg *Liver Than You'll Ever Be*, would be individually stamped by band members and anybody else who happened to drop by Track's Old Compton Street offices. The label lettering was designed by freelance artist Beadrall Sutcliffe.

SUNDAY, 12 APRIL

Keith and mentor, Carlo Little, teamed up with Ritchie Blackmore (guitar), Nicky Simper (bass), and Matthew Fisher (piano) to form a one-off backing group for Screaming Lord Sutch at the Country Club, Hampstead, North West London.

Billed as "Lord Sutch And His Heavy Friends," it was Sutch`s first British show in four years.

Keith and Carlo drummed on the Little Richard medley "Jenny Jenny" and "Good Golly Miss Molly." Pete, John, Viv Stanshall, and Spencer Davis were among the audience members. The gig was recorded on the Pye mobile, eventually released by Atlantic in July 1972 as part of *Hands Of Jack The Ripper*, credited to Lord Sutch and Heavy Friends.

MONDAY, 13 APRIL

Recording/mixing IBC Studio A: Material exclusively for broadcast on BBC Radio 1. The session may have been indirectly motivated by a recent exchange in *Radio Times* (the Beeb's listings paper), dated 19 March, between Pete, critic/author George Melly, and Douglas Muggeridge, Controller of Radio 1 and 2.

Muggeridge bemoaned the dearth of top groups willing to broadcast for the corporation. Townshend: "Well, they have to come in and use BBC studios." Muggeridge: "You're worried about the quality of the sound?" Townshend: "If I was going to give a performance that was impromptu, then I would put myself in the hands of BBC engineers. But not if I'm being asked to recreate, penny for penny, a record that took me perhaps two months, in four hours in a BBC studio... Why can't master tapes be made by groups and supplied to you? There could be BBC supervision, and it could be BBC produced..." Muggeridge: "It is my understanding that very few groups would be willing to do such a thing. But if you, or the Beatles, or the Rolling Stones are willing to provide us with a tape, you can be quite sure we'll put it on the air!"

The Who taped versions (produced by Paul Williams) of "I'm Free," "The Seeker," "Heaven And Hell," "Substitute," "Pinball Wizard," and "Shakin' All Over," the last incorporating a few lines from Willie Dixon's "Spoonful." All premiered on *Dave Lee Travis*, Sunday, 19 April, 10:00 am—12:01 pm, and individual tracks were repeated daily on the *Johnnie Walker* slot, Monday, 11—Friday, 15 May, 9:00—10:00 am, and again from 25—29 May (same times). "I'm Free" and "Heaven And Hell" aired on *Sounds Of The '70's* with David Symonds, 25 May, 6:00—7:01 pm. The group received £10 per transmission.

In future, the Who licensed "dry" mixes of various tracks recorded "OS" (i.e., at their own studio) for broadcast on Radio 1, occasionally featuring slight variations of the released mixes.

SATURDAY, 18 APRIL
University, Leicester, with Viv Stanshall's Big Grunt.

Pete required eight stitches to a head wound when a group of Hell's Angels invaded the stage. In the *NME*, Pete described *Live At Leeds* to Richard Green: "People always talk about the Who being good on stage. We're all about visual pop flash and in the past when we've recorded shows, tapes have sounded very grotty at best. When I should have been playing guitar, I'd have been waving my arms about like a windmill or when Keith should have been playing, he'd have been yelling 'ooh-ya, ooh-ya' like Lennie Hastings [an eccentric British jazz drummer] ... he's so deafening. If we do a two-and-a-half-hour show, he just starts playing like a machine. I'm sure he puts out more watts than the rest of us put together!"

SATURDAY, 25 APRIL
University, Nottingham.

"*Tommy* was written with the idea that it would musically bridge the gap between the Who on stage and the Who on record—a gap that was getting wider by the moment..." Pete told Penny Valentine. "In the end, *Tommy* swept away both sides of the argument. It got rid of the aggressive guitar bashing non-musical Who and the recording studio Who. That album earned us a whole new batch of fans—a lot of them quite honestly, I'd be pleased to lose again. Especially the American pseudo-intellectuals who kept reading things into it. I would have thought that was impossible—for God's sake, it *was* a story and very clear at that."

MONDAY, 27 APRIL
Civic Hall, Dunstable, with Writing On The Wall.

FRIDAY, 1 MAY
University, Exeter, with Mighty Baby.

SATURDAY, 2 MAY
University, Sheffield.

FRIDAY, 8 MAY
Elliot College, University of Kent, Canterbury, with Genesis.

SATURDAY, 9 MAY
University, Manchester.

MONDAY, 11—FRIDAY, 15 MAY
The Who rehearsed at the Granada Theatre, Wandsworth, booked from 1:30—6:30 pm. It was a familiar venue; almost six years earlier as the High Numbers, the group had rehearsed their act here for the Arthur Howes package show dates.

FRIDAY, 15 MAY
University, Bailrigg, Lancashire, with Quintessence, whom Keith apparently assisted in their production.

SATURDAY, 16 MAY
Derwent College, University of York, with Jan Dukes De Grey.

Live At Leeds was released in the U.S. by Decca a week in advance of Track's 22 May release date in Britain. The album reached #4 and #3 in each respective territory. Exactly twenty-five years to the day of the original concert, a remixed and greatly expanded (77 minutes) CD version of the album was released, launching Polygram's reissue programme of the Who's output.

SATURDAY, 23 MAY
In *Record Mirror*, John spoke about the recording in progress: "They are all separate tracks this time. *Tommy* took two years, and we couldn't begin anything like that without a rest. We want to work on changing the act, because although a lot of people want to hear *Tommy*, we don't want to bore them by carrying on with it too long. The music will always be heavy, for we're a loud group. That's another reason why I'd never consider putting an orchestra behind us with some intricate arrangements. I don't think people would be able to hear them. I play loud, Pete plays a lot of loud chords, and Keith just plays his own solo behind us. It would drown out an orchestra."

SUNDAY, 7 JUNE
The Who commenced their seventh American tour—and first lucrative one, grossing twice as much as any previous visit—with two shows, 2:30 & 8:00 pm, at the Metropolitan Opera House, Lincoln Center, New York City.

Promoted by Nathan Weiss and New Action Ltd., in association with Bill Graham, the concerts were attended by a total 8000 and grossed $55,000. The Who made history by being the first and last group, British or American, to play at this prestigious home of the classics. "All productions of quality come to the Met," said assistant manager Herman Krawitz, who was responsible for the booking. Fans queued over the weekend of 15 May for tickets, which sold out in eight frantic hours of box office activity, and were available only from the Fillmore. This was a gesture of respect to the Who's hardcore New York following who, on the night of the show, mingled with the tuxedos and bow ties.

The Met shows were intended as the Deaf, Dumb, and Blind Boy's swan song as Roger told Richard

Green: "The [Met] will be the last time we will feature it [*Tommy*], although we may play parts of it, perhaps a bit different, other times. It's becoming a bit of a monkey, like the breaking of the gear, people expected it." Keith was more succinct: "We're trying to get off it, although we've said that before. But when we get down to rehearsing without doing *Tommy*, we only have two numbers left!"

The New York Times devoted a whole page to the group and both concerts received standing ovations,

BELOW and PAGES 184–185: ANAHEIM, 14 JUNE.

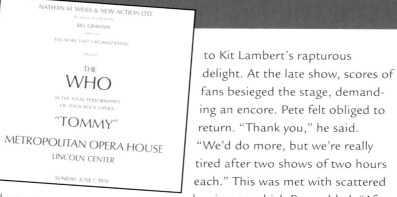

to Kit Lambert's rapturous delight. At the late show, scores of fans besieged the stage, demanding an encore. Pete felt obliged to return. "Thank you," he said. "We'd do more, but we're really tired after two shows of two hours each." This was met with scattered booing, to which Pete added, "After two fucking hours, boo to you, too!" With that, he angrily threw the mike into the audience and stormed offstage.

A report by Hughes Rudd, broadcast that evening on CBS News, included footage of "Amazing Journey," "Sparks," and "We're Not Gonna Take It" from the early show, mixed with pre- and post-show audience opinion. CBS also conducted an unbroadcast half-hour interview with Pete and vox pops interviews backstage with the rest of the group.

TUESDAY, 9 and WEDNESDAY, 10 JUNE
Mammoth Gardens, Denver, Colorado.

SATURDAY, 13 JUNE
Convention Hall, Community Concourse, San Diego, California.

SUNDAY, 14 JUNE

Anaheim Stadium, Oakland, California.

An elevated stage was constructed at home plate on the playing field for a five-hour (1:00—6:00 pm) concert promoted by Concert Associates. The Who headlined over the Blues Image, Leon Russell, and John Sebastian.

MONDAY, 15 and TUESDAY, 16 JUNE

Community Theater, Berkeley, California.

FRIDAY, 19 JUNE

Dallas Memorial Auditorium, Dallas, Texas, with Cactus.

SATURDAY, 20 JUNE

Hofheinz Pavilion, University of Houston, Houston, Texas.

SUNDAY, 21 JUNE

Ellis Auditorium, Memphis, Tennessee.

MONDAY, 22 JUNE

Municipal Auditorium, Atlanta, Georgia.

The flight from Memphis International Airport was yet another in a series of nightmare plane journeys for Pete. As John recalled: "We were on the plane waiting a long time for take off. The pilot had switched on the intercom to announce the delay, then had left it on and you could hear him whistling. We were really drunk, and the whistling was driving us crazy, so all of a sudden Pete jumps up and shouts, 'All right, all right, I'll tell you where the bomb is!' This stewardess overheard him, and next thing, the FBI took us out, searched all our luggage and detained Pete for questioning. We were scheduled to play in Atlanta at nine o'clock, and he didn't get in until ten thirty. Keith and I were sitting around in the dressing room, getting drunk, saying we didn't care and we'd take it out of his share, but Roger was really pissed off. At the time, Pete got out of it by saying that he'd only said, 'We ought to go down a bomb,' but for a while, things looked pretty bad."

To add to their woes, the group's P.A. and lighting equipment got stuck along a road enroute. Consequently, the 8:30 pm concert didn't take place until midnight, to a remaining diehard crowd of 6000.

1
9
7
0

THURSDAY, 25 and FRIDAY, 26 JUNE
Music Hall, Cincinnati, Ohio.

SATURDAY, 27 JUNE
Music Hall, Cleveland, Ohio, with additional support James Taylor.

MONDAY, 29 JUNE
Merriweather Post Pavilion, Columbia, Maryland.

WEDNESDAY, 1 JULY
Auditorium Theatre, Chicago, Illinois.

THURSDAY, 2 JULY
Freedom Palace, Kansas City, Missouri.

FRIDAY, 3 JULY
Minneapolis Auditorium, Minneapolis, Minnesota.

SATURDAY, 4 JULY
Auditorium Theatre, Chicago, Illinois.

SUNDAY, 5 JULY
Cobo Arena, Detroit, Michigan, with the James Gang.

WEDNESDAY, 24 JUNE
The Spectrum, Philadelphia, Pennsylvania, with the James Gang, who supported over the next four nights.

The sleepless entourage had flown in from Atlanta with hotel reservations to find all seven rooms had been given to an Eastern Star convention. "I want to tell Philadelphia how they've been treating us," Peter Rudge raged to the local press. "How could they do this to us? Philadelphia's one of our home towns in America, and now we can't even get a hotel room." A pioneering video screen was installed to project the concert, but the images emerged blurred and in black and white. Backstage, promoter Larry Magid presented the group with plaques commemorating over $5 million worth of *Tommy* sales.

TUESDAY, 7 JULY
"Music Shed," Tanglewood, Lenox, Massachusetts, promoted by Bill Graham, with Jethro Tull and It's A Beautiful Day, before a crowd of more than 18,000.

Joshua White, formerly head of the Fillmore's Joshua Light Show, had set up his own Joshua Television company, which filmed the Cincinnatti Pop Festival on 13 June. Company producer Lee Erdman videotaped the entire concert on closed circuit in colour, and it was simultaneously projected onto a 15x21-foot screen on the lawn outside the 6000 capacity shed, while Eddie Kramer engineered the sound on 8-track. The footage was originally intended for a television special of edited highlights from three "Fillmore at Tanglewood" summer concerts but remains largely unseen. Graham's introduction, "Heaven And Hell," "I Can't Explain," and "Water" feature in *Thirty Years of Maximum R&B Live* and a clip of the end of the show briefly appears during *The Kids Are Alright* end credits.

FRIDAY, 10 JULY
"Summertime Blues" was released, reaching #38, (#27 in the U.S.). Track's decision to extract it from *Live At Leeds*, a move the group was not altogether happy with, was made during the Who's absence in America.

The B-side, "Heaven And Hell," was an unfinished rough mix from the 13 April IBC/BBC session. "'Heaven and Hell' was a good song to tune up to," said Entwistle, "a lot of open strings, which is why we always started the act with it." At the same time, Pete completed and mixed Thunderclap Newman's *Hollywood Dream* at Eel Pie Sound. A year in the making, the album was finally released by Track on 2 October.

FRIDAY, 17 JULY
Pete appeared in the first of a three-part BBC-2 programme, *The Timeless Moment*, transmitted 10:30—11:00 pm. Presenter Geoffrey Moorhouse talked to people about insights into reality glimpsed through drugs, madness, or mysticism: "Were these experiences a genuine contact with God, or merely delusion?" Part One ("Experienced Through Drugs") included an interview (filmed late-1969) at the London centre for the Meher Baba Association, actually Pete's old fifth-floor flat at 87 Wardour Street, Soho.

Pete, Mike, and Katie McInnerney, as well as leader Don Stevens and several other devotees, described the experiences that in turn led them to Baba. The head of the movement, Dr. Allen Cohen, a psychiatrist at Berkeley University, was also interviewed. Other contributors included Steve Abrams, Charles Cameron, Rosalind Heywood, Father Kenneth Leach, and Dr. Alan Watts.

SATURDAY, 25 JULY

Civic Hall, Dunstable, with Wishbone Ash and Roger Ruskin Spear.

AUGUST

Pete (guitar), Keith (drums), and Ronnie Lane (bass) recorded with Mike Heron from the Incredible String Band at Sound Techniques Studio, Chelsea. "Warm Heart Pastry," credited to "Tommy and the Bijoux," appeared on Heron's first solo album, *Smiling Men With Bad Reputations*, which was released May 1971 on Island Records.

Producer Joe Boyd, whom Pete had met at the UFO Club in 1967, remembered the session: "Pete had arranged it with Mike about a week before, and he, Keith, and Ronnie came down to the studio. Mike played Pete the song, and he started to get an arrangement in his head. They rehearsed it for a few hours, and I remember Pete being very meticulous. He would stop the song if he heard the slightest thing amiss. It could be a little thing with Keith's drums, or whatever... he knew exactly how he wanted it to sound, so when we came to record, it was relatively easy to put down. The idea to call it 'Tommy and the Bijoux' was Pete's, as a way of bypassing the usual record company red tape." John Cale (viola) and backing vocalists, Liza Strike and Sue and Sunny, were overdubbed separately.

SATURDAY, 8 AUGUST

The Belfry, Sutton Coldfield, Birmingham.

SATURDAY, 15 AUGUST

The Who were advertised as appearing at the Yorkshire Folk, Blues and Jazz Festival, Krumlin, Barkisland, near Halifax.

A Track spokesman told the press: "The organisers billed the Who in advance before they contacted us. They asked us about the group and we said no, but they carried on advertising. They definitely won't be appear-

ing." Brian Highley, of Northern Entertainments, countered: "We were given a written go-ahead from Track Records to bill the Who after we spoke to them, but we had a phone call last week from them saying the Who wouldn't sign their contract." A spokesman for Fiery Creations, organisers of the Isle of Wight Festival, claimed they had an exclusive contract with the Who for festival appearances in 1970.

MONDAY, 24 AUGUST

Civic Hall, Wolverhampton, supported by Trapeze, featuring future Deep Purple bassist, Glenn Hughes.

John Sebastian, in town for the Isle of Wight Festival and currently a houseguest of the Townshends, attended the show. He repaid the hospitality by tie-dying Roger's fringed jacket, Keith's shirt, and one of Pete's boiler suits. Sebastian was also filmed at Eel Pie Sound, performing "Blues for J.B." which later appeared in *Playing The Thing*, Chris Morphet's 30 minute history of the harmonica, distributed by Fair Enterprises (1972).

SATURDAY, 29 and SUNDAY, 30 AUGUST

3rd Isle of Wight Festival of Music, East Afton Farm, near Freshwater, Isle of Wight.

The five-day event was again promoted by Rikki Farr and Raymond and Ronald Foulk for Fiery Creations Ltd. The Who headlined the third night over Cat Mother and the All Night Newsboys, Spirit, Mungo Jerry, and the Doors.

As at Woodstock, production manager John Wolff was appointed fee negotiator, as he recalled: "I had the thankless task of asking Rikki Farr for more money after Kit and Chris had already agreed a fee. I said, 'What am I to go for?' Kit said, 'See if you can get ten grand,' which was like ten times more! So I went down there with Cy [Langston] on his motorbike and as we rode off, Farr spotted us and, there must have been something about my face, because he went white, saying, 'Oh no, they're not going to play, are they? It's money, isn't it'" I went, 'Only ten

grand, Rikki.' He went, 'My god, that's blackmail!' 'Yeah, I'm afraid so.'"

Backstage, Pete held court from "Maxine," the new Dodge motor home he and wife Karen had brought over and the inspiration for "Goin' Mobile" from *Who's Next*. "The Who had two black trucks immediately behind the stage where they spent the weekend, hanging out," MC Jeff Dexter recalled. "Like the year before, they brought their own PA down to supplement the Charlie Watkins system we were using."

With acts inevitably running over, the Who didn't appear until approximately 2:00 am on Sunday morning, when Dexter finally announced, "And now...a nice little band from Shepherd's Bush...the 'Oo!" to the 600,000-strong crowd, technically the Who's largest-ever audience.

"We come 'ome and find ourselves playing to a load of bloody foreigners!" Pete joked in reference to Jean-Jacques Lebel and his Situationists from Paris who had "liberated" the festival site. "I had these 25,000 watt spotlights which operated from the back of the stage," said Wolff. "They had their own generator and during 'See Me, Feel Me,' we turned them on full into the crowd. All the moths in the Isle of Wight flew into the beams!"

Having played for nearly two hours, the Who's set anticlimactically fizzled out. "We didn't play it quite right" Pete wrote in *Melody Maker*. "We had trouble with the ending. We ended once and it was perfect. Then for some reason, Roger carried on singing. Well, the group can't walk off, so we had to go on. I'd thrown me guitar up and bounced it on the ground, and of course it was grossly out of tune. It took me five minutes to get it in tune, five minutes to get me head together because me adrenalin had gone down, five minutes to get enough energy to get Moon to end. You very much have to play the end of an act right. It's probably far more important for the Who than the rest of it put together." Sly and the Family Stone had the unenviable task of playing to a weary but exhilarated crowd. (Ironically, the Who had to follow Sly's prolonged set at Woodstock.)

Music and interviews taped at the festival by Johnny Moran were included in a special Isle of Wight edition of Radio 1's *Scene And Heard*, broadcast Monday, 31 August, 6:00—7:00 pm. The Who's set was recorded on the 8-track CBS Mobile and documented by Murray Lerner as part of an intended feature film. However, it took some twenty-five years for the footage to see the light of day, when negotiations to sell the film rights broke down. "Fiery Creations Ltd. was wound up in the High Court with debts of around £40,000," said Dexter. "The Who were one of the creditors because they didn't get all of their money. They got their advance, and the gig money, but they didn't get all of what they were owed in total, because the whole thing lost money. So technically, the rights actually belonged to the creditors."

Despite being credited, Dexter's introduction was bizarrely replaced by an anonymous voiceover, both for Castle's *Live At The Isle Of Wight* CD and the accompanying Warner video *Listening To You* (1996), which re-edited the set order. "Young Man Blues" and "I Don't Even Know Myself" first appeared in *Thirty Years of Maximum R&B Live* (1994).

Lerner's festival documentary *Message To Love*, released in 1995, featured (in edited form) "Young Man Blues" and "Naked Eye," the latter not included in *Listening To You*. Keith and his Track signing, comedian Murray Roman, can also be seen animatedly discussing the mating habits of the average festivalgoer!

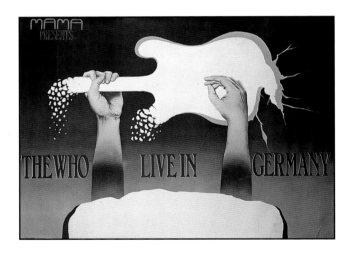

SATURDAY, 12 SEPTEMBER
Münsterland Halle, Münster, West Germany.

SUNDAY, 13 SEPTEMBER
Oberrheinhalle, Offenbach, West Germany.

WEDNESDAY, 16 SEPTEMBER
De Doelen, Rotterdam, Holland.

THURSDAY, 17 SEPTEMBER
Concertgebouw, Amsterdam, Holland.

SUNDAY, 20 SEPTEMBER
Falkoner Centret Teatret, Copenhagen, Denmark.

MONDAY, 21 SEPTEMBER
Veslby Risskov Hallen, Aarhus, Denmark.

THURSDAY, 24 SEPTEMBER
Double Pisces, an experimental Austrian film commissioned for the Montreaux Festival, opened at the ICA in London. Written, produced, and directed by Dick Fontaine and produced by Tattooist for ORF films, the soundtrack included Pete's demo for "I Don't Even Know Myself" and "Piledriver," an instrumental with Pete on organ and guitar and Speedy Keene on drums and percussion. *Double Pisces* formed part of an ICA programme of Tattooist productions and shorts, including Richard Stanley's *The Seeker* (see 26 March).

OCTOBER
At Trident Studios, 17 St. Anne's Court, off Wardour Street, Keith produced ("I supplied the booze") and drummed on Viv Stanshall's rendition of "Suspicion," a hit for Terry Stafford in 1964, intended as part of the pair's "comedy—rock 'n' roll" album. John Entwistle played bass and brass, Paul Curtis (from Gun) and "Bubs" White, guitars, while Viv contributed extra brass. Keith and "Vic" brought "the dregs of the Speakeasy" back to do backing vocals, in one 10 pm–5 am session.

Credited to Vivian Stanshall's Gargantuan Chums, the single was released on 11 December by Fly, a Track Records offshoot set up by company executive David Ruffell. The accompanying publicity pictures, photographed by Barrie Wentzell, depicting Moon as Hitler and Stanshall as Himmler, provoked predictably strong reactions from all quarters.

TUESDAY, 6 OCTOBER
Sophia Gardens, Cardiff, Wales.

"The Most Exciting Stage Act In The World" ballroom and university tour commenced, supported by the James Gang, whose Speakeasy showcase Pete and Keith had attended the previous evening. "It's only natural for a group like the Who to ask itself 'where do we go from here?'" said Peter Rudge. "Well, it seems to us that the business has now turned full circle, and that the fans would welcome the opportunity of seeing the Who in some of the venues it played in its early days."

WEDNESDAY, 7 OCTOBER
Free Trade Hall, Manchester.

THURSDAY, 8 OCTOBER
Orchid Ballroom, Purley.

FRIDAY, 9 OCTOBER
With a cover of "Overture From *Tommy*" by Assembled Multitude being a surprise Stateside hit (#16) in July on Atlantic, Track extracted the Who's version, with "See Me, Feel Me" as an A-side, to boost extra sales. Four weeks later, the single was withdrawn in favour of an EP. (See 6 November.)

SATURDAY, 10 OCTOBER
University of Sussex, Brighton, with additional guest, Roger Ruskin Spear and his Giant Kinetic Wardrobe. The gig was held in the Old Refectory, a building suited for about 1000, which in this instance had an extra 400 crammed into it.

SUNDAY, 11 OCTOBER
Odeon Cinema, Birmingham.

TUESDAY, 13 OCTOBER
Locarno Ballroom, Leeds.

A charity Rock Relics Auction, the first of its kind, was staged by Bill Graham at the Fillmore East, New York, with all proceeds being donated to political candidates running for office on an anti-war platform. The Who lots proved to be the most popular. Two of Entwistle's T-shirts fetched $65, and Moon's trousers, cigarette lighter, and drumsticks a bargain at $50. A beaming fan left wearing Daltrey's tie-dyed Isle of Wight fringed jacket, after paying $340 for the privilege. Most expensive of all was a seventeen-foot (5m) sign announcing the group's week-long run of 1969 shows at the venue, selling for $400 to rock promoter Aaron Russo, who intended to display it in his house.

ABOVE and PAGES 190–191: Hammersmith Palais, 29 October.

FRIDAY, 16 and SATURDAY, 17 OCTOBER
Concerts at Trentham Gardens, Stoke-on-Trent and University of East Anglia, Norwich, were postponed to 26 October and 5 December, respectively, after Roger caught bronchial flu.

SUNDAY, 18 OCTOBER
Odeon Cinema, Lewisham, South East London.

THURSDAY, 22 OCTOBER
ABC Cinema, Stockton-on-Tees, Durham.

FRIDAY, 23 OCTOBER
Green's Playhouse, Glasgow, Scotland.

SATURDAY, 24 OCTOBER
University, Sheffield.

SUNDAY, 25 OCTOBER
Empire Theatre, Liverpool.

MONDAY, 26 OCTOBER
Trentham Gardens, Stoke-on-Trent. Rescheduled from 16 October.

THURSDAY, 29 OCTOBER
Palais, Hammersmith, London, with Roger Spears Giant Kinetic Wardrobe replacing the James Gang.

FRIDAY, 6 NOVEMBER
Track released a 33 rpm EP of *Tommy* tracks priced at six shillings as a counter measure against the rising price of singles. Those who had already bought the "See Me, Feel Me" single (see 9 October) could exchange it at Track's Old Compton Street address.

A set of three *Tommy* promotional singles, issued in July 1969, never reached the shops due to a lack of interest from Polydor. "I think Kit and Chris got together and said *Tommy*'s been out, done its thing—it was incredibly highly priced in England—how about releasing everything from *Tommy* on singles," Townshend told *Zigzag*, "so that if somebody wanted to buy *Tommy* as a serial, as it were, they could do it... It was a nice idea, but the public didn't really want to buy *Tommy* on singles."

1970

An EP of four tracks ("Water," "I Don't Even Know Myself," "Postcard," and "Now I'm A Farmer") was scheduled for Christmas release, to retail at 9 shillings 3 pence, the current price for singles. "Basically the mood of the group has always been keeping record prices down to a rational level," said Pete. "We are still one of the lowest priced groups. This EP idea came from Roger, and the four tracks for the price of two is a reflection of that mood."

Roger explained the fate of his idea to *Record Mirror*. "We didn't release the maxi-single after all, because the tracks were about ten minutes long, and we couldn't get them all on. We could have cut it down and made it shorter, but it wouldn't have been right. We even tried recording shorter versions, but that wouldn't work either."

SUNDAY, 8 NOVEMBER
Keith sat in on congas at an East of Eden gig at the Lyceum, London. During the *Who's Next* sessions, he "produced" fiddle player Dave Arbus' violin solo overdub on "Baba O'Riley."

ABOVE: PETE BACKSTAGE WITH HIS YOUNGER BROTHERS SIMON (LEFT) AND PAUL (RIGHT), HIS WIFE KAREN, AND KIT LAMBERT.

THURSDAY, 12 NOVEMBER
Keith jammed onstage with the Beach Boys at the Winter Gardens, Bournemouth, after being recruited on the train journey enroute. The following summer, after drummer Dennis Wilson put his hand through a window, severing the tendons, Keith was approached to fill in on certain dates during the Beach Boys' November 1971 European tour. The offer had to be declined because of Who commitments.

SATURDAY, 21 NOVEMBER
University, Leeds.

THURSDAY, 26 NOVEMBER
Fillmore North, Mayfair Ballroom, Newcastle.
Keith, John, and Pete had travelled up earlier, but Roger was unable to reach the venue because of thick fog on the M1. Promoter Jeff Docherty explained the situation to the disappointed audience of 3000 and a make-up show was scheduled for 15 December. Support group Curved Air played a full set using the Who's lights and PA, with the sound mixed by Bob Pridden.

SATURDAY, 28 NOVEMBER
Lanchester College, Coventry.

DECEMBER
At Mick Jagger's invitation, Pete, Ronnie Lane, and Billy Nicholls contributed (uncredited) backing vocals to the Rolling Stones' "Sway" at Olympic Sound Studios, Barnes. The track appeared on *Sticky*

Fingers, released by Rolling Stones Records on 23 April 1971.

SATURDAY, 5 DECEMBER
The Lads' Club, Norwich. Rescheduled from 5 and 17 October.

TUESDAY, 15 DECEMBER
Mayfair Ballroom, Newcastle. Rescheduled from 26 November.

WEDNESDAY, 16 DECEMBER
Futurist Theatre, Scarborough, Yorkshire.

SUNDAY, 20 DECEMBER
The Roundhouse, London. "Implosion" show, 3:30–11:30 pm, with America, Patto, Chalk Farm District Salvation Army (carol singing with a fifty-piece choir), and Elton John.

The concert was a special Christmas charity benefit put together by the Implosion organisers, Camden Borough Council, Track Records, and the Who, to provide a party for the needy on Christmas Day. Tickets were priced at just eight shillings with only 2500 available. "This is the very last time we'll play *Tommy* on stage," Pete solemnly announced. "Thank Christ for that!" Keith bellowed in response.

WEDNESDAY, 30 DECEMBER
In Studio A, Television Centre, the Who pre-recorded an insert for *Into '71*, a 55-minute BBC-1 New Year's Eve special, featuring Blue Mink, CCS, Georgie Fame, Elton John, Alexis Korner, Pan's People, Alan Price, Labi Siffre, Cat Stevens, Sue and Sunny, Livingston Taylor, Peter Thorup, and Traffic, broadcast 10:55–11:50 pm.

Introduced by Lulu, the Who appeared as the final act, miming to pre-recorded backing tracks for "I Don't Even Know Myself" and "Naked Eye" with live vocals, before a studio audience. Curiously, the opening lyric of "Naked Eye" ("Take a little dope") was excised, yet Townshend's line ("you can cover up your guts, but when you cover up your nuts") remained intact. Pete wore a full Cockney Pearly King outfit, while a strapped-up Keith, suffering a fractured collarbone, mimed behind a transparent Perspex drumkit, used mainly for television appearances.

there once was

The Who, or more precisely Pete Townshend, faced a quandary. The runaway success of *Tommy* created unenviable pressure to produce an equally remarkable follow-up in terms of originality and commercial favour. The Who were at the top of their form, consistently drawing maximum-capacity audiences due to their reputation as the ultimate live experience, aurally confirmed by *Live At Leeds*.

However, the group urgently needed to progress, as much of their stage act seemed to revolve around the sensory-impaired Walker boy. Townshend had sincere faith in rock music's potential to cut through barriers and communicate on all levels. "At rock concerts you can achieve those rare moments where both group and audience completely forget themselves and become completely ego-less," he told *Disc and Music Echo* in 1972. "The most precious moments of my life are those moments on the stage when all is one."

Looking beyond the usual single-album-tour cycle, Pete aimed to steer the Who into the untried medium of film. The previous December, *Billboard* jumped the gun by reporting the group were to embark on two major film productions: an adaptation of *Tommy* and a new project, provisionally dubbed *Your Turn In The Barrel* or *Barrel One And Barrel Two*. (Townshend later explained these were simply working titles for the project, based on one barrel holding fiction while the other contained fact in the form of live performance.) Finally titled *Lifehouse*, the film was a multi-media blend of science fiction, mysticism, technology, and live action. It was Pete's most ambitious project to date and one that would cause him considerable frustration over the next thirty years.

On 13 January, a press conference was held at the Young Vic Theatre, Waterloo, South London, during which Pete and theatre director Frank Dunlop unveiled the modus operandi behind *Lifehouse* and discussed how the Who would go about presenting it. The group planned to stage a regular series of experimental concerts at the Young Vic where the film's fictional element would be developed in conjunction with the audience, which Townshend expected to remain constant. (Ironically, just a few years later, this very scenario forced him to question his commitment to stage work.) By using such an unorthodox method, Pete hoped that interesting, charismatic characters would emerge to take their natural place within the script. "Each participant is both blueprint and inspiration for a unique piece of music or song," he later wrote, taking his inspiration from the Sufi music teachings of Inayat Khan.

The setting for *Lifehouse* was modern England, albeit an England devastated by an ecological disaster, where pleasures such as music were prohibited. The majority of the population in urban centres are forced to live indoors wearing "experience suits," while those in rural areas subsist as farmers and gypsies. So far, so good. However, the suits are linked to a government Grid, a kind of Matrix that provides the people with all their needs. Enter a government dissident, Bobby, who hijacks the Grid to broadcast liberating rock and roll (courtesy of the Who) from the Lifehouse, enabling listeners to shed their experience suits and attain a higher spirituality. Throw into this conceptual cauldron the fact that much of the Who's material was to incorporate the pioneering use of synthesisers and quadrophonic sound, and things started to look overly complex. With the benefit of hindsight, one can see how visionary some of Townshend's ideas actually were. The Grid is certainly an accurate prototype of the Internet, at the time still a secret U.S. military project, while "grid sleep" is an uncanny reflection of virtual reality. But this was 1971 and technology wasn't anywhere near so advanced!

Pete used every opportunity to speak about the project openly and at great length, seeing the film as a natural progression for the Who. However, the Young Vic shows proved frustrating and unsatisfactory, for both the band and the motley crew of "freaks and 13-year-old skinheads" that had been lured in off the street. The audiences were not aware of what was expected of them in terms of interactivity, and it's likely that, despite Pete's best efforts, the rest of the band didn't fully understand their role either.

A substantial deal had been struck with Universal Pictures to bankroll the film but, unbeknownst to Townshend, Kit Lambert had actually sold the idea on the back of his beloved *Tommy* movie being realised. With Lambert's *Tommy* script failing to resemble coherency, Universal's funds were suddenly withdrawn. "I blamed the frustration [*Lifehouse*] caused me on its innate simplicity and my innate verbosity; one cancelled out the other," Pete later wrote in *The Lifehouse Chronicles* (published 2000). As simple as it may have seemed to the Who's composer-in-chief, to his more Luddite workmates, it was nigh on impossible. John held the impression that group and audience were expected to coexist together indefinitely, while Roger wondered whether there would be enough wire in the world to link everybody up!

"I was at my most brilliant and I was at my most effective," Pete reflected thirty years on, "and when people say I didn't know what the fuck I was talking about what they're actually doing is revealing their own complete idiocy, because the idea was so fucking simple!"

As his unwieldy extravaganza came crashing down around him, Pete could at least take solace in the twenty or so quality songs he'd written and demoed specifically for the venture. Experiencing a period of low morale, the Who relocated to New York to record at the Record Plant, an idea suggested by Lambert, whose guidance and inspiration Pete sought in the depths of a serious crisis of confidence. It didn't take long for him to realise his estranged muse had succumbed to the lure of hard drugs. With Keith also demonstrating his own unhealthy predilictions, and Townshend drowning his demons in Rémy Martin, the sessions were cut short. Back in London, the job of remixing the tapes was handed to Glyn Johns, who suggested the group start from scratch—firstly at "Stargroves," Mick Jagger's country mansion, and then at Johns' favoured workbase, Olympic Studios, in Barnes. The

Lifehouse concept was dropped and Johns pared down the best songs to form an ordinary single album. The result became *Who's Next*, pithily referred to by Pete as "the best non-concept album based on a concept the Who ever made!"

Although outward appearances may have proved deceiving, the Who's confidence took a knock with the stillbirth of *Lifehouse*. After all, they were members of rock's pantheon. They had lasted out the Sixties with the same line-up and had created the first successful rock opera in *Tommy*. How could they fail to deliver?

"What we have to do now is rebuild ourselves because we were so heavily involved in the film idea," Townshend admitted to *Melody Maker*. In May, the group cautiously embarked on a series of low-key, minimally advertised gigs around Britain, breaking in the new material as it was being recorded. Of the new songs, several rapidly became live staples with the aid of pre-recorded backing tapes.

The album's powerful opener, "Baba O'Riley," featuring a hypnotic pattern played on a Lowrey electric organ fed through a synthesiser, sprang from the twin inspirations of Meher Baba and minimalist avant-garde composer Terry Riley. "Bargain," again utilising an inspired and intelligent Moog arrangement, took its opening line, "I'd gladly lose me to find you" from a Baba tenet. Oddly enough, Johns left out the "central pivot" of *Lifehouse*, "Pure and Easy," designed to be heard at the end of the film as the audience transcended into the Universal Note. (The song appeared three years later on *Odds and Sods*.) Its incandescent opening lines were repeated in the moving finale to "The Song Is Over."

"Behind Blue Eyes," the original candidate for single honours though ultimately rejected for being "out of character" (although it did appear in this format in North America), was sung from the point of view of *Lifehouse*'s villainous character, Brick. "Won't Get Fooled Again" (trailered in truncated form in June as a single and credited prematurely in the U.S. as "from the motion picture *Lifehouse*") told of the negative effects of revolution. "A song against the revolution," Pete explained, "because the revolution is only a revolution in the long run and a lot of people are going to get hurt."

With their confidence restored on record, the Who returned to America in July with material strong enough to replace *Tommy*, although a selection from the opera was retained in the act to

appease the fans. Commencing with two sell-out concerts at New York's Forest Hills Tennis Stadium, the tour grossed $1.25 million from twelve venues over three weeks. In September, the Who headlined an outdoor Bangladesh benefit before 35,000 at London's Oval cricket ground and received the distinction of opening the new-look Rainbow Theatre, Finsbury Park, over three nights in November. At the conclusion of the second leg of a box office–breaking U.S. tour in December, *Los Angeles Times* columnist Robert Hilburn spoke for many when he dubbed the Who "the Greatest Show on Earth."

Offstage, Keith took a cameo role as an overdosing nun in Frank Zappa's incomprehensible *200 Motels*, invested over £60,000 in his dream home, Tara House, and concluded the year by compèring a Sha Na Na concert in drag. Onstage, the effects of his self-abuse became alarmingly apparent when he had to be helped through a Who show in San Francisco with the aid of morphine jabs.

Frustrated by not having an outlet for his songs, John became the first band member to release a solo album. Taking a mere fortnight to record, *Smash Your Head Against The Wall* was full of the bizarre humour so familiar to Who fans from "Boris The Spider," "Fiddle About," and lately, "My Wife," a dark ode to the less-than-delightful joys of connubial bliss and an instant stage favourite. The Ox's album threw down the gauntlet to the rest of the band. "We learned more about John from him making an album than we did in all the years he'd ever played bass with us," admitted Pete. "Because he did it, and it spoke to us. I got a lot of feedback from John's record."

In October the Who released a single in Europe, "Let's See Action," a jaunty, motivational anthem salvaged from *Lifehouse*—its original title being the Baba-inspired "Nothing Is Everything," and *Meaty, Beaty, Big, and Bouncy*. The album's appearance marked the end of a long-standing legal dispute with original producer Shel Talmy and rendered all previous Who compilations obsolete at a stroke. Pete called it "possibly the best ever Who album" and contributed an in-depth, informative, and witty essay for *Rolling Stone*, providing a neat outline to the previous six years of Who history unfamiliar to most Americans.

"This album is as much for us as for you, it reminds us who we really are. The Who."

1971

JANUARY

John recorded his first solo album, *Smash Your Head Against The Wall*, in just two weeks at Trident Studios. Session time was booked by Cy Langston from midday to 6:00 am, and engineered by future Queen producer, Roy Thomas Baker. "The first album was very difficult to mix," John told Chris Welch. "You needed six hands to do it properly. We spent much longer mixing than recording. We weren't used to tidying stuff up then, so we kept cutting out bits we didn't want. There was no such thing as 'dropping in.'"

As well as producing and arranging, John played an extensive variety of instruments, including bass, trumpet, trombone, flugelhorn, organ, and piano, and sang and wrote each track, with the exception of Neil Young's "Cinnamon Girl," which remained unreleased until appearing as a bonus track on the 1997 CD reissue. Cy played lead guitar and Jerry Shirley (Humble Pie) was recruited on drums. Keith Moon played bongos on "Number 29" (with ex-Bonzo's Neil Innes and Viv Stanshall on additional percussion) and lead a boisterous sing-a-long of "Rudolf The Rednose Reindeer" on the fade of "I Believe In Everything."

FRIDAY, 1 JANUARY

Who material was included in a BBC Radio 3 programme *Study On 3*, devoted to "Making A Pop Recording," broadcast 6:30–7:00 pm. In Part One ("Recording Techniques") of two programmes, host Ian Grant described the changes in recording techniques from the early days of direct disc cutting to present day multi-tracking, and demonstrated with illustrations from the Who how, stage by stage, a musical number was built up.

MONDAY, 4 JANUARY

The Young Vic Theatre, Waterloo, South East London.

The first unpublicised rehearsal for a series of experimental *Lifehouse* concerts, or "total music," as Pete Townshend described them. "Pete came along here some months ago to see *Waiting For Godot*," explained artistic director Frank Dunlop, "and then he brought the rest of the Who, and they were enthusiastic too." (In mid-1970, Dunlop had made

overtures to Townshend and Kit Lambert about staging *Tommy* as the theatre's first production when it opened on 10 September 1970.)

WEDNESDAY, 13 JANUARY

A press conference was held at the Young Vic, as Townshend and Dunlop formally announced *Lifehouse*. "We shall not be giving the usual kind of Who rock show," said Townshend. "The audience will be completely involved in the music, which is designed to reflect people's personalities. We shall try to induce mental and spiritual harmony through the medium of rock music." The project was the initial step in preparations for a movie, financed by Universal Pictures, to be filmed largely at the Young Vic, based on "an experiment in relationship between the Who and its audience."

SUNDAY, 24 JANUARY

Following a *Lifehouse* rehearsal, Pete and Keith were unwinding at the Speakeasy when, overhearing their conversation at the next table, Frank Zappa "leaned over and said in true Hollywood fashion, 'Wanna be in a movie?'" Moon told *Sounds*. "He said, 'Be at the Kensington Palace Hotel at seven o'clock

tomorrow morning,' and that was it." Acting on Zappa's casual invitation, Keith assembled with the rest of the *200 Motels* cast (Pete sent his apologies, as he was preoccupied with *Lifehouse*) for a week of dress rehearsals at Pinewood Studios, Iver, Buckinghamshire.

MONDAY, 1—SUNDAY, 7 FEBRUARY

200 Motels was shot in a mere seven days in Studio A at Pinewood, using the Vidtronic process, meaning it was edited and transferred from videotape and blown up to 35-mm film. The movie was financed with a budget of more than $600,000 from United Artists, directed by Tony Palmer (who later claimed to have attempted getting his name removed from the credits), and co-produced by Jerry Good and Zappa's manager, Herb Cohen.

This unhinged road movie, set in "Centerville USA," starred the Mothers of Invention (with Flo and Eddie, a.k.a. ex-Turtles vocalists Howard Kaylan and Mark Volman), Theodore Bikel (Narrator), Ringo Starr (Frank Zappa), and the Royal Philharmonic Orchestra. Keith cameoed as the overdosing "Hot Groupie Nun," a part originally offered to Mick Jagger.

"I'm really only doing this film to get the hang of working before cameras," Keith told *Melody Maker*'s Chris Charlesworth. "I've never been on a film set before so the experience will come in useful for our own film... each of us in the group is being given a section to write for themselves, so I'm thinking of having my bit shot in Bermuda so we can all go over there. I don't know what the film company will think of it though!"

200 Motels opened in America at the Doheny-Plaza, Beverly Hills, California, Friday, 29 October, and in England at the Classic Cinema, Piccadilly Circus, London, on Thursday, 16 December.

SUNDAY, 14 and MONDAY, 15 FEBRUARY

Lifehouse rehearsal and concert, Young Vic Theatre, London.

£30,000 had been spent on quadrophonic sound equipment, with each show attended by a 400-strong audience made up of special invites from youth clubs and similar organisations. A limited number of tickets were made available to the general public, although the shows were not advertised in the press.

SATURDAY, 20 FEBRUARY

Keith was a guest MC at the "Viv Stanshall, Neil Innes and Freaks" show at the Roundhouse, Dagenham, Essex.

MONDAY, 22 FEBRUARY

Lifehouse concert, Young Vic Theatre, London.

MONDAY, 1 MARCH

Lifehouse concert, Young Vic Theatre, London.

THURSDAY, 11 MARCH

Keith was a surprise participant in the All-Star Jam Session, organised by drummer Pete York (ex-Spencer Davis Group, Hardin and York) at Bumpers Club, Coventry Street, London, featuring Jon Lord, Roger Glover, and Ian Paice (Deep Purple), as well as various members of the Keef Hartley Band. The event was successful enough to warrant Keith's return for the follow-up, held at the same club with the same musicians on Monday, 5 April. York was encouraged to take the show on the road, although Keith was not involved.

RIGHT: ROGER AT THE YOUNG VIC THEATRE.

MONDAY, 15 MARCH

A week of *Lifehouse* sessions commenced at the Record Plant Studios, 321 West 44th Street, New York City.

The idea to relocate to the Big Apple came from Kit Lambert, who was co-producing Labelle's debut album there with Vicki Wickham. His suggestion got him credited as producer, although, according to Pete, this mainly entailed him "rolling up at half past seven in the evening, disrupting everything, but by then we had enough to get it together."

The group were augmented by Al Kooper (organ), Ken Ascher (piano), and Mountain's Leslie West (guitar). West had given Pete a Les Paul Junior with a single pickup. This, along with a 1947 orange Gretsch, a gift from Joe Walsh, were the main guitars Pete used on *Who's Next*.

TUESDAY, 16 MARCH

Initial takes of "Won't Get Fooled Again" and, delving back to their Marquee past, an eight minute cover of Marvin Gaye's "Baby Don't You Do It," featuring Leslie West on lead guitar, recorded during a two day warm-up in Studio Two, produced by West's Mountain cohort, Felix Pappalardi.

WEDNESDAY, 17 AND THURSDAY, 18 MARCH

"Pure And Easy" (logged as "The Note"), "Love Ain't For Keeping," "Getting In Tune" (logged as "I'm In Tune"), and "Behind Blue Eyes." These were recorded during a four-day session in newly opened Studio One, with Jack Adams and assistant engineer, Jack Douglas, who went on to produce Aerosmith, Cheap Trick, and John Lennon.

While at the Record Plant, Pete and a wasp-dressed Moon met their idol Link Wray recording in the adjoining studio. The bizarre but humourous encounter was recalled by Townshend in his sleeve note for *The Link Wray Rumble*, released by Polydor in July 1974. "Waspman," the June 1972 B-side to "Join Together," was dedicated to Wray.

LATE MARCH

Back in London, the 16-track Record Plant tapes required mixing, but Kit Lambert proved unequal to the task. Enter Glyn Johns, who made safety copies of the material at Olympic on 23 April. "Glyn was originally brought in to remix the stuff we had done in New York and do overdubs," Pete told *Zigzag*. "So he listened to it and said it was great, it was good,

ABOVE: FINAL *LIFEHOUSE* CONCERT, YOUNG VIC, 5 MAY.

but if we started again, he could do better. We said, 'Let's do it on the Stones mobile' because we wanted to test it for the Young Vic, because we were gonna go back in again and do it all live."

APRIL

"Won't Get Fooled Again" (remake) was recorded in the hallway of "Stargroves," Mick Jagger's Victorian mansion in Newbury, Berkshire, produced by Glyn Johns on the Rolling Stones 16-track Mobile Studio. According to a contemporary report, "Going Mobile" was also recorded at "Stargroves." Whether this was the released take on *Who's Next* has proved difficult to substantiate. "Won't Get Fooled Again" received further overdubs at Olympic and was mixed at newly opened Island Studios, 8 Basing Street, West London.

THURSDAY, 1 APRIL

At his specific request, Track issued John's first solo single, "I Believe In Everything" B/W "My Size," on April Fools' Day. The A-side was a different mix from the forthcoming *Smash Your Head Against The Wall* album version. Although failing to chart in the U.K., the single sold respectably in America, where some fans were under the misguided belief it was the latest Who single. "Decca soon put them right about that!" the Ox lamented.

FRIDAY, 2 APRIL

A multi-media ballet adaptation of *Tommy* by the Montreal-based Les Grands Ballets Canadiens opened at the City Center Theatre, New York City, for a fortnight's run. Choreographed by Fernand Nault, it featured a company of sixty, with light show effects, films by the Quebec Film Bureau, and music from the Who's original album. (The response was enthusiastic enough for a further run in October.) A similar presentation, but with a new musical interpretation, was staged by the Seattle Opera Company, running for three weeks from 28 April at the Moore Theatre, Seattle, Washington.

MONDAY, 12 APRIL

Recording moved to Olympic Sound Studios, 117 Church Road, Barnes, South West London, with Glyn Johns. "Bargain" was first attempted and subsequently returned to on 5 June. "Too Much Of Anything," featuring Nicky Hopkins on piano, remained in rough mix form until 1974 when Roger re-recorded his vocals, and John remixed it for inclusion on *Odds and Sods*.

SATURDAY, 24 APRIL

Pete's daughter Aminta Alice was born at Queen Charlotte's Maternity Hospital, Hammersmith.

MONDAY, 26 APRIL

Lifehouse concert, Young Vic Theatre, London.

Recorded on 16-track for reference purposes on the Rolling Stones Mobile by Andy Johns, Glyn's younger brother. An impromptu jam on Larry Williams' "Bony Moronie," first released in 1988 as the B-side to a reissue of "Won't Get Fooled Again,"

appeared again, along with "Naked Eye" on the *Thirty Years of Maximum R&B* box set (1994). "Naked Eye" and "Water" were included as bonus tracks on the expanded *Who's Next* CD (1995).

MAY–JUNE

Who's Next sessions at Olympic Sound Studios. "We were just getting astounded at the sounds Glyn was producing... For the first time, the Who were recorded by someone who was more interested in the sound than in the image of the group," Pete told Penny Valentine. "Glyn's not particularly interested in the Who image, whereas when Kit Lambert was producing us, that was all he cared about." Despite such praiseworthy remarks, Johns only received an associate producer's credit for his work.

Songs recorded and mixed included "Time Is Passing," "Pure And Easy" (remake), "Love Ain't For Keeping" (acoustic remake), "Behind Blue Eyes" (remake), "Nothing Is Everything" (the working title for "Let's See Action"), featuring Nicky Hopkins on piano, and "Baba O'Riley," featuring Pete on piano and Dave Arbus on violin.

Entwistle's "My Wife," featuring John on brass and piano, was recorded almost as an afterthought. "After the *Lifehouse* idea was scrapped and it was decided to make just a single album," he explained, "it was decided that I'd have a track on the album. I only really had the one song ["My Wife"], which I wanted to keep for my album. We ended up recording it, but I felt the Who's version didn't swing like I'd intended." Entwistle re-recorded the track the following year for his second solo album, *Whistle Rymes*.

WEDNESDAY, 5 MAY

Lifehouse concert, Young Vic Theatre, London.

Pete's growing disillusion with the project meant further planned *Lifehouse* shows were scrapped.

His disappointment was still palpable three months later in an interview with *Sounds*' Steve Peacock: "We originally wanted the Young Vic for six weeks, and this was to be a trial period in which we were going to make the film, but the Young Vic is a government sponsored bloody organisation, and it turned out that we could only have it every Monday, and then everybody started to think that it should be every Monday—I could never see it like that, I always figured it would be something where you woke up and went to bed with it; either that or you came and went every day.

"But it failed, more I think because we, the Who, couldn't really find the energy to cope with the technical problems, and by the time it came to doing it we couldn't fully identify with the idea. We proved that it was all possible, but by the time we'd done that, we just didn't have it in us to do it. We'd had so much of it, I mean I was getting slightly... hallucinogenic I think is the word, and the whole thing eventually just fell apart."

FRIDAY, 7 MAY

"Fillmore North," Top Rank Suite, Sunderland.

The first in a series of "secret" shows; each given little or no advance publicity with a cut-price admission charge of 50p.

SATURDAY, 8 MAY

Record Mirror featured an interview with Roger. Describing the current state of the Who: "We were never nearer to breaking up than we were three months ago. It's not through lack of interest in the group; it's just a desperation feeling... We've got enough material recorded for a single album, which would be fantastic, but we'll go on to make it a double, like we did with *Tommy*. It's got a theme because it works best for the Who. It builds where just a series of songs never seems to."

On the proposed Universal Pictures film: "We aim to have the album finished by mid-July, but the stumbling block we're up against is that we can't go out on stage and play a whole new act based on the album. So the best thing is to wait until the album is out and then do the stage act and film it. That will give the audience a chance to know the numbers. We've got the forty minutes of new material for on stage, but at the moment we are stuck for a beginning! We've got a really good film deal, but we had to work hard to get their interest. They don't understand that you can't tie yourself down to a set time... you can't say exactly when the album will be released and when you'll be onstage."

On future shows, Roger jokingly suggested the Oldfield Hotel: "We're going to loon along to gigs and take second billing. It will be just a rehearsal to us. The people will be doing us a favour, so we won't expect to get any money for it."

THURSDAY, 13 MAY

Kinetic Circus, Mayfair Suite, Birmingham.

1971

FRIDAY, 14 MAY
University, Liverpool.

Track released the first Who solo album, John Entwistle's *Smash Your Head Against The Wall*. In keeping with the Ox's macabre sense of humour, the sleeve featured a picture of his face, covered by a flesh-toned plastic mask, transposed against the X-ray of a terminal heart patient. In juxtaposition, the inside sleeve showed a pregnancy test X-ray.

"I'd been thinking about this album for two years," he told Michael Watts. "Until recent months, I didn't have quite enough numbers and I was too lazy to complete anymore, but since the Who have not been performing I had time to make this album..."

It was released in a remixed form in the U.S. on 9 October, due to Entwistle's displeasure with the original mastering. Thanks to the Who's touring presence, the album eventually reached #134 in *Billboard*, selling approximately 100,000 copies.

SATURDAY, 22 MAY
Pete's visage appeared in an experimental, 35-minute silent feature, *Heads*, directed by Peter Gidal, screened at the National Film Theatre, London. The film (shot in late-1969) consisted of tight, hand-held close-ups of thirty-one well-known faces gazing consecutively into a zoom lens. These ranged from artists (Richard Hamilton, Claes Oldenburg, Francis Bacon, David Hockney), to Rolling Stones connections (Charlie Watts, Marianne Faithfull, Anita Pallenburg), to television personalities (Linda Thorson of *The Avengers*).

SUNDAY, 23 MAY
Caird Hall, Dundee, Tayside, Scotland.

SATURDAY, 5 JUNE
Recording/mixing Olympic: Further takes of "Bargain," which was returned to on 18 and 19 June.

MONDAY, 7 JUNE
Recording/mixing: "Getting In Tune" (remake with Nicky Hopkins on piano), John's "Time Waits For No Man" (the working title for "When I Was A Boy"), and "Naked Eye," recorded at Eel Pie Sound in 1970 in rough mix form. The latter was considered a contender for *Lifehouse* in its originally proposed incarnation as a double, but was not released until *Odds and Sods* in 1974.

FRIDAY, 25 JUNE
After a year's silence, the Who's first new material appeared—"the annual single which we try to release every two years," as Townshend described it.

"Won't Get Fooled Again" was a 3:35 edit of the full-length *Who's Next* cut, while "I Don't Even Know Myself" came from the 1970 Eel Pie sessions. The original choice of A-side, "Behind Blue Eyes," was vetoed because "we thought it was too much out of character." (Nevertheless it became a U.S. single in November.) Somewhat jumping the gun, Decca issued "Won't Get Fooled Again" in the States on 17 July, with the label credit reading "from the motion picture *Lifehouse*." The single reached #9 and #15 in the U.K. and U.S., respectively. Publicity material depicted a brazen Keith in drag, dressed in a corset, brandishing a whip!

SATURDAY, 26 JUNE
Dressed in a Sha Na Na T-shirt, Keith introduced that band's headlining set on the second night of the annual Reading Festival. His fervour for the twelve-piece satirical 50s rock and roll revival act was such that he flew to New York later in the year to MC their Carnegie Hall concert. (See 28 December.)

THURSDAY, 1 JULY
Assembly Hall, Worthing.

SATURDAY, 3 JULY
City Hall, Sheffield.

The memorable sleeve shot for *Who's Next*—a composite, with the sunset background from a rejected idea showing Pete's motor home on an unobstructed hillside added later—was taken the following day by Ethan Russell on the drive to Leicester. The group stopped to relieve themselves against a giant concrete monolith Russell had spied standing amid a slag heap. (Those unable to urinate on cue were aided by small film cans filled with rainwater.)

Apparently, a similarly tasteless idea of the group urinating against a giant Marshall stack was vetoed. Though vulgar, the idea was not nearly as offensive as the original design planned, as Townshend told *Zigzag*. "*Who's Next* nearly came out with the most revolting pornographic cover you've ever seen. In the end, it turned out to be mildly pornographic, but slightly boring at the same time. Dave King [responsible for *The Who Sell Out* and Hendrix's *Electric Ladyland* sleeves] was commissioned to do a cover and he

came up with one with a huge fat lady with her legs apart and where the woman's organ was supposed to be, would be a head of the Who grinning out from underneath the pubics."

SUNDAY, 4 JULY
De Montfort Hall, Leicester.

Ethan Russell took a series of shots showing the band sitting among the debris of a backstage storage room as a further idea for the *Who's Next* cover. One photo was eventually used on the rear sleeve. (This photo session has previously been documented as occurring at Liverpool University on 14 May.)

WEDNESDAY, 7 JULY
The Who went to Television Centre to pre-record an insert for *Top Of The Pops*, miming to the single edit of "Won't Get Fooled Again," broadcast Thursday, 15 July, 7:15—7:50 pm. The band were originally booked to return on 14 July to pre-record two songs in the show's "Album Slot," but this did not occur as the group attended Keith's housewarming. The Moody Blues appeared in their place.

THURSDAY, 8 JULY
The Pavilion, Bath.

SATURDAY, 10 JULY
Civic Hall, Dunstable.

MONDAY, 12 JULY
The Winter Garden, Eastbourne.

WEDNESDAY, 14 JULY
All of the group attended Keith's housewarming at his £65,000 ultra-modern glass bungalow, Tara House, bought from sci-fi film director Peter Collinson, in St. Ann's Hill, Chertsey, Surrey. The party also doubled as a press launch for *Who's Next*.

A fireworks display threatened to ignite the trees on the seven acre property, and police were inevitably summoned after irate neighbours complained about the noise—the shape of things to come. While there, Pete was accosted by Chris Rowley, Mick Farren, and J. Edward Barker, all writers for *International Times* who felt confused by the negative sentiments expressed in "Won't Get Fooled Again" and demanded to know where he stood in the so-called "revolution."

Pete's convoluted reply appeared in the 9-23 September edition of *IT*: "'Won't Get Fooled Again' is partly a personal song, but mainly a song which screams defiance at those who feel that any cause is better than no cause, that death in a sick society is better than putting up with it, or resigning themselves to wait for change. It mainly screams defiance at those who try to tell us [the Who] what we have to do with money that isn't ours, power that belongs not to us but our audiences, and lives that long ago were handed to the rock world on platters. We fight to remain. Merely remain... You have no need to fret, you're not losing a rock band, you're not gaining new leaders, you're keeping the Who."

THURSDAY, 15 JULY
Town Hall, Watford.

SATURDAY, 17 JULY
Viv Stanshall was offered his own four part BBC Radio 1 series by producer John Walters to fill the *Top Gear* slot vacated by a holidaying John Peel. Viv Stanshall's *Radio Flashes*—"Melody and mirth on the high wireless"—was recorded at Broadcasting House.

In "Breath From The Pit," Viv played clever dick detective "Colonel Knutt," an updated version of the "Dick Barton" radio serials. John Walters played the owl and Keith the part of Lemmie, Knutt's Cockney sidekick. The first instalment was broadcast in the second programme, Saturday, 14 August, 3:00—5:00 pm, with the other two instalments following over the next fortnight (same times.)

"I still feel that the group should be making a film," Pete told the *NME*'s Nick Logan. "There is so much that the whole Who organisation, our whole team could do in a film. This may sound like blowing our own trumpets, but I don't think there are very many other groups who have the knowledge of stage rock theatre, but at the same time the necessary lack of ego to carry it off. At the moment, we are leaning

heavily on the fact that we are good experienced musicians and can put on a good stage act but... and I hate to rub it in... what we really need is a film."

MONDAY, 19 JULY
Roger married his long-standing girlfriend, 24-year old Heather Taylor, at Battle Registry Office, East Sussex. Witnesses included ex-Love Affair singer Steve Ellis, and the ceremony was performed by registrar Daisy Field!

Keith and Viv Stanshall went to EMI's Abbey Road Studios where Liverpudlian comic trio the Scaffold (consisting of Roger McGough, John Gorman, and Mike McGear, neé McCartney) were recording "Do The Albert," the theme to a BBC-1 programme commemorating the Royal Albert Hall's centenary. Les Harvey (of Stone The Crows) played bass, Stanshall provided backing vocals, his Bonzo's compatriate Neil Innes tinkled the ivories, and Moon bashed away on drums. The track was released as a Parlophone single on 1 October.

SATURDAY, 24 JULY
"We get very neurotic during down periods," Pete told *Disc*. "We really came close to splitting. We just didn't know what to do. I had to commandeer the situation and steer the group in a new direction to try and gain enthusiasm. It'll be very interesting when we get back to the same situation again. We'll have to look very closely at things."

THURSDAY, 29 and SATURDAY, 31 JULY
The Who commenced the Northeast and Midwest leg of their 1971 North American tour, supported by Labelle, with two sell-out concerts—a total of 28,000 seats, previously equalled only by Frank Sinatra, the Beatles, and Simon and Garfunkel—at the Forest Hills Music Festival, Forest Hills Tennis Stadium, Forest Hills, New York City.

An extra show was added by promoter Ron Delsener when tickets for the 31st sold out in record time from the Carnegie Hall box-office. The first show was delayed 45 minutes when a cloudburst threatened a cancellation. The group tied rubber pads to their shoes to avoid electrocution, and Townshend compensated for the crowd's wait in torrential rain by reducing two Gibson SGs to matchwood. Moon also spurred Entwistle into destroying his favourite red Gibson Thunderbird. "If you dropped a Gibson Thunderbird," John explained,

"the neck always used to bust right off at the nut. When we were playing Forest Hills, I left the last note ringing, and lent it up against the amplifier, and Moon knocked it over on his way off stage... the head fell off, so I smashed it to smithereens!" The show was marred by the fatal stabbing of a twenty-one-year-old usher by a youth attempting to gatecrash.

8-mm colour footage of both concerts was shot by fan Ira Zadikow, some of which was used in the 1997 VH-1 cable special *Legends: The Who*.

ABOVE: 1971 U.S. AND U.K. TOUR PROGRAMME.

SUNDAY, 1 AUGUST

Members of the Who attended the evening Bangladesh charity concert starring George Harrison and friends at Madison Square Garden, and jammed at the post-concert party held at Ungano's, located at West 70th Street.

MONDAY, 2 AUGUST

Center For The Performing Arts, Saratoga Springs, New York.

The concert was projected via a closed-circuit videoscreen to a capacity audience of 31,000. New York Who freaks Jeff Stein and Chris Johnston were permitted to photograph the band close-up. Their candid pictures from this show, Rochester a week later, and Dallas on 2 December were published in book form as *The Who* in 1973. Stein went on to direct *The Kids Are Alright* (see 30 May 1977).

TUESDAY, 3 AUGUST

The Spectrum, Philadelphia, Pennsylvania.

WEDNESDAY, 4—SATURDAY, 7 AUGUST

Music Hall, Boston, Massachusetts.

Mylon supported on the 4th & 5th; Labelle on the 6th and 7th.

MONDAY, 9 AUGUST

War Memorial Auditorium, Rochester, New York.

TUESDAY, 10 AUGUST

Civic Arena, Pittsburgh, Pennsylvania.

THURSDAY, 12 AUGUST

Public Music Hall, Cleveland, Ohio.

FRIDAY, 13 AUGUST

O'Hara Arena, Dayton, Ohio.

SATURDAY, 14 AUGUST

Cobo Arena, Detroit, Michigan.

As a reflection of the Who's Stateside popularity, *Who's Next* was released by Decca a full fortnight before its U.K. release on 27 August. Paradoxically, while reaching only #4 in the *Billboard* chart, it

became the Who's only #1 album in Britain. A six minute pre-recorded interview with Pete by Michael Wale was broadcast on BBC Radio 1's *Scene And Heard*, 2:00—3:00 pm.

SUNDAY, 15 AUGUST

Metropolitan Sports Center, Minneapolis, Minnesota.

MONDAY, 16 AUGUST

Mississippi River Festival, Edwardsville Campus, Southern Illinois University, Edwardsville, Illinois.

TUESDAY, 17—THURSDAY, 19 AUGUST

Auditorium Theatre, Chicago, Illinois.

SEPTEMBER

Pete Townshend hadn't entirely given up on the idea of a Who film in whatever form it should take. To this end, a conference to discuss and exchange ideas was arranged at Roger's home in Burwash, Sussex. Townshend engaged Richard Stanley and Chris Morphet to film the talks with the aim of possibly incorporating them into the finished feature. From the outset, Townshend's dominance was obvious in what was ironically supposed to be a democratic forum.

With soundman Paul Robinson, Stanley and Morphet filmed the group seated around a table, generally clowning and discussing making a documentary. Pete talked about the business of film making and what the Who had and hadn't done: "What made us want to go and conquer America was being English... Because we've got obsessed with the money we're taking, we've got obsessed with the circus aspect. Let's admit we want the money for what it'll get us." Keith disagreed: "I can't play it straight—the circus bit is part of it." (This sequence included Keith's "circus act" stunt, which was edited for *The Kids Are Alright.*)

Each member individually expounded how he thought the documentary should develop. Entwistle wanted the film to deglamourise the rock business. Moon talked about the theatrics of the group, disagreeing with Pete, feeling that a Who encore should be the highpoint of the film: "I'm leaving the band to join a bigger one... the rest of the band are humourless—three of the most miserable sods I've ever met... To get four of us talking around a table is an achievement."

Typically, Daltrey made no effort to conceal his true feelings. He found Pete's ideas "very abstract and risky," calling him "too dictatorial." Townshend advised the viewer to disregard what the others had said: "I have RESPONSIBILITY!" The Who, he felt, had come to the end of their tether. "We'd come upon the point where we realised that [his arm whirling]—it's no good, you can't go on doing that, it's beyond the beyond... so we've decided to make a film."

Although filmed in colour, Jeff Stein selected clips for *The Kids Are Alright* from a 16-mm B&W slash print made for editing purposes.

MONDAY, 6 SEPTEMBER

The pencilled-in date for shooting to commence on Universal Pictures' *Tommy* film. The Who were required to be on set for filming commitments lasting through each working week to the eve of their British tour on 18 October. Universal, as owners of MCA Records, had first option on the film rights, which they dropped after the band lost interest in the idea and Kit Lambert's script was rejected.

Meanwhile, rehearsals commenced at the Granada, Wandsworth, London, with the band's new £20,000 seven-and-a-half ton American built Sunn PA and lighting system. Roger's cousin, Graham Hughes, was hired to design a sleeve for the forthcoming *Meaty, Beaty, Big, and Bouncy* compilation. "I'd already taken the gatefold shot of the Railway Hotel," Hughes remembered. "I made a mock-up of a poster and pasted it onto the hoarding. By sheer coincidence, while I was preparing the shot, this guy came walking up the side path who looked just from the period so it fitted perfectly. For the cover, Bill Curbishley and I searched around schools and housing estates in the East End for kids who looked like the Who as youngsters. The album was originally going to be called *The Who Looks Back*, and I'd seen these old derelict buildings near to where the band were rehearsing at a bingo hall on Wandsworth Road. I shot the kids, one of whom was Bill's younger brother Paul, and the band on separate days, using the window frame to emphasise the "looking back" aspect. I'm then told that Track were changing the title *to Meaty, Beaty, Big, and Bouncy*—a line from a dog food commercial!"

RIGHT: KEITH AT THE OVAL WITH CRICKET BAT, **18 SEPTEMBER.**

4th Hyde Park ??? Tentative

5th) Start Filming of TOUR
7th)
3th) All four members required
9th)
9th)

3th)   )
4th)   ) Pete/John/Keith
5th) Roger)
6th)   )
7th)

0th Roger

1st Roger

3rd   ) Pete/John/Keith
4th Roger)

5th Bristol University ??? Tentative

8th)
9th) Roger
0th)

1st Roger

2nd Reading University

4th   )
5th Roger) Pete
6th John)
7th Keith)

9th Surrey University

          OR

0th Kent University

2th)
3th) All Group - Holiday Camp
4th)
5th)

UK TOUR

8th Southampton Guildhall

20th Birmingham Odeon

21st Cardiff Capitol

23rd Blackpool Opera House

SATURDAY, 18 SEPTEMBER

The Oval Cricket Ground, Kennington, South East London.

"Goodbye Summer" charity concert, co-promoted by Raymond and Ronald Foulk, in aid of the Bangladesh Relief Fund, commencing at 11:00 am, with over 31,000 attending. The Who headlined over Cochise, the Grease Band, Lindisfarne, Quintessence, Mott The Hoople, America, Eugene Wallace, Atomic Rooster, and the Faces.

An hour behind schedule, the Who's 90 minute set ended with an extended "Magic Bus," featuring Keith bashing away with a cricket bat. "I'd been loaned this valuable bat as part of my stage uniform from the Surrey Cricket Club," MC Jeff Dexter recalled. "Keith nicked it off me, and started playing the drums with it. Much to my horror, when he'd finished, he just lobbed it into the crowd. Fortunately, all the people from the club who were watching from up in the members room loved it and didn't seem to care!"

The event raised a total profit of £18,336, and the Who donated 25% of the gross box office receipts. The entire concert was recorded on 8-track Dolby Sound, using the Pye Mobile unit, but none of the material has surfaced, ostensibly due to insufficient technical quality.

SATURDAY, 25 SEPTEMBER

The production master for *Meaty, Beaty, Big, and Bouncy* was compiled at Apple Studios, 3 Savile Row, London, and released by U.S. Decca on 30 October (reaching #11); 26 November in the U.K. (reaching #9). "We were going to call it *The Who Looks Back*," said Pete, "but Kit thought it made it sound as if we were all dead! Much of the material is from the old Brunswick days, and it means a lot to me personally and the group to own our songs again. It means a lot to me that the Who now own 'My Generation' and oldies like 'La La La Lies,' 'A Legal Matter,' and 'It's Not True.' None of that material has ever been re-released and now it's available for those new friends we have made since *Tommy*."

Kit Lambert was livid, claiming the album had been pressed and released without his final approval, while he was absent in America. He attempted to have it withdrawn on the grounds that it was improperly sequenced, and because he disagreed

with the song selection. Lambert actually succeeded in getting Polydor to withdraw the album for 48 hours, but too many copies had been distributed for the changes he desired to be made, so the original went back on sale.

TUESDAY, 28 SEPTEMBER

Free Trade Hall, Manchester.

SATURDAY, 2 OCTOBER

University, Reading.

The first of three unpublicised university dates, supported by Ron Geesin. "He did two test gigs with us," Pete told *Zigzag*, "and to put it mildly, he wiped the floor with the Who—just him and his bits of paper and his piano playing. He's so far ahead of his time as a performer that people just can't pick up on it."

SATURDAY, 9 OCTOBER

University of Surrey, Guildford, Surrey.

Halfway through the set, there was an unscheduled guest appearance from John Sebastian, who apologised for not bringing a guitar. He had flown into Britain that morning to be unexpectedly met at the airport by Keith posing as a chauffeur, who insisted Sebastian and his wife Catherine be his houseguests during their week-long stay. At the Who's Boston concerts in August, Moon had delighted in mimicking Sebastian, dressing up in tie-dye jeans and spectacles, telling the audience what "wonderful people they were."

"I went to the show and had a few harmonicas with me," remembered Sebastian. "Keith said, 'Come on up with us!' I said, 'Great, you know, we can jam on a little blues thing in A,' or something like that. Well, Pete leans into me and says in a loud stage whisper, 'We can't because I'm afraid Keith can't

ABOVE: John Sebastian with Pete at Guildford, 9 October.

play the blues!' Keith's standing behind him, nodding and saying, 'I can't, you know!'—feeling proud of himself. It was so funny because I was this New York kid brought up to know how to play the blues whenever the occasion demanded it, and it was so refreshing to find that here's this guy who didn't know how and more besides, couldn't care less. I thought, 'Yeah, I want to play with these guys!'"

SUNDAY, 10 OCTOBER

Eliot College, University of Canterbury, Kent.

FRIDAY, 15 OCTOBER

"Let's See Action" B/W "When I Was A Boy," the first in a trilogy of singles featuring material leftover from *Lifehouse*, was released in the U.K. and Europe only, reaching #16 on the *NME* chart.

MONDAY, 18 OCTOBER

Guildhall, Southampton.

The commencement of an eleven city British tour promoted by John and Tony Smith, in association with Track International. Support on each date was Quiver.

WEDNESDAY, 20 OCTOBER

Odeon Theatre, Birmingham.

THURSDAY, 21 OCTOBER

Green's Playhouse, Glasgow, Scotland.

A near riot had occurred when 6000 fans fought for 3000 tickets, all of which were sold within ninety minutes, so a second show was added on 9 November.

FRIDAY, 22 OCTOBER

Opera House, Blackpool.

SATURDAY, 23 OCTOBER

University, Liverpool.

```
ODEON THEATRE
BIRMINGHAM
THE WHO
EVENING 7-30 p.m.
WEDNESDAY
OCTOBER      20
FRONT STALLS
£1·25
B16
No Ticket exchanged nor money refunded
THIS PORTION TO BE RETAINED        (P.T.O.
```

SUNDAY, 24 OCTOBER

Trentham Gardens, Stoke-on-Trent.

THURSDAY, 28 OCTOBER

Odeon Cinema, Manchester.

FRIDAY, 29 OCTOBER

ABC Cinema, Hull.

SATURDAY, 30 OCTOBER

Odeon Cinema, Newcastle.

THURSDAY, 4—SATURDAY, 6 NOVEMBER

The Who played the grand opening of the Rainbow Theatre, Finsbury Park, North London. (It was previously known as the Astoria Cinema when the group played there on 4 February 1966.)

The venue was re-opened by John Morris, who as American director of production, had crossed paths with the Who at the Fillmore East and Woodstock. Nine thousand seats for three shows, supported by Quiver, sold out at the rate of 1000 an hour. The Rainbow held 3500 but each house was packed to 4000, with an extra 500 "standing only" tickets. Joe's Light Show was imported from the Fillmore East, as well as on-screen slide projections and a chorus line of dancing "can-can" girls who led the Who onstage.

An opening night report, featuring "See Me, Feel Me," was featured in Thames news magazine programme *Today*, broadcast 5 November in the London ITV region only.

TUESDAY, 9 NOVEMBER

Green's Playhouse, Glasgow, Scotland.

THURSDAY, 18 NOVEMBER

The Who flew to New York, missing the launch of the Mini Cooper S they were sponsoring in the RAC *Daily Mirror* Rally of Great Britain, starting in Harrogate, Yorkshire on the 20th. Stan Griffin and co-driver Chris Dickenson (both CID policemen) posed at the starting point with female models wearing *Meaty, Beaty, Big, and Bouncy* T-shirts.

The rally ended four days later, but the Who's car was out of the running, having broken down in Scotland. A 37 minute film, *From Harrogate It Started*, directed by Brian Llewelyn and Alan Ross, released the following year by United Motion Pictures, featured a soundtrack of Who hits. (See 5 October 1972.)

LEFT and ABOVE: RAINBOW PROGRAMME AND POSTERS.

1
9
7
1

The following May, the car was entered in the International Welsh Rally, and Keith, accompanied by Track promo man Vernon Brewer and accountant John Field, was on hand to launch the leg commencing in Penmachno, North Wales, renamed "The Who Special." The Who's car came in third.

SATURDAY, 20 NOVEMBER
The Southern and West Coast leg of the Who's North American tour commenced at the Charlotte Coliseum, Charlotte, North Carolina. Support on the first ten dates was Bell and Arc. Accompanying the entourage was journalist/writer Nik Cohn, ostensibly to gather background information for a proposed film script. His experiences on the road, written in Cohn's inimitable style, appeared in the February 1973 issue of *Cream* as "Be Happy, Don't Worry!" While in Carolina, Pete specially chartered a plane to visit Myrtle Beach, South Carolina, home to the world's largest Baba centre.

MONDAY, 22 NOVEMBER
University Of Alabama Memorial Coliseum, Tuscaloosa, Alabama.

TUESDAY, 23 NOVEMBER
Municipal Auditorium, Atlanta, Georgia.

THURSDAY, 25 and FRIDAY, 26 NOVEMBER
Miami Beach Convention Hall, Miami, Florida.

SUNDAY, 28 NOVEMBER
Mid-South Coliseum, Memphis, Tennessee.

MONDAY, 29 and TUESDAY, 30 NOVEMBER
The Warehouse, New Orleans, Louisiana.

WEDNESDAY, 1 DECEMBER
Sam Houston Coliseum, Houston, Texas.

THURSDAY, 2 DECEMBER
Dallas Memorial Auditorium, Dallas, Texas.

SATURDAY, 4 and SUNDAY, 5 DECEMBER
Denver Coliseum, Denver, Colorado.
Support on the remaining dates was gospel act Mylon Le Fevre and Holy Smoke.

TUESDAY, 7 DECEMBER
Veterans Memorial Coliseum, Phoenix, Arizona.

WEDNESDAY, 8 DECEMBER
San Diego Sports Arena, San Diego, California.

THURSDAY, 9 DECEMBER
Inglewood Forum, Los Angeles, California.

18,000 tickets sold-out in ninety minutes flat, breaking the Rolling Stones' record from two years previous. MCA arranged a midnight awards presentation by president Mike Maitland at an invitation-only party at the Top of the Strip, on the top floor of the Continental Hyatt House. Guests included Cass Elliot, John and Catherine Sebastian, and Mick and Bianca Jagger. Any formality the ceremony warranted was instantly dispelled when Townshend, grabbing a handful of the twenty-eight gold and four platinum discs, screamed, "They're all mine! They're all mine!" The others promptly jumped on top of him.

FRIDAY, 10 DECEMBER
Civic Arena, Long Beach, California.

Three numbers in, Pete responded to the crush at the front of the stage by bellowing, "Either sit down, or lay down, but shut up!... This is a rock and roll concert not a fucking tea party!" This now infamous outburst was selected as an apt introduction for the *Thirty Years of Maximum R&B* box set.

SUNDAY, 12 and MONDAY, 13 DECEMBER
Civic Auditorium, San Francisco, California.

Keith had to be trundled onto the San Francisco-bound plane in a wheelchair, after drinking a near-lethal cocktail of brandy and barbiturates. The opening show suffered as a still-groggy Moon had to be propped up behind his drums and pumped full of stabilisers. On two occasions, he was pulled off stage for quick morphine shots. After floundering through the first few numbers, he miraculously returned to his usual dynamic form, collapsing exhausted across his cymbals at the final flourish. "A fucking star," Pete grudgingly praised.

Both shows were recorded for possible live release, but after the 16-track tapes were remixed by Glyn Johns, the glaring fact remained that only one song had not appeared on record before. The song in question, a revived cover of Marvin Gaye's "Baby Don't You Do It," was released in edited form the following June as the B-side to "Join Together." The remainder of the show stayed in the vaults until "Bargain," "My Wife," and an impromptu jam on Freddie King's "Going Down" first appeared on the MCA compilations *Who's Missing* (1987) and *Two's Missing* (1988).

ON STAGE

, December 8, 1971/7:30 PM/San Diego Sports Arena

, December 10, 1971/8 PM/Long Beach Arena

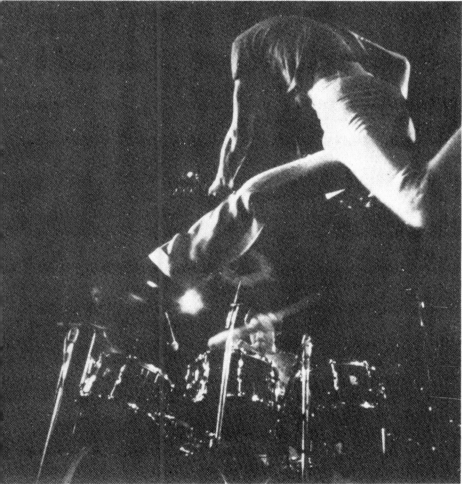

THE WHO

introducing

MYLON

WEDNESDAY, 15 DECEMBER
Center Coliseum, Seattle, Washington.

"It's always the same at the end of a tour. The last gig is awful," Pete told *Melody Maker* the following September. "At the end of the [last] American tour, we played Seattle and one of the trucks carrying our equipment crashed. We had to borrow the other group's stuff for it. It could have been worse though."

TUESDAY, 28 DECEMBER
Keith flew back to New York from England for one night's work, guest emceeing Sha Na Na's two concerts at Carnegie Hall. Introducing the opening act, comedy duo Cheech and Chong, he appeared in full drag, dressed in a full-length gold lamé gown, black wig, heavily padded bra, and a foot-long cigarette holder. Moon made at least three other costume changes for the occasion, including a traditional English lord's outfit in top hat and tails, a gold lamé outfit (to match Sha Na Na's), and leotards for a run and head-over-heels tumble routine. He also sat in with the band for a crazed drum solo during "Caravan."

ROCK IS DEAD... LONG LIVE ROCK

1972

By Who standards, 1972 was quiet. For the first time in eight years, the group took a lengthy sabbatical from the road. Apart from a brief European sojourn in August, including an outdoor show in Paris that attracted close to half a million people, the relentless touring of previous years was put on hold. This was to be the rule rather than exception, much to the chagrin of certain band members. "The live shows stay exciting because we're always working on doing something different," John told *Record Mirror*. "Work's more concentrated in America… There you're just the group, and that's all that matters. My bass playing has got better each year, but I'm never really satisfied."

Thanks to the cumulative financial success of *Tommy* and *Who's Next* and the attendant trailblazing tours, the band could now afford to indulge themselves. The fiscal debt that had threatened to rent them asunder almost seemed like a distant memory. For Pete, it was a chance to sit back and take stock of the Who's situation, especially after the associated stresses involved with the *Lifehouse* project.

Baba activities preoccupied much of his time. He spent the early part of the year in India visiting the Avatar's tomb, coinciding with the release of a second privately pressed devotional album, *I Am*. (The first such album, *Happy Birthday*, was released in 1970.) An earnest television appearance on a Sunday religious programme, *How Can You Be So Sure?*, coupled with the fact that pirate copies of these limited edition albums were changing hands for exorbitant sums in America, prompted him to compile his first solo album proper, *Who Came First*. Despite it's deliberate un-Wholike nature, the record enjoyed critical plaudits and modest sales, the proceeds of which went to the Meher Baba Trust.

John became a father and concentrated on recording two more solo albums displaying his dark humour, *Whistle Rymes* and *Rigor Mortis Sets In*, the latter planting the seed for a touring outfit during the frustrating periods of Who inactivity. His whole world being a stage, Keith turned his Surrey home, Tara House, into a twenty-four-hour party zone and became an honorary member of satirical 50s rock and roll troupe, Sha Na Na. In October, he furthered his acting ambitions by appearing in *That'll Be The Day*, playing maniacal drummer J.D. Clover, a supporting role requiring little method acting! He also gave perhaps his most notorious (and hilarious) interview to Jerry Hopkins of *Rolling Stone*, from which such self-perpetuating myths as "the Rolls-Royce in the swimming pool" entered rock and roll's hall of excess. As the Who's unofficial PR man, Moon was a master. Roger occupied himself with the upkeep of his Burwash estate. Always the group member most loathe to stray beyond the confines of the Who, he nevertheless hatched plans for his own solo album, to be overseen the following year by singer/actor Adam Faith at Daltrey's own Barn studio.

The Who regrouped in May to begin recording sessions with Glyn Johns for *Rock Is Dead—Long Live Rock*, a proposed double concept-album loosely concerning the band's roots that would also integrate some of the ideas left over from *Lifehouse* in an attempt to bring that experiment to fruition. However, it rapidly became evident that the work was turning into "the shadow of *Who's Next*." A new approach and set of ideas were required. Two songs, "Is It In My Head?" and "Love Reign O'er Me," were retained as part of a more ambitious project that looked back to the Who's origins, albeit through different eyes. In the interim, "Join Together" and "Relay" were released as "interest maintaining" singles. Ironically, the promotional film accompanying "Join Together" was perhaps the closest Pete got to a celluloid realisation of band and audience co-existing as one.

While Townshend toiled, as if on cue his first opus unexpectedly came back to haunt him. If it wasn't Kit Lambert making concerted efforts to turn *Tommy* into a grand cinematic extravaganza, it was some fawning theatrical impresario bent on selling his vision of the project to Pete. The original story had already taken on a life of its own in the form of plays and a ballet. Even the lightweight singing outfit the New Seekers took a revived medley of "Pinball Wizard"/ "See Me, Feel Me" into the Top 20. For a character, now three years old, that Deaf, Dumb, and Blind Boy sure paid a mean windfall! Earlier in the year, Pete gave his approval to a West Coast stage production, though had no direct involvement. Now, respected American producer Lou Reizner was intent on reviving the rock opera as an all-star vehicle, financed by industry mogul Lou Adler.

Initially wary, both Pete and Roger became enthusiastically involved in the enterprise, which featured an all-star cast of Sandy Denny, Graham Bell, Steve Winwood, Maggie Bell, Richie Havens, Merry Clayton, Ringo Starr, and Richard Harris, with the London Symphony Orchestra and Chamber Choir. Reizner had originally envisaged Rod Stewart (whom he produced) in the lead role, but after some discreet persuading from Townshend, the job was handed to a delighted Daltrey, who reprised his role both on record and at two December charity shows at London's Rainbow Theatre, in which most of the cast were involved. While John appeared as Cousin Kevin, Keith stole the show as a larger-than-life Uncle Ernie, who the *NME*'s Roy Carr memorably described as "the epitome of warped depravity to the extent you could all but smell him." Sipping brandy stage left, Pete was visibly tense as the Narrator, missing cues, insulting the audience, and at the end, feigning to wipe his rear with the script. He later expressed personal regret in taking part and donated his profits to the Music Therapy Children's Charity. Roger, who had taken his fringed '69/'70 stage costume out of mothballs, revelled in the occasion, leading the entire audience in the "Listening To You" finale.

"A lot of the Who has been lost in volume since we left *Tommy* out of the live show," he admitted to *Record Mirror*, "it's lost some of the light and shade, and I've found it a lot less rewarding without the character of Tommy. There will definitely be another *Tommy*. We said we never would but we will, and it will be about one person with quadrophenia, and will probably form one-half of a double album."

ABOVE: Pete as the Narrator at the Rainbow production of *Tommy*.

1972

1972

JANUARY–FEBRUARY

Pete travelled to Arangaon, India, meeting with Meher Baba's disciples and family members.

"I visited his tomb and there is a ritual there when all his followers stand around the tomb and sing [Cole Porter's] 'Begin The Beguine,' which was one of his favourite songs. It totally zapped me out when I was there. I stood up after all this and was crying and everything."

To mark the third anniversary of the Avatar's passing, a second, limited-edition devotional album, *I Am*, was issued. The package featured a forty-eight-page broadsheet, "Wallpaper," with photos, poetry, and lyrics. Pete's contribution featured his original twelve-minute ARP synthesiser loop for "Baba O'Riley" and "O Pavardigar" ("Distant God"), Baba's Universal Prayer adapted to music and later included on *Who Came First*. (An unreleased version sung by Pete in German was recorded for the opening of a Baba centre in Switzerland.)

In addition, Pete played synthesiser on "Dragon" by Dave Hastilow, guitar and drums behind poet Mike Da Costa on "Affirmation," and synthesised flute on "This Song Is Green," written and sung by Billy Nicholls. Nicholls' other contribution, "Forever's No Time At All," co-written with Katie McInnerney, and featuring Caleb Quaye on lead guitar, was engineered by Pete and also included on *Who Came First*. (See 29 September.)

SUNDAY, 23 JANUARY

John's son, Christopher Alexander, was born at Queen Charlotte's Maternity Hospital, Hammersmith.

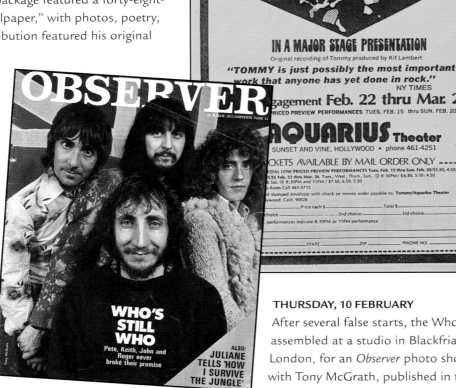

THURSDAY, 10 FEBRUARY

After several false starts, the Who assembled at a studio in Blackfriars, London, for an *Observer* photo shoot with Tony McGrath, published in the colour supplement dated 19 March. The session was originally to have taken place in North London earlier that day, but Keith was late in arriving from a *Disc and Music Echo* party at Hatchett's Club, Piccadilly, where he and John accepted the Who's award for Best Live Band.

TUESDAY, 22 FEBRUARY

Joel Rosensweig's production of *Tommy* opened at the Aquarius Theatre, on Hollywood's Sunset and Vine, promoted by Concert Associates and KRLA. It was the first major stage presentation of the work to earn Pete's approval, after receiving considerable critical acclaim when presented at the University of Southern California in March 1971. The show ran through 26 March.

MONDAY, 27 MARCH

At Television Centre, Pete pre-recorded the second of a six-part BBC-1 religious television series, *How Can You Be So Sure?*, chaired by Michael Dornan. In each programme, a person with a sure answer to everything faced a small group of contemporaries who regarded such answers with suspicion. Pete's faith in Baba was questioned by Bill Nicholson, Heather Mansfield, John Farnell, and Leyla Kenter-Akean. The programme was transmitted Sunday, 16 April, 6:15–6:45 pm, and repeated the following afternoon, 1:00–1:30 pm.

Pete's appearance on the show helped inspire his own personalised tribute to Baba, *Who Came First*, as he told the *NME*'s Nick Logan: "After I did that television programme talking about Baba, a lot of people came up to me and said, 'Listen, nobody wants to sit for half an hour listening to you talking about it... If you've got anything to say about Baba, do it through music. You're a musician—that's why you got on the programme in the first place—so play, sing songs, do what you were bloody born to do.' So I had that in mind."

TUESDAY, 28 MARCH

An interview with Pete in his Twickenham home studio was included in *Whatever Happened To Tin Pan Alley?*, an hour-long ATV documentary on popular music similar in scope to Tony Palmer's *All My Loving*. (See 10 March 1968). It was screened over the ITV network, 10:30–11:30 pm.

As well as providing a brief visual history, the four-minute Who segment showed Pete mixing Billy Nicholls' "Forever's No Time At All" and doodling on his ARP 2600-P synthesiser. "The Song Is Over" was played over the programme's end credits.

FRIDAY, 28 APRIL

Keith and DJ Jeff Dexter appeared before a studio audience at Television House, Kingsway, on Thames' local news-magazine programme *Today*, hosted by Eamonn Andrews. The pair were debating the merits of open-air festivals against Tory politician James Wentworth-Day. (A recent proposed Night Assemblies Bill threatened to restrict or stop pop festivals altogether.) The show was broadcast live (in the London ITV region only) from 6:00–6:30 pm.

APRIL—MAY

John recorded his second solo album, *Whistle Rymes*, at Island Studios, 8 Basing Street, West London, to the tune of £12,000. Produced by John Alcock, the musicians included Alan Ross (acoustic guitar), Peter Frampton and Jimmy McCulloch (electric guitars), Rod Coombes and Gordon Barton (drums), John Weider (violin), Neil Sheppard (electric piano, organ), Bryan Williams (John's carpenter!—trombone/trumpet), and the Ox himself on vocals, bass, piano, French horn, and synthesiser bass.

The songs were written on piano in two months at Entwistle's home studio at 28 Corringway, Ealing. "I just showed the musicians what I wanted," he told Richard Green. "They wrote out their chords, and that was it. It was pretty free and easy, we were drunk most of the time..."

Roger produced *Riding On The Crest Of A Slump*, the debut album by the Ellis Group, fronted by ex-Love Affair singer Steve Ellis, with Zoot Money, Andy Gee, and Dave Lutton. "We rehearsed the album at Mitch Mitchell's studio and in Roger's front room at Sussex for three days," Ellis remembered. "Then it was recorded in about five weeks at Olympic. Roger did the mixing, but then CBS mislaid the masters, so it took another week starting from scratch to re-mix, by which time, they suddenly found the original tapes!" The album was released by Epic in September.

FRIDAY, 19 MAY

First documented session at Olympic Sound Studios for *Rock Is Dead—Long Live Rock*, a projected album about the Who's history intended for October release, produced by the Who and associate producer Glyn Johns. Among the demos Pete submitted for the project were "Get Inside," "Women's Liberation" (a.k.a. "Riot In The Female Jail"), and "Can't You See I'm Easy?"

MONDAY, 22 MAY

Recording Olympic: "Join Together" (logged as "Join Together With The Band").

FRIDAY, 26 MAY

Recording Olympic: "Relay."

MAY—JUNE

While on call for Who sessions, John oversaw the mixing of *Whistle Rymes*, the title a sarcastic pun on the common mispelling of his surname, at Nova Sound Recording Studios, 27 Bryanston Street, Marble Arch. Because of problems with the artwork, the album's release was delayed until Friday, 3 November.

At Olympic, Pete mixed tracks recorded at Eel Pie Sound for *Who Came First*, explaining his motivation to Nick Logan: "..there had been two limited edition Baba albums out already and in America they were getting bootlegged at fantastic fees... I've got a copy of one of them and the quality is incredible, but the thing is that on *I Am*, the second one, I only did two bloody songs... and the album was being described as the Pete Townshend Solo Album. It meant that I was getting credited, in some cases, with doing really strange songs... songs I had bugger all to do with apart from the fact that I edited the album together." (Unbeknownst to all but the faithful, both albums could still be obtained via mail order from the Baba Information centres.)

Ronnie Lane and Ron Wood of the Faces were engaged in recording the incidental music to Alexis Kanner's Canadian film, *Mahoney's Last Stand*. While at Olympic, Pete contributed percussion to "Car Radio" and guitar on "Tonight's Number." Both tracks featured Lane on bass, Wood on guitars, Ian McLagan on piano, Bobby Keys on sax, Jim Price on brass, and Kenny Jones/Bruce Rowlands on drums. The soundtrack, given the working title *Wood Lane*, was mixed in August 1973, but not released until September 1976. Glyn Johns credited Townshend as "provider of special effects." Pete also played bass harmonica on a Gallagher and Lyle track, "Give The Boy A Break," released on their *Willie And The Lapdog* album in April 1973.

SATURDAY, 3 JUNE

Keith compèred the Garden Party concert, starring the Beach Boys, Sha Na Na, Joe Cocker, Melanie, and Richie Havens, before 15,000 at the Crystal Palace Bowl, South East London.

The show was filmed by Ron Delsener for network screening in the States on Tuesday, 18 July as an hour-long NBC syndicated special, *Good Vibrations From London*, a follow-up to his earlier ABC special, *Good Vibrations From Central Park*.

ABOVE RIGHT: Keith in costume.
BELOW RIGHT: Keith and "Legs" Larry Smith at Crystal Palace, 3 June.

Although scheduled to run from 12:30—6:00 pm, massive delays occurred due to heated arguments over the appalling PA system between promoter John Smith, the NBC crew, and sound engineers from Marshall Sound.

Keith was first seen sprinkling confetti as he and "Legs" Larry Smith arrived by helicopter. They were then driven a short distance by Rolls-Royce to the artificial lake surrounding the stage. Moon crossed to the stage on his miniature hovercraft when, reaching the edge, he slipped and fell, announcing Sha Na Na in a dripping wet tuxedo!

As the audience waited in the pouring rain during the interminable changeovers, Keith and Legs did their best to entertain with sketches involving several costume changes. Reprising his Carnegie Hall personas (see 28 December 1971), Keith dressed head-to-toe in drag and reappeared in a matching gold lamé outfit. During a ninety-minute lull between Richie Havens and the Beach Boys, he severely cut his foot during a spirited attempt to enliven proceedings and was carried off to hospital for stitches. He was discharged in time for the Beach Boys encore, running onstage to hug singer Mike Love and guest pianist Elton John, both of whom carried him (hopping) offstage.

MONDAY, 5 JUNE
Recording Olympic: "Long Live Rock."

TUESDAY, 6 JUNE
Recording Olympic: "Put The Money Down."

The sessions proceeded no further as Townshend felt the resemblance to *Who's Next* was too obvious. "What we've done really is looked at the Who and said, 'O.K. in order to shake it up, let's turn the whole thing upside down and start again," Townshend told *Sounds*. "I don't think it's going to be easy." The tracks recorded to date were either released as interim singles or remained in the can until being exhumed the following year by John for *Odds and Sods*. Pete's demos for "Is It In My Head?" and "Love Reign O'er Me" were incorporated into *Quadrophenia*.

FRIDAY, 9 JUNE
Sha Na Na commenced a U.K. tour at the Mayfair Ballroom, Newcastle. Keith popped up at regular intervals with assistant/driver Peter "Dougal" Butler to offer his support and patronage, appearing at their Speakeasy reception and at odd stops on the following itinerary: University, Hull (10), Kinetic Circus, Kenilworth (11), Belle Vue, Manchester (12), University, Sheffield (16), Stadium, Liverpool (17), South Parade Pier, Portsmouth (18), University, Cardiff (21), Guildhall, Plymouth (22), University, Exeter (23), Belfry, Birmingham (24), and two concerts at the Roundhouse, Chalk Farm (25).

He even followed the troupe to Europe, where they represented the U.K. at the Gulden Zeezwaluw '72 (Golden Sea Swallow) International TV Festival in Knokke, Belgium, broadcast 22 July. Moon couldn't resist joining in as a leather-clad MC but during rehearsals, his attempt at a double somersault and jackknife, ended in a back flop off the stage. He was taken to a Belgian hospital for three days and re-admitted to Weybridge Hospital on Wednesday, 12 July to undergo a minor operation for an abcess on the base of the spine. "Keith had bruised the base of his spine previously from another accident, but he just neglected it," said Who publicist Keith Altham. "He said himself it was from years of falling off barstools."

FRIDAY, 16 JUNE
"Join Together" B/W "Baby Don't You Do It" (recorded live in San Francisco in December 1971) was released, reaching #9. The single was the last to be issued on Decca in America on 8 July, where it reached #17. Henceforth, all U.S. Who product would appear through new Stateside distributors, MCA Records.

SUNDAY, 25 JUNE
A promotional clip for "Join Together," directed by Michael Lindsay-Hogg, was shot on 35-mm at the London Weekend Television Studios, Wembley (not Shepperton studios as previously documented). Filming lasted from 1:00—9:00 pm and ten takes were run through on a mobile stage, before an invited audience of Track staff and Who Fan Club members. The film first aired Thursday, 13 July on BBC-1's *Top Of The Pops*, 7:25—8:00 pm, and was repeated the following week (same times).

Joe Boyd, who had worked with Pete on Mike Heron's album (see August 1970), was present to conduct an interview for a Jimi Hendrix documentary he was making. Not for the first time, as Boyd recalled. "Pete had agreed to talk about Jimi for the movie, and we'd caught a great fifteen minute interview with him, down by the river near his home in Twickenham. While we were in New York, all the London interviews we'd done on 16-mm were sent off to Hollywood to be blown up to 35 mm. Unfortunately, they didn't think to put the stuff in film cans, they just packed it all into a cardboard box, and when it arrived, the guy at Universal Studios didn't know what it was and threw the box away! So there was nothing we could do but to beg for all of the interviews to be redone.

"We tracked Pete down, told him our problem, but he didn't sound hopeful. However, he worked out the only time he might be free was after a video shoot the Who were doing. On the day, to get the kids in the mood, the Who plugged in and played a proper gig for an hour as a warm-up, and then promised to play again for another hour after the shoot, as a reward. Sure enough, when they'd finished filming, the group started playing again.

"While Pete was spinning his arm, he badly gashed his hand and had to be taken off to hospital. He told everybody to sit tight, saying he'd carry on as soon as he got back! After about half an hour, he came back with his hand all stitched up and bandaged, and to my amazement, they finished the show for all the kids who'd waited.

"Now as time went on, the crew were starting to take everything down, so we had to keep handing them five pound notes to keep the lights on, as we needed them for background. There was still no sign of Pete, so I went upstairs to the dressing room, to see what was happening. He was drinking brandy, looking absolutely shattered. He just glared at me, as if to say, 'I've promised to do your interview, and I will in my own time,' in other words, 'fuck off!' About three quarters of an hour later, he came down, looking a mess and I thought, 'This isn't going to happen.' He pointed to the camera and said, 'How much is in there?' 'About eleven minutes,' I said. 'Then that's what you're getting!'

"So he started talking, and he just completely transformed himself. He was just as sparkling as in the first interview, even more so. That's why we put him at the very start of the film."

Jimi Hendrix premiered in London on Thursday, 14 June, 1973 at the Warner West End, Leicester Square.

TRACK RECORDS 439 1741
The who
TELEVISION SPECTACULAR
SUNDAY 25th JUNE 1pm
London Weekend TV Studios
Wickham Rd (Nth Circular rd) Wembley
Bakerloo Line to Stonebridge Park
Buses 112 & 212
REFRESHMENTS AVAILABLE
ADMIT ONE

SUNDAY, 16 JULY

Members of the Anti-Apartheid Movement held a champagne supper and celebrity concert on the grounds of Keith's home, Tara House, in Chertsey. More than 100 people paid £10 a head to attend and entertainment was provided by singer Blossom Dearie, satirist John Bird, actress Eleanor Bron, and the Scaffold. Just out of hospital (see 9 June), Keith did his best to disrupt pro-

The Who in Concert:

FRANKFURT	HAMBURG	BERLIN	ESSEN	WIEN	MÜNCHEN
11. Aug.,	12. Aug.,	30. Aug.,	31. Aug.,	2. Sept.,	4. Sept.,
21 Uhr,	20 Uhr,	20 Uhr,	21 Uhr,	19.30 Uhr,	20 Uhr,
Festhalle	E.-Merck.-H.	Deutschl.-H.	Grugahalle	Stadthalle	Deutsch. Museum

ceedings by parading around in his gold lamé Sha Na Na outfit, miming to rock and roll favourites that blasted from his jukebox.

MONDAY, 7 AUGUST

Recording Olympic: "Waspman." "All the band ever says to me when they're in the studio singing is 'Get Out!'" Moon told Richard Green. "Then I act as barman, 'cause they all get terrible dry throats, and I have to keep on pouring out the brandy all the time. Also, if I'm in the studio looning about while they're trying to lay down a vocal track, they can't sing if they're laughing at me dressed up as a wasp. You know, there's nothing worse, when you're trying to be serious, than to have a human wasp flying all over the studio."

FRIDAY, 11 AUGUST

The Who commenced their first European tour in almost two years at the Festhalle, Frankfurt, West Germany, with Track signings Golden Earring supporting on all dates. Having not played together for several months, a series of prior rehearsals did not prevent opening night mishaps. "On the European tour, I had forgotten how to control the volume on my bass because I was so used to playing in a studio," John told Chris Charlesworth, "and on the first night Pete did his knees in because he'd forgotten to put on shin pads for his jumping act."

SATURDAY, 12 AUGUST

Ernst Merck Halle, Hamburg, West Germany.

In England, the first part of a half-hour interview featuring Pete discussing *Who Came First* with Michael Wale, was transmitted on Radio 1's *Scene And Heard*, 4:00—5:00 pm; the second followed 19 August (same times).

TUESDAY, 15 AUGUST

Keith filmed a brief cameo in Ringo Starr's film *Count Downe*, drumming on "Jump Into The Fire" in a concert scene shot over three days in a warehouse at Surrey Docks, South East London. "The Count Downes" included Klaus Voormann (bass), Peter Frampton (guitar), Bobby Keyes (sax), Jim Price (trumpet), Rikki Farr as MC, and vocalist Harry Nilsson in the title role, with Ringo as Merlin. John Bonham replaced Keith for the remaining live sequences.

Directed by horror veteran Freddie Francis and produced by Ringo for Apple Films, the film's title was changed to *Son Of Dracula* when given a limited cinematic release, premiering at the Atlanta Film Festival, in Georgia on 19 April, 1974.

WEDNESDAY, 16 AUGUST

Forest Nationale, Brussels, Belgium.

THURSDAY, 17 AUGUST

Oude Rai, Amsterdam, Holland.

MONDAY, 21 AUGUST

KB Hallen, Copenhagen, Denmark.

A second show at the venue, scheduled for the following day, was moved to the 25th.

WEDNESDAY, 23 AUGUST

Kungliga Tennishallen, Stockholm, Sweden.

Shots of the Who's arrival at Arlanda Airport, interviews by Urban Lasson with Bob Pridden and roadie Alan Smith, and Keith and Pete clowning backstage, as well as 2 minutes 30 seconds of "Won't Get Fooled Again" from this evening's concert closed *Roadies*, a self-explanatory Sverige Television documentary, broadcast Sunday, 22 April, 1973, 9:15—9:55 pm.

THURSDAY, 24 AUGUST

Scandinavium, Gothenburg, Sweden.

FRIDAY, 25 AUGUST

KB Hallen, Copenhagen, Denmark.

WEDNESDAY, 30 AUGUST

Deutschlandhalle, Berlin, West Germany.

THURSDAY, 31 AUGUST

Grugahalle, Essen, West Germany.

SATURDAY, 2 SEPTEMBER

Stadhalle, Vienna, Austria.

MONDAY, 4 SEPTEMBER

Deutsches Museum, Kongressaal, Munich, West Germany.

The Who were voted "Star Of The Week" by the *Munich Abendzeitung*, described as "extraordinary performers in the cultural and political field during the Olympic Games."

TUESDAY, 5 SEPTEMBER

Mehrzweckhalle, Wetzikon, Zurich, Switzerland.

SATURDAY, 9 SEPTEMBER

Fête de L'Humanité (French Workers Festival), Paris, France, with Country Joe McDonald.

An estimated 400,000 people attended this open-air event, with all funds going to the French

Communist Party. The concert was filmed in colour by Freddy Hausser and footage was first screened the following year as part of an ORTF documentary, *Pop Galerie*.

A reclusive Eric Clapton and girlfriend Alice Ormsby-Gore were present, having been discreetly invited along by Pete, who, with Bob Pridden, was currently sorting through the tapes for Derek and the Dominoes' aborted second album.

SUNDAY, 10 SEPTEMBER
Palais des Sports, Lyon, France.

THURSDAY, 14 SEPTEMBER
Palasport, Rome, Italy.

As it was the last European show and in response to the hall's atrocious PA system and rowdy audience, Townshend sacrificed his guitar—the only occasion this happened on the tour.

MONDAY, 25 SEPTEMBER
Unhappy with the available studios in London, the Who resolved to build their own.

The group purchased and began renovating a large, disused warehouse (formerly St. Andrew's Parish Hall) at 115 Thessaly Road, Battersea, South West London. As well as a recording studio, the building functioned as a storage facility for the Who's thirty tons of sound and lighting equipment.

FRIDAY, 29 SEPTEMBER
Pete's Baba devotional album, *Who Came First*, was released by Track. (Its appearance was delayed from 18 August because of problems over the elaborate sleeve design.) Apart from contributions by Ronnie Lane ("Evolution," on which Pete played acoustic guitar) and Billy Nicholls ("Forever's No Time At All"), it was a bona fide Townshend solo effort. Pete sang, played guitar, bass, drums, keyboards, and synthesiser, and engineered, mixed, and produced "in one gynormouse ego trip."

Three tracks: "Pure And Easy," "Let's See Action" (under it's original title "Nothing Is Everything"), and "Time Is Passing" were Pete's original *Lifehouse* demos. Jim Reeves' hit "There's A Heartache Following Me," like Cole Porter's "Begin The Beguine," was one of Baba's favourite ditties. "Sheraton Gibson," about Pete's dislike of touring, was written in Cleveland on the Who's 1970 tour.

The album was housed in a gatefold sleeve featuring photos of the Avatar and a poster reproduction of a "very expensive" Mike McInnerney painting. Graham Hughes took the cover shot in a Chelsea scout hall. "The title gave me the 'what came first, the chicken or the egg?' idea so Vernon Brewer of Track and I went out and bought all these eggs and lit them from underneath," Hughes said. "We also had to go and get a boiler suit for Pete because he didn't have one! I took the shot very quickly because Pete was in a hurry. We suspended him from a winch with his Doc Martens just out of reach of the eggs which he was trying to kick!" Press copies of the album came with several sheets of Townshend's notes behind each song. All proceeds went towards a special trust fund to further Baba's teachings, to which both Decca and Track generously donated 15% of the record's retail sales.

OCTOBER
Final vocal and overdubbing in Studio One, Olympic Studios, on Lou Reizner's all-star reworking of *Tommy*, with the London Symphony Orchestra and English Chamber Choir, conducted and directed by David Measham.

The cast featured (in order of appearance): Pete Townshend (Narrator), Sandy Denny (Nurse), Graham Bell (Lover), Steve Winwood (Father), Maggie Bell (Mother), Richie Havens (Hawker), Merry Clayton (Acid Queen), Roger Daltrey (Tommy), John Entwistle (Cousin Kevin), Ringo Starr (Uncle Ernie), Rod Stewart (Local Lad), and Richard Harris (Doctor).

The orchestral parts were arranged by Wil Malone, with additional arrangements scored by session guitarist "Big" Jim Sullivan. Reizner's project had taken an exhaustive year of planning and a total of

eight months solid studio work, financed to the tune of £60,000 by producer Lou Adler.

Daltrey and Townshend attended most sessions, adding vocal parts and acoustic guitar where necessary. When pressed for extra material by Reizner, Townshend donated "Love Reign O'er Me" for Maggie Bell to sing. "It didn't go on in the end," he recalled, "because he [Reizner] wanted to put his album out before we put out *Quadrophenia*—a full year before—so I said, 'no, it's got to come off.' We were hoping Maggie would put it out, but she didn't."

Adler's company, Ode Records, released the double album in the U.S. on 27 November, where it sold 400,000 copies, going gold within a week. Radio Luxembourg heralded the record's official 8 December U.K. release date with an exclusive preview in its entirety, from 10:30 pm—12 midnight on Friday, 1 December. The following day, the whole of Radio 1's *Scene And Heard* (4:00—5:00 pm) was devoted to the album, with the show extending 30 minutes into the *David Simmons* slot.

THURSDAY, 5 OCTOBER
Keith and Pete attended a press party at the Europa Hotel, Grosvenor Square, to launch their sponsored £6000 Group 2 Ford Escort RS 1600. (The car was entered in the annual RAC *Daily Mirror* Rally of Great Britain, starting that December in Leeds.)

John was in America on a three-week *Whistle Rymes* promotional jaunt, while Roger was celebrating the birth of his first daughter, Rosie Lea, born 3 October at Pembury Hospital, Kent.

At the party, Moon arrived in a bear costume and was led around by parson Viv Stanshall. Toastmaster Townshend poured champagne, while he, Moon, and two scantily-clad models posed with drivers Stan Griffin and Chris Dickenson. Moon offered his services as a member of the rally backup team! Like the previous year (see 20 November 1971), Brian Llewelyn directed a 30 minute film *RAC '72—A Record After 13 Years*, which again featured a soundtrack of Who music.

FRIDAY, 13—20 OCTOBER
That'll Be The Day soundtrack sessions at Olympic Studios, London, produced by Lou Reizner. An all-

The Who requests the pleasure of the company of ____ at the Europa Hotel, Grosvenor Sq., London, W1 on Thursday, 5th October, 1972 at 7.30 Full Bar & Buffet Dress Informal This invitation is not transferable without prior arrangement For further information—please telephone: 01-439 1741

TRACK DELUXE 2408 201

star line-up consisting of Billy Fury (vocals), Keith Moon (drums), Pete Townshend and Ron Wood (guitars), Graham Bond (sax), and John Hawken (piano) recorded "Rock Is Dead—Long Live Rock." The song appeared in the film and on the double soundtrack album, released by Ronco Records in May 1973. Moon shared a "Music Supervisor" credit with Beatles aide, Neil Aspinall.

MONDAY, 23 OCTOBER—FRIDAY, 8 DECEMBER
Keith filmed his scenes in *That'll Be The Day* on location at Warners Holiday Camp, Puckpool, and the Lakeside Inn, Wootton Bridge, Isle of Wight. Directed by Claude Whatham and starring David Essex and Ringo Starr, with a screenplay written by *Evening Standard* columnist Ray Connolly, the film revolved around the exploits of Jim MacLaine, a rock and roll-obsessed youth growing up in 1950s Britain.

Keith slicked his hair back to play drummer J.D. Clover in Stormy Tempest and the Typhoons, a part specially written into the film for him by Connolly. Tempest (Billy Fury) and the Typhoons, featuring Graham Bond on sax, John Hawken on piano, and Keith's assistant, Peter "Dougal" Butler, and drum tech Mick Double on guitar and bass respectively, mimed to "Rock Is Dead—Long Live Rock." Viv Stanshall cameoed as a fading rock and roll singer in the same sequence. Co-produced by David Puttnam and Sanford Lieberson for Goodtimes Enterprises Ltd., the film premiered in London on 12 April, 1973. Keith went on to appear in the inevitable sequel, *Stardust.* (see 18 February, 1974.)

OCTOBER—NOVEMBER
John's *Rigor Mortis Sets In*, co-produced by John Alcock, was completed in less than three weeks at Nova Sound Studios, Marble Arch. *Rigor Mortis* featured Entwistle on bass, Alan Ross and Graham Deakin (from Ro Ro), on guitar and drums respectively, Bryan Willams on piano/trombone, and Tony Ashton on keyboards. Backing vocals were courtesy of the Ladybirds (formerly the Vernons Girls).

MONDAY, 6—THURSDAY, 9 NOVEMBER
During the week, an all-star jam occured at an Alice Cooper session at Morgan

RIGHT: Pete and Keith with friends at the Europa, 5 October.

Studios, Willesden, North London, featuring Keith Moon, Marc Bolan, Harry Nilsson, and Rick Grech. Producer Bob Ezrin kept the tapes rolling, but nothing was used for the completed *Billion Dollar Babies* album, released March 1973.

SATURDAY, 25 NOVEMBER
"The Relay" B/W "Waspman" was issued by MCA in the States a month before its 22 December U.K. release date, peaking at #39 in *Billboard*; #21 in the U.K.

Keith was in Los Angeles as "Surprise Super Star Guest Host" of a disastrous benefit for the Southern California Council of Free Clinics, sponsored by KROQ-FM, at Memorial Coliseum. Billed as "the Ultimate ROQ Concert/Festival," the show featured co-headliners Chuck Berry, the Bee Gees, Sly and the Family Stone, the Eagles, and Stevie Wonder. Further down the bill were the Raspberries, Frankie Valli and the Four Seasons, Yellowstone, Merry Clayton, and Mott The Hoople. Keith, dressed as usual in drag, introduced Wonder and "Special Added Attraction" Sha Na Na.

A poor turnout of 32,000 were subjected to innumerable delays, and an overzealous police unit of 500 (only fifty were expected) had a field day with drug busts. Despite hovering near bankruptcy, KROQ, which videotaped the concert, pledged $100,000 to the cause.

TUESDAY, 28 NOVEMBER

From 4:15—6:15 pm in Studio B12, Broadcasting House, Pete rehearsed and recorded an interview with Johnny Moran regarding Lou Reizner's *Tommy* for *Scene And Heard*, broadcast Saturday, 2 December, 4:00—5:00 pm.

FRIDAY, 1 DECEMBER

In Studio B7, Broadcasting House, Pete rehearsed from 3:30 pm and appeared as a guest with Tony Blackburn on Radio 1's *Roundtable*, hosted by Emperor Rosko, broadcast live 5:00—7:00 pm.

TUESDAY, 5—
THURSDAY, 7 DECEMBER

Dress rehearsals for the *Tommy* cast (including the London Symphony Orchestra and the English Chamber Choir) at the Rainbow Theatre. During a break, the *NME*'s Roy Carr chatted with Townshend, who was confident that Reizner's production would finally lay *Tommy* to rest: "Actually, I don't think people will expect us to perform it, but I think it will undoubtedly widen our audience, and we may pull in a few fans who wouldn't normally listen to the group. Naturally, we're excited about the new activity around the group, but *Tommy* is now his own master. Anyway, we're now working on a 'Jimmy.'"

SATURDAY, 9 DECEMBER

After just under a dozen hours of rehearsal, two sell-out *Tommy* shows, 6:00 & 9:30 pm, in aid of the Stars Organisation for Spastics, were staged at the Rainbow, Finsbury Park, North London.

Reizner had originally intended to hold the concerts at the Royal Albert Hall on the same date. The London Symphony Orchestra had booked the hall through the normal channels, but the venue's management refused permission when it was discovered that rock artists would also be

ABOVE : *Tommy* finale at London's Rainbow Theatre. From left: Merry Clayton, Richie Havens, Peter Sellers, Sandy Denny, Rod Stewart, Graham Bell, Steve Winwood, Roger, conductor David Measham, Pete, John, and Keith.

appearing. (Unsurprisingly, in light of what happened the last time the Who appeared there on 5 July, 1969.) "The manager of the Albert Hall told me he considered *Tommy* to be unsavoury and that, in his estimation, it isn't an opera," said Reizner. "I am amazed that he is able to set himself up in judgement in this way." To add insult to injury, the LSO were charged the standard £500

booking fee, which was deducted from the concert proceeds, despite the production having moved to the more hospitable Rainbow free of charge. When learning of this, Townshend pledged to cover the difference if the allocated charity sum failed to realise £10,000.

The Rainbow stage was redesigned to resemble a giant pinball machine, with perspex lighting

consoles and flashes to simulate the movement of a pinball. Visual effects by Joe's Lights were projected above the stage onto a giant screen. (Stage producer Don Hawkins' original plan to turn the entire theatre into a gigantic pinball table in which the audience would sit was vetoed by the GLC.)

Each artist repeated his or her role as played on Reizner's album. Due to filming commitments,

Ringo Starr's Uncle Ernie character was played most convincingly by Keith, while Peter Sellers replaced Richard Harris as the Doctor. Rod Stewart was accompanied on guitar by Faces side-kick Ron Wood.

Despite a sum in excess of £12,000 spent on production costs, both shows were an unqualified success, raising £15,000—£20,000 for charity. Reizner's grandiose plans included staging the

production in London each Christmas for charity and turning the extravaganza into a full-length feature film. Despite his best intentions, negotiations to restage the event the following year were thwarted by the Albert Hall, who refused permission again on the same grounds, and by the unavailability of certain guest artists, including the Who. (See 11–14 February and 13 December, 1973.)

1 9 7 2

FOUR FACES 1973

Apart from a couple of television slots and a one-off, last-minute Dutch concert in March, the Who effectively disappeared from view for the early part of 1973. "I've got to get a new act together for the Who," Pete told *Melody Maker*. "And I don't care if it takes me two years before you see the Who again, we've got to get something fresh... We've tried going through all the hits, basing a show on that, but that doesn't work. It's all in the past now, people don't really want to sit and listen to all our past." In the interim, the restless band members killed time with various non-group activities while waiting to commence work on *Quadrophenia*.

Always a magnet for eccentrics, Pete produced John Otway's first recordings for Track and personally involved himself in the rehabilitation of Eric Clapton, culminating in two all-star concerts at the Rainbow Theatre in January, subsequently released as a live album. Reclusive and overcoming a heroin addiction, Clapton had apparently conceded only after Townshend agreed to appear. "I thought, 'Right mate, we've got ya!'" Townshend recalled. "I'd been asked to help Eric finish an album of Derek and the Dominoes tapes that had been lying around for years, and instead I found it was turning into a social occasion. I knew appearing live he'd have to work." Thanks to Townshend's efforts, Clapton eventually kicked

LEFT: PETE WITH ERIC CLAPTON AT THE RAINBOW THEATRE.

his addiction using Dr. Meg Patterson's patented electric acupuncture treatment.

John released his third solo album, *Rigor Mortis Sets In*, a collection of dark ditties parodying 50s rock and roll. Keith went globetrotting, including a return to Australia, where he reprised his role of Uncle Ernie in Lou Reizner's *Tommy*. He was also given his own four-part BBC Radio 1 series, providing proof of his natural talent for Python-esque humour—a direction that he was unfortunately diverted from. In April, Roger released his eponymous solo album, a collection of professionally crafted, un-Who-like pop, co-penned by star-in-waiting Leo Sayer. "I haven't done it just to have a solo album; it was a period of learning," said Roger. "It gives me, as singer for the Who, a much bigger dimension, because it helped me discover me and what I can sing, and how I should sing. As long as I keep getting better, that's what it's all about, because it benefits the Who."

An unexpected hit single, "Giving It All Away," provided the first significant success from any non-group activity. When the Reizner version of "I'm Free" also made in-roads into the British charts as a single in August, Roger suddenly had an independent power base within the Who—a fact that a vulnerable Townshend, still reeling from the failure of *Lifehouse* and entrenched in *Quadrophenia*, was acutely aware of.

Dissatisfied with the studio situation in London, the Who invested in an old church hall in Battersea, with the intention of building their own state of the art studio and rehearsal room. Ramport Studio

(nicknamed "the Kitchen") was still in an unfinished state as the *Quadrophenia* sessions commenced. The control room was ripped out, waiting to be replaced with a 16-track desk. Meanwhile, the group utilised Ronnie Lane's Mobile Studio, employing the services of its designer, Ron Nevison. "Typically, Pete was trying to record the most ambitious and complex album of [the Who's] career in a studio that was still being built, without a producer

and in quadrophonic sound, a medium that had not yet been perfected," Richard Barnes wrote, in an eloquent summation of affairs. (The idea for quadrophonic sound was eventually discarded along the way.)

"I've really had more control over this album than any other Who album we've ever done," Pete told the *NME*, "from the beginning right through to the very end. I've directed it, if you like." Townshend described *Quadrophenia* to *Circus* as "a sort of musical *Clockwork Orange*." Ironically, the comparison was more applicable to its unrealised predecessor, *Lifehouse*, but the theme of "ultra-violence" such as that perpetrated by rival youth cults—in this case, Mods and Rockers—was relevant. For the story, Townshend dug back to the Who's formative years to create the character of Jimmy, an amalgam of six people Pete knew from their early mod audience, namely "Irish" Jack Lyons, Paddy Keene, Chrissie Colville, Mike Quinn, and brothers Lee and T.K. Gaish.

Buried in a whirl of uppers and downers, beach fights, and unrequited love, the story concentrated on the quest for spiritual redemption, using four musical themes—"quadrophenia"—to reflect each of the Who's personalities. Jimmy is a working class kid, disillusioned with a life of dead-end jobs, unsympathetic parents, and a psychiatrist who doesn't understand him. He's a loser, but at least he's "one of us," i.e., a mod. Even then, a self-conscious need to keep up with the pack fills him with despair. He loses the girl of his dreams to his best mate, smashes up his GS scooter, and considers suicide beneath the wheels of a train. Instead, he takes the 5:15 back to the scene of previous triumphs and frustrations, Brighton, only to find that the "ace face" he looked up to now scrapes a living as a hotel bellboy. Based on a true life epiphany Pete experienced while in the Sea Scouts, Jimmy finally finds what he's seeking, far out to sea on a rock. Like *Tommy* before it, the ending is deliberately left vague. Did Jimmy reach safety, or did he drown at the moment of God realisation? (The numerous water references connect to Baba's philosophies, and Townshend would continue to use water as a metaphor for salvation.)

For the stereo sound effects used throughout the complex recording, Pete and Ron Nevison took Ronnie Lane's mobile unit down to Cornwall and stuck microphones out on a rock to record the sea crashing. At Goring, Berkshire, Pete spent evenings paddling along in a punt behind a flock of coots,

ABOVE: PETE, (WITH HIS FATHER CLIFF), RECORDING SOUND EFFECTS FOR *QUADROPHENIA* AT GORING.

getting them to fly away so he could record the sound of birds taking off from water—at one point, even dropping an expensive tape recorder and microphone into the Thames.

While *Quadrophenia* was being recorded, the festering situation between the band and their management came to a head. The previous year, Daltrey had instigated an audit of the group's accounts and found a serious black hole that needed explaining. To add insult to injury, Lambert and Stamp rejected his solo album, no doubt concerned that its success could jeopardise the Who's future.

After Lambert and Stamp's callous rebuke, Roger brought in Bill Curbishley to handle his affairs. An East End schoolfriend of Chris Stamp and Mike Shaw, Curbishley had worked his way up through Track's ranks since being employed by Stamp in 1971, proving himself by renegotiating the Who's European concert percentages the following year. Increasingly, Lambert and Stamp were content to leave the day-to-day involvement with their charges to the likes of Curbishley, Shaw, and Peter Rudge, while indulging in their own personal (and destructive) vices. Lately, Curbishley and Stamp had

1
9
7
3

been dealing with Robert Stigwood regarding funding for the revived idea of a *Tommy* movie, a subject dear to the heart of Lambert, who proceeded to unravel the negotiations with his own demented demands. The last straw came when emergency funds were required for some essential work on Ramport Studio. A cheque was duly issued by Lambert and Stamp out of back royalties owing, but Lambert invalidated it before departing to his palazzo in Venice. Curbishley consequently quit his job at Track to set up his own company, Five One Productions Ltd., 69 New Bond Street, to oversee the Who's affairs.

At first, Pete refused to be drawn into the matter, based partly on loyalty, but in particular, because he feared he'd lose the creative catalyst he saw in Lambert—although there hadn't been much evidence of it lately. However, the situation soon became intractable. "Kit went a bit mad straight away," Townshend recalled. "He decided his role for *Quadrophenia* was to bring in trays of food! We fell out simply because he let me down, I felt. I wanted to beat him up. And I think I did hit him once. But I stopped before things went too far."

Townshend reached the end of his tether when he discovered that a large amount of his American publishing money had vanished. When Daltrey finally issued an ultimatum of "them or me," Pete joined Roger and John in instigating legal proceedings against his managers. Moon refused to be drawn into the mire.

By October, the fruits of six months work on *Quadrophenia* were realised, but certain band members had gripes. Having tracked the album's brass arrangements for hours at a stretch, John felt his bass wasn't mixed to a satisfactory level. (In 1978 he subsequently remixed the tapes for the *Quadrophenia* film soundtrack.) Not being privy to the mixing, Roger complained about the sterility of the sound and how his vocals had been buried. Townshend felt Daltrey was being ungrateful, as he wrote four years later in *Rolling Stone*: "Fundamentally, I had taken on too much as always and couldn't handle the strain when things went wrong and people blamed me." During the subsequent English and American tours, their first in two years, animosities between the two boiled over during rehearsals, ending with Daltrey punching Townshend into hospital. All was forgiven, but it was an ill omen.

The clamour for concert tickets was frenzied. At the Lyceum, the police sent a seemingly endless line of ticket-buyers around the back of the build-

ings in the Strand; the line ultimately reaching Charing Cross Station, a good three quarters of a mile away.

The initial *Quadrophenia* shows were less than smooth, partly because the record was delayed in reaching the shops because of problems at the press. Townshend and Daltrey felt obliged to resort to lengthy explanations between numbers. Roger's continued protests about the disruption of the shows' flow resulted in a number of songs being dropped after the first few concerts. Above all, the *Quadrophenia* material relied on complex backing tapes, which refused to function in sync, sending Townshend into a tailspin.

Midway through a show in Newcastle, Pete exploded into a rage (unfairly directed against the band's hapless sound man, Bob Pridden) smashed his guitar, and tore into the offending tapes, which had taken weeks to assemble, before temporarily storming offstage. The high-profile Lyceum shows were criticised for poor crowd handling and obstructed views.

The headaches followed them across the Atlantic, not least due to the continued technical problems, band in-fighting, and the very Englishness of the subject matter, which required even lengthier dissertations between numbers. Keith's behaviour had grown increasingly erratic, triggered by his long-suffering wife Kim finally walking out on him with their daughter Mandy. During the opening concert in San Francisco, he collapsed after consuming a drink spiked with an animal tranquilliser, requiring the services of an audience member to complete the show. In Montreal, an after-show party turned into a destructive release, resulting in most of the touring party (including the band) ending up behind bars. After playing some French dates the following February, at least one band member was relieved to see *Quadrophenia* laid to rest from the Who's act. (The bulk of the work remained unperformed for more than twenty-two years.)

In December, due to the mayhem surrounding tickets for the Lyceum shows, the group played four Christmas concerts in Edmonton, North London, which Pete considered to be among the Who's finest. However, his enthusiasm was to be short-lived. With the perceived indifference directed towards *Quadrophenia* shaking his confidence, Pete was experiencing feelings of insecurity at failing to break through his own self-imposed boundaries. Ever restless, he began to question the group's continued relevance.

1973

JANUARY—FEBRUARY

Six weeks of recording and mixing for Roger's first solo album, *Daltrey*, produced by pop singer/actor Adam Faith (née Terry Nelhams). The two Actonians met the previous autumn when Faith brought his protégé Leo Sayer down to Daltrey's 8-track Barn studio to record Sayer's debut album, *Silverbird*. "He kept talking about what would I like to do if I ever did a solo album," Daltrey recalled. "I never really had it in my head to do one, but the Who weren't doing anything, and I thought, 'well if I'm ever going to do one, it might as well be now.'" (Faith worked with Keith the following year on *Stardust*. See 18 February, 1974.)

Sayer composed the songs with partner Dave Courtney, while "You And Me" and "The Way Of The World" were co-written with Faith. Musicians on the album included Courtney (piano), Russ Ballard (guitar, keyboards), Bob Henrit (drums), B.J. Cole (steel guitar), Dave Arbus (violin), and Dave Wintour (bass). Del Newman arranged the strings.

The backing tracks were recorded at Roger's Burwash studio, while vocals and mixing were completed in Apple's basement studio at 3 Savile Row

and Nova Sound, London. Looking for the best acoustics, the vocals to "One Man Band (Reprise)" were recorded on the Apple rooftop (scene of the Beatles' last informal concert in 1969). A non-album, gospel-flavoured track, "There Is Love," featuring Jimmy Page on guitar, appeared in September as the B-side to "Thinking."

WEDNESDAY, 3 JANUARY

The Who pre-recorded an appearance on the Saturday night chat show, *Russell Harty Plus*, at the London Weekend Television Studios on the South Bank. In Studio 3, an insert for "Relay" (with camera effects) was taped and host Harty interviewed the group, sitting along the stage edge, before a studio audience.

Harty struggled valiantly to maintain order as the conversation soon degenerated into chaos, thanks to Keith and Pete's unscripted antics, including a clothes-ripping tussle and Moon striptease. (Clips were used in *The Kids Are Alright*.)

The programme, directed by Michael Lindsay-Hogg, featured additional guests Miss World, Lord Weymouth, and Christopher Lee, and was broadcast three nights later, 10:40—11:40 pm, over the LWT and Anglian regions only. "Relay" reappeared in a special *Russell Harty Plus Pop*, broadcast 19 January, 1974, and was featured in *Who's Better, Who's Best*.

WEDNESDAY, 10 JANUARY

At Chertsey Court, Keith was fined £15 for possessing a firearm without a license. His gardener, Ian Smith, had borrowed the antique shotgun without Keith's knowledge. Moon admitted the offence, claiming the gun had been left behind at his home by the previous occupants. Asked by chairman Mr. Olivier Hacking when he could pay, Keith enquired, "Do you take American Express cards? I haven't used money for years!"

SATURDAY, 13 JANUARY

Pete headed the stellar cast of musicians backing Eric Clapton at the Rainbow Theatre, Finsbury Park, London. Two shows, 5:30 & 8:30 pm, supported by the Average White Band, were staged as part of a series of concerts promoted by Great Western Festivals to mark Britain's entry into the Common Market.

Ten days of rehearsals were held at Ron Wood's Richmond home, "The Wick," where the ad hoc

backing band loosely fell together. "The Palpitations" featured Pete playing rhythm, Wood on bass, Steve Winwood on keyboards, and Jim Karstein of the Crickets touring band on drums. Townshend's additional choice of drummer, Jim Keltner, was unavailable, so Winwood suggested Traffic bandmates drummer Jim Capaldi and percussionist Rebop. After a few days, Rick Grech, who'd played with Clapton and Winwood in Blind Faith, showed up and was invited to play bass, allowing Wood to move to slide guitar.

Clapton had found the rehearsals daunting: "I honestly thought they'd kill him," Townshend told Mark Plummer. "It was such a long time since he'd worked." There was no guarantee that, strung out and nerve-stricken, he'd show on the night. As showtime for the first concert came and went, these became very real fears. Clapton eventually turned up fifteen minutes late, meekly mumbling an excuse about his girlfriend, Alice Ormsby-Gore, having to let out his white stage suit a couple of inches!

Both shows were recorded by Glyn Johns on Ronnie Lane's Mobile Studio, but additional vocal overdubs were required. "That was due to the fact that we should have had a 16-track, but we only had an eight track, which would be great for a Faces or Who live gig, but there were so many people doing so many things," Townshend explained to Charles Shaar Murray. The best of the tapes, remixed and produced by Bob Pridden, were released in September as *Eric Clapton's Rainbow Concert*.

MONDAY, 15 JANUARY

Keith flew to Paris on Pete's behalf to collect the prestigious Grand Prix de l'Académie du Disque Français awards for both the *Tommy* album and stage production.

FRIDAY, 19 JANUARY

In Studio B7, Broadcasting House, Keith appeared as a guest on Radio 1's *Roundtable*, produced by John Walters, transmitted live, 5:00—7:00 pm. Instead of discussing the merits of each new record, Moon insisted on reading from a book entitled *Eating in Africa* and disrupted the filming for *Radio Wonderful*, a 30-minute documentary made by Richard Loncraine, in conjunction with Goodtimes Enterprises. Goodtimes was also the company behind *That'll Be The Day*; *Radio Wonderful* was that film's supporting feature. (See 12 April.)

ABOVE: Russell Harty, Miss World, and the Who, 3 January.

TUESDAY, 23 JANUARY

Keith drummed on a Dave Carlsen session at Studio 3, CBS Studios, 31 Whitfield Street, London, playing on "Death On A Pale Horse" and one other cut which remains unreleased. All proceeds from the track, featuring Carlsen (née Dave Clarke—vocals/guitar/organ), Noel Redding (bass), and Alan Dickenson (piano), were donated to the National Society for Mentally Handicapped Children.

"I knew Keith from the Speakeasy and asked him along to play," Clarke recalled. "He missed the first session and when he showed up for the second, he broke down on the way in from Chertsey. When I first saw him, he and Dougal were pushing the lilac Roller round the corner!" The sessions were abruptly terminated when Keith and studio manager Dave Margereson viciously fell out. As an act of faith, Moon paid for session time at Trident over the weekend of 2–3 February. Carlsen's album *Pale Horse* was released by Spark Records in November.

FRIDAY, 26 JANUARY

"Made In Japan" B/W "Hound Dog" was released by John Entwistle's band Rigor Mortis. The record was launched with a reception held at a Japanese steakhouse in Soho. Black-edged invitations printed with a wreath were personally delivered by Track promo man Vernon Brewer. While the forthcoming *Rigor Mortis Sets In* album was played, three Asian beauties in bikinis, with "Made In Japan" stamped on their navels, served saki, and a "Professor Suzuki" gave karate demonstrations.

MONDAY, 29 JANUARY

For a fee of £125, the Who pre-taped a two song insert for BBC-2's late night rock series *The Old Grey*

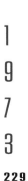

Whistle Test in Presentation Studio B, Television Centre. The group mimed to "Relay" and "Long Live Rock," with live vocals over pre-recorded backing tracks. "Relay," which opened the programme, lasted a full 4 minutes 50 seconds, while "Long Live Rock" was notable for Townshend and Daltrey trading verses, unlike the released version on *Odds and Sods*. Introduced by "Whispering" Bob Harris, the show was broadcast the following evening, 10:45—11:15 pm.

SUNDAY, 11—WEDNESDAY, 14 FEBRUARY

Four New York dates for Lou Reizner's *Tommy* stageshow scheduled to occur at the Albert Hall were scrapped. (See 9 December, 1972.) A charity concert was scheduled for Radio City Music Hall on the 11th followed by three nights at Nassau Coliseum, Long Island. Dave Mason was tipped to narrate, leaving Pete free to play guitar. Townshend could only commit to the charity show, and many of the original London cast were also unavailable. A planned show at the L.A. Forum in March was also abandoned, although an Australian production went ahead. (See 31 March.)

WEDNESDAY, 28 FEBRUARY

At the London A&M offices, Keith, John, and Roger were on hand to receive Gold Discs for Ode Record's *Tommy*, marking worldwide sales of over one million. Also present were Lou Reizner, David Measham, Steve Winwood, and Sandy Denny.

SATURDAY, 3 MARCH

Rehearsals commenced at the Who's own Ramport Studio, christened "the Kitchen," at 115 Thessaly Road, Battersea, South London. A fire had badly damaged the premises on New Year's Eve, but builders worked overtime to make the start of the group's recording schedule. Initial recording was experimental in nature to determine how well the 16-track console operated; it was found to be wanting. Until a replacement could be installed, Ronnie Lane's Mobile Studio was converted from 8 to 16-track and utilised as a control room, with a two-way video system and mike linkup, operated by designer-engineer Ron Nevison and assistant Ron Fawcus, who were retained for the *Quadrophenia* sessions.

ABOVE: A&M AWARD CEREMONY FOR *TOMMY*, 28 FEBRUARY, WITH (FROM LEFT) DAVID MEASHAM, LOU REIZNER, THE PRESIDENT OF A&M, SANDY DENNY, ROGER, JOHN, AND KEITH.

SATURDAY, 10 MARCH

De Vliegermolen Sportshal, Voorburg, The Hague, Holland.

The Who replaced scheduled headliners Roxy Music at the eleventh hour, topping the second day of the annual "Popgala" over the Faces, Rory Gallagher, and Gary Glitter. The concert, staged and filmed by VARA-TV, was edited down and broadcast Friday, 16 March, 8:20—9:50 pm, on Nederland 2. The Who filled the closing twenty-minute segment with "Pinball Wizard," "Won't Get Fooled Again," "My Generation," and "See Me, Feel Me."

More highlights were shown on *Popgala Zien* (Friday, 11 May, 7:05—7:55 pm, Nederland 2), featuring "Summertime Blues" and a brief Keith interview, and again on Friday, 3 August, with a repeat of "See Me, Feel Me" on Nederland 1 (same times). Parts of "Popgala" were also broadcast in stereo on VARA Radio as *Hilversum 1* (Wednesday, 14 March, 5:00—5:55 pm). "Magic Bus" appeared (in part) in *Who's Better, Who's Best*, and "My Generation" in *Thirty Years of Maximum R&B Live*. A five-minute interview with Roger by Anne Nightingale was broadcast on Radio 1's *Scene And Heard* on Saturday, 17 March, 4:00—5:00 pm.

MONDAY, 12 MARCH

Roger and band (Bob Henrit—drums, Russ Ballard—guitar, Dave Wintour—bass, and Dave Courtney—piano) pre-taped "One Man Band" and "Giving It All Away" for *The Old Grey Whistle Test* in Presentation Studio B, Television Centre. The programme was broadcast the following evening, 11:35—12:05 pm. Daltrey was also booked as a guest on the 17 March *Russell Harty Plus* but did not appear.

"Giving It All Away" B/W "The Way Of The World" was released as a single on 16 March, eventually reach-

ABOVE: FROM LEFT, ADAM FAITH, PRODUCER MIKE APPLETON, RUSS BALLARD, AND ROGER ON THE *OLD GREY WHISTLE TEST*, 12 MARCH.

ing #5 on the *NME* chart. Both tracks were taken from *Daltrey*, released Friday, 20 April.

SUNDAY, 18 MARCH

Keith collapsed at Tara House and was rushed to St. Peter's Hospital, Chertsey, after a "magic wand gun" loaded with blank cartridges exploded on impact. A faulty spring in the gun caused a pellet to strike Keith in the chest, grazing his stomach and causing minor bruising. "Keith has decided to leave magic for the fairies," quipped his publicist Keith Altham.

THURSDAY, 29 MARCH

Roger made a live *Top Of The Pops* appearance plugging "Giving It All Away" from Television Centre, transmitted by BBC-1, 6:45—7:15 pm.

SATURDAY, 31 MARCH

Keith reprised his role as Uncle Ernie in the Australian stage version of Lou Reizner's *Tommy*, promoted by Jim McKay. The first show, before 30,000 at the outdoor Myer Music Bowl, Melbourne, was originally scheduled for the previous night but heavy rain put it back a day. Roger had been offered the starring role, but no doubt mindful of the Who's

experiences there in 1968, declined the offer. "I went over there and just generally intimidated the Australian cast," Moon explained. "Graham Bell came over with me. It was a good idea really, because any experience we'd got from the London show, we were able to help the others because we'd seen how it had worked in London." Reizner and conductor David Measham were also involved in the production.

The cast, which rehearsed at the Braite Institute Hall, Prahran, Victoria, featured Daryl Braithwaite (Tommy), Colleen Hewitt (Mrs. Walker), Broderick Smith (Mr. Walker), Jim Keays (the Lover), Wendy

ABOVE: "POPGALA," 10 MARCH.

Saddington (the Nurse), Doug Parkinson (formerly of the Questions, who supported the Who on the 1968 tour—the Hawker), Ross Wilson (Cousin Kevin), Linda George (the Acid Queen), Billy Thorpe (the Pinball Wizard), and Bobby Bright (the Doctor). Graham Bell, originally the Lover in the London production, played the Narrator. Keith received unanimously good reviews, and promoter Jim McKay sent a "thank you" letter, praising him as an "extremely shrewd showman."

SUNDAY, 1 APRIL

The second Australian *Tommy* show (with Ian "Molly" Meldrum replacing Keith) took place at the Royal Randwick Racecourse, Sydney, commencing at 8:15 pm. The concert was filmed and screened Friday, 13 April by Channel 7, 8:00—10:00 pm, sponsored by Ford. It received the Australian TV award for the year's most outstanding creative effort.

THURSDAY, 12 APRIL

That'll Be The Day premiered at the ABC-2 cinema, Shaftesbury Avenue, London. Keith and wife Kim attended, as did Pete, who was disconcerted to find that Ray Connolly's screenplay bore a strong resemblance to his ideas for *Quadrophenia*.

"When I went to see *That'll Be The Day*, I got about halfway through to the bit where he was on the beach and then I walked out in complete disgust," he told Charles Shaar Murray. "I said to Keith, 'You've been making this film all this time. Why couldn't you tell me that the story was very similar?'" *That'll Be The Day* premiered in America at the Beverley Canon Theatre, Beverly Hills, California, on Wednesday, 30 October, 1974.

FRIDAY, 13 APRIL

On the *Daltrey* promotional trail, Roger appeared as a guest on Radio 1's *Roundtable*, broadcast live from Broadcasting House, 5:00—7:00 pm.

THURSDAY, 19 APRIL

A six-minute filmed insert of Keith in his study at Tara House, playing and talking about pinball machines with Derek Hart, was featured in BBC-2's *Europa*, broadcast 8:00—8:30 pm. Subtitled "Enthusiasts? Dreamers? Nuts?," the insert featured Hart innocently enquiring, "Can you explain the kind of satisfaction you get from pinball?" Moon: "Yeah, sexual! I've always loved balls..."

TUESDAY, 24 APRIL

Roger was interviewed at his Burwash farm by Steve Dixon for Radio 1's *Scene And Heard*, broadcast 27 April, 7:00—8:00 pm. John appeared on the 4 May edition in an interview with Johnny Moran, pretaped Friday, 27 April.

MAY

Prior to *Quadrophenia* recording sessions at Ramport Studio, Kit Lambert arranged a return visit to Stargroves (see April 1971), Mick Jagger's Newbury mansion, for preproduction work on structuring the story and to record basic tracks with Record Plant engineer Jack Adams on the Ronnie Lane Mobile.

ABOVE: KEITH AS UNCLE ERNIE IN AUSTRALIA.
BELOW: DEREK HART AND KEITH AT TARA HOUSE, 19 APRIL.

FRIDAY, 11 MAY

John's *Rigor Mortis Sets In* was released. The considerable delay was over a problem getting the links between tracks cleared—a parody of the children's character Andy Pandy spitting and vomiting. These had to be removed, thus requiring the revamping of the original sleeve copy and artwork.

Roger flew to Amsterdam, Holland, to plug his unexpected hit, "Giving It All Away," on AVRO's *Top Pop*, transmitted three nights later on Nederland 1. On Wednesday, 30 May, he appeared in Hamburg, Germany, on Radio Bremen's *Muzikladen*. Daltrey was originally booked as a guest on the 20 May edition of BBC-2's *The John Denver Show*, but American singer Paul Williams appeared in his place.

SATURDAY, 19 MAY

Keith began rehearsing and recording material for his own four-part BBC Radio 1 series at Studio B6, in the basement of Broadcasting House, Portland Place. Each show was written and produced by John Walters, who had previously worked with Keith on Viv Stanshall's *Radio Flashes* (see 17 July, 1971), and so was fully aware of the lunacy in store. "Producing Keith Moon was rather like producing Dracula," Walters remembered. "You had to get them both before the sun went down. The first time he came down to the studios at night, that was the first thing I discovered. You didn't work with Moon at night. The further he got into the day, the further he got from any sort of reality."

Keith was becomingly modest about his own contribution: "The whole thing was his [Walters] idea. He wrote them on the train coming up to Broadcasting House every day. I added things or deleted them as necessary." Uncertain of his own abilities, Keith originally wanted the shows to include guest pals such as Ringo Starr, Harry Nilsson, Marc Bolan, and the Faces. Walters vetoed the idea after playing the pilot to Derek Chinnery, head of Radio 1, who thought it funny as it was. "After the first two shows, it had taken so long that I thought, 'Christ, we're never going to get this together.' Then the second week, I booked the studio in the morning. Keith came in perfectly straight, very eager to work and eager to please. He really became concerned with the work and gave up all his Saturdays and a lot of free time."

MONDAY, 21 MAY

Quadrophenia sessions commenced at Ramport, running through into June, initially produced by Kit Lambert. The album was originally to be recorded and mixed in a new untried medium: quadrophonic sound. Many of the stereo sound effects, as well as Pete's synthesiser tracks and some of the piano parts on his demos, were retained on the finished mixes, after the tapes were transferred from 8 to 16-track at Olympic Studios.

Roger, John, and Keith each laid down their separate parts, and Townshend assembled them into the finished product. As their individual tracks were overdubbed onto the demos, they wiped out his original

LEFT: BBC PRODUCER JOHN WALTERS AND KEITH, 19 MAY.

work. John spent long hours at a stretch arranging and multi-tracking the album's horn arrangements. Pete played banjo and all string parts, using as many as six over-dubs with twenty or thirty synthesiser channels behind that so he could be in total control of the arrangement. "Most of the guitar solos I just did at three o'clock in the morning, raving drunk," he said.

FRIDAY, 25 MAY
John became the last Who member to appear as a guest reviewer on Radio 1's *Roundtable*, broadcast live from Studio B15, Broadcasting House, 5:00—7:00 pm. Unlike the others, he made a return appearance the following year on 6 September.

JUNE
With Nicky Hopkins unavailable, Chris Stainton, of the Grease Band, was enlisted to play piano on "The Dirty Jobs," "5:15," and "Drowned." (Townshend lifted the piano riff for "Drowned" from Joe Cocker's "Hitchcock Railway.")

Ken Russell was a frequent visitor to the *Quadrophenia* sessions for *Tommy* film script consultations. A screenplay was finalized, dated 18 July. Russell happened to be present at a memorable session for "Drowned." He floridly described the scene to David Litchfield in *Image*: "We were there the night they recorded a number called "Rain" [sic], and there was a cloudburst, and they wanted a stereo rain effect. We were in this caravan outside, and bit by bit, the playing stopped except for the piano, and I went in and the floor and the roof had caved in as they were singing and the rain had really deluged them. They were soaking wet, and there were firemen with a hose pumping it out except for the actual man in the cubicle playing the piano, and he was gamely playing on, and he was up to his neck in water, and when they opened the door, it poured like a waterfall."

SATURDAY, 2 JUNE
Keith arrived at Broadcasting House directly from Ron Wood's twenty-sixth birthday party. "He had to be carried into the studio by Dougal," Walters remembered, "and had some difficulty reading lines. Suddenly, he started to get into a character which might be described as Son of Hancock. He adopted a role that was basically a twit. A Shepherd's Bush confident idiot, full of opinions, a kind of Pearly

King of the Speakeasy. Once we got that Ealing comedy cockney, it all fell into place."

MONDAY, 11 JUNE
John and Rigor Mortis (Eddie Jones—guitar, Graham Deakin—drums, and Tony Ashton—keyboards) taped "Peg Leg Peggy" and "My Wife" for BBC-2's *The Old Grey Whistle Test* in Presentation Studio B, Television Centre. The programme was broadcast the following evening, 11:35—12:05 pm.

SATURDAY, 7 JULY
Keith recorded material for the final part of his "A Touch Of The Moon" radio series at Broadcasting House. The first programme was transmitted Tuesday, 21 August in Radio 1's vacant *Sounds Of The '70's* slot (John Peel was on holiday), 11:02—12:00 pm. The following three shows were broadcast over each successive Tuesday (same times). Keith received a payment of £35 per programme and several skits left on the cutting room floor still reside in the BBC sound archives. Plans to record a Christmas album with Walters that year never came to fruition although the two did work together again, albeit briefly. (See 11 October, 1975.)

TUESDAY, 17 JULY
Quadrophenia overdubbing at Ramport. During a downpour, Pete decided to use authentic storm effects as an overdub. Keith stood outside the studio banging a Paiste gong to simulate thunder, until a loud burst of the genuine article resolved matters. At the same time, a hapless roadie risked electrocution recording the rainfall in stereo on several microphones under an umbrella. Roger, recovering from a bout of German measles, completed "Love Reign O'er Me" by taping his climatic vocal.

FRIDAY, 20 JULY
"I'm Free" B/W "Overture (From *Tommy*)," extracted from Lou Reizner's *Tommy*, was released, reaching #13 on the *NME* chart in August. A 16-mm BBC colour promotional film, shot on Roger's Burwash farm, was first aired on the 10 August edition of *Top Of The Pops*, and repeated 31 August.

SATURDAY, 21 JULY
Keith flew to Frankfurt, Germany, invited by Ian McLagan to introduce the Faces, who headlined a two-day rock festival at the Radstadion the following

evening. "Here they are with their new bass player from Japan," he bellowed, "but don't let that put you off. The Faces!" During the encore of "Borstal Boys," Keith reappeared, hitting a cymbal alongside drummer Kenny Jones.

TUESDAY, 31 JULY
Keith was interviewed by Anne Nightingale for Radio 1's *Scene And Heard*, broadcast Thursday 2 August, 7:00—8:00 pm.

AUGUST—SEPTEMBER
Pete and Ron Nevison locked themselves away at Pete's 24-track Eel Pie Sound studio in Goring, Berkshire, for the considerable task of mixing *Quadrophenia*.

"We Close Tonight," written by Pete and sung by John, with varispeed vocals from Keith, was discarded in rough mix state, showing up later on the expanded *Odds and Sods* CD (1998). Not leaving anything to chance, Pete flew to Los Angeles with the tapes to personally oversee the mastering with Arnie Arcosta at The Mastering Lab.

Meanwhile, at Ramport and Nova Sound, John made stereo remixes of "Postcard," "Now I'm A Farmer," "I Don't Even Know Myself," "Water," and "Naked Eye"—all recorded on 8-track at Eel Pie Sound, Twickenham, in 1970—as well as "Pure And Easy" and "Too Much Of Anything" for the *Odds and Sods* collection he was compiling. "Water," originally selected to appear on the album, was instead hived off as the B-side to "5:15," released Friday, 5 October.

TUESDAY, 7 AUGUST
Rushes from July footage shot at Shepperton by AIOK Films' Dave Speechly was shown at De Lane Lea Studios, Wembley, at 4:00 pm, with the group present. For their return to the stage, the Who were considering using a film backdrop, incorporating a screen on winches that could be lowered whenever necessary. The idea foundered due to a major problem in constructing and fabricating a screen large enough. To recoup the filming costs, it was proposed that some of Speechly's footage be used as a promo film for *Quadrophenia*, but this never came about. Instead, Peter Neal was hired for a similar, ill-fated undertaking. (See 17 August.)

Quadrophenia stage rehearsal at Emerson, Lake, and Palmer's rehearsal studio, Manticore, at 396—400 North End Road, Fulham, South West London. Filmmaker Peter Neal and his crew were commissioned to intersperse triple 16-mm stop frame images of the group as a backdrop, after Townshend saw a similar venture Neal had undertaken for Jethro Tull's *A Passion Play*. The Who were to play in front of three giant film screens. Keith, wearing cans, would drum to the soundtrack, and the rest would play to him, and thus, be in time with the film. The idea was eventually rejected after proving technically unworkable.

FRIDAY, 24 AUGUST

The Who (and extras) assembled outside the Hammersmith Odeon for a 5:00 am *Quadrophenia* photo shoot with Ethan Russell. "The Who In Concert—All Tickets Sold" was billed in lights. "It had to be in the early morning or we would have had thousands of people queuing up for tickets," a Track spokesman told *Sounds*. The group then made their way over to Graham Hughes' photographic studio at 9 Rathbone Place, London.

"We had to carry... almost drive this scooter up the stairs to my first floor studio," Hughes remembered.

The front cover picture was taken against a special sky blue canvas. Roger thought of the idea of painting the Who logo on the back of the kid's parka. I still hadn't figured out where the group were going to appear, when the idea of the wing mirrors suddenly dawned on me. I asked Pete, John, and Roger to crouch down and stare into the glass while I shot each image. Keith had disappeared, so I had to go down to Tara and photograph him seperately in his greenhouse to get the same effect."

The gatefold packaging, costing £10,000, featured a forty-four-page tableaux of monochrome photos taken over two weeks by Russell in London, Brighton, Goring, and Cornwall. The Mod kid was played by Chad, alias Terry Kennett, a twenty-one-year-old paint sprayer from Battersea, who had been discovered by Townshend in The Butcher's Arms pub, a few yards from Ramport Studios.

SATURDAY, 25 AUGUST

The music press revealed that *Tommy*, produced by Track in association with the Robert Stigwood Organisation, was to be made into a major feature film early the following year by Ken Russell. Each of the Who would have acting roles, it was confirmed.

THURSDAY, 6 SEPTEMBER

A group meeting to discuss the bands' management and business affairs was held at the offices of Goodman, Michaels, and Rosten, Sparc House, 86 Gloucester Place, London.

WEDNESDAY, 19 SEPTEMBER

At Television Centre, Roger pre-recorded a slot for *Top Of The Pops*, miming his new single "Thinking," solo with acoustic guitar, broadcast 7:25—8:00 pm the following evening.

TUESDAY, 2 OCTOBER

The Daily Mail revealed the breakdown of Keith's seven year marriage to Kim, who had left Tara House over the weekend with their daughter Amanda, and was staying with friends.

"I suppose she was like any woman," Moon said, "they fall in love with a guy. But all the same, they can't help wanting to change him. She tried to get me to change because she didn't like people laughing at me. But if you're a clown, you've got to put up with that, haven't you? I tried. I really did." Citing "unreasonable behaviour," Kim was granted an uncontested decree nisi, custody of Mandy, and a

ABOVE: *TOP OF THE POPS* REHEARSALS AND TAPING.

one-time settlement of £40,000, at the London Divorce Court on 11 April, 1975.

The Who had agreed to appear on the hour-long 500th edition of *Top Of The Pops* for a fee of £100. The group expected to simply mime, but under a Musicians Union ruling, this wasn't permitted. (Pete had announced his displeasure at this firmly in print three years earlier via his *Melody Maker* column.) To satisfy the powers that be, the Who went through the motions of recording a track for "5:15" at Ramport before an MU and BBC representative—all for a slot of less than five minutes.

WEDNESDAY, 3 OCTOBER

Camera rehearsals and taping "5:15" on *Top Of The Pops* at Television Centre.

Introduced as the final act by Noel Edmonds, all vocals were recorded live, with the group playing along to a tape-copy of the backing track. At the fade, Townshend tore into the amps and Moon's kit, smashed his Gretsch, and then turned on show producer Robin Nash and demonstrated his dim view of the BBC and the programme's organisation by giving him the fingers—all while wigs taken from the prop room were thrown about. This was cut from the following evening's transmission, aired 7:00—8:00 pm, but can be seen during *The Kids Are Alright* end credits sequence. Townshend's outburst and Moon's behav-

iour in the "Green Room" earned the Who a life-time BBC ban—lifted after a letter of apology was accepted by the corporation.

FRIDAY, 5 OCTOBER

"5:15" was released in the U.K, reaching #20. In the U.S., "Love Reign O'er Me" was favoured for A-side honours on 27 October.

The first in an exclusive three-part Pete Townshend interview with Michael Wale was broadcast on Radio 1's *Rockspeak*, between 10:00—12:00 pm in the *Sounds Of The 70's* slot. The initial eighteen-minute conversation centred on Eric Clapton's Rainbow concert, while the following two programmes (recorded on location and broadcast 19 and 26 October) were devoted to *Quadrophenia*. Around this time, Pete recorded an interview with Nicky Horne for *Your Mother Wouldn't Like It,* the first of numerous Who-related exclusives on newly established Capital Radio, London's first legal commercial station, which began broadcasting 16 October.

SATURDAY, 6 OCTOBER

An interview with Roger by Tony Stewart appeared in the *NME*, giving the first hints of his dissent with the Who's business affairs. "The Who's suffered," Roger said, "and we're starting to suffer internally, which really is bad... This is what worries me. It's happened

to the Stones and the Beatles, and it's the same bloody problem." Stewart was treated to an advance preview of two *Quadrophenia* tracks in Daltrey's Barn studio.

CIVIC HALL
WOLVERHAMPTON

John and Tony Smith
in association with
Five One Productions
present
THE WHO
in concert
STALLS
£2.20

L15

Mon. Oct. 29
at 7.30 p.m.

cial programmes
sale only inside the hall.
ES CAN MONEY BE REFUNDED
TO BE RETAINED

MONDAY, 8 OCTOBER

From 4:00—7:00 pm, in Studio B7, Broadcasting House, Roger rehearsed and recorded Radio 1's *My Top 12*. As well as picking his favourite dozen, Daltrey was interviewed between songs by host Brian

ABOVE: Pete, Keith, and John being filmed by Richard Stanley in Manchester, 1 November.

British shops until Friday, 2 November due to pressing problems, both he and Daltrey felt it necessary to run a self-conscious commentary throughout. Over the course of the tour, some five songs were eventually dropped. "We trimmed it to what we felt was the best live presentation," Keith told Roy Carr. "It's very difficult when you're in the studio to determine what will actually work on stage... When we first started doing it on stage, we were just finding out for ourselves what numbers should be left in—and even more important, what parts to drop. The only way we could ever do that was by playing most of it before an audience and carefully noting their reactions."

THURSDAY, 1 and FRIDAY, 2 NOVEMBER
King's Hall, Belle Vue, Manchester.

Support on the rest of the British dates were Kilburn and the High Roads, a London six-piece, featuring singer Ian Dury. A documentary short, filmed by Richard Stanley for the BBC, showed concert shots, the crowd arriving, the band backstage tuning-up, Bob Pridden with Pete's guitars, and the end-of-concert party. The item was included on BBC-1's regional news magazine programme *Nationwide—Look North* slot on the 2nd, 6:00–6:55 pm. A close-up shot of Keith leering through a glass of brandy was used in *The Kids Are Alright*.

Matthew. The programme was broadcast Sunday, 21 October, 10:00–11:00 am.

TUESDAY, 9 OCTOBER
Keith's father, Alfred, died of a heart attack at the age of fifty-three.

WEDNESDAY, 10—FRIDAY, 12 OCTOBER and MONDAY, 15—FRIDAY, 19 OCTOBER
Rehearsals on D Stage at Shepperton Studios in preparation for the tour opening on the 28th. 4-track stage backing tapes for the *Quadrophenia* material were made at the Lane Mobile Studio on 11 October.

MONDAY, 22 OCTOBER
Chaotic scenes ensued when box offices around the country opened for the Who's first British concerts in two years. In London, more than 400 spent Sunday night queuing along the Strand for tickets, the number swelled to more than 1000 by 10:00 am. Eventually, some 20,000 had gathered for only 9000 available tickets to three Lyceum shows.

Who rehearsals continued to the 24th at Shepperton. Richard Stanley and Chris Morphet were on hand to film the band for an unreleased

MCA-funded promo. Their cameras weren't operating when underlying resentments boiled to the surface, and a violent row erupted between Pete and Roger. After a remark from Daltrey, an enraged Townshend bashed him with his guitar. Daltrey knocked Townshend out cold with a single uppercut, landing him in hospital with temporary amnesia.

WEDNESDAY, 24 OCTOBER
Quadrophenia debuted on New York radio three days before its U.S. issue by MCA, going gold on the day of release and platinum after two days, representing one million sales. The album reached #2 in both the U.S. and U.K. markets.

SUNDAY, 28 OCTOBER
Trentham Gardens, Stoke-on-Trent.

The premiere of *Quadrophenia* on the "Fallout Shelter" tour, promoted by John and Tony Smith in association with Five One Productions.

MONDAY, 29 OCTOBER
Civic Hall, Wolverhampton.

"We played *Quadrophenia* for the first time last night and it was bloody horrible," Townshend informed the audience. With the album not reaching

ABOVE: Keith and Pete on *Look North*.

MONDAY, 5—WEDNESDAY, 7 NOVEMBER
Odeon Theatre, Newcastle.

The uncooperative backing tapes being used to present *Quadrophenia*, coupled with the audiences' unfamiliarity with the material, was a time bomb waiting to explode. During the first concert, Townshend snapped. Stopping the show in a rage, he

ABOVE: Backstage at Belle Vue, Manchester, 1 November.

bawled out hapless soundman Bob Pridden and hauled him to centre-stage, smashing his guitar and attacking the amps and damaging the backing tapes before storming off. The others followed in stunned silence and the curtain was dropped. Ten minutes later, without explanation or apology, the group reappeared to play an "oldies" set which terminated with Townshend smashing another Les Paul, while Keith scattered his kit.

With the incident making local news, Keith and Pete went to Broadcasting Centre, on Barrack Road, the following evening to appear live on *Look North*, broadcast 6:00—6:55 pm. During the jovial exchange, both alleviated fears that the remaining concerts might be cancelled.

SUNDAY, 11—TUESDAY, 13 NOVEMBER
"It's good to be back in Leeds," Keith quipped as the Who opened the first of three London concerts in

two years at the Lyceum. In accommodating all the group's vast equipment, the venue offered a poor view of the stage to much of the audience, causing a crush at the front. More than a dozen people fainted at the first show, which had to be halted momentarily after three numbers. "We don't want anything like this to ever happen again," said Daltrey.

Such was the tide of general ill-feeling that Townshend felt compelled to apologise through the letters page of *Melody Maker* (dated 24 November): "To all the people who inevitably will complain about the organisation at the Lyceum, the Who say, please, please hang on. Next year we will be playing larger, more suitable places, with cheaper seats. And to those who were hurt, or even just disgusted at not being able to see, nobody feels as bad about it as ourselves."

TUESDAY, 20 NOVEMBER

The U.S. and Canadian *Quadrophenia* tour, supported by Lynyrd Skynyrd, commenced with an ill-fated show at the Cow Palace, San Francisco, California.

Having had his backstage drink spiked with animal tranquilliser, Keith collapsed midway through "Won't Get Fooled Again" and was carried off by drum tech Mick Double and Skip Johnson, a rigger from PA company Heil Sound (and future husband of Grace Slick). The band left the stage for fifteen minutes. After being revived, Moon came back on, only to collapse again at the conclusion of "Magic Bus."

Rather than end the show, Townshend asked if there was an available drummer in the audience of 15,000. Nineteen-year old Scott Halpin, from Muscatine, Iowa, volunteered and played through three numbers ("Smokestack Lightning," "Spoonful," and "Naked Eye") before the show finally ended. The concert was broadcast as an FM simulcast over KSAN San Francisco, KOME San Jose, and KZAP Sacramento and was unofficially filmed on B&W videotape for promoter Bill Graham's archive. (Clips were used in *Thirty Years of Maximum R&B Live*.) Back at the St. Francis Hotel, Keith slept solidly for ten hours and spent the evening of the 21st in L.A., sheepishly watching television in his suite at the Century Plaza.

THURSDAY, 22 and FRIDAY, 23 NOVEMBER

Inglewood Forum, Los Angeles, California.

Both 19,500-capacity shows broke the record for the fastest-ever sell-out at the venue, previously held by Led Zeppelin. 40,000 fans crowded the box office; many had camped out in the parking lot for up to four days before tickets went on sale. A special "Magic Bus" greeted them with a PA blasting out

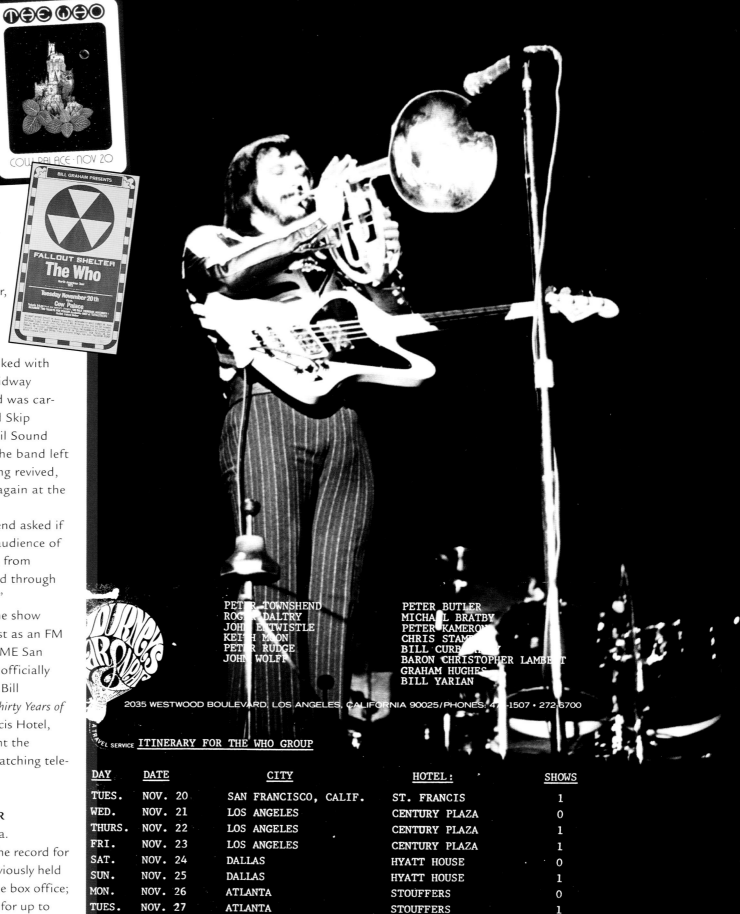

PETER TOWNSHEND
ROGER DALTRY
JOHN ENTWISTLE
KEITH MOON
PETER RUDGE
JOHN WOLFF

PETER BUTLER
MICHAEL BRATBY
PETER KAMERON
CHRIS STAMP
BILL CURBISHLEY
BARON CHRISTOPHER LAMBERT
GRAHAM HUGHES
BILL YARIAN

2035 WESTWOOD BOULEVARD, LOS ANGELES, CALIFORNIA 90025/PHONES: 477-1507 • 272-5700

TRAVEL SERVICE **ITINERARY FOR THE WHO GROUP**

DAY	DATE	CITY	HOTEL:	SHOWS
TUES.	NOV. 20	SAN FRANCISCO, CALIF.	ST. FRANCIS	1
WED.	NOV. 21	LOS ANGELES	CENTURY PLAZA	0
THURS.	NOV. 22	LOS ANGELES	CENTURY PLAZA	1
FRI.	NOV. 23	LOS ANGELES	CENTURY PLAZA	1
SAT.	NOV. 24	DALLAS	HYATT HOUSE	0
SUN.	NOV. 25	DALLAS	HYATT HOUSE	1
MON.	NOV. 26	ATLANTA	STOUFFERS	0
TUES.	NOV. 27	ATLANTA	STOUFFERS	1
WED.	NOV. 28	ST. LOUIS	CHASE PARK PLAZA	1
THURS.	NOV. 29	CHICAGO	WATER TOWER	1
FRI.	NOV. 30	DETROIT	ST. REGIS	1
SAT.	DEC. 1	MONTREAL	BONAVENTURE	0
SUN.	DEC. 2	MONTREAL	BONAVENTURE	1
MON.	DEC. 3	BOSTON	COLONADE	1

Quadrophenia. On the 22nd, after a fifteen-minute wait, the audience were treated to a rare encore of "Baby Don't You Do It" and "Spoonful," with Townshend smashing yet another Les Paul.

SUNDAY, 25 NOVEMBER

Dallas Memorial Auditorium, Dallas, Texas.

TUESDAY, 27 NOVEMBER

The Omni, Atlanta, Georgia.

WEDNESDAY, 28 NOVEMBER

St. Louis Arena, St Louis, Missouri.

THURSDAY, 29 NOVEMBER

International Ampitheatre, Chicago, Illinois.

Backstage, Graham Hughes shot the *Odds and Sods* sleeve. "I'd stayed up the night before with a letraset," Hughes recalled, "designing the letters on the American football helmets with each of the band's names printed on. When I finally managed to get them together in one place, which happened to be the bathroom, Pete and Roger's helmets didn't quite fit so that's why they're wearing each other's. That *Quadrophenia* tour wasn't very pleasant and the band were arguing a lot. When I showed Pete the blow-up of the cover, he didn't like it and told me so. I was so frustrated by this time, I started ripping it up…. That's when he decided he liked it! I stuck it back together with adhesive tape and Roger said, 'call it a bunch of odds and sods.'"

FRIDAY, 30 NOVEMBER

Cobo Arena, Detroit, Michigan.

SUNDAY, 2 DECEMBER

The Forum, Montreal, Canada.

The Who and French Canada were like oil and water. "It all started when we walked off the plane wearing paper hats on our heads made out of these French in-flight newspapers, singing the French National Anthem," remembered Graham Hughes. "Straight away, there was a definite vibe against us."

MCA Records threw an after-show press party in the hospitality suite at the Bonaventure Hotel. At the height of the friviolities, Moon grabbed a painting off the wall, kicked the canvas out, and replaced it with his own abstract ketchup design. "Everybody was laughing and egging each other on," remembered John Wolff. "Keith and Pete picked up a mar-

ble coffee table and smashed through a wall between the bedroom and the sitting room, before sending it through the window. Next the television set went out into the swimming pool, and there was glass everywhere. The record company execs were getting nervous, so we all scarpered to our rooms about 4 am."

"I got this mysterious phone call in the early hours, saying, 'How would you like to photograph Hiroshima?!'" said Hughes. "I went down to the room, the lights were on, but it was locked. The hotel detective happened to be passing. He was horrified at what he found. MCA's PR man, Bill Yarian, was in there, looking absolutely distraught amongst this complete devastation. I got one quick flash shot off and legged it with the hotel manager and detective chasing after me."

The Canadian Mounted Police were promptly summoned. Peter Rudge was roused and escorted to collect all members of the tour party, sixteen of whom wound up behind bars at Station Police Numero 10. Despite Rudge's best efforts, the hotel manager Fernand Roberge refused to be placated by offers of reimbursement. Rudge ended up sharing a cell with Townshend, while Graham Hughes was paired with his furious cousin. (Daltrey had not partaken in the carnage, having retired to bed early.)

MONDAY, 3 DECEMBER

Boston Garden, Boston, Massachusetts.

The entourage missed their scheduled 1:22 pm Air Canada flight due to spending seven hours in a Montreal police cell, narrowly causing the cancellation of the show. After local promoter Donald Tarlton paid $6000 in cash to cover all damages, the entourage were released in time to catch a rescheduled 4:00 pm flight to Boston. Entwistle, who shared

PAGES 240–241:
BOSTON GARDEN, 3 DECEMBER.

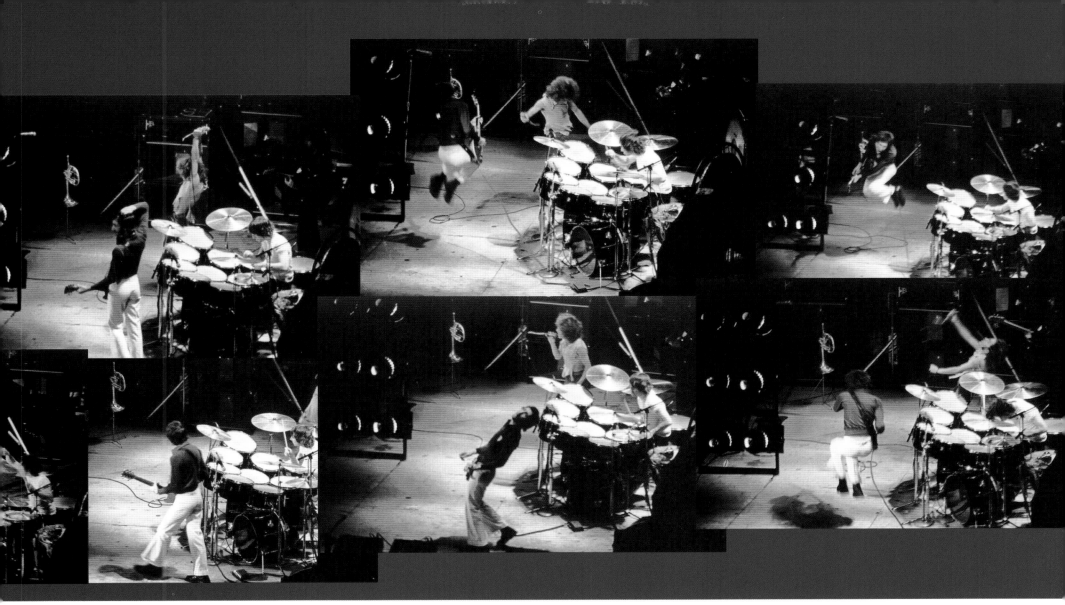

a cell with Moon, immortalised the experience in "Cell No.7" on his 1975 album, *Mad Dog*.

TUESDAY, 4 DECEMBER

The Spectrum, Philadelphia, Pennsylvania.

This was the closest the tour came to New York, deliberately avoiding the media spotlight while *Quadrophenia* was being road-tested. The show was recorded on the Record Plant 16-track mobile for broadcast by DIR Radio on *The King Biscuit Flower Hour*. Edited highlights were transmitted nationwide in Metromedia Stereo, 9:00—10:30 pm, on Sunday, 31 March, 1974 and repeated on 29 December. The band and entourage travelled by train to Washington, D.C., the following day.

THURSDAY, 6 DECEMBER

Capital Center, Largo, Maryland.

28,000 people attended this final U.S. *Quadrophenia* concert, again recorded by the Record Plant mobile. A

Graham Hughes shot from the end of the show graces the inner sleeve of *Odds and Sods*. The Who flew back to London via New York on the 7th.

THURSDAY, 13 and FRIDAY, 14 DECEMBER

After just one rehearsal, Lou Reizner presented *Tommy* for the second time at the Rainbow Theatre, in aid of the Richmond Fellowship for Autistic Children. However, this time, Roger was the only Who member involved. The rest of the cast included David Essex (the Narrator), Marsha Hunt (the Nurse), Roger Chapman (in place of Steve Marriott—Father), Elkie Brooks (Mother), Graham Bell (the Lover), Richie Havens (replaced on the second night by Ron Charles—the Hawker), Bill Oddie (Cousin Kevin), Merry Clayton (the Acid Queen), Viv Stanshall (Uncle Ernie), Roy Wood (Local Lad), and Jon Pertwee (the Doctor), with the London Symphony Orchestra and English Chamber Choir, again conducted and directed by David Measham. The production was recorded

and broadcast as a Capital Radio special on 30 December, 6:00—8:00 pm.

Keith turned up on opening night ("to keep Viv Stanshall sober") straight from a screen test for *Stardust*, the sequel to *That'll Be The Day*; he was dressed in some of Ringo Starr's original Beatles gear. The ex-Beatle was understandably reluctant to relive his immediate past and advised Moon to go for the part, only to find screenwriter Ray Connolly had brought back his J.D. Clover character. Adam Faith landed Starr's role. (See 18 February, 1974.)

TUESDAY, 18 and WEDNESDAY, 19; SATURDAY, 22 and SUNDAY, 23 DECEMBER

Sundown Theatre, Edmonton, North London.

"Who's Christmas Party?" concerts, promoted by Tony Smith, supported by Babe Ruth. To avoid the chaotic scenes experienced at the Lyceum box office on 22 October, tickets for the four shows were made available only via mail order application.

HOW many friends 1974

Fresh from the chastening *Quadrophenia* debacle and with the painful

spectre of *Lifehouse* still lingering in the back of his mind, Pete commit-

ted himself, against his better judgement, to the role of musical director

on Ken Russell's *Tommy*. Prior to shooting, he agreed to Russell's proviso

that there be no scripted dialogue, with the soundtrack to consist

entirely of music.

Thus, six weeks of studio time was spent re-recording the score at Ramport, with the sessions engineered by Ron Nevison on the Lane Mobile Studio and produced by Townshend, in association with John Entwistle. An all-star crew of musicians and backing singers were enlisted to match the on-screen glitz and glamour.

The sessions were disrupted by the current energy crisis, the three-day working week, and a noise complaint lodged against the studio, resulting in a midnight curfew. Pete specially composed four new songs for the project, as well as restructuring much of the original album material.

In addition to radically reorganising the plot (the lover now killed Tommy's father rather than the other way round), Russell cast Oliver Reed and Jack Nicholson in leading roles, neither of them blessed with passable singing voices, and Ann-Margret, who had never sung rock before, much to Townshend's horror.

Apart from some French dates in February, recording and filming occupied all the band's time. A low-key gig in Oxford acted as a warm-up to a major live summer event on 18 May at Charlton Athletic Football Ground, South London, which was filmed by the BBC and recorded for radio. Four days later, the band played a closed gig in Portsmouth especially for the *Tommy* extras. In June, four record-breaking nights were slotted in at Madison Square Garden in New York—a city deliberately omitted from the previous year's *Quadrophenia* schedule.

Although the shows were well-received, some saw the group as simply going through the motions, particularly at Charlton, where Entwistle later confessed he was ready to quit, such was the lack of empathy between the band members. The fact hadn't gone unnoticed by Pete Townshend, who found the growing Pavlovian response to Who shows disturbing: "At Charlton, I got completely pissed... I was so happy to get out of it. For Madison Square Garden, we had to fight and snatch the time off from the film and consequently when we got there it wasn't really all that wonderful from our point of view... I felt really guilty I couldn't explode into the exuberant and happy energy our fans did. I screwed up every inch of energy doing it, then would be brought down by a monitor whistling or something, and I'd have to work myself up again..."

Always painfully honest, Pete felt he'd become little more than a caricature, and as a result, had to force himself into performing. What disconcerted him most was looking down to find the same old faces in the front rows staring back at him. "I don't know what's happening sometimes. All I know is that when we last played Madison Square Garden, I felt acute shades of nostalgia. All the Who freaks had crowded around the front of the stage and when I gazed out into the audience all I could see were those same sad faces that I'd seen at every New York Who gig. It was dreadful and they were telling us what to play. Every time I tried to make an announcement, they all yelled "Shurrup Townshend and let Entwistle play "Boris The Spider!" And, if that wasn't bad enough, during the other songs they'd all start chanting 'jump, jump, jump...' I was so brought down by it all. I mean is this what it had all degenerated into?!" Daltrey drily noted that the Who played these shows "running on three cylinders."

Apart from *Tommy*, various Who projects were bandied about over the summer, including a television adaptation of *Quadrophenia*, which got as far as the drawing board stage, and an unlikely venture, also designated for the small screen, involving the Who playing specially composed material from such contemporary songwriters as Ray Davies, Frank Zappa, and even Sweet svengalis, Chinn & Chapman.

Inevitably, individual pursuits took over. Pete made his first solo appearance onstage when he played an Easter charity gig at London's Roundhouse, revealing a different performing persona from the leaping, windmilling axe hero. Playing acoustic guitar for much of the evening, he performed a mix of originals and cover versions. "That show was a tiny hiccup in the middle of all the *Tommy* work," Pete recalled, "I ran up the backing tracks in a single night." In August, he and Keith turned up to lend their drunken support on the last dates of Eric Clapton's U.S. comeback tour.

As well as reprising his role as J.D. Clover in *Stardust*, the sequel to *That'll Be The Day*, Keith and his new buddy Oliver Reed planned to collaborate in a West End play, but the idea got lost between hangovers. Following the Clapton guest appearances, Keith and new girlfriend, Annette Walter-Lax, relocated to Los Angeles, where they became regulars on

ABOVE: PETE'S SOLO SHOW AT THE ROUNDHOUSE.

Who—there's no split

THE WHO are not splitting up, despite rumours circulating in the music business.

Pete Townshend took time out this week to put the record straight. He stated: "It seems at the moment that various people in the music business have got nothing better to do than disseminate rumours about a Who split.

"I would just like to say that at the moment I am writing the material for a new Who album to be recorded as soon as the "Tommy" film has been released in February. Glyn Johns has been asked to produce.

If I get any free time from writing and editing the music for the "Tommy" film, I too would love to do a solo album. However, one of the reasons we are all engaged in apparently individual pursuits is quite simply that to us the Who is too precious to hurry. Our future work on record and on stage is being planned now. Farewell."

the social circuit. Such was Keith's assimilation into the city's musical community that he followed through on ill-advised plans to record his own solo album, produced by ex-Beatles aide Mal Evans. This was apparently concocted after fellow skinsman Ringo Starr told Keith he had a great voice—proof, if any were needed, that rock drummers shouldn't heed each others' professional advice. MCA record company executives were horrified at what they

heard and brought in producers Skip Taylor and John Stronach to salvage what they could, starting the rest from scratch.

With more time on his hands than the others, John compiled and completed *Odds and Sods*, a collection of unused Who tracks sitting in the Track vaults, neatly illustrating that the Who's leftovers were superior to many a band's output. He also completed his fourth solo album, *Mad Dog*.

"I play far better on stage," said John. "I like to do concerts. If the Who don't give me the opportunity to do that, I'll find other ways of getting in front of an audience." Making good on his word and not heeding Roger's advice against touring solo, John took a stripped-down version of his own band, Ox, on a financially foolhardy tour of the U.K. and U.S., which eventually left him more than £30,000 poorer.

While Pete's self-confidence continued to erode, Roger's was on the ascendant. His untried acting abilities impressed Ken Russell enough for him to be offered the lead role in Russell's next extravaganza, *Lisztomania*, to be filmed early the following year. Required on-set for most of *Tommy* and its post-production, Roger had to wait until November before he could get into the studio to record *Ride A Rock Horse*, a more soulful, R&B-influenced effort than the commercial balladeering of his first.

At Robert Stigwood's financial inducement, Pete was spending tortuous hours in seclusion at his home studio, scoring the complex incidental music for *Tommy*, which later secured him an Oscar nomination for Best Score Adaptation. As he recalled, "I went into my home studio to do four weeks of film composing on miniscule edit changes chucked at me about every hour by film editor Terry Rawlings, and then the Elstree dubbing theatre for three weeks grappling with Quintophonic sound, the rightful precursor of Dolby Surround." The laborious experience made Pete vow to never get involved in the film side of the business again.

All of this individual activity led to wide speculation that the Who had broken up, cajoling Pete into making an official press statement in November to the contrary. Privately, the rigours of the *Tommy* film, the dilemma of the Who as artists versus nostalgia act, and his marital problems had led him into a downward spiral of drink and depression, and had made him seriously question his commitment to the group. The following year was to be a turning point.

1974

1974

THURSDAY, 10 JANUARY

For the *Tommy* soundtrack, Pete, John, and Keith started off by recording a basic track for "I'm Free," and "Pinball Wizard," though in Townshend's estimation "they came out sounding like a cliché." Alternatively, in Moon's absence due to "illness" an array of guest musicians were enlisted, including Faces drummer Kenny Jones, who participated in a warm-up jam with John and Pete on 12 January. For the ensuing sessions at Ramport, the contributing musicians included: Ron Wood, Eric Clapton, Mick Ralphs, Alan Ross, Caleb Quaye (guitars), Nicky Hopkins, Chris Stainton (keyboards), Tony Stevens, Dave Wintour, Phillip Chen, Fuzzy Samuels (bass), and Tony Newman, Graham Deakin, Richard Bailey, Mike Kellie (drums).

FEBRUARY

Each of the *Tommy* cast were called upon to pre-record their individual parts to be lip-synched to in the movie. Coached by Pete, Ann-Margret commenced recording her vocals, as did Roger. Pete, John, Billy Nicholls, Jess Roden, and Paul Gurvitz recorded three- and four-part vocal harmonies in several marathon sessions, some lasting into the following day, while John commenced taping the score's brass arrangements.

SATURDAY, 9 FEBRUARY

In the midst of the *Tommy* sessions, the Who played seven dates in France, supported by John "Speedy" Keene and band, starting at the Palais des Grottes, Cambrai, Lille.

SUNDAY, 10 FEBRUARY

Parc des Expositions, Paris, France.

The Who were the first band to play this newly opened venue, which held 20,000. The concert was scheduled to begin appropriately enough at 5:15 pm, but the venue's glass doors were opened eight hours beforehand because of the large crowd pressing dangerously against them. Because of the early admission, the path of the Who's equipment lorries was effectively blockaded. After some choice Anglo-French exchanges, the crew were eventually able to clear a pathway. Of the 25,000-strong crowd, 6000

were let in free after an extension of the house limit had been obtained.

The lights were raised after three songs when the Who's transformer exploded. The group remained on stage while emergency repairs were carried out. Roy Carr, reviewing the show for the *NME*, duly noted: "Daltrey twirled his mike, Townshend attempted to kick a hole in the stage, Moon swigged brandy, banged his gong and looned about, and Entwistle looked on, impassive as ever." Fifteen minutes later, the house lights dimmed and the group continued playing. At the conclusion of "Drowned," a thoroughly adrenalised Townshend demolished his Les Paul. Following a tremendous ovation, the crowd were treated to an extended encore of "Substitute," "Magic Bus," "Naked Eye," "Let's See Action," and "My Generation Blues."

THURSDAY, 14 FEBRUARY

Keith performed as a member of the Intergalactic Elephant Band, the name given to an all-star aggregation backing Roy Harper at his "Valentine's Day

Massacre" concert at the Rainbow, Finsbury Park. Also appearing were Jimmy Page, Robert Plant, John Bonham, Ronnie Lane, and Max Middleton. The concert appeared as Side Four ("The Great Divider") of Harper's *Flashes From The Archives Of Oblivion*, released by Harvest in November.

FRIDAY, 15 FEBRUARY

Palais des Sports Armes, Poitiers, France.

SUNDAY, 17 FEBRUARY

Foire de Toulouse, Toulouse, France.

MONDAY, 18 FEBRUARY

Nine weeks of production commenced on *Stardust*, the sequel to *That'll Be The Day*. (See 25 October, 1972.) It starred David Essex, Adam Faith, Marty Wilde, Paul Nicholas, and Larry Hagman. As before, Ray Connolly wrote the screenplay and David Puttnam and Sanford Lieberson produced for Goodtimes Enterprises Ltd; the new blood was director Michael Apted.

Keith reprised his role as drummer J.D. Clover with Jim MacLaine and the Stray Cats. Location scenes were shot in London and Manchester. (See 17 March.) Location filming (not requiring Keith) also took place in Spain and the United States.

FRIDAY, 22 FEBRUARY

Parc des Expositions, Nancy, France.

SUNDAY, 24 FEBRUARY

Palais des Sports, Lyon, France.

Apart from a few numbers, the bulk of *Quadrophenia* was laid to rest. "I could never work out quite what was going on there," Pete told Dave Schulps. "Roger thought that *Quadrophenia* wouldn't stand up unless you explained the story—and he's not the most verbose character. It was done sincerely, but I found it embarrassing, and I think it showed, so I was glad when we dropped it. I couldn't really work out what must be going on in the audience's mind when they were being told, 'There's this kid and he's just like you and me...' and then the music began; and then, 'Then this kid, he....' The whole thing was a disaster. Roger ended up hating *Quadrophenia*—probably because it had bitten back."

MARCH

Tommy recording continued at Ramport. John completed overdubbing the score's brass arrangements. The crowd vocal cacophony at the conclusion of "We're Not Going To Take It" was contributed by a group of recruited boys and girls plus female session choristers the Breakaways, who sang back-up harmonies on several tracks. Pete, Vicki Brown, and Margo Newman recorded the vocal chorus to "It's A Boy" at Apple studios. The pipe organ overdubs for "Tommy's Holiday Camp," played by Gerald Shaw, were recorded on the Island mobile at Notre Dame de France, 5 Leicester Place. (The church's adjoining hall was the site of several early Detours and Who appearances.) The cast continued to record their vocals, including Oliver Reed (who required considerable coaching!), Paul Nicholas, Arthur Brown, Barry Winch (playing Tommy as a child), Alison Dowling on "Bernie's Holiday Camp" and "Christmas," and thirteen-year-old Simon Townshend as the newsboy on "Miracle Cure."

SUNDAY, 17 MARCH

The hysterical, Beatles-like 1965 Pollwinners concert scene in *Stardust*, featuring Jim MacLaine and the Stray Cats, was filmed at King's Hall, Belle Vue, Manchester, using the Who's PA. The Stray Cats consisted of David Essex, Keith Moon, Dave Edmunds (the film's musical director), and actors Karl Howman and Peter Duncan.

THURSDAY, 21 MARCH

An interview with Keith on location for *Stardust* at Edgewarebury Country Club was broadcast a week later on BBC-2's *Film Night*, Wednesday, 27 March, 11:00—11:30 pm.

"I don't think I've ever not been an actor," Moon told *Sounds*' Steve Peacock. "I've always been an actor that plays the drums. I haven't been a film actor, but there are many aspects of acting—it's just a different approach. On a screen that's maybe 70 foot wide, you may only have to lift your little finger, whereas to get the same effect on stage you'd have to swing your whole arm. I seldom stop acting, except...well, when I'm asleep."

Stardust premiered at the ABC, Shaftesbury Avenue, London, on Thursday, 24 October.

MONDAY, 1—FRIDAY, 19 APRIL

Keith and Dougal Butler flew to Los Angeles for a three-week break. On 10 April, Moon moved out of their Beverly Wilshire suite into a $5000 a month rented beachfront house on the Pacific Coast Highway, Santa Monica, with Ringo Starr, Harry Nilsson, and John Lennon.

Lennon was producing Nilsson's *Pussycats* at Record Plant West and Burbank Studios. Moon drummed with Ringo and Jim Keltner on "Loop de Loop" and "Rock Around The Clock," played congas on "Mucho Mungo"/"Mt. Elga," and Chinese wood blocks on "All My Life." The album was released by RCA in August.

TUESDAY, 2—FRIDAY, 5 APRIL

Tommy sync pulses and playback mixdowns for Ken Russell and the film choreographers were prepared at Ramport, Eel Pie, Goring, and CTS Studio, The Music Centre, Wembley.

WEDNESDAY, 10 APRIL

Pete attended a special reception thrown by Robert Stigwood at China Garden, Berwick Street, Soho, formally celebrating Eric Clapton's return to active work. Among the guests were Elton John, Rick Grech, and Ron Wood.

SUNDAY, 14 APRIL

Pete performed his first solo concert, a special Easter benefit at the Roundhouse, Chalk Farm, London—in aid of the Camden Square Community Play Centre, staged between 3:30—10:00 pm.

Also appearing were Keith Christmas, Coast Road Drive, and Byzantium. When original billtopper Tim Hardin pulled out, Townshend hurriedly prepared tapes to fill an hour's set.

He surrounded himself with six guitars, two effects boxes, a rhythm box, a clavinet, two vocal mikes (one fed through a Leslie to provide a vibrato vocal), and two tape decks, as well as a lamp and table with sheets of lyrics and a running order.

Set List: "The Seeker," Jimmy Reed's "Big Boss Man," "Substitute," Veronique Sanson's "Amoreuse," Tim Hardin's "If I Were A Carpenter," "Happy Jack," "Tattoo," "Join My Gang," "Behind Blue Eyes," Jimmy Reed's "Talkin' New York Blues," the original demo tapes to "My Generation," covers of Bob Dylan's trad arranged "Girl From The North

ABOVE: PETE'S SOLO SHOW AT THE ROUNDHOUSE, 14 APRIL.

Country" and "Corrina, Corrina," Traffic's "No Face, No Name, No Number," "Let's See Action," "Pinball Wizard," "See Me, Feel Me," and an encore of "Magic Bus"/"My Generation."

Advance publicity went from promoting a low-key, one-man show to hawking a keenly anticipated rock event, which, understandably, made Pete incredibly nervous. Happily, the show was well-received, raising £1000, and marred only by a notorious local character, "Irish" Kevin, who repeatedly shouted for "Underture," much to Pete's annoyance. After several warnings, Townshend climbed from the stage, lunged through the crowd, and physically threatened him.

In Los Angeles, Keith and Ringo Starr appeared on *The Flo And Eddie Show*, live from KROQ's Pasadena headquarters, with DJ Rodney Bingenheimer. (Keith became a frequent habitué of Bingenheimer's English Disco on Sunset Strip.) Moon, accompanied by Dougal, played the Bonzo's and surf music and then at midnight, Ringo appeared, taking listeners' calls, and making the show run over by 40 minutes. Because of this and the frequent expletives that ran unchecked, Flo and Eddie were hauled before the disciplinary board and suspended.

MONDAY, 15—SUNDAY, 21 APRIL
Overdubbing and sound mixing at Ramport and CTS, including the master of "Pinball Wizard" by Elton John (and band), with vocal harmonies from the Breakaways, independently produced by Gus Dudgeon.

MONDAY, 22 APRIL
Tommy went into production, directed by Ken Russell and co-produced by Russell and Robert Stigwood for Columbia Pictures. Executive Producers: Beryl Vertue and Chris Stamp. Associate Producer: Harry Benn.

Cast: Ann-Margret (Nora Walker), Oliver Reed (Frank Hobbs), Roger Daltrey (Tommy), Elton John (the Pinball Wizard), Eric Clapton (the Preacher), Keith Moon (Uncle Ernie), Jack Nicholson (in place of Richard Chamberlain—the Specialist), Robert Powell (Group Captain Walker), Paul Nicholas (Cousin Kevin), Tina Turner (the Acid Queen), and Arthur Brown (the Priest).

"I don't think anybody could do it except Ken Russell," said Daltrey. "We need a guy who we can relate to, feed information in to him, and get something back. Ken's the first bloke that's done that since our manager Kit Lambert dropped out of the scene. There's been a lot that's changed, little things that make it valid as a complete story—plus the old freedom that allows your mind to add its own interpretations. Personally, I think it's going to be amazing, bloody incredible."

Returning from America, Keith walked off the set in a fit of pique when he discovered Russell had rewritten his Uncle Ernie part to highlight Reed's character. The first week was occupied with shooting interior scenes at Harefield Grove, a country estate in Middlesex, featuring Nora, Frank, Captain Walker, and young Tommy (Barry Winch). Pete had his own caravan on the set, closely monitoring scene alterations that required changes to the incidental music.

WEDNESDAY, 24 APRIL; MONDAY, 29 APRIL— WEDNESDAY, 1 MAY
Filming of the "Cousin Kevin" sequence at Harefield Grove with Paul Nicholas. Roger was dragged around by his hair, dunked in a bath of evil smelling yellow liquid, and blasted by a full-pressure hose full of pond water for several takes, prompting his anguished outcry, "This is the first and last bloody film I make!"

SATURDAY, 27 APRIL; THURSDAY, 2 and SATURDAY, 4 MAY
Filming of Keith's perverted "Fiddle About" sequence at Harefield Grove.

WEDNESDAY, 1 and THURSDAY, 2 MAY
The Who squeezed in two evenings of rehearsals at Shepperton, booked from 5:00 pm—12 midnight, in preparation for forthcoming concerts. In light of the group's recent touring schedule, rehearsing hardly seemed necessary, but by common consent, the act needed reworking now that *Quadrophenia* had been dropped. Although some of that album was included, the emphasis was on older material as a representational history of the band.

THURSDAY, 2 and FRIDAY, 3 MAY
Jack Nicholson's vocal for "Go To The Mirror" was recorded at Ramport.

SUNDAY, 5 MAY
Recording and mixing at Ramport: Saxes were overdubbed onto "Bernie's Holiday Camp" by Geoff Daley, Bob Efford, and Ronnie Ross. Keith recorded his "Tommy's Holiday Camp" vocal during an evening session.

MONDAY, 6 MAY
New Theatre, Oxford. Unannounced "warm-up" concert.

Tommy location filming moved to Hayling Island and Portsmouth, Hampshire. (Ken Russell had retained an affection for the area after shooting *The Boyfriend* there.)

WEDNESDAY, 8—FRIDAY, 10 MAY
The "Pinball Wizard" sequence, featuring Elton John and 1500 extras hired from the Portsmouth Polytechnic, was shot at the King's Theatre, Albert

ABOVE: PETE, ANN-MARGRET, AND KEITH ON THE *TOMMY* SET.

Young Times for teenage

Who were here on Monday

BACK IN the days of free pop concerts in Hyde Park we were waiting in a nearby pub for the rain to stop and the Stones to start.

An old wrinkled woman behind the bar with a cigarette in her mouth and fag ash all down her front said it was all a waste of time.

"Just a lot of bloody noise, the Stones. Bloody rubbish," she said, through a grey drift of ash. "You want to listen to some real music." Someone asked sarcastically who she would like to see. "The Who," she said. "That's a real group."

It's as good an introduction as any. On Monday the old woman's favourite group came to the New Theatre and she would have fully approved of their reception.

Sue Hackett-Jones, the assistant manager, said she had never seen

anything like the rush for tickets: the box office was sold out within a few hours of opening and when all the tickets had gone there were all kinds of plans to get in for nothing. Someone

was hoping to get through with the help of an old St John Ambulance uniform.

Inside the theatre before the show, the supporting group dutifully played, but it was proba-

bly about as rewarding as trying to sell ice-creams in a snow storm. Fans walked up and down restlessly wearing Who badges. A girl sat in front of us clutching a case plastered with Who

stickers.

There were growing rumours that the Who weren't coming at all. But they did and with the first challenging chords of "Can't Explain" the people in the

stalls moved in one body, leaving their £1.80 seats to stand as near the stage as possible. I spent most of the performance trying to catch a glimpse of Roger Daltry or Pete Townsend

---

Road, Portsmouth. To complicate matters, an amateur dramatic society were booked in during the evenings, which required the crew to dismantle the set at 6:00 pm, only for it to be reassembled at 5:00 am in time for the following day's shoot.

The scene required rival factions of supporters to storm the stage and mob their hero as the Who methodically destroyed their gear. Pete, John (both wearing Bermans & Nathans–designed pound note suits), and Keith initially mimed to playback, but then insisted on plugging in for authenticity's sake. After one retake, there was an anxious moment when Townshend's falling Les Paul grazed a young extra's head. "There was blood everywhere," he told Richard Barnes, "and she was carried off to hospital. But she came back a few hours later and told us she was 'very honoured' to have been smashed over the head by Pete Townshend's guitar. I gave her the guitar."

MONDAY, 13—WEDNESDAY, 15 MAY

The "Eyesight To the Blind," Church of St. Marilyn sequence with Eric Clapton and Arthur Brown, using blind and disabled extras, was filmed at the Royal Marine Church, Eastney.

In the build-up to Charlton, Keith and John appeared on Capital Radio's *Your Mother Wouldn't Like It*, transmitted live from Euston Tower, London, on the 13th, 6:30—8:30 pm. They were interviewed by Nicky Horne and took listeners' calls. When one female admirer professed an interest in meeting him, Keith suggested they rendezvous under the club's clock tower!

THURSDAY, 16 and FRIDAY, 17 MAY

The "Sally Simpson" concert sequence, featuring Victoria Russell, was filmed at Wesley Central Hall, Portsmouth.

SATURDAY, 18 MAY

"Summer Of '74," Charlton Athletic Football Ground, The Valley, South East London.

Promoted by Michael Alfandary for John Smith Productions and Trinifold Ltd., the concert ran from 12:00 midday—11:00 pm. From the outset, the Who were strongly involved with the event's initiation and helped select the acts appearing, which were (in order): Montrose, Lindisfarne, Bad Company, Lou Reed, Humble Pie, and Maggie Bell. Originally, Dave Mason and Townshend favourites, the Sweet, were billed to appear but cancelled. Yes were put forward, but manager Brian Lane declined on their behalf.

"We considered a number of venues, including various football grounds," Townshend explained. "We finally selected Charlton because of its particular acoustic qualities and the excellent views of the stage from the terraces." Although an attendance limit was set at 50,000, an estimated 80,000 flooded into the Valley because of a security breakdown. The Who used a thirty-man sound crew and thirty-five tons of equipment, incorporating quadrophonic sound and a specially designed and constructed lighting console flown in from Philadelphia.

Originally, Ken Russell had planned to film the concert as the finale to *Tommy*, or for simultaneous release as a separate cinematic venture. In the event, the Who's hour and 45 minute set was tele-recorded by the BBC for a fee of £750—band and management receiving £600 and £150 respectively—with the final terms only agreed upon the day before. Their cameras were sited on a track below the platform, behind the stage, and alongside the mixing board, causing an hour's delay before the Who's arrival on stage at 8:45 pm.

The footage was edited and screened as the first in a new series of BBC-2's arts programme *2nd House* on Saturday, 5 October, 9:10—10:40 pm. Entitled *2nd House: The Who*, it included an interview with Pete by presenter Melvyn Bragg (taped Thursday 29, August at Television Centre) in the first half hour, followed by an hour of concert material. The following year, viewers had another chance to see an edited 75 minute version of the programme on *2nd House 2nd Run*, screened Saturday, 7 June. Clips from the Bragg interview were used in *The Kids Are Alright*, while "Substitute," "Drowned," "Bell Boy," and part of "My Generation Blues" appeared in *Thirty Years of Maximum R&B Live*. An out-take of "Behind Blue Eyes" from the Who's archive appeared in *Classic Albums: Who's Next* (1999).

Capital Radio's Tommy Vance introduced a special, *The Who In Concert*, from 7:00 pm, with live inserts and interviews by Nicky Horne, Roger Scott, and Dave Symonds. The concert feed was recorded on the Rolling Stones Mobile and mixed by Townshend and Ron Nevison. "Young Man Blues"

and "Baba O'Riley," together with a recorded Townshend interview, were first broadcast in October during Capital's *Your Mother Wouldn't Like It* slot. In December, virtually the entire show (sans a deficient "I Can't Explain" and "5:15") was broadcast in FM stereo, 10:00—12:00 pm, during Capital's *Rock Pile* programme.

TUESDAY, 21 MAY

At Phonogram studios, London, four-track master copies were made of the three High Numbers tracks recorded in 1964: "I'm The Face," "Zoot Suit," and "Here 'Tis"—provisionally to be included on *Odds and Sods*. John made stereo remixes of each at Ramport on Thursday, 20 June, but in the end, only "I'm The Face" was selected for the album. Remixed and remastered stereo versions of all three tracks saw the light of day exactly twenty years later as part of the Who's *Thirty Years of Maximum R&B* box set.

WEDNESDAY, 22 MAY

Guildhall, Portsmouth, supported by Gypsy.

Private "thank you" concert for the 1500 student extras who worked on *Tommy*, promoted by the Portsmouth Polytechnic Students Union, in association with the Robert Stigwood Organisation.

Set List: "I Can't Explain," "Young Man Blues," "Baba O'Riley," "Behind Blue Eyes," "Substitute," "I'm A Boy," "Tattoo," "Boris The Spider," "Drowned," "Bell Boy" (with false start), "Doctor Jimmy," "Won't Get Fooled Again," "Pinball Wizard," "See Me, Feel Me," and a lengthy encore of "5:15," "Magic Bus," "My Generation Blues" (segueing into the usual version), "Naked Eye," "Feelin'" (a cover of a Johnny Kidd and the Pirates song from 1959), "Eyesight To The Blind" (the film arrangement), a reprise of "My Generation Blues," and "Let's See Action."

Although he rated it as one of the best gigs the Who ever played, due to complete emotional overload, Townshend's grip on reality was tenuous at best. "At that gig, I signed several managerial and recording contracts, in a complete black fog," he wrote in *Rolling*

Stone three years later. "The only event I remember is quietly screaming for help deep inside as I asked John Entwistle if it had ever happened to him."

THURSDAY, 23 MAY

Filming of the "Tommy's Holiday Camp" sequence, featuring Keith driving a mobile pipe organ prop, at Fort Purbrook, Portsmouth.

SATURDAY, 25 MAY

A scheduled concert at Shawfield Stadium, Glasgow, Scotland, was cancelled because promoter Michael Alfandary was unable to secure an adequate license. "The fact is that Shawfield turned down the show until they had the opportunity of assessing what happened at Charlton," he explained. "The Who are determined to play Scotland particularly as they missed playing there on their last tour. However this cannot now take place until after the conclusion of the *Tommy* film, which puts it at mid-July at the earliest." A planned outdoor Welsh concert also failed to materialise, ostensibly due to *Tommy* commitments running over. Rumours of two joint supershows featuring the Who, Deep Purple, Beck, Bogert, Appice, Humble Pie slated for the August Bank Holiday weekend were vehemently denied by Bill Curbishley.

THURSDAY, 30 MAY

Tommy filming at Harry Pound Scrapyard, Portsmouth, continuing from 3—7 June. For the "We're Not Going To Take It" sequence, dozens of gigantic harbour buoys painted silver were set on fire with gas jets. Daltrey lost all the hair on one arm after walking through the banks of flames wearing just a thin T-shirt.

Russell's crew remained in Portsmouth for scenes not requiring the Who. On 11 June, while filming the "Bernie's Holiday Camp" interior ballroom scenes at South Parade Pier, all were hastily evacuated when a fire broke out. Not one to miss an opportunity, Russell manoeuvred his cameras into place on the beach and directed the building's destruction, seen briefly during the movie's climactic sequence. Film equipment and personal belongings totalling thousands of pounds were lost in the blaze.

CONGRATULATIONS
To the Greatest Rock Band in the World
PETE · ROGER JOHN · KEITH

TRACK RECORD

From everyone at TRACK RECORDS, London
Kit Lambert · Chris Stamp · Mike Shaw Vernon Brewer · Bill Curbishley John Field · Chris Chappel · Edwin Matzenik Keith Swallow · Judy Franks · Barbara Taylor Eamonn Sherlock · Florence Eldridge
◆ ◆ ◆ ◆
FROM MAXIMUM R&B TO ULTIMATE ROCK

MONDAY, 10 and TUESDAY, 11; THURSDAY, 13 and FRIDAY, 14 JUNE

The Who snatched time off from *Tommy* to play four nights at Madison Square Garden, their first New York appearances in almost three years. (The group was originally pencilled in to play the Garden on 14 March and Nassau Coliseum, Long Island, on the 15th.)

Within fifteen hours, three of the four shows at the 22,000-capacity arena sold out on the strength of a single sixty-second radio spot, broadcast on 31 March at the end of a special 90 minute Who edition of *The King Biscuit Flower Hour*. (There was talk of adding three more dates, from the 15th to the 17th.)

Whomania gripped the Big Apple with its usual intensity. Fans checked into the Navarro, forcing Pete to move to the Hotel Pierre. A walkie-talkie system of radio transmitters had to be rigged up for the band and crew to communicate, because fans tied up all the phone lines trying to get through. "We decided to include some of the old stuff," Pete told *Melody Maker*'s Chris Charlesworth, "because we felt initially that a good five or six thousand of the front row seats at the Garden would be old Who devotees who enjoy the old stuff... These fans feel that they own the Who. They were there in the front row at the Murray the K Show and now that the Who have reached this stage, they feel that as they've been so loyal, they have a prior claim to what numbers we're going to play and things like that. New York to us is like what the Goldhawk Club is like to us in England."

Support on the first two shows were Golden Earring. At the end of Monday's concert, despite an announcement that the Who would not be returning, 20,000 stomped, screamed, and cheered for an encore. "The thought ran through my head that it had been such a boring day and the least I could do was smash a guitar,"

Townshend told Charlesworth, "but in those circumstances it wouldn't really be right. On my first day in New York, I felt a great feeling of being back and a great respect and kinship for that audience." Daltrey was more blunt. "We was fucking 'orrible. It just shows that we are human, though. We can have a terrible night just like everybody else." Tuesday's show was an improvement, with Townshend reducing a Les Paul to matchwood, later explaining he was pleased at the way the show went.

On the 13th and 14th, Maggie Bell and Montrose, respectively, supported. Thursday's show progressed into an improvised "My Generation" jam featuring "Gloria," "You Really Got Me," and "Big Boss Man." Moving into "The Punk and the Godfather," Roger's mike cut out and he stormed off. The others carried on for a few minutes with Pete singing before he shook his head, took off his guitar, and left the stage seething, with the others following. A rowdy mob responded by exploding cherry bombs and raining bottles onto the stage. On the final night, Townshend brought the proceedings to a climax by smashing three guitars, letting Keith smash a fourth.

MCA threw a "Manhattan Madness" party for the group at the Manhattan Center, covered by CBS-TV cameras and featuring a roller derby rink, go-go dancers, fire eaters, and sword swallowers. Ronnie Spector and the Ronettes provided the cabaret for 1500 guests, including Elton John, the Beach Boys, Bette Midler, and Johnny and Edgar Winter. 8-mm colour film shot at three of the four MSG shows by Joel Naftelberg was used in *The Kids Are Alright* end credits sequence.

SUNDAY, 16 JUNE

At Ramport, Tina Turner overdubbed her "Acid Queen" vocal in time for a four day shoot at Lee International Studios, Kensal Road, West London.

MONDAY, 17 JUNE

Filming of the "Go To The Mirror" sequence with Jack Nicholson at Harefield Grove.

FRIDAY, 21 and SATURDAY, 22, MONDAY, 24— WEDNESDAY, 26 JUNE

Filming of the "Champagne" and "Smash The Mirror" sequences at Harefield Grove.

MONDAY, 1—THURSDAY, 4 JULY

Tommy location filming moved to Keswick in the Lake District, Cumbria.

THURSDAY, 4 JULY

John completed final remixing and production on *Odds and Sods* at Nova Sound, and the album was mastered at Apple studios on Wednesday, 17 July. With *Tommy* taking longer than expected and not being required on the film set, he was able to indulge in extracurricular projects.

His fourth solo album, *Mad Dog*, begun at the start of the year, was completed and mixed at Nova Sound and Scorpio Studios, co-produced by John Alcock. Rigor Mortis had changed its name—"due to public demand— they thought it was sick!"—to John Entwistle's Ox.

Musicians included Jim Ryan (guitars), Tony Ashton (keyboards), Graham Deakin (drums), Eddie Jobson (violin/synthesiser), Howie Casey and Dick Parry (saxes), Dave Caswell (trumpet), and John Mumford (trombone). Irene and Doreen Chanter and Juanita Franklin (a.k.a. session choristers Thunderthighs) sang backing vocals and lead on "Mad Dog," with strings by the Nashville Katz and Mike Wedgewood.

SATURDAY, 13 JULY

The music press announced that Roger had been offered the title role in Ken Russell's upcoming film biography of Hungarian composer-pianist Franz Liszt, due to go into production in the New Year. (Mick Jagger and David Bowie were originally under consideration for the part.)

At the same time, Keith and Oliver Reed were reported to be collaborating on a film, *The Two Clowns*, and writing a non-musical dramatic play in which they would co-star when staged in London's West End the following year. Working titles included *The Dinner Party*, *An Evening Of British Rubbish*, and *A Night Of British Lunacy*.

TUESDAY, 23 JULY

Pete Meaden took Pete to see Birmingham group the Steve Gibbons Band perform at Dingwalls, Camden Town, North London, after Meaden had raved about them. Townshend recommended the band to Roger, and the following year, they were signed to Goldhawke, the label formed by Daltrey and his personal manager, Bill Curbishley. Meaden and Curbishley became the band's co-managers as Fireball Ltd.

THURSDAY, 1—SUNDAY, 4 AUGUST

Pete and Keith guested unannounced on the last dates of Eric Clapton's American tour. On the 1st, at the Omni, Atlanta, Georgia, Pete played on "Layla" and "Baby Don't You Do It," and Keith joined in on "Little Queenie." On the 2nd, at the Coliseum, Greensboro, North Carolina, Pete played on "Willie And The Hand Jive" and "Get Ready," while Keith joined in on "Layla," "Badge," and "Little Queenie." On the 4th, at the International Raceway, West Palm Beach, Florida, Pete and Joe Walsh came on for the encore of "Layla" and "Little Queenie." Keith wandered onstage between numbers and sang "I Can't Explain," with Clapton vamping the riff. Bob Pridden was employed behind the soundboard, and "Legs" Larry Smith acted as tap-dancing, ukelele-playing MC for "Eric Cleptomaniac and the Diddicoys."

WEDNESDAY, 21 AUGUST

Principal photography on *Tommy* was completed, with sequences shot on Hayling Island and Southsea beach, near the Lifeboat Café. The original budget had been set at approximately £1million for a twelve-week shooting schedule. It ended up costing Columbia and the Stigwood Organisation $3.5 million (approximately £2.4 million), with shooting taking up eighteen weeks.

THURSDAY, 29 AUGUST

As the British press announced his intention of quitting Britain for America, Keith flew back to London for dubbing work on *Tommy*. Editing started at Lee International Studios on 30 September.

WEDNESDAY, 4 SEPTEMBER

Back in Los Angeles, Keith videotaped two American television commercials to promote the *Odds and Sods* album and conveniently, his forthcoming single, "Don't Worry Baby." For the first, in a Wild West setting, he wore his American football helmet used on the album sleeve. The second depicted him as a bleached blond surfer, complete with woodie, surfboard, and old-style bathing costume, trampling through children's sand castles before paddling out into the ocean. (The camera pulled back to reveal him in a child's paddling

pool!) The adverts never made it to the tube as MCA executives deemed them distasteful.

Also during this month, Keith agreed to appear in *Sonic Boom*, a comedy short made by UCLA film student Eric Louzil, about a supersonic jet that lands in a small town and creates hysteria about an impending sonic boom that never happens. Keith's cameo as a mad professor, complete with false mask, cotton wool beard, and walking cane, was shot in a single day at the Burbank Court House. The film, which also featured a motley crew of Ricky Nelson, George Kennedy, Sal Mineo, Jonathan Winters, Johnny Crawford, and Chuck Woolery, was released in the U.S. as a supporting feature to Jack Gold's *Man Friday* in March 1976.

FRIDAY, 6 SEPTEMBER

At Broadcasting House, John appeared as a guest on Radio 1's *Roundtable*, broadcast live from 5:00—7:00 pm. Also during this time, he was interviewed on location by Michael Wale for *Rockspeak*, broadcast Friday, 27 September, 10:00 pm—12 midnight.

FRIDAY, 13 SEPTEMBER—MONDAY, 7 OCTOBER

At Ramport and Nova Sound, John and John Alcock co-produced *Music Breakup*, the unreleased third album by Sharks. "They've got the same line-up as the Who," Alcock explained, "and they want to get a live sound to the record, so John asked me to co-produce." However, the group split before its completion.

At the same time, a twelve-piece version of "The Ox" rehearsed at the Royal Ballroom, Tottenham, featuring John on bass and vocals, Roy Young and Mike Deacon (keyboards), Graham Deakin (drums), and Memphis guitarist Robert A. Johnson, who had previously worked with Isaac Hayes and Ann Peebles. A four-piece horn section and backing vocalists Thunderthighs completed the line-up.

SATURDAY, 28 SEPTEMBER

As a foretaste of what to expect from Keith's current Record Plant sessions, which had begun in a loose fashion in late August, "Don't Worry Baby" B/W "Teenage Idol" was released (in the U.S. only) with heavy publicity from MCA. Both tracks were produced by former Beatles roadie, Mal Evans, and the release was the only concrete result of his labours.

Thanks to an almost universal thumbs-down (Bobby Abrams in *Phonograph* described it as "a turkey, both artistically and commercially"), Evans

was fired from the project soon after and the just-completed album was scrapped. "I admit that was a really shitty record," Keith told *Sounds'* Andy McConnell the following January. "That was my first attempt at singing and let's say it got better every minute after that!" (A re-recorded version of "Don't Worry Baby" appeared on the *Two Sides Of The Moon* album.)

FRIDAY, 4 OCTOBER

Odds and Sods was released in the U.K. (#10) and in the U.S. on 12 October (#15). Pete contributed extensive liner notes (published unabridged in the 21 September edition of *NME*) and Track executive Mike Shaw came up with the idea of printing the song titles in Braille.

"A lot of bootlegs were being put out, and the kids were being ripped off because the mix on them was very rough," said John, who oversaw the project. "We found that we had a huge amount of unreleased material, stuff that we either wanted to use as singles or on albums but had got left by the wayside, so we decided to use it."

SATURDAY, 5 OCTOBER

"Who Day" on the BBC. As well as their appearance on the first in a new series of the Beeb's arts programme *2nd House* (see 18 May), Radio 1 broadcast the first of four 20-minute weekly interviews with each band member (interspersed with music and comments from the others) in a series entitled *Who's Who*, produced by interviewer Stuart Grundy.

Each hour-long programme ran successive Saturdays, 2:00—3:00 pm. Pete appeared first (recorded 26 September), followed by John (12th, recorded 7 October at Ramport), Keith (19th, recorded in L.A. on 14 October), and Roger (26th, recorded 21 October).

WEDNESDAY, 9 OCTOBER

On his thirtieth birthday, John commenced recording his contribution to the stage musical score of *Flash*

Fearless versus The Zorg Women Parts 5 & 6, over two weeks at Wessex Studios, Highbury New Park, North London, with John Alcock producing.

Parts of the album were recorded in New York, Memphis, and L.A, featuring Robert A. Johnson, Mick Grabham, Justin Hayward, John Weider, Steve Pettican (guitars), Nicky Hopkins, Chick Churchill, Kirk Duncan, Mike Deacon (keyboards), Bill Bruford, Carmine Appice, Kenny Jones, Graham Deakin (drums/percussion), Jim Frank (harmonica), Howie Casey (sax), John Weider and Eddie Jobson (violin/synthesiser), and Lesley Duncan, Doreen Chanter, Kay Garner, Jill Mackintosh, and Thunderthighs (backing vocals). Featured vocalists were Alice Cooper, Jim Dandy, Elkie Brooks, Maddy Prior, James Dewar, and Frankie Miller (on the U.S. version only).

John, as Zilch, sang lead on "The Chop," while Keith Moon played Long John Silver. "It may well be another concept album," John told Roy Carr, "but I just approached the project as a bunch of rock and roll songs. Basically, I saw it as a perfect opportunity to play some funky bass with a lot of other musicians while getting sloshed. Chrysalis spent a packet on booze. I alone went through eight dozen bottles of wine…" The album was released in May 1975. Concurrently, Ox, now streamlined to a four-piece, rehearsed at Shepperton. The equipment and rehearsals cost John £20,000.

FRIDAY, 8 NOVEMBER

Keith, with a little help from his friend Ringo Starr, was guest host of ABC's *Wide World In Concert* second anniversary television special, which was aired live in two consecutive 90-minute segments from the ABC Television Studios, North Hollywood, 11:30 pm–2:30 am EST.

Taped highlights from past shows and in-studio performances, including the Allman Brothers Band, Bachman Turner Overdrive, Loggins and Messina, Elvin Bishop, James Brown, Three Dog Night, and Sparks, were linked by the hosts' zany introductions. In one, Ringo slinked from his dressing room with a pair of scissors to cut off Keith's tie!

Moon, with red-painted whiskers, also got to indulge in a manic, five-minute drum solo on his perspex kit, a water-filled floor tom complete with swimming goldfish, to the enragement of animal lovers, who called in to complain. He then took questions from the studio audience. Asked what

would happen to the fish, he quipped "even the best drummers get hungry."

MONDAY, 11 NOVEMBER

Roger commenced work on his second solo album, *Ride A Rock Horse,* at Ramport, produced and arranged by Russ Ballard, who, as on Daltrey's first album, played guitar and keyboards. Musicians included Dave Wintour (bass), Stuart Francis and Henry Spinetti (drums), Paul Korda and Philip Goodhand-Tait (piano), Dave "Clem" Clempson (guitar on "Feeling"), Nick Newell (sax on "Hearts Right"), Alan Bown (trumpet on "Proud"), plus Sweedies and American funk rocksters Kokomo on backing vocals. Tony Meehan played percussion and handled the string and

ABOVE: RINGO AND KEITH, 8 NOVEMBER.

brass arrangements, except for "Get Your Love," arranged by John Barham.

Keith was re-recording his *Like A Rat Up A Pipe* album at the Record Plant, later retitled *Two Sides Of The Moon* by accomplice Ringo Starr. At the insistence of MCA's Mike Maitland, Mal Evans was replaced by Canned Heat producer, Skip Taylor, as well as John Stronach, engineer on Motown sessions for Berry Gordy. The pair had to virtually start from scratch in a salvage operation.

Of the final ten tracks, Keith drummed on only three, with Jim Keltner handling the bulk of percussive duties. "I just find the whole L.A. atmosphere much easier to work in, much easier to have fun in as well," Moon explained to *Beat Instrumental*. "I just had a bit of spare time, and I thought I might as

well book some studio time. It was not a matter of hiring various musicians, it was just seeing who was around and willing to drop in for a jam."

Among the sixty (!) credited musicians who "dropped in" were Joe Walsh, Danny Kortchmar, and Jesse Ed Davis (guitars), Bobby Keys (sax), Klaus Voorman (bass), Jim Keltner (drums), and Flo and Eddie (backing vocals). Additional guests included John Sebastian, Spencer Davis, Johnny Rivers, Jim Gilstrap, members of Fanny, Jo Jo Gunne, Rick Nelson and the Stone Canyon Band, and Keith's hero, surf guitarist Dick Dale. The L.A. Philharmonic strings and choir were conducted and arranged by veteran producer Jimmie Haskell.

The recording alone cost horrified MCA executives more than $200,000. "Five years ago, this album would have been a two-year project for me, because the Who weren't such a big band then," Keith gleefully told *Sounds*' Andy McConnell. "People like MCA are on my side now, and it's a lot easier to work that way." MCA did veto the release of Keith's planned Christmas single, recorded at the Record Plant and featuring such characters as Joe Walsh and Larry Hagman.

MONDAY, 25 NOVEMBER

Keith flew to London for last-minute dubbing work on *Tommy* at EMI Elstree Studios, Hertfordshire. Concurrently, Pete completed final editing and sound mixing at CTS, Wembley.

SUNDAY, 8 DECEMBER

John Entwistle's Ox (consisting of Entwistle—bass/vocals, Robert A. Johnson—guitar, Mike Deacon—keyboards, and Graham Deakin—drums) played the first date of a financially disastrous tour of Britain and America, at the City Hall, Newcastle.

Only 300 hardcore fans filed into a venue that accomodated more than 2000. For the English dates, John had originally planned to augment the band with a brass section, but settled instead for sax player Geoff Daly and two backing singers, Ireen and Doreen Chanter, from Thunderthighs. The Who's crew and PA were used for the tour, with the sound mixed by Bob Pridden. Support was Joe Vitale's Madmen.

FRIDAY, 13 DECEMBER

John Entwistle's Ox, Odeon Theatre, Southport.

TUESDAY, 17 DECEMBER

John Entwistle's Ox, City Hall, Sheffield.

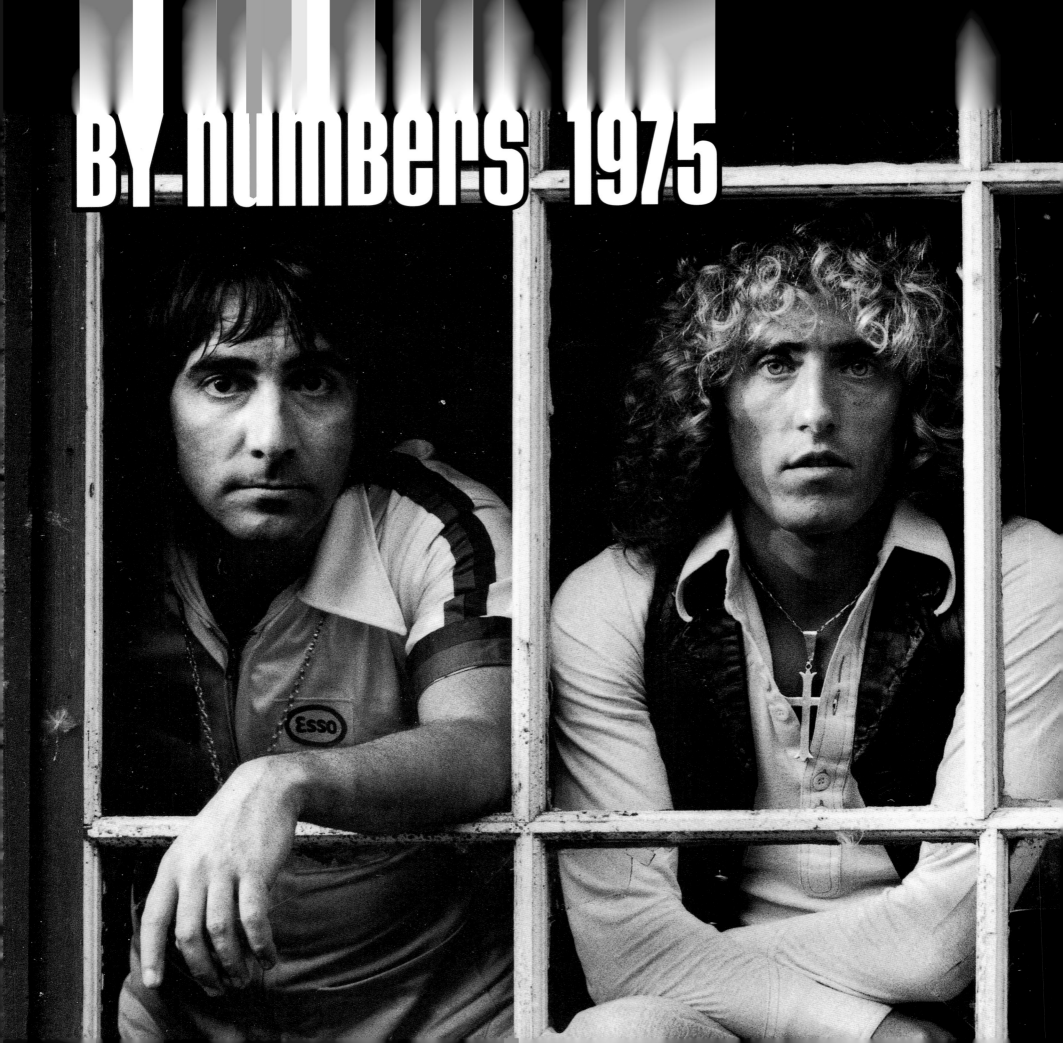

BY numBers 1975

Frustrated by the lack of information regarding group activity and with a preponderance of solo projects, Who fans could be forgiven for believing the widely-circulating rumour that the group was no longer. However, 1975 was to prove a pivotal year because of the world-wide success of the group's first venture into celluloid, *Tommy*, which brought with it a whole new audience eager to see the Who's existence continue.

Tommy opened on both sides of the Atlantic in March with lavish, star-studded premieres, organised by Allan Carr and Bobby Zarem to the tune of over $100,000. It was one of the first movies to be exploited with a merchandising campaign running alongside it. In a direct echo of the climactic "We're Not Gonna Take It" scene, fans could purchase *Tommy* badges, T-shirts, stickers, and mirrors in the cinema foyer. The film (a massive box-office smash, of course) was judged a success in introducing a new, non-rock-oriented audience to the original work, while to the average rock fan, it was a banal travesty. In the former camp was respected *Village Voice* film critic Andrew Sarris, who presciently noted, "We [non-rock] fans like what we see in *Tommy* because it confirms our belief that Rock has entered its mindlessly decadent phase, all noise and glitter and self-congratulation." Most opted for the latter view and were surprised, and more than a little disappointed, at how Pete had happily allowed Ken Russell, with his visually bombastic style, take credibility-damaging liberties with his creation. However, Townshend, who'd originally envisaged Russell as the man for the job, merely saw this as a means to an end. "If I had ever dug my heels in about *Tommy* and said no one has the right to change my conception, it would have killed *Tommy* dead as a concept," he argued. In our post-modern age, some now view the film as a 70s kitsch classic.

Ironically, the person who should have been partaking in a large share of the spoils didn't even receive a screen credit. Kit Lambert was rapidly going from bad to worse. Mortally offended, in a news piece printed in the 19 July edition of the *NME*, he made public his intended legal measures against Robert Stigwood, Chris Stamp, and the Who's de facto manager, Bill Curbishley, ending by somewhat disingenuously claiming he found *Tommy* "a superb film."

Tommy propelled Roger to superstardom in his own right, particularly in America where, at the age of thirty, he became a teen heartthrob. During an August visit to promote the film and his second solo album, *Ride A Rock Horse*, he was mobbed wherever he appeared. If art imitates life, Daltrey had become Tommy.

Undeterred by the unanimous negative reaction to his first solo offering, *Two Sides Of The Moon* (released that spring), Keith entered the studio again in September to record an ill-fated album with the same recipe of star pals, including David Bowie and Ron Wood.

In April, the band reunited at Shepperton studios, initially without Roger, who was occupied filming Russell's *Lisztomania* on an adjacent soundstage, to begin recording the first Who album in two years. "They are anxious to show the public that the Who have not disbanded," said a press spokesman, refuting the rumours. "Because of their various solo commitments, there have been many reports to this effect. Even Warner Brothers Pictures have fallen into this trap, describing Daltrey in their publicity blurbs as 'former pop star.' But they will be back in live action before long."

Pete was still heavily disillusioned with his role within the Who, the *Tommy* fiasco, and the rock scene in general. The songs he wrote for *The Who By Numbers* candidly reflected this inner turmoil, with the kind of honesty displayed on comparable works such as *John Lennon/Plastic Ono Band* and Bob Dylan's *Blood On The Tracks*. The lyrics covered his drinking and wenching ("However Much I Booze"), impotence and marital breakdown ("Imagine A Man"), business pressures ("They're All In Love"), and the corrupt, two-faced world of the money-driven music business machine ("How Many Friends"), revealing the true extent of his disharmony. The demos, circulated as usual to the other members before recording, reportedly moved Keith to tears. Even Entwistle's contribution, "Success Story," a darkly ironic tale about stardom, kept with the bleak mood. Pete subsequently looked back to this time as the point when he should have left the Who to strike out on his own. (To all intents and purposes, loyalty and financial considerations held him back.) Certainly, the lyrical preoccupations were better suited to a Townshend solo album, which is how many view *The Who By Numbers*.

Having turned thirty during the recording, and tormented by the words he'd written ten years earlier about wishing for a premature demise, Pete sat down with *NME* journalist Roy Carr, an old friend within the business, and let flow a remarkable outpouring of rage, frustration, and self-loathing, aiming barbs at the business of rock and its audience, his contemporaries, and inevitably his bandmates, Roger in particular. Even Carr was disturbed enough to conclude the feature with a disclaimer that Pete either wanted to end the Who there and then or was "just after a bit of public feedback."

Weeks later, it was Roger's turn to reply through the pages of the same paper. Talking to Tony Stewart, he rebuked Pete's claims about the Who and the passivity of their audience. "I never read such a load of bullshit in my life," he snorted, "he's talked himself up his own arse. And there are quite a lot of disillusioned and disenchanted kids about now after reading that...." His main bone of contention was Pete's criticism of the recent live shows. "The Who weren't bad. I think we've had a few gigs where Townshend was bad, and I'll go on record as saying that. On a few of the last gigs, Townshend was pissed and incapable. So don't talk to me about booze, because I've never been onstage drunk in the last seven years, Mr. Townshend! I'm just getting a bit fed up with these left-handed attacks." The only common ground in both interviews was the excellence of Pete's new material. To an outsider, it appeared bizarre that the pair had been in close proximity during recent recording sessions and business meetings, yet felt compelled to wash their dirty linen in public. But then such a state of affairs seemed oddly normal within Who circles.

When the album was released in October, many saw it as a further sign of the band's imminent demise. Carr was moved to describe it as "Pete Townshend's Suicide Note." But Pete had just returned from a Baba sabbatical with his family in America. Having bared his soul to Baba confidante,

Murshida Ivy Duce, he was advised, in effect, to "keep playing guitar in the Who until further notice."

Under normal circumstances, with a successful movie and a lucrative new deal with Polydor, there should have been little to worry about financially. This, however, was the Who, and a cash crisis seemed to always lurk in the background. Legal proceedings had been instigated against Track Records for mismanagement, and effectively, the band's finances were frozen. More out of fiscal necessity than anything else, the group embarked on a year-long tour, playing for maximum capacity audiences throughout Britain, Europe, and the United States.

On 3 October, the "Greatest Rock And Roll Band In The World" tour opened at Stafford's Bingley Hall, with the Who out to reclaim that title from the Rolling Stones. Although the shows were greeted with enthusiastic reviews and were a predictable box office success, a few dissenting voices were disappointed at how conservative the act had become. *Quadrophenia* had all but vanished, and because of the film, a large chunk was redevoted to *Tommy*. With Pete's frequently aired wish to progress and see the Who age with dignity notwithstanding, this seemed like a step backwards. But why fix what isn't broken? With a rejuvenated Townshend having made peace with his inner demons (for now), it's doubtful anyone left the shows less than ecstatic. The Leicester concerts saw the introduction of the band's innovative laser display, engineered by their long-standing production manager, John "Wiggy" Wolff. Due to the uncertain nature of their potentially dangerous effect, the group were prohibited from using lasers at some venues.

After the first leg of a successful U.S. tour, the year ended with three Christmas shows at London's Hammersmith Odeon. Ticket demand was so high that allocation was made via a lottery. The lucky ones that attended attest that they were some of the best gigs the Who ever played. Free balloons and badges lay on each seat, Moon descended in his Esso Jump Suit on a harness from the top of the stage while Roger wore a "George Davis Is Innocent" T-shirt, which was ironic, as later events proved he wasn't!

1975

FRIDAY, 10 JANUARY
After poorly attended shows at larger venues, John Entwistle's Ox played a string of modest university gigs—the first in Edinburgh, Scotland—supported by Unicorn.

SATURDAY, 11 JANUARY
John Entwistle's Ox, University, Leeds.

TUESDAY, 14 JANUARY
John Entwistle's Ox, Guildhall, Plymouth.

WEDNESDAY, 15 JANUARY
John Entwistle's Ox, University, Exeter.

FRIDAY, 17 JANUARY
John Entwistle's Ox, Brunel University, Uxbridge.

WEDNESDAY, 22 JANUARY
John Entwistle's Ox, University, Liverpool.

FRIDAY, 24 JANUARY
John Entwistle's Ox, University of East Anglia, Norwich.

SATURDAY, 25 JANUARY
John Entwistle's Ox, University, Leicester.

WEDNESDAY, 29 JANUARY
Keith and David Essex attended the U.S. premiere of *Stardust* at the Sack Cheri Complex, Boston. Afterwards, a cocktail party was thrown by Columbia Pictures at the Ritz-Carlton. Keith announced to assembled reporters he'd suffered an "emotional collapse" from the film and had spent a week in hospital convalescing. "It was almost my life re-lived," he said, "more than just a movie, it was almost like a real band."

Keith flew on to New York to do press for his forthcoming solo album, *Two Sides Of The Moon*, including a special guest appearance on Scott Muni's WNEW-FM show, chatting between tracks and acting as DJ. On 31 January, he attended a party to celebrate Lynyrd Skynyrd's Academy of Music gig.

The group was now being managed by Who tour organiser, Peter Rudge.

ABOVE: RINGO AND ROGER IN *LISZTOMANIA*.

MONDAY, 3 FEBRUARY—FRIDAY, 23 MAY

Ken Russell's *Lisztomania* went into production at Shepperton Studios, produced by Roy Baird, with co-producers David Puttnam and Sanford Lieberson for Goodtimes Enterprises. Executive Producers were: Brian Lane and Bill Curbishley.

Roger starred as Franz Liszt, Sara Kestelman as Princess Carolyn, Paul Nicholas as Wagner, Fiona Lewis as the Countess, with guest appearances from Ringo Starr as the Pope and Rick Wakeman (who composed and arranged the film score) as Thor.

During the first weeks of filming, Daltrey completed his second solo album, *Ride A Rock Horse*, at Ramport and CBS Studios. "I would get up at 6:45 and be at the film studios by 7:15," Roger recalled. "I'd be there till seven at night and then go into the recording studio from eight till ten, or eleven, and be back at the hotel and in bed by midnight." Initially, the film was allocated an eleven week shoot, but another four weeks were added, delaying Roger's active involvement in *The Who By Numbers* sessions.

FRIDAY, 14 FEBRUARY

A pre-taped insert of Ox performing their new single, "Cell Number 7" and "Mad Dog," appeared on BBC-2's *The Old Grey Whistle Test* (8:10—9:00 pm). John's fourth solo album, *Mad Dog*, followed on 28 February. The sleeve featured frenzied stills from an 8-mm film of his Irish wolfhounds, Hamish and Jason, while the poster featured the canines sitting posed in Entwistle's open-topped Cadillac. Due to impending legal action against Track, both single and album were released on a one-off deal with Decca.

Ox flew to Europe for media promotion in France and Germany. In Hamburg, John walked out of a press preview of *Tommy* when the projectionist got the reels the wrong way round!

FRIDAY, 21 FEBRUARY

Itching to be back on the road, John took Ox on an eighteen-city U.S. trek, commencing at the Memorial Auditorium, Sacramento, California, as "Special Guest Stars" to the J. Geils Band.

SATURDAY, 22 FEBRUARY

The original movie soundtrack to *Tommy* was released in the States by Polydor, who had acquired worldwide rights, prior to the premieres in New York and L.A. on 18 and 19 March. Thanks to all the surrounding hoopla, the double album reached #2 in *Billboard* and #21 when released in England on 21 March.

SUNDAY, 22 and MONDAY, 23 FEBRUARY

Ox, Winterland, San Francisco, California, supporting the J.Geils Band.

WEDNESDAY, 26 FEBRUARY

Ox, Long Beach Arena, Long Beach, California.

SATURDAY, 1 MARCH

Ox, Massey Hall, Toronto, Ontario.

SUNDAY, 2 MARCH

Ox, Masonic Temple Hall, Detroit, Michigan.

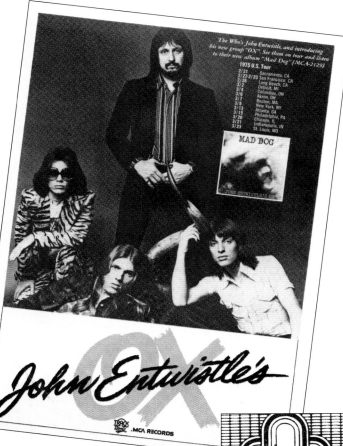

MONDAY, 3 MARCH

Ox, Agora Ballroom, Columbus, Ohio.

WEDNESDAY, 5 MARCH

Ox, Civic Theatre, Akron, Ohio.

FRIDAY, 7 MARCH

Ox, Orpheum Theater, Boston, Massachusetts, co-billed with Roy Buchanan.

At Broadcasting House, London, Pete recorded an interview with John Peel, previewing the *Tommy* soundtrack for a two-and-a-half-hour Radio 1 "Rock Week" special, broadcast 5:00—7:30 pm the following day.

SATURDAY, 8 MARCH

Ox, Academy Of Music, New York City, with Carmine Appice's Astroport.

SUNDAY, 9 MARCH

Ox, Century II, Buffalo, New York.

TUESDAY, 11 MARCH

Ox, Constitution Hall, Washington, D.C.

THURSDAY, 13 MARCH

Ox, Municipal Auditorium, Atlanta, Georgia. Cancelled due to poor ticket sales.

FRIDAY, 14 MARCH

An interview with Roger in his dressing room at Shepperton was broadcast on *The Old Grey Whistle Test* (8:10—8:40 pm). Despite its taking place on the *Listzomania* set, the conversation with Bob Harris centred firmly on *Tommy*, with the "Pinball Wizard" sequence being shown.

SATURDAY, 15 MARCH

Ox, The Spectrum, Philadelphia, Pennsylvania.

The show was recorded by DIR Radio for broadcast on *The King Biscuit Flower Hour*, but was subsequently not aired. It was given an official CD release in 1997.

SUNDAY, 16 MARCH

Ox, Calderone Theatre, Hempstead, Long Island, New York.

MONDAY, 17 MARCH

Ox, Billero Hall, Allentown College, Allentown, Pennsylvania.

Keith's lone solo album, *Two Sides Of The Moon*, was released by MCA (Polydor in the U.K.) on 25 April.

TUESDAY, 18 MARCH

A *Tommy* morning press call was held in the Casino Ballroom of the Essex House Hotel, New York City, with the main cast present except for Oliver Reed and Jack Nicholson. (Daltrey and Ken Russell were in England working on *Lisztomania*.) The world premiere followed that evening at the Ziegfeld Theatre. Problems with the special Quintophonic sound system occured right up to opening night. (Similiar to quadrophonic sound, Quintophonic had the addition of a fifth speaker behind the screen, from which the vocal tracks issued.)

Townshend had spent three frustrating hours at the theatre the previous day, attempting to fix the delay between the front and back speakers, and groaned in horror when it was still not right at the opening. He leapt from his seat in the darkness to help correct the sound from the booth. Much to his

ABOVE: JOHN AND KEITH CHECK THE REVIEWS AT THE NEW YORK *TOMMY* PREMIERE, 18 MARCH.

evident relief, the film received a standing ovation and some 30 minutes later, an enthusiastic rabble were still in their seats, demanding the projectionist re-show it. By then, the VIP's were being wined and dined at an elaborate midnight party thrown in a special sealed off section of the New York subway, under the IND Station at 57th Street and Sixth Avenue.

WEDNESDAY, 19 MARCH

The 8:00 pm West Coast premiere of *Tommy* at Mann's Wilshire Theatre, Los Angeles with Pete, Keith, Ann-Margret, Tina Turner, Elton John, and Robert Stigwood in attendance. All were interviewed by David Frost for an ABC *Wide World Special*, broadcast 26 March, 11:30 pm—1:00 am EST, and repeated 8 August. Columnist Army Archerd interviewed guests arriving at the premiere and the party held afterward at the Studio One Club. These included Paul and Linda McCartney, Ron Wood, Kenny Jones, Sally Kellerman, Dean Martin, Tommy Smothers, and Ryan and Tatum O'Neal.

The Allan Carr publicity parties in Hollywood cost $25,000, while the premieres in New York, L.A., and Chicago (on 20 March) cost an astonishing $100,000. Within a month, *Tommy* had grossed more than $2 million at thirteen selected cinemas across the continent.

THURSDAY, 20 MARCH

Ox, Arie Crown Theater, Chicago, Illinois, supporting Joe Walsh's Barnstorm.

In England, Roger's youngest daughter, Willow Amber, was born at Pembury Hospital, Kent.

FRIDAY, 21 MARCH

Ox, Convention Centre, Indianapolis, Indiana.

SATURDAY, 22 MARCH

Ox, Milwaukee Arena, Milwaukee, Wisconsin, supporting J.Geils Band with James Cotton.

SUNDAY, 23 MARCH

Ox, Kiel Auditorium, St Louis, Missouri.

The last date on a tour that ended in recriminations, costing John more than $70,000 out-of-pocket.

WEDNESDAY, 26 MARCH

Tommy European gala premiere at the Leicester Square Theatre, London.

All the Who were present, as were Ken Russell, Robert Stigwood, Elton John, Ringo Starr, Eric Clapton, Lulu, David Essex, Rod Stewart, and Britt Ekland.

Nicky Horne's Capital Radio show *Your Mother Wouldn't Like It* was broadcast live from the foyer, 9:00—11:00 pm, with on-the-spot reports and interviews. Stigwood threw a post-premiere party at the Inn on the Park, Mayfair. For its first London week, the film set an all-time house record of £26,978, the previous best being £20,440. Additional revenue was garnered from *Tommy* merchandise (programmes, mirrors, stickers, T-shirts, etc.) on sale at selected theatres.

THURSDAY, 27 MARCH

Roger, with Ken Russell, pre-recorded an appearance on the *Russell Harty* chat show, transmitted 10:40—11:25 pm the following evening over the LWT network.

RIGHT: KEITH AND GIRLFRIEND ANNETTE WALTER-LAX ARRIVE IN LONDON, 29 APRIL.

Elton John appeared during the first half of the programme and the "Pinball Wizard" sequence was shown. Asked by Harty how the film had affected his relationship with the Who, Daltrey declared his main ambition was to now get back on the road with "the 'orrible 'Oo—the worst rock and roll group in the world." The "I'm Free" sequence was used to introduce Ken Russell, who was his usual animated self, calling Townshend "the new Shakespeare" and ranting about how the Who could raise Britain "out of its ambient, decadent state more than Wilson or those crappy people could ever hope to achieve!" Kiki Dee closed the programme.

FRIDAY, 18 APRIL

The original commencement date set for the Who's recording schedule, although Keith did not return to Britain until 29 April.

MONDAY, 21 APRIL

A limbering-up jam at Ramport with Ox drummer Graham Deakin sitting in.

ROGER DALTREY IS TOMMY

WEDNESDAY, 30 APRIL

The Who By Numbers sessions commenced over four weeks on Shepperton J Stage, using the Island Mobile Studio.

"When we got together before recording again," John said, "Pete was obviously not into it, so we went down to Shepperton for two days to rehearse without Roger singing, just Pete, Keith, and myself playing Shadows instrumentals out-of-tune, all those old things. We had such a good time that we turned around completely and found ourselves playing better than we had in years." Glyn Johns was back after Townshend had handled all production duties on *Quadrophenia*, supplemented by Nicky Hopkins on piano. Roger's filming commitments on *Lisztomania* overran, but this conveniently coincided with the initial backing tracks being laid down. His vocals were recorded solo, supervised by Johns, who mixed the album at Island studios, Basing Street.

"Blue, Red, And Grey" was recorded solo by Pete at his Eel Pie studio. "Glyn wanted it on the album," Pete told Dave Schulps in *Trouser Press*. "I cringed when he picked it. He heard it on a cassette and said, 'What's that?' I said, 'Nothing.' He said, 'No. Play it.' I said, 'Really, it's nothing. Just me playing a ukelele.' But he insisted on doing it. I said, 'What? That fucking thing. Here's me, wanting to commit suicide, and you're going to put that thing on the record!'" John's brass arrangement was overdubbed at Ramport.

FRIDAY, 16 MAY

At Television Centre, Keith chatted with Bob Harris about *Two Sides Of The Moon* and the Who's plans for BBC-2's *The Old Grey Whistle Test*, broadcast live 8:10–9:00 pm. A Moon-related project that failed to get off the ground during this time was a Sam

Peckinpah remake of *Soldiers Three*, casting Keith, Ringo Starr, and Harry Nilsson in straight roles as army lieutenants in Victorian India. "It will be like the teaming of Redford and Newman for *Butch Cassidy and the Sundance Kid*," Moon gushed to the *Evening Standard*. "I can already ride horses, but I'm going to have to learn to ride elephants and camels."

FRIDAY, 23 MAY

Tommy was shown as the closing film at the 1975 Cannes Film Festival. Keith was among the cast who flew in for promotional purposes.

FRIDAY, 30 MAY

"Get Your Love" B/W "World Over" was the first single taken from Roger's *Ride A Rock Horse*. Because of legal proceedings being instituted against Track, a separate production company, Goldhawke, was formed by Daltrey and manager Bill Curbishley for the release of the album through Polydor on 4 July; MCA (U.S.) on 26 July.

Ride A Rock Horse turns Roger Daltrey into a Living Legend

New Album
8 Track Cartridge & Musicassette

New single 'Walking The Dog' b/w 'Proud'

MONDAY, 2 and TUESDAY, 3 JUNE

A 30-minute *Ride A Rock Horse* promotional feature, consisting of videos for "Get Your Love," "Near To Surrender," "Walking The Dog," "Oceans Away," "Milk Train," "Heart's Right," and "Proud," was produced by Gavrick Losey at Shepperton. The film mixed straight lip-synch performances with animation

sequences by Ian Emes. A press preview was held Monday, 30 June at the Starlite cinema, Mayfair Hotel, London.

SATURDAY, 19 JULY

The dispute between the Who and their management went public. Kit Lambert told the *NME* that, on behalf of the Track group of companies, he was preparing final documents for "drastic and far-reaching" legal action against Robert Stigwood and associates in connection with the *Tommy* film and soundtrack album. He alleged he'd been denied access to relevant documents and that money had been withheld: "Although I own the world copyright and wrote the original scenario, I had no screen credit and have received no financial return. I have been trying to resolve this matter for ten months but have got nowhere, so I am now forced into action."

Lambert further alleged that Stigwood had "alienated the affections of my former partner Chris Stamp, whose resignation I am now demanding from the board of all companies associated with the Who." He said he had dismissed Bill Curbishley from his title of managing director of Track, claiming that Curbishley was never duly appointed to the board of directors. "I want to make it clear that I consider *Tommy* to be a superb film," he added somewhat bizarrely. "However, my action is not concerned with that aspect. It is directed against what I consider to be a lack of business equity and what I am claiming to be an unacceptable slur."

FRIDAY, 8 AUGUST

Roger was in Los Angeles at the start of a seven city, coast-to-coast promotional jaunt for *Ride A Rock Horse*, taking in Dallas, Atlanta, Chicago, Boston, New York, and Philadelphia. At a party in Beverly Hills (attended by Keith), he received the ABC Interstate Theatres "New Star Of The Year" award, previously won by Paul Newman, Steve McQueen, Warren Beatty, and Dustin Hoffman, presented to him by *Tommy* co-star Ann-Margret.

SATURDAY, 9 AUGUST

Roger and Keith were guest presenters at the heavily-criticised First Annual Rock Music Awards, hosted by Elton John and Diana Ross, at the Santa Monica Civic Auditorium. Roger and Ann-Margret presented the "Best Female Vocalist" award while Keith accepted an award for Bad Company as "Best New Group," and presented the "Best Male Vocalist" category with Olivia Newton-John. As Daltrey and Ann-Margret went to receive the award for *Tommy* as "Best Rock Movie or Theatrical Production," presented by actors Brenda Vaccaro and Michael Douglas, Keith ran ahead of them, ape-fashion, and stole the medal. He eventually returned to the stage the same way to hand it back. Produced by Don Kirshner and Bob Wynn, the 90-minute special was taped and broadcast from 10:00 pm by CBS (Channel 2).

THURSDAY, 14 AUGUST

Keith appeared during the finale of Eric Clapton's concert at the Inglewood Forum, L.A., playing percussion on "Why Does Love Got To Be So Sad?" He reappeared with fellow guests Carlos Santana and Joe Cocker for "Eyesight To The Blind" and the closing jam.

TUESDAY, 19 AUGUST

Reaching New York on his media tour, Roger was interviewed live on ABC's *AM America*, the daily forerunner to *Good Morning America*, broadcast 8:00–10:00 am EDT.

While in the Big Apple, he taped appearances on the 22 August edition of NBC's *Midnight Special*, miming "Get Your Love" and "Walking The Dog" as well

as duetting with guest hostess Helen Reddy in a salute to *Tommy*, and WNEW/Metromedia's *Wonderama*, a Sunday morning children's television programme, presented by Bob McAllister, broadcast 24 August. The "Listening To You" *Tommy* sequence and "Walking The Dog" and "Proud" promos were shown, and Roger provided a microphone swinging demonstration. During a press conference at the Plaza Hotel, Daltrey scotched abundant rumours of a Who split after the recent barbed exchanges between Townshend and himself through the pages of the *NME*.

SATURDAY, 23 and SUNDAY, 24 AUGUST

The dates for two scheduled Led Zeppelin concerts at Alameda County Coliseum Stadium, Oakland, California. Zeppelin were forced to cancel after singer Robert Plant was injured in a car smash while on holiday in Greece. Promoter Bill Graham apparently offered the Who $800,000 to fill in, but the offer was declined, despite three quarters of the group being in the States at the same time.

While Roger was promoting his album, Pete arrived on a Baba sabbatical with his family, starting in Myrtle Beach, South Carolina, before travelling to Sufi leader Murshida Ivy Duce's retreat in Walnut Creek, California.

MONDAY, 25 AUGUST

At Television City, L.A., Keith taped an appearance on *The Merv Griffin Show*, a popular Metromedia syndicated afternoon chat show, broadcast Wednesday, 3 September.

MONDAY, 8 SEPTEMBER

Keith took it upon himself to arrange a session for comedian Peter Cook at Clover Recorders, Hollywood, featuring members of the Band and Ricky Nelson, who tried arranging Cook's woefully inept non-vocals. The unproductive session soon degenerated into a marathon binge. The unreleased track in question, "Rubber Ring," was among songs Keith selected from the Warner Brothers catalogue for his own ill-fated second album—begun around the same time at Clover.

The sessions were produced by Booker T and the M.G.s guitarist Steve Cropper, with Jim Keltner drumming, and Cropper's sidekick, Donald "Duck" Dunn on bass. Ringo Starr, David Bowie, and Ron Wood were among the star names who dropped by

to help. Three completed tracks: "Do Me Good," "Real Emotion," and Randy Newman's "Naked Man" appeared in 1997 as bonus tracks on the *Two Sides Of The Moon* CD reissue.

The session for "Do Me Good" was filmed by producer Tony Palmer for his mammoth, seventeen-part television history of popular music, *All You Need Is Love*. The four-minute segment appeared in Part 16 ("Whatever Gets You Through The Night—Glitter Rock"), transmitted Saturday, 28 May 1977, over the LWT network, 10:30–11:30 pm.

Keith was seen recording his vocal track, listening to playbacks with Cropper, and kissing girlfriend Annette Walter-Lax for the camera. Keith was also interviewed (clad in a red bathrobe) at his Sherman Oaks home about the Who's early years. Although not included in Palmer's documentary, a clip was used by Jeff Stein in *The Kids Are Alright*.

SATURDAY, 20 SEPTEMBER

Keith flew into London for two weeks of intensive Who rehearsals on D Stage at Shepperton. "Keith later told me I had walked into the rehearsal hall smiling," Townshend wrote in *Rolling Stone*, "he related this because he had found it remarkable. Something positive had happened to me."

WEDNESDAY, 1 and THURSDAY, 2 OCTOBER

Keith and John appeared on respective nights as guests on John Peel's new Radio 1 programme,

ABOVE: PETER COOK AND KEITH, 8 SEPTEMBER.

broadcast 11:00—12:00 pm, previewing a side each of *The Who By Numbers*. Neither of them had heard the final mixes. (Final mastering occurred at IBC on 16 September). "This will be as much of a surprise for me as it will be for you," said Keith, confessing he hadn't heard most of the vocals. The following night, John revealed that Pete had made changes to several titles up to the last minute.

THURSDAY, 2 OCTOBER

Keith was interviewed by guest presenter Marc Bolan on *Today*, the London regional news magazine programme, broadcast live, 6:00—6:35 pm, from Thames Television studios, on Euston Road. According to reports, Keith's barbed humour reduced the "boppin' elf" to tears.

FRIDAY, 3 and SATURDAY, 4 OCTOBER

The Who By Numbers was issued in the U.K. reaching #7 (in the U.S. on the 25th reaching #8.) The release coincided with the start of a "Greatest Rock And Roll Band In The World" U.K. tour, promoted by Harvey Goldsmith for John Smith Entertainments and Trinifold Ltd. Polydor spent some £20,000 on promotion and the Steve Gibbons Band supported on each date.

The Who were the first act to appear at the recently completed 8000 capacity New Bingley Hall, Stafford County Showground, with two warm-up

shows, their first performances in fourteen months. £6000 was spent on risers for the equipment and drums, to give the group more room on stage. Unfortunately, they only succeeded in cutting them off from each other and were jettisoned after opening night.

"The Who is a band that's got to hear each other," said Entwistle. "If we don't, the whole thing falls to pieces. We've got to be on the floor with the amps close, so we can hear what we're doing. When we haven't been working for a long time we try to do something new, and every time, the whole sound goes."

MONDAY, 6 and TUESDAY, 7 OCTOBER

King's Hall, Belle Vue, Manchester.

WEDNESDAY, 8 OCTOBER

A week's break in the tour itinerary had been specially arranged to allow Pete to make a pilgrimage to India for a Meher Baba gathering, and for Roger to fly to America to attend the premiere of *Lisztomania* at New York's Ziegfeld Theatre on 10 October. (The film opened in L.A at the Fox-Wilshire on the 17th.) In fact, neither made the journey; Daltrey was recovering from a chest fever, while Townshend put his visit back to the following February.

The November issue of *19* magazine carried a free flexi-single containing excerpts ("Wagner's Dream," "Count Your Blessings," and "Love's Dream") from Rick Wakeman's *Lisztomania* score, released 21 November on A&M Records, as well as an interview with Daltrey discussing his success in *Tommy* and his role as Liszt.

The "Love's Dream" sequence was previewed on *The Old Grey Whistle Test*, Tuesday, 4 November, while the film opened at the Warner West End, Leicester Square, on Thursday, 13 November.

SATURDAY, 11 OCTOBER

Keith used the tour break to record material for an unissued comedy album at the BBC's Maida Vale studios, with producer John Walters. This followed on

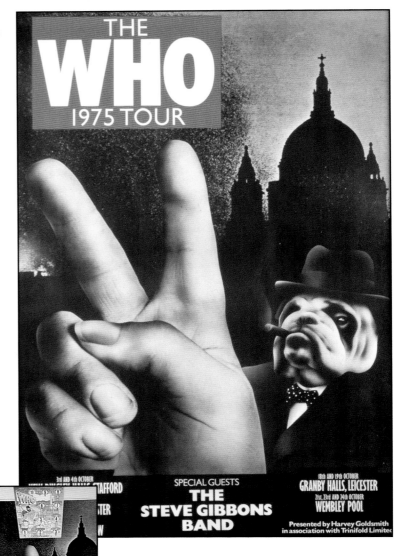

from their earlier endeavours together. (See 17 July 1971 and 19 May 1973.)

"Now we've got some more time," said Moon, "there's some stuff that was written then and John's been writing since. It's in the process of being worked out." When Keith failed to appear at several booked sessions, the idea was quietly abandoned.

WEDNESDAY, 15 and THURSDAY, 16 OCTOBER

Apollo, Glasgow, Scotland.

Because the Who omitted Scotland from their last British tour, the clamour for tickets was so great that the venue's manager had to go on local television to formally announce that both shows were completely sold out and that no further bookings could be accepted. (Apparently, they had received enough applications to stage fourteen concerts!)

FOG SPELLS TROUBLE FOR KEITH MOON

PRESTWICK AIRPORT'S first fog-bound day in three years caused rock star Keith Moon to lose his head and start shouting and bawling in the terminal. And when he could not get information about his flight for London he punched a computer at an airline desk, causing it to cease to operate.

Ayr Sheriff Court was told this last Saturday when Moon, who is the drummer of the 'Who,' pleaded guilty to charges of breach of the peace and maliciously damaging a computer.

The 30-year-old musician who gave his address as Sherman Oaks, California, had been playing in Glasgow last Thursday and was due to fly from Abbotsinch on Friday for London.

FOG BOUND

But the city airport was fog bound and by the time Moon and his fellow Who members reached Prestwick it too had closed due to the fog.

Procurator fiscal Robert Cruickshank said that Moon became incensed with the situation. He had been drinking but was not drunk, and he began to shout and bawl. He was warned about his behaviour but continued to shout and he then punched a computer at the British Airways ticket desk.

An agent for Moon said that he had been unfortunate to arrive at the airport on its first fog bound day in three years.

Honorary Sheriff Substitute Hugh Hunter, fining Moon £30 on each charge, told him his behaviour was disgraceful.

After leaving the court Moon told reporters that he had been well treated while being held in custody. He said: "It's the best night's sleep I've had in years.

"I became angry at the airport and started shouting — other passengers were shouting but I was louder than them. I'm sorry now about what happened but I won't fly British Airways again."

After breakfasting at a Prestwick hotel, Moon flew from the airport on a specially chartered aircraft to Leicester where his group were appearing on Saturday night.

EMPIRE POOL, WEMBLEY

Harvey Goldsmith for John Smith Entertainments by arrangement with Trinifold presents

THE WHO

FRIDAY, 24 OCTOBER, 1975

at 8 p.m.

WEST ARENA TIER

£2.75

TO BE RETAINED   See conditions on back

OCTOBER
24

ENTER AT NORTH DOOR

WEST ARENA TIER

ROW C

THE WHO EUROPE '75

SIGNED ....

---

to charter their own jet for the remainder of the tour at an estimated cost of £300,000, as commercial airlines refused to have them.

SATURDAY, 18 and SUNDAY, 19 OCTOBER
Granby Halls, Leicester.

The debut of the Who's pioneering laser effects involved a bit of skullduggery for lighting operator John Wolff. "I used a 4 watt laser with all moving effects because potentially, if a beam stands still, it can blind someone," Wolff recalled. "A guy from Health and Safety came down to do an inspection. Everytime he went to do a measurement, I'd shift the beam a fraction. I was told not to shine the lasers in the audience, so I said I'd block them out, but as soon as this jobsworth left, I took them off and the audience loved it, especially during 'See Me, Feel Me.'" The GLC prevented Wolff from using the lasers at the following Wembley shows.

TUESDAY, 21; THURSDAY, 23; and FRIDAY, 24 OCTOBER
Empire Pool, Wembley, London.

Despite being a sell-out, the gigs were marred by crowd violence and overzealous security. During the first show, Townshend pointedly referred to the latter as "pricks in white shirts," while homeboy Moon stood on his drums, bellowing, "Don't you know, you're on my domain?!" Townshend also made acerbic reference to an article published in *The Sunday Times* on 19 October by Derek Jewell, who wrote

---

FRIDAY, 17 OCTOBER
Keith was at the centre of a fracas at Prestwick International Airport after the Who's London flight was diverted from fogbound Glasgow. He was held in custody overnight and appeared in Ayr Sheriff's Court the following morning, pleading guilty to charges of breaching the peace and maliciously damaging a British Airways computer. He was fined £30 on each charge, cheekily commenting to reporters that his cell stay was "the best night's sleep I've had in years, everyone was terrific." Thanks to his antics, the Who had

"the Who are trapped playing ageing music for the ageing young."

MONDAY, 27 OCTOBER
The Ahoy, Rotterdam, Holland.

TUESDAY, 28 OCTOBER
Stadthalle, Vienna, Austria.

WEDNESDAY, 29 OCTOBER
Stadthalle, Bremen, West Germany.

THURSDAY, 30 and FRIDAY, 31 OCTOBER
Philipshalle, Düsseldorf, West Germany.

SUNDAY, 2 and MONDAY, 3 NOVEMBER
Messehalle, Sindelfingen, West Germany.

THURSDAY, 6 and FRIDAY, 7 NOVEMBER
Eherthalle, Ludwigshafen, West Germany.

TUESDAY, 18 NOVEMBER
The Who and entourage flew to New York.

THURSDAY, 20 NOVEMBER
The first leg of the 1975/76 American tour, supported by Toots and the Maytals, was kicked off in Houston, Texas, before 18,000 at The Summit, a newly opened basketball arena.

The entire concert, including the encore of "My Generation," "Naked Eye," "Magic Bus," and "My Generation Blues," was filmed in stereo sound, incorporating a three camera pro-system, relaying live visuals and added effects to two large back projection screens. The Cleveland show on 9 December was filmed in the same fashion.

After the show, promoter Bob Cope threw a party at a local club, where a troupe of actors/dancers enacted song titles from *The Who By Numbers*. Spurred on by John, a drunken Keith joined in on a concertina. Police arrived after complaints of Moon's all too literal translations during "Squeeze Box." When Entwistle went to John Wolff's aid, the pair were arrested and charged with disorderly conduct. They were fingerprinted and spent two hours in a cell before being bailed out. The charges were later dropped.

SUNDAY, 30 NOVEMBER
Indiana University Assembly Hall, Bloomington, Indiana.

MONDAY, 1 DECEMBER
Kemper Arena, Kansas City, Missouri.

TUESDAY, 2 DECEMBER
Veterans Memorial Auditorium, Des Moines, Iowa.

THURSDAY, 4 and FRIDAY, 5 DECEMBER
Chicago Stadium, Chicago, Illinois.

ABOVE: PETE WITH TOOTS HIBBERT, 20 NOVEMBER.

against football teams, comedians, wrestlers, one hit wonders. It's degrading. In fact, having a hit is extremely embarrassing!"

SUNDAY, 23 NOVEMBER
Mid-South Coliseum, Memphis, Tennessee.

MONDAY, 24 NOVEMBER
The Omni, Atlanta, Georgia.

TUESDAY, 25 NOVEMBER
M.T.S.U. Murphy Center, Murfreesboro, Tennessee.

THURSDAY, 27 NOVEMBER
Hampton Coliseum, Hampton Roads, Virginia.

FRIDAY, 28 NOVEMBER
Coliseum, Greensboro, North Carolina.

FRIDAY, 21 NOVEMBER
L.S.U. Assembly Center, Baton Rouge, Louisiana.

SATURDAY, 22 NOVEMBER
MCA released "Squeeze Box" B/W "Success Story," restoring the Who to the *Billboard* Top 20 at #16. It stayed on the listings for four months and fared even better in Britain, reaching the Top 10 when released on 16 January, 1976. "I wouldn't mind if we never released another single, ever!" Entwistle complained to *Sounds'* John Ingham. "I hate releasing a poor little song to compete

SATURDAY, 6 DECEMBER

Metropolitan Stadium, Pontiac, Michigan.

The Who set a record at the Silver Dome for the largest ever indoor rock concert attendance, drawing 78,000 people and grossing $614,998. (The record was broken by Led Zeppelin at the same venue two years later.) Due to the arena's vast size, a thirty-by-forty foot (9m x 12m) closed circuit video screen was installed, nowadays standard practice for such an event.

The stereo feed was recorded on 2-inch colour videotape for the Who's archives. Part of the "Join Together"/"Road Runner"/"My Generation Blues" medley was remixed by John Entwistle and appeared in *The Kids Are Alright* movie and soundtrack.

MONDAY, 8 DECEMBER

Riverfront Coliseum, Cincinnati, Ohio.

TUESDAY, 9 DECEMBER

Richfield Coliseum, Cleveland, Ohio.

WEDNESDAY, 10 DECEMBER

Memorial Auditorium, Buffalo, New York.

THURSDAY, 11 DECEMBER

Maple Leaf Gardens, Toronto, Canada.

The Who flew back to New York after the show. Roger, Keith, and John were staying at the Navarro under thinly disguised pseudonyms: Roger as "D. Rogers," Keith as "M. Keith," and John as "E. Johnson." Pete stayed at the Pierre as "T. Peters."

SATURDAY, 13 DECEMBER

Civic Center, Providence, Rhode Island.

SUNDAY, 14 DECEMBER

Civic Center, Springfield, Massachusetts.

MONDAY, 15 DECEMBER

The Spectrum, Philadelphia, Pennsylvania.

The last show on the first leg of the American tour, returning the following March.

SUNDAY, 21—TUESDAY, 23 DECEMBER

Odeon, Hammersmith, London.

Three "Merry Xmas From The 'Orrible 'Oo" concerts were arranged after overwhelming ticket demand for the October British dates. A party atmosphere prevailed with each seat receiving a "Christmas Pack" containing a streamer, mask, and

Who By Numbers badge. The shows were supported by the group Charlie and compèred by Graham Chapman. Unfortunately, the Monty Python man bombed night after night, attempting a comic monologue over loud, impatient shouts for "the 'Oo!" (Keith had recently approached Chapman to star in a Moon-produced film version of *Dick Whittington*.)

Moon made his entrance descending via winch to his drums—ascending in the same fashion at show's end. As "Won't Get Fooled Again" climaxed, balloons and "snow" showered over the audience. Backstage on the final night, Roger, wearing a topical "George Davis Is Innocent" T-shirt, revealed plans for the Who to headline at least two major open-air concerts at leading British football grounds the following summer.

goodbye all you punks
1976

Because the Who's finances were effectively tied up in litigation with their previous management, road work continued out of necessity, urged on by Bill Curbishley. Peter Rudge had organised the Who's American tours via his Sir Productions company in New York, but an intolerable working situation between the two men resulted in Curbishley's confirmation as the Who's full-time manager in May. (He had been acting *de facto* in this capacity with Rudge since 1973.)

The Who By Numbers tour, begun the previous October, took up most of the Who's time in 1976. Polydor wanted the group to promote the album, but it became obvious that the set list had turned into a "greatest hits" celebration of the Who's history, so much so that Moon had it written in permanent marker on his floor tom. Apart from an occasional jam before the finale of "Won't Get Fooled Again," no attempt was made to deviate from a safe

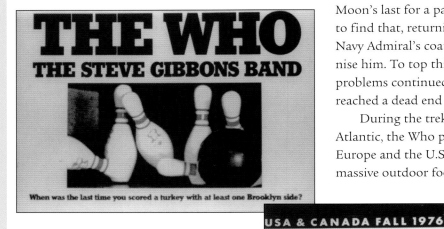

pattern during shows—a state of affairs that was never satisfactorily resolved.

The year began quietly enough, with Pete in a contemplative mood. In February, he flew to India on his second Baba pilgrimage, documented in the film *The God Man*, while a third privately pressed devotional album, *With Love*, was released. Putting his money where his cause was, Pete opened the Meher Baba Oceanic Centre in Twickenham during a break in the touring schedule.

The Who covered America on extensive, neatly planned coast-to-coast assaults, playing in large indoor basketball and hockey arenas or outdoor football stadiums. Such streamlined touring didn't pass without incident. On opening night in Boston, Keith collapsed after a near-lethal intake of brandy and barbiturates, forcing the band to move the show to the end of the schedule. The following night, in a desperate cry for attention, he kicked the glass out of a framed painting, sustaining a serious injury to his heel in the process. In August, his excessive behaviour finally caught him up when he was hospitalised for eight days in Miami.

Rolling Stone awarded each group member a pair of red suspenders in recognition of being voted "Best

Band of 1976." Because the level of touring became the most extensive undertaken since 1971, the band were regaining the same level of power they'd attained in their glory years. At least three quarters of the band were happy to devote their time to the road. "We'd have good nights and bad nights like any other band, but we found ourselves playing better than ever," said Entwistle. "To me, that last tour with Keith was the peak of the Who's career."

After the final Toronto show on 21 October, Moon's last for a paying audience, Pete was horrified to find that, returning home wearing an American Navy Admiral's coat, his own daughters didn't recognise him. To top things off, Townshend's hearing problems continued to worsen. The road had reached a dead end as far as he was concerned.

During the treks back and forth across the Atlantic, the Who played to capacity audiences in Europe and the U.S. In Britain, they played three massive outdoor football stadium shows, including a return to Charlton, where their entry into the *Guinness Book Of Records* as "World's Loudest Band" was assured. The official figures recorded the audience as 50,000 but far more flooded into the grounds. Thanks to an abundance of forged tickets on the market, many genuine ticket-holders couldn't gain admittance. The same problem had occurred at the first Charlton event where the gates were simply opened to accommodate the crowds outside. The atmosphere was wet and uncomfortable, with much fighting. At one point, a spectator climbed the floodlights for a better view and fell. Just before the Who went on, the rain miraculously stopped—the only wet day in a temperature record–breaking English summer.

After the Who's show, the GLC (Greater London Council) authorities banned any more concerts from taking place at Charlton because so many by-laws had been broken.

While massive events like this had become standard practice among rock's upper echelon, a younger generation started to question the validity of such remote and cynical circuses. Although the music press were slow to give "punk rock" any major coverage, this street movement, spearheaded by the Sex Pistols, three of whom hailed from West London, was making its presence felt at venues such as the 100 Club and the Marquee, from which the Who had sprung. Ironically, "Substitute" figured in their early repertoire. To Pete, it was the rallying call he'd been waiting for. "I used to wake up in the night, praying to be destroyed. 'Get me out of this bloody whirlpool,'" he wrote in *Rolling Stone* the following year. "I thought the hypocrisy of the position the Who was in was just unbelievable. In the end, I actually thought of inventing a new form of music that would take over from where the Who left off. In my imagination, I invented punk rock a thousand times."

Punk was still a mere whisper, but by the end of the year, thanks to the publicity generated from the Sex Pistols' controversial appearance on live television, that whisper turned into a vengeful scream.

FEBRUARY

Delayed from the previous October, Pete visited Baba's crypt in India for the second time. He was filmed performing "Drowned" on acoustic guitar for a gathering of devotees at the Pilgrim Centre. The performance was featured in *The God Man*, a documentary produced by the Australian Baba chapter. The following month, a third devotional album, *With Love*, was issued, featuring three unique Townshend contributions: "In His Hands," "Sleeping Dog," and "Lantern Cabin."

SATURDAY, 21 FEBRUARY

The *NME* announced that the Who were planning to film their own showcase for *Supersonic* producer Mike Mansfield, as part of a series of specials for London Weekend Television. The concert would take place in March at either LWT's South Bank studios or at a specially arranged event. Due to conflicting schedules, however, the idea never bore fruit.

ABOVE: Boston Garden, 1 April.

FRIDAY, 27 FEBRUARY

Hallenstadion, Zurich, Switzerland, supported by the Steve Gibbons Band.

SATURDAY, 28 FEBRUARY

Olympiahalle, Munich, West Germany.

MONDAY, 1 and TUESDAY, 2 MARCH

Pavillion de Paris, Paris, France.

TUESDAY, 9 MARCH

The second leg of the American tour, supported by the Steve Gibbons Band, commenced at the Boston Garden, Boston, Massachusetts, before 18,000. The show was abandoned after just two songs when Keith collapsed over his drums and crashed to the floor. He was rushed to Massachusetts General Hospital.

Officially diagnosed as having flu, it was thought he had mixed brandy with barbiturates. A "make up" show was scheduled at tour's end on 1 April.

THURSDAY, 11 MARCH

Madison Square Garden, New York City.

The show was put back a day to allow Keith to fully recover. After the Boston scare, all eyes were on Moon, who had severely cut his foot the previous evening in his suite at the Navarro. Miraculously, he allayed fears by playing with his usual stamina. This time, the Who played only one night at the Garden, because, as Daltrey explained, "[MSG] is such a bad place for rock and roll, and we don't want to prostitute it more than we have to." The group rewarded the packed house with an encore of "Road Runner," "Let's See Action," and "Naked Eye."

SATURDAY, 13 MARCH

Dane County Memorial Coliseum, Madison, Wisconsin.

Local mayor, Paul R. Soglin proclaimed "Who-Mania Day": "I urge all conscientious music lovers,

ABOVE AND RIGHT: THE WHO AT
WINTERLAND, 27 AND 28 MARCH.

whether or not they still have their hearing, to engage
in observance of Who-Mania Day, throughout the
City of Madison."

SUNDAY, 14 MARCH
Civic Center Arena, St. Paul, Minnesota. Rescheduled
from 12 March.

MONDAY, 15 MARCH
Myriad Convention Center, Oklahoma City,
Oklahoma.

TUESDAY, 16 MARCH
Tarrant County Convention Center, Fort Worth,
Texas.

THURSDAY, 18 MARCH
Salt Palace Convention Center, Salt Lake City, Utah.

FRIDAY, 19 MARCH
A show at McNichols Sports Arena, Denver, Colorado,
had to be put back to 30 March due to the Who's
equipment trucks being held up by snowstorms.

SUNDAY, 21 MARCH
Anaheim Stadium, Anaheim, California, with Little
Feat and Rufus and Chaka Khan.
    While in L.A., Pete played guitar on "The
Path," an unissued track from Eric Clapton's *No
Reason To Cry* album sessions at Shangri-La
Studios, Malibu.

WEDNESDAY, 24 MARCH
Memorial Coliseum, Portland, Oregon.

THURSDAY, 25 MARCH
Seattle Center Coliseum, Seattle, Washington.

SATURDAY, 27 and SUNDAY, 28 MARCH
Winterland, San Francisco, California.

TUESDAY, 30 MARCH
McNichols Sports Arena, Denver, Colorado.
Rescheduled from 19 March.

THURSDAY, 1 APRIL
Boston Garden, Boston, Massachusetts. Rescheduled
from 9 March.

SATURDAY, 15 MAY

Telling waiting pressmen of his plans to build his own £200,000 hotel in Bora-Bora, Tahiti (so he could wreck it in peace), Keith flew into London for Who rehearsals at Shepperton.

SATURDAY, 22 MAY

Parc des Expositions, Colmar, France.

TUESDAY, 25 MAY

Palais des Sports, Lyon, France.

MONDAY, 31 MAY

Charlton Athletic Football Ground, London.

The first of three "Who Put The Boot In" shows, supported on each by Widowmaker, the Outlaws, Chapman-Whitney's Streetwalkers, Little Feat, and the Sensational Alex Harvey Band. Marred by incessant rain and crowd violence, the Who's return before 50,000 earned them an entry in the *Guinness Book Of Records* as "World's Loudest Pop Group" with a 120-decibel reading at 50 metres.

Backstage, Norman Gunston (alias zany Australian media personality, Garry McDonald) caught individual chats with Roger, John, and Keith for *The Norman Gunston Show*, his top-rated television comedy show, broadcast over the Australian ABC network on Tuesday, 14 September.

Gunston's interviewing technique (such as it was) involved throwing oddball questions to

Harvey Goldsmith presents

THE WHO
and their friends

Monday 31st May 1976 2.00 p.m. – 10 p.m.
Gates open at 12 noon
see music press for other artists appearing

Tickets
£4.00
inc VAT

CHARLTON ATHLETIC
FOOTBALL CLUB
THE VALLEY
LONDON S.E.7

No re-admission
for conditions see reverse
to be retained and produced
on demand.

No. 015341

confound his celebrity victims. A bearded Moon wasn't playing the game, and emptied a bottle of vodka over Gunston, bellowing "You Australian slag, piss off!"

While in London, Keith was reunited with Lou Reizner to record an inimitable rendition of "When I'm Sixty-Four" for *All This And World War II* at Olympic Studios. An Interglobal Films/VPS production, the film set B&W and colour archive footage of the years before and during World War II to the music of the Beatles, performed by a proverbial kitchen sink of groups and singers, rounded up by Reizner as musical director. These included Ambrosia, Elton John, the Bee Gees, Roy Wood, the Four Seasons, the Brothers Johnson, Status Quo, Rod Stewart, Tina Turner, Leo Sayer, Lynsey De Paul, Jeff Lynne, Henry Gross, Peter Gabriel, Bryan Ferry, and David Essex—all accompanied by the LSO and the Royal Philharmonic. Produced by Sanford Lieberson, directed by Susie Winslow, and edited by Colin Berwick, the film was dubbed and edited at Delta Sound and Lee International Studios, London, in August. Both the movie and accompanying soundtrack album were released through 20th Century Fox in October. The film had a limited run in selected U.K. cinemas the following year as a memoriam to Reizner, who died of stomach cancer at the age of forty-four.

SATURDAY, 5 JUNE

Celtic Football Club, Celtic Park, Glasgow, Scotland.

Backstage, during Alex Harvey's set, a young boy who'd won a Sunday newspaper competition helped Moon destroy the Uncle Ernie pipe organ prop from the *Tommy* movie.

SATURDAY, 12 JUNE

Swansea City Football Club, Vetch Field, Swansea, Wales.

A special train was laid on for those still holding Charlton tickets who'd been denied admission due to overcrowding and ticket forgeries. The concert was engineered by Ron Nevison on the Lane Mobile Studio and material was first transmitted later in the year on Capital Radio's *Your Mother Wouldn't Like It*.

"My Wife" and "Dreaming From The Waist" first officially appeared on the *Thirty Years of Maximum R&B* box set. These, plus "Squeeze Box" and "Behind Blue Eyes," were added as bonus tracks on *The Who By Numbers* remastered CD (1996).

WEDNESDAY, 7— SUNDAY, 11 JULY

A week of events was organised to mark the opening of the Meher Baba Oceanic Centre, set up by Pete at The Boathouse, Ranelagh Drive, Twickenham. Guest of honour was one of Baba's original English devotees, Adi K. Irani.

During the final evening, *Delia*, a Townshend-produced film about follower Delia de Leon, was shown, featuring footage from the *Tommy* premiere, a Baba party at Kew Gardens, and Pete's February visit to India. A half-hour concert featuring Pete on guitar, Billy Nicholls on acoustic, and Steve Humphreys on bass, wound up the festivities.

SUNDAY, 1 AUGUST

The Who checked into the Watergate Hotel, Washington, D.C., before starting a four-date American Whirlwind Tour, covering cities bypassed in March.

TUESDAY, 3 and WEDNESDAY, 4 AUGUST

Capital Center, Largo, Maryland, supported by Law.

SATURDAY, 7 AUGUST

Gator Bowl, Jacksonville, Florida, supported by Law, Black Oak Arkansas, and Labelle.

Roger, John, and Keith caught a delayed chartered

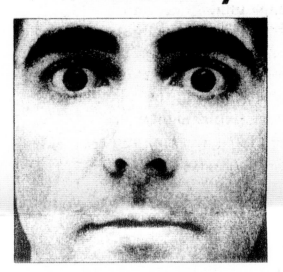

Keith Moon Hospitalized: 'I Felt Dizzy'

But he's out again. Be warned.

MIAMI—The call went out to police as a "41 Baker," August 11th. "41" refers to a sick or injured person; "Baker" means restraining people who are "mentally disturbed."

By the time an ambulance arrived at the Fontainebleau Hotel, Who drummer Keith Moon, the object of the police call, had already collapsed—though not before trashing his room and running around the hotel in what one security guard described as a "very agitated state."

It was the second time Moon had been rushed to an American hospital this year. In March, he collapsed onstage at Boston Garden, two songs into the Who's first show of their March-April tour. At the time, Roger Daltrey blamed Moon's collapse on "the flu," and Moon was able to perform two nights later in Madison Square Garden. The latest collapse occurred two days after the Who's show at Miami's City Baseball Stadium, the fourth date in their three-city minitour.

"I'm fine," Moon reported five days later from his hospital bed at Hollywood (Florida) Memo-

rial Hospital. Talking to Miami disc jockey Dave Ryder, he said, "I don't really remember much about it. I felt dizzy . . . and I just blacked out and woke up here. They [the doctors] said [it was] a breakdown . . . from overwork, pressure, just getting wound up over the shows. I've been working quite steadily over the past two years and eventually it just catches up with you."

Moon was released from the hospital August 19th, and he flew to Los Angeles. Earlier, he'd told Ryder, "I got a house to build in Malibu, so I can't spend much time here."

On the heels of a less-than-sellout tour (including a reported 15,000 at Jacksonville's 70,000-capacity Gator Bowl), the Who are still looking forward to a penciled-in tour this fall. According to one publicity spokesperson, Moon would be "perfectly fit for the forthcoming tour." In the interim, while Moon recuperates in Malibu, Peter Townshend and John Entwistle are on holiday and Roger Daltrey has returned to England to record his next solo album. ♫

flight from Miami; Pete had already arrived from Washington, D.C. Because of the intense heat, only 35,000 showed to a venue capable of holding twice that amount. Despite, or because of this, the Who put on a memorable show.

"Instead of ignoring the circumstances, they reacted to them," wrote *NME* reviewer Al Rudis. "When the Who had taken the stage that night, they weren't performing for the people there. They were performing for the audience that didn't show up. They were playing out the disappointment and resentment, and it was almost a kind of hatred that motivated them." The entourage returned to Miami after the show; the 8th had been set aside as a raindate.

MONDAY, 9 AUGUST
Miami Baseball Stadium, Miami, Florida, with Law, Montrose, and the Outlaws.

The following day was set aside as a raindate, with the possibility of adding an extra show on the 11th also set aside in the event of a sell-out. This didn't occur due to Keith being hospitalised for eight days after collapsing from nervous exhaustion in his hotel suite at the Fontainebleau. "I was drinking two bottles of brandy a day, champagne and wine at night," he said. "My doctor told me if I didn't stop, I'd be dead in three months. Now I'm down to a few glasses a day."

SEPTEMBER
Rough Mix, the joint collaboration between Pete and ex-Small Faces and Faces bassist, Ronnie Lane began in a loose fashion, with the demos being laid down using Lane's Mobile Studio. "I was eager to do something in the studio with our producer Glyn Johns, without the pressure of it being a Who gig," Townshend explained. "When Ronnie came to me and asked me to produce his next album, I said I'd rather do a joint album."

SATURDAY, 18 SEPTEMBER
Keith and Ron Wood were guest presenters at the *2nd Annual Rock Music Awards*, hosted by Diana Ross and Alice Cooper, broadcast live from the Hollywood Palladium, Los Angeles, 10:30–11:00 pm on CBS.

In England, Eric Clapton appeared as a guest, playing the dobro at country-and-western singer Don Williams' concert at the Hammersmith Odeon. Backstage, he introduced Williams to Pete and Ronnie Lane. Williams' hit, "Till The Rivers All Run Dry," was subsequently covered on *Rough Mix*. An enthusiastic Clapton asked promoter Harvey Goldsmith to organise a series of Christmas shows (which proved to be

ABOVE: BACKSTAGE AT THE HAMMERSMITH ODEON, 18 SEPTEMBER. CLOCKWISE FROM LEFT ARE RONNIE LANE, DON WILLIAMS, PETE, ERIC CLAPTON, AND DANNY FLOWERS, DON WILLIAMS' GUITARIST.

ill-fated) at the venue, with Townshend and Lane among the guests.

Townshend later discussed his introduction to Williams and country-and-western music with Melvyn Bragg in the second programme of London Weekend Television's long-running arts series, *The South Bank Show*, transmitted 10:15–11:15 pm, over the ITV region, 18 March, 1978.

FRIDAY, 24 SEPTEMBER

The Story Of the Who was released by Polydor. The sleeve image of a pinball machine exploding was taken from a television advertisement to promote the double album. Due to litigation, many crucial tracks were excluded, but it still charted at #2.

"It's not really a story of the Who," said John. "It was just a case of whatever tracks we could get on it, tracks we actually owned. We're still going through this thing with Shel Talmy, so we had to sort of skirt around a bit. I think it caters to the new breed of fan who hasn't got the old material."

"Substitute" B/W "I'm A Boy" and "Pictures Of Lily" was extracted in both 7-inch and 12-inch formats, the first 12-inch maxi-single to be released in the U.K. on 22 October. "It's amazing that 'Substitute' got back in the charts," said John. "I got a kick out of it because we didn't have to do *Top Of The Pops*—they used a film instead." The clip in question, extracted from *2nd House* (see 18 May, 1974), was shown 4 November, helping push the single to #7.

MONDAY, 4 OCTOBER

The Who flew into Phoenix to begin the last American leg of the year-long tour, supported by Mother's Finest. A full rehearsal involving band and crew took place at Veterans Memorial Coliseum the following day.

WEDNESDAY, 6 OCTOBER

Veterans Memorial Coliseum, Phoenix, Arizona.

THURSDAY, 7 OCTOBER

Sports Arena, San Diego, California.

SATURDAY, 9 and
SUNDAY, 10 OCTOBER

Alameda County Stadium, Oakland, California.

"Day On The Green" shows with the Grateful Dead, promoted by Bill Graham. The 11th and 12th were set aside as raindates. Gates opened at 9:00 am, with the Dead on stage at 11:00 am.

Over two days, the Who played before 93,000 fans.

WEDNESDAY, 13 OCTOBER
Memorial Coliseum, Portland, Oregon.

THURSDAY, 14 OCTOBER
Seattle Center Coliseum, Seattle, Washington.

SATURDAY, 16 OCTOBER
Northlands Coliseum, Edmonton, Alberta, Canada.

The Who flew in during the afternoon and travelled on to Winnipeg the following day.

MONDAY, 18 OCTOBER
Winnipeg Arena, Winnipeg, Manitoba, Canada.

THURSDAY, 21 OCTOBER
Maple Leaf Gardens, Toronto, Canada.

Keith Moon's last official show, before an audience of 20,000. An end-of-tour party was thrown at the Hyatt Regency, which left an impression on Pete. "The road crew had thrown a party for us, and it happened to be the first party I had been to for at least five years that meant anything to me," he wrote the following year. "I don't go to a lot of parties as a rule, but I'm glad I made this one. I suddenly realised that behind a Who show are people who care as much as, or more than, we do. It enabled me, talking to the individuals who help get the show together, to remember the audiences care too."

A second night in Toronto booked for the 22nd was cancelled, as was a show in Montreal on the 23rd (due in no small part to the Who's previous troubles there—see 2 December, 1973.) A provisional date was set, for a third Toronto concert on the 24th but that show never came to be.

SATURDAY, 23 OCTOBER
The English press announced that Keith was getting hitched to his girlfriend, Swedish model Annette Walter-Lax, with Pete as best man, in Los Angeles on 15 December. Keith had bought a $15,000 gold ring from Tiffany's, announcing, "I've finally met a woman who loves everything I do and claps in all

the right places." Three of the four ex-Beatles were set to attend, and a special jet had been chartered to fly guests from London. Typical of the chaos surrounding Keith, Annette hadn't even been informed, and the so-called wedding was postponed only five days beforehand. (The two remained a couple.)

NOVEMBER
Sessions commenced at Ramport for Roger's third solo album, *One Of The Boys*, produced by Dave Courtney and Tony Meehan over the original choice of Jerry Leiber and Mike Stoller. Songs were contributed by Paul McCartney, Steve Gibbons, Andy Pratt, Colin Blunstone, Paul Korda, and Philip Goodhand-Tait. Three tracks were co-written by Daltrey and Courtney: "Satin and Lace," "Doing It All Again" and "The Prisoner," inspired by armed robber John McVicar's autobiography, *By Himself*, to which the Who's management had acquired the movie rights. Roger invited students from the local Battersea technical school to film the sessions as an educational project.

MONDAY, 1 – MONDAY, 15 NOVEMBER
Rough Mix recording sessions at Olympic Studios, under the original working title *April Fools* (See September, 1976.) The album was produced and engineered by Glyn Johns and his assistant engineer, Jon Astley, Pete's brother-in-law.

Guest musicians at these initial sessions included Eric Clapton (lead and acoustic guitar, dobro), John "Rabbit" Bundrick (organ, piano, Fender Rhodes), Ian 'Stu' Stewart (piano), Boz Burrell (bass), and Henry Spinetti (drums).

MONDAY, 6 DECEMBER—FRIDAY, 25 MARCH, 1977
Shooting schedule at Paramount Studios, Hollywood, for *Sextette*, starring eighty-three-year-old movie star, Mae West in her last-ever role, as Marlo Manners. Keith cameoed as Roger, a campy dress designer. Produced by Dan Briggs and Bob Sullivan, directed by Ken Hughes, and executive produced by Warner G. Toub, the film was based on West's original stage play. The all-star vehicle featured Timothy Dalton, George Raft, Dom DeLuise, Tony Curtis, Ringo Starr, Alice Cooper, George Hamilton, Rona Barrett, and Keith Allison. The movie, an unmitigated box-office disaster, was given a limited American cinema release in 1978.

For all the momentum gained

from the previous year, Pete

Townshend was determined that

his family, his hearing, and his

sanity should come first. Always

eager to communicate whatever

thoughts or theories gripped him,

he uncharacteristically turned

down all interview requests,

retreating for most of the year into

Twickenham domesticity in

between writing songs for the next

Who album. While Britain was

gripped by Jubilee madness and

punk rock, the Who remained idle,

until they finally reconvened, with-

out fanfare, in September.

As far as Pete was concerned, there was to be no talk of live shows, and during a group business meeting, he made this point official. Surprisingly, Roger was understanding and sympathetic to his reasons. To Keith and John, touring was their lifeblood, but it was a Catch-22 situation. Moon was so visibly out of condition that live work would have proved almost a physical impossibility.

At the start of the year, both Roger and Pete completed solo endeavours they had begun the previous year. Although critically acclaimed as his best effort to date, Daltrey's third solo album, *One Of The Boys*, failed to garner the same commercial success as its predecessors. He declined a lucrative offer to perform two Stateside solo shows, saying he "wouldn't be able to provide the same passion as he did for Who shows."

Pete released *Rough Mix*, his acclaimed collaboration with fellow Baba lover Ronnie Lane. Despite their status as spiritual godfathers to the nascent punk scene, the album was light years away from the prevailing spirit of visceral energy and raw adrenaline—though not to its detriment. Townshend's songs were in a much lighter, upbeat vein than the

outpouring of bile on *The Who By Numbers*. Although originally coerced into collaborating by Lane, the album stands as a testament to both songwriters' skills and Glyn Johns' ability to draw the best from each. In April, Pete made a surprise onstage appearance at the Rainbow with Eric Clapton, who'd guested on *Rough Mix*.

While John laid low in his home studio, Keith slid into the terminal stages of decline, overindulging in every vice the City of Angels had to offer. Pete later revealed that he would ring in the early hours just to say goodnight and to tell him that he loved him. "Yeah, but you're still a pain in the arse," was the guitarist's typical response. Once when ringing collect, Moon fell asleep mid conversation. Sensing their chat was over, Pete put the receiver down, but forgot to replace it properly. Eight hours later, when his wife Karen tried to make a call, Pete found he was still footing a considerable bill for Moon's transatlantic snores. An apocryphal story perhaps, but one that illustrates the misery Moon felt and how desperately he missed his bandmates. Apart from a recent cameo as Roger, a gay dress designer in the all-star turkey *Sextette*, his much-trumpeted movie career had come to nothing, thanks to his unpredictable behaviour. Between periods of attempted detoxification, he continued to run wild.

The protracted legal wrangling between the Who and their former managers, Kit Lambert and Chris Stamp, was finally settled in January following a lengthy business meeting in a Poland Street office. "Back when the trouble first started between the band and myself and Kit," Stamp recalled, "David Platz [of Essex Music, Townshend's publishers] panicked and had gone and sold some of his shares in Pete's American publishing, behind his back, to a company owned by Allen Klein, which Klein to this day still owns."

To find his nemesis was involved in the negotiations was the final straw. A full settlement of £575,000 was arrived at for Townshend's U.S. copyrights to date, along with an additional sum covering back royalties. The rights to the Who's recordings would revert to the Who group of companies. (Lambert and Stamp came out with virtually nothing, and Track Records went into liquidation the following year.) Pete now had more control over his catalogue, but it felt like a hollow victory. He went straight to the Speakeasy, with Stamp in tow, intent on obliterating himself. In the murk, he found two of the Sex Pistols. Townshend launched into his usual tirade about the corrupt state of the rock business and how the Who had compromised their position, insisting that these young upstarts should finish the job once and for all. Instead of confrontation or debate, Pete was dismayed to find both were Who fans. "'Ere, the 'Oo aren't breaking up, are they Pete?" drummer Paul Cook innocently inquired. "We love 'em, don't we, Steve?" Guitarist Steve Jones voiced his agreement. This only made it worse. Pete took his publishing cheque, tore it into shreds, and staggered into the West End night, later getting roused in a Soho doorway by a young policeman who recognised him. If he could stand up and walk away, he wouldn't be run in, he was told.

Although absent from the stage, Townshend and Daltrey made regular media appearances to plug solo work. After two years, both were gearing up for the next Who album, and Pete took the opportunity to preview some of the demos for his new songs over Capital Radio's airwaves. (Townshend later revealed most of these were originally destined for a projected update of *Lifehouse*.)

"Who Are You," a song that had been kicking around for a year, described that day of teeth-pulling business foibles and his memorable encounter with the Sex Pistols. In September, with the resumption of Who business, Keith bid L.A. adieu and moved back to Britain and into Ramport with Glyn Johns and his assistant, Jon Astley (Pete's brother-in-law, who'd worked on *Rough Mix*), to commence recording *Who Are You*.

Behind the scenes the group invested a considerable amount in buying a stake of Shepperton Film Studios, where they regularly rehearsed and recorded.

It was at Shepperton where the band assembled in July to shoot footage intended for their first self-financed cinematic venture. *The Kids Are Alright*, directed by long-term Who freak Jeff Stein, was to be an authorised biopic of the group's career, combining a wealth of archive footage with newly filmed material. The shooting schedule went overtime and overbudget, resulting in much acrimony, but ultimately, the results were to prove far more rewarding than a vehicle like *Tommy*, even though the films were radically different in nature.

Requiring quality footage of certain tracks otherwise unavailable, a hastily arranged concert took place at North London's Kilburn State Gaumont on 15 December. The effects of brandy consumption and not having played together onstage for more than a year were immediately apparent. Townshend repeatedly voiced his disapproval at proceedings. "There's a guitar up 'ere if any bigmouthed little git wants to come and fucking take it off me!" he snarled, climaxing a familiar setlist by hurling his Les Paul aloft. They would have to do better than that....

JANUARY—MARCH

Roger completed and mixed *One Of The Boys* at Ramport. Because of tax complications, all vocals were recorded at EMI's Pathe Marconi Studios in Paris. Featured musicians were Rod Argent (keyboards), Brian Odgers and John Entwistle (bass), Phil Kenzie and Jimmy Jewell (sax), Andy Fairweather-Low (backing vocals/guitar), Stuart Tosh (drums), and a host of guest guitarists including Eric Clapton, Alvin Lee, Jimmy McCulloch, Paul Keogh, Hank Marvin, and Mick Ronson. Clapton's contribution (taped 24 January) was not used thanks to Daltrey's gift, a barrel of Fuller's Superstrong Ale, being consumed by "Slowhand" and his men during the session.

ABOVE: RONNIE LANE AND PETE.

Pete and Ronnie Lane's *Rough Mix* collaboration continued at Olympic Studios, with guest musicians including Charlie Watts (drums), John Entwistle (bass, brass), Peter Hope Evans (harmonica), Mel Collins (sax), Charlie Hart (violin), Benny Gallagher (accordion), and Graham Lyle (acoustic guitar).

The orchestral accompaniment to "Street In The City" was scored by Pete's father-in-law, Edwin Astley. Townshend and Lane played and sang together on just three tracks: "Rough Mix," "Heart To Hang Onto," and "Till The Rivers All Run Dry," featuring vocal support from Billy Nicholls and John Entwistle.

THURSDAY, 20 JANUARY

A tired, emotional (and very drunk) Pete turned up at the Speakeasy to see John Otway perform. As Pete recalled: "'Who Are You' was the product of one particular day on which two things happened: I met the Sex Pistols, and I discovered that somehow Allen Klein had managed to buy into my American publishing. It was an eleven-hour meeting in this Poland Street office, and I left with a seven-figure cheque feeling angry and frustrated. I was with Chris Stamp, and we went to the Speakeasy and lo and behold, two of the Sex Pistols [guitarist Steve Jones and drummer Paul Cook] were there."

In his inebriated state, Pete mistook Cook for lead singer Johnny Rotten. A scuffle occurred when Townshend attempted to physically prevent *NME* photographer Steve Davis taking pictures, assuming some kind of set-up. "He thinks he's past it," Cook said later, "but he ain't really. He's still great." "He was a really great geezer," agreed Jones, "even though he was like, paralytic."

SATURDAY, 5 FEBRUARY

Roger appeared on *Jim'll Fix It*, a popular BBC-1 series (screened 5:45—6:20 pm) in which celebrity DJ Jimmy Savile helps to fulfil a child's wild ambition. Since she couldn't see the restricted film, youngster Sally Anne Pearson had written in, wanting to meet "Tommy." Roger was happy to oblige and an insert was filmed on his Burwash estate, intercut with the "I'm Free" sequence from the movie.

SATURDAY, 12 MARCH

The *NME* reported rumoured plans for the Who to headline a season of nine concerts at the Rainbow Theatre to coincide with the Queen's Silver Jubilee

ABOVE: JOHN WOLFF AND "LIGHT FANTASTIC."

celebrations, set for either late May or early June. Who publicist Keith Altham commented: "They have a very busy time ahead in the studios, with a new Who album and various solo LPs to make, and I've heard nothing about London concerts. But that doesn't mean they won't do them!"

Who lighting engineer John Wolff was currently experimenting with holograms to project a 3-D laser image of the group into the air and onto an audience. His pioneering exhibition "Light Fantastic," costing £750,000, ran at London's Royal Academy of Art 14 March—7 April.

THURSDAY, 21 and FRIDAY, 22 APRIL

A promotional film for "One Of The Boys" was directed by Tony Klinger on location around West London, starring Roger and actress Madeline Smith. Daltrey tucked his long tresses under a wig to pose as a Teddy boy, a Hell's Angel, a skinhead, and a punk rocker, complete with safety pin through nostril!

Each sequence required forty-minute make-up calls at Lee International Studios, where parts of *Tommy* had been filmed. Klinger had made promo clips for Deep Purple and was associate producer on

ABOVE: ROGER AS A PUNK, 21 APRIL.

such feature films as *Gold* and *Shout At The Devil*. The "One Of The Boys" promo received the ultimate exposure by being blown up and shown as a short along with *Star Wars* across America that summer. Thanks to his work with Daltrey, Klinger and producer Sydney Rose were selected by Bill Curbishley to work on *The Kids Are Alright*. (See 30 May.)

FRIDAY, 29 APRIL

Pete appeared as an unannounced guest at Eric Clapton's Rainbow concert, playing guitar on "Layla" and the encore, "Crossroads."

WEDNESDAY, 4 MAY

From 9:00 to 11:00 pm, Roger appeared live on Capital Radio's *Your Mother Wouldn't Like It*, promoting *One Of The Boys*, released Friday, 20 May.

As well as being interviewed by host Nicky Horne, Roger exhibited good taste by selecting the following as his "Desert Island Discs": Larry Williams ("Short Fat Fannie" and "Bony Maronie"), Eddie Cochran ("C'mon Everybody"), Jerry Lee Lewis ("Great Balls Of Fire"), Creedence Clearwater Revival ("Born On The Bayou"), the Ronettes ("The Best Part Of Breaking Up"), the Kinks ("All Day And All Of The Night"), Buddy Holly ("Rave On"), and the

Big Bopper ("Chantilly Lace"). He finished by taking listeners' calls, the last questioning Daltrey's recent decision to turn down a lucrative half-million-dollar offer for two Stateside solo concerts.

Roger also pre-recorded an interview with Stuart Grundy for Radio 1's *Rock On*, broadcast Saturday, 7 May, 1:31—2:30 pm.

SATURDAY, 28 MAY

The *NME* reported that after two weeks of widespread speculation, the Who had rejected an offer to headline an open-air concert being staged in the grounds of Longleat House in September. "The Who are still working out exactly when they'll be recording their new album," said Keith Altham, "and until that is sorted out, it's impossible to fix any dates. So regretfully, they've had to decline Longleat and it now seems they won't be making any live appearances in Britain this summer."

MONDAY, 30 MAY

Production started on *The Kids Are Alright*, directed by Jeff Stein and produced by Tony Klinger and Bill Curbishley for the Who's company, Rock Films Ltd. Executive Producer: Sydney Rose. Editor: Ed Rothkowitz.

Stein, a twenty-two-year-old New York filmmaker specialising in commercials, initially approached Pete in March 1975, with the idea of a Who biopic. A year later, after the group viewed a seventeen-minute showreel that met with their approval, Stein was given the go-ahead. A forty-eight week schedule was allocated, with an initial budget pegged at £300,000. The first weeks were occupied in locating film library material in London, Los Angeles, and New York.

THURSDAY, 23 JUNE

Keith guested with Led Zeppelin during their six-night stand at the Inglewood Forum, Los Angeles. He appeared during drummer John Bonham's lengthy "Moby Dick" drum solo, hammering away on a spare timpani and again during the encores. "I'll be back at the Forum later in the year with my back-up band," he informed the sell-out audience.

MONDAY, 11 JULY

The Who began rehearsing at Shepperton Film Studios. The band invested a £350,000 stake in the old manor house, the core of the site, and two acres of property, planning extensive renovations that

ABOVE: KEITH AND ZEP, AT THE INGLEWOOD FORUM, 23 JUNE.

would cost several hundred thousand pounds. To date, they had spent around a million pounds developing laser and video equipment and intended to hire the studios out to other artists wanting to make use of the facilities.

During the first week of rehearsal, Roger shot a mimed promotional video for his latest solo single, "Say It Ain't So Joe" featuring John and a topless, overweight Keith among the backing band.

WEDNESDAY, 20 JULY

The first day's shooting on *The Kids Are Alright* at Shepperton, 2:00–8:00 pm.

Each member was filmed arriving at the complex (Roger flew in by helicopter from Sussex) and rehearsing on J Stage.

Songs rehearsed: "The Real Me," "Bell Boy," "The Kids Are Alright" (one take turning into a reggae version!), The Newbeats' "Run, Baby, Run," "Smokestack Lightning / Spoonful," "God Knows" (an instrumental), and "Won't Get Fooled Again."

THURSDAY, 21 JULY

Second day of shooting *The Kids Are Alright* at Shepperton. A sequence featuring Keith was first to be filmed, showing him arriving in a hired fire truck, dressed as a fireman, and entering the studio through a wall of coloured smoke from several sulphur bombs let off inside by technicians. The madcap scene continued to show Keith clambering onto the stage and playing a demented solo enveloped amid the dense smoke (this was cut from the finished production).

Stein's cameras again captured the group's separate arrivals and various discussions within the studio booth, while listening to playbacks. Songs rehearsed: "Who Are You," "Baba O'Riley," "Shakin' All Over," Cliff Richard and the Shadows' "Travellin' Light," the Beatles' "I Saw Her Standing There," and "Water." Jan and Dean's "Barbara Ann" from this day's rehearsal was seen in the movie, as was part of a humorous dialogue between Keith and Pete about the state of the latter's hearing.

MONDAY, 8—FRIDAY, 12 AUGUST

A week-long shoot in Los Angeles, filming Keith's scenes for *The Kids Are Alright*.

MONDAY, 8 AUGUST

Filming at the Moon residence at 31504 Victoria Point Road, Malibu, was delayed until early afternoon because the master of the house was still asleep. Keith sat answering questions on how he saw the Who's future, without a hint of seriousness. When finally asked for the truth by crewman Pete Nevard, Keith soberly snapped to attention: "The truth as you want to hear it?... You couldn't afford me!" Additional filming took place on Malibu Beach, including an unscripted moment when Keith and assistant Dougal Butler threw executive producer Sydney Rose into the ocean fully clothed and held him underwater. Returning to the house, Stein filmed Rose blowdrying $6000 of production money. Keith then dressed up in biker gear, with a lifesize blow-up doll spread out on the kitchen table. Another scene, featuring Keith playing cards with Annette and Rick Danko of the Band, had to

be deleted as Danko never signed a release form. By then, it was too late to remove his name from the film's credits.

TUESDAY, 9 AUGUST

Filming was again disrupted by Keith's nocturnal habits, so the crew filmed him asleep in bed as their first set-up. Interviews continued in the lounge throughout the afternoon.

WEDNESDAY, 10 AUGUST

Unused scenes of Keith's night life were shot outside The Crazy Horse and Alice's Restaurant. Location filming then moved to The Pleasure Chest, an erotic emporium. The scene featuring Keith dressed in various bondage paraphernalia with Mary Ann Zabresky as a dominatrix—"what's your opinion of your public image?"—was shot inside the dungeon, as was a link for the "Barbara Ann" Shepperton sequence. (See 20 July.)

THURSDAY, 11 AUGUST

A raucous party to celebrate Keith's upcoming birthday was arranged in the evening at Trancas Restaurant and Bar, Malibu. While Who tapes blared, a giant cake with a special "Jack in the Box" spring was wheeled in, from which a hired stripper popped out to Keith's undisguised delight. An ordinary cake was then presented, which he karate chopped in half, spreading the resulting mess over himself, the girl, and the carpets, causing $100 worth of damage.

FRIDAY, 12 AUGUST

During the early afternoon, Keith was filmed walking along Malibu Beach, proclaiming loudly as Julius Caesar. A swift costume change and Keith was in his Robert Newton pirate outfit as Long John Silver, complete with rubber parrot perched on his shoulder, which fell off mid-shot. A scene with a dead chicken prop was not used. Filming moved back inside the house when Ringo Starr and his children arrived. (Keith was filmed phoning Starr, inviting him to participate on the 8th.) Ringo quizzed Keith on camera about the group ("I've just been sitting in"), the other members, and his hotel exploits for several hours, though most of it was not used. With this in the can, the American shoot was completed.

LATE AUGUST

Over two days at CBS Studios, Hollywood, Keith rehearsed and videotaped a guest segment for *Rolling Stone...The 10th Anniversary*, a two-hour television special, networked and simulcast in FM stereo on Friday 25 November. Keith appeared in a ten-minute "Life In The Fast Lane" segment, describing one of his over-the-top hotel escapades to Phoebe Snow, Melissa Manchester, and Billy Preston. This segued into a hotel-wrecking sketch before a studio audience with *Saturday Night Live* comedian Steve Martin. The segment appeared, in edited form, in *The Kids Are Alright*. Made on a million dollar budget by producer Steve Binder, the special also featured Jerry Lee Lewis, Richie Havens, Art Garfunkel, Sissy Spacek, Bette Midler, and Gladys Knight and the Pips.

MONDAY, 12 SEPTEMBER

Prior to recording after a two year layoff, Keith moved from Los Angeles back to London for Who rehearsals. "It took awhile for the band to get together again in a studio situation," Keith told Scott Muni the following August. "We'd always been on the road and come into the studio and been able to get the albums done. But there'd been this delay, when we hadn't worked together closely as a band. Eventually, we had to go down to Shepperton just to find out how to be the Who again, and then we could go into the studio."

FRIDAY, 16 SEPTEMBER

Rough Mix by Pete Townshend and Ronnie Lane was released. "When it boils down to it," said Townshend, "this is one thing this album is about, after ten years of the bloody rock business with its corruption, rip-offs, everything else. People fleecing us, stealing from us, screwing us, exploiting us, insulting us. After all that we get together, do an album, we enjoy it, and it's good music. That's really all we care about."

MONDAY, 19 SEPTEMBER

Rehearsals commenced at Ramport prior to recording *Who Are You*. Initially produced by Glyn Johns, assistant engineer Jon Astley completed the task after Johns opted out in the New Year, ostensibly due to a prior commitment to produce Joan Armatrading. Additional overdubs were recorded by Pete and Astley at Eel Pie Sound, Goring. Pete's father-in-law,

Edwin Astley, overdubbed the string arrangements in December. Final mixing occurred the following April, but the recording period took only about a month in actual studio time. Rod Argent played piano on "Who Are You," "Love Is Coming Down," and synthesiser on "Had Enough."

MONDAY, 26 SEPTEMBER

Pete and Ronnie Lane were interviewed in Studio A, Television Centre by Bob Harris for BBC-2's *The Old Grey Whistle Test*, broadcast the following evening, 11:15—11:55 pm. The seven-minute segment was preceded by film inserts of the Boomtown Rats and the Dictators illustrating the "New Wave" of bands from both sides of the Atlantic. (Townshend preferred the former.) "Rough Mix" was played (cut to unrelated Filmfinders footage) and several humourous references to future Who keyboardist, John "Rabbit" Bundrick, were made within his earshot. (Bundrick's band, Crawler, were waiting to close the programme.)

MONDAY, 3 OCTOBER

A pre-recorded interview with Pete to promote *Rough Mix* was broadcast on Capital Radio's *Your Mother Wouldn't Like It*. "I get ten offers a week to produce punk bands," he snorted, indicating he had no desire of taking any up. Of the Who, he said, "although I love the band, we've got to the end of what we can do."

SATURDAY, 15 OCTOBER

Pete appeared on Radio 1's *Rock On*, broadcast 1:31—2:30 pm, via a pre-recorded interview with Stuart Grundy at Broadcasting House to plug *The Story Of Tommy* book. Co-written with Richard Barnes and published by Townshend's own company, Eel Pie Publishing, he revealed he originally began making notes on the film set with Ken Russell.

MONDAY, 24 and THURSDAY, 27 OCTOBER

Recording/mixing: "New Song," with backing vocals by Andy Fairweather-Low and Billy Nicholls.

During this time, a playback of "Sister Disco" made Roger and Glyn Johns come to blows. "Pete and I had spent the weekend at Goring preparing the synthesised strings," explained Jon Astley. "We thought it sounded great, but Roger thought it was over-produced and said so. Glyn made a remark back and the next thing, they were out in the studio hall fighting."

MONDAY, 31 OCTOBER

Pete appeared being interviewed at his Twickenham home by Jeremy Paxman on BBC-1's current affairs programme *Tonight*, broadcast 11:15—11:55 pm. Illustrated with clips of "My Generation" from *All My Loving* (see 10 March, 1968), plus "Sensation" and "Welcome" from the *Tommy* film, Townshend discussed how his music was influenced by his own frustration and later, the audience's frustration, as well as guitar and hotel smashing, drugs, the New Wave, and politics. "I'm a desperate old fart now," he told Paxman. "Not boring though!"

MONDAY, 7 NOVEMBER

Pete appeared again on Capital Radio's *Your Mother Wouldn't Like It*, broadcast 9:00—11:00 pm. As well as being interviewed by Nicky Horne, the demos for "Sister Disco," "Who Are You," "Love Is Coming Down," and an unreleased song, "Like It The Way It Is," were previewed behind the station's company jingle, in an unsuccessful attempt to deter bootlegging.

MONDAY, 14 NOVEMBER

Twenty-four weeks in, production work on *The Kids Are Alright* moved from America to Shepperton. The group rehearsed in preparation for filming scheduled to take place at the Gaumont State, Kilburn, on 15 December.

MONDAY, 21 NOVEMBER

Keith took journalist Chris Welch to school with a crash course on punk rock for a *Melody Maker* article, accompanied by press agent Keith Altham, manager Bill Curbishley, driver Richard Dorse, and Billy Idol and Tony James of Generation X. Introduced by mutual friend, producer Phil Wainman, at a Chrysalis reception, Keith had recently sat in with the group when he and Graham Chapman dropped in to their Atlanta rehearsal studio in Chalk Farm. Always the showman, Moon insisted the party drive the short distance from the Marquee Club down Wardour Street to the Vortex Club in his pink Rolls Royce. "This is style," he shouted at the orderly queuing punks as he boisterously shoved his way into the club.

MONDAY, 12 DECEMBER

Pete and Keith went to the Vortex, where Wayne County and the Electric Chairs, Backlash, and the Skunks were appearing. The latter Brixton band impressed Townshend to the extent that he had 2000 copies of their single, "Good From The Bad" B/W

"Back Street Fightin'," pressed and distributed at his own expense, as the debut release on his Eel Pie label the following June.

TUESDAY, 13 DECEMBER

Pete broke his silence, granting a rare interview to American journalist Dave Schulps of *Trouser Press*, in which he categorically stated his intention of not touring with the Who in the foreseeable future. Later, he, Roger, and John (Keith was absent with a hangover) listened to playbacks at Ramport. Daltrey also overdubbed his vocal on "Who Are You"; the backing track had been cut in October.

WEDNESDAY, 14 DECEMBER

The Who and crew spent the afternoon rehearsing at the Gaumont State, Kilburn, North West London, in readiness for the following day's film shoot. Keith astounded the others by appearing in his planned stage outfit, a tight-fitting, puce-coloured, rhinestone-bedecked tap dancing suit made especially for

ABOVE: KILBURN REHEARSAL, 14 DECEMBER.
LEFT: KEITH WITH CHRIS WELCH, 21 NOVEMBER.

him in Nashville. "All my other clothes are at the cleaners," he quipped.

During a break, Roger told Schulps: "I can't wait to get back on stage again... Every time I get out on a stage I want to go back. That's what rock's about, especially the 'Oo. I mean, Pete has bad problems with his ears, it's true, but we all want to go back. We'll work on him!"

THURSDAY, 15 DECEMBER

Gaumont State Cinema, Kilburn, London. A privately staged 75-minute concert at this 2000 seat theatre, filmed on 16-mm for *The Kids Are Alright*.

A single, vague announcement made during the morning on Capital Radio brought more than 800 people to the venue within half an hour, despite it stating that only 500 would be admitted. Producer Tony Klinger had to phone Capital and officially deny his own story, asking that nobody else show up. Having been absent from the concert stage for more than a year, unsurprisingly, virtually nothing was used by Jeff Stein in the finished film.

Post-gig, Stein's cameras risked all by continuing to film the surly group backstage, climbing the stairs and in their dressing room, seen during the end credits sequence. "My Wife" was used for *The Kids Are Alright* soundtrack but did not appear in the film.

not to be taken away 1978

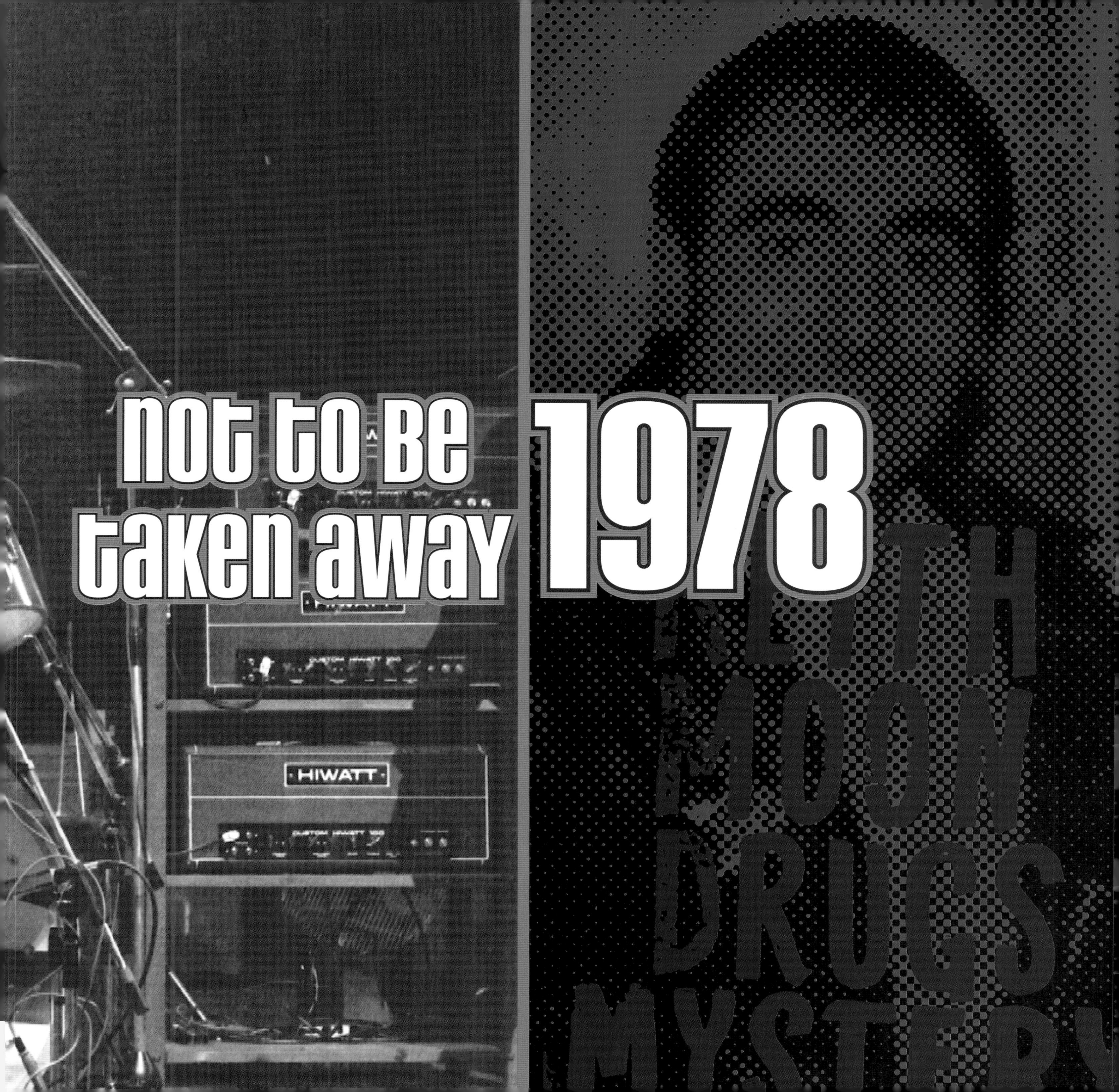

If the Who had gone to ground throughout "the summer of hate," which punk rock came to symbolise, 1978 promised a renewal. The group were preparing to release their first album in three years, had film projects in the pipeline, and Pete permitting, there was even talk of touring. However, all these events were to be overshadowed by a sudden but not entirely unexpected tragedy.

While John mixed the soundtrack to *The Kids Are Alright*, the protracted recording sessions for *Who Are You* finally staggered their way to an unsteady conclusion. Despite being one of the few to escape the barbed criticism the New Wave was directing at his contemporaries, Pete had written songs with slick arrangements and glossy production (tailored for U.S. radio, according to co-producer Jon Astley). After the relative simplicity of *By Numbers*, *Who Are You* saw an unexpected return to the grandiose arrangements of *Quadrophenia*. Only the album's title track retained some of the Who *sturm und drang* of old. John contributed an unprecedented three tracks, one of which, "905," was salvaged from a science fiction opera he'd been working on at some length. Roger recorded his vocals away from the unproductive carousing, in between filming a supporting role in an undistinguished horror flick, *The Legacy*. Above all, the sessions revealed the extent to which Keith had let himself go, his lost L.A. sojourn extracting a high physical price. At one point, troubles with a difficult time signature prompted his now infamous quip, "I'm probably the best Keith Moon-type drummer in the world." Not in the best of conditions himself, Townshend issued a blunt ultimatum to shape up or ship out, but he knew his threat held no water. How could the Who survive without Keith Moon?

As a result of the group's growing business interests, Keith was installed as director of promotion and publicity for the Who Group Ltd. It was hoped the role would give him a new sense of purpose.

The Kids Are Alright was wrapped up, bar the final concert sequence. Due to the poor results Kilburn had generated, another private show was hastily arranged at Shepperton on 25 May for the benefit of Jeff Stein's cameras. This time, things came together. Pete's undeniable enthusiasm at being back on the boards is evident in the final print. He leapt, windmilled, and executed a floor slide that was the envy of the invited punks in the audience. Roger was in fine voice, while John's musicianship simply astounded. Despite his condition, Keith gamely kept up behind his outsized kit. Climaxing a transcendent "Won't Get Fooled Again," he jumped unsteadily into Pete's outstretched arms. Warm hugs, an audience acknowledgement, and the show was over. Little did anyone realise its significance.

On 7 August, the Who's original publicist Pete Meaden was found dead. The news came as a shock, particularly to Pete. Thanks to Meaden's recommendation, Townshend had got Roger and Bill Curbishley involved with the Steve Gibbons Band and apparently thought nothing of giving his original mentor a generous sum each year as an undying debt of gratitude. (Sadly, he was to suffer the loss of his most important muse on 7 April, 1981, when Kit Lambert died of head injuries sustained from a fall down his mother's staircase.)

Several days before Meaden's death, Pete and Keith had attended the opening of a celebratory "Who's Who" exhibition at London's Institute of Contemporary Arts.

On 6 September, Keith attended a star-studded reception at Peppermint Park, London, with girlfriend Annette to mark "Buddy Holly Week," an annual event thrown by Paul McCartney. Making their excuses, the couple returned early to their Mayfair flat, where Keith fell asleep after consuming an excess of heminevrin, a prescribed drug aiding alcohol withdrawal that should have been taken under supervision. He'd inadvertently swallowed a staggering thirty-two sedatives, although more sensationalistic reports claim he choked on his own vomit. Ironically, Keith died at a time when it seemed like he was curbing his excessive lifestyle. With this in mind, it's poignant to consider the way he died—by his normal standards, he would have at least taken a hotel with him!

Pete was at his Eel Pie studio with Baba associate Billy Nicholls when the afternoon call came through from Jackie Curbishley, Bill's wife and partner in Trinifold, the Who's management company. Such was Townshend's stoic poise that Nicholls only heard the news after returning home. Pete's conversation with Roger left no room for misinterpretation: "'He's gone and done it.' 'Done what?' 'Moon.'" Journalist Raja Prem and photographer Mick Oliver were interviewing John for the Irish rock paper *Hot Press* when he was called away to the phone on two occasions. The conversation carried on as normal until the indomitable Ox façade cracked when asked about the Who's future. The following day's newspapers carried eulogies for the "wild man of rock" and "Moon the Loon": tributes to an unparalled life of eccentric hell-raising. Few bothered to mention just what an incredible and instinctive musician he was. That same day, the remaining members of the band emerged from a lengthy meeting with a prepared statement: "The Who? We are more determined than ever to carry on, and we want the spirit of the group to which Keith contributed so much to go on..."

For many, however, the death of Keith Moon could only signal the end to one of rock and roll's longest, most exhilarating, and most unlikely soap operas. In Keith's own somewhat prophetic words from 1972, "Once we feel we've achieved all we can together, then there's no point in carrying on, because we'd have nothing more to give..."

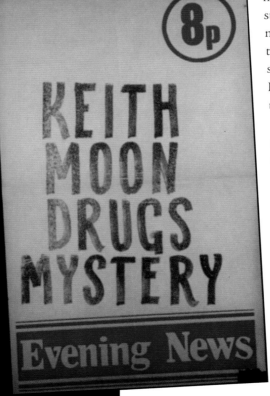

JANUARY—MARCH

Production on *Who Are You* was hampered due to various calamities. In February, Pete injured his hand during a family argument and was unable to play guitar for a month. Roger, who recorded his vocal tracks in the others' absence, was out for a fortnight after a throat infection required an operation. Meanwhile, John, as Musical Director, worked into the early hours at Studio Four, CTS Studios, Wembley, remixing *The Kids Are Alright* soundtrack with Cy Langston and engineer Pete Wandless.

ABOVE: FILMING AT THE ENTWISTLE ESTATE, 5 JANUARY.

THURSDAY, 5 and FRIDAY, 6 JANUARY

John's country squire solo sequence for *The Kids Are Alright* was shot over two days at his home in Stow-on-the-Wold, Gloucestershire. An impressive array of guitars from his collection of more than 200 was set up throughout the hallway and on the stairs, filmed in one shot on a Steadicam by Richard Stanley, Chris Morphet, and John Metcalfe.

John descended with an armful of gold records for a simulated clay pigeon shoot—first with a rifle, then a machine gun. He was also filmed talking about his Who songs, Rigor Mortis, how he and Keith almost created Led Zeppelin, the Who's sound, and finances ("now I'm too old to enjoy my money"). One Oxlike idea for a scene (filmed in the bar but not used) showed Stein asking questions on camera, which when pulled back, revealed the answers being given by a skeleton.

Like Keith's interview in Los Angeles (see 12 August, 1977), most of this material ended up on the cutting room floor. Because of lack of time and disputes over funding, the opportunity to conduct similar filming sessions with Roger and Pete did not arise.

SATURDAY, 7 JANUARY

The press reported that Monty Python's Graham Chapman was producing and starring in *The Odd Job* at Shepperton, with Cliff Owen directing. Keith's name was mentioned in the supporting cast, but when the film went into production on 27 February, David Jason appeared in the role. (Moon pleaded recording commitments.) Another film project in which Chapman sought Keith's involvement was the Python's own *Life Of Brian*, currently without a backer after EMI had pulled out.

MONDAY, 16 JANUARY—FRIDAY, 31 MARCH

Eleven-week (originally eight) production schedule for *The Legacy*, featuring Roger, at Bray Studios, Berkshire, and on location in and around London and the Home Counties. The film was produced by David Foster and Lawrence Turman and directed by Richard Marquand for Pethurst Ltd.

The screenplay, co-written by Jimmy Sangster, Patrick Tilley, and Paul Wheeler, and loosely based on Agatha Christie's *And Then There Were None*, concerned an American designer (Katharine Ross) and her boyfriend (Sam Elliott) coming to England to start an assignment. The couple reluctantly agree to stay at their new employer's ancestral home, Ravenhurst. There they meet a strange assortment of guests who meet horrible fates, including Roger (hair dyed dark brown for a typecast role as rock singer Clive Jackson), who graphically chokes to death on a chicken bone. The movie was edited at Pinewood in June and opened at the Warner West End 4 cinema, London, on 1 October.

MONDAY, 6 MARCH

Rehearsal at Shepperton on M Stage. John "Rabbit" Bundrick auditioned for the group as a potential keyboard player. After a boisterous drinking session with Keith, he fell out of a taxi at 2:00 am in Oxford Street, breaking his wrist.

MONDAY, 13; TUESDAY, 14; and THURSDAY, 16 MARCH

Recording at RAK Studios, 42—48 Charlbert Street, St. John's Wood, North West London.

APRIL—MAY

Overdubbing (including Keith's drum tracks) and final mixing of *Who Are You* at Ramport. A further set of mixes were prepared at Olympic during May and June but these were rejected.

"Music Must Change" nearly didn't make the album due to Keith's problems with its 6/8 time. "Keith's relationship with Glyn was not the slickest," said Pete. "One great exchange was where he had some difficulty getting some break on the track. We'd done about 3 or 4 takes, and he kept apologising, and in the end he stood up and he said, shouting, 'I'm the best Keith Moon-type drummer in the world!'" Apart from some cymbal crashes, all that remained of the original track was Roger's vocal. The backing was created by Pete and Jon Astley at Eel Pie, Goring.

SATURDAY, 1 APRIL

Melody Maker reported that Track Records had gone into liquidation under growing pressure from creditors, with total debts estimated at £70,000.

WEDNESDAY, 26 APRIL

The first professional theatre production of *Tommy* since Ken Russell's film adaptation opened at the Queens Theatre, Hornchurch, Essex, starring Dana Gillespie, Alan Love, Paul da Vinci, and Richard Barnes (no relation to Pete's long-time friend), running until 20 May. Receiving rave notices, the run was further extended from 13 to 30 June. Initially uninterested in any direct endorsement, Pete was persuaded to attend the show on 15 June and was impressed enough to return the following night. With Townshend's help, theatre director John Hole transferred the production to the West End the following January.

TUESDAY, 9 MAY

Jeff Stein filmed an insert for "Who Are You" at Ramport. The original intention was for the group to mime along to the pre-recorded backing track with live vocals. Instead, guitar, piano, and drum overdubs were all specially re-recorded. The clip first premiered, 8:50–11:30 am, during LWT's *The Saturday Banana* on 15 July and was included unedited in *The Kids Are Alright*. After forty-eight weeks, production on the film was officially completed, bar the final Shepperton concert sequence.

THURSDAY, 25 MAY

Keith Moon's final curtain. A privately staged afternoon rehearsal/concert shot on 35 mm on B Stage at Shepperton, in front of a specially invited, bussed-in audience of 500. Among them were members of Generation X, the Rich Kids, the Pretenders, and the Sex Pistols. Meet the new boss...

Filming was arranged to complete *The Kids Are Alright* after Stein's dissatisfaction with the Kilburn rushes. (See 15 December, 1977.) For continuity's sake, everyone except Keith wore the same stage clothes. The original plan was to run through just three numbers ("Baba O'Riley," "My Wife," and "Won't Get Fooled Again"), but after numerous retakes, the group played a complete show as a reward for the audience's patience.

Before commencing filming, the audience were asked to assemble on the studio lawn in four equal lines, with a member of the Who at the helm of each, for the benefit of lensman Terry O'Neill. His aerial shot of the assembly became a proposal for the *Who Are You* sleeve (though this idea was rejected in the end.)

FRIDAY, 26 MAY

At Shepperton, an alternative photograph for the album sleeve was taken by O'Neill at the side of I Stage in the car park. The Who's crew spent the morning assembling the group's masses of sound equipment in preperation for the shoot. Ironically, the instruction inscripted on Keith's chair read "Not To Be Taken Away."

John Wolff's elaborate tunnel laser display during "Won't Get Fooled Again" was filmed again, separately, at Twickenham Film Studios with the band in the shot.

MONDAY, 3 JULY

Flying home after a month-long business holiday in Mauritius, Keith was removed from the plane in the Seychelles after drunkenly disrupting the British Airways flight. He was held overnight and put on a Kenyan Airlines flight back to London the following day.

TUESDAY, 4 JULY

Having officially moved back to Britain, Keith took up his post as director of promotion and publicity for the Who Group Ltd. This was a newly formed company (previously Ramport Enterprises Ltd.) that managed the Who's businesses from The Old House, Shepperton. His duties involved promoting various Who ventures and activities, which included a trucking company, films, and the laser division, run by John Wolff, as well as developing the sound stages as rehearsal rooms and recording studios complete with residential and restaurant facilities. The company's managing director, Tony Prior, told the press: "We believe Keith is aptly suited to directing promotion and attaining publicity for the various business ventures that members of the Who are now involved in."

WEDNESDAY, 12 JULY

Nicky Horne interviewed Keith in the Shepperton boardroom for the London regional news programme, *Thames at 6*. Keith showed Horne around the Who's laser display, Soundstage One (where the band's sound equipment was stored), and invited him onto the luxury touring coach for a preview of *Who Are You*. The five-minute item, shown during the programme from 6:00 to 6:35 pm, became Keith's last British television interview.

BELOW: Private Shepperton concert, 25 May.

FRIDAY, 14 JULY

"Who Are You" B/W "Had Enough" was released in the U.K., reaching #18. The single was originally scheduled for 30 June as a double A-side. In the U.S., it climbed to #14 when issued on 5 August.

SATURDAY, 15 JULY

John appeared via a pre-recorded interview on Radio 1's *Rock On*, talking about *Who Are You* and the New Wave with host Stuart Grundy, transmitted 1:31—2:30 pm.

TUESDAY, 1 AUGUST

Pete and Keith attended the opening of "Who's Who," a fifteenth anniversary exhibition staged at London's Institute of Contemporary Arts, in the Mall. The event was organised by Steve Margo, Peter Johns, and "Irish" Jack Lyons, with Chris Chappel of Trinifold Ltd.

The band's history was depicted through cuttings, Gold Discs, video monitors screening continuous film clips, a slide show, plus a stage set-up with the group's equipment. John Wolff demonstrated the group's laser technology and projected holograms onto the ceiling and walls. Guests at the opening included Ian Dury and twelve-year-old Zak Starkey (Ringo Starr's son), escorted by Keith, who was giving the youngster drum lessons. The exhibition ran from noon to 8:00 pm, admission 25p, until 31 August.

FRIDAY, 4 AUGUST

While John remained behind to finish mixing *The Kids Are Alright* soundtrack at Ramport, Pete, Roger, and Keith flew to New York to do promotion for *Who Are You*.

Radio interviews included WNEW-FM with Scott Muni and WLIR-AM Hempstead with Denis McNamara. A live interview by David Hartman with Keith and Pete at the Navarro (Roger was absent visiting his in-laws) was screened on ABC-TV's *Good Morning America*, Monday, 7 August. This broadcast included clips of the "I Can't Explain" and "Who Are You" promos, and a preview of "Barbara Ann" from *The Kids Are Alright,* on which dubbing and editing commenced at Goldwyn Studios, Los Angeles, the following month. A two-part interview with Moon and Townshend by Joel Siegel, taped the same morning, aired over the following consecutive nights on ABC's *Eyewitness News*.

SATURDAY, 5 AUGUST

Peter Meaden, the Who's original publicist and mentor, was found dead of barbiturate poisoning at his parents' home in Edmonton, North London, aged thirty-six. The coroner, failing to find evidence of intended suicide, delivered an open verdict.

THURSDAY, 10 AUGUST

Roger, Keith, and Pete arrived separately at a lavish *Who Are You* press launch at Universal Studios,

ABOVE: NICKY HORNE INTERVIEWING KEITH FOR *THAMES AT 6*, 12 JULY.

Hollywood. Dayglo "Who Are You?" signs posted along streets pointed guests to the party. An elite gathering were wined and dined while listening to the album in a studio soundstage, decked out as a futuristic sci-fi fantasy with padded silver armchairs, giant cogs, and capsules. Transparent cylindrical sculptures twenty feet high bore the illuminated message "Who Are You." As part of a major media blitz, MCA Records arranged simultaneous free "listen-ins" for the album in seven major cities around the States on 20 August, with tickets distributed via local radio stations. An added visual attraction was John Wolff's laser show at theatres including Griffith Park Observatory's planetarium in Hollywood, and the Palladium, New York.

FRIDAY, 18 AUGUST

Who Are You was released in the U.K. (#6); 21 August in the U.S. (#2).

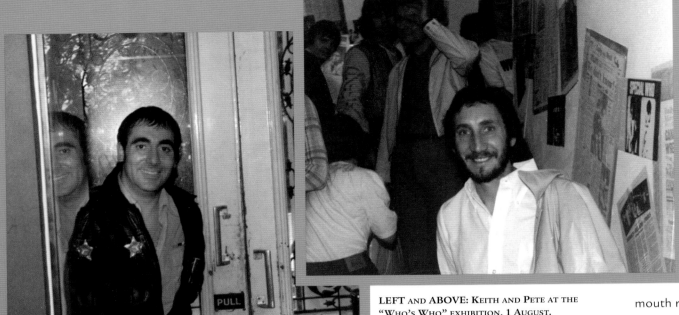

approximately 7:30 am, he awoke hungry and insisted Annette cook him his regular steak breakfast. After wolfing down the food, he swallowed more tablets before drifting off. Sometime that morning, Keith succumbed in his sleep, having consumed a total of thirty-two sedatives.

Annette was sleeping on the living room couch, thanks to Keith's incessant snoring. She awoke around 3:40 pm to find him lying lifeless, face down on the bed. After calling for an ambulance and Keith's doctor, Geoffrey Dymond, she attempted to revive him by beating his chest and administering mouth-to-mouth resuscitation, but to no avail. The big heart that had sustained Keith through years of self-abuse had finally given out. He was found to be dead on arrival at Middlesex Hospital, Westminster. He was only thirty-two.

A pre-recorded interview with Nicky Horne, "An Evening with Pete Townshend," was broadcast on Capital Radio's *Your Mother Wouldn't Like It* slot, 9:00–11:00 pm. As well as the album, Pete discussed *The Story Of Tommy* book, *The Kids Are Alright* and *Quadrophenia* movies, and his ongoing hearing problems, while an excerpt from the "Who Are You" demo was played.

WEDNESDAY, 30 AUGUST

Requiring authentic drum-smashing sounds to overlay onto mute footage destined for *The Kids Are Alright*, John called Keith into CTS Studios, Wembley, to record some overdubs. "We set his kit up and Keith came in and started to play what was required," recalls Cy Langston. "Then after about two or three hours, he just got more and more sluggish, he could barely hold a drumstick."

WEDNESDAY, 6—THURSDAY, 7 SEPTEMBER

Keith and Annette attended a party hosted by Paul McCartney at Peppermint Park, 13 Upper St. Martin's Lane, Covent Garden, to mark the beginning of "Buddy Holly Week." McCartney owned the publishing rights to Holly's music and held an annual function to celebrate his birthday. (Roger had attended the first of these at the Lyceum, two years earlier, on 7 September.)

Keith was both unusually subdued and sober, sharing a booth with the McCartneys, David Frost, actor John Hurt, and, ironically, ex-Faces drummer Kenny Jones. The gathering then transferred to the Odeon, Leicester Square, for the midnight film premiere of *The Buddy Holly Story*, starring Gary Busey.

After forty-five minutes, Keith felt restless, so he and Annette made their excuses and caught a taxi to their flat at 12 Curzon Place, Mayfair. Pete had lent Keith £15,000 to buy the property from Harry Nilsson. Eerily, Mama Cass Elliot had died in that same flat four years earlier.

Annette prepared a meal, which they ate in bed while Keith watched a video of *The Abominable Dr. Phibes*. Having taken several Chlormethiazole (heminevrin) sedatives, prescribed to aid alcohol withdrawal, he fell asleep with the film still running. At

FRIDAY, 8 SEPTEMBER

As a post-mortem was conducted, a lengthy meeting between band and management took place behind closed doors at Shepperton. In an official press statement, Pete wrote: "We have lost our great comedian, our supreme melodramatist, the man, who apart from being the most unpredictable and spontaneous drummer in rock, would have set himself alight if he thought it would make the audience laugh or jump out of its seats... We loved him and

ABOVE and OPPOSITE, BELOW: KEITH AND ANNETTE ARRIVING IN LEICESTER SQUARE FOR *THE BUDDY HOLLY STORY* FILM PREMIERE, 6 SEPTEMBER.

he's gone. The Who? We are more determined than ever to carry on, and we want the spirit of the group to which Keith contributed so much to go on, although no human being can ever take his place."

MONDAY, 11 SEPTEMBER

The same day that Keith's body was cremated at Golders Green crematorium, North London, the official inquest was opened and immediately postponed for a week.

WEDNESDAY, 13 SEPTEMBER

A private afternoon ceremony at Golders Green crematorium was attended by 120 mourners, including Keith's immediate family, ex-wife Kim, and twelve-year-old daughter Mandy, as well as Roger, John, and Pete. Annette collapsed with grief in the Garden of Remembrance and was helped away by Who aide, Bill Harrison. Eighty-five bouquets had been laid out, including Roger's ingenious white daisy and yellow chrysanthemum tribute featuring a champagne bottle embedded in a television screen. Wreaths were sent from, among others, Oliver Reed, Led Zeppelin, the Rolling Stones, David Bowie, Fleetwood Mac, and Keith's favourite charity, Make Children Happy. Musician friends present at the service and wake held at Hendon Hall included Eric Clapton, Bill Wyman, and Charlie Watts.

MONDAY, 18 SEPTEMBER

At the inquest, after hearing evidence from Annette, Dr. Geoffrey Dymond, and pathologist Professor Keith Simpson, who confirmed the number of tablets consumed, Inner West London coroner Dr. Gavin Thurston recorded an open verdict. Thurston reported that though Keith had self-administered a massive overdose, there was no evidence to suggest he had intended to commit suicide.

The *selected* Who discography which follows limits itself to important studio and live recordings, spanning 1964-1978, featuring the late Keith Moon, along with posthumous archive releases (as of June 2001).

It primarily concerns official releases in the U.K./U.S. and thus discards promos, interview discs, bootlegs, etc. The information below each entry refers to the relevant territory, the first occasion the release was made commercially available, and its subsequent chart position (if any). Reissues of the same product have not been included unless the tracks and artwork substantially differ from their original form.

In the case of the Who's CD reissues, the release information refers to their most current or comprehensive form, not necessarily their first appearance in this particular format. Release dates are based on research gleaned from the contemporary music press, trade advertisements, diaries, and recognised charts such as the *New Musical Express, Melody Maker, Record Retailer*, and *Music Week* in the U.K., *Billboard, Record World*, and *Cash Box* in the U.S. These were cross-checked with reference sources such as *The Guinness Book Of British Hit Singles*, its companion volume of *British Hit Albums*, as well as Joel Whitburn's various *Billboard* chart compilations. A release date can prove subjective, depending on location and how efficiently a record company's distribution system worked, particularly in the United States. The information presented here subsequently updates all previous discographies I have attempted. If any significant discrepancies have arisen, written evidence would be welcomed c/o the publisher's address.

Perhaps this listing will be updated in the future—or when Andy and Matt are revising the script for a film version!

Rock on!
Ed Hanel

SINGLES

Title (A-side)/Title (B-side)
(Territory) Label & Cat. No./Release Date/Chart Position

Zoot Suit/I'm The Face
(The High Numbers)
(U.K.) Fontana TF 480/ 3 Jul 64/
Backdoor Door 4/ 1980 reissue/
(A and B sides reversed)

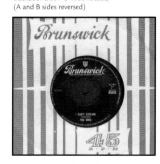

I Can't Explain/Bald Headed Woman
(U.K.) Brunswick 05926/ 15 Jan 65/-8-
(U.S.) Decca 31725/ 13 Feb 65/-93-
Date based on Billboard chart;
Cash Box first reviewed the single 19 Dec 64, implying Bald Headed Woman as the A-side.

Anyway Anyhow Anywhere/Daddy Rolling Stone
(U.K.) Brunswick 05935 21 May 65/-10-

Anyway Anyhow Anywhere/Anytime You Want Me
(U.S.) Decca 31801/ 5 Jun 65/-

My Generation/ Shout And Shimmy
(U.K.) Brunswick 05944/ 29 Oct 65/-2-

My Generation/ Out In The Street
(B-side subtitled *'You're Going To Know Me'*)
(U.S.) Decca 31877/ 20 Nov 65/-74-

Substitute/(a) Circles (b) Instant Party
(U.K.) Reaction 591001 (both issues)/ 4 Mar 66/-5-
B-sides same song version with different titles.

A Legal Matter/Instant Party
(U.K.) Brunswick 05956/ 7 Mar 66/-32-
B-side original Talmy version.

Substitute/Waltz For A Pig
(U.K.) Reaction 591001/ 14 Mar 66/-5-
(U.S.) Atco 45-6409/ 2 Apr 66/-(reissued 19 Aug 67/-)
A-side lyric altered, various B-sides credit the Who or Who Orchestra.

The Kids Are Alright/A Legal Matter
(U.S.) Decca 31988/ Jul 66/-
A-side—edited version.

The Kids Are Alright/ The Ox
(U.K.) Brunswick 05965/ 12 Aug 66/-41-
Original release intended as Brunswick 05956 above.

I'm A Boy (single version)**/In The City**
(U.K.) Reaction 591004/ 26 Aug 66/-2-
(U.S.) Decca 32058/ 10 Dec 66/-

READY STEADY WHO (EP)
(U.K.) Reaction 592001/ 11 Nov 66/-1-
(Record Mirror EP chart.)

La La La Lies/The Good's Gone
(U.K.) Brunswick 05968/ 11 Nov 66/-

Happy Jack/I've Been Away
(U.K.) Reaction 591010/ 9 Dec 66/-3-

Happy Jack/ Whiskey Man
(U.S.) Decca 32114/ 18 Mar 67/-24-
Ralph Steadman picture sleeve.

Pictures Of Lily/Doctor, Doctor
(U.K.) Track 604 002/ 21 Apr 67/-4-
(U.S.) Decca 32156/ 24 Jun 67/-51-

The Last Time/ Under My Thumb
(U.K.) Track 604 006/ 30 Jun 67/-44-

I Can See For Miles/
Mary-Anne With The Shaky Hands *(sic)*
(U.S.) Decca 32206/ 18 Sep 67/-9-

I Can See For Miles/Someone's Coming
(U.K.) Track 604 011/ 13 Oct 67/-10-

Call Me Lightning/Dr. Jekyll & Mr. Hyde
(U.S.) Decca 32288/ 16 Mar 68/-40-

Dogs/Call Me Lightning
(U.K.) Track 604 023/ 14 Jun 68/-25-

Magic Bus (single version)**/Someone's Coming**
(U.S.) Decca 36322/ 27 Jul 68/-25-

Magic Bus (single version)**/**
Dr. Jekyll & Mr. Hyde (alt. mix)
(U.K.) Track 604 024/ 11 Oct 68/-26-

Pinball Wizard/Dogs Part Two
(U.K.) Track 604 027/ 7 Mar 69/-4-
(U.S.) Decca 732465; Decca 32465/ 22 Mar 69/-19-
Who's first stereo 45; picture sleeve states, "From The Soon To Be Released Rock Opera Tommy (1914/1984)."

I'm Free/We're Not Gonna Take It
(U.K.) Decca 732519/ 5 Jul 69/-37-

The Seeker/Here For More
(U.K.) Track 604 036/ 20 Mar 70/-19-
(U.S.) Decca 32670/ 25 Apr 70/-44-

Summertime Blues/Heaven And Hell
(U.K.) Track 2094 002/ 10 Jul 70/-38-
(U.S.) Decca 32708/ 11 Jul 70/-27-

See Me, Feel Me/ Overture From *Tommy*
(U.S.) Decca 732729/ 26 Sep 70/-12-
Picture sleeve states, "From The TOMMY Finale We're Not Gonna Take It."
(U.K.) Track 2094 004/ 9 Oct 70/-

TOMMY (EP)
(U.K.) Track 2252 001/ 6 Nov 70/-
Replaced withdrawn Track 2094 004 above.

Won't Get Fooled Again/Don't Know Myself
(U.S. title *I Don't Even Know Myself*)
(U.K.) Track 2094 009/ 25 Jun 71/-9-
(U.S.) Decca 32846/ 17 Jul 71/-15-
Label states: "From The Motion Picture Lifehouse."

Let's See Action/When I Was A Boy
(U.K.) Track 2094 012/ 15 Oct 71/-16-

Behind Blue Eyes/My Wife
(U.S.) Decca 32888/ 6 Nov 71/-34-

Join Together/Baby Don't You Do It
(U.K) Track 2094 102/ 16 Jun 72/-9-
(U.S.) Decca 32983/ 8 Jul 72/-17-

Relay (*U.S. title, The Relay*)**/Waspman**
(U.K.) Track 33041/ 25 Nov 72/-39-
(U.K.) Track 2094 106/ 22 Dec 72/-21-

5.15/Water
(U.K.) Track 2094 115/ 5 Oct 73/-20-

Love, Reign O'er Me (different mix)**/Water**
(U.S.) Decca 40152/ 27 Oct 73/-76-

The Real Me/I'm One
(U.K.) Track 40182/ 12 Jan 74/-92-

Postcard/Put The Money Down
(U.K.) Track 40330/ Nov 74/-

Listening To You, See Me Feel Me/Overture from *Tommy*
(*Tommy* Soundtrack)
(U.S.) Polydor 15098/ Mar 75/ -
(U.K.) Polydor 2001 561/ 11 Apr 75/-

Squeeze Box/Success Story
(U.S.) MCA 40475/ 22 Nov 75/-16-
(U.K.) Polydor 2121 275/ 16 Jan 76/-10-

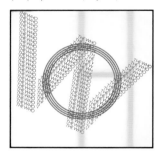

Slip Kid (edited version)**/ Dreaming From The Waist**
(U.S.) MCA 40603/ 7 Aug 76/-

Substitute/I'm A Boy (album version)**/Pictures Of Lily**
(U.K.) Polydor 2058 803/ 22 Oct 76/-7-
Both 7" and 12" versions issued.

Who Are You/Had Enough
(U.K.) Polydor 2121 361/ 14 Jul 78/-18-
(U.S.) MCA 400948/ 5 Aug 78/-14-

Won't Get Fooled Again/Boney Maronie *(sic)*
(*Live Young Vic 26/4/71*)
(U.K.) Polydor POSP 917/Aug 88/-
Won't Get Fooled Again
(U.K) CD single Polydor POCD 917/ Aug 88/-
includes **Boney Maronie** *(sic) (Young Vic)* and **Mary-Anne With The Shaky Hand**
(erroneously credited as live New York, 1967)

My Generation/Pinball Wizard
(B-side, otherwise unavailable, live at Leeds University 14/2/70)
(U.K) Polydor 8639187/ Jun 96/-
My Generation
(U.K.) CD single Polydor 8546372/ Jun 96/-
includes **Pinball Wizard** *(B-side, otherwise unavailable, live at Leeds University 14/2/70)*

ALBUMS

Title
Track Listing
(Territory) Label & Cat. No./
Release Date/Chart Position

MY GENERATION
1. Out In The Street /2. I Don't Mind (Brown)/3. The Good's Gone/4. La La La Lies / 5. Much Too Much (Townshend; Pavey, Doonican credit on reissues) /6. My Generation 7. The Kids Are Alright/8. Please, Please, Please (Brown, Terry)/ 9. It's Not True/10. I'm A Man/ 11. A Legal Matter/ 12. The Ox (Townshend, Moon, Entwistle, Hopkins)
(U.K.) Brunswick LAT 8616 *(mono)/* 3 Dec 65/-5-

THE WHO SINGS MY GENERATION
Track 7 is 2:49 edit, 10. deleted, and last three tracks are ordered: 10. The Ox/ 11. A Legal Matter/ 12. Instant Party (Shel Talmy's production of Circles)
(U.S.) Decca DL 4664 *(mono)*
Decca DL 74664 *(stereo)/* Apr 66/-
CD MCAD-31330/ Sep 88
(Original CD issue, remixed MCAD-31330-3-IT 21)

A QUICK ONE
1. Run Run Run/2. Boris The Spider (Entwistle)/3. I Need You (Moon)/4. Whiskey Man (Entwistle)/5. Heatwave (sic) (Holland/ Dozier/ Holland)/6. Cobwebs And Strange (Moon) 7. Don't Look Away/8. See My Way (Daltrey)/9. So Sad About Us/10. A Quick One, While He's Away
(U.K.) Reaction 593 002 *(mono)/* 9 Dec 66/-4-
CD Polydor 527 758-2/ Jun 95 *
(U.S.) CD MCA MCAD-11267/ Jun 95 *
* = Remastered reissue w/ extra tracks:
Batman(Hefti)/Bucket 'T'(Atfield/Christian/Torrance)/Barbara Ann (Fassert)/Disguises/ Doctor, Doctor (Entwistle)/I've Been Away (Entwistle)/In The City (Moon/Entwistle)/Happy Jack (Acoustic Version)/ Man With Money(Everly, Everly)/My Generation - Land Of Hope And Glory (Townshend/ Elgar)

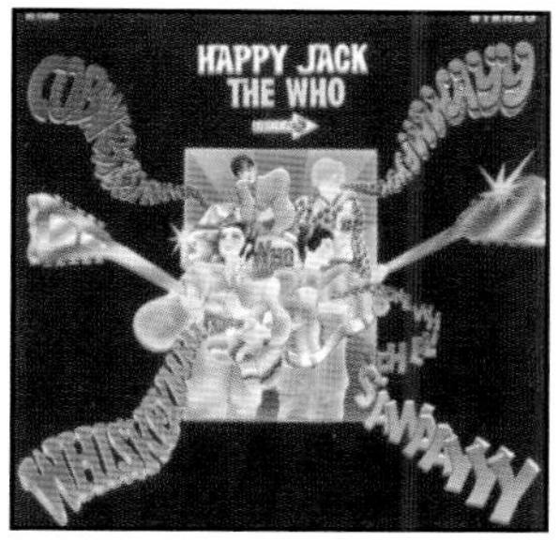

HAPPY JACK
Deletes* Heat Wave, *adds title song.
(U.S.) Decca DL 4892 (*mono*)
Decca DL 74892 (*stereo*)/ May 67/-67-
CD MCAD-31331 (*adds* Heat Wave)

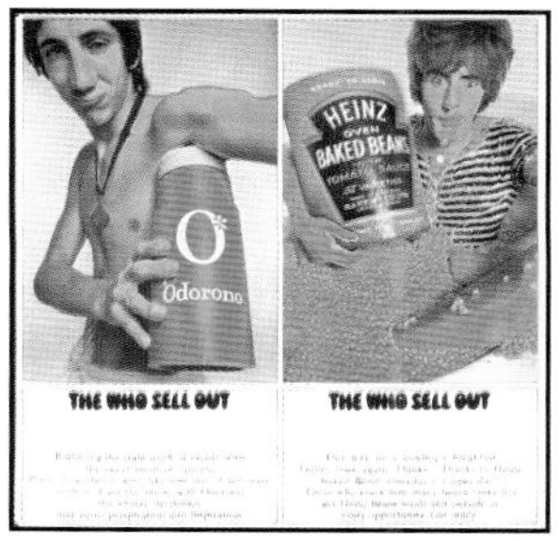

THE WHO SELL OUT
1. Armenia City In The Sky (Keene)/2. Heinz Baked Beans (Entwistle)/3. Mary Anne With The Shaky Hand (album version)/4. Odorono/ 5. Tattoo/6. Our Love Was/7. I Can See For Miles/8. I Can't Reach You/9. Medac (in U.S., Spotted Henry) (Entwistle)/10. Relax/11. Silas Stingy /12. Sunrise/ 13. Rael, 1 And 2 (in U.S., Rael)
(U.K.) Track 612 002 (*mono*)
Track 613 002 (*stereo*)/ 15 Dec 67/-13-
Mono/stereo versions contain different mixes
CD Polydor 527 759-2 *
(U.S.) Decca DL 4950 (*mono*)
Decca DL 74950 (*stereo*)/ 6 Jan 68/-48-
CD MCAD-11268/ Jun 95 *
** =Remastered reissue w/ extra tracks: Rael 2/Top Gear ad/ Glittering Girl/Coke 2 ad/Melancholia/Bag O'Nails ad/Someone's Coming (Entwistle)/John Mason's Cars ad (Rehearsal)/Jaguar/ John Mason's Cars (Reprise) ad/Early Morning Cold Taxi (Langston, Daltrey)/ Coke 1 ad/Hall Of The Mountain King (Grieg)/Radio One (Boris Mix) ad/ Girl's Eyes (Moon)/ Odorono (Final Chorus) /Mary Anne With The Shaky Hand (Alt. version)/Glow Girl/ Track Records ad*

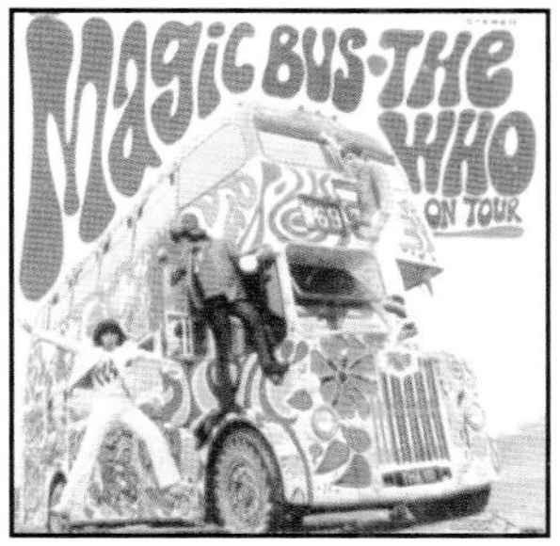

MAGIC BUS—THE WHO ON TOUR
1. Disguises/2. Run Run Run/3. Dr. Jekyll & Mr. Hyde (Entwistle) /4. I Can't Reach You /5.Our Love Was, Is (Stereo version)/6. Call Me Lightning/7. Magic Bus (long studio version)/8. Someone's Coming (Entwistle)/9. Doctor, Doctor (Entwistle)/10. Bucket 'T' (Altfield, Christian, Torrance)/ 11. Pictures Of Lily
(U.S.) Decca 5064 (*mono*)
Decca 75604 (*stereo*)/ Sept. 68/-39-
CD MCAD-31333.

DIRECT HITS
1. Bucket 'T' (Altfield, Christian, Torrence)/2. I'm A Boy (single version)/ 3.Pictures Of Lily/4. Doctor Doctor (Entwistle)/ 5. I Can See For Miles/6. Substitute/7. Happy Jack/8. The Last Time (Jagger, Richard)/9. In The City (Moon, Entwistle)/ 10. Call Me Lightning/11. Mary Anne with The Shaky Hand (album version)/12. Dogs
(U.K.) Track 612 006 (*mono*)
Track 613 006 (*stereo*) 18 Oct 68/-

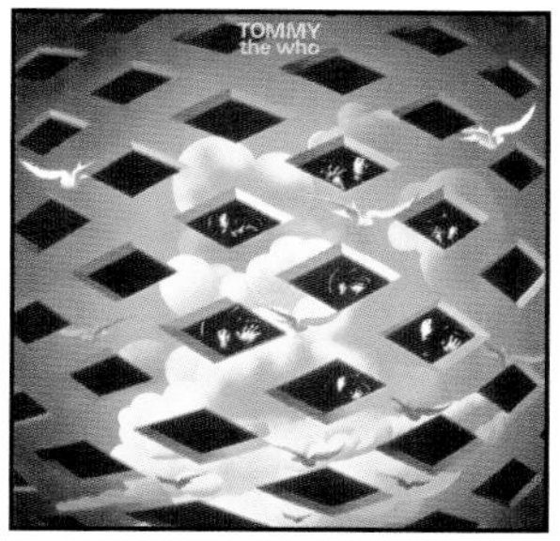

TOMMY
1.Overture/2. It's A Boy/3. 1921/4. Amazing Journey/ 5. Sparks/6. Eyesight To The Blind (on U.K cover, The Hawker) (Williamson) 7. Christmas/8. Cousin Kevin (Entwistle)/9. The Acid Queen/10. Underture/11. Do You Think It's Alright?/12. Fiddle About (Entwistle)/13. Pinball Wizard/14. There's A Doctor/15. Go To The Mirror!/16. Tommy, Can You Hear Me?/17. Smash The Mirror/18. Sensation/19. Miracle Cure/20. Sally Simpson/21. I'm Free/22. Welcome/23. Tommy's Holiday Camp(Moon)/ 24. We're Not Gonna Take It
(U.S.) Decca DXSW 7205/ 17 May 69/-4-
Alt.vocal track of Eyesight To The Blind - MFSL UDCD 533
CD (*Remastered*) MCAD 11417/ Mar 96
(U.K.) Track 613 013/4 - 23 May 69/-2-
Track 2657 002/ 1973. *Alt.vocal track for* Eyesight To The Blind.
CD (*Remastered*) Polydor 531 043-2/ Mar 96

THE HOUSE THAT TRACK BUILT
Various Artists, features studio version of Young Man Blues.
(U.K.) Track 613 016/ Jul 69/-

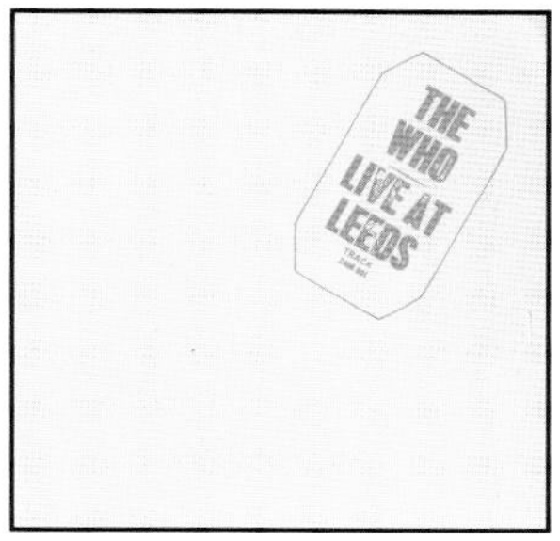

LIVE AT LEEDS
1.Young Man Blues (Allison)/2. Substitute/3. Summertime Blues (Cochran/Capehart) /4. Shakin' All Over (Heath)/ 5.My Generation/6. Magic Bus
(U.S.) Decca DL 79175/ 16 May 70/-4-
MCAD-11230/ Feb 95 *
(U.K.) Track 2406 001/ 22 May 70/-3-
CD Polydor 527 169-2/ Feb 95 *
** = Remastered CD is virtually a reconstructed release as follows: 1.Heaven And Hell (Entwistle)/2. I Can't Explain/3. Fortune Teller (Neville)/4. Tattoo/ 5. Young Man Blues (Allison)/ 6. Substitute/7. Happy Jack/8. I'm A Boy/9. A Quick One While He's Away/10. Amazing Journey-Sparks/11. Summertime Blues (Cochran, Capehart)/ 12. Shakin' All Over (Heath)/13.My Generation/14. Magic Bus*

LIVE AT LEEDS (Deluxe Edition)
Complete 14/2/70 concert, featuring the entire performance of Tommy.
CD MCA 088 112 618-2
To be released September 2001.

BACKTRACK 1, 2, 3, 4, 5
Sampler LP's with various Who tracks. Volume 3 features previously unreleased stereo mixes.
(U.K.) Track 2407 001
Track 2407 002
Track 2407 003
Track 2407 004
Track 2407 005/ 22 May 70/

WOODSTOCK
Various Artists, features We're Not Gonna Take It
(U.S.) Cotillion SD 3-500/ May 70/-1-
Cotillion CD SD 500-2
(U.K.) Atlantic 2663 001/ 29 May 70/-35-

BACKTRACK 7: MIXED BAG
Several Who tracks
BACKTRACK 8: A QUICK ONE
BACKTRACK 9: THE WHO SELL OUT
BACKTRACK 14: THE OX
Who songs by Entwistle

(U.K.) Track 2407 007
Track 2407 008
Track 2407 009
Track 2407 014/ 6 Nov 70/

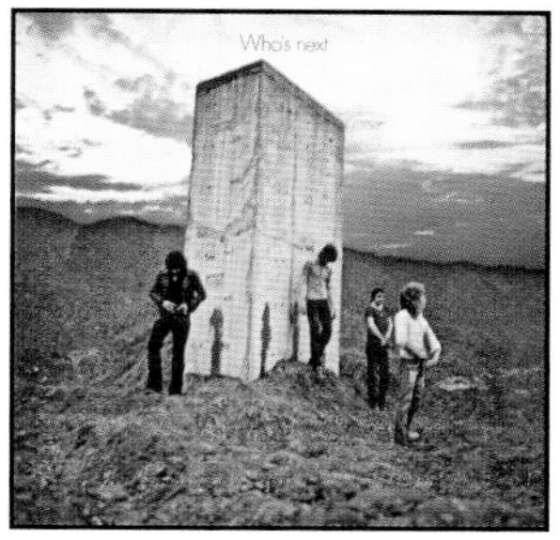

WHO'S NEXT
1.Baba O'Riley/2. Bargain/3. Love Ain't For Keeping/4. My Wife (Entwistle)/5. The Song Is Over/6. Getting In Tune/ 7. Going Mobile /8. Behind Blue Eyes/9. Won't Get Fooled Again (long version)
(U.S.) Decca 79182/ 14 Aug 71/-4-
CD MCAD 11269/ Nov 95 *
(U.K.) Track 2408 102 27 Aug 71/-1-
CD Polydor 527 760-2/ Nov 95 *
** = Remastered reissue w/ extra tracks: Pure And Easy (Alt. version)/Baby Don't You Do It (Holland, Dozier, Holland)/ Naked Eye/Water/Too Much Of Anything/ I Don't Even Know Myself/Behind Blue Eyes (Alt. version)*

MEATY, BEATY, BIG, AND BOUNCY
1. I Can't Explain/2. The Kids Are Alright (edited version)/ 3.Happy Jack/4. I Can See For Miles/5. Pictures Of Lily/ 6. My Generation/7. The Seeker 8. Anyway Anyhow Anywhere (Townshend, Daltrey)/9. Pinball Wizard/10. A Legal Matter/ 11. Boris The Spider (Entwistle)/12. The Magic Bus (sic) (long studio version)/13. Substitute/14. I'm A Boy (album version)
(U.S.) Decca DL 79184/ 30 Oct 71/-11-
CD MCAD-37001 (DIDX-348)
(cover indicates 4:28 version of Magic Bus, *but in fact has the single mix)*
(U.K.) Track 2406 006/ 26 Nov 71/-9-

TOMMY *Part 1*
(U.K.) Track 2406 007/ 12 May 72/
Reissue of Sides 1 & 2 of Track 613 013/4

TOMMY *Part 2*
(U.K.) Track 2406 008/ 16 Jun 72/
Reissue of Sides 3 & 4 of Track 613 013/4

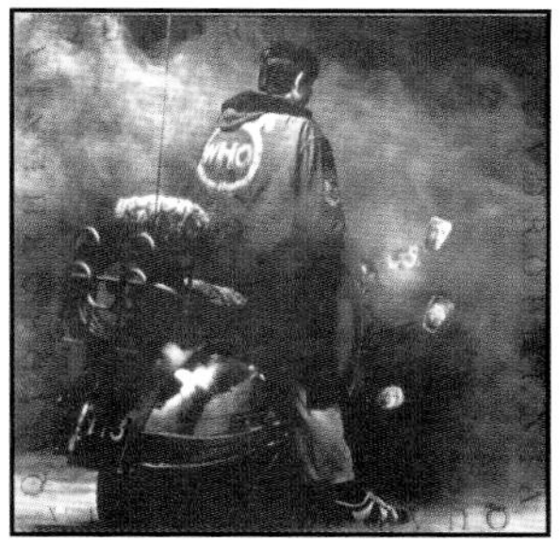

QUADROPHENIA
1. I Am The Sea/2. The Real Me/3. Quadrophenia/4. Cut My Hair/5. The Punk And The Godfather 6. I'm One/7. The Dirty Jobs/8. Helpless Dancer/9. Is It In My Head?/10. I've Had Enough/11. 5.15/12. Sea And Sand/13. Drowned/14. Bell Boy 15. Doctor Jimmy/16. The Rock/17. Love, Reign O'er Me

(U.S.) MCA2 10004/ 27 Oct 73/-2-
CD (*Remastered*) MCAD2-11463/ Jul 96
(U.K.) Track 2657 013/ 2 Nov 73/-2-
CD (*Remastered*) Polydor 531 971-2/ Jul 96

TRACK ALLSORTS:
ANISEED, PEPPERMINT, COCONUT
Samplers with various Who tracks.
(U.K.) Track 2409 205
Track 2409 206
Track 2409 207/ 17 May 74/-

A QUICK ONE/THE WHO SELL OUT
(U.K.) Track 2409 209/10 - 24 May 74/-

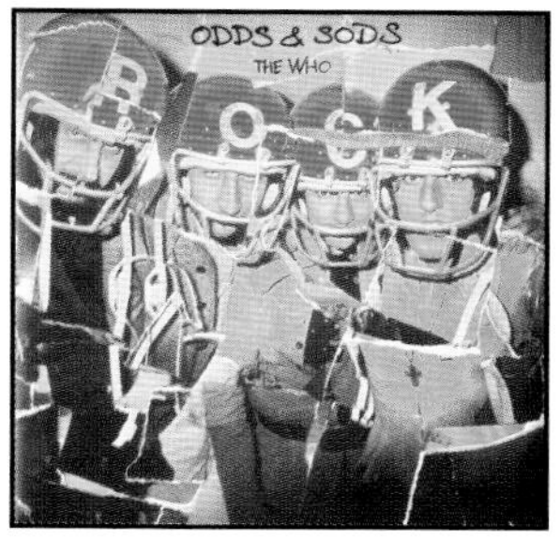

ODDS AND SODS
1. Postcard (Entwistle)/2. Now I'm A Farmer/3. Put The Money Down/4. Little Billy/5. Too Much Of Anything/6. Glow Girl 7. Pure And Easy/8. Faith In Something Bigger/9. I'm The Face/10. Naked Eye/ 11. Long Live Rock
(U.K.) Track 2406 116/ 4 Oct 74/-10-
CD Polydor 539 791-2/ Mar 98 *
(U.S.) MCA 2126/ 12 Oct 74/-15-
CD MCAD-11718/ Mar 98 *
** = Remastered CD is virtually a reconstructed release as follows: 1. I'm The Face (Meaden)/2. Leaving Here (Holland,Dozier, Holland)/3. Baby Don't You Do It (Holland, Dozier, Holland)/ 4. Summertime Blues (Studio) (Cochran,Capehart)/5. Under My Thumb (Alt. version)(Jagger, Richards)/6. Mary Anne With The Shaky Hand (2nd alt. version)/ 7. My Way (Cochran, Capehart)/ 8. Faith In Something Bigger/9. Glow Girl/10. Little Billy/11. Young Man Blues (Alt. studio version) (Allison)/ 12. Cousin Kevin Model Child (Entwistle)/13. Love Ain't For Keeping (Alt. version)/14. Time Is Passing/15. Pure And Easy/16. Too Much Of Anything/17. Long Live Rock/18. Put The Money Down/19. We Close Tonight/20. Postcard (Entwistle)/21. Now I'm A Farmer/22. Water/23. Naked Eye*

A QUICK ONE (HAPPY JACK)/ THE WHO SELL OUT
(U.S.) MCA 2-4067/ 30 Nov 74/-

MY GENERATION/MAGIC BUS
(U.S.) MCA 2-4068/ 30 Nov 74/-185

TOMMY (SOUNDTRACK)
1. Prologue/2. Captain Walker, It's A Boy/3. Bernie's Holiday Camp/4. 1951, What About the Boy/5. Amazing Journey/6. Christmas/7. Eyesight To The Blind (Williamson) 8. Acid Queen/9. Do You Think It's Alright? (1)/10. Cousin Kevin (Entwistle)11. Do You Think It's Alright?(2)/12.Fiddle About(Entwistle)/13. Do You Think It's Alright? (3)/14. Sparks / 15. Extra, Extra, Extra/16. Pinball Wizard/17. Champagne/18. There's A Doctor/19. Go To The Mirror/20. Tommy Can You Hear Me /21. Smash The Mirror /22. I'm Free/23. Mother And Son/24. Sensation /25. Miracle Cure/26. Sally Simpson/27. Welcome/28. TV Studio /29. Tommy's Holiday Camp (Moon)/ 30. We're Not Gonna Take It/31. Listening to You; See Me, Feel Me
(U.S.) Polydor PD2-9505/ 22 Feb 75/-2-
CD Polydor 841 121-2
(U.K.) Polydor 2657 014/ 21 Mar 75/-21-
CD Polydor 841 121-2

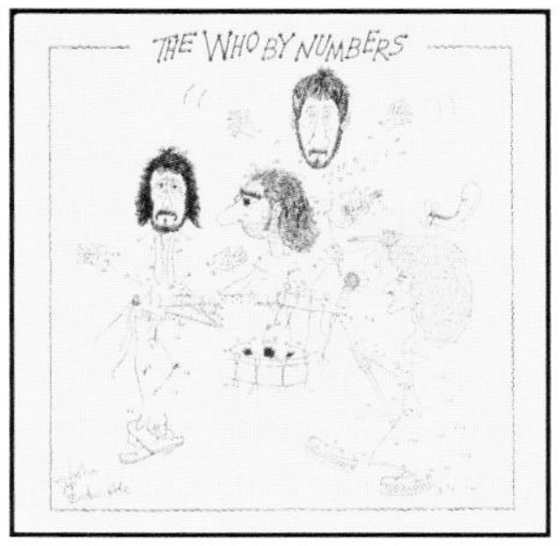

THE WHO BY NUMBERS
1. Slip Kid/2. However Much I Booze/3. Squeeze Box/ 4. Dreaming From The Waist/6. Imagine A Man 7. Success Story (Entwistle)/8. They Are All In Love/9. How Many Friends/10. In A Hand Or A Face
(U.K) Polydor 2490 129/ 3 Oct 75/-7-
CD Polydor 533 844-2/ Nov 96 *
(U.S.) MCA 2161/ 25 Oct 75/-8-
CD MCAD-11493/ Nov 96 *
** = Remastered reissue w/ extra tracks: Squeeze Box/ Behind Blue Eyes/Dreaming From The Waist (live Swansea, 12/6/76)*

THE STORY OF THE WHO
Magic Bus (long studio version)/2. Substitute/3. Boris The Spider (Entwistle) /4. Run Run Run/5. I'm A Boy (album version) /6. Heat Wave (Holland, Dozier, Holland)/7. My Generation (Live At Leeds edit) 8. Pictures Of Lily/9. Happy Jack/10. The Seeker/ 11. I Can See For Miles/12. Bargain/ 13. Squeeze Box/14. Amazing Journey/ 15. The Acid Queen/ 16. Do You Think It's Alright?/ 17. Fiddle About (Entwistle)/18. Pinball Wizard/19. I'm Free/20. Tommy's Holiday Camp (Moon)/21. We're Not Gonna Take It/22. Summertime Blues (Cochran/Capehart; Live At Leeds edit) 23. Baba O'Riley/24. Behind Blue Eyes/25. Slip Kid/26. Won't Get Fooled Again
(U.K.) Polydor 2683 069/ 24 Sep 76/-2-

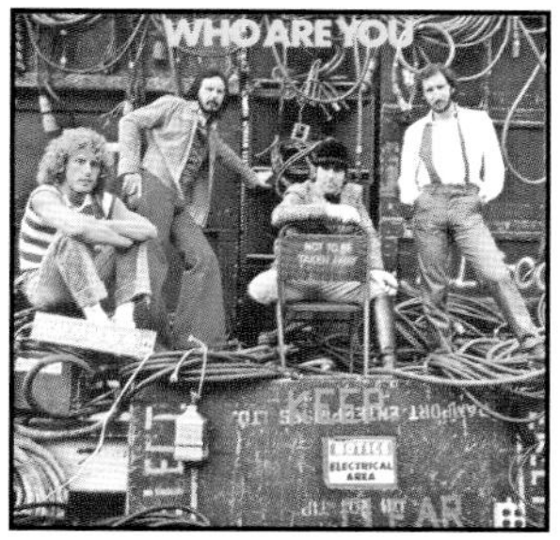

WHO ARE YOU
1. New Song/2. Had Enough (Entwistle)/3. 905 (Entwistle)/ 4. Sister Disco/5. Music Must Change/6. Trick Of The Light (Entwistle)/7. Guitar And Pen/8. Love Is Coming Down/9. Who Are You
(U.K.) Polydor 2683 084/ 18 Aug 78/-6-
CD Polydor 533 845-2/ Nov 96 *
(U.S) MCA 3050/ 21 Aug 78/-2-
CD MFSL UDCD 561. *Alt. version of* Guitar And Pen
CD MCAD-11492/ Nov 96 *
** = Remastered reissue w/ extra tracks: No Road Romance/Choir Boy/ Empty Glass/Guitar And Pen/ Love Is Coming Down/ Who Are You*

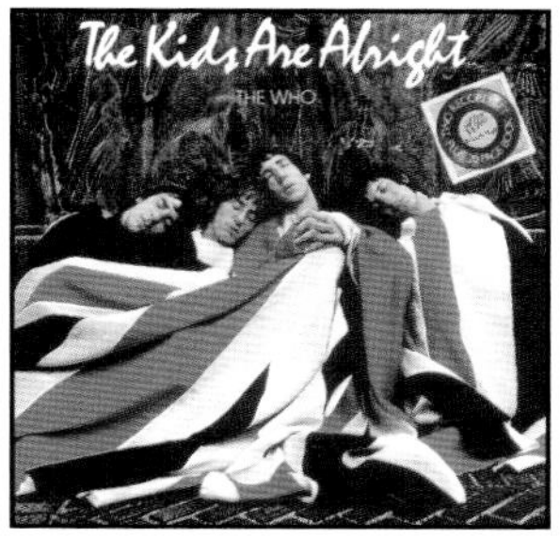

THE KIDS ARE ALRIGHT (SOUNDTRACK)
1. My Generation (Smothers Brothers)/2. I Can't Explain (Shindig)/ 3. Happy Jack (live, Leeds)/4. I Can See For Miles (Smothers Brothers)/5. Magic Bus (Beat Club)/6. Long Live Rock 7. Anyway Anyhow Anywhere (Ready Steady Go!)/8. Young Man Blues (live, London Coliseum)/9. My Wife (live, Kilburn)/10. Baba O'Riley (live, Shepperton)/11. A Quick One While He's Away (live, Rolling Stones R&R Circus)/12. Tommy, Can You Hear Me? (Beat Club)/13. Sparks/14. Pinball Wizard/15. See Me, Feel Me (live- Woodstock)/16. Join Together, Road Runner, My Generation Blues (live, Pontiac Stadium)/17. Won't Get Fooled Again (live, Shepperton)
(U.K.) Polydor 2675 179/ 8 Jun 79/-26-
CD (*remastered*) Polydor 543 694-2/ Mar 2001
(U.S.) MCA 2-11005/ 23 Jun 79/-8-
CD (*remastered*) MCA 314 543 694- 2/ 17 Apr 2001

QUADROPHENIA (SOUNDTRACK)
1. I Am The Sea/2. The Real Me/3. I'm One/4. 5.15/5. Love Reign O'er Me/ 6. Bell Boy/7. I've Had Enough/8. Helpless Dancer/9. Doctor Jimmy/ 10. Zoot Suit (Meaden)/11. non-Who track/12. Get Out And Stay Out/13. Four Faces/14. Joker James / 15. The Punk And The Godfather.
Keith Moon credited on Who tracks.
Sides 1 & 2 remixed by John Entwistle.
Side 4 contains non-Who soundtrack selections.
(U.K) Polydor 2625 037/ 5 Oct 79/-23-
CD Polydor 543 691-2/ March 2001
(U.S.) Polydor PD2-6235/ 6 Oct 79/-46-
CD Polydor 314 543 691-2/ 17 Apr 2001

WHO'S MISSING
1. Shout & Shimmy (Brown)/2. Leaving Here (Holland/Dozier/Holland)/3. Anytime You Want Me (Ragavoy/Mimms) /4. Lubie (Come Back Home) (Revere/Lindsay) /6. Barbara Ann (Fassert) /7. I'm A Boy/ 8. Mary-Anne With The Shaky Hands (sic) /9. Heaven And Hell (Entwistle) /10. Here For More (Daltrey) /11. I Don't Even Know Myself/12. When I Was A Boy (Entwistle) /13. Bargain ('72 dating incorrect, act. San Francisco 13/12/71)
(U.S.) MCA-5641/ 30 Nov 85/-116-

TWO'S MISSING
1. Bald Headed Woman (Talmy)/2. Under My Thumb (Jagger/Richards)/3. My Wife (Entwistle)(live, San Francisco 13/12/71)/4. I'm A Man (McDaniel)/5. Dogs/6. Dogs Part Two (Moon/Towser/Jason)/7. Circles/8. The Last Time (Jagger/Richards)/9. Water/10. Daddy Rolling Stone (Blackwell)/11. Heat Wave (Holland/Dozier/Holland)/12. Goin' Down (sic) (Nix) ('72 dating incorrect, San Francisco 13/12/71)/13. Motoring (Holland/Dozier/Holland)/14. Wasp Man (Moon)
(U.S) MCA-5712/ Mar 87/

MONTEREY POP FESTIVAL
(4 CD Box Set of June '67 festival. Who tracks: 1. Substitute 2. Summertime Blues 3. Pictures Of Lily 4. A Quick One While He's Away 5. Happy Jack 6. My Generation)
(U.S.) Rhino R70596/ Oct 92/-
(U.K.) Essential ROKCD 102/ 1994/-

THIRTY YEARS OF MAXIMUM R&B
(4 CD Box Set)
CD 1: 1. Pete Dialogue (live, Long Beach 10/12/71)/2. I'm The Face (Meaden)/3. Here 'Tis (McDaniel)/4. Zoot Suit (Meaden)(stereo remixes)/5. Leaving Here (Holland/Dozier/Holland)/6. I Can't Explain/7. Anyway Anyhow Anywhere (Townshend/Daltrey)/8. Daddy Rolling Stone (Blackwell, previously credited to Martin)/9. My Generation/10. The Kids Are Alright/11. The Ox (Townshend /Moon/Entwistle/Hopkins)/ 12. A Legal Matter/13. Pete Dialogue/14. Substitute (both live, Leeds 14/2/70)/15. I'm A Boy (single version -alt.stereo mix)/16. Disguises (stereo mix)/17. Happy Jack Jingle/18. Happy Jack/19. Boris The Spider (Entwistle)/20. So Sad About Us/ 21. A Quick One, While He's Away (combines studio cut and Rock & Roll Circus rehearsal 11/12/68)/22. Pictures Of Lily/

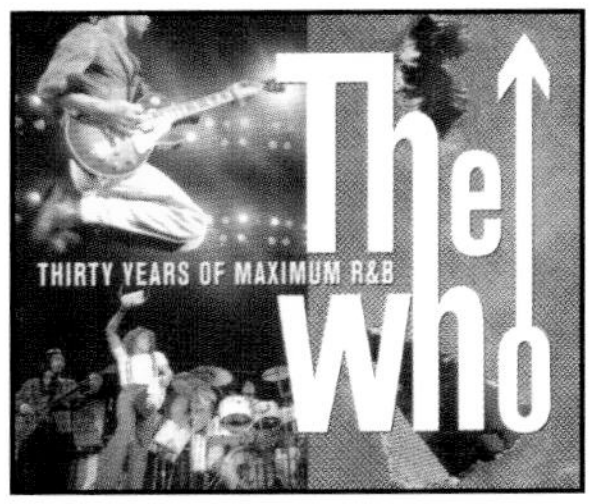

23. Early Morning Cold Taxi (Langston/Daltrey)/24. Coke 2/ 25. (This Could Be) The Last Time (Jagger/Richards)/26. I Can't Reach You/27. Girl's Eyes (Moon)/28. Bag O'Nails/29. Call Me Lightning

CD 2: (N.B:The Who Sell Out tracks are fresh remixes) 1. Rotosound Strings/2. I Can See For Miles/3. Mary Anne With The Shaky Hands (sic) (Album version)/4. Armenia City In The Sky (Keene)/5. Tattoo/6. Our Love Was/7. Rael 1/8. Rael 2/ 9. Track Records/Premier Drums/10. Sunrise/11. Russell Harty Dialogue/12. Jaguar (edited)/13. Melancholia/14. Fortune Teller (Neville)/15. Magic Bus (Single version)/16. Little Billy/ 17. Dogs/18. Overture/19. Acid Queen/20. Abbie Hoffman incident/21. Underture (both live, Woodstock 17/8/69)/ 22. Pinball Wizard/23. I'm Free/ 24. See Me Feel Me (live, Leeds 14/2/70)/25. Heaven And Hell (Entwistle)/26. Pete Dialogue/ 27. Young Man Blues (Allison) (live, Leeds 14/2/70)/28. Summertime Blues (Cochran/Capehart) (Leeds, 14/2/70).

CD 3: 1. Shakin' All Over (Heath) (Leeds 14/2/70)/2. Baba O'Riley/3. Bargain (edited live, San Francisco 13/12/71)/ 4. Pure And Easy/5. The Song Is Over/6. Studio Dialogue/ 7. Behind Blue Eyes/8. Won't Get Fooled Again/9. The Seeker/ 10. Bony Moronie (Williams) (live, Young Vic 26/4/71 - 2nd mix)/11. Let's See Action/12. Join Together/13. Relay/14. The Real Me (1979 remake, Kenney Jones- drums)/15. 5:15 (single edit)/16. Bell Boy/17. Love Reign O'er Me (edited)

CD 4: 1. Long Live Rock/2. Life With The Moons/3. Naked Eye (live, Young Vic 26/4/71)/4. University Challenge/5. Slip Kid (edited)/6. Poetry Cornered/7. Dreaming From The Waist (live, Swansea 12/6/76)/8. Blue Red And Grey/9. Life With The Moons 2/10. Squeeze Box/11. My Wife (Entwistle) (live Swansea 12/6/76)/12. Who Are You (single edit)/13. Music Must Change/14. Sister Disco (2nd mix)/15. Guitar And Pen (3rd mix).
Tracks 16–21 consists of post-Moon material bar Track 20. Pete Dialogue (Fillmore West, San Francisco 16/6/69).
(U.K.) Polydor 521 751-2/May 94/-
(U.S.) MCA 11020/5 Jul 94/-170-

MESSAGE TO LOVE: THE ISLE OF WIGHT FESTIVAL 1970
(2 CD set. Various Artists, features uncredited Murray Roman & Keith Moon intro and edited versions of Young Man Blues and Naked Eye from 30/8/70 concert)
(U.K) Castle/Essential EDF CD 327/1995/-

THE WHO LIVE AT THE ISLE OF WIGHT FESTIVAL 1970
(2 CD set from 30/8/70 concert)
CD 1: 1. Heaven And Hell (Entwistle)/2. I Can't Explain/ 3.Young Man Blues (Allison)/4. I Don't Even Know Myself/ 5. Water/6. Overture/7. It's A Boy/8. 1921/9. Amazing Journey/10. Sparks/11. Eyesight To The Blind (The Hawker) (Williamson)/ 12. Christmas
CD 2: 1. The Acid Queen/2. Pinball Wizard/3. Do You Think It's Alright?/4. Fiddle About (Entwistle)/5. Tommy Can You Hear Me?/6. There's A Doctor/7. Go To The Mirror!/ 8. Smash The Mirror/9. Miracle Cure/10. I/Free/11. Tommy's Holiday Camp (Moon)/12. We're Not Gonna Take It/13. Summertime Blues (Cochran/Capehart)/14. Shakin' All Over (Heath)/Spoonful (Burnett)/Twist And Shout (Russell,Medley)/ 15. Substitute/16. My Generation/17. Naked Eye/18. Magic Bus
(U.K.) Castle/Essential EDF CD 326/1996/
(U.S.) Columbia C2K 65084/29 Oct 96/

BBC SESSIONS
1. My Generation (Radio 1 Jingle)/2. Anyway Anyhow Anywhere (Townshend/Daltrey)/3. Good Lovin' (Clark/ Resnick)/4. Just You And Me, Darling (Brown)/5. Leaving Here (Holland/Dozier/Holland)/6. My Generation/7. The Good's Gone/8. La La La Lies/9. Substitute/10. Man With Money (Everly/Everly)/11. Dancing In The Street (Stevenson/Gaye/ Hunter)/12. Disguises/ 13. I'm A Boy/14. Run Run Run/ 15. Boris The Spider (Entwistle)/16. Happy Jack/17. See My Way (Daltrey)/18. Pictures Of Lily/19. A Quick One (While He's Away)/20. Substitute (Version 2)/21. The Seeker/22. I'm Free/ 23. Shakin' All Over (Heath)/Spoonful (Dixon)/24. Relay/ 25. Long Live Rock/26. Boris The Spider (Radio 1 Jingle) (Entwistle)
(U.K) Polydor CD 547 727-2/14 Feb 00
LP 547 727-1
(U.S) MCA 088 111 960-2/15 Feb 00
Track 10 deleted and Spoonful from track 23 edited out. A bonus CD of additional BBC sessions (Point PNT 9019) was available exclusively via the Best Buy chain of stores, featuring: 1. Townshend Talks Tommy/2. Pinball Wizard/3. See Me, Feel Me/4. I Don't Even Know Myself/5. I Can See For Miles/6. Heaven And Hell/7. The Seeker/8. Summertime Blues

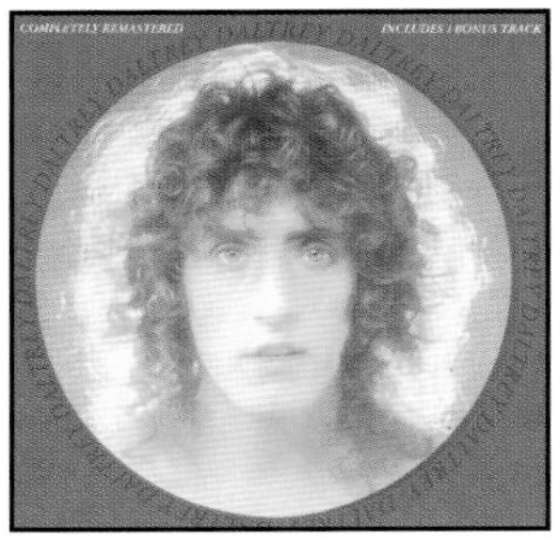

SELECTED SOLO DISCOGRAPHY 1971–1978

ROGER DALTREY

ALBUMS

DALTREY
1.One Man Band/2. The Way Of The World/3. You Are Yourself/4. Thinking/5. You And Me/6. It's A Hard Life/ 7. Giving It All Away/8. The Story So Far/9. When The Music Stops/10. Reasons/11. One Man Band (Reprise). All tracks Courtney, Sayer, except 2 & 5 — Faith, Courtney.
(U.K.) Track 2406 107/20 Apr 73/
Original release had picture centre label and omitted credit for last track.
(U.S.) MCA 328/19 May 73/-45-
(EURO) CD RE 4636-WY, *includes bonus track: There is Love (Courtney, Sayer)*

RIDE A ROCK HORSE
1. Get Your Love (Ballard)/2. Hearts Right (Korda)/3. Oceans Away (Goodhand-Tait)/4. Proud (Ballard)/5. World Over (Korda)/6. Near To Surrender (Ballard)/7. Feeling (Korda)/ 8. Walking The Dog (Thomas)/9. Milk Train (Bugatti, Musker)/ 10. Born To Sing Your Song (Neal, Marchand)
(U.K.) Polydor 2442 135/4 Jul 75/-14-
(U.S.) MCA 2147/26 Jul 75/-28-
(EURO) CD Repertoire REP 4642-WY, *includes bonus tracks: You Put Something Better Inside Me (Rafferty/ Egan)/Dear John (Courtney)/Oceans Away (Goodhand-Tait) (alt. version)*

ONE OF THE BOYS
1. Parade (Goodhand/Tait)/2. Single Man's Dilemma (Blunstone)/3. Avenging Annie (Pratt)/4. The Prisoner (Courtney/Todd/Daltrey)/5. Leon (Goodhand/Tait)/6. One Of the Boys (Gibbons)/7. Giddy (McCartney)/8. Written On The Wind (Korda) in US, Say It Ain't So Joe (Head)/9. Satin And Lace (Courtney/Meehan/Daltrey)/10. Doing It All Again (Courtney/Meehan/Daltrey)
(U.K.) Polydor 2442 146/20 May 77/45-
(U.S.) MCA 2271/11 Jun 77/-46-
(EURO) CD Repertoire REP 4643-WY, includes bonus tracks: *Martyrs And Madmen (Swindells)/Treachery(Swindells)/ Say It Ain't So Joe (Head)*

SINGLES

Giving It All Away/ The Way Of The World
(U.K.) Track 2094 110/16 Mar 73/-5-
(U.S.) MCA Track 40053 31 Mar 73/-83-
From DALTREY

Thinking/There Is Love
(U.K.) Track 2094 014/14 Sept 73/-
(U.S.) MCA Track 40084/Sept 73/-
From DALTREY – *B-side non-album track*

Get Your Love/World Over
(U.K.) Polydor 2058 593/30 May 75/-
From RIDE A ROCK HORSE

Walking The Dog/Proud
(U.K.) Polydor 2058 628/8 Aug 75/-
From RIDE A ROCK HORSE

(Come And) Get Your Love/Hearts Right
(U.S.) MCA 40453/4 Oct 75/-68-
From RIDE A ROCK HORSE

Oceans Away/Feeling
(U.S.) MCA 40512/Jan 76/-
From RIDE A ROCK HORSE

Written On The Wind/Dear John
(U.K.) Polydor 2121 319/22 Apr 77/-
From ONE OF THE BOYS – *B-side non-album track*

One Of The Boys/You Put Something Better Inside Me
(U.K.) Polydor 2058 896/24 Jun 77/-
From ONE OF THE BOYS – *B-side non-album track*

Say It Ain't So Joe/ Satin & Lace
(U.S.) MCA 40765/30 Jul 77/-
From ONE OF THE BOYS

Avenging Annie/The Prisoner
(U.S.) MCA 40800/1 Oct 77/-88-
From ONE OF THE BOYS

Say It Ain't So Joe/Satin & Lace
(U.K.) Polydor 2058 948
Release cancelled

Say It Ain't So Joe/The Prisoner
(U.K.) Polydor 2058 986/17 Feb 78/-
From ONE OF THE BOYS

Leon/The Prisoner
(U.S.) MCA 40862/Apr 78/-
From ONE OF THE BOYS

JOHN ENTWISTLE

ALBUMS

SMASH YOUR HEAD AGAINST THE WALL
1. My Size/2. Pick Me Up (Big Chicken)/3. What Are We Doing Here?/4. What Kind Of People Are They/5. Heaven And Hell 6. Ted End/7. You're Mine/8. No.29 (Eternal Youth)/10. I Believe In Everything (all Entwistle.)
(U.K.) Track 2406 005/14 May 71/-
(U.S.) Decca 79183/9 Oct 71/-126-
CD Sundazed SC 6116 *includes bonus tracks: Cinnamon Girl and alt. version of What Are We Doing Here?*
(EURO) CD Repertoire REP 4613-WY *includes extra track: Cinnamon Girl (Young)*

WHISTLE RYMES
1. Ten Little Friends /2. Apron Strings/3. I Feel Better/ 4. Thinkin' It Over/5. Who Cares? 6. I Wonder/7. I Was Just Being Friendly/8. The Window Shopper/9. I Found Out/ 10. Nightmare (Please Wake Me Up) (all Entwistle.)
(U.K.) Track 2406 104/3 Nov 72/-
(U.S.) Decca DL 79190/4 Nov 72/-138-
CD Sundazed SC 6117
(EURO) CD Repertoire 4618-WY

RIGOR MORTIS SETS IN (U.K. title)
JOHN ENTWISTLE'S RIGOR MORTIS SETS IN (U.S. title)
1. Gimme That Rock 'N' Roll/2. Mr. Bassman (Cymbal)/3. Do The Dangle/4. Hound Dog (Lieber/Stoller)/5. Made In Japan/ 6. My Wife/7. Roller Skate Kate/8. Peg Leg Peggy/9. Lucille (Penniman)/10. Big Black Cadillac (all Entwistle, unless otherwise stated.)
(U.K.) Track 2406 106/11 May 73/-
(U.S.) MCA 321/9 Jun 73/-174-
U.K./U.S. sleeves reversed
(EURO) CD Repertoire REP 4621-WY

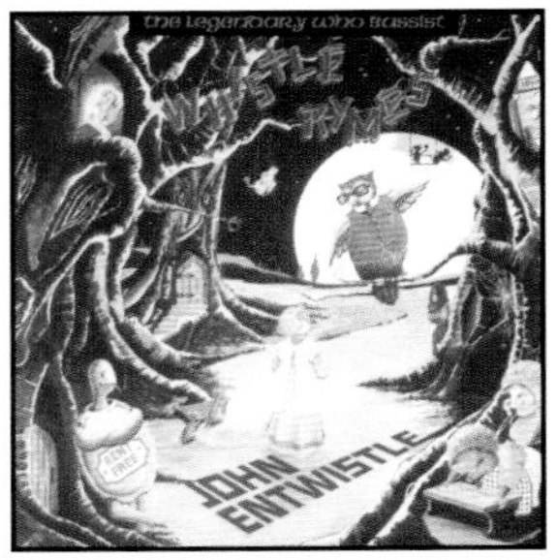

MAD DOG
1. I Fall To Pieces/2. Cell Number 7/3. You Can Be So Mean/ 4. Lady Killer/5. Who In The Hell?/6. Mad Dog/7. Jungle Bunny/8. I'm So Scared/9. Drowning (all Entwistle.)
(U.S.) MCA 2129/Feb 75/-192-
(U.K.) Decca TXS 114/28 Feb 75/-
(EURO) CD Repertoire REP 4629-WY

JOHN ENTWISTLE (U.S.)
JOHN ENTWISTLE LIVE ON THE KING BISCUIT FLOWER HOUR (U.K.)
1. Heaven And Hell/2. Whiskey Man/3. My Size /4. Boris The Spider/5. Not Fade Away/6. Cell Number Seven/7. Who Cares?/ 8. Give Me That Rock And Roll/9. My Wife/10. Interview
(U.K.) KBFH Records KBFHCD006/1997
(U.S.) BMG 70710-88030-2/1997
Different U.S./U.K sleeves.
Concert recorded 15 Mar 75 at The Spectrum, Philadelphia

SINGLES

I Believe In Everything /My Size
(U.K.) Track 2049 008/1 Apr 71/-
(U.S.) Decca 32896/May 71/-
From SMASH YOUR HEAD

I Wonder/Who Cares
(U.S.) Decca Track 33052/Nov 72/-
From WHISTLE RYMES

Made In Japan/Hound Dog
(U.K.) Track 2049 107/26 Jan 73/-
From RIGOR MORTIS SETS IN

Made In Japan/Roller Skate Kate
(U.S.) MCA 40066/Jun 73/-
From RIGOR MORTIS SETS IN

Mad Dog/Cell Number Seven
(U.K.) Decca FR 13567/7 Feb 75/-
From MAD DOG

KEITH MOON

ALBUMS

TWO SIDES OF THE MOON
1. Crazy Like A Fox (Staehely)/2. Solid Gold (Barclay)/3. Don't Worry Baby (Wilson- Christian)/4. One Night Stand (Larden)/ 5. The Kids Are Alright (Townshend)/6. Move Over Ms. L (Lennon)/ 7. Teenage Idol (Lewis)/8. Backdoor Sally (Marascalco)/9. In My Life (Lennon- McCartney)/10. Together (Nilsson)
(U.S.) MCA 2136/17 Mar 75/-155-
CD Mausoleum 60038-2
(U.K.) Polydor 2442 134/25 Apr 75/-
(EURO) CD Repertoire REP 4635-WY
CD includes bonus tracks: Radio Spot/I Don't Suppose (unknown)/ Naked Man (Newman)/Do Me Good (Cropper)/Real Emotion (Cropper)/Don't Worry Baby (Wilson-Christian) (first mix)/ Teenage Idol (Lewis) (first mix)/Together Rap (Moon-Starr)

SINGLES

Don't Worry Baby/ Teenage Idol
(U.S.) MCA 40316/28 Sep 74/-
First mix, produced Mal Evans.

Don't Worry Baby/ Together
(U.K.) Polydor 2058 584/2 May 75/-
From TWO SIDES OF THE MOON.
Skip Taylor/John Stronach produced versions.

Solid Gold/Move Over Miss L
(U.S.) MCA 40387/Apr 75/-
From TWO SIDES OF THE MOON.

Crazy Like A Fox/In My Life
(U.S.) MCA 40433/Jul 75/-
From TWO SIDES OF THE MOON.

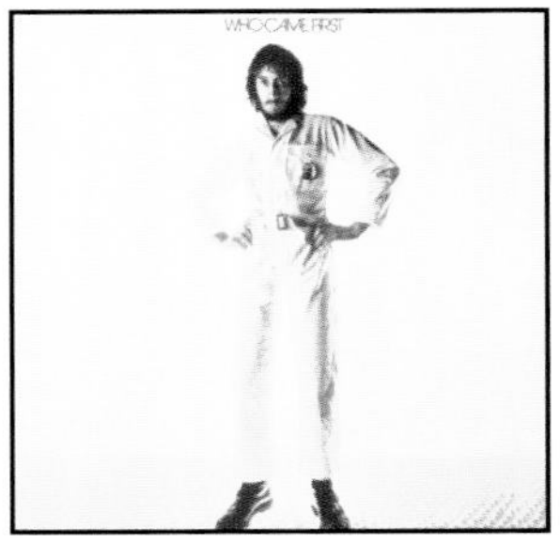

PETE TOWNSHEND

ALBUMS

HAPPY BIRTHDAY
USL 001/Feb 70 Reissued as MBO-1
Contributed and played on several tracks.

I AM
USL 002/Feb 72 Reissued as MBO-2
Contributed and played on several tracks.

The above albums were only available via mail order from the Meher Baba Spiritual League.

WHO CAME FIRST
1. Pure & Easy/2. Evolution (Lane)/3. Forever's No Time At All (Nicholls/McInnerney)/4. Nothing Is Everything (Let's See Action)/ 5. Time Is Passing/6. There's A Heartache Following Me (Baker)/ 7. Sheraton Gibson/8. Content (Kennedy/Townshend)/ 9. Parvardigar
(U.K.) Track 2408 201/ 9 Sep 72/-30-
(U.S.) Decca 79189/Oct 72/-69-
Ryko RCD 10246 – *features bonus tracks from Meher Baba albums: His Hands/The Seeker (Demo)/ Day Of Silence/Sleeping Dog/The Love Man/ Lantern Cabin*

WITH LOVE
USL 003-76/ Mar 76 Re-issued as MBO-3
Contributed three tracks.
The above album was only availiable via mail order from the Meher Baba Spiritual League.

ROUGH MIX (with Ronnie Lane)
1. My Baby Gives It Away/2. Nowhere To Run (Lane)/3. Rough Mix (Townshend/Lane)/4. Annie (Lane)/5. Keep Me Turning/ 6. Cat Melody (Lane)/7. Misunderstood/8. April Fool(Lane)/ 9. Street In The City/10. Heart To Hang Onto/11. Till The Rivers All Run Dry (Holyfield, Williams)
(U.S.) MCA 2295/Sep 77/-45-
CD ATCO 7 90097-2/Jun 89
(U.K.) Polydor 2442 147/16 Sep 77/-44-

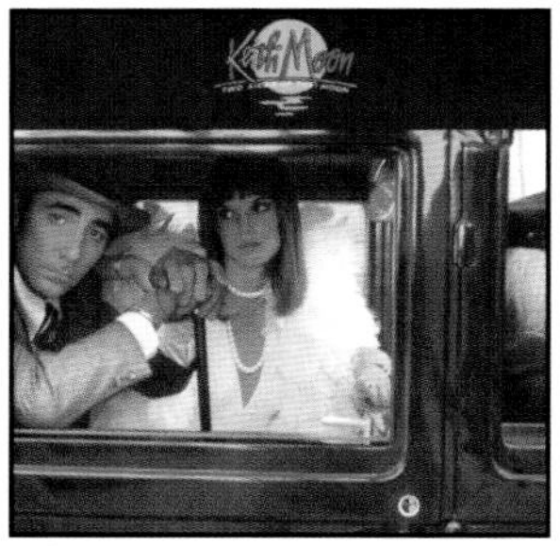

SCOOP
(U.S.) ATCO 7 90063-1-F/19 Mar 1983/-
CD ATCO 7 90063-2/
(U.K) ATCO 79-0063-1/1983
Includes demos recorded for the Who.

ANOTHER SCOOP
(U.S) ATCO 7 90539-1-G/ 7 Mar 87/-
CD ATCO 7 90539-2
(U.K.) ATCO 79-0539-1/ 1989/-
Includes demos recorded for the Who.

AVATAR
U.K. Eel Pie (No. Cat. No.)/7 Feb 2000
Limited CD box set of 2000, available only via Pete Townshend's official website. Includes Happy Birthday, I Am, and With Love plus bonus fourth CD.

THE LIFEHOUSE CHRONICLES
U.K. Eel Pie EPR 002-1/6-7 Feb 2000
Limited edition 6 CD box set, available only via Pete Townshend's official website. Includes demos recorded for the Who.

SINGLES

Street In The City/ Annie (Ronnie Lane)
(U.K.) Polydor 2058 944/11 Nov 77/-
From ROUGH MIX
7" and 12" format pressed; only 12" officially released.

My Baby Gives It Away/ April Fool (Ronnie Lane)
(U.S.) MCA 40818/19 Nov 77/-
From ROUGH MIX

Keep Me Turning/Nowhere To Run (Ronnie Lane)
(U.S.) MCA 40878/18 Mar 78/-
From ROUGH MIX

My Generation/Pinball Wizard
Eel Pie Publishing/Sept 82
*1-sided flexi-disc of Who demos, included with
The Who: Maximum R&B by Richard Barnes.*

PRODUCTIONS AND
GUEST APPEARANCES

ROGER DALTREY

BACKTRACK 7: MIXED BAG
(U.K.) Track 2407 007/6 Nov 70
Producer of Bent Frame track, It's Only Me

RIDING THE CREST OF A SLUMP (Ellis)
(U.K.) Epic EPC 64878/29 Sep 72
(U.S.) Epic KE 31945/17 Jan 73
Producer

TOMMY (Various Artists, with London
Symphony Orchestra and Chambre Choir)
(U.S.) Ode 99 001/27 Nov 72
        Ode QU 89001 (Quad Mix)/Dec 72
(U.K. Ode SP 88 001/8 Dec 72
Vocals — see also John Entwistle, Pete Townshend.

I'm Free/Underture (with London Symphony Orchestra
and Chambre Choir)
(U.S.) Ode 66040/Sep 72
I'm Free/Overture (with London Symphony Orchestra
and Chambre Choir)
(U.K.) Ode 66302/20 Jul 73
(from Tommy)

TOMMY (SOUNDTRACK)
(U.S.) Polydor PD2-9502/22 Feb 75
(U.K.) Polydor 2657 014/21 Mar 75
Vocals

**Listening to You, See Me, Feel Me/ Overture
From Tommy**
(U.S.) Polydor 15098/Mar 75
(U.K.) Polydor 2001 561/4 Apr 75
(from Tommy soundtrack)

LISZTOMANIA (SOUNDTRACK)
(U.S.) A&M SP-4546/ Nov 75
(U.K.) A&M AMLH 64546/ 21 Nov 75

Love's Dream/Orpheus Song
(U.S.) A&M 1779-S/Nov 75
(U.K.) A&M AMS 7206/28 Nov 75
(from Lisztomania soundtrack)

JOHN ENTWISTLE

So Sad About Us/Love Will Continue
(The Merseys)
(U.K.) Fontana TF 732 29/Jul 66
French horn on B-side (see also Pete Townshend).

Suspicion (Vivian Stanshall's Gargantuan Chums)/
Blind Date (Big Grunt)
(U.K.) Fly Bug 4/11 Dec 70
Bass, brass A-side (see also Keith Moon).

TOMMY (Various Artists, with the London
Symphony Orchestra and Chambre Choir)
(U.S.) Ode 99 001/25 Nov 72
        Ode QU 89001 (Quad Mix)/Dec 72
(U.K.) Ode SP 88 001/8 Dec 72
Vocal, Cousin Kevin.

TOMMY (SOUNDTRACK)
(U.S.) Polydor PD2-9502/22 Feb 75
(U.K.) Polydor 2657 014/21 Mar 75
Co-producer. Vocals, bass, and brass.

**FLASH FEARLESS VS. THE ZORG
WOMEN PARTS 5 AND 6** (Various Artists)
(U.S.) Chrysalis 1072/May 75
(U.S.) Chrysalis 1081/23 May 75
*Bass, brass, and vocals.
U.S./U.K. versions differ in one track (see also Keith Moon).*

ANY ROAD UP (Steve Gibbons Band)
(U.K.) Polydor Goldhawke 2383 381/7 May 76
(U.S.) MCA 2178/1976
*Producer (with Cy Langston).
Recorded at Ramport and Eel Pie.*

ROLLIN' ON (Steve Gibbons Band)
(U.K.) Polydor Goldhawke 2383 433/11 Feb 77
(U.S.) MCA 2243/1977
*Thanked in credits (with Cy Langston).
Recorded at Eel Pie, Goring.*

ONE OF THE BOYS (Roger Daltrey)
(U.K.) Polydor 2442 146/20 May 77/-45-
(U.S.) MCA 2271/ 11 Jun 77/-46-
EURO CD Repertoire REP 4643- WY
Bass on several tracks.

FABULOUS POODLES (Fabulous Poodles)
(U.K.) Pye NSPL 18530/9 Sep 77
*Producer (engineer: Cy Langston), bass.
Recorded at Ramport Studios.*

ROUGH MIX (with Ronnie Lane)
(U.S.) MCA 2295 Sep 77
        CD ATCO 7 90097-2/Jun 89
(U.K.) Polydor 2442 147/16 Sep 77
Back-up vocals on Till The Rivers All Run Dry.

KEITH MOON

I Stand Accused/All My Life (Merseybeats)
(U.K.) Fontana TF 645/3 Dec 65
Gong on A-side.

Hi Ho Silver Lining/ Beck's Bolero (Jeff Beck)
(U.K.) Columbia DB 8151/24 Mar 67
(U.S.) Epic 5-10157/3 Apr 67
Drums on B-side.

All You Need Is Love/Baby You're A Rich Man
(The Beatles)
(U.K.) Parlophone R 5620/7 Jul 67
(U.S.) Capitol 5964/17 Jul 67
Backing vocals on A-side.

TRUTH (Jeff Beck)
(U.S.) Epic BN 26413/29 Jul 68
(U.K.) Columbia SCX 6293/4 Oct 68
Drums on Beck's Bolero. Credited as "You Know Who"on timpani.

Witchi Tai To/Jam (Topo D. Bil)
(U.K.) Charisma CB 116/9 Jan 70
Percussion on A-side.

Suspicion (Vivian Stanshall's Gargantuan Chums)/
Blind Date (Big Grunt)
(U.K.) Fly Bug 4/11 Dec 70
Producer, drums A-side (see also John Entwistle).

SMILING MEN WITH BAD REPUTATIONS
(Mike Heron)
(U.K.) Island 9146/7 May 71
(U.S.) Electra 74093/1971
*Drums on Warm Heart Pastry, credited as Tommy and the
Bijoux. (see also Pete Townshend).*

SMASH YOUR HEAD AGAINST THE WALL
(John Entwistle)
(U.K.) Track 2406 005/14 May 71
(U.S.) Decca 79183/9 Oct 71
        CD Sundazed SC 6116
(EURO) CD Repertoire REP 4613-WY
*Percussion on Number 29 and vocals in chorus on I Believe In
Everything.*

Do The Albert/Commercial Break (Scaffold)
(U.K.) Parlophone R 5922/1 Oct 71
Drums on A-side.

SOMETIME IN NEW YORK CITY
(John Lennon & Yoko Ono)
(U.S.) Apple SVBB 3392/12 Jun 72
(U.S.) Apple PCSP 716/15 Sep 72
*Drums on Live Jam - Cold Turkey and Don't Worry, Kyoko.
Credited by Lennon as Keif Spoon.
Recorded live at the Lyceum, London, Dec 69.*

HANDS OF JACK THE RIPPER
(Lord Sutch And Heavy Friends)
(U.K.) Atlantic K 40313/14 Jul 72
(U.S.) Cotillion 9040/1972
*Drums on Jenny, Jenny and Good Golly, Miss Molly medley.
Recorded live at Hampstead Country Club, Apr 70.*

PALE HORSE (Dave Carlsen)
(U.K.) Spark Records SRLP 110/Nov 73
Drums on Death On A Pale Horse.

THAT'LL BE THE DAY (SOUNDTRACK)
(U.K.) Ronco MR2002/3 - 25 May 73
*Drums on Long Live Rock (track credited to Billy Fury).
(See also Pete Townshend.)*

VALENTINE (Roy Harper)
(U.K.) Harvest SHSP 4027/14 Feb 74
(U.S.) Chrysalis CHR 1163/1974
Drums on Male Chauvinist Pig Blues.

FLASHES FROM THE ARCHIVES OF OBLIVION
(Roy Harper)
(U.K.) Harvest SHDW 405/15 Nov 74
*Drums on The Great Divider (Side 4).
Recorded live, Rainbow Theatre Valentine's Day Concert 74.*

PUSSY CATS (Harry Nilsson)
(U.S.) RCA CPL-1 0570/19 Aug 74
(U.K.) RCA APL1 0570/30 Aug 74
*Chinese wood blocks on All My Life, drums on
Loop De Loop and Rock Around The Clock,
congas on Mucho Mungo/Mt. Elga.*

REEL TO REAL (Love)
(U.S.) RSO 4804/Nov 74
(U.K.) RSO 2394 145/17 Jan 75
Keith's unknown contribution cited in credits.

TOMMY (SOUNDTRACK)
(U.S.) Polydor PD2-9502/22 Feb 75
(U.K.) Polydor 2657 014/21 Mar 75
Drums/vocals Uncle Ernie.

**FLASH FEARLESS VS. THE ZORG WOMEN
PARTS 5 AND 6** (Various Artists)
(U.S.) Chrysalis 1072/May 75
(U.S.) Chrysalis 1081/23 May 75
*Contributed drums on two tracks.
U.S./U.K. versions differ in one track.*

20th ANNIVERSARY OF ROCK 'N' ROLL
(Bo Diddley)
(U.S.) RCA APL 1-1229/Jan 76
(U.K.) RCA RS 1042/Mar 76
*Percussion on Diddley Jam. Recorded early 75, Record Plant
West, L.A.*

ALL THIS AND WORLD WAR II
(Various Artists)
(U.S.) 20th Century 2T 522/25 Oct 76
(U.K.) Riva RVLP-2/5 Nov 76
Vocals on When I'm Sixty-Four.

ROCK ROLLS ON (Michael Bruce)
(Germany) Euro-Tec ET 4-27-1/1983
Re-issued on CD as IN MY OWN WAY
(U.S.) One-Way Records OW 34486/Oct 97
*Ex-Alice Cooper solo effort, recorded late 74 Record Plant West,
L.A. Drums on As Rock Rolls On credited to Rikki Fataar, but
includes mixed down Moon drum track. Moon thanked in credits.*

PETE TOWNSHEND

So Sad About Us/Love Will Continue
(The Merseys)
(U.K.) Fontana TF 732/29 Jul 66
*A-side written and produced by PT prior to Who's version, although
label production credits Kit Lambert. (See also John Entwistle.)*

Devil's Grip/Give Him A Flower
(The Crazy World of Arthur Brown)
(U.K.) Track 604 008/15 Sep 67
Co-producer credit with Kit Lambert.

Fire/Rest Cure (The Crazy World of Arthur Brown)
(U.K.) Track 604 022/14 Jun 68
(U.S.) ATCO Track 2556/7 Sep 68
Associate Producer credit. Rhythm guitar on B-side.

THE CRAZY WORLD OF ARTHUR BROWN
(The Crazy World of Arthur Brown)
(U.K.) Track 612 005 (Mono)
        613 005 (Stereo)/21 Jun 68
(U.S.) ATCO 8198/7 Sep 68
Associate Producer credit.

Nightmare/What's Happening
(initial copies listed Music Man as B-side)
(The Crazy World of Arthur Brown)
(U.K.) Track 604 026/15 Nov 68
Associate Producer credit.

Something In The Air/Wilhelmina
(Thunderclap Newman)
(U.K.) Track 604 031/23 May 69
*Producer, bass. Single version A-side, non-album B-side.
On all Thunderclap Newman associated releases, PT used
the pseudonym Bijou Drains.*

Something In The Air/I See It All
(Thunderclap Newman)
(U.S.) ATCO Track 45 2769/1969

Accidents/I See It All
(Thunderclap Newman)
(U.K.) Track 2094 001/15 May 70
Producer, bass. Single version A-side, non-album B-side.

The Reason/Stormy Petrel
(Thunderclap Newman)
(U.K.) Track 2094 003/28 Aug 70
*Producer, bass. Single version A-side. B-side recorded live at
Hammersmith Town Hall and produced by Townshend and
Richard Cardboard.*

HOLLYWOOD DREAM
(Thunderclap Newman)
(U.K.) Track 2406 003/2 Oct 70
(U.S.) Atlantic Track SD8264/ 1970
Producer, bass, pedal steel guitar on title track.

Wild Country/ Hollywood Dream
(Thunderclap Newman)
(U.K.) Track 2094 005/13 Nov 70
*From HOLLYWOOD DREAM. Producer, bass, pedal steel
on B-side.*

SMILING MEN WITH BAD REPUTATIONS
Mike Heron,
(U.K.) Island ILPS 9146/7 May 71
(U.S.) Electra 74093/1971
*Guitar on Warm Heart Pastry, as Tommy and the Bijoux
(see also Keith Moon).*

STICKY FINGERS (The Rolling Stones)
(U.K.) Rolling Stones COC 59100/23 Apr 71
(U.S.) Rolling Stones 59100/15 May 71
*Uncredited backing vocals on Sway, with Mick Jagger, Ronnie
Lane and Billy Nicholls.*

WOMAN CHILD (Marsha Hunt)
(U.K.) Track 2410 101/17 Dec 71
Guitar/backing vocals on Long Black Veil and Wild Thing.

REVELATIONS (Various Artists)
(U.K.) Rev 1/2/3-4 Aug 72
*Glastonbury Fayre triple album set. Contributed one studio track,
Classified.*

RAINBOW (Andy Newman)
(U.K.) Track 2406 103/11 Aug 72
Overseer and Executive Producer.

TOMMY (Various Artists, with the London Symphony
Orchestra and Chambre Choir)
(U.S.) Ode 99 001/25 Nov 72
        Ode QU 89001 (Quad Mix)/Dec 72
(U.K.) Ode SP 88 001/8 Dec 72
Narrator (see also Roger Daltrey, John Entwistle).

Forever's No Time At All/This Song Is Green
(Billy Nicholls)
(U.K.) Track 2094 109/16 Feb 73
*A-side from WHO CAME FIRST. Recording engineer,
synthesised flute on B-side.*

WILLIE AND THE LAPDOG (Gallagher and Lyle)
(U.K) A&M AMLH 68148/7 Apr 73
Bass harmonica on Give The Boy A Break.

Murder Man/If I Did
(John Otway & Wild Willy Barrett)
(U.K.) Track 2094 111/20 Apr 73
(U.S.) MCA Track 40081/1973
Producer, bass. Recorded at Eel Pie Sound for Community Music.

THAT'LL BE THE DAY (SOUNDTRACK)
(U.K.) Ronco MR2002/3–25 May 73
*Guitar on Long Live Rock (Track credited to Billy Fury).
(See also Keith Moon.)*

I Can't Explain/Hawaii (Yvonne Elliman)
U.K Purple PUR 114/3 Aug 73
Guitar on A-side, also included on: FOOD OF LOVE album.
(U.K.) Purple PUR TPS 3504/ 26 Oct 73
(U.S.) MCA 356/ 1973

ERIC CLAPTON'S RAINBOW CONCERT
(Eric Clapton)
(U.K.) RSO 877/Sep 73
(U.S.) RSO 2394 116/28 Sep 73
Guitar, backing vocals.

LOVE SONGS (Billy Nicholls)
(U.K.) GM GML 1011/2 Aug 74
*Engineer on Helpless, Helpless.
Recorded at Eel Pie Sound.*

TOMMY (SOUNDTRACK)
(U.S.) Polydor PD2-9502/22 Feb 75
(U.K.) Polydor 2657 014/21 Mar 75
Producer, vocals, guitar, and keyboards.

MAHONEY'S LAST STAND
(Ron Wood/Ronnie Lane)
(U.S.) ATCO SD 36 136/Sep 76
(U.K.) Atlantic K 50308/17 Sep 76
Percussion on Car Radio and guitar on Tonight's Number.

Louisa On A Horse/ Misty Mountain
(John Otway & Wild Willy Barrett)
(U.K.) Track 2094 133/27 Aug 76
Producer, bass. Recorded 73 at Eel Pie Sound.

ROLLIN' ON (Steve Gibbons Band)
(U.K.) Polydor Goldhawke 2383 433/11 Feb 77
(U.S.) MCA 2243/1977
*Townshend engineered at Eel Pie Sound, Goring, Berkshire (see
also John Entwistle).*

JOHN OTWAY & WILD WILLY BARRETT
(John Otway & Wild Willy Barrett)
(U.K.) Extracted EXLP 1/1 Jul 77
(reissued as Polydor SUPER 2383 453)/5 Aug 77
(U.S.) Stiff USE 5/1977
*Includes Murder Man, If I Did, Louisa On A Horse,
Misty Mountain.*

CONCERT INDEX: 1961–1977

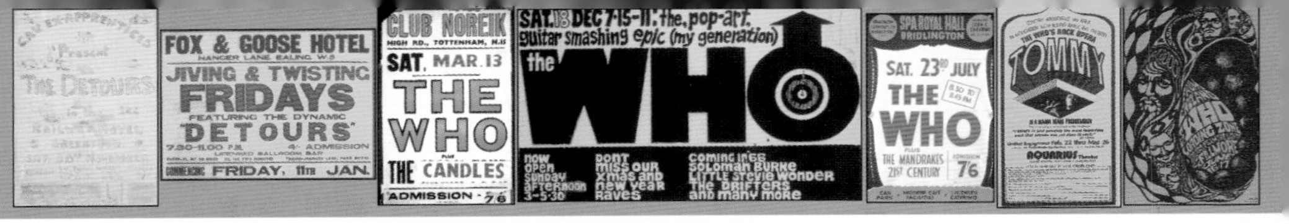

Solo performances by individual band members are denoted by their initials, i.e., (KM) indicates a performance featuring Keith Moon. When the band played a venue multiple times in one year, the year is included in the sequence's final date, i.e., 10/10, 24/10, 27/10/64.
(c) stands for "cancelled"
(p) stands for "postponed"

AUSTRALIA
Adelaide Centennial Hall: 27/1/68 (2)
Brisbane Festival Hall: 20/1/68 (2)
Melbourne Festival Hall: 25–26/1/68 (2 per day)
Melbourne Myer Music Bowl: 31/3/73 (KM)
Sydney Stadium: 22–23/1/68 (2 per day)

AUSTRIA
Vienna Stadhalle: 2/9/72, 28/10/75

BELGIUM
Brussels Forest Nationale: 16/8/72
Woluwe Festival: 20/5/67

CANADA
Calgary Stampede Corral: 13/7/67 (2), 10/7/68 (2)
Edmonton Civic Centre: 16/10/76
Edmonton New Edmonton Gardens: 21/8/67, 2/3/68
Fort William Gardens: 26/8/67
Kingston Memorial Centre: 15/7/68
Montreal Autostade: 17/7/68 (2)
Montreal Forum: 27/3/68, 2/12/73
Ottawa Capitol Theatre: 21/5/69 (2) (c), 15/10/69
Ottawa Civic Centre: 16/7/68
Saskatchewan Saskatoon Arena: 11/7/68
Toronto CNE Coliseum: 7/4/68, 14/10/69
Toronto Maple Leaf Gardens: 9/8/67, 11/12/75, 21/10/76
Toronto Massey Hall: 1/3/75 (JE)
Toronto Rock Pile Club: 19/5/69 (2)
Vancouver The Agrodome: 17/7/67, 1/3/68
Winnipeg Arena: 22/8/67, 18/10/76

DENMARK
Aalborg Fredrikstorv: 26/9/65
Aarhus Hallen: 26/9/65
Aarhus Veslby Risskov Hallen: 21/9/70
Copenhagen Falkoner Centret Teatret: 20/9/70
Copenhagen Herlev Hallen: 20/10/66
Copenhagen Hit House: 7/6/66
Copenhagen KB Hallen: 25/9/65, 21/8/72, 22/8/72 (p), 25/8/72
Copenhagen Royal Theatre: 24/1/70
Helsingor Folkets Hus: 25/9/65
Odense Fyens Forum: 7/6/66, 23/10/66

FINLAND
Helsinki Jäähallissa: 30/4/67

FRANCE
Colmar Parc des Expositions: 22/5/76
Lille Palais des Jrottes, Cambrai: 9/2/74
Lyon Palais d'Hiver de Lyon: 28/10/66
Lyon Palais des Sports: 10/9/72, 24/2/74, 25/5/76
Nancy Parc des Expositions: 22/2/74
Paris Fête de L'Humanite: 9/9/72
Paris La Locomotive: 13/11/65 (2), 2/4/66 (2)
Paris Le Club au Golf Drouot: 2/6/65
Paris Parc des Expositions: 10/2/74
Paris Pavillion de Paris: 1-2/3/76
Paris Theatre des Champs Elysses: 16-17/1/70
Poitiers Palais des Armes: 15/2/74
Toulouse Foire De Toulouse 17/2/74

GERMANY (WEST)
Berlin Deutschlandhalle: 30/8/72
Berlin Opernhaus: 28/1/70
Berlin Sportpalast: 30/10/66
Bremen Stadthalle: 19/4/67, 29/10/75
Cologne Kongresshalle: 6/11/66 (2)
Cologne Opernhaus: 26/1/70
Düsseldorf Philipshalle: 30-31/10/75
Düsseldorf Rheinhalle: 7/11/66, 11/4/67
Essen Grugahalle: 31/8/72
Frankfurt Festhalle: 11/8/72
Frankfurt Radstadion: 22/7/73 (KM)
Hamburg Ernst Merck Halle: 12/8/72
Hamburg Opernhaus: 27/1/70
Herford Jaguar-Club: 10/4/67
Ludwigshafen Eherthalle: 6-7/11/75
Ludwigshafen Friedrich-Ebert-Halle: 12/4/67
Munich Circus-Krone-Bau: 13/4/67 (2)
Munich Deutsches Museum, Kongressaal: 4/9/72
Munich Olympiahalle: 28/2/76
Münster Münsterland Halle: 14/4/67, 12/9/70
Nuremburg Messehalle: 8/4/67
Offenbach Oberrheinhalle: 13/9/70
Ravensburg Oberschwabenhalle: 16/4/67
Saarbrücken Messehalle: 5/11/66
Siegen Siegerlandhalle: 15/4/67
Sindelfingen Messehalle: 2-3/11/75
Ulm Donauhalle: 16/4/67
Wiesbaden Rhein-Main Halle: 15/4/67
Wuppertal Thalia-Theater: 9/4/67

IRELAND
Cork Arcadia Ballroom: 8/5/66
Dublin National Stadium: 7/5/66

ITALY
Bologna Palazzetto dello Sport: 24/2/67 (2)
Milan Palalido: 25/2/67
Milan Piper Club: 25/2/67
Rome Palasport: 14/9/72
Rome Palazzetto dello Sport: 26/2/67
Rome Piper Club: 26/2/67
Turin Palazzetto dello Sport: 23/2/67 (2)

THE NETHERLANDS
Amsterdam Concertgebouw: 29/9/69, 30/1/70, 17/9/70
Amsterdam Oude Rai: 17/8/72
The Hague Club 192: 12/10/66
The Hague De Marathon: 21/9/65
The Hague De Vliegermolen Sportshal: 10/3/73
Rotterdam Ahoy: 27/10/75
Rotterdam De Doelen: 16/9/70

NEW ZEALAND
Auckland Town Hall: 29/1/68 (2)
Wellington Town Hall: 31/1/68 (2)

NORWAY
Oslo Njardhallen: 2/5/67

SWEDEN
Eskilstuna Sporthallen: 5/5/67
Gothenburg Cirkus: 10/10/65 (2), 3/5/67 (2)
Gothenburg Konserthallen: 21/10/66 (2)
Gothenburg Scandinavium: 24/8/72
Halmstad Folkparken: 24/10/66
Höör Jagersbo-Höör: 22/10/66
Jonköping Rigoletto: 4/5/67
Kristianstad Sommarlust: 7/5/67
Kungliga Tennishallen: 23/8/72
Kungsor Kungsparken: 3/6/66
Malmö MFF-Stadion: 23/10/66, 7/5/67
Nyköping Traffen: 5/6/66
Norrköping Masshallen: 4/5/67
Örebro Idrottshuset: 5/6/66
Sandviken Högbo Bruk: 4/6/66
Simrishamn Gislovs Stjarna: 22/10/66
Söderhamn Berget: 4/6/66
Stockholm Club Nalen: 25/10/66
Stockholm Grona Lund: 2/6/66
Stockholm Johanneshovs Isstadion: 10/10/65
Stockholm Kungliga Tennishallen: 6/5/67
Uppsala Liljekonvaljeholmen: 3/6/66

SWITZERLAND
Zurich Hallenstadion: 27/2/76
Zurich Mehrzweckhalle Wetzikon: 5/9/72

UNITED KINGDOM: ENGLAND
Note: The county designations refer to the location *prior* to the 1 April, 1974, reorganisation act.

BEDFORDSHIRE
Bedford Corn Exchange: 10/9/66
Dunstable California Ballroom: 7/12/63, 4/4/64 (Detours), 3/9/65, 4/3/67, 19/10/68
Dunstable Civic Hall: 14/5/65, 27/4/70, 25/7/70, 10/7/71
Luton Majestic Ballroom: 24/5/64 (Who), 20/8/64 (High Numbers), 11/4/65

BERKSHIRE
Newbury Plaza Ballroom: 4/4/65
Newbury Corn Exchange: 20/5/66
Reading Festival: 26/6/71 (KM)
Reading Majestic Ballroom: 24/5/65
Reading Olympia Ballroom: 10/10, 24/10, 27/10/64 (High Numbers), 14/11/64, 8/4/65, 8/7/65
Reading University: 12/12/68, 2/10/71
Windsor Ricky Tick Club: 30/10/64 (High Numbers), 28/5/65, 25/6/65, 17/12/65
Windsor 6th National Jazz and Blues Festival: 30/7/66

BRISTOL
Colston Hall: 10/11/68 (2)
Corn Exchange: 19/5/65, 8/12/65, 11/5/66
Hippodrome Theatre: 4/12/69
Locarno Ballroom: 21/7/66, 26/1/67, 18/5/67, 10/7/69 (KM)
Silver Blades Ice Rink: 8/1/68
University: 7/12/68

BUCKINGHAMSHIRE
Bletchley Wilton Hall: 31/7/65
High Wycombe Town Hall: 15/6/65, 26/6/65, 24/8/65, 30/11/65, 25/4/67
Slough Adelphi Cinema: 10/11/67 (2), 9/11/68 (2)
Slough Carlton Ballroom: 24/10/65

CAMBRIDGESHIRE
Cambridge Christ's College: 12/6/67
Cambridge Corn Exchange: 14/3/69
Cambridge Dorothy Ballroom: 23/11/65
March Marcam Hall: 5/3/66

CHESHIRE
Altrincham Stamford Hall: 9/4/65
Nantwich Civic Hall: 6/1/68, 18/1/69
Northwich Memorial Hall: 19/2/66
Stockport Manor Lounge: 13/6/65

CORNWALL
Camborne Skating Rink: 14/10/65
Redruth Flamingo Club: 27/7/66

CUMBERLAND
Carlisle Cosmopolitan Club: 9/1/66, 7/9/69
Carlisle Market Assembly Hall: 9/10/65, 18/6/66, 19/11/66

DERBYSHIRE
Buxton Pavilion Gardens Ballroom: 29/5/65, 9/4/66
Chesterfield Victoria Hall: 15/4/65, 24/2/66 (p), 3/3/66
Derby Corporation Hotel: 29/5/64
Derby Odeon Cinema: 22/4/66 (2), 16/9/66 (2)

DEVONSHIRE
Barnstaple Queen's Hall: 4/11/65 (c), 28/7/66
Devonport Forum Cinema: 18/3/67
Devonport Van Dike Club: 11/7/69 (KM)
Exeter University: 17/3/67, 1/5/70, 15/1/75 (JE)
Plymouth Guildhall: 9/12/65, 14/1/75 (JE)
Torquay Town Hall: 17/7/65, 20/8/66

DURHAM
Durham University: 8/12/67, 21/6/68
Stockton-on-Tees ABC Cinema: 22/10/70
Sunderland Empire Theatre: 10/12/66 (2)
Sunderland Top Rank Suite: 7/5/71
Sunderland Whitburn Bay Hotel: 28/4/69, 28/7/69

ESSEX
Basildon Locarno: 9/7/65, 18/3/66, 2/9/66
Brentwood Bubbel's Club: 14/12/68
Chelmsford Corn Exchange: 28/11/64, 23/1/65, 4/12/65, 30/4/66, 15/10/66
Colchester Corn Exchange: 23/8/65
Colchester Essex University: 10/2/68
Dagenham Roundhouse: 20/2/71 (KM)
Grays Marquee Meadow Festival: 23/8/69 (c)
Hadleigh Kingsway Theatre: 25/1/67 (2)
Ilford Palais: 6/9/66, 31/1/67
Loughton Youth Centre: 2/4/65
Romford County Technical School: 18/5/66 (KM)
Romford Shandon Hall Dance Club: 2/10/64 (High Numbers)
Southend-on-Sea Odeon Cinema: 5/2/66 (2)

GLOUCESTERSHIRE
Cheltenham Whaddon Football Ground: 16/7/65
Cheltenham Blue Moon Club: 11/8/65

HAMPSHIRE
Basingstoke Carnival Hall: 26/8/65
Basingstoke Galaxy Club: 26/12/64
Bournemouth Le Disque A Go!Go! Club: 3/3/65, 12/5/65 (KM)
Bournemouth Pavilion Ballroom: 20/8/65, 2/3/69 (p), 2/4/69, 29/8/69
Bournemouth Winter Gardens Theatre: 12/11/70 (KM)
Farnborough Town Hall: 30/6/65, 8/9/65, 9/3/66
Portsmouth Birdcage Club: 18/12/65, 12/3/66, 4/2/67
Portsmouth Brave New World Club: 9/1/68
Portsmouth Savoy Ballroom: 11/7/65, 19/9/65
Southampton Gaumont Cinema: 14/4/66 (2)
Southampton Guildhall: 18/10/71
Southampton Top Rank Ballroom: 20/10/65
Southampton University: 11/12/65, 26/11/68
Southampton Waterfront Club: 31/10/64 (High Numbers), 18/12/64, 13/2/65, 22/4/65

HEREFORDSHIRE
Hereford Hillside Ballroom: 15/10/65

HERTFORDSHIRE
Barnet All Saints' Hall: 8/8/64 (High Numbers)
Bishop's Stortford Rhodes Centre: 27/3/65, 23/10/65
Boreham Wood Lynx Youth Club (a.k.a. Links International Club): 26/2/65, 24/4/65, 26/4/66
Carpenders Park Labour Hall (a.k.a. "The Mine"): 12/8/64, 2/9/64, 7/10/64 (High Numbers), 4/11/64
Cheshunt Wolsey Hall: 11/10/64 (High Numbers), 18/11/64, 13/1/65, 1/12/65, 2/3/66
Hemel Hempstead Dacorum College: 7/4/65
Hertford Corn Exchange: 25/3/66
Royston Public Baths: 19/3/65
St. Albans City Hall: 22/11/68
Stevenage Bowes Lyon Youth House: 17/6/65
Stevenage Locarno Ballroom: 14/7/65, 3/11/65, 26/1/66, 21/4/66, 7/9/66, 17/5/67
Watford Odeon Cinema: 16/4/66 (2)
Watford Top Rank Suite: 29/4/68
Watford Town Hall: 15/7/71
Watford Trade Union Hall: 11/7, 18/7 (Who), 25/7, 1/8, 22/8, 19/9, 13/10, 18/10 (High Numbers), 7/11, 29/11/64, 21/3, 25/4, 25/10/65, 1/1/66

HUNTINGDONSHIRE
Ramsey Gaiety Ballroom: 3/7/65, 21/12/68

KENT
Broadstairs Grand Ballroom: 23/11, 30/11/62, 4/1, 18/1, 22/2, 22/3, 24/5, 31/5/63 (Detours)
Bromley Bal Tabarin Club: 3/1/68
Bromley Court Hotel: 31/3/65, 28/4/65
Canterbury Kent University: 8/5/70, 10/10/71
Chatham Town Hall: 4/4/66
Folkestone Toft's Club: 28/1/67
Maidstone Granada Cinema: 9/11/67 (2)
Margate Dreamland Ballroom: 12/8/65, 12/2/66, 25/8/66, 13/1/68
Ramsgate Marina Ballroom: 4/7/66
Rochester Corn Exchange: 5/10/64, 19/10/64 (High Numbers), 9/11/64
Rochester Odeon Cinema: 23/4/66 (2)
Tunbridge Wells Assembly Hall: 5/7/65

LANCASHIRE
Ashton-under-Lyne Locarno Ballroom: 26/5/66
Barrow-in-Furness Public Hall: 13/5/65
Blackburn Locarno Ballroom: 23/5/66
Blackpool Opera House: 16/8/64 (2) (High Numbers), 22/10/71
Blackpool Queen's Theatre: 30/8/64 (2), 6/9/64 (2) (High Numbers)
Blackpool South Pier: 28/5/66 (2)
Bolton Institute of Technology: 22/4/69
Bury Palais de Danse: 14/5/66
Lancaster University: 15/5/70
Leigh Beachcomber Club: 30/1/66
Liverpool Cavern Club: 31/10/65
Liverpool Empire Theatre: 6/2/66 (2), 1/11/67 (2), 20/11/68 (2), 12/12/69, 25/10/70
Liverpool University: 14/2/66, 4/5/68, 22/2/69, 14/5/71, 23/10/71, 22/1/75 (JE)
Manchester Belle Vue: 4/9/66, 1-2/11/73, 6-7/10/75
Manchester Faculty of Technology Union: 17/2/68
Manchester Free Trade Hall: 7/10/70, 28/9/71
Manchester Jigsaw Club: 8/1/66
Manchester New Century Hall: 21/10/67
Manchester Oasis Club: 23/4/65, 12/9/65, 28/11/65, 20/2/66
Manchester Odeon Cinema: 28/10/71
Manchester Palace Theatre: 5/12/69
Manchester "The Twisted Wheel" Club: 3/10/65
Manchester University: 30/10/65, 31/5/68, 30/11/68, 9/5/70, 14/5/71, 23/10/71
Morecambe Central Pier: 13/8/65, 27/3/66, 22/7/66, 6/1/67
Morecambe Floral Hall Ballroom: 18/6/65
Morecambe Winter Gardens: 29/5/66 (2)
Nelson Imperial Ballroom: 11/9/65, 29/1/66, 1/10/66, 17/12/66, 11/11/67
Preston Beachcomber Club: 21/2/66
Rawtenstall Astoria Ballroom: 22/5/65
Southport Floral Hall: 21/5/66, 3/6/67
Southport Odeon Cinema: 13/12/74 (JE)
Warrington Parr Hall: 22/3/65
Warrington Co-Op Hall: 23/1/66

LEICESTERSHIRE
Hinckley St. George's Hall: 6/11/65, 26/3/66
Leicester College of Arts and Technology: 1/5/65
Leicester De Montfort Hall: 9/5/65 (2), 4/7/71
Leicester Granby Halls: 19/6/64 (High Numbers), 5/3/65, 27/5/66, 13/3/67, 25/10/68, 18-19/10/75
Leicester Il Rondo Club: 14/4/65, 9/6/65
Leicester University: 14/6/68, 18/4/70, 25/1/75 (JE)

LINCOLNSHIRE
Boston Starlight Room Gliderdrome: 26/2/66
Grantham Drill Hall: 18/9/65, 3/9/66
Grimsby Gaiety Ballroom: 17/9/65, 10/2/67
Lincoln Football Ground: 30/5/66
Scunthorpe Baths Hall: 16/10/65

LONDON
From 1961–1964, the Who performed countless times in the greater London area as the Detours, the High Numbers, and the Who. Because pop music was regarded as ephemeral, many of these gigs were not advertised in the local press. Promoters preferred to post flyers or leaflets in surrounding areas. In some instances, fans like "The 100 Faces" would hear of shows or last-minute cancellations via word-of-mouth. Inevitably, this listing is restricted to what was documented or could be otherwise substantiated, and thus is only a conservative representation of gigs the Who actually played in their home town from 1961–1964.

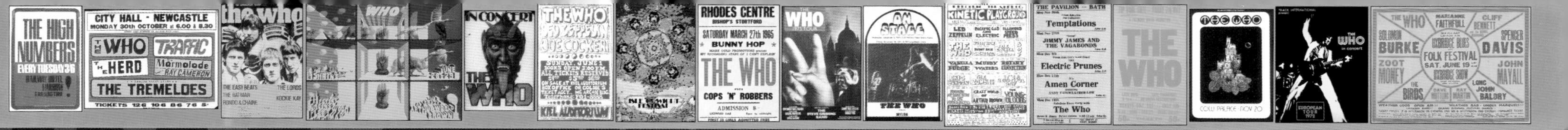

Bumpers Club: 11/3/71, 5/4/71 (KM)
Cavern Club (see also Notre Dame Hall): 10/4/65, 19/6/65, 11/3/66
College of Distributive Trade: 29/3/63 (Detours)
Coliseum Theatre: 14/12/69
London School Of Economics: 27/11/65
Lyceum Ballroom: 18/10/68, 15/12/69 (KM), 28/12/69 (KM), 8/11/70 (KM), 11-13/11/73
Marquee Club: 24/11, 1/12, 8/12, 15/12, 22/12, 29/12/64; 5/1, 12/1, 19/1, 26/1, 2/2, 9/2, 16/2, 23/2, 2/3, 9/3, 16/3, 23/3, 30/3, 6/4, 13/4, 20/4, 27/4, 25/5, 7/6, 13/7, 2/11, 21/12/65; 15/4, 23/4/68, 17/12/68
Notre Dame Hall (see also Cavern Club): 26/7, 30/8, 27/9/63 (Detours)
100 Club: 13/4/64, 27/4/64
Regent Polytechnic: 8/2/69
Royal Albert Hall: 5/7/69 (2)
Saville Theatre: 29/1/67 (2), 22/10/67 (2)
Scene Club: 22/7, 29/7, 5/8, 19/8, 26/8, 2/9/64 (High Numbers)
Technical College: 18/1/65, 9/7/66
Thames Riverboat Shuffle: 15/8/64 (High Numbers)
Tiles Club: 29/4/66, 29/7/66

LONDON (East)
Clerkenwell The City University: 24/5/68
Forest Gate Upper Cut Club: 21/12/66
Hackney In Crowd Club: 15/1/66
Leytonstone The Red Lion PH: 14/12/64, 21/12/64, 28/12/64, 4/1/65
Stratford Town Hall: 16/5/65
Stratford Two Puddings PH: 15/1/66
Walthamstow Granada Cinema: 4/11/67 (2), 8/11/68 (2)

LONDON (North)
Chalk Farm Roundhouse: 31/12/66, 5/10/68, 15-16/11/68, 9/2/69 (p), 23/2/69, 20/12/70, 14/4/74 (PT)
Edmonton Cooks Ferry Inn: 25/3/65
Edmonton Regal Theatre: 17/4/66 (2)
Edmonton Sundown Theatre: 18-19, 22-23/12/73
Finsbury Park Astoria Cinema: 4/2/66 (2)
Finsbury Park Rainbow Theatre: 4-6/11/71, 9/12/72 (2), 13/1/73 (2) (PT), 13-14/12/73 (RD), 14/2/74 (KM), 29/4/77 (PT)
Golders Green Refectory: 26/6/64
Hampstead Country Club: 12/4/70 (KM)
Hendon Lakeside Ballroom: 5/4/65
Highgate St. Joseph's Hall: 6/6/65
Kilburn Mazenod Church Hall: 13/3/63 (Detours)
Manor House Club: 7/7/65
Stamford Hill Loyola Hall: 5/6/65, 7/8/65,
Tottenham Club Noreik: 9/1, 13/3, 24/4, 26/6/65
Tottenham Royal Ballroom: 12/1/68

LONDON (South)
Brixton Ram Jam Club: 10/3/66
Catford Witchdoctor Club: 28/4/66
Charlton Athletic Football Ground: 18/5/74, 31/5/76
Crystal Palace Bowl: 3/6/72 (KM)
Elephant and Castle London College Of Printing: 19/12/64, 3/4/65, 15/6/68
Eltham Hill Eltham Baths: 6/12/65, 28/2/66
Forest Hill Glenlyn Ballroom: 13/9, 4/10, 11/10, 1/11, 6/12, 20/12/63, 3/1, 24/1, 31/1, 14/2 (Detours), 16/3, 23/3, 3/4, 6/4, 10/4, 20/4, 24/4, 4/5, 11/5, 15/5, 18/5, 25/5, 1/6, 8/6, 15/6, 22/6, 29/6/64; 21/1/66
Greenwich Town Hall: 23/9/64, 30/9, 14/10, 28/10/64 (High Numbers), 24/6/65
Kennington The Oval Cricket Ground: 18/9/71
Lewisham Odeon Cinema: 18/10/70
Putney Pontiac Club: 28/7/65
Putney St. Mary's Ballroom: 6/10, 27/10, 17/11, 1/12, 8/12, 15/12, 22/12/63 5/1, 26/1, 2/2, 9/2 (Detours), 23/2, 1/3, 8/3/64
Streatham Locarno Ballroom: 8/7/66, 15/12/66
Wimbledon Palais: 26/11/65, 11/2/66, 13/5/66

LONDON (West)
Acton Town Hall: 1/9/62, 26/11/63 (Detours)
Acton The White Hart PH: 17/2, 18/2, 24/2, 25/2, 3/3, 4/3, 11/3, 18/3, 25/3, 1/4, 8/4, 15/4, 22/4, 29/4, 5/5, 9/5, 26/5, 6/6, 9/6, 13/6, 23/6, 30/6, 7/7, 14/7, 11/8, 15/8, 18/8, 25/8, 1/9, 8/9, 15/9, 22/9, 29/9, 24/11, 29/12/63; 12/1, 19/1 (Detours), 15/3, 5/4, 12/4, 26/4, 31/5, 26/7/64 (High Numbers)
Bayswater Douglas House: 17/2, 24/2, 3/3, 10/3, 17/3, 24/3, 31/3, 7/4, 14/4, 21/4, 28/4, 5/5, 12/5, 19/5, 26/5/63 (Detours)
Ealing Ealing Club: 21/11/64, 27/12/64; 2/1, 9/1, 30/1, 11/2, 18/2, 25/2, 4/3, 10/3, 17/3, 24/3, 26/3/65
Ealing Evershed Sports Pavilion: 29/2/64
Ealing Feathers Hotel: 15/11, 13/12/63 (Detours)
Ealing Fox and Goose PH: 11/1/63 (Detours)
Ealing Mead Hall: 7/3/64
Hammersmith Odeon: 21-23/12/75
Hammersmith Palais: 29/10/70
Hanwell Community Centre: 27/11/65
Hanwell Park Hotel: 17/5/63 (Detours)
Shepherd's Bush Goldhawk Social Club: 7/6, 5/7, 12/7, 16/8, 6/9, 25/10, 8/11, 22/11, 29/11/63 (Detours); 7/2, 28/2, 6/3, 11/4, 17/4, 8/5 (Who), 31/7/64 (High Numbers); 12/3, 20/3, 16/4, 3/12/65

MIDDLESEX
Edgware The White Lion PH: 5/12/65
Greenford The Oldfield PH: 21/2, 23/2, 28/2, 7/3, 14/3, 21/3, 28/3, 4/4, 11/4, 13/4, 18/4, 25/4, 27/4, 30/4, 11/5, 18/5, 23/5, 28/5, 1/6, 8/6, 15/6, 20/6, 27/6, 29/6, 4/7, 6/7, 11/7, 18/7, 20/7, 23/7, 25/7, 10/8, 17/8, 20/8, 22/8, 27/8, 29/8, 5/9, 7/9, 19/9, 26/9, 28/9, 3/10, 10/10, 12/10, 17/10, 24/10, 26/10, 31/10, 7/11, 9/11, 14/11, 21/11, 28/11, 5/12, 12/12, 14/12, 19/12/63; 2/1, 11/1, 14/1, 16/1, 18/1, 21/1, 23/1, 25/1, 30/1, 6/2, 13/2 (Detours), 20/2, 27/2, 5/3, 17/3, 19/3, 26/3, 2/4, 16/4, 23/4, 7/5, 14/5, 21/5, 28/5/64
Greenford Railway Hotel: 30/11/63 (Detours)
Greenford Starlite Ballroom: 14/3/65, 27/6/65, 29/10/65, 13/3/66, 15/7/66, 12/2/67
Harrow Technical College: 12/12/64
Hayes Blue Moon Club: 20/6/65
Hayes Botwell House: 19/4/65
Isleworth Borough Road College: 25/1/69
Isleworth Osterley Hotel: 9/3/63 (Detours)
Kenton New Fender Club: 30/7/65
Northolt CAV Sports Ground: 19/1/63, 6/4/63 (Detours)
Pinner (venue unknown): 31/12/64
Southall Community Centre: 4/7/65, 13/2/66
Southall The White Hart PH: 4/6, 11/6, 18/6, 25/6, 6/8/64 (High Numbers)
Twickenham Eel Pie Island: 30/10/68
Wealdstone Railway Hotel PH: 30/6/64 (Who), 7/7, 14/7, 21/7, 28/7, 4/8, 11/8, 18/8, 25/8, 8/9, 15/9, 22/9, 29/9, 6/10, 20/10 (High Numbers), 2/11/64
Wembley Empire Pool: 19/11/65, 1/5/66, 21/10, 23-24/10/75
Wembley GEC Pavilion: 14/6/63 (Detours)
Wembley St. Joseph's Hall: 21/2/65
Wembley Town Hall: 1/4/65
Uxbridge Brunel University: 17/1/75 (JE)
Uxbridge Burton's Ballroom: 29/6/65
Uxbridge The New Georgian Club, Cowley: 14/8/65
Uxbridge Uxbridge Show: 19/6/65

NORFOLK
Cromer Royal Links Pavilion: 11/2/67
Great Yarmouth Brittania Theatre: 1/8, 8/8, 15/8, 22/8/65, 26/6/66 (2)
Great Yarmouth Tower Ballroom: 23/3/66
Norwich Federation Club: 13/12/65
Norwich The Lads' Club: 5/12/70
Norwich St. Andrew's Hall: 29/11/65 (p)
Norwich University of East Anglia: 5/10/70 (p), 17/10/70 (c), 24/1/75 (JE)

NORTHAMPTONSHIRE
Kettering Granada Cinema: 8/11/67 (2)
Northampton Maple Ballroom: 2/7/65
Peterborough Palais: 21/8/65, 8/10/66

NORTHUMBERLAND
Newcastle-upon-Tyne City Hall: 30/10/67 (2), 18/11/68 (2), 19/12/69, 8/12/74 (JE)
Newcastle-upon-Tyne Club A Go Go: 17/2/66
Newcastle-upon-Tyne Majestic Ballroom: 3/5/65
Newcastle-upon-Tyne Mayfair Ballroom: 26/11/70 (p), 15/12/70
Newcastle-upon-Tyne Odeon Cinema: 30/10/71, 5-7/11/73
Newcastle-upon-Tyne University: 1/2/69

NOTTINGHAMSHIRE
Kirkby-in-Ashfield Festival Hall: 13/1/67
Nottingham Brittania Rowing Club: 1/2/66
Nottingham Dungeon Club: 2/5/65
Nottingham Sherwood Rooms: 23/8/66, 12/11/68
Nottingham Theatre Royal: 5/11/67 (2)
Nottingham University: 25/4/70

OXFORDSHIRE
Headington Technical College: 7/3/69
Oxford New Theatre: 17/1/65 (2), 6/5/74
Oxford Pembroke College: 27/5/67

PEMBROKESHIRE
Milford Haven Pill Social Centre: 22/10/65

SHROPSHIRE
Shrewsbury Music Hall: 22/8/69
Wellington Majestic Ballroom: 25/2/66

SOMERSET
Bath Pavilion: 17/5/65, 15/11/65, 25/4/66, 10/10/66, 24/4/67, 18/12/67, 9/12/68, 4/8/69, 8/7/71
Bath Regency Ballroom: 20/6/64
Bath University: 7/2/69
Bridgwater Town Hall: 26/4/65
Yeovil Liberal Hall: 14/7/66

STAFFORDSHIRE
Hanley Gaumont Cinema: 15/9/66 (2)
Hanley Gaumont Top Rank Suite: 1/9/65
Smethwick Baths Ballroom: 22/1/66
Stafford New Bingley Hall: 3-4/10/75
Stoke-on-Trent King's Hall: 19/3/66
Trentham Gardens 4/6/65 (c), 16/10/70 (p), 26/10/70, 24/10/71, 28/10/73

Walsall Town Hall: 19/4/66
West Bromwich Adelphi Ballroom: 22/1/66
Wolverhampton Civic Hall: 24/1/69, 24/8/70, 29/10/73

SUFFOLK
Felixstowe Pier Pavilion: 9/9/66
Ipswich Baths Hall: 1/11/65
Ipswich Manor House Ballroom: 28/6/65

SURREY
Camberley Agincourt Ballroom: 28/2/65, 2/10/65, 16/1/66
Cheam Baths Hall: 30/12/66
Croydon Fairfield Hall: 15/4/66 (2), 21/9/69
Guildford Ricky Tick Club: 21/5/65, 19/12/65
Guildford University of Surrey: 9/10/71
Kingston-on-Thames Granada Cinema: 3/11/67 (2)
Purley Orchid Ballroom: 24/8/66, 18/1/67, 8/10/70
Richmond-upon-Thames 5th National Jazz & Blues Festival: 6/8/65
Wallington Wallington Public Hall: 8/6/65

SUSSEX
Brighton Brighton Dome: 21/4/67
Brighton Florida Rooms: 29/3, 18/4, 10/5, 16/5, 17/5, 7/6, 28/6 (Who), 12/7, 19/7, 2/8 (High Numbers), 25/11, 2/12, 9/12, 16/12, 23/12/64; 17/4/65, 20/11/65
Brighton Hippodrome Theatre: 9/8/64 (2) (High Numbers), 23/8/64 (2) (High Numbers)
Brighton New Barn Club: 12/12/65
Brighton University of Sussex: 10/10/70
Chichester College Of Further Education: 25/6/66
Crawley Civic Hall: 18/4/65
Crawley Starlight Ballroom: 24/3/66, 11/2/68
Eastbourne The Winter Garden: 1/7/66, 2/8/69, 12/7/71
Hassocks Ultra Club: 2/1/66, 11/9/66
Hastings Pier Ballroom: 24/12/65, 21/8/66, 30/12/67, 20/7/69
Hastings Witchdoctor Club: 4/8/65
Lewes 9th National Jazz & Blues Festival: 9/8/69
Worthing Assembly Hall: 27/5/65, 19/8/65, 11/1/68, 7/8/69, 1/7/71
Worthing Pavilion Ballroom: 23/12/65, 12/5/66, 24/11/66, 19/12/68

WARWICKSHIRE
Birmingham Birmingham Theatre: 24/4/66 (2), 17/11/68 (2)
Birmingham Brum Kavern Club: 28/3/65
Birmingham Gay Tower Ballroom: 20/6/66
Birmingham Mayfair Suite: 13/5/71
Birmingham Midnight City Club: 3/12/66
Birmingham Mothers Club: 19/1/69, 1/3/69, 19/7/69
Birmingham Odeon Cinema: 11/10/70, 20/10/71
Birmingham Town Hall: 6/11/67 (2)
Birmingham University: 28/1/66, 21/2/69
Coventry Lanchester College: 14/2/69, 28/11/70
Coventry Locarno Ballroom: 1/9/66, 2/2/67
Coventry Matrix Hall: 28/8/65
Coventry Theatre: 29/10/67 (2)
Nuneaton Co-Op Ballroom: 11/6/65
Sutton Coldfield The Belfry: 13/9/69, 8/8/70

WILTSHIRE
Chippenham Neeld Hall: 15/5/65
Devizes Corn Exchange: 23/11/68
Salisbury City Hall: 26/8/65
Salisbury University: 24/6/66
Swindon Locarno Ballroom: 28/10/65
Swindon McIlroy's Ballroom: 18/5/65
Trowbridge Town Hall: 30/4/65

WORCESTERSHIRE
Dudley Town Hall: 12/6/65
Kidderminster Town Hall: 20/5/65, 16/12/65, 5/5/66
Malvern Winter Gardens: 16/11/65, 3/5/66 (p), 21/6/66, 29/11/66
Stourbridge Town Hall: 16/6/65, 24/11/65, 4/5/66

YORKSHIRE
Barnsley Civic Hall: 16/7/66
Bridlington Spa Royal Hall: 4/9/65, 23/7/66, 26/11/66
Hull ABC Cinema: 29/10/71
Hull University: 16/6/66, 6/12/67, 3/5/68, 15/2/70
Leeds Locarno Ballroom: 13/10/70
Leeds Queen's Hall: 8/4/66, 14/10/66
Leeds University: 23/6/66, 21/1/67, 14/2/70, 21/11/70
Middlesbrough Mister McCoy's Club: 7/1/66
Redcar Coatham Hotel: 2/2/69, 27/7/69
Scarborough Futurist Theatre: 6/12/70
Sheffield City Hall: 28/10/67 (2), 17/12/74 (JE)
Sheffield Esquire Club: 15/2/66
Sheffield King Mojo Club: 30/5/65, 29/8/65, 7/11/65
Sheffield University: 29/6/66 (c), 16/2/68, 12/10/68, 2/5/70, 24/10/70, 3/7/71
York University: 11/10/68, 16/5/70

UNITED KINGDOM: ISLE OF MAN
Douglas Palace Theatre: 18/8/66, 10/6/67

UNITED KINGDOM: ISLE OF WIGHT
2nd Isle of Wight Festival Of Music: 30/8/69
3rd Isle of Wight Festival Of Music: 29/8/70
Ventnor Winter Gardens: 10/7/65

UNITED KINGDOM: NORTHERN IRELAND
Belfast Ulster Hall: 8/6/67 (2)
Lisburn Top Hat Ballroom: 6/5/66
Magilligan Golden Slipper Ballroom: 9/6/67

UNITED KINGDOM: SCOTLAND
Aberdeen Beach Ballroom: 7/10/67
Auchinleck Community Centre: 26/4/69
Dumfries Assembly Hall: 9/12/66
Dundee Caird Hall: 23/5/71
Dunfermline Kinema Ballroom: 6/10/65, 8/10/67, 27/4/69, 6/9/69
Edinburgh University: 10/1/75 (JE)
Elgin Two Red Shoes Ballroom: 6/5/65
Galashiels Volunteer Hall: 18/2/66
Kirkcaldy Raith Ballroom: 7/5/65
Glasgow Apollo: 15-16/10/75
Glasgow Celtic Park: 5/6/76
Glasgow Green's Playhouse: 23/10/70, 21/10/71, 9/11/71
Glasgow Kelvin Hall: 4/9/64 (2) (High Numbers)
Glasgow Locarno Ballroom: 17/11/66, 29/5/67
Glasgow Paisley Ice Rink: 19/11/68
Glasgow Strathclyde University: 11/5/68, 25/4/69
Greenock New Palladium Ballroom: 8/5/65
Nairn Ballerina Ballroom: 6/10/67
Perth City Halls: 8/10/65, 17/6/66, 18/11/66

UNITED KINGDOM: WALES
Ammanford Regal Ballroom: 13/1/66
Cardiff Sophia Gardens: 30/8/65, 6/10/70
Cardiff Top Rank Suite: 8/7/66, 10/3/67
Cwmbran Coed Eva Community College: 31/1/66
Llanelli Glen Ballroom: 15/7/65
Pontypool British Nylon Spinners Club: 4/3/66
Pontypridd Municipal Hall: 14/1/66
Skewen Ritz Ballroom: 15/7/65, 13/1/66
Swansea City Football Ground, Vetch Field: 12/6/76
Swansea University College: 15/12/65

UNITED STATES (by state)

ALABAMA
Montgomery Garrett Coliseum: 28/7/67
Birmingham Auditorium: 29/7/67 (3)
Tuscaloosa University Of Alabama Memorial Coliseum: 22/11/71

ARIZONA
Phoenix Municipal (Giants) Stadium: 17/8/68
Phoenix Veteran's Memorial Coliseum: 7/12/71, 6/10/76

CALIFORNIA
Anaheim Convention Center: 8/9/67
Anaheim Stadium: 14/6/70, 21/3/76
Berkeley Community Theater: 15-16/6/70
Fresno Selland Arena: 16/8/68, 12/6/70 (c)
Los Angeles Hollywood Bowl: 19/11/67
Los Angeles Hollywood Palladium: 13/6/69
Los Angeles Inglewood Forum: 9/12/71, 22-23/11/73, 14/8/75 (KM), 23/6/77 (KM)
Los Angeles Memorial Coliseum: 25/11/72 (KM)
Los Angeles Shrine Exposition Hall: 28-29/6/68
Long Beach Civic Arena: 10/12/71, 26/2/75 (JE)
Monterey International Pop Festival, Monterey Fairgrounds: 18/6/67
Oakland Alameda County Stadium: 9-10/10/76
Sacramento Memorial Auditorium: 16/7/67 (2), 8/7/68, 21/2/75 (JE)
San Diego Convention Hall: 27/8/68, 13/6/70
San Diego Sports Arena: 8/12/71, 7/10/76
San Francisco Civic Auditorium: 12-13/12/71
San Francisco Cow Palace: 18/11/67, 20/11/73
San Francisco Fillmore Auditorium: 16-17/6/67, 22/2/68
San Francisco Fillmore West: 13-15/8/68, 17-18/6/69 (2 per night), 19/6/69
San Francisco Winterland Ballroom: 23-24/2/68, 22-23/2/75 (JE), 27-28/3/76
San Jose Civic Auditorium: 21/2/68, 26/8/68
Santa Barbara Earl Warren Showgrounds: 29/8/68
Santa Monica Civic Auditorium: 28/8/68

COLORADO
Colorado Springs Kelker Junction Concert Hall: 18/8/68
Denver Coliseum: 4-5/12/71
Denver Mammoth Gardens: 9-10/6/70
Denver McNichols Sports Arena: 19/3/76 (p), 30/3/76

CONNECTICUT
Hartford Bushnell Auditorium: 4/11/69
Wallingford Oakdale Music Theatre: 21/7/68

DISTRICT OF COLUMBIA
Washington, D.C. Constitution Hall: 13/8/67 (2), 31/3/68, 11/3/75 (JE)
Washington, D.C. Georgetown University: 2/11/69

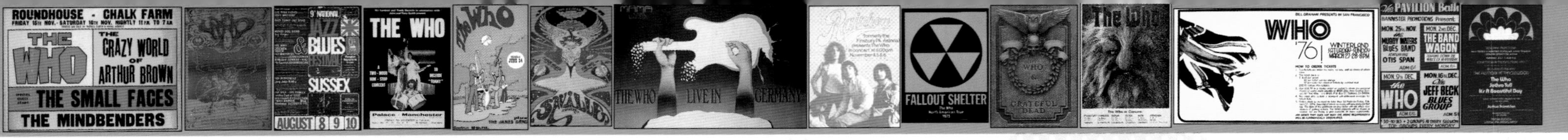

FLORIDA
Fort Lauderdale "Code 1": 23/3/68
Jacksonville Gator Bowl: 7/8/76
Miami Baseball Stadium: 9/8/76
Miami Beach Convention Hall: 30/7/67, 25-26/11/71
Miami Beach Marine Stadium: 28/7/68
Orlando Coliseum: 24/3/68
Orlando Sports Stadium: 27/7/68
St. Petersburg Bayfront Center: 31/7/67
Tampa Curtis Hixon Hall: 22/3/68
West Palm Beach International Raceway: 4/8/74 (PT & KM)

GEORGIA
Atlanta Municipal Auditorium: 29/8/67 (2), 22/6/70, 23/11/71, 13/3/75 (JE)(c)
Atlanta The Omni: 27/11/73, 1/8/74 (PT & KM), 24/11/75

HAWAII
Honolulu International Center Arena: 9/9/67

ILLINOIS
Algonquin The New Place: 31/7/68
Arlington Heights The Cellar: 15/6/67
Chicago Arie Crown Theater: 20/3/75 (JE)
Chicago Auditorium Theatre: 1 & 4/7/70, 17-19/8/71
Chicago The 'Lectric Theatre: 1/8/68
Chicago International Amphitheatre: 5/8/67, 29/11/73
Chicago Kinetic Playground: 29-31/5/69, 31/10/69
Chicago Stadium: 4-5/12/75
Edwardsville Mississippi River Festival, Southern Illinois University: 16/8/71
Peoria Opera House, Exposition Gardens: 10/3/68
St. Charles Jaguar Club: 10/8/68
Springfield Illinois State Fairgrounds: 9/8/68

INDIANA
Bloomington Indiana University Assembly Center: 30/11/75
Fort Wayne The Swinging Gate: 24/11/67
Indianapolis Convention Center: 21/3/75 (JE)
Indianapolis Indiana State Fair Coliseum: 1/9/67 (2)
Monticello Indiana Beach Ballroom: 12/7/68 (2)
Muncie The New Barn, Lions Delaware County Fairgrounds: 23/11/67

IOWA
Des Moines Veterans Memorial Auditorium: 2/12/75

LOUISIANA
Baton Rouge Louisiana State University Assembly Center: 21/11/75
Baton Rouge Redemptorist High School Football Stadium: 26/7/67
Chalemette Saint Bernard Civic Auditorium: 26/7/68 (2)
New Orleans The Warehouse: 29-30/11/71

MARYLAND
Baltimore Civic Center: 11/8/67
Columbia Merriweather Post Pavilion: 25/5/69, 29/6/70
Largo Capital Center: 6/12/73, 3-4/8/76

MASSACHUSETTS
Boston The Boston Tea Party: 13-15/5/69, 11-12/11/69
Boston Commonwealth Armory: 10/10/69
Boston Boston Garden: 3/12/73, 9/3/76 (p), 1/4/76
Boston Music Hall: 6/8/68 (2), 4-7/8/71
Boston Orpheum Theater, Boston: 7/3/75
Lenox Tanglewood Music Shed: 12/8/69, 7/7/70
Springfield Civic Center: 14/12/75
Worcester Holy Cross College Gymnasium: 17/10/69

MICHIGAN
Ann Arbor Fifth Dimension Club: 14/6/67
Detroit Cobo Hall (Arena): 5/7/70, 14/8/71, 30/11/73
Detroit Grande (Riviera) Ballroom: 9/3/68, 13/7/68 (2), 9-11/5/69, 11-12/10/69
Detroit Masonic Temple Hall: 2/3/75 (JE)
Flint Atwood High School Stadium: 23/8/67
Pontiac Metropolitan Stadium: 6/12/75
Southfield High School: 22/11/67

MINNESOTA
Duluth Arena: 26/8/67
Minneapolis Auditorium: 20/8/67, 3/7/70
Minneapolis Metropolitan Sports Center: 8/3/68, 15/8/71
Minneapolis Tyrone Guthrie Theatre: 8/6/69 (2)
St. Paul Civic Center: 12/3/76 (p), 14/3/76

MISSISSIPPI
Jackson Mississippi State Coliseum: 1/8/67

MISSOURI
Kansas City Freedom Palace: 2/7/70
Kansas City Kemper Arena: 1/12/75
Kansas City Music Hall: 22/8/68
Kansas City Shawnee Mission South High School Gymnasium: 17/11/67
St. Louis St. Louis Arena: 28/11/73
St. Louis Kiel Auditorium: 1/6/69, 23/3/75 (JE)
St. Louis Kiel Opera House: 25/8/67 (2), 8/11/69

NEBRASKA
Omaha Rosenblatt Stadium: 4/8/67

NEW JERSEY
Asbury Park Convention Hall: 12/8/67 (2)
Madison Baldwin Gymnasium, Drew University: 29/3/68
Scotch Plains Union Catholic High School Gymnasium: 29/11/67

NEW YORK
Albany Palace Theater: 10/11/69
Bethel Woodstock Music and Art Fair: 17/8/69
Buffalo Century Theatre, Buffalo, New York: 9/3/75 (JE)
Buffalo Kleinhans Music Hall: 15/11/69
Buffalo Melody Fair, Wurlitzer Park, North Tonawanda: 4/8/68
Buffalo Memorial Auditorium: 10/12/75
Ellenville Tamarack Lodge: 29/7/68
Long Island Calderone Theatre, Hempstead: 16/3/75 (JE)
Long Island New Commack Arena: 1/12/67
Long Island Malibu Beach and Shore Club, Lido Beach: 7/7/67
Long Island Westbury Music Fair: 30/3/68
New York Academy of Music: 8/3/75 (JE)
New York Carnegie Hall: 28/12/71 (KM)
New York Fillmore East: 5-6/4/68, 16/5/69 (2—one p), 17-18/5/69 (2 per day), 5-6/6/69 (2 per day), 20-25/10/69 (2 per day)
New York Forest Hills Tennis Stadium: 29 & 31/7/71
New York Madison Square Garden: 10-11/6/74, 13-14/6/74, 11/3/76
New York Metropolitan Opera House: 7/6/70 (2)
New York RKO Radio Theatre: 25/3-2/4/67 (5 per day)
New York The Schaefer Music Festival, Wollman Skating Rink, Central Park: 7/8/68 (2)
New York Singer Bowl: 2/8/68
New York Village Theatre: 8/7/67, 25/11/67 (2), 26/11/67
New Paltz New York State University Gymnasium: 13/11/69
Rochester War Memorial Auditorium: 30/8/67, 9/8/71
Saratoga Springs Center for the Performing Arts: 2/8/71
Stony Brook New York State University Gymnasium: 18/10/69
Syracuse Onondaga War Memorial Auditorium: 16/11/69
White Plains Westchester County Center: 3/11/69

NORTH CAROLINA
Charlotte Coliseum: 20/11/71
Greensboro Coliseum: 2/8/74, 28/11/75

NORTH DAKOTA
Fargo Civic Auditorium: 20/8/67, 21/11/67

OHIO
Akron Civic Theatre: 5/3/75 (JE)
Athens Ohio State University: 7/11/69
Cincinnati Music Hall: 27/8/67 (2), 25-26/7/70
Cincinnati Riverfront Coliseum: 8/12/75
Cleveland Musicarnival: 14/7/68
Cleveland Music Hall: 14/11/69, 27/6/70
Cleveland Public Music Hall: 31/8/67 (2), 12/8/71
Cleveland Richfield Coliseum: 9/12/75
Columbus Agora Ballroom: 3/3/75 (JE)
Columbus Ohio State Fairgrounds: 2 - 4/9/67 (2 per day)
Columbus Veterans Memorial Auditorium: 1/11/69
Dayton O'Hara Arena: 13/8/71
Granville Livingston Gymnasium, Dennison University: 6/11/69
Lorain The Big Moose Showcase: 18/8/67 (c)

OKLAHOMA
Oklahoma City Myriad Convention Center: 15/3/76
Oklahoma City State Fair: 21/7/67
Oklahoma City Wedgewood Village Amusement Park: 23/8/68, 24/8/68 (2)

OREGON
Portland Memorial Coliseum: 14/7/67, 24/3/76, 13/10/76

PENNSYLVANIA
Allentown College, Billero Hall: 17/3/75 (JE)
Philadelphia Convention Hall: 24/8/67
Philadelphia Electric Factory: 23-24/5/69, 19/10/69 (2)
Philadelphia JFK Stadium: 24/7/68
Philadelphia The Spectrum: 24/6/70, 3/8/71, 4/12/73, 15/3/75 (JE), 15/12/75
Pittsburgh Civic Arena: 3/9/67, 10/8/71
Pittsburgh Syria Mosque: 26/10/69

RHODE ISLAND
Providence Rhode Island Auditorium: 14/8/67, 18/7/68
Providence Civic Center: 13/12/75

SOUTH DAKOTA
Sioux Falls Arena: 28/8/67

TENNESSEE
Chattanooga Memorial Auditorium: 17/8/67 (2)
Memphis Ellis Auditorium: 21/6/70
Memphis Mid-South Coliseum: 28/11/71, 23/11/75
Murfreesboro MTSU Murphy Center: 25/11/75

TEXAS
Beaumont City Auditorium: 16/3/68 (2)
Dallas Dallas Memorial Auditorium: 23/7/67, 19/6/70, 2/12/71, 25/11/73
Fort Worth Tarrant County Convention Center: 16/3/76
Houston Hofheinz Pavilion, University of Houston MTSU: 20/6/70
Houston Music Hall: 17/3/68 (2)
Houston Sam Houston Coliseum: 22/7/67, 1/12/71
Houston The Summit: 20/11/75
San Antonio Municipal Auditorium: 15/3/68

UTAH
Salt Lake City The Lagoon Terrace Ballroom: 19/7/67 (2)
Salt Lake City Salt Palace Convention Center: 18/3/76

VIRGINIA
Hampton Roads Coliseum: 27/11/75
Richmond The Mosque: 23/7/68 (2)
Virginia Beach Civic Center (The Dome): 20/7/68 (2)

WASHINGTON
Seattle Center Coliseum: 15/7/67, 15/12/71, 25/3/76, 14/10/76

WISCONSIN
Lake Geneva Majestic Hills Theater: 3/8/68, 7/6/69
Madison Dane County Memorial Coliseum: 3/8/67, 13/3/76
Milwaukee Arena: 22/3/75 (JE)

OTHER ENGAGEMENTS PLAYED
The following is a chronology of gigs and venues known to have been played by the Detours, the High Numbers, and the Who up to 1969, the dates of which cannot (as of this writing) be traced. Following the success of *Tommy*, live performances became less regular and were faithfully reported in the music press, as was befitting a group of the Who's stature.

1962–63 (The Detours)
Abbey Hotel, Park Royal, West London.
Boseley's church hall, Shepherd's Bush.
Evershed and Bignoles Apprentice Association Social Club Dance, The Boston Manor PH, Hanwell.
Ealing JYC (Jewish Youth Club), 15 Grange Road, Ealing.
Eel Pie Island, Twickenham, Middlesex.
Hammersmith Palais, Hammersmith. Talent Contest with Wainwright's Gentlemen and the Joe Loss Orchestra.
New Labour Hall, Ealing Road, Wembley.
The Queen of Hearts PH, Honeypot Lane, Stanmore.
The Red Lion PH, Acton.
St. Mary's College Social Dance, Town Hall, Acton.

1964
(The High Numbers)
The Zambezi, Hounslow, Middlesex.
The Bruce Grove Ballroom, Tottenham, North London.
Publicist Pete Meaden persuaded columnist June Southworth from the weekly pop magazine Fabulous *to attend this Friday night gig in the hopes of a future article. She came away bemused rather than impressed, after witnessing Meaden stop a bouncer from throttling Roger, and arranged for a feature, which was published 10 October.*
Town Hall, Poplar, East London.

1965
(The Who)
Gliderdrome, Boston, Lincolnshire.
Lotus Ballroom, Forest Gate, East London.
This popular bingo hall featured "groups and discs" every Tuesday and Saturday, promoted by Ken Johnson. With his brother Eddie, Johnson promoted Who gigs at the Stratford Town Hall and Two Puddings Club. A February 1967 advertisement for the venue lists the Who among the acts that had appeared to date.
University Ball, Victoria Rooms, Bristol.
University, Exeter, Devonshire.

1967–1968
University, Swansea, Wales, with the Dream.

ENGAGEMENTS NOT PLAYED
The following is a list of gigs that were scheduled, publicised, advertised, or announced as upcoming, but not played. Some have been subsequently documented in *The Who Concert File*, but extensive research shows they did NOT occur.

1964
2 August: Hippodrome, Brighton, Sussex. *The High Numbers played The Florida.*
7 October: Town Hall, Greenwich, London.
22 November: Goldhawk Social Club, Shepherd's Bush, London.
25 November: California Ballroom, Dunstable, Bedfordshire.
27 November: Railway Arms, Neasden, North West London.
The above three erroneous dates seem to have originated from Guy Peellaert's 1974 book, Rock Dreams.

1965
5 February: Town Hall, Bath, Somerset.
18 March: Civic Hall, Crawley, Sussex. *Rescheduled to 18 April.*
26 March: Railway Hotel, Wealdstone, Harrow, Middlesex.
28 March: Ritz Ballroom, King's Heath, Birmingham. *An all-Midlands R&B show was held.*
15 April: Locarno Ballroom, Swindon, Wiltshire. *The Who had been provisionally booked for an Easter gig, but the owner feared for his venue (correspondence stating as such from agent Barry Perkins was packaged with Live At Leeds). The Riot Squad and Tony Rivers and the Castaways appeared instead.*
5 May: City Hall, Perth, Scotland.
12 May: Palais de Danse, Bury, Lancashire. *Originally advertised, but The Four Pennies appeared.*
18 May: Railway Hotel, Wealdstone, Harrow, Middlesex. *This date stems from a fictitious poster on the Meaty, Beaty, Big, and Bouncy sleeve.*
11 June: St. George's Ballroom, Hinckley, Leicestershire.
3 July: Thorngate Ballroom, Gosport, Portsmouth, Hampshire.
27 August: Town Hall, Torquay, Devonshire.
6 October: Palais de Danse, Cowdenbeath, Scotland.
10 October: The Lido, Lennoxbank House Hotel, Balloch, Scotland.
11 October: Parr Hall, Warrington, Lancashire.
14 October: Birdcage Club, Portsmouth. *When this popular mod club moved to a new site at Eastney Road, the Who were advertised as headlining the official opening party with Jimmy James and the Vagabonds. The Action appeared instead.*

1966
13 January: Embassy Ballroom, Swansea, Wales.
31 January: Youth Centre, Newport, Wales.
8 February: Town Hall, Farnborough, Hampshire. *Rescheduled to 9 March.*
18 February: Drill Hall, Dumfries, Scotland.
11 March: Market Hall, St. Albans, Hertfordshire.
21 March: Beachcomber Club, Preston, Lancashire. *Cancelled due to contractual difficulties.*
4 April: Top Rank Ballroom (a.k.a. The Majestic), Reading, Berkshire.
23 April: Gaumont, Sheffield, Yorkshire. (2)
11 April: Floral Hall, Southport, Lancashire.
2 May: The Pavilion, Bath, Somerset.
19 June: Britannia Theatre, Brittania Pier, Great Yarmouth, Norfolk.
28 June: South Pier, Blackpool, Lancashire.
3, 10, 17, 24 and 31 July: Brittania Theatre, Brittania Pier, Great Yarmouth.
9 July: Shea Stadium, Queens, New York, U.S. *A Disc news report (dated 11 June) mentioned the Who were being sought for a show (with the Merseys) at this large baseball stadium famed for staging two Beatles concerts. "We are trying to get visas," said Chris Stamp, "and if they are granted, the show is definitely on." This may have been yet another example of Lambert and Stamp's attempts to keep the Who's name in the news, but interestingly, an early advertisement for an all-star "Sound Blast '66" concert held on 10 June at Yankee Stadium lists "Who?" at the foot of the artists bill.*
15 July: Tiles Club, London. *Rescheduled to 29 July.*
20 August: Imperial Ballroom, Nelson, Lancashire.
21 August: Brittania Theatre, Brittania Pier, Great Yarmouth.
22 August: Odeon Cinema, Glasgow, Scotland. (2)
28 August: Ultra Club, Downs Hotel, Hassocks, Sussex. *Rescheduled to 11 September.*
17 September: Odeon Cinema, Cheltenham. *Cancelled package tour.* (2)
18 September: De Montfort Hall, Leicester. (2)
22 September: Odeon Cinema, Glasgow, Scotland. (2)
23 September: Caird Hall, Dundee, Scotland. (2)
24 September: Odeon Cinema, Sunderland. (2)
25 September: Palace Theatre, Manchester. (2)
29 September: Town Hall, Maidstone, Kent. *Postponed to 1 December, then cancelled due to contractual difficulties.*
30 September: Guildhall, Portsmouth. (2)
2 October: Hippodrome, Birmingham. (2)
6 October: Odeon Cinema, Luton. (2)
8 October: Odeon Cinema, Southend-on-Sea. (2)
9 October: Winter Gardens, Bournemouth. (2)
16 October: Starlite Ballroom, Greenford.
20 October: Locarno Ballroom, Ashton-under-Lyne, Lancashire.
26 October: Mayfair Ballroom, Newcastle.
4 November: Kassel, West Germany.
5 December: Locarno Ballroom, Streatham, South London. *A Concert File typo—actually played 15 December.*

1967
5 February: Waterfront Club, Cliff Hotel, Southampton.
18 February: Pavilion Gardens Ballroom, Buxton, Derbyshire.
21 February: Town Hall, High Wycombe. *Rescheduled to 28 March then 25 April.*
27 February: Locarno Ballroom, Glasgow, Scotland. *Rescheduled to 29 May.*
10 March: Top Rank Ballroom, Swansea, Wales. *Rescheduled to 10 May then 5 June before being cancelled.*
11 March: King's Hall, Stoke-on-Trent.
20 March: The Pavilion, Bath. *Rescheduled to 24 April.*
10-15 April: Saville Theatre, London. *A planned week-long season of shows featuring the Who, the Koobas and the Jimi Hendrix Experience, was scrapped.*

13 May: Shoreline Club, Bognor Regis, Sussex. *Bob Pridden recalls the Who not appearing at this "all-nighter", due to the inadequate space the venue's small stage afforded their equipment.*

18 May: Locarno Ballroom, Bristol. *Advertised but cancelled due to John's hand injury, although no subsequent apology was made in* The Bristol Evening Post.

4 June: Guildhall, Southampton.

5 June: Top Rank Suite, Swansea, Wales. *Advertised but cancelled to allow John's hand to further heal.*

16 June: University of Sussex, Brighton. *The Evening Argus reported that the student union were attempting to claim £100 compensation from NEMS Enterprises after the cancellation of the Who's appearance at the summer ball. This was due to the booking clashing with the group's forthcoming visit to America for the Monterey International Pop Festival. A student spokesman claimed the Who had a £550 contract for a 45-minute appearance, while NEMS said only a verbal agreement had been entered into. By way of compensation, Cream replaced the Who, playing a 90 minute set for only £350.*

7 August: Westbury Music Fair, Long Island, New York, U.S. (2 shows, 5:00 & 8:30 pm). *The Herman's Hermits tour played this annual event but judging from reviews in both Billboard and Cashbox, the Who did not appear, as they were in the recording studio.*

18 August: The Big Moose Showcase, Lorain, Ohio, U.S. *Cancelled in accordance with promoter Dick Clark's wishes that the Hermits' tour not play in Ohio prior to his 27 and 31 August bookings.*

6 December: Skyline Ballroom, Hull, Yorkshire.

22 December: "Christmas On Earth Continued," Olympia Grand Hall, Kensington, London. *The Who were originally billed to appear at this underground event with the Jimi Hendrix Experience, Eric Burdon and the Animals, the Move, Pink Floyd, Keith West, and Tomorrow. The Who pulled out when Pete injured his hand.*

31 December: Upper Cut Club, Forest Gate, London, with the Troggs and the Herd.

1968

3 January: Locarno Ballroom, Streatham, London.

13 February: Swansea University Pajama Dance, Glen Ballroom, Llanelli, Wales.

15 February: University, Hull, Yorkshire.

4 April: "Fillmore North", Vancouver, Canada. *The English music press reported the Who were to be the opening act at this prestigious new underground club, but the local papers make no mention of the event.*

12 May: Locarno Ballroom, Wakefield, Yorkshire.

3 July: Albuquerque, New Mexico, U.S.

9 July: Exhibition Hall, Regina, Alberta, Canada.

28 July: Municipal Auditorium, Nashville, Tennessee, U.S.

5-6 August: Electric Factory, Philadelphia, Pennsylvania, U.S.

10 August: Aragon Ballroom, Chicago, U.S.

11 August: Indianapolis, U.S.

31 August: Salt Lake City, Utah, U.S.

25 October: Mayfair Ballroom, Newcastle.

1969

17 January: Great Hall, Kings College, The Strand, London. *Cancelled because the contract was made with a hoaxer, not the Social Secretary.*

15 February: Dreamland Ballroom, Margate, Kent.

2 March: Pavilion Ballroom, Bournemouth. *Rescheduled to 2 April.*

7 April: Alexandra Palace, North London. *A cancelled, multi-artist Easter show.*

24 April: Mayfair Ballroom, Newcastle.

26 April: City Hall, Perth, Scotland.

6 June: State Fair Grounds, Detroit, Michigan, U.S. *The Who were due to appear with The Stooges and Arthur Brown at a Russ Gibb-promoted festival.*

14 June: Rose Palace, Pasadena, California, U.S.

3 August: Cosmopolitan Club, Carlisle, Cumberland.

1970

8 May: University, Liverpool.

16 May: Keele University, Staffordshire.

9 June: Center Coliseum, Seattle, Washington, U.S.

12 June: Selland Arena, Convention Center, Fresno, California, U.S. *Cancelled due to problems transporting the Who's gear from Denver in time.*

27 October: University of East Anglia, Norwich. *Originally booked for 5 October, then postponed to 17 October and then further to 5 December at an alternate venue.*

1971

7 August: Yale Bowl, New Haven, Connecticut, U.S. *Cancelled due to campus riots.*

21 August: Civic Center, Baltimore, Maryland, U.S.

22 and 24 August: Red Rocks Amphitheatre, Denver, Colorado.

29 August: Central Park, New York City. *Free concert blocked by local authorities.*

4 September: Hyde Park, London. *As above, the Who had negotiated to headline a free concert but restrictions imposed by the GLC (Greater London Council) forced the group to pull out, although the event went ahead without them, albeit on a much smaller scale. Similarly, an attempt to stage an outdoor concert in Manchester amounted to nothing, until the Oval show in London on 18 September.*

25 September: University, Bristol.

1972

4 February: Lanchester Arts Festival, Coventry. *Keith was originally billed among the guests appearing as part of Viv Stanshall's multi-media show. However, Keith was on a safari holiday in Mombasa, Africa, on this date.*

8 September: The Ahoy, Rotterdam, The Netherlands.

TELEVISION APPEARANCES

This appendix lists the Who's appearances as a group on British television from 1964 to 1974. It excludes news coverage, solo appearances, and the screening of their promotional films/videos. It is arranged in order of transmission date, not by filming/recording date.

FILM DATE	FIRST TRANS	PROGRAMME TITLE	STATION
20/8/64	24/8/64	The Beat Room	BBC 2
live	29/1/65	Ready, Steady, Go!	Rediffusion
live	11/3/65	Top Of The Pops	BBC 1
15/3/65	15/3/65	Gadzooks! It's All Happening!	BBC 2
24/3/65	25/3/65	Top Of The Pops	BBC 1
1/4/65	1/4/65	Top Of The Pops	BBC 1
unknown	20/5/65	Three Go Round	Southern
live	21/5/65	Ready Steady Goes Live!	Rediffusion
23/5/65	29/5/65	Thank Your Lucky Stars	ABC
7/6/65	7/6/65	Gadzooks! It's The In Crowd	BBC 2
live	10/6/65	Top Of The Pops	BBC 1
live	17/6/65	Top Of The Pops	BBC 1
1/7/65	2/7/65	Ready, Steady, Go!	Rediffusion
3/65	26/7/65	Workshop	BBC 2
live	6/8/65	Ready, Steady, Go!	Rediffusion
live	3/9/65	Ready, Steady, Go!	Rediffusion
live	5/11/65	Ready, Steady, Go!	Rediffusion
live	11/11/65	Top Of The Pops	BBC 1
live	18/11/65	Top Of The Pops	BBC 1
live	19/11/65	Ready, Steady, Go!	Rediffusion
live	25/11/65	Ready, Steady, Go!	Rediffusion
live	2/12/65	Top Of The Pops	BBC 1
live	3/12/65	Ready, Steady, Go!	Rediffusion
19/11/65	8/12/65	Glad Rag Ball	ABC
unknown	16/12/65	Three Go Round	Southern
17/12/65	24/12/65	Ready, Steady, Go!	Rediffusion
live	31/12/65	The New Year Starts Here	Rediffusion
5/1/66	5/1/66	A Whole Scene Going	BBC 1
27/1/66	28/1/66	Ready, Steady, Go!	Rediffusion
7/3/66	7/3/66	Scene at 6:30	Granada
live	18/3/66	Ready, Steady, Go!	Rediffusion
24/3/66	24/3/66	Top Of The Pops	BBC 1
live	1/4/66	Ready, Steady, Allez!	Rediffusion
14/4/66	14/4/66	Top Of The Pops	BBC 1
1/5/66	8/5/66	Poll Winners Concert	ABC
15/6/66	15/6/66	A Whole Scene Going	BBC 1
live	19/8/66	Ready, Steady, Go!	Rediffusion
6/9/66	9/9/66	Ready, Steady, Go!	Rediffusion
15/9/66	15/9/66	Top Of The Pops	BBC 1
21/9/66	21/9/66	Top Of The Pops	BBC 1
18/10/66	21/10/66	Ready, Steady, Go!	Rediffusion
20/12/66	23/12/66	Ready, Steady, Goes!	Rediffusion
29/12/66	29/12/66	Top Of The Pops	BBC1
11/1/67	12/1/67	Top Of The Pops	BBC 1
live	1/2/67	Scene	Granada
26/4/67	27/4/67	Top Of The Pops	BBC 1
21/10/67	15/10/67	Twice A Fortnight	BBC 1
live	26/10/67	Top Of The Pops	BBC 1
live	2/11/67	Top Of The Pops	BBC 1
unknown	9/11/67	Top Of The Pops	BBC 1
17/12/67	23/12/67	Twice A Fortnight	BBC 1
16/12/67	25/12/67	Top Of The Pops	BBC 1
17/6/68	20/6/68	Top Of The Pops	BBC 1
11/10/68	11/10/68	How It Is	BBC 1
10/3/68	3/11/68	All My Loving	BBC 1
15/11/68	18/11/68	Time For Blackburn	Southern
21/11/68	22/11/68	Crackerjack	BBC 1
22/11/68	22/11/68	How It Is	BBC 1
14/3/69	14/3/69	How Late It Is	BBC 1
live	27/3/69	Top Of The Pops	BBC 1
live	28/3/69	Today	Thames
live	10/4/69	Top Of The Pops	BBC 1
16/4/69	20/4/69	This Is... Tom Jones	ATV
live	24/4/69	Top Of The Pops	BBC 1
16/12/69	31/12/69	Pop Go The Sixties!	BBC 1/ZDF
live	26/3/70	Top Of The Pops	BBC 1
30/12/70	31/12/70	Into '71	BBC 1
7/7/71	14/7/71	Top Of the Pops	BBC 1
3/1/73	6/1/73	Russell Harty Plus	LWT
29/1/73	30/1/73	The Old Grey Whistle Test	BBC 2
18/5/74	5/10/74	2nd House: The Who	BBC 2

RADIO APPEARANCES

This appendix lists the Who's British radio appearances as a group from 1965 to April 1970, excluding interviews and solo appearances. It is arranged in order of transmission, not by recording date, and excludes repeated material.

REC DATE	FIRST TRANS	PROGRAMME TITLE	STATION
live	22/1/65	Ready, Steady, Radio!	Luxembourg
live	2/4/65	The Joe Loss Pop Show	BBC Light
live	11/5/65	Ready, Steady, Radio!	Luxembourg
live	25/5/65	Ready, Steady, Radio!	Luxembourg
25/5/65	29/5/65	Saturday Club	BBC Light
live	8/6/65	Ready, Steady, Radio!	Luxembourg
24/5/65	19/6/65	Top Gear	BBC Light
live	27/7/65	Ready, Steady, Radio!	Luxembourg
22/11/65	27/11/65	Saturday Club	BBC Light
live	5/12/65	Ready, Steady, Radio!	Luxembourg
15/3/66	19/3/66	Saturday Club	BBC Light
live	13/5/66	The Joe Loss Show	BBC Light
13/9/66	17/9/66	Saturday Club	BBC Light
17/1/67	21/1/67	Saturday Club	BBC Light
10/10/67	15/10/67	Top Gear	BBC Radio1
10/10/67	15/11/67	Top Gear	BBC Radio 1
13/4/70	19/4/70	Dave Lee Travis	BBC Radio 1

INDEX

PHOTO CREDITS

The publishers are indebted to the authors and their numerous friends for providing all the memorabilia and newspaper clippings that appear in this book. The authors have also provided a large number of the photographs, and together we have made every effort to correctly credit the original photographers and copyright holders of the photographs. If any errors have occurred, we will be happy to correct them in future printings of this book.

ABC Television Ltd.: 57 (top)
BBC Photo Stills Archive: 124
CBS Photo Archive: 123
©Tim Bartlett: 17 (left and middle)
Courtesy Peter Butler: 143 (left), 263
©Richard Chase: 144
©Dianne Corcoran: 240-241 (all), 251 (all)
Courtesy of the Daltrey Family Archive: 8

©Carl K. Davis: 119
Courtesy Decca Records: 44
©Henry Diltz: 168
Robert Druce: 12-13, 34 (top left, bottom left)
Courtesy EMI Records: 17 (right)
The Entwistle Family Archive: 10 (left four)
©Mike Evans: 10 (right, both)
Courtesy *The Evening Post*: 136
©Graham Hughes: 197, 198 (both), 242
Hulton Getty/Archive Photos: 116, 117, 141, 165, 171
Courtesy Joe Giorgianni: 38 (right top and bottom)
Courtesy of Bill Graham: 113, 144 (bottom), 154 (bottom), 186 (bottom), 277 (bottom)
©Ross Halfin: 257, 267 (bottom), 286-287, 290 (bottom two), 291 (bottom)
©Colin Jones: 30, 76 (right), 80, 212 (*Observer Newspapers*)
Courtesy Max Ker-Seymer: 62, 69 (all)
London Features International: 45, 46 (top), 49, 61 (both), 65, 67, 74, 82, 87, 109 (both), 127, 130-131, 132, 133 (left), 134, 135 (left), 147 (all), 152, 153, 158 (both), 160, 161 (left top and bottom), 170 (all), 172-173, 176, 181 (right), 203, 211, 219 (bottom), 224, 225 (both), 232 (right), 230, 231, 232 (both), 233 (top), 236, 242, 268, 292 (bottom), 293 (top)
Courtesy Olle Lundin: 63, 73 (bottom), 75, 84 (right), 85 (all), 86, 110 (bottom), 210
©Dennis McCoy: 142, 239, 272 (left), 272-273
©David Montgomery: 96-97 (all)
©Chris Morphet: 84 (left), 89 (all), 90 (bottom two), 91, 94, 95 (both), 98, 103 (bottom), 105, 107, 108 (all), 110-111, 111, 112 (middle, right), 125 (middle and right), 126 (both), 140, 141 (left), 177 (all), 189, 190 (all), 191 (all), 194, 207, 218, 225 (both), 237 (both), 289
Michael Ochs Archives: 50, 73 (top), 113, 114, 121, 122, 138, 185 (bottom, ©Joel Axelrod), 238 (©Harry Godwin), 253, 258, 259 (right), 271 (©Larry Hult), 276-277, 293 (right)
©Terry O'Neill: 3, 254-255
©Don Paulson: 99, 106, 128, 129
©Jan Persson (courtesy Olle Lundin): 93 (both)
Photo Features: 56 (top)
Pictorial Press: 24-25, 76 (left), 86 (right), 88-89, 101, 105, 159
©Barry Plummer: 213 (both), 280, 282 (both), 285 (left), 291 (top)
©Michael Putland/Retna Pictures Ltd.: 64 (both), 149 (both), 175, 192-193, 196, 208-209, 216-217 (all), 220-221, 233 (bottom), 260, 268-269
Redferns: ©K&K Ulf Kruger Ohg: 94 (right), 102, 178; ©Chuck Boyd: 143; ©Dave Ellis: 222-223; ©David Redferns: 226-227
Retna Pictures Ltd.: 47, 103 (top), 133 (right), 134 (©Peter Simon), 150-151 (©Ray Stevenson), 163, 164, 167, 179 (©Ray Stevenson), 180 (both, ©Ray Stevenson), 184 (top and right: ©Joel Axelrod), 228, 235 (©Chris Walter), 248 (©Joe Gafney)
Rex Features: 6, 42 (left), 53, 60, 68, 70, 79, 135, 166, 169 (top and bottom), 230, 266 (right), 278, 285 (right)
Courtesy Brad Rodgers: 104 (both), 125 (left)
©Peter Rudge: 112 (left)
©Keith Smart: 292 (top two)
Courtesy Bob Solly: 31
Courtesy Richard Stanley: 188 (right)
©Sandy Steel: 56 (bottom five)
©Anthony Stern: 92 (bottom)
©Amie Stoppard: 5
Topham/Picturepoint: 72 (top), 261
Courtesy of the Townshend Family Archive: 9
Courtesy Track Records: 183, 229
Trinifold Ltd.: 27, 118, 204 (©Robert Ellis), 281, 275, 283, 290
©Peter Vernon-Kell: 16 (bottom)
©Chris Walter: 245, 247
©David Wedgbury/Not Fade Away: 42-43, 46 (bottom), 48, 52, 54 (top)
Courtesy Mary Williams: 20 (right)
©Tom Wright: 137, 138 (upper right), 139, 161 (right)